Food and Drink in American History

Food and Drink in American History

• A "Full Course" Encyclopedia •

Volume 3: Background, Documents, and Resources

Andrew F. Smith

Santa Barbara, California   Denver, Colorado   Oxford, England

Library of Congress Cataloging-in-Publication Data

Food and drink in American history : a "full course" encyclopedia / [edited by] Andrew F. Smith.
pages cm
Includes bibliographical references and index.
ISBN 978-1-61069-232-8 (hardback) — ISBN 978-1-61069-233-5 (ebook)
1. Food—Encyclopedias. 2. Cooking, American—Encyclopedias. 3. Food habits—United States—Encyclopedias. I. Smith, Andrew F., 1946–
TX349.F5716 2013
641.597303—dc23 2013007323

ISBN: 978-1-61069-232-8
EISBN: 978-1-61069-233-5

17 16 15 14 13 1 2 3 4 5

This book is also available on the World Wide Web as an eBook.
Visit www.abc-clio.com for details.

ABC-CLIO, LLC
130 Cremona Drive, P.O. Box 1911
Santa Barbara, California 93116-1911

This book is printed on acid-free paper ♾
Manufactured in the United States of America

· Contents ·

Volume 1

Volume 2

Volume 3

• List of Primary Sources •

Documents, 1539–2012

• Introduction •

With the exception of the historical recipes, the entries in Volumes 1 and 2 are all secondary sources—material collected, evaluated, and interpreted. Many entries were based on primary sources. These included firsthand accounts written by explorers and visitors, poets and novelists, promoters and advertisers, magazine and newspaper writers, politicians and government officials, and supporters and critics of various views related to food and beverages. These accounts were recorded in many ways, including in diaries, logs, poems, songs, manuscripts, letters, advertisements, articles, books, cookbooks, laws, and government documents, to name a few. Documents written at the time of the events are called primary sources. Primary sources are at the core of culinary history. Historians interpret and evaluate primary sources to write articles and books.

Volume 3 has a selected sample of 129 documents that reflect the diversity of these sources and the great variety of views about the foods and beverages that Americans have consumed. These documents are primary sources. They permit the reader to form his or her own opinion about what really happened in history. In addition to the content conveyed in the documents, the selection also reflects the perspective of the authors, the authors' biases, and the times in which the authors lived.

Historical documents generate various questions: Who was the author? What is the author's perspective? How might someone else who lived at the same time have a different perspective? What are the author's biases? How do historians use bias to understand history? What was the author's purpose in writing the document? Who was the intended audience? How might readers at later times interpret or evaluate documents differently?

This volume includes a glossary of important terms and appendices on food history organizations and associations; important culinary history listservs and websites; food newsletters, periodicals, journals, and magazines; libraries with large culinary- or agriculture-related collections; food-related museums; and universities with food studies programs. The volume also includes a selected bibliography of the most significant writing on American food and drink and a comprehensive index.

Historical Overview of Documents

Pre-Columbian Food and Drink

The American Indians living in North America in prehistoric times did not develop written languages. Part of what we know about their foodways comes from archaeological excavations and from oral histories of American Indians that were recorded hundreds of years after their ancestors' first contact with Europeans. Most of our knowledge is derived from the writings of European explorers and colonists, who clearly judged the Native Americans in light of their own European perspectives. The first European account dates to 1511, when Spanish explorer Juan Ponce de León first visited Florida. According to Antonio de Herrera y Tordesillas, who later wrote an account of the expedition, the Indians in Florida ate mainly "Herbs, Roots, the Products of the Earth and Fish." They also made bread from roots—possibly sweet potatoes or yucca.

Another Spanish expedition, led by Hernando de Soto (1496–1542), arrived in Florida in 1539. His party traveled from there all the way to Texas. The explorers' records show that American Indians ate maize, beans, pumpkins, squash, chestnuts, fowl, dogs, buffalo, grapes, "plums" (probably persimmons), wild game, fish, walnuts, pecans, and other nuts, including acorns, which the Indians made into something like butter (see Document 1).

The first permanent European settlement in America—at St. Augustine in Florida—was founded by the Spanish in 1565. Twenty years later, the English tried to establish a colony on Roanoke Island in what is today North Carolina. The naturalist Thomas Hariot accompanied the colonists. Upon returning to England, he wrote of the native flora and fauna and of the foods that the American Indians ate. He reported that they barbecued and smoked fish and ate corn, beans, deer, and other game (see Document 2).

The colony at Roanoke failed, and in 1607 the English attempted to establish a colony at Jamestown, Virginia. John Smith, one of the colony's leaders, was captured by the Algonquin Indians. He reported that they ate bread, which they made from corn; game, especially deer and hares; wildfowl, especially wild turkeys and partridges; seafood, including fish, crabs, oysters, and tortoises; various roots; and strawberries, mulberries, and nuts, especially acorns and chestnuts (see Document 3).

Later European explorers, visitors, and colonists recorded their impressions of the American Indian diet, but by this time native peoples had been heavily influenced by Europeans. A Dutch colonist, Adriaen van der Donck, wrote of the American Indians in and around Manhattan Island that they mainly drank water. No alcoholic beverages were consumed by American Indians prior to the arrival of Europeans (see Document 6). Europeans introduced alcoholic beverages, which caused havoc with the social structure of the Indians. As colonial historian Robert Beverly noted in 1705, American Indians in Virginia were "so greedy of it, that most of them will be drunk as often as they find an opportunity; notwithstanding which it is a prevailing humor among them, not to taste any strong drink at all, unless they can get enough to make them quite drunk, and then they go as solemnly about it as if it were part of their religion" (see Document 9). The Swedish botanist Pehr Kalm, who visited America in the mid-18th century, was fascinated by the American Indians, and he wrote extensive reports about what they ate (see Document 13).

Few, if any, original American Indian foodways survived to become part of the mainstream American diet. Due to the loss of their hunting grounds, the destruction of their societies, and the eventual abundance of plants and domesticated animals introduced by European colonists, American Indians generally adopted European foodways. Many iconic American Indian foods, such as Navajo fry bread, are traditions that date only from the 19th century.

EUROPEAN COLONISTS AND ENSLAVED PEOPLES

From the beginning of European colonization, the population of eastern North America included culturally, linguistically, religiously, and racially diverse groups. There were hundreds of Native American groups as well as British, Dutch, Swedish, German, and French immigrants. Slaves were brought from Africa to the North and the South; by the early 17th century.

Throughout the colonial period, most Americans lived in rural areas, where they worked on farms or plantations. Those who lived in small towns bought their food in public markets or general stores and sometimes grew their own vegetables in home gardens. The few colonists who lived in cities, such as Philadelphia, Boston, and New York, had access to fairly sophisticated foods, both native-grown and imported.

In addition to the rural and urban differences, diverse climatic and soil conditions created roughly demarcated culinary regions: the Northern Colonies (New Hampshire, Massachusetts, Rhode Island, and Connecticut), the Middle Colonies (New York, New Jersey, and Pennsylvania), and the Southern Colonies (Delaware, Maryland, Virginia, North and South Carolina, and Georgia). A fourth culinary region was the frontier, which began about 100 miles inland from the Atlantic coast. Those living on the frontier basically survived on what they could shoot, trap, or catch with a hook and line.

The seeds that colonists brought with them from the Old World did not immediately thrive in North American soil, and hunger, malnutrition, and starvation took their toll on the early settlers. Their survival owed much to the American Indians, who supplied them with food and taught them how to hunt, fish, forage, and cultivate New World plants. Within a decade of the first successful settlements, however, food was plentiful. Domesticated animals, particularly swine, chickens, and dairy cows, were common throughout the colonies. Agricultural staples such as corn, wheat, and later rice were produced in abundance, and colonists could avail themselves of a considerable variety of vegetables and fruits.

By far the most important food in colonial America was corn. Fresh corn was boiled or roasted in hot ashes or dried and ground into cornmeal, which was cooked into mush, hasty pudding, porridge, and bread (see Documents 8, 57). The second most important New World crop was beans. Pre-Columbian Indians had domesticated numerous types of beans, many of which had been widely distributed throughout the Americas before the Europeans arrived. Pumpkins and squash, also of New World origin, were baked into breads and cakes and were used in making puddings, pies, tarts, and pancakes.

Many vegetables from Africa and South America found their way to colonial tables via the slave trade. In the South, slaves were often allowed to have gardens to supplement their basic rations, and they planted seeds they had brought with them from their homelands: okra, cassava, sweet potatoes, peanuts, sesame seeds, tomatoes, and chili peppers.

Colonists, especially in frontier areas, harvested the abundant game, wild fowl, fish, and seafood. Three game animals predominated in their diet: deer, bear, and buffalo. Deer were by far the most important. Bear meat was an important food in the East, but most important was the animal's fat, which when rendered was as good as lard and less expensive than scarce olive oil. Some buffalo roamed throughout some of the English colonies from New York to Georgia, though never in the quantities found on the Great Plains. Other game found on colonial tables included beaver, muskrats, rabbits, raccoons, squirrels, wild turkeys, cranes, swans, ducks, and geese.

Shellfish were plentiful. The most important was oysters, which were eaten raw, boiled, baked, or broiled. Next in importance were crabs, which were particularly favored in the Chesapeake Bay area and along New England's shores. Clams were eaten throughout the colonies. American lobsters were large and abundant. During colonial times they were not considered a delicacy but were mainly used to stave off hunger when choicer foods were unavailable. Turtles were taken for food in the area from the Florida Keys to the Chesapeake Bay and were made into soup.

Pigs and hogs thrived throughout the English colonies but particularly in the South because of the mild winters. Pork was easy to preserve by salting, pickling, or smoking. In the early years, imported cows supplied milk, butter, and cheese and occasionally meat and hides. Eventually dairy cows became a mainstay in agriculture in New England and the Middle Colonies. In the warmer South, fresh milk spoiled quickly; it kept better in the form of buttermilk, butter, and cheese. Domesticated poultry, particularly chickens, ducks, geese, and turkeys, were also important food sources during this period. Unlike beef, lamb, and pork, a chicken or goose could be eaten in one or two meals, so preserving the meat was not an issue. Fowl also provided feathers for pillows and bedding. Poultry was abundant but expensive, as a bird's chief value was in its eggs. A caponized rooster or a tender hen was a great luxury.

Wheat was also introduced by early colonists. By the mid-17th century, the Middle Colonies had become known as the Bread Colonies. Rice, introduced from Africa during the latter part of the 17th century, became the most important grain in the Southern Colonies and was used to make bread and puddings. Colonists transplanted many common European vegetables, such as beets, cabbage, carrots, onions, peas, and turnips, to their American gardens. Colonists also planted asparagus, chives, cabbage, cauliflower, cucumbers, endives, garlic, leeks, lettuce, shallots, and spinach in kitchen gardens. The white potato, introduced by the Spanish to Europe from South America, was then returned to the Americas in North American colonies during the late 17th century.

Old World fruits, such as apples, cherries, currants, peaches, pears, plums, pomegranates, and quince, were eaten fresh, made into tarts and pies (see Document 8), fermented and distilled into alcoholic beverages, and dried for winter use. Colonists planted melon and watermelon seeds shortly after colonization, and these proliferated throughout America, as did figs, nectarines, oranges, and pomegranates.

There were few natural sweeteners available to the North American colonists. By the 18th century, maple sap and later maple syrup and sugar were used in limited quantities in the Northern and Middle Colonies.

Colonial agriculture differed little from European farming practices of the same period, which had not changed much since the Middle Ages. Farming was arduous labor, requiring plenty of manpower and long hours of work during three seasons of the year. But during the late 18th century, methods of growing, raising, and processing food began to change. Some farmers adopted enhanced European agricultural practices, such as the use of organic fertilizers, crop rotation, and systematic livestock breeding. This interest in so-called scientific farming would revolutionize American agriculture during the 19th century.

Water was the main beverage of the colonial period, particularly in rural areas. As cows became common, milk became an important drink. The English, Dutch, and German colonists were partial to beer, and breweries were established early on. Hard cider and applejack became the most important alcoholic drinks in New England and the Middle Colonies. Native New World grapes were abundant, but early attempts to make wine from them were unsuccessful. Wealthy colonists imported sweet wines, such as canary, claret, madeira, port, and sherry, which traveled well, but most colonists did not drink wine and considered its use pretentious. Colonists invented a wide variety of mixed beverages—combinations of alcohol and other ingredients—as noted by Israel Acrelius (see Document 15). Rum was first introduced into North America around 1651 from the West Indies. When New Englanders began importing cheap molasses, they also started to distill their own rum. It was a common drink in taverns, where men of all classes socialized and discussed the news of the day.

The greatest military threat to the English colonies in North America was France, which controlled Canada and much of the territory west of the Alleghenies. The French menaced the American westward expansion into what is today the Midwest. When British and colonial American forces won the French and Indian War (1754–1763), the French treat ended. But the British Parliament wanted American colonists to help pay for the war and the expense of stationing British troops in Canada and preventing American Indians from raiding colonial settlements on the frontier.

In 1765 Parliament passed the Sugar Act, which levied a tax on North American imports of five products, notably molasses. New England's legislators, merchants, and distillers felt that the molasses tax would destroy rum production—the region's second most important industry—and strongly opposed it. Although the Sugar Act was eventually rescinded, disagreements between the British Parliament and the colonies continued. The tax on imported tea—and the arrogance of Bostonians who dumped British tea in the city's harbor—sparked the American Revolution (see Document 16).

During the war, both British and American forces had problems feeding their troops. The British military occupiers of New York had to import supplies from Ireland, as most farmers in the region refused to sell them food. The Continental Army had few resources for buying food, and its commander, George Washington, turned to patriotic citizens for help in feeding his army (see Document 17).

THE EARLY REPUBLIC

After the war, the new nation faced many difficulties, including the question of how to pay debts incurred by the states that had borne the brunt of the fighting. Congress finally agreed that the federal government should assume the responsibility of paying those debts, but how was it to do so?

Along with many other Americans, Benjamin Rush, the country's foremost medical practitioner, was concerned with the amount of spirituous liquor that Americans imbibed (see Document 18). This led Alexander Hamilton, the secretary of the treasury, to propose a tax on spirituous liquors manufactured in the United States (see Document 19). After much haggling, this proposal was accepted by Congress. When the new tax went into effect, it caused a rebellion among those living in the western parts of Pennsylvania, Maryland, and Virginia, for whom whiskey was a major source of income. The rebellion was put down with a minimum of loss of life, and the federal government's right to tax was established. Although the tax was removed when Thomas Jefferson became president, it would later be reestablished.

The amount of alcohol that Americans consumed continued to rise with each passing decade. The United States had 2,579 registered distilleries in 1792; 18 years later there were 14,191, which churned out 25 million gallons of spirits annually. In addition, there were numerous unlicensed commercial stills throughout the country, many in private homes. In 1810, Americans drank more than four and a half gallons of pure alcohol per capita, and it was estimated that about 6,000 Americans died each year as a consequence of their drinking. American men drank and socialized in taverns and bars, which were also places where travelers could find a simple meal and a room for the night (see Documents 25, 41, 42).

America's most consumed alcoholic drink during the early 19th century was whiskey. Many Americans did not like the taste of pure whiskey, and as a result the cocktail—a mixture of a distilled spirit and other ingredients—increasingly grew in importance as the century progressed. The bar as a drinking counter (it was initially a long narrow table on which liquor was served) was an invention of the 19th century (see Document 41). Jerry Thomas was the nation's best-known bartender, and his accomplishments were described by an English traveler who observed him at work in San Francisco (see Document 72).

Beginning in the 1830s, Germans began to immigrate en masse to the United States, and they brought with them lager beer, which quickly became popular (see Document 55).

As alcohol consumption increased, the temperance movement, which at first was interested only in reducing the amount of spirits that Americans drank, picked up steam during the early 19th century (see Document 34). Two strong temperance advocates were Dr. William Alcott and Sylvester Graham. They were also vegetarians and supported a simple diet devoid of elaborate or stimulating food and beverages, including alcohol, coffee, and tea (see Documents 37, 39). Their prescriptions were followed by tens of thousands of Americans (see Document 60). But the outbreak of the Civil War dampened support for temperance and vegetarianism, and the movement stalled.

Eating at Home

Throughout the colonial period and the early 19th century, most Americans ate their meals at home. City dwellers bought their food in public markets where farmers, butchers, cheesemongers, and other purveyors brought their goods to sell. Frances Trollope's description of a Cincinnati market in the 1830s (see Document 27), Thomas Devoe's description of New York markets (see Document 80), and a description of markets in New Orleans (see Document 88) provide a detailed picture of how urban Americans bought their food up until the 1930s. The late 20th-century resurrection of farmers' markets in American cities is an attempt to re-create this farm-to-table way of shopping.

Traditionally, an American girl learned to cook at her mother's side in their home kitchen. During the early 19th century, many Americans left farms and moved into cities. As families fragmented, the connection between mother and daughter was often broken. Cookbooks became the means of transmitting this vital knowledge.

British cookbooks had been republished in the American colonies since 1742. The first cookbook by an American-born author was Amelia Simmons's *American Cookery* (see Document 21), and many more cookbooks were to follow. Sarah Josepha Hale, the editor of the most popular women's magazine of the mid-19th century, published more than a dozen cookbooks (see Document 59). More than 280 historical recipes can be found in Volumes 1 and 2 of this work.

Of particular interest are southern cookbooks, which reflected a sophisticated culinary style. There were several reasons for this. The long southern growing season fostered a greater diversity of produce, and the wealthy denizens of the plantation South could afford to import food and drink from Europe and spices from Asia. And, of course, the plantation South had a plentiful supply of free labor, in the form of enslaved people.

Slaves were brought from Africa to all the North American colonies, but the institution prevailed only in the South. where cash-crop agriculture, such as tobacco and cotton, emerged. Northern states gradually abolished slavery during the early 19th century. How slaves were treated varied from region to region and from plantation to plantation. In some places they were permitted to grow food in gardens, and they grew a wide variety of non-European produce that became part of southern cuisine.

Field slaves were engaged in the heavy labor required to grow cotton, tobacco, and food crops, while other slaves ran plantation kitchens. Slaves received regular food allotments, and southerners claimed that their slaves were well fed (see Document 48). However, accounts of escaped slaves (see Documents 32, 45, 48, 101) and later interviews with former slaves (see Document 48) proved otherwise. Harriet Beecher Stowe's *Uncle Tom's Cabin* (1852) describes meals served by slaves to their masters, which provide a stark contrast to Stowe's descriptions of what the slaves themselves ate (see Document 52).

In the South, the desire to extend slavery gave impetus to a major push westward, beyond Louisiana. Americans migrated to Texas, which in 1836 won its independence from Mexico. The United States annexed Texas in 1845 and the following year went to war with Mexico. The Mexican-American War resulted in the U.S. acquisition of California and the Southwest. The foods of the native and Spanish peoples in this area were new to Americans, and many Americans wrote about the unfamiliar dishes they encountered (see Documents 42, 94). In the late 19th century, tremendous waves of German, Irish, and Chinese immigration took place. Most of the newcomers settled in the North and introduced Americans to their culinary traditions, as would subsequent immigrant groups who came to the United States.

Eating Outside the Home

During the early 19th century, Americans began to eat some meals away from home. Upscale restaurants such as Delmonico's and the Astor House in New York, the Mansion House in Philadelphia, and the Occidental Hotel in San Francisco catered to the well-to-do (see Documents 41, 72, 87), while boardinghouses provided food as well as lodging to the lower classes. Their tables were not always the most hospitable, as Asa Greene notes in his description of a New York boardinghouse (see Document 29).

Foreign visitors to the United States who recorded their impressions often wrote about the food and drink they sampled. Most were appalled by what they encountered, but others were delighted by some aspects of American culinary life. The French gastronome Jean Anthelme Brillat-Savarin, who lived in America for two years, was delighted with his own preparation of a wild turkey that he shot and cooked in Hartford, Connecticut (see Document 20). Constantin-François de Volney (1757–1820), a French historian and philosopher, lived in Philadelphia for three years beginning in 1795; his writings make clear his total disgust with American food and drink (see Document 23). Adam Hodgson, a businessman from Liverpool, England, was distressed with the waste in American kitchens (see Document 25). Frances Trollope's view of Cincinnati in the early 1830s included praise for that city's food market (see Document 27). British aristocrat Thomas Hamilton was unimpressed with Niblo's, one of New York's most popular taverns (see Document 25). Harriet Martineau, a British journalist who visited America in the early 1830s, described a Southern plantation dinner (see Document 33).

American journalists and novelists also included descriptions of food in their works. Just a few examples are included in this volume. James Fenimore Cooper, for example, described shooting the Christmas turkey (see Document 24). In a later work, Cooper proclaimed that Americans were ignorant of cookery (see Document 35). British writer Frederick Marryat disagreed with Cooper and offered his own more complex assessment (see Document 41). Asa Greene was put off by the food served in a boardinghouse (see Document 29), while Abram C. Dayton recollected culinary life at the City Hotel in New York during the 1830s (see Document 86). Herman Melville wrote about New England chowder (see Document 49), Nathaniel Hawthorne described an American dinner—no French food—and the accompanying wine (see Document 50), and Louisa May Alcott wrote about squash (see Document 81).

The Erie Canal, completed in 1825, connected New York City with the Great Lakes. This made it possible to ship agricultural goods from the Midwest to the Eastern Seaboard. This marked the beginning of huge improvements in food distribution from rural to urban areas. Railroads became an important means of conveyance during the following decade, and by the time the Civil War broke out in 1861, the Midwest was tied to the East Coast by four major railroads. These railroads—and the food they transported—made an important contribution to the Union's eventual victory.

CIVIL WAR AND VICTORIAN AMERICA

From a food standpoint, the Northern states had many advantages during the Civil War (1861–1865). Agricultural production was increasing thanks to mechanization, and the North had railroads and shipping lines in place to transport food when necessary. The North was able to feed its million-man army and its civilian population without resorting to rationing (see Document 75). The Confederacy, on the other hand, had imported food extensively before the war, and although the South was the nation's preeminent agricultural region, plantations mainly grew cash crops, such as cotton and tobacco. Despite attempts to change over to food crops, the South was unable to feed either its armies in the field or its civilians in urban areas. Food shortages resulted in bread riots in Confederate cities and in the eventual disintegration of Confederate armies. When it became clear that the South was unable to produce and distribute enough food, the Union armies targeted Southern agriculture in hopes of starving out the enemy (see Documents 68, 73, 77, 78).

In many ways, the Civil War set the stage for the industrial food system that developed during the next century. In 1862 the U.S. Congress passed three important pieces of legislation that established the U.S. Department of Agriculture (USDA), created agricultural colleges in every state, and funded the transcontinental railroad, completed in 1869. All of these improved American agriculture and helped to create a national food system (see Documents 69, 70, 71).

The Civil War ended slavery in the United States, and many former slaves moved northward and westward, where they worked in restaurants and helped to create an American cuisine (see Document 110).

Holidays

During the early 19th century, there were a number of regional holidays in the United States but only two national holidays: President George Washington's birthday (February 22) and Independence Day (July 4), the latter of which Americans celebrated with gusto and often with barbecues (see Documents 36, 101). Thanksgiving became an official holiday in the New England states in the early 19th century. Sarah Josepha Hale, one of the most influential women of the mid-19th century, wrote about a traditional New England Thanksgiving in her novel *Northwood* (see Documents 4, 26). When she became the editor of *Godey's* magazine, she launched a campaign to make Thanksgiving a national holiday. Beginning in 1841, New England historians had designated an event that occurred in 1621 at Plimoth Plantation as the First Thanksgiving (see Document 4). In November 1864, civilians in the North sent Thanksgiving provisions to the Union armies (see Document 77). After the Union victories at the Battle of Gettysburg and the Siege of Vicksburg in 1863, President Abraham Lincoln declared Thanksgiving a national holiday. After the Civil War, Thanksgiving became one of America's most important national holidays. The focus of Thanksgiving is, of course, on food.

Americans also celebrated religious holidays with special foods. Christians in New York and the South celebrated Christmas, but it did not become a national holiday until 1870 (see Documents 24, 53). Easter was celebrated by most Christians (see Document 84). Other religious holidays such as Passover were also celebrated (see Document 116).

Mechanization and Industrialization of the American Food System

American agriculture began to automate during the antebellum period. Cyrus McCormick and other inventors designed devices that mechanized agriculture, making it possible to expand agricultural production (see Document 51). Production soared during the Civil War and continued to increase throughout the rest of the century. Farmers' profits rose, and the price of staples declined. This period in American farming history through the end of World War I is called the "Golden Age of Agriculture." Entrepreneurs launched new commercial products, and professional advertising experts jumped in to help them build sales.

Commercial canning began in the early 19th century, but canned food was expensive and was largely served in fancy restaurants. When the Civil War began, the Union Army and the Union Navy were confronted with feeding a million-man military stretched across thousands of miles. One solution was to let contracts to commercial canners, who promptly found ways to lower production costs by improving the manufacturing process (see Document 79). By the time the war ended, canned goods were affordable for most Americans (see Document 82).

The transcontinental railroad, which began construction in 1862 and was completed seven years later, made it possible to ship fresh food, such as citrus fruit, from California to the East Coast, thus making a major contribution to the national food system.

THE EARLY 20TH CENTURY

During the late 19th century as agriculture became more and more mechanized, food processing was increasingly industrialized. The new processed and manufactured foods were subject to adulteration, and there were no laws in place to prevent unsafe products from entering the market. Many people became sick, and some died. Individual states passed pure food laws, but they were difficult to enforce. Pure food legislation was introduced into Congress beginning in 1879 but never made it out of Senate and House committees. The pure food movement strengthened in the 1880s but by the turn of the century had still not succeeded in passing a federal law against impurities in processed foods.

One strong advocate for diet reform was John Harvey Kellogg, a Seventh-day Adventist who became the director of a sanitarium in Battle Creek, Michigan (see Document 91). He invented a number of vegetarian foods that he promoted as healthful, such as grain-based ready-to-eat breakfast cereals, and campaigned around the country for pure food. Others, such as C. W. Post, picked up on Kelloggs's ideas and began manufacturing their own versions of his products. Post's claims for his products were exaggerated, and his advertising was eventually branded as false (see Document 105).

It was the publication of Upton Sinclair's novel *The Jungle* (1906) that finally pushed Congress to pass the Food and Drug Act (see Documents 102, 103, 104). Under this legislation, a federal regulatory body would set and enforce safety standards for thousands of different foods to prevent their adulteration or mislabeling. Although imperfect, the Food and Drug Act did make the federal government responsible for abuses perpetrated by businesses. As Americans became more confident that meat and processed foods were safe, sales soared. The profitability of large food companies increased, making it easier for them to comply with the legislation; as a result, many smaller companies folded. Applications of this law to food products continue today, assuring Americans of a safe food supply.

The temperance movement, determined to stop the manufacture, sale, and consumption of alcoholic beverages, picked up steam during the early 20th century, leading to the rise of soft drinks and alternatives to bars and saloons, such as coffeehouses, tearooms, and soda fountains. Flavored sodas had been manufactured during the late 19th century and became very popular during the early 20th century. These family-friendly beverages were not always as benign as they seemed; at one time Coca-Cola actually contained cocaine (see Document 114).

World War I

World War I began in Europe in July 1914, and soon European nations increased their orders of food from the United States—a boon to American agriculture. When the United States entered the war in 1917, domestic rationing and conservation went into effect. Wheat and food prices rose, and in New York City riots protesting food shortages broke out. The federal government printed posters admonishing Americans to eat less meat and avoid wasting food and encouraging them to plant vegetable gardens (see Document 112). Americans were also encouraged to eat more fish, and many Americans tried sportfishing (see Document 117).

During the war, American soldiers overseas sampled unfamiliar foods, and when they came back home they craved more varied menus. World War I also brought attention to chocolate as a favorite American food. The U.S. Quartermaster Corps ordered 40-pound blocks of chocolate and sent them to American troops in Europe, where the chocolate was a prized luxury for the soldiers. In the post–World War I era, the American appetite for sweets seemed limitless.

Prohibition

When the United States declared war on Germany on April 6, 1917, patriotic fever swept the nation, and leaders of prohibition organizations linked prohibition and patriotism. Congress passed legislation to prevent grain from being distilled into alcohol, and brewing was also restricted. In December 1917 Congress passed the Eighteenth Amendment to the Constitution, prohibiting "the manufacture, sale, or transportation of intoxicating liquors within, the importation thereof into, or the exportation thereof from the United States and all territory subject to the jurisdiction thereof for beverage purposes" (see Document 115).

By January 16, 1919, three-fourths of the states had ratified the amendment. Congress passed the National Prohibition Act, commonly called the Volstead Act, over President Woodrow Wilson's veto. The act defined intoxicating beverages as containing more than 0.5 percent alcohol (see Document 118). Beginning on January 16, 1920, it became illegal to manufacture, transport, import, or sell such beverages. Distilleries, wineries, and breweries closed or began making different products, such as grape juice, near beer, and alcohol for medicinal and industrial purposes. Saloons, bars, and liquor stores closed, and speakeasies—illegal drinking establishments—opened. There were also newly launched clubs, offering food, (illegal) drink, and entertainment. By 1930, U.S. authorities estimated that there were 250,000 speakeasies in the country. The New York City police commissioner estimated that there were 32,000 speakeasies in that city alone—more than twice the number of legal bars and saloons that existed prior to Prohibition. The alcohol ban remained in effect for 14 years.

Political opposition to Prohibition had begun even before the Eighteenth Amendment became law. Thousands of Americans joined organizations such as the Association Against Prohibition and the Women's Organization for National Prohibition Reform, which by November 1932 had a membership of more than 1.1 million. In February 1933 Congress proposed and approved the Twenty-first Amendment, repealing Prohibition. The amendment was ratified by the last of the required number of states on

December 5, 1933 (see Document 120). Breweries, distilleries, and wineries reopened. Speakeasies closed. Bars opened, but for the most part saloons were a thing of the past (except in Hollywood movies about the Old West).

Prohibition had lasting effects on American drinking habits. During the dry years, nonalcoholic beverages became commonplace. Fruit juices, such as grape, orange, and lemon, were advertised as healthful, and their sales accelerated. The sale of carbonated soft drinks also increased, partly because sodas—such as ginger ale and Coca-Cola—were used as mixers for foul-tasting bootleg liquor.

A number of new beverages came on the scene during Prohibition. Edwin Perkins, head of the Perkins Products Company of Hastings, Nebraska, marketed a bottled soft drink concentrate called Fruit Smack. Intended to be combined with water and sugar, Fruit Smack was popular, but the heavy bottles were expensive to ship. Perkins tried something else—a powdered concentrate packed in paper envelopes. He called the product Kool-Ade (later renamed Kool-Aid). This helped create a new category of beverages—children's drinks—that still flourishes today.

Changing Meal Patterns

Until the mid-19th century, most Americans engaged in hard manual labor on farms. Even those living in towns and cities had to perform some amount of physical work just to accomplish their daily activities. Whether on farms or in cities, most Americans went home for their midday meal, which was often the biggest meal of the day. Industrialization and urban life made this difficult, as workers had limited time to eat lunch and often worked far from home. Many workers brought their lunch from home, but others took their meals at a cafeteria, lunchroom, bar, coffee shop, diner, or lunch counter.

Different eating habits, an abundance of food, and less physical labor added up to an imbalance between calories consumed and calories burned, and Americans began to gain weight. In 1918, Los Angeles physician Dr. Lulu Hunt Peters promoted calorie counting as a method of weight reduction in her book *Diet and Health, with a Key to the Calories.* Using her own system, which began with a fast and then worked up to 1,200 calories per day, Peters had lost 50 pounds. Her plan had the endorsement of governmental agencies, and the book eventually sold more than 2 million copies. Calorie counting has been part of most weight-loss diets ever since.

The 1930s saw the advent of fad diets, some fairly sensible and others quite bizarre. Dr. Stoll's Diet-Aid, the Natural Reducing Food, was promoted through beauty parlors. The product consisted of one teaspoon each of milk chocolate, starch, whole wheat, and bran mixed with one cup of water, to be drunk for breakfast and lunch. The grapefruit diet appeared in the early 1930s. It was credited to William H. Hay, who believed that starches, proteins, and fruits should be consumed separately. The regimen was limited to a few select vegetables, protein sources, and grapefruit, which Hay said supplied a fat-burning enzyme. The grapefruit diet, renamed the Hollywood Diet, found new popularity in the 1970s.

Eating Out

For many Americans, the post–World War I period was one of unprecedented discretionary income. The stock market was booming, and jobs were plentiful in cities. Many Americans chose to spend their money in restaurants and not necessarily fine-dining establishments; diners and coffee shops were emblematic of the era. The quality of the food was perhaps beside the point, as suggested by such descriptors as "hash house," "greasy spoon," "chew and choke," and "slop house."

A new type of eating place appeared in the 1920s. White Castle, the nation's first fast-food chain, was launched in 1921. Its limited menu of short-order foods and beverages was soon emulated by other companies. Associated with fast-food chains was the rise of drive-ins, places where Americans could eat lunch or dinner in the comfort of their cars.

This was also a boom time for soda fountains and for the sale of products such as grape juice that could easily be made into alcoholic beverages. It was also a period of improvements in the manufacture of food products, especially the application of continuous processing techniques that greatly improved efficiency and lowered the cost of production.

Processed Foods

Processed foods increasingly became part of the American food scene. Thousands of new canned foods and other packaged foods appeared on store shelves. Some were entirely new categories of food, such as breakfast cereals and snacks. Historically Americans rarely ate between meals, and if they did their choice would probably be a piece of fruit. This changed in the early 20th century. Cracker Jack, a mixture of caramel-coated popcorn and peanuts, made its debut in 1896 as America's first commercial snack food (see Document 98). Thanks to a cascade of advertising campaigns, by 1916 Cracker Jack was the largest-selling confection in the world. Other manufactured foods, such as Jell-O, appeared early in the century, and by the 1920s commercial snacks had become an American habit.

One new way of advertising the new commercial products was through a new medium: radio. From a marketing standpoint, radio's immense power lay in its national audience and its relatively low cost. There was no denying that products advertised on the radio sold. As American gathered around to listen to their favorite programs, food companies commissioned radio personalities such as Jack Benny to promote their products. Breakfast cereal makers were among the earliest to avail themselves of radio advertising. In 1926 General Mills was the first advertiser to use a singing radio commercial, and in 1933 Wheaties sponsored the program *Jack Armstrong, the All-American Boy,* on NBC.

Other new technologies changed industrial food production and the way Americans ate. Until the 1920s, people brought home a loaf of bread from the bakery in a paper bag and sliced the bread as needed. The bread went stale fairly quickly, and there was also danger in using the requisite sharp knife—particularly if a child did the cutting. Then someone devised a way to slice loaves mechanically as they came out of commercial ovens, and wrapping the sliced loaf part of the process. The Chillicothe Baking Co. of Chillicothe, Ohio, may have been the first company to market wrapped loaves of sliced bread. The emblematic commercial food product of this period was Wonder Bread, which was advertised as a health food for children. The fact that children could make their own sandwiches without handling a knife was a bonus. By the 1930s, processed foods dominated the American foodscape.

The Great Depression

As soon as World War I ended the demand for American farm products sharply declined, and agriculture went into a depression that lasted for the next 20 years. Commodity prices declined, and farmers abandoned their farms. Factory farms (large farms owned and operated as businesses) and co-ops (with many farmers pooling their resources to improve production, marketing, and sales) became more common (see Documents 113, 119).

On October 29, 1929, the stock market crashed, setting off a panic that led to the decade-long Great Depression. Agriculture, already in decline, deteriorated even more rapidly as more and more farmers lost their farms or set out for cities in search of employment. Eventually unemployment rose as high as 25 percent; breadlines and soup kitchens sprang up in cities. The federal government as well as state and city governments developed programs to feed the poor, put Americans back to work, and assist struggling farmers with price supports.

The few fine restaurants that had survived Prohibition closed during the Depression. Americans were eating at cheap fast-food chains, drive-ins, cafés, cafeterias, and lunchrooms—and at home, where they depended on thrifty dishes such as macaroni and cheese, spaghetti and meatballs, casseroles, and canned soups. (Decades later, Americans would return to these recipes with nostalgia, calling them "comfort food.") Many people went hungry, and American writers, such as John Steinbeck, wrote about their experiences. The industrial food system was still up and running, but many Americans simply couldn't afford to buy its products (see Documents 121, 122).

The Depression hastened the rise of the supermarket. Consumers wanted lower prices, and since supermarkets could buy in bulk, they could charge less than small grocery stores. The smaller stores couldn't compete with supermarket prices, and many of them closed. Supermarkets reshaped the way food is marketed. Impulse buying (unplanned buying) has been attributed to the rise of supermarkets. As a greater variety of products became available, shoppers had a harder time making smart choices, even when, much later, unit pricing became standard and nutrient labeling became the law. Advertising and promotion leveraged consumers' purchases, and today food companies as a category are among the largest advertisers. Foods that weren't advertised disappeared from supermarkets, while those that were promoted successfully survived to claim optimal shelf placement.

World War II

War broke out in Europe in September 1939, and as in World War I, European nations began ordering American agricultural products. American farming rebounded as shipments of food to England rose. After the United States entered the war in December 1941, meats, grains, and sugar, among other things, were rationed, and imported products were hard to come by. Faced with the rigors of rationing, Americans on the home front turned to nutritious substitutes, such as corn, potatoes, and peanuts, that were not rationed. These became the basis for many wartime meals.

Just when the demand for food crops was rising, many farmers were leaving their fields to enlist. The government encouraged Americans to grow fruits and vegetables in backyard Victory Gardens, and an estimated 80 percent of the population responded; in 1943 these gardens produced 40 percent of the fresh produce on American tables (see Document 123).

The Food and Drug Administration (FDA) encouraged the enrichment of white bread with vitamins. In 1943 the War Foods Administration temporarily required bread to be made with enriched flour, and most white flour and breads sold in the United States today are enriched with several nutrients.

During World War II, the federal government first published nutritional standards—called Recommended Dietary Allowances (RDA)—for energy, protein, and eight essential vitamins and minerals. These were the levels of nutrients required by an average adult for good health. During the war, the USDA also promoted the "Basic Seven"—a special version of these guidelines modified to help people deal with rationing and shortages. After the war this became the "Basic Four," which stressed dairy products, meats, fruits and vegetables, and grains. Nutrition experts advised planning balanced meals with meat or poultry at the core along with vegetables and a starch, such as potatoes or rice. Eggs, milk, and orange juice were among the foods advocated as being particularly healthful.

POST–WORLD WAR II

World War II ushered in important changes in the American food system. The growth of supermarkets had slowed down as wartime restrictions halted construction, foods were rationed, and food processors focused on military contracts. Before the war, most grocery clerks were young men; as they enlisted and left their jobs, women filled their places. After the war, women continued to work as cashiers. The postwar period saw tremendous growth in the number of supermarkets—from 10,000 in 1946 to 17,000 in 1953. Their capital resources gave them the edge in building new suburban markets as they abandoned less profitable inner-city stores.

Food transportation changed as a result of techniques developed by the military during the war. The U.S. military transported goods in shipping containers and employed a roll-on–roll-off technique for driving vehicles on and off ships. These systems were greatly improved after the war, and today nonbulk agricultural goods and packaged foods are transported thousands of miles across borders and oceans at relatively low cost. This has made imported comestibles, such as wines, cheeses, and spices, more affordable; has broadened the range of choices for American consumers; and has also encouraged the export of American foods to other countries.

Long-haul trucks equipped with roof-mounted refrigeration systems first hit American roads in 1948. This enabled refrigerated and frozen foods to be distributed easily and efficiently to the most isolated communities. The increased use of trucks also set in motion the decentralization of food processing, enabling processing plants to be built where labor costs were lowest and where local and state zoning and taxing policies were most advantageous. The creation of the interstate highway system greatly increased the efficiency of truck transportation and also facilitated the growth of fast-food chains, which clustered around on- and off-ramps (see Document 124).

Yet another development resulting from World War II was how to feed personnel traveling long distances. Air crews began freezing prepared meals and reheating them aboard the planes. After the war, companies such as Frozen Dinners, Inc., in Pittsburgh prepared meals to be served on Pan Am's overseas flights. Applications of this idea to commercial food gave rise to the TV dinner and thousands of other frozen foods.

As women entered the workforce, they were less able or willing to spend as much time shopping or cooking. Supermarkets came to the rescue, making shopping more efficient and offering new convenience foods, including frozen products. These had been on the market prior to the war, but they were not widely adopted until the postwar period. Frozen juices, TV dinners, and desserts became mainstays of family meals. As the 20th century came to a close, however, supermarkets had to face a sociological fact. In families where both parents worked outside the home, kitchen-table suppers were being replaced by restaurant meals and takeout food. This fostered the proliferation of quick-service chains as well as gourmet shops selling high-quality prepared food.

Radar technology that was developed during World War II led to the creation of a new type of oven that cooked food with unprecedented speed. After the war, these microwave ovens gradually became commonplace in restaurants. Microwave ovens began to appear in home kitchens beginning in the 1960s.

During World War II, with millions of Americans in the military and millions more doing war work stateside, restaurants faced a shortage of trained chefs and culinary professionals. A group of New Haven restaurateurs decided to open a school for training restaurant staff, but the war ended before they accomplished their goal. At that point, the labor problem changed. There were plenty of workers but few with the skills needed to work in food service. The New Haven restaurant school opened its doors in May 1946. A few years later the school changed its name to the Culinary Institute of America; it was the first modern American culinary school.

World War II also changed the nation's food orientation by exposing Americans to other cuisines. The service personnel who had served overseas and the many tourists, businessmen, and government officials who visited Europe after the war enjoyed the fine food and wines of France, Italy, and other countries, and they wanted more of the same when they returned home. Experts came forward to teach Americans the art of preparing foreign cuisines, and many were able to do so using a new technology: television.

Television

Television technology had been perfected by the late 1930s, but monetary and technological demands during World War II stopped early experimentation. When the war ended, television burst on the scene, but few Americans could afford to buy TV sets. In the 1950s. the price of televisions dropped. Disposable income rose for many middle-class families during this period, so that most could afford television sets. By 1956, 40 million sets were in American homes. By the end of the decade, 86 percent of American homes had a TV. Television also created opportunities for people such as James Beard and Julia Child to create cooking shows for the new medium. Thanks in part to Child, who popularized classic French cooking in the 1960s, gourmet cookery emerged as a popular hobby.

Fast Food

Richard and Maurice McDonald created a radical new fast-food operation in San Bernardino, California. The brothers designed an efficient assembly line to make hamburgers and french fries, providing customers with fast, consistent, cheap meals. The brothers began franchising their operation in the 1950s. Ray Kroc acquired the rights to franchise their operation nationally. Kroc's successful franchise system was the prototype for other fast-food chains, which readily adopted the McDonald's model. Other fast-food chains, such as Burger King, Kentucky Fried Chicken, Taco Bell, Wendy's, and Pizza Hut, rapidly opened outlets throughout the United States and many other countries.

Obesity and Dieting

As fewer Americans engaged in less strenuous exercise and as food became abundant for many Americans, weight gain was the result. Dieting began in earnest after World War I, but it was not until after World War II that dieting became an obsession. America's first national organization that focused on weight loss was Take Off Pounds Sensibly (TOPS), started in 1948, which was modeled after Alcoholics Anonymous in the belief that peer support could be a key to successful weight loss. Other weight-loss programs emerged, such as Overeaters Anonymous and Weight Watchers. Today, an estimated 25 percent of Americans are on a diet at any one time.

Sugar-free products had been manufactured for the needs of diabetics since the 1920s. It wasn't until the 1950s that the market for diet products mushroomed. Tasti-Diet Foods, the first such line, was created in 1951 by Tillie Lewis; the company's canned fruits were sweetened with saccharin. Diet beverages are a multibillion-dollar business today, but the first diet soda was not marketed until 1951. In 1963 a study estimated that 28 percent of Americans were dieting.

Despite numerous diet programs and products, Americans have continued to gain weight. Today 61 percent of Americans are judged as being overweight. Obesity rates have risen from 12 percent to 20 percent of the population since 1991. Nowhere has this been more of concern than with the increase in weight for children.

Beverages

After the war, American beverages changed as well. Coffee, America's most consumed beverage after water, was a cheap beverage for the masses, routinely brewed at home or picked up on the run from a coffee shop or vending machine. In the 1960s, soft drinks became the most consumed category of beverages. Soft drink manufacturers increased the number of their products, while the industry was generally consolidated into three major companies—the Coca-Cola Company, PepsiCo, and the Dr Pepper Snapple Group. These companies expanded into other beverages, including fruit juices, sports beverages, energy drinks, and bottled water.

New wineries were established in different parts of the United States. In 1945 Marvin Sands established the Canandaigua Industries Company in the Finger Lakes region of New York. This winery mainly produced bulk and fortified wines, especially dessert wines. The company grew rapidly by acquiring other wineries and soon began marketing a wide number of brands. The production of quality wines was greatly enhanced by the victories of California wines in a tasting in Paris in

1976. The American wine industry has expanded ever since, and today most states have wineries.

American beer production also increased after the war. Three major beer companies emerged: Budweiser, Miller, and Pabst. During the 1980s, microbrewing became an important part of the beer scene in America.

America's traditional spirit of choice, whiskey, slipped in consumption, while vodka, which had been manufactured in the United States only since the 1930s, became America's most consumed spirit. Rum made a comeback, and tequila became a popular beverage.

Food Magazines

Gourmet magazine began publication in 1941, but its subscription base rapidly expanded after the war. By its second decade, *Gourmet* was an established presence on the American food scene and in many ways was an arbiter of taste. Since the 1950s, the number of American magazines focusing on food has grown tremendously. There were fewer than 20 in the early 1960s, but by 2002 the number of magazines, quarterlies, journals, and newsletters had swelled to 145. In addition to *Gourmet,* the upscale glossy American food magazines of this period were *Bon Appétit, Food & Wine,* and *Saveur.* Occupying more specialized niches were *Cook's Illustrated, Fine Cooking, Good Food,* and *Eating Well.*

Haute Cuisine

In October 1941, Henri Soulé opened Le Pavillon in New York City; the luxurious restaurant specialized in French haute cuisine. Soulé's great legacy was his nurturing of restaurateurs and other influential individuals on America's food scene. Restaurants that appealed to the well-to-do with quality food opened in every large city and many smaller cities.

After World War II many more Americans visited France, and some sojourned there for years. Some first saw France while in the military, while others were on assignment in the Foreign Service. Still others—the newly affluent upper middle class—took advantage of the strong U.S. dollar and vacationed in France, where they discovered simple but excellent food at modest prices in provincial restaurants, superior produce at outdoor markets, and a dazzling array of cheeses and wines they had never heard of back home.

Feeding the Poor

Some states had school lunch programs in the 1920s; the federal government began supporting such programs in the 1930s. In 1946 the School Lunch Act established federally subsidized lunches for the nation's schoolchildren. Since then, other programs have been developed to support nutritious meals for students.

During the 1960s, Americans became more concerned about the poor, particularly those who were malnourished. One result was the the Food Stamp Act, passed in 1964, which instituted a federal-assistance program administered by individual states to provide help to people and families with little or no income (see Document 125). The program was funded through the USDA. Qualified individuals and families could redeem the stamps in grocery stores and supermarkets. The program was subsequently renamed the Supplemental Nutrition Assistance Program (SNAP). The system has shifted from stamps to electronic benefits transfer (EBT) cards that operate like credit cards and debit cards.

Counterculture Food

Great strides were made in American agriculture during the 20th century, but with progress came protest. As farming and food processing became more centralized, mechanized, and chemically enhanced, some Americans voiced concerns about the quality, safety, and palatability of the food supply. The dangers of pesticides, fertilizers, hormones, and additives became apparent and were made known to the public at large during the 1960s. Many counterculture advocates were people who had lost faith in the government and the capitalist system. The counterculture also established food co-ops, as mainstream health-food stores were plagued by charges of fraud and hucksterism. Critical appraisals of American food appeared in the 1970s.

Food co-ops, self-run by their members, were initially no-frills sources for staples such as brown rice, whole-grain breads, herbal teas, nuts, seeds, beans, dried fruits, honey, and soy products. As co-ops became more commercial, they began offering natural cheeses, yogurt, organically grown fruits and vegetables, pure juices, granolas, oils, and vitamin and mineral supplements.

Some people in the counterculture saw a vegetarian diet as a route to better health and a way to help fight hunger in America and around the world. The North American Vegetarian Society was founded in 1974, and several vegetarian magazines, such as *Vegetarian Times,* now have large subscriber bases.

In 1971 Alice Waters opened a small restaurant called Chez Panisse in Berkeley, California. As Chez Panisse matured, becoming a touchstone of American cuisine, Waters found willing partners in her mission of promoting local, fresh, seasonal ingredients. She joined fine cooking with community activism, supporting local farmers, organic food, and sustainable agriculture. Cooking was a product of agriculture as well as a part of culture. Reflecting Waters's heartfelt endorsement of small-scale local food production, such operations gained new respect. Artisans milking their own herds to make goat cheese or stoking wood ovens to bake hearty peasant breads and farmers growing heirloom tomatoes and subtly flavored strains of basil were celebrated for their accomplishments. Upscale farm stands and city shops specializing in fine local foods proliferated around the country. Waters championed organic farms, humane animal husbandry, and sustainable fisheries, and they too became common throughout the United States. This was first called California cuisine and then, as it spread across the country, American cuisine.

Another impact of the counterculture food movement was a burgeoning interest in organic gardening, which has blossomed during the past few decades. Associated with organic gardening is a movement to preserve small farms by connecting consumers in cities with farmers in surrounding areas. One such effort led to the growth of urban farmers' markets, where local growers truck in their produce and sell it directly to customers, thus eliminating the middlemen and establishing a connection between city dwellers and farmers. One example is New York City's Greenmarkets, founded in 1976 by Barry Benepe. Today there are 66 Greenmarket sites in the city, and Benepe's efforts have served as a model for hundreds of other urban farmers' markets around the nation.

Some enterprises launched by those in the counterculture food movement have survived and thrived, such as Erewhon Foods, Celestial Seasonings, and Whole Foods. Another successful innovation is community-supported agriculture, in which members pay in advance for a season's worth of produce, thereby providing the farmer with money for seed and whatever else is needed to bring the produce to market.

Immigrant Food

Successive waves of immigrants have arrived in the United States during the past century, but it wasn't until after World War II that mainstream Americans began to adopt versions (usually bastardized) of ethnic foods, newly enriching the traditional American diet. Mexican culinary influences spread slowly around the United States in the early 20th century. Small Mexican American roadside restaurants, often called taco stands, sprang up throughout California and the Southwest. In addition to such fast-food chains as Taco Bell, today there are more than 7,000 Mexican restaurants throughout the United States. Mexican food is now the second most popular ethnic cuisine in the United States and it is a close runner-up to Italian food.

Italians, Greeks, Japanese, East European Jews, Chinese, Koreans, Latinos, Africans, Caribbeans and many other immigrants introduced or popularized particular fruits, vegetables, seafoods, or traditional dishes while serving as cooks, truck gardeners, fishermen, delicatessen and restaurant owners, vendors, or wholesalers. Many common American dishes—hot dogs, hamburgers, chili con carne, chop suey, Swedish meatballs, gyros, tacos, tamales, bagels, pizza, spaghetti, sushi, and pad thai, to name but a few—owe their origins to immigrants. The immigrant experience in this country has thus created a cornucopia of ethnic or ethnic-inspired foods that have enriched and expanded the scope of American cuisine.

Globalization

Americans have imported and exported food since the early colonial days. Until the mid-20th century, food imports were greatly restricted by tariffs and quotas. Since World War II, the United States has joined with other nations to lower tariffs and other barriers to trade. This has been accomplished through various multilateral agreements, such as the General Agreement on Tariffs and Trade (GATT), the World Trade Organization (WTO), and the North American Free Trade Agreement (NAFTA) as well as a number of bilateral agreements with specific nations.

The WTO has made it easier for American food manufacturers and distributors to launch and sustain operations in other countries. NAFTA binds the United States, Canada, and Mexico together economically, and since its ratification in 1994 American companies have flooded into Mexico and Canada. Some Canadian and Mexican companies have also expanded their operations into the United States.

THE 21ST CENTURY

In 1992 the FDA established guidelines for testing the safety of foods using all methods of plant breeding, including transgenic ones. The FDA concluded that transgenic foods posed no new or special safety risks, and therefore the FDA guidelines exempted transgenic plants from case-by-case review. Since 1996, the planting of biotech crops has experienced double-digit growth every year. By 2008, transgenic plantings had swelled to 92 percent of the soybeans and 80 percent of the corn grown in the United States. Similar percentages are common for other crops, such as cotton and canola. These first-generation products will soon be joined by second-generation transgenic foods. During the past few years alone, the USDA has approved more than 1,000 new biotech plants for use by farmers.

Many cooking series, such as James Beard's *I Love to Cook, Dione Lucas's Cooking Show,* Graham Kerr's *The Galloping Gourmet,* and Julia Child's *The French Chef,* had aired on television since the 1940s, but the launch of the Food Network in 1993 changed everything. The Food Network spawned such personalities as Emeril Lagasse, Bobby Flay, Sara Moulton, Ming Tsai, and Rachael Ray, who have become some of America's most influential tastemakers. While the Food Network's initial audience was primarily female, more men began watching the network as time passed. By 2012, almost half of the viewers were male. Some of this can be attributed to celebrity chefs such as Lagasse, Flay, and Kaga Takeshi, who made it culturally appropriate for American men to take an interest in cooking—traditionally a woman's domain.

Large retail general-merchandise chains, such as Costco and Walmart, began selling grocery items in the late 20th century. Founded in Seattle, Washington, in 1983 by James Sinegal and Jeffrey Brotman, Costco specialized in packaged foods in large economy sizes but has since expanded into fresh produce, meats, seafood, baked goods, and liquor (where permitted by state or local laws). Walmart Stores, started in Bentonville, Arkansas, by Sam Walton in 1962, began as a discount department store. Walmart sold virtually no food in 1993; by 2001 it was the second-largest food retailer in America. Today the company is the largest seller of groceries in the world. Walmart went from selling $66.5 billion in groceries in 2004 to selling $135 billion in groceries four years later, which was more than the next three chains combined.

Inventions

The Internet has also revolutionized the American food system by creating unprecedented opportunities for food producers to sell their products. Virtually any food product is available for sale on the Internet, and people with the funds to do so can have even exotic products delivered promptly.

Websites with recipes and related food matters sprang up, such as Allrecipes.com. Virtually every food company has a presence on the Internet to supply information about its products. Many companies offer other services as well, such as online ordering and gift certificates. Corporate websites also promote their products in a variety of ways, such as offering money-saving coupons for those who fill out surveys. The information thus collected is then used to enhance the company's marketing strategy, often by targeting those who fill out the survey for special promotions. Finally, food companies have begun to advertise extensively online, especially through social media. The Internet has created an unprecedented means of marketing products directly to particular audiences.

Hundreds of culinary applications have been developed for a number of different platforms, including tablets, iPads, Kindles, Nooks, and smartphones (iPhone, Android, BlackBerry, etc.). These culinary apps fall into several categories: shopping assistants (where to locate food stores and where to find particular products); restaurant listings and reviews; food truck locators, often with advice on what to order; recipe databases and interactive cookbooks with video clips on how to prepare recipes; food ordering assistance for takeout or delivery; nutrition information; inventory control for restaurants and bars; and games. Kindles, iPads, and Nooks can be used to download cookbooks.

Food trucks have been around for decades. An outgrowth of pushcarts, they mainly sold coffee, sandwiches, doughnuts, or ice cream. In the 1980s they began serving a wider range of foods, such as pizza, subs, fries, falafel, hot dogs, tacos, hamburgers, and waffles, and are now common in many American cities. Recently food trucks have proliferated, offering unusual specialties, fusion food, and trendy dessert items. They have also become more sophisticated in their marketing, using Twitter and Facebook to tell customers where they will be on a given day.

Criticism and New Policies

Criticism of the American food system has been constant since the counterculture food movement began in the 1970s. Eric Schlosser took on the fast-food industry. Writers such as Marion Nestle and Michael Pollan have criticized big agriculture, food processors, and food distributors and promoted organic foods. In part as a result of this criticism, many new laws have been passed that have improved aspects of the American food system. The Nutrition Labeling and Education Act was passed in 1990, and the National Organic Program was approved in 2000. The Food Allergy Labeling and Consumer Protection Act, passed in 2004, requires manufacturers to disclose known allergens in their products (see Documents 126–129).

The Nutrition Labeling and Education Act of 1990 requires nutrition labels to be placed on food products but exempts restaurants from printing such information on their menus. The Patient Protection and Affordable Care Act was signed into law on March 23, 2010. The act includes a provision that created a national, uniform nutrition-disclosure standard for restaurants and requires chain restaurants, drive-thrus, convenience stores, vending machines, and retail stores with 20 or more locations to post nutrition information in plain sight. Stores must also display, according to the legislation, "a succinct statement concerning suggested daily caloric intake." The FDA prepared the standards, which went into effect in 2011 (see Document 129).

The American foodscape remains vibrant. Immigrant populations and émigré chefs continue introducing new foods to America's table. Global trade has given Americans wider food choices than ever before and has inspired a dizzying array of places to buy and enjoy that food: chic restaurants using exotic imported ingredients, fast-food chains serving vegetarian alternatives, thriving supermarkets offering tens of thousands of products, and newly revived old-fashioned food sources such as farmers' markets, local artisan bakers, and farmstead cheese makers, while American food corporations continue to produce a wide variety of foods and a more abundant supply.

· Documents, 1539–2010 ·

1539 · 1 · Hernando de Soto's Expedition

Introduction: *Hernando de Soto (1496–1542) was born in Spain and sailed to the New World in 1514. After a number of governmental positions and campaigns, he outfitted an expedition and landed on the west coast of Florida in 1539. His expedition explored Florida and parts of the present-day states of Georgia, South Carolina, Tennessee, Alabama, Mississippi, Arkansas, Louisiana, and Texas. De Soto was killed in 1542 along the banks of the Mississippi River. Three accounts of this expedition survive. Each account mentions food encountered along the way. This document is from an otherwise unknown writer who identifies himself modestly as "A Gentleman of Elvas." The peafowl mentioned by the author refers to the turkey, a distant relative of the Old World peafowl. As there were no plums in the Americas at the time, the author is likely referring to persimmons. There were chestnuts in eastern North America, and they were an important food consumed by American Indians and later by European colonists. When Asiatic chestnuts were introduced into the United States in 1904, they brought a fungal parasite that completely destroyed the American chestnuts, and none survived. There were—and are—American walnuts that derive from the tree commonly called the black walnut. These is no consensus on what the fruit is that the author calls "ligoacam." Some botanists believe that it is the Asimina triloba, more commonly known as the pawpaw, a fruit-bearing tree that is common to eastern America.*

Certain Diversities and Peculiarities of the Land of Florida; and the Products and Birds and Animals of That Land

The bread which is eaten in all the land of Florida is of maize which resembles coarse millet. This maize is found in all the islands and Indies of Castile from the Antilles on. In Florida, there are also many walnuts, plums, mulberries, and grapes. They sow and harvest the maize, each one cultivating his own.

The fruits are common to all, for they grow very abundantly in the open fields, without it being necessary to plant or cultivate them. Wherever there are mountains, there are chestnuts. They are somewhat smaller than those of Spain.

From the great river westward, the walnuts differ from the others, for they are easier to crush and shaped like acorns. From the great river to the port, they are, for the most part, hard and the trees and walnuts seem similar to those of Spain.

In all parts of the country is a fruit which comes from a plant like "ligoacam," which the Indians sow. The fruit resembles the royal pear, and has an excellent smell and a delicious taste. Another plant grows in the open field, which produces a fruit near the ground like the strawberry, which is very tasty.

The plums are of two kinds, red and gray, of the form and size of walnuts. They have three or four stones. They are better than all those of Spain and they make much better dried ones of them. Only in the grapes can one perceive the lack of cultivation, which although they are large have large seeds.

All the other fruits are very perfect and less harmful than those of Spain. In Florida, are many bears and lions, wolves, deer, jackals, cats, and rabbits.

There are many wild fowl there, as large as peafowls, small partridges like those of Africa, cranes, ducks, turtledoves, thrushes, and sparrows.

There are certain black birds which are larger than sparrows and smaller than starlings. There are goshawks, falcons, sparrowhawks, and all the birds of prey found in Spain. The Indians are well proportioned. Those of the flat lands are of taller stature and better built than those of the mountains. Those of the interior are better supplied with maize and clothing native to the country than those of the coast.

Source: A Gentleman of Elvas, "True Relation of the Hardships Suffered by Governor Hernando De Soto & Certain Portuguese Gentlemen during the Discovery of the Province of Florida." Translated by James Alexander Robertson. Florida State Historical Society–Deland, 1933.

1590 • 2 • Thomas Hariot's Description and Depiction of Inhabitants

Introduction: *The first English colony in what is today the United States was established on Roanoke Island, in North Carolina, in 1585. Thomas Hariot (1560–1621), a naturalist, was one of the colonists who arrived in 1685, and he collected a large amount of information about minerals, flora, fauna, and the American Indians living on the island. He returned to England in 1586 and published his report about the colony in 1588. In that year Spain and England were at war, and no relief supplies were sent to the Roanoke colony. When English ships finally arrived on the island, the colony with its 90 men, 17 women, and 11 children had completely disappeared. Below are some excerpts from Hariot's report regarding the food eaten by the Algonquin Indians living on the island.*

After they have taken store of fish, they get them unto a place fit to dress it. There they stick up in the ground 4 stakes in a square room, and lay 4 postes upon them, and others over thwart the same like unto an hurdle, of sufficient height, and laying their fish upon this hurdle, they make a fire underneath to broile the same, not after the manner of the people of Florida, which do but scorch, and harden their meat in the smoke only to reserve the same during all the winter. For this people, reserving nothing for store, they do broil, and spend away all at once, and when they have further need, they roast or seethe fresh, as we shall see herafter. And when as the hurdle can not hold all the fish, they hang the Rest by the fires on sticks set up in the ground against the fire, and then they finish the rest of their cookery. They take good heed that they be not burnt. When the first are broiled they lay others on, that were newly brought, continuing the dressing of their meat in this sort, until they think they have sufficient.

Wickonzówr, called by us Peaze [beans]. . . . They make them victuall either by boyling them all to pieces into a broth; or boiling them whole untill they bee soft and beginne to breake as is used in England, eyther by themselves or mixtly together: sometime they mingle of the wheate with them. Sometime also beeing whole soddeu, they bruse or pound them in a morter, & thereof make loaves or lumps of dowishe bread, which they use to eat for varietie.

Their manner of feeding is in this wise. They lay a mat made of bents on the ground and set their meat on the midst therof, and then sit down Round, the men upon one side, and the women on the other. Their meat is Maize sodden [boiled], in such sort as I described it in the former treatise of very good taste, deer flesh, or of some other beast, and fish. They are very sober in their eating, and drinking, and consequently very long lived because they do not oppress nature.

Source: Thomas Hariot, *A Briefe and True Report of the New Found Land of Virginia* (1590; reprint, New York: Dodd, Mead, 1903), 101.

1608 • 3 • JOHN SMITH, *THE GENERALL HISTORIE OF VIRGINIA*

Introduction: *John Smith (1580–1631), one of the leaders of the Jamestown colony, the first successful English settlement in North America, was captured by the Algonquin Indians in January 1608. In 1624 he published* The Generall Historie of Virginia, *an account of the colony's early years. Smith told the story to John Studley, who wrote it down. It not only tells about the food and customs of Algonquin Indians living in Virginia but also tells of the relationship between Smith and Pocahontas, the Algonquin chief's daughter who was later popularized in books and movies.*

Ere long there was brought to him enough venison and bread to have served twenty men. I think his appetite at that time was not very good. They put what he left in baskets and tied it over his head. About midnight they again set the meat before him. All of this time not one of them would eat a bite with him. The next morning they brought him as much more, and then they ate all the old, and reserved the new as they had done the other, which made him think they wanted to fat him to eat him. Yet in this desperate condition one brought him his gown to protect him from the cold, in return for some beads and toys which Smith had given him on his first arrival in Virginia. . . .

The king's brother invited him to his house, whereto he bade him welcome, and as many platters of bread, fowl, and wild beasts as surrounded him. Not any of the Indians would eat with him, but would put away all that remained in baskets. On his return all the king's women and their children flocked about him for their part of the food, as it was a custom to be merry with such fragments. . . . [Smith returned to Jamestown.]

Now every once in four or five days, Pocahontas, with her attendants, brought Captain Smith enough provisions to save many of their lives.

Thus from numb death our good God sent relief,
The sweet assuager of all other grief.

Captain Smith's narrative of the plenty he had seen, and of the state and bounty of Powhatan (which till that time was unknown), so revived their dead spirits (especially the story of the love of Pocahontas), that all fear was abandoned. Thus you may see what difficulties still hindered any good endeavor, yet you see by what strange means God hath still delivered it. . . .

Men, women, and children have their several names according to the humor of their parents. The women, they say, love their children very dearly. To make them hardy, they wash them in the rivers in the coldest mornings, and by painting and ointments so tan their skins, that after a year or two no weather will hurt them. The men pass their time in fishing, hunting, wars, and such manlike exercises, scorning to be seen doing any womanlike work. The women and children do all the work. They make mats, baskets, pots, mortars; pound their corn, make their bread, prepare their victuals, plant and gather their corn, and bear all kinds of burdens.

They readily kindle their fire by rubbing a dry pointed stick, in a hole made in a little square piece of wood, which taking fire will kindle moss, leaves, or any dry thing that will quickly burn. In March and April they live much upon their fishing weirs; and feed on fish, turkeys, and squirrels. In May and June they plant their fields, and live mostly on acorns, walnuts, and fish. But to change their diet, some scatter in small companies, and live upon fish, beasts, crabs, oysters, land tortoises, strawberries, and mulberries. In June, July, and August, they feed upon roots, berries, fish, and green wheat. It is strange to see how their bodies change with their diet (even as the deer and wild beasts), for with the different seasons they seem fat and lean, strong and weak. Powhatan, their great king, and some others that are provident, roast their flesh and fish, and keep it till time of need.

For fishing, hunting, and wars they use their bows and arrows. They bring their bows to the form of ours by scraping with a shell. Their arrows are made, some of straight young sprigs, which they head with bone two or three inches long. These they use to shoot at squirrels on trees. Another sort of arrow is made of reeds. These are pierced with wood headed with splinters of crystal or some sharp stone, the spurs of a turkey, or the bill of some bird. For a knife they use the splinter of a reed to cut their feathers in form. With this knife they will joint a deer or any beast, shape their shoes, buskins, and mantles. To make the notch of their arrows they have the tooth of a boar set in a stick. The arrow-head they quickly make with a little bone, or with any splint of a stone, or glass in the form of a heart. With the sinews of deer and the tops of deers' horns boiled to a jelly they make a glue that will not dissolve in cold water, and with this they glue the head to the end of their arrows.

For their wars they use targets that are round and made of the bark of trees, and wear a sword of wood at their backs, but oftentimes they use the horns of a deer, put through a piece of wood in the form of a pickaxe for swords. Some have a long stone sharpened at both ends and used in the same manner. This they were wont to use for hatchets also, but now by trading they have plenty of iron. Such are their chief instruments and arms. They fish much in boats, which they make of one tree by burning and scratching away the coals with stones and shells till they have made it in the form of a trough. Some of them are an ell[1] deep, forty or fifty feet in length, and will bear forty men. But the most ordinary are smaller, and will bear ten, twenty, or thirty men. Instead of oars they use paddles and sticks, with which they will row faster than we can our barges.

Betwixt their hands and thighs their women spin the bark of trees, deer sinews, or a kind of grass, into thread, which they make very even. This thread serves for many uses about their houses and apparel. They also make nets and lines of it for fishing. Their hooks are either of bone, in the form of a crooked pin or fish-hook, or of the splinter of a bone tied to a little stick. At the end of the line they tie on the bait.

They use also long arrows tied to a line wherewith they shoot at fish in the rivers, but they of Accawmack use staves like javelins headed with bone. With these they dart fish swimming in the water. They have also many artificial weirs in which they get abundance of fish. In their hunting and fishing they take the greatest pains; and as it is their ordinary exercise from infancy, they esteem it a pleasure, and are very proud to be expert in it. By their continual ranging and travel they know all the advantages and places most frequented with deer, beasts, fish, fowl, roots, and berries. In their hunts they leave their habitations, and forming themselves into companies, go with their families to the most desert places, where they spend their time in hunting and fowling up the mountains, or by the heads of the rivers, where there is plenty of game. For betwixt the rivers the ground is so narrow, that little game comes there which they do not devour. It is a marvel that they can so accurately pass three or four days' journey through these deserts without habitation. Their hunting houses are like unto arbors covered with mats.

The women follow after them, with corn, acorns, mortars, and all the baggage they use. When they come to the place of exercise, every man does his best to show his dexterity, for by excelling in those qualities they get their wives. They will shoot forty yards level, or very near the mark, and one hundred and twenty yards is their best at random. In their hunts in the desert they commonly go two or three hundred together. Having found the deer, they surround them with many fires, and betwixt the fires they place themselves. Some take their stand in the midst. They chase the deer, thus frightened by the fires and the voices, so long within the circle that they often kill six, eight, ten, or fifteen at a hunting. They also drive them onto some narrow point of land and force them into the river, where with their boats they have ambuscades to kill them. When they have shot a deer by land, they track it like bloodhounds by the blood, and so overtake it. Hares, partridges, turkeys, fat or lean, young or old, they devour all they can catch.

Note

1. A unit of measure equal to about 45 inches.

Source: Thomas Studley, "Proceedings of the English Colony in Virginia," in *History of the Settlement of Virginia* (New York: Effingham Maynard, 1890). 26–30, 34–36. Originally published in John Smith, *The Generall Historie of Virginia* (1624).

1621 • 4 • Edward Winslow, "Letter Sent from New-England to a Friend"

Introduction: *English colonists arrived in Plimouth Plantation, Massachusetts, in 1620. One of the colonists, Edward Winslow (1595–1655), wrote a letter home in December 1621 that was published the following year in England in a book titled*

Mourt's Relation. *The letter describes the early life at Plimouth Plantation and also describes a feast with the American Indians. In 1841 Alexander Young (1800–1854), a Unitarian minister in Boston, republished Winslow's letter in his compilation of early records,* Chronicles of the Pilgrim Fathers of the Colony of Plymouth, from 1602–1625. *Young added a footnote to Winslow's description of the 1621 event, claiming that this "was the first thanksgiving, the harvest festival of New England. On this occasion they no doubt feasted on the wild turkey as well as venison." The footnote was picked up by other New England writers, who embellished it and presented it as fact. During the 1870s, the First Thanksgiving myth became enshrined in school textbooks.*

A Letter Sent from New England to a friend in these parts, setting forth a brief and true Declaration of the worth of that Plantation; As also certain useful Directions for such as intend a VOYAGE into those Parts.

Loving, and old Friend,

Although I received no letter from you by this ship, yet forasmuch as I know you expect the performance of my promise, which was, to write unto you truly and faithfully of all things, I have therefore at this time sent unto you accordingly. Referring you for further satisfaction to our more large relations.

You shall understand, that in this little time, that a few of us have been here, we have built seven dwelling-houses, and four for the use of the plantation, and have made preparation for divers others. We set the last spring some twenty acres of Indian corn, and sowed some six acres of barley and peas, and according to the manner of the Indians, we manured our ground with herrings or rather shads, which we have in great abundance, and take with great ease at our doors. Our corn did prove well, and God be praised, we had a good increase of Indian corn, and our barley indifferent good, but our peas not worth the gathering, for we feared they were too late sown, they came up very well, and blossomed, but the sun parched them in the blossom. Our harvest being gotten in, our governor sent four men on fowling, that so we might after have a special manner rejoice together after we had gathered the fruit of our labors; they four in one day killed as much fowl, as with a little help beside, served the company almost a week, at which time amongst other recreations, we exercised our arms, many of the Indians coming amongst us, and among the rest their greatest King Massasoit, with some ninety men, whom for three days we entertained and feasted, and they went out and killed five deer, which they brought to the plantation and bestowed on our governor, and upon the captain, and others. And although it be not always so plentiful as it was at this time with us, yet by the goodness of God, we are so far from want that we often wish you partakers of our plenty.

We have found the Indians very faithful in their covenant of peace with us; very loving and ready to pleasure us; we often go to them, and they come to us; some of us have been fifty miles by land in the country with them, the occasions and relations whereof you shall understand by our general and more full declaration of such things as are worth the noting, yea, it has pleased God so to possess the Indians with a fear of us, and love unto us, that not only the greatest king amongst them, called Massasoit, but also all the princes and peoples round about us, have either made suit unto us, or been glad of any occasion to make peace with us, so that seven of them at once have sent their messengers to us to that end. Yea, an Isle at sea, which we never saw, hath also, together with the former, yielded willingly to be under the protection, and subjects to our sovereign lord King James, so that there is now great peace amongst the Indians themselves, which was not formerly, neither would have been but for us; and we for our parts walk as peaceably and safely in the wood as in the highways in England. We entertain them familiarly in our houses, and they as friendly bestowing their venison on us. They are a people without any religion or knowledge of God, yet very trusty, quick of apprehension, ripe-witted, just. The men and women go naked, only a skin about their middles.

Edward Winslow, one of the leading colonists at Plimoth Plantation, wrote the letter describing what would be identified in 1842 as "the first Thanksgiving." (Cirker, Hayward and Blanche Cirker, eds. *Dictionary of American Portraits,* 1967)

For the temper of the air, here it agreeth well with that in England, and if there be any difference at all, this is somewhat hotter in summer, some think it to be colder in winter, but I cannot out of experience so say; the air is very clear and not foggy, as hath been reported. I never in my life remember a more seasonable year than we have here enjoyed; and if we have once but kine, horses, and sheep, I make no question but men might live as contented here as in any part of the world. For fish and fowl, we have great abundance; fresh cod in the summer is but coarse meat with us; our bay is full of lobsters all the summer and affordeth variety of other fish; in September we can take a hogshead of eels in a night, with small labor, and can dig them out of their beds all the winter; we have mussels and othus[1] at our doors: oysters we have none near, but we can have them brought by the Indians when we will; all the spring-time the earth sendeth forth naturally very good sallet herbs: here are grapes, white and red, and very sweet and strong also. Strawberries, gooseberries, raspas, etc. Plums of three sorts, with black and red, being almost as good as a damson: abundance of roses, white, red, and damask; single, but very sweet indeed. The country wanteth only industrious men to employ, for it would grieve your hearts (if as I) you had seen so many miles together by goodly rivers uninhabited, and withal, to consider those parts of the world wherein you live to be even greatly burdened with abundance of people. These things I thought good to let you understand, being the truth of things as near as I could experimentally take knowledge of, and that you might on our behalf give God thanks who hath dealt so favorably with us.

Our supply of men from you came the ninth of November 1621, putting in at Cape Cod, some eight or ten leagues from us. The Indians that dwell thereabout were they who were owners of the corn which we found in caves, for which we have given them full content, and are in great league with them. They sent us word that there was a ship near unto them, but thought it to be a Frenchman, and indeed for ourselves, we expected not a friend so soon. But when we perceived that she made for our bay, the governor commanded a great piece to be shot off, to call home such as were abroad at work; whereupon every man, yea, boy that could handle a gun, were ready, with full resolution that if she were an enemy, we would stand in our just defense, not fearing them, but God provided better for us than we supposed; these came all in health, not any being sick by the way (otherwise than sea sickness) and so continue at this time, by the blessing of God; the good-wife Ford was delivered of a son the first night she landed, and both of them are very well.

When it pleaseth God, we are settled and fitted for the fishing business, and other trading; I doubt not but by the blessing of God the gain will give content to all; in the mean time, that we have gotten we have sent by this ship, and though it be not much, yet it will witness for us that we have not been idle, considering the smallness of our number all this summer. We hope the merchants will accept of it, and be encouraged to furnish us with things needful for further employment, which will also encourage us to put forth ourselves to the uttermost.

Now because I expect your coming unto us with other of our friends, whose company we much desire, I thought good to advertise you of a few things needful; be careful to have a very good bread-room to put your biscuits in, let your cask for beer and water be iron-bound for the first tire if not more; let not your meat be dry-salted, none can better do it than the sailors; let your meal be so hard trod in your cask that you shall need an adz or hatchet to work it out with: trust not too much on us for corn at this time, for by reason of this last company that came, depending wholly upon us, we shall have little enough till harvest; be careful to come by some of your meal to spend by the way, it will much refresh you. Build your cabins as open as you can, and bring good store of clothes and bedding with you; bring every man a musket or fowling-piece, let your piece be long in the barrel, and fear not the weight of it, for most of our shooting is from stands; bring juice of lemons, and take it fasting; it is of good use; for hot waters, aniseed water is the best, but use it sparingly; if you bring any thing for comfort in the country, butter or sallet oil, or both is very good; our Indian corn, even the coarsest, maketh pleasant meat as rice, therefore spare that unless to spend by the way; bring paper and linseed oil for your windows, with cotton yarn for your lamps; let your shot be most for big fowls, and bring store of powder and shot: I forbear further to write for the present, hoping to see you by the next return, so I take my leave, commending you to the Lord for a safe conduct unto us. Resting in Him,

Your loving friend,
E. W. [Edward Winslow]
Plymouth in New England this 11th of December, 1621.

Note

1. Most likely a misprint in the original; probably means "others."

Source: Edward Winslow, "Letter Sent from New-England to a Friend," in *A Relation or Iournall of the Beginning and Proceeding of the English Plantation Setled at Plimoth in New England* (London: Iohn Bellamie, 1622), 60–65.

1630 • 5 • "Francis Higginson's New-England's Plantations"

Introduction: *Francis Higginson (1588–1630) was a Puritan minister who left England along with 350 other Puritans in February 1629. They arrived in Salem, Massachusetts, where they settled. He wrote down this description in the following months. His glowing report, which he sent to England for publication, was intended to draw other Puritans to the colony. Higginson caught a fever and died in 1630.*

The fertility of the soil is to be admired at, as appeareth in the abundance of grass that groweth everywhere, both very thick, very long, and very high in divers places. But it groweth very wildly, with a great stalk, and a broad and ranker blade, because it never had been eaten with cattle, nor mowed with a scythe, and seldom trampled on by foot. It is scarce to be believed how our kine and goats, horses and hogs do thrive and prosper here, and like well of this country.

In our Plantation we have already a quart of milk for a penny. But the abundant increase of corn proves this country to be a wonderment. Thirty, forty, fifty, sixty, are ordinary here. Yea, Joseph's increase in Egypt is outstripped here with us. Our planters hope to have more than a hundredfold this year. And all this while I am within compass; what will you say of two hundred fold, and upwards? It is almost incredible what great gain some of our English planters have had by our Indian corn. Credible persons have assured me, and the party himself avouched the truth of it to me, that of the setting of thirteen gallons of corn he hath had increase of it fifty-two hogsheads, every hogshead holding seven bushels of London measure, and every bushel was by him sold and trusted to the Indians for so much beaver as was worth eighteen shillings; and so of this thirteen gallons of corn, which was worth six shillings eight pence, he made about £327 of it the year following, as by reckoning will appear; where you may see now God blesseth husbandry in this land. There is not such great and plentiful ears of corn I suppose any where else to be found but in this country, being also of variety of colors, as red, blue, and yellow, &c.; and of one corn there springeth four or five hundred. I have sent you many ears of divers colors, that you might see the truth of it.

Little children here, by setting of corn, may earn much more than their own maintenance.

They have tried our English corn at New Plymouth Plantation, so that all our several grains will grow here very well, and have a fitting soil for their nature.

Our Governor hath store of green pease growing in his garden as good as ever I eat in England.

This country aboundeth naturally with store of roots of great variety and good to eat. Our turnips, parsnips and carrots are here both bigger and sweeter than is ordinarily to be found in England. Here are also store of pumpions, cowcumbers,[1] and other things of that nature which I know not. Also, divers excellent pot-herbs grow abundantly among the grass, as strawberry leaves in all places of the country, and plenty of strawberries in their time, and penny-royal, winter-savory, sorrel, brooklime,[2] liverwort,[3] carvel, and watercresses;[4] also leeks and onions are ordinary, and divers physical herbs. Excellent vines are here up and down in the woods. Our Governor hath already planted a vineyard, with great hope of increase.

Also, mulberries, plums, raspberries, currants, chestnuts, filberts, walnuts, small-nuts, hurtleberries,[5] and haws of white-thorn,[6] near as good as our cherries in England, they grow in plenty here. . . .

The abundance of sea-fish are almost beyond believing; and sure I should scarce have believed it except I had seen it with mine own eyes. I saw great store of whales, and grampuses, and such abundance of mackerels that it would astonish one to behold; likewise codfish, abundance on the coast, and in their season are plentifully taken. There is a fish called a bass, a most sweet and wholesome fish as ever I did eat; it is altogether as good as our fresh salmon; and the season of their coming was begun when we came first to New-England in June, and so continued about three months' space. Of this fish our fishers take many hundreds together, which I have seen lying on the shore, to my admiration. Yea, their nets ordinarily take more than they are able to haul to land, and for want of boats and men they are constrained to let a many go after they have taken them; and yet sometimes they fill two boats at a time with them. And besides bass, we take plenty of scate and thornback, and abundance of lobsters, and the least boy in the Plantation may both catch and eat what he will of them. For my own part, I was soon cloyed with them, they were to so great, and fat, and luscious. I have seen some myself that have weighed sixteen pound; but others have had divers times so great lobsters as have weighed twenty-five pound, as they assured me.

Also, here is abundance of herring, turbot, sturgeon, cusks, haddocks, mullets, eels, crabs, muscles, and oysters. Besides, there is probability that the country is of an excellent temper for the making of salt; for, since our coming, our fishermen have brought home very good salt which they found candied by the standing of the sea-water and the heat of the sun upon a rock by the seashore; and in divers salt marshes that some have gone through, they have found some salt in some places crushing under their feet, and cleaving to their shoes.

Fowls of the air are plentiful here, and of all sorts as we have in England, as far as I can learn, and a great many of strange fowls which we know not. Whilst I was writing these things, one of our men brought home an eagle which he had killed in the wood; they say they are good meat. Also here are many kinds of excellent hawks, both sea hawks and land hawks; and myself walking in the woods with another in company, sprung a partridge so big that through the heaviness of his body could fly but a little way; they that have killed them say they are as big as our hens. Here are likewise abundance of Sept' turkeys often killed in the woods, far greater than our English turkeys, and exceeding fat, sweet, and fleshy; for here they have abundance of feeding all the year long, as strawberries (in summer all places are full of them) and all manner of berries and fruits. In the winter time I have seen flocks of pigeons, and have eaten of them. They do fly from tree to tree, as other birds do, which our pigeons will not do in England. They are of all colors, as ours are, but their wings and tails are far longer; and therefore it is likely they fly swifter to escape the terrible hawks in this country. In winter time this country doth abound with wild geese, wild ducks, and other sea-fowl, that a great part of winter the planters have eaten nothing but roast meat of divers fowls which they have killed.

Notes

1. "Cowcumbers" refers to cucumbers, an Old World plant, but which plant this refers to in America is unclear.
2. *Veronica beccabunga.*
3. A type of *Marchantiophyta* that was thought to cure liver diseases.

4. Probably *Cardamine rotundifolia* or *Cardamine micranthera.*
5. Huckleberries, members of *Vaccinium* and *Gaylussacia* genera.
6. Hawthorn, a member of the *Crataegus* genera, with small berrylike fruit.

Source: "Francis Higginson's New-England's Plantations," in *Chronicles of the First Planters of the Colony of Massachusetts from 1623 to 1636,* edited by Alexander Young (Boston: Little, Brown, 1844), 245–258.

1665 • 6 • Van Der Donck, Description of New Netherland

Introduction: *The Dutch settled Manhattan beginning in 1624. Adriaen van der Donck (1618–1655) arrived in 1641. While in America, he explored the surrounding areas and kept a faithful record of his observations. He returned to the Netherlands in 1647 and published his observations of New Netherland in 1650. His motives for his writing were in part to encourage others to move to North America. His book* Be-schryvinge van Nieuw-Nederlant (Description of New Netherland) *was published in 1655. New Netherland was captured by the British in 1664 in the lead-up to the Second Anglo-Dutch War (1865–1867) when the British sent four warships into the harbor. New Amsterdam surrendered before a single shot was fired, and the city was renamed New York, in honor of James Stuart, Duke of York, the future King James II.*

Of the Food and Subsistence of the Indians.

In eating and drinking the Indians are not excessive, even in their feast-days. They are cheerful and well satisfied when they have a sufficiency to support nature, and to satisfy hunger and thirst. It is not with them as it is here in Holland, where the greatest, noblest, and richest live more luxuriously than a *Calis,* or a common man; but with them meat and drink are sufficient and the same for all. Their common drink is water from a living spring or well, when it can be had, wherein they seldom fail, as in days of old. Sometimes in the season of grapes, and when they have fresh meat or fish, and are well pleased, they will press out the juice of the grapes and drink it new. They never make wine or beer. Brandy or strong drink is unknown to them, except to those who frequent our settlements, and have learned that beer and wine taste better than water.

In the Indian languages, which are rich and expressive, they have no word to express drunkenness. Drunken men they call fools. When they associate much with our people, and can obtain liquor, they will drink to excess, when they become insolent and troublesome, and are malicious. To prevent this, the government has forbidden the sale of spirituous liquors to the Indians. Most of them however will not taste liquor. Before they are accustomed to spirituous liquor, they are easily made drunk, for which a small glass or two is sufficient; but in time they become accustomed to it, and bear it as well as our own people do. The rheumatic gout, red and pimpled noses, are snares unknown to them; nor have they any diseases or infirmities which are caused by drunkenness.

Their common food is meat, and fish of every kind, according to the seasons, and the advantages of the places where they reside. They have no pride, or particular methods in preparing their food. Their fish or meat they usually boil in water, without salt, or smout[1] and nothing more than the articles yield. They know of no stewing, fricasseeing, baking, frying, or the like methods of cooking, and seldom do they warm up or boil any food, unless it be small pieces of meat or fish, when they travel or are hunting, and have no other opportunity to prepare their food.

For bread they use maize, or Turkey corn, which the women pound fine into meal, (as the Hebrews did their manna in the wilderness,) of which they bake cakes, for they know nothing of mills. They also use pounded maize, as we do rice, and samp,[2] with their boiled meat. Their common food, and for which their meal is generally used, is pap, or mush, which in the New-Netherlands is named sapaen.[3] This is so common among the Indians, that they seldom pass a day without it, unless they are on a journey or hunting. We seldom visit an Indian lodge at any time of the day, without seeing their sapaen preparing, or seeing them eating the same. It is the common food of all; young and old eat it; and they are so well accustomed to it, and fond of it, that when they visit our people, or each other, they consider themselves neglected unless they are treated with sapaen. Without sapaen they do not eat a satisfactory meal. And when they have an opportunity, they frequently boil fish or meat with it; but seldom when the meat or fish is fresh, but when they have the articles dried hard, and pounded fine. This food they usually prepare at the close of the winter and in the spring, when the hunting season is past, and their stock of provisions is nearly exhausted. They also use many dry beans, which they consider dainties. Those they boil soft with fresh meat. They use for their subsistence every kind of fish and flesh that is fit for food, which the country and the places of their settlements afford, and that they can obtain. They observe no stated times for their meals, as our people do, but they suppose it best to eat when they are hungry. They can control their appetites, bodies and stomachs in a wonderful manner; for with very little or no food, they can pass two, three, or four days, and when afterwards they again have it plenty, they will make up for the arrears lost without overcharging their stomachs, or becoming sick; and although they eat freely, they have no excessive caters or gluttons among them.

Ceremonies of high or low seats, or of beginning to eat their meals first or last, or to be waited upon, I have never seen among them. Seldom will they invite each other to eat with them, except at great feasts, but every person who is with them at meal time, without exception, can partake of their fare without pay or compensation. It is not customary with them to receive compensation for their hospitality. On extraordinary occasions, when they wish to entertain any person, then they prepare beavers' tails, bass heads, with parched corn meal, or very fat meat stewed with shelled chestnuts bruised.

When they intend to go a great distance on a hunting excursion, or to war, where they expect to find no food, then they provide themselves severally with a small bag of parched corn meal, which is so nutritious that they can subsist on the same many days. A quarter of a pound of the meal is sufficient for a day's subsistence; for as it shrinks much in the drying, it also swells out again with moisture. When they are hungry, they eat a small handful of the meal, after which they take a drink of water, and then they are so well fed, that they can travel a day. When they can obtain fish or meat to eat, then their meal serves them as well as fine bread would, because it needs no baking. . . .

Of their Sustenance and Medicines.

Famine they do not fear, nor do they regard medicines and purgatives much. When they are unwell, they fast; if that will not remove the complaint, they then have recourse to sweating and drinks; but the latter they take very sparingly. Their sweating places are made of clay, and enclosed tight in the earth, with a small entrance to admit the patients within the apartments. Where the place is needed there many stones are heated, and placed around and within the same; and then the patient enters and sits down, naked and singing, wherein he remains as long as it is possible to endure the heat, and on leaving the stewing apartment, they usually lay down in cold spring water. By those means they say that they gain relief, and cure most diseases. They can heal fresh wounds and dangerous bruises in a most wonderful manner. They also have remedies for old sores and ulcers, and they also cure venereal affections so readily, that many an Italian master who saw it, would be ashamed of his profession. All their cures are made with herbs, roots and leaves, (with the powers of which they are acquainted,) without making any compounds. Still it must be admitted that nature assists them greatly, for they indulge in no excesses of eating or drinking, otherwise they could not accomplish so much with such simple and small means. When any of them are very sick, and they apprehend the disease to be of a deadly character; then, they all, or at least the nearest relatives of the sick persons, have recourse to devil-hunting or driving, and make noise enough to frighten a person in extremity to death; which they say they do to learn from the devil whether the patient will live or die, and when hope of recovery is given, what remedies are to be used for the restoration of the sick. They seldom however receive any positive answers, but directions to use remedies, and when their hope for the recovery of the sick, then food is presented to the person, who is persuaded to eat heartily, whether the food is relished or not.

BESCHRYVINGE
Van
NIEUVV-NEDERLANT,
(Gelijck het tegenwoordigh in Staet is)
Begrijpende de Nature, Aert, gelegentheyt en vruchtbaerheyt van het selve Landt; mitsgaders de proffijtelijcke ende gewenste toevallen, die aldaer tot onderhoudt der Menschen, (soo uyt haer selven als van buyten ingebracht) gevonden worden. Als mede de maniere en ongemeyne Eygenschappen vande Wilden ofte Naturellen vanden Lande. Ende een bysonder verhael vanden wonderlijcken Aert ende het Weesen der BEVERS.
Daer noch by-gevoeght is
Een Discours over de gelegentheyt van Nieuw-Nederlandt, tusschen een Nederlandts Patriot, ende een Nieuw Nederlander.
Beschreven door
ADRIAEN vander DONCK,
Beyder Rechten Doctoor, die tegenwoordigh noch in Nieuw-Nederlandt is.
En hier achter by gevoeght
Het voordeeligh Reglement vande Ed: Hoog. Achtbare Heeren de Heeren Burgermeesteren deser Stede/ betreffende de saken van Nieuw Nederlandt.
Den tweeden Druck.
Met een pertinent Kaertje van 't zelve Landt verçiert, en van veel druck-fouten gesuyvert.

t'AEMSTELDAM,
By Evert Nieuwenhof, Boeck-verkooper / woonende op 't Ruslandt / in 't Schrijf-boeck / ANNO 1656.
Met Privilegie voor 15 Jaren.

Title page of Adriaen van der Donck's book *Be-schryvinge van Nieuw-Nederlant* (Description of New Netherland), 1656 edition.

Of their Agriculture, Planting, and Gardening.

All their agriculture is performed by their women. The men give themselves very little trouble about the same, except those who were old. They, with the young children will do some labor under the direction of the women. They cultivate no wheat, oats, barley or rye, and know nothing of ploughing, spading and splitting up the soil, and are not neat and cleanly in their fields. The grain which they raise for bread, and mush or sapaen, is maize or turkey-corn, and they raise various kinds of beans as before remarked. They also plant tobacco for their own use, which is not as-good as ours, and of a different kind, that does not require as much labour and attendance. Of garden vegetables, they raise none, except pumpkins and squashes, as before observed. They usually leave their fields and garden spots open, unenclosed, and unprotected by fencing, and take very little care of the same, though they raise an abundance of corn and beans, of which we obtain whole cargoes in sloops and galleys in trade.

Of manuring and proper tillage they know nothing. All their tillage is done by the hand and with small adzes, which they purchase from us. Although little can be said in favour of their husbandry, still they prefer their practice to ours, because our methods require too much labour and care to please them, with which they are not well satisfied.

A Relation of their H.unting and Fishing.

To hunting and fishing the Indians are all extravagantly inclined, and they have their particular seasons for these engagements. In the spring and part of the summer, they practise fishing. When the wild herbage begins to grow up in the woods, the first hunting season begins, and then many of their young men leave the fisheries for the purpose of hunting; but the old and thoughtful men remain at the fisheries until the second and principal hunting season, which they also attend, but with snares only. Their fishing is carried on in the inland waters, and by those who dwell near the sea, or the sea-islands. The latter have particular advantages. Their fishing is done with seines, set-nets, small fikes,[4] wears, and laying hooks. They do not know how to salt fish, or how to cure fish properly. They sometimes dry fish to preserve the same, but those are half tainted, which they pound to meal to be used in chowder in winter. Their young and active men are much engaged in hunting bears, wolves, fishers, otters, and beavers. Near the sea-shores and rivers where the Christians mostly reside, they hunt deer, where many are killed. Those are mostly caught in snares, they also shoot them with arrows and guns. The Indians sometimes unite in companies of from one to two hundred, when they have rare sport. On those occasions, they drive over a large district of land and kill much game. They also make extensive fikes with palisades, which are narrow at their terminating angles, wherein they drive multitudes of animals and take great numbers. At a word, they are expert hunters for every kind of game, and know to practise the best methods to insure success. The beavers are mostly taken far inland, there being few of them near the settlements—particularly by the black Minquas, who are thus named because they wear a black badge on their breast, and not because they are really black, by the Senecas, by the Maquas, and by the Rondaxes or French Indians, who are also called Euyrons (Hurons). For beaver hunting the Indians go in large parties, and remain out from one to two months, during which time they subsist by hunting and on a little corn meal which they carry out with them, and they frequently return home with from forty to eighty beaver skins, and with some otter, fishers and other skins also, even more than can be correctly stated. We estimate that eighty thousand beavers are annually killed in this quarter of the country, besides elks, bears, otters, deer and other animals. There are some persons who imagine that the animals of the country will be destroyed in time, but this is unnecessary anxiety. It has already continued many years, and the numbers brought in do not diminish. The country is full of lakes, seas, rivers, streams and creeks, and extends very far, even to the great south sea; hence we infer, that there will not be an end to the wild animals, and also because there are large districts where the animals will remain unmolested.

Of the Agricultural Productions.

The pursuit of agriculture is not heavy and expensive there, as it is in the Netherlands. First, because the fencing and enclosing of the land does not cost much; for instead of the Netherlands dykes and ditches, they set up post and rail, or palisado fences,[5] and when new clearings are made, they commonly have fencing timber enough on the land to remove, which costs nothing but the labour, which is reasonably cheap to those who have their own hands, and without domestic labour very little can be effected. The land whereon there are few standing trees, and which has been grubbed and ploughed twice, we hold to be prepared for a crop of winter grain. For summer grain one ploughing is sufficient. If it is intended to sow the same field again with winter grain, then the stubble is ploughed in, and the land is sowed with wheat or rye, which in ordinary seasons will yield a fine crop.

I can affirm that during my residence of nine years in the country, I have never seen land manured, and it is seldom done. The land is kept in order by tillage, which is often done to keep down weeds and brush, but for which it would have rest. Some persons, (which I also hold to be good management,) when their land becomes foul and weedy, break it up and sow the same with peas, because a crop of peas softens the land and makes it clean; but most of the land is too rich for peas, which when sown on the same grow so rank that the crop falls and rots on the land. Some of the land must be reduced by cropping it with wheat and barley, before it is proper to sow the same with peas. We have frequently seen the straw of wheat and barley grow so luxuriant that the crops yielded very little grain.

I deem it worthy of notice, that with proper attention, in ordinary seasons, two ripe crops of peas can be raised on the same land in one season, in the New-Netherlands. It has frequently been done in the following manner, viz. The first crop was sown in the last of March or first of April, which will ripen about the first of July; the crop is then removed, and the land ploughed, and sowed again with peas of the first crop. The second crop will ripen in September, or about the first of October, when the weather is still, fine and warm. The same can also be done with buckwheat, which has frequently been proved; but the first crop is usually much injured by finches and other birds, and as wheat and rye are plenty, therefore there is very little buckwheat sown. The maize (Indian corn) is carefully attended to, and is sufficient to the wants of the country.

The Turkey wheat, or maize, as the grain is named, many persons suppose to be the same kind of grain which Jesse sent parched by his son David to his other sons of the army of Israel. This is a hardy grain, and is fit for the sustenance of man and animals. It is easily cultivated, and will grow in almost every kind of land, in the worst and strongest in the country, even in a foul and worn-out soil. It is a good crop to subdue new land, and to prepare it for other purposes. When the timber has been removed, and the brush burnt up, then we take a broad hoe, and cut out hills about six feet apart, and plant five or six grains in a hill, with which some persons also plant Turkey beans (as before noticed). After the grain shoots up and grows, it requires two dressings. The weeding and cleaning is done with a broad adze, without breaking up the ground, and is not very laborious work. The weeds and trash in the first dressing, are cut off and placed in a row between the hills. The second dressing is easier. Then the weeds and sprouts are cut off around the hills, and the weeds and rubbish of the first cleaning, are drawn round the corn-hills, which afterwards grow high and tall, and smother all the weeds, stumps, and trash, and kill all other vegetation except pumpkins; those will grow among the maize.

When the land has been treated as above described for one summer, it is fit for any other use; or it may be planted with maize again, which will then grow better than in the first year, and be easier kept clean, and with less labour. Tobacco may be planted on the land, or it may be ploughed and broken up for other purposes, which can then be easily done, because the roots are in a state of decay and easily broken up. After a corn crop is gathered, the land may be sowed with winter grain in the fall without previous ploughing. When this is intended, the corn is gathered, the stalks are pulled up and burnt, the hills levelled, and the land sown and harrowed smooth and level. Good crops are raised in this manner. I have seen rye sown as before described, which grew so tall that a man of common size would bind the ears together above his head, which yielded seven and eight schepels.[6]

The Rev. Johannis Megapolensis, Junior, minister of the colony of Rensselaorwyck, in certain letters which he has written to his friends, which were printed (as he has told me) without his consent, but may be fully credited, he being a man of truth and of great learning, who writes in a vigorous style,—states, with other matters, that a certain farmer had cropped one field with wheat eleven years in succession, which to many persons will seem extraordinary, and may not be credited. Still it is true, and the residents of the place testify to the same, and they add, that this same land was ploughed but twelve times in the eleven seasons—twice in the first year, and once in every succeeding year, when the stubble was ploughed in, the wheat sown and harrowed under. I owned land adjoining the land referred to, and have seen the eleventh crop, which was tolerably good. The man who did this is named Brandt Pelen; he was born in the district of Utrecht, and at the time was a magistrate (schepen) of the colony of Rensselaerwyck. We acknowledge that this relation appears to be marvellous, but in the country it is not so, for there are many thousand morgens[7] of as good land there, as the land of which we have spoken.

During the period when I resided in the New Netherlands, a certain honorable gentleman, named John Everts Bout, (who was recommended to the colonists by their High Mightinesses, &c.) laid a wager that he could raise a crop of barley on a field containing seven morgens of land, which would grow so tall in every part of the field, that the ears could easily be tied together above his head. I went to see the field of barley, and found that the straw, land by land, was from six to seven feet high, and very little of it any shorter. It has also been stated to me as a fact, that barley has frequently been raised, although not common, which yielded eleven schepel, Amsterdam measure, per vin of 103 sheaves.[8] Therefore, all persons who are acquainted with the New-Netherlands, judge the country to be as well adapted for the cultivation of grain, as any part of the world which is known to the Netherlanders, or is in their possession.

With the other productions of the land we must include tobacco, which is also cultivated in the country, and is, as well as the maize, well adapted to prepare the land for other agricultural purposes, which also, with proper attention, grows fine, and yields more profit. Not only myself but hundreds of others, have raised tobacco, the leaves of which were three-fourths of a yard long. The tobacco raised here is of different kind, but principally of the Virginia kind, from which it differs little in flavour, although the Virginia is the best. Still it does not differ so much in quality as in price. Next to the Virginia it will be the best; many persons esteem it better, and give it a preference. It is even probable, that when the people extend the cultivation of the article, and more tobacco is planted, that it will gain more reputation and esteem. Many persons are of opinion that the defect in flavour arises from the newness of the land, and hasty cultivation, which will gradually be removed.

Barley grows well in the country, but it is not much needed. Cummin seed, canary seed, and the like, have been tried, and Commander Minuit testifies that those articles succeed well, but are not sought after. Flax and hemp will grow fine, but as the women do not spin much, and the Indians have hemp in abundance in the woods from which they make strong ropes and nets, for these reasons very little flax is raised; but the persons who do sow the seed, find that the land is of the proper quality for such articles.

Notes

1. A type of oil.
2. Hulled corn made from yellow corn softened with water.
3. A mush made from pounded dried corn.
4. Spikes.
5. Wall typically made with wood or tree trunks.
6. One schepel equals about two grain scoops or three pecks.
7. An imprecise measure of land that could equal about an acre.
8. Units of measure.

Source: Jeremiah Johnson, trans., "Van der Donck's Description of the New Netherlands," *Collections of the New York Historical Society*, 2nd Series, Vol. 1 (New York: Printed for the Society, 1841), 157–160, 192–194, 207–210.

1672 • 7 • JOHN JOSSELYN, *NEW-ENGLAND RARITIES DISCOVERED*

Introduction: *John Josselyn (fl. 1638–1675) was an English explorer who traveled and lived in New England. His descriptions of the flora and fauna are considered some of the best for the colonial period. Below are excerpts about four food items: wild turkeys, which were highly valued in all the European colonies in eastern North America; watermelons (Citrullus lanatus), which originated in Africa and were introduced into North America by European colonists; sarsaparilla (Smilax regelii), which was consumed as a tea and was used with sassafras in making root beer; and corn (Zea mays), the single most important domesticated food in the Americas.*

The *Turkie,* who is blacker than ours; I have heard several credible persons affirm, they have seen *Turkie Cocks* that have weighed forty, yea sixty pounds; but out of my personal experimental knowledge I can assure you, that I have eaten my share of a *Turkie Cock,* that when he was pull'd and garbidg'd, weighed thirty pound, and I have also seen threescore broods of young *Turkies* on the side of a Marsh, sunning of themselves in a morning betimes, but this was thirty years since, the *English* and the *Indian* having now destroyed the breed, so that 'tis very rare to meet with a wild *Turkie* in the Woods;

but some of the *English* bring up great share of the wild kind, which remain about their Houses as tame as ours in *England.*

Squashes, but more truly *Squontersquashes,* a kind os Mellon, or rather Gourd, for they oftentimes degenerate into Gourds; some of these are green, some yellow, some longish like a Gourd, others round like an Apple, all of them pleasant food boyled and buttered, and season'd with Spice; but the yellow Squash called an Apple Squash, because like an Apple, and about the bigness of a Pome-water is the best kind; they are much eaten by the Indians and the English, yet they breed the small white Worms (which Physitians call Ascarides,) in the long Gut that vex the Fundament with a perpetual itching, and a desire to go to stool.

Water-Mellon, it is a large Fruit, but nothing near so big as a Pompion, colour, smoother, and of a sad Grass green rounder or more rightly Sap-green; with some yellowness admixt when ripe; the feeds are black, the flesh or pulpe exceeding juicy.

Sarsaparilia, a Plant not yet sufficiently known by the English: Some say it is a kind of Bind Weed; we have, in New-England two Plants, that go under the name of Sarsaparilia: the one not above a foot in height without Thorns, the other having the same Leaf, but is a shrub as high as a Goose Berry Bush, and full of sharp Thorns; this I esteem as the right, by the shape and savour of the Roots, but rather by the effects answerable to that we have from other parts of the World; It groweth upon dry Sandy banks by the Sea side, and upon the banks of Rivers, so far as the Salt water flowes; and within Land up in the Country, as some have reported.

Indian Wheat, of which there is three forts, yellow, red, and blew; the blew is commonly Ripe before the other a Month: Five or Six Grains of Indian Wheat hath produced in one year 600. It is hotter than our Wheat and clammy; excellent in Cataplasms to ripen any Swelling or impostume. The decoction of the blew Corn, is good to wash sore Mouths with: It is light of digestion, and the English make a kind of Loblolly of it to eat with Milk, which they call Sampe; they beat it in a Morter, and fist the flower out of it: the remainder they call Homminey, which they put into a Pot of two or three Gallons, with Water, and boyl it upon a gentle Fire till it be like a Hasty Pudden; they put of this into Milk, and so eat it. Their Bread also they make of the Homminey so boiled, and mix their Flower with it, cast it into a deep Bason in which they form the Loaf, and then turn it out upon the Peel, and presently put it into the Oven before it spreads abroad; the Flower makes excellent Puddens.

Source: John Josselyn, *New-England Rarities Discovered* (London: G. Widdowes, 1672), 8–9, 101, 109, 112.

1704 • 8 • Leonard Welsted, "Of Apple-Pyes"

Introduction: *While many different ethnic and national groups settled North America, English settlers put down the deepest roots. Not only were English settlers most numerous, but many considered themselves forever English and maintained strong connections with Great Britain. One of the important contributions of English cookery* *was the apple pie. European colonists planted apple trees shortly after their arrival in America. As their orchards bore fruit, apples were consumed in a variety of ways, including in pies. Leonard Welsted (1688–1747) was an English writer who wrote this poem when he was 16 years old while in school. Although he never visited America, his poem was widely circulated. The phrase "As American as apple pie" did not become common until the 1930s.*

Of APPLE-PYES: *A poem, by Mr.* WELSTED.

OF all the delicates which *Britons* try,
To please the palate, or delight the eye;
Of all the several kinds of sumptuous fare,
There's none that can with apple-pye compare,
For costly flavour, or substantial paste,
For outward beauty, or for inward taste.

WHEN first this infant dish in fashion came,
Th' ingredients were but coarse, and rude the frame;
As yet, unpolish'd in the modern arts,
Our fathers eat brown bread instead of tarts:
Pyes were but indigested lumps of dough,
'Till time and just expence improv'd them so.

KING *Coll* (as ancient annals tell)
Renown'd for fiddling and for eating well,
Pippins in homely cakes with honey stew'd,
Just as he bak'd (the proverb says) he brew'd.

THEIR greater art succeeding princes shew'd,
And model'd paste into a nearer mode;
Invention now grew lively, palate nice,
And sugar pointed out the way to spice.

BUT here for ages unimprov'd we stood,
And apple-pyes were still but homely food;
When god-like *Edgar,* of the *Saxon* line,
Polite of taste, and studious to refine,
In the dessert perfuming quinces cast,
And perfected with cream the rich repast:
Hence we proceed the outward parts to trim,
with crinkumcranks adorn the polish'd rim,
And each fresh pye the pleas'd spectator greets
With virgin fancies and with new conceits.

DEAR *Nelly,* learn with care the pastry art,
And mind the easy precepts I impart;
Draw out your dough elaborately thin,
And cease not to fatigue your rolling-pin:
Of eggs and butter, see you mix enough;

For then the paste will swell into a puff,
Which will in crumbling sound your praise report,
And eat, as housewives speak, exceeding short:
Rang'd in thick order let your quincies lie;
They give a charming relish to the pye:
If you are wise, you'll not brown sugar slight,
The browner (if I form my judgment right)
A tincture of a bright vermil' will shed
And stain the pippin, like the quince, with red.

WHEN this is done, there will be wanting still
The just reserve of cloves, and candy'd peel;
Nor can I blame you, if a drop you take
Of orange water, for perfuming sake;
But here the nicety of art is such,
There must not be too little, nor too much;
If with discretion you these costs employ,
They quicken appetite, if not they cloy.

NEXT in your mind this maxim firmly root,
Never o'er-charge your pye with costly fruit:
Oft let your bodkin thro' the lid be sent,
To give the kind imprison'd treasure vent;
Lest the fermenting liquors, mounting high
Within their brittle bounds, disdain to lie;
Insensibly by constant fretting waste,
And over-run the tenement of paste.

TO chuse your baker, think and think again,
You'll scarce one honest baker find in ten:
Adust and bruis'd, I've often seen a pye
In rich disguise and costly ruin lie;
While the rent crust beheld its form o'erthrown,
Th' exhausted apples griev'd their moisture flown,
And syrup from their sides run trickling down.

O BE not, be not tempted, lovely *Nell,*
While the hot piping odours strongly swell,
While the delicious fume creates a gust,
To lick th' o'erflowing juice, or bite the crust:
You'll rather stay (if my advice may rule)
Until the hot is temper'd by the cool;
Oh! first infuse the luscious store of cream,
And change the purple to a silver stream;
That smooth balsamick viand first produce,
To give a softness to the tarter juice.

Source: Leonard Welsted, "Of APPLE-PYES: A Poem," in William Ellis, *Country Housewife's Family Companion* (London: James Hodges and B. Collins, bookseller, at Salisbury, 1730).

1705 • 9 • Robert Beverly, *History of Virginia*

Introduction: *Robert Beverly (1673–1722) was born in Jamestown, Virginia, and was a planter and historian. His work History of Virginia is one of the best histories of life in early Virginia. His account below looks at what and how American Indians ate.*

Of Their Cookery and Food

[American Indian] . . . cookery has nothing commendable in it, but that it is performed with little trouble. They have no other sauce but a good stomach, which they seldom want. They boil, broil, or toast all the meat they eat, and it is very common with them to boil fish as well as flesh with their homony; this is Indian corn soaked, broken in a mortar, husked, and then boiled in water over a gentle fire for ten or twelve hours, to the consistence of frumenty: the thin of this is what my Lord Bacon calls cream of maise, and highly commends for an excellent sort of nutriment.

They have two ways of broiling, viz., one by laying the meat itself upon the coals, the other by laying it upon sticks raised upon forks at some distance above the live coals, which heats more gently, and dries up the gravy; this they, and we also from them, call barbecueing.

They skin and paunch all sorts of quadrupeds; they draw and pluck their fowl; but their fish they dress with their scales on, without gutting; but in eating they leave the scales, entrails and bones to be thrown away. They also roast their fish upon a hot hearth, covering them with hot ashes and coals, then take them out, the scales and skin they strip clean off, so they eat the flesh, leaving the bones and entrails to be thrown away.

They never serve up different sorts of victuals in one dish; as roast and boiled fish and flesh; but always serve them up in several vessels.

They bake their bread either in cakes before the fire, or in loaves on a warm hearth, covering the loaf first with leaves, then with warm ashes, and afterwards with coals over all. . . .

15. Their food is fish and flesh of all sorts, and that which participates of both; as the beaver, a small kind of turtle, or terrapins, (as we call them,) and several species of snakes. They likewise eat grubs, the nymphae of wasps, some kinds of scarabaei, cicadae, &c. These last are such as are sold in the markets of Fess, and such as the Arabians, Lybians, Parthians and Ethiopians commonly eat; so that these are not a new diet, though a very slender one; and we are informed that St. John was dieted upon locusts and wild honey.

They make excellent broth of the head and umbles of a deer, which they put into the pot all bloody. This seems to resemble the jus nigrum of the Spartans, made with the blood and bowels of a hare. They eat not the brains with the head, but dry them and reserve them to dress their leather with.

They eat all sorts of peas, beans, and other pulse, both parched and boiled. They make their bread of the Indian corn, wild oats, or the seed of the sunflower. But when they eat their bread, they eat it alone, and not with their meat.

They have no salt among them, but for seasoning use the ashes of hickory, stickweed,[1] or some other wood or plant affording a salt ash.

They delight much to feed on roasting ears; that is, the Indian corn, gathered green and milky, before it is grown to its full bigness, and roasted before the fire in the ear. For the sake of this diet, which they love exceedingly, they are very careful to procure all the several sorts of Indian corn before mentioned, by which means they contrive to prolong their season. And indeed this is a very sweet and pleasing food.

They have growing near their towns, peaches, strawberries, cushaws, melons, pompions, macocks, &c. The cushaws and pompions they lay by, which will keep several months good after they are gathered; the peaches they save by drying them in the sun; they have likewise several sorts of the phaseoli.[2]

In the woods, they gather chinkapins,[3] chestnuts, hickories and walnuts. The kernels of the hickories they beat in a mortar with water, and make a white liquor like milk, from whence they call our milk hickory. Hazlenuts they will not meddle with, though they make a shift with acorns sometimes, and eat all the other fruits mentioned before, but they never eat any sort of herbs or leaves.

They make food of another fruit called cuttanimmons, the fruit of a kind of arum,[4] growing in the marshes: they are like boiled peas or capers to look on, but of an insipid earthy taste. Captain Smith in his History of Virginia calls them ocaughtanamnis, and Theod. de Bry in his translation, sacquenummener.

Out of the ground they dig trubs, earth nuts,[5] wild onions,[6] and a tuberous root they call tuckahoe,[7] which while crude is of a very hot and virulent quality: but they can manage it so, as in case of necessity, to make bread of it, just as the East Indians and those of Egypt are said to do of colocassia, or the West Indians of cassava. It grows like a flag in the miry marshes, having roots of the magnitude and taste of Irish potatoes, which are easy to be dug up.

16. They accustom themselves to no set meals, but eat night and day, when they have plenty of provisions, or if they have got any thing that is a rarity. They are very patient of hunger, when by any accident they happen to have nothing to eat; which they make more easy to themselves by girding up their bellies, just as the wild Arabs are said to do in their long marches; by which means they are less sensible of the impressions of hunger.

17. Among all this variety of food, nature hath not taught them the use of any other drink than water; which though they have in cool and pleasant springs every where, yet they will not drink that if they can get pond water, or such as has been warmed by the sun and weather. Baron Lahontan tells of a sweet juice of maple, which the Indians to the northward gave him, mingled with water; but our Indians use no such drink. For their strong drink they are altogether beholden to us, and are so greedy of it, that most of them will be drunk as often as they find an opportunity; notwithstanding which it is a prevailing humor among them, not to taste any strong drink at all, unless they can get enough to make them quite drunk, and then they go as solemnly about it as if it were part of their religion.

18. Their fashion of sitting at meals is on a mat spread on the ground, with their legs lying out at length before them, and the dish between their legs; for which reason they seldom or never sit more than two together at a dish, who may with convenience mix their legs together and have the dish stand commodiously to them both, as appears by the figure.

The spoons which they eat with do generally hold half a pint; and they laugh at the English for using small ones, which they must be forced to carry so often to their mouths that their arms are in danger of being tired before their belly.

Notes

1. Common ragweed (*Ambrosia artemisiifolia*).
2. Beans.
3. Acorns from a species of an oak tree.
4. A name given to plants of eastern North America belonging to the order Araceæ, such as the arrow-arum (*Peltandra virginica*), the dragon-arum (*Arisæma dracontium*), and the water-arum (*Calla palustris*).
5. Jerusalem artichoke (*Helianthus tuberosus*), a species of sunflower.
6. *Allium canadense.*
7. *Wolfiporia extensa,* a large underground fungus from which American Indians made bread.

Source: Robert Beverley, *The History of Virginia, in Four Parts . . . History and Present State of Virginia* (1705; reprint, Richmond, VA: J. W. Randolph, 1855), 138–141.

1714 • 10 • John Lawson, *The History of Carolina*

Introduction: *John Lawson (1674?–1711) was an English explorer. He arrived in Charleston in August 1700 and began a 1,000-mile exploration of the Carolinas on December 28, 1700. His description below is from South Carolina.*

As we row'd up the River we found the Land towards the Mouth, and for about sixteen Miles up it, scarce any Thing but Swamp and Percoarson, affording vast Ciprus-Trees, of which the *French* make Canoes, that will carry fifty or sixty Barrels. After the Tree is moulded and dug, they saw them in two Pieces, and so put a Plank between, and a small Keel, to preserve them from the Oyster-Banks, which are innumerable in the Creeks and Bays betwixt the *French* Settlement and *Charles*-Town. They carry two Masts, and Bermudas Sails, which makes them very handy and fit for their Purpose; for although their River fetches its first Rise from the Mountains, and continues a Current some hundreds of Miles ere it disgorges it self, having no sound Bay or Sand-Banks betwixt the Mouth thereof, and the Ocean. Notwithstanding all this, with the vast Stream it affords at all Seasons, and the repeated Freshes it so often allarms the Inhabitants with, by laying under Water great Part of their Country, yet the Mouth is barr'd affording not above four or five Foot Water at the Entrance. As we went up the River, we heard a great Noise, as if two Parties were engag'd against each other, seeming exactly like small Shot. When we approach'd nearer the Place, we found it to be some *Sewee Indians* firing the Cane Swamps, which drives out the Game, then taking their particular Stands, kill great Quantities of both Bear, Deer, Turkies, and what wild Creatures the Parts afford.

Tuesday Morning we set towards the *Congerees,* leaving the *Indian* Guide *Scipio* drunk amongst the *Santee-Indians.* We went ten Miles out of our Way, to head a great Swamp, the Freshes having fill'd them all with such Quantities of Water, that the usual Paths were render'd unpassable. We met in our Way with an *Indian* Hut, where we were entertain'd with a fat, boil'd Goose, Venison, Racoon, and ground Nuts. We made but little Stay; about Noon, we pass'd by several large Savannah's, wherein is curious Ranges for Cattel, being green all the Year; they were plentifully stor'd with Cranes, Geese, *&c.* and the adjacent Woods with great Flocks of Turkies. This Day we travell'd about 30 Miles, and lay all Night at a House which was built for the *Indian* Trade, the Master thereof we had parted with at the *French* Town, who gave us Leave to make use of his Mansion. Such Houses are common in these Parts; and especially where there is *Indian* Towns, and Plantations near at hand, which this Place is well furnish'd withal.

At the Sight of this fair Prospect, we stay'd all Night; our *Indian* going about half an Hour before us, had provided three fat Turkeys e're we got up to him. . . .

The next Day it prov'd a small drisly Rain, which is rare, there happening not the tenth Part of Foggy-falling Weather towards these Mountains, as visits those Parts. Near the Sea-board, the *Indian* kill'd 15 Turkeys this Day; there coming out of the Swamp, (about Sun-rising) Flocks of these Fowl, containing several hundred in a Gang, who feed upon the Acorns, it being most Oak that grow in these Woods. There are but very few Pines in those Quarters.

Early the next Morning, we set forward for the *Congeree-Indians,* parting with that delicious Prospect. By the Way, our Guide kill'd more Turkeys, and two Polecats, which he eat, esteeming them before fat Turkeys. Some of the Turkeys which we eat, whilst we stay'd there, I believe, weigh'd no less than 40 Pounds.

The Land we pass'd over this Day, was most of it good, and the worst passable. At Night we kill'd a Possum, being cloy'd with Turkeys, made a Dish of that, which tasted much between young Pork and Veal; their Fat being as white as any I ever saw.

Our *Indian* having this Day kill'd good store of Provision with his Gun, he always shot with a single Ball, Missing but two Shoots in above forty; they being curious Artists in managing a Gun, to make it carry either Ball, or Shot, true. When they have bought a Piece, and find it to shoot any Ways crooked, they take the Barrel out of the Stock, cutting a Notch in a Tree, wherein they set it streight, sometimes shooting away above 100 Loads of Ammunition, before they bring the Gun to shoot according to their Mind. We took up our Quarters by a Fish-pond-side; the Pits in the Woods that stand full of Water, naturally breed Fish in them, in great Quantities. We cook'd our Supper, but having neither Bread, or Salt, our fat Turkeys began to be loathsome to us, altho' we were never wanting of a good Appetite, yet a Continuance of one Diet, made us weary.

The next day, still passing along such Land as we had done for many days before, which was, Hills and Vallies, about 10 a Clock we reach'd the Top of one of these Mountains, which yielded us a fine Prospect of a very level Country, holding so, on all sides, farther than we could discern. When we came to travel through it, we found it very stiff and rich, being a sort of Marl. This Valley afforded as large Timber as any I ever met withal, especially of Chesnut-Oaks, which render it an excellent Country for raising great Herds of Swine. Indeed, were it cultivated, we might have good hopes of as pleasant and fertile a Valley, as any our *English* in *America* can afford. At Night, we lay by a swift Current, where we saw plenty of Turkies, but perch'd upon such lofty Oaks, that our Guns would not kill them, tho' we shot very often, and our Guns were very good. Some of our Company shot several times, at one Turkey, before he would fly away, the Pieces being loaded with large Goose-shot.

At the other House, where our Fellow Travellers lay, they had provided a Dish, in great Fashion amongst the *Indians,* which was Two young Fawns, taken out of the Doe's Bellies, and boil'd in the same slimy Bags Nature had plac'd them in, and one of the Country-Hares, stew'd with the Guts in her Belly, and her Skin with the Hair on. This new-fashion'd Cookery wrought Abstinence in our Fellow-Travellers, which I somewhat wonder'd at, because one of them made nothing of eating *Allegators,* as heartily as if it had been Pork and Turneps. The *Indians* dress most things after the Wood-cock Fashion, never taking the Guts out. At the House we lay at, there was very good Entertainment of Venison, Turkies, and Bears; and which is customary amongst the *Indians,* the Queen had a Daughter by a former Husband, who was the beautifullest *Indian* I ever saw, and had an Air of Majesty with her, quite contrary to the general Carriage of the *Indians.* She was very kind to the *English,* during our Abode, as well as her Father and Mother.

At night . . . we saw plenty of Turkies, but pearch'd upon such lofty oaks, that our Guns would not kill them, tho' we shot very often, and our Guns were very good. . . .

As soon as it was day, we set out for the *Achonechy*-Town, it being, by Estimation, 20 Miles off, which, I believe, is pretty exact. We were got about half way, (meeting great Gangs of Turkies) when we saw, at a Distance, 30 loaded Horses, coming on the Road, with four or five Men, on other Jades, driving them. We charg'd our Piece, and went up to them: Enquiring, whence they came from? They told us, from *Virginia.* The leading Man's name was *Massey,* who was born about *Leeds* in *Yorkshire.* He ask'd, from whence we came? We told him. Then he ask'd again, Whether we wanted anything that he had? telling us, we should be welcome to it. We accepted of Two Wheaten Biskets, and a little Ammunition. He advised us, by all means, to strike down the Country for *Ronoack,* and not think of *Virginia,* because of the *Sinnagers,* of whom they were afraid, tho' so well arm'd, and numerous. They persuaded us also, to call upon one *Enoe Will,* as we went to *Adshusheer,* for that he would conduct us safe among the *English,* giving him the Character of a very faithful *Indian,* which we afterwards found true by Experience. The *Virginia*-Men asking our opinion of the Country we were then in? we told them, it was a very pleasant one. They were all of the same Opinion, and affirm'd, That they had never seen 20 Miles of such extraordinary rich Land, lying all together, like that betwixt *Hau*-River and the *Achonechy* Town. Having taken our Leaves of each other, we set forward; and the Country, thro' which we pass'd, was so delightful, that it gave us a great deal of Satisfaction. About Three a Clock we reach'd the Town, and the *Indians* presently brought us good fat Bear, and Venison, which was very acceptable at that time. Their Cabins were hung with a good sort of Tapestry, as fat Bear, and barbakued or dried Venison; no *Indians* having greater Plenty of Provisions than these. The Savages do, indeed, still possess the Flower of *Carolina,* the *English* enjoying only the Fag-end of that fine Country. We had not been in the Town 2 Hours, when *Enoe Will* came into the King's Cabin; which was our Quarters. We ask'd him, if he would conduct us to the *English,* and what he would have for his Pains; he answer'd, he would go along with us, and for what he was to have, he left that to our Discretion.

The next Day, early, came two *Tuskeruro Indians* to the other side of the River, but could not get over. They talk'd much to us, but we understood them not. In the Afternoon, *Will* came with the Mare, and had some Discourse with them; they told him, The *English,* to whom he was going, were very wicked People; and, That they threatened the *Indians* for Hunting near their Plantations. These Two Fellows were going among the *Shoccores* and *Achonechy Indians,* to sell their Wooden Bowls and Ladles for Raw-Skins, which they make great Advantage of, hating that any of these Westward *Indians* should have any Commerce with the *English,* which would prove a Hinderance to their Gains. Their Stories deterr'd an Old *Indian* and his Son, from going any farther; but *Will* told us, Nothing they had said should frighten him, he believing them to be a couple of Hog-stealers; and that the *English* only sought Restitution of their Losses, by them; and that this was the only ground for their Report. *Will* had a Slave, a *Sissipahau-Indian* by Nation, who killed us several Turkies, and other Game, on which we feasted.

Source: John Lawson, *The History of Carolina: Containing an Exact Description of the Inlets, Havens, Corn, Fruits, and Other Vegetables of That Country* (London: Printed for W. Taylor and J. Baker, 1714), 18–19, 25–27, 45, 53, 55.

1728 • 11 • William Byrd, Diary Entry on an Expedition to Mark the North Carolina–Virginia Border

Introduction: *William Byrd (1674–1744) was born in Virginia but was educated in England. He returned to Virginia and was a plantation owner. Byrd was a bibliophile and collected the largest library in colonial America. He was particularly interested in natural history. Also a surveyor, he led expeditions to mark the border between North Carolina and Virginia. Byrd kept a diary of this expedition. Below is an except from November 1, 1728.*

As we marcht along, we had the fortune to kill a Brace of Bucks, as many Bears, and one wild Turkey. But this was carrying Sport to wantonness, because we butchered more than we were able to transport. We ordered the Deer to be quarter'd and divided amongst the Horses for the lighter Carriage, and recommended the Bears to our dayly attendants, the Turkey-Buzzards.

We always chose to carry Venison along with us rather than Bear, not only because it was less cumbersome, but likewise because the People cou'd eat it without Bread, which was now almost spent. Whereas the other, being richer food, lay too heavy upon the stomach, unless it were lightened by something farinaceous. This is what I thought proper to remarque, for the service of all those whose Business or Diversion shall oblige them to live any time in the Woods.

And because I am persuaded that very usefull Matters may be found out by Searching this great Wilderness, especially the upper parts of it about the Mountains, I conceive it will help to engage able men in that good work, if I recommend a wholesome kind of Food, of very small Weight and very great Nourishment, that will secure them from Starving, in case they shou'd be so unlucky as to meet with no Game. The Chief discouragement at present from penetrating far into the Woods is the trouble of carrying a Load of Provisions. I must own Famine is a frightful Monster, and for that reason to be guarded against as well as we can. But the common precautions against it, are so burthensome, that People can't tarry long out, and go far enough from home, to make any effectual Discovery.

The Portable Provisions I would furnish our Foresters withal are Glue-Broth and rockahomini: one contains the Essence of Bread, the other of Meat.

The best way of making Glue-Broth is after the following method: Take a Leg of Beef, Veal, Venison, or any other Young Meat, because Old Meat will not so easily Jelly. Pare off all the fat, in which there is no Nutriment, and of the Lean make a very strong

Broth, after the usual Manner, by boiling the meat to Bags till all the Goodness be out. After Skimming off what fat remains, pour the Broth into a wide Stew-Pan, well tinn'd, & let it simmer over a gentle, even Fire, till it come to a thick Jelly. Then take it off and set it over Boiling Water, which is an Evener Heat, and not so apt to burn the Broth to the Vessel. Over that let it evaporate, stirring it very often till it be reduc'd, when cold, into a Solid Substance like Glue. Then cut it into small Pieces, laying them Single in the Cold, that they may dry the Sooner. When the Pieces are perfectly dry, put them into a Cannister, and they will be good, if kept Dry, a whole East India Voyage.

This Glue is so Strong, that two or three Drams, dissolv'd in boiling Water with a little Salt, will make half a pint of good Broth, & if you shou'd be faint with fasting or Fatigue, let a small piece of this Glue melt in your Mouth, and you will find yourself surprisingly refreshed.

One Pound of this cookery wou'd keep a man in good heart above a Month, and is not only Nourishing, but likewise very wholesome. Particularly it is good against Fluxes, which Woodsmen are very liable to, by lying too near the moist ground, and guzzling too much cold Water. But as it will be only us'd now and then, in times of Scarcity, when Game is wanting, two Pounds of it will be enough for a Journey of Six Months.

But this Broth will be still more heartening, if you thicken every mess with half a Spoonful of Rockahominy, which is nothing but Indian Corn parched without burning, and reduced to Powder. The Fire drives out all the Watery Parts of the Cora, leaving the Strength of it behind, and this being very dry, becomes much lighter for carriage and less liable to be Spoilt by the Moist Air.

Thus half a Dozen Pounds of this Sprightful Bread will sustain a Man for as many Months, provided he husband it well, and always Spare it when he meets with Venison, which, as I said before, may be very Safely eaten without any Bread at all.

By what I have said, a Man needs not encumber himself with more than 8 or 10 Pounds of Provisions, tho' he continue half a year in the Woods.

These and his Gun will support him very well during that time, without the least danger of keeping one Single Fast. And tho' some of his days may be what the French call Jours madgres, yet there will happen no more of those than will be necessary for his health, and to carry off the Excesses of the Days of Plenty, when our Travellers will be apt to indulge their Lawless Appetites too much.

Source: John Spencer Basset, ed., *The Writings of Colonel William Byrd of Westover in Virginia* (New York: Doubleday, Paige, 1902), 191–194.

1733 • 12 • Food in the *Pennsylvania Gazette*

Introduction: *The* Pennsylvania Gazette *was one of the most important newspapers in colonial America. Below is an article from the newspaper of November 5, 1733, that included items of food, including Thanksgiving proclaimed by the colonial governor.*

Boston, Novem. 5. On Friday last His Excellency the Governor was pleased to give his Assent to the Bill for the Supply of the Treasury and to two other Bills. About a Week ago several Vessels coming from Martha's Vineyard for this Port, were taken short by the Wind upon the Shoals, and in coming into Homes's Hole in the Night, a Sloop from North-Carolina, ran foul of Capt. Howel, in a Scooner from Philadelphia, with Wheat and Flour, and did him so much Damage that he sunk soon after, by which Accident most of the Cargo was lost. The Men took to the Boat in so great a Hurry, that they forgot or had not Time to take in the Oars, but the Wind happening to be out, it carried the Boat directly to the Shore. We hear that the Vessels lately arrived from Ireland have brought above Five Hundred Casks of Butter, and that a great deal more is expected so that 'tis hoped it will be reduced to Sixteen Pence a Pound in a short Time. We hear also, that great Quantities of Wheat will be brought in the Ships yet expected from London, it being sold there for Two Shillings per Bushel.

'Tis expected a Proclamation will speedily be published by His Excellency the Governour, to warn the Inhabitants of this Province against taking any of the new Emission of Bills of Credit on the Colony of Rhode-Island, agreeable to the Report of a Committee of the General Court appointed to consider of that Affair.

His Excellency the Governour, with the Advice of His Majesty's Council, has issued out a Proclamation appointing the 22d of this Instant November to be observed as a Day of publick Thanksgiving throughout this Province.

Source: *Pennsylvania Gazette,* November 16, 1733.

1749 • 13 • Pehr Kalm, *Travels into North America*

Introduction: *Pehr Kalm (1716–1779) was a Swedish botanist who was a good friend of Carl Linnaeus. In 1748 Kalm came to America, where he remained for three years. He kept careful observations of what he saw and wrote them down in a journal, which was published after his return to Sweden. His observations on flora and fauna provide a wide description of North America. He also offered descriptions of the people he met, especially Swedes. His comments about the food of American Indians is particularly enlightening.*

March the 17th [1749]. At the first arrival of the Swedes in this country, and long after that time it was filled with Indians. But as the Europeans proceeded to cultivate the land, the Indians fold their land, and went further into the country. But in reality few of the Indians really left the country in this manner; most of them ended their days before, either by wars among themselves, or by the small-pox, a disease which the Indians were unacquainted with before their commerce with the Europeans, and which since that time has killed incredible numbers of them. For though they can heal wounds and other external hurts, yet they know not how to proceed with fevers, or in general with internal diseases. One can imagine, how ill they would succeed with the cure of the small-pox, when as soon as the pustules appeared, they leaped naked into the cold water of the rivers, lakes, or fountains, and either dived over head into it, or poured it over their body in great abundance, in order to cool the heat of the fever. In the same manner they carry their children, when they have the small-pox, into the water and duck them.

But brandy has killed most of the Indians. This liquor was likewise entirely unknown to them, before the Europeans came hither; but after they had tasted it, they could never get enough of it. A man can hardly have a greater desire of a thing, than the Indians have of brandy. I have heard them say, that to die by drinking brandy, was a desirable and an honourable death; and indeed 'tis no very uncommon thing to kill themselves by drinking this liquor to excess. The food of these Indians was very different from that of the inhabitants of the other parts of the world. Wheat, rye, barley, oats, and rice-groats, were quite unknown in America. In the same manner it is with regard to the fruits and herbs which are eaten in the old countries. The maize, some kinds of beans, and melons, made almost the whole of the Indian agriculture and gardening; and dogs were the only domestic animals in North America. But as their agriculture and their gardening were very trifling, and they could hardly live two months in a year upon their produce, they were forced to apply to hunting and fishing, which at that time, and even at present, are their chief subsistence, and to seek some of the wild plants and trees here. Some of the old Swedes were yet alive, who in their younger years had an intercourse with the Indians, and had seen the minutiæ of their Economy. I was therefore desirous of knowing which of the spontaneous herbs they made use of for food at that time; and all the old men agreed that the following plants were what they chiefly consumed:

Hopniss or Hapniss[1] was the Indian name of a wild plant, which they ate at that time. The Swedes still call it by that name, and it grows in the meadows in a good foil. The roots resemble potatoes, and were boiled by the Indians, who eat them instead of bread. Some of the Swedes at that time likewise ate this root for Want of bread. Some of the English still eat them instead of potatoes. Mr. Bartram told me, that the Indians who live farther in the country do not only eat these roots, which are equal in goodness to potatoes, but likewise take the pease which lie in the pods of this plant, and prepare them like common pease. Dr. Linnaeus calls the plant Glycine Apios.

Katniss is another Indian name of a plant, the root of which they were likewise accustomed to eat, when they lived here. The Swedes still preserve this name. It grows in low, muddy and very wet ground. The root is oblong, commonly an inch and an half long, and one inch and a quarter broad in the middle; but some of the roots have been as big as a man's fists. The Indians either boiled this root or roasted it in hot ashes. Some of the Swedes likewise eat them with much appetite, at the time when the Indians were so near the coast; but at present none of them make any use of the roots. A man of ninety-one years of age, called Nils Gustafson, told me, that he had often eaten these roots when he was a boy, and that he liked them very well at that time. He added that the Indians, especially their women, travelled to the islands, dug out the roots, and brought them home; and whilst they had them, they desired no other food. They said that the hogs, which are amazingly greedy of them, have made them very scarce. The cattle are very fond of its leaves. I afterwards got some of these roots roasted, and in my Opinion they tasted well, though they were rather dry: The taste was nearly the same with that of the potatoes. When the Indians come down to the coast and see the turneps of the Europeans, they, likewise give them the name of katniss. Their katniss is an arrow-head or Sagittaria, and is Only a variety of the Swedish arrow-head or Sagittaria sagittifolia, for the plant above the ground is entirely the same, but the root Under ground is much greater in the American than in the European, Mr. Osheck in his voyage to China, Vol. I. p. 334, of the English edition, mentions, that the Chinese plant a Sagittaria; and eat its roots. This seems undoubtedly to be a variety of this katniss. Further in the north of this part of America, I met with the other species of Sagittaria which we have in Sweden. Taw-ho and Taw-him was the Indian name of another plant, the root of which they eat. Some of them likewise call it Tuckah; outmost of the Swedes still knew it by the name of Taw-Bo. It grows in moist ground and swamps. Hogs are very greedy of the roots, and grow very fat by feeding on them. Therefore, they often visit the places where these roots grow; and they are frequently seen rooting up the mud, and falling with their whole body into the water, so that only a little of the back part was out of the water. It is therefore very plain, that these roots must have been extirpated in places which are frequented by hogs. The roots often grow to the thickness of a man's thigh. When they are fresh, they have a pungent taste, and are reckoned a poison in that fresh state. Nor did the Indians ever venture to eat them raw, but prepared them in the following manner: They gathered a great heap of these roots, dug a great long hole, sometimes two or three fathoms and upwards in length, into which they put the roots, and covered them with the earth that had been taken out of the hole; they made a great fire above it, which burnt till they thought proper to remove it; and then they dug up the roots, and Consumed them with great avidity. These roots, when prepared in this manner, I am told, taste like potatoes. The Indians never dry and preserve them; but always take them fresh out of the marshes, when they want them. This Taw-ho is the Arum Virginicum, or Virginian Wake-robin. It is remarkable, that the Arums, with the plants next akin to them, are eaten by men in different parts of the world, though their roots, when raw, have a fiery pungent taste, and are almost poisonous in that state. How can men have learnt, that plants so extremely opposite to our nature were eatable; and that their poison, which burns on the tongue, can be conquered by fire. Thus the root of the Calla palujlris, which grows in the north of Europe, is sometimes used instead of bread on an exigency. The North American Indians consume this species of Aram. Those of South America and of the West Indies, eat other species of Arums. The Hottentots, at the Cape of Good Hope, in Africa, prepare bread from a species of Arum or Wake-robin,—which is as burning and poisonous as the other species of this plant. In the same manner, they employ the roots of some kinds of Arum as a food, in Egypt and Asia. Probably, that severe but sometimes useful mistress, necessity, has first taught men to find out a food, which the first taste would have rejected as useless. This Taw-ho seems to be the same with what the Indians in Carolina call Tuckahoo. . . .

Taw-kee is another plant, so called by the Indians, who eat it. Some of them call it Taw-kirn, and others Tackvim. The Swedes call it always by the name of Tawkee.[2] The plant grows in marshes, near moist and low grounds, and is very plentiful in North America. The cattle, hogs and stags, are very fond of the leaves in spring; for they are some of the earliest. The leaves are broad, like those of the Convallariai or Lilly of the Valley, green on the upper side, and covered with very minute hair, so that they looked like a fine velvet. The Indians pluck the seeds, and keep them for eating. They cannot be eaten fresh or raw, but must be dried. The Indians were forced to boil them repeatedly in water, before they were fit for use; and then they ate them like pease. When the Swedes gave them butter or milk, they boiled or broiled the seeds in it. Sometimes they employ these seeds instead of bread; and they taste like pease. Some of the Swedes likewise ate them; and the old men among them told me, they liked this food better than any of the other plants which the Indians formerly made use of. This T'aw-kee was the Orontium aquaticum.

Bilberries were likewise a very common dish among the Indians. They are called Huckleberries by the English here, and belong to several species of Vaccinium, which are all of them different from our Swedish Bilberry-bush, though their berries, in regard to colour, shape, and taste, are so similar to the Swedish bilberry, that they are distinguished from each other with difficulty. The American ones grow on shrubs, which are from two to four feet high; and there are some species which are above seven feet in height. The Indians formerly plucked them in abundance every year, dried them either in the sun-shine or by the fireside, and afterwards prepared them for eating, in different manners. These huckleberries are still a dainty dish among the Indians. On my travels through the country of the Iroquese,[3] they offered me, whenever they designed to treat me well, fresh maize-bread, baked in an oblong shape, mixed with dried Huckleberries, which lay as close in it as the raisins in a plumb-pudding. I shall write more at large about it in the sequel. The Europeans are likewise used to collect a quantity of these berries, to dry them in ovens, to bake them in tarts, and to employ them in several other ways. Some preserve them with treacle. They are likewise eaten raw, either quite alone or with fresh milk. . . .

[March 27, 1749] The old Swede, whom I came to visit, seemed to be still pretty hearty and fresh, and could walk by the help of a stick; but he complained of having felt in these latter years, some pains in his back, and limbs, and that he could keep his feet warm in winter only by sitting near the fire.

He said he could very well remember the state of this country, at the time when the Dutch possessed it, and in what circumstances it was in before the arrival of the English. He added, that he had brought a great deal of timber to Philadelphia, at the time that it was built. He still remembered to have seen a great sorest on the spot where Philadelphia now stands. The father of this old man had been one of the Swedes who were sent over from Sweden, in order to cultivate and inhabit this country. He returned me the following answers to the questions I asked him.

Quere, Whence did the Swedes, who first came hither, get their cattle? The old man answered, that when he was a boy, his father and other people had told him, that the Swedes brought their horses, cows, and oxen, sheep, hogs, geese, and ducks, over with them. There were but few of a kind at first, but they multiplied greatly here afterwards. He said, that Maryland, New York, New England, and Virginia, had been sooner inhabited by Europeans than this part of the country; but he did not know whether the Swedes ever got cattle of any kind, from any of these provinces, except from New York. Whilst he was yet very young, the Swedes, as well as he could remember, had already a sufficient stock of all these animals. The hogs had propagated so much at that time, there being so great a plenty of food for them, that they ran about wild in the woods, and that the people were obliged to shoot them, when they intended to make use of them. The old man likewise recollected, that horses ran wild in the woods, in some places; but he could not tell whether the other kind of cattle turned wild. He thought that the cattle grow as big at present as they did when he was a boy, supposing they get as much food as they want. For in his younger years, food for all kinds of cattle was so plentiful, and even so superfluous, that the cattle were extremely well fed by it. A cow at that time gave more milk, than three or four do at present; but she got more and better food at that time, than three or four get now; and, as the old man said, the scanty allowance of grass, which the cattle get in summer, is really very pitiful. The causes of this scarcity of grass have already been mentioned.

Quere, Whence did the English in Pennsylvania and New Jersey get their cattle? They bought them chiefly from the Swedes and Dutch, who lived here; and a small number were brought over from Old England. The form of the cattle, and the unanimous accounts of the English here, confirmed what the old man had said.

Quere, Whence did the Swedes here settled get their several sorts of corn, and likewise their fruit-trees and kitchen herbs? The old man told me that he had frequently heard, when he was young, that the Swedes had brought all kinds of corn, and fruits, and herbs, or feeds of them, with them. For, as far as he could recollect, the Swedes here were plentifully provided with wheat, rye, barley, and oats. The Swedes, at that time, brewed all their beer of malt made of barley, and likewise made good strong beer. They had already got distilling vessels, and made good brandy. Every one among them had not a distilling vessel, but when they intended to distil, they lent their apparatus to one another. At first they were forced to buy maize of the Indians, both for sowing and eating. But after continuing for some years in this country, they extended their maize-plantations so much that the Indians were obliged some time after to buy maize of the Swedes. The old man likewise assured me, that the Indians formerly, and about the time of the first settling of the Swedes, were more industrious and laborious in every branch of business, than they are now. Whilst he was young, the Swedes had a great quantity of very good white cabbage. Winter cabbage, or Caje, which Was left on the ground during winter, was likewise abundant. They were likewise well provided with turnips. In winter they kept them in holes under ground. But the old man did not like that method; for when they had lain too long in these holes in winter, they became spungy. He preferred that method of keeping them which is now commonly adopted and which consists in the following particulars. After the turnips have been taken out of the ground in autumn, and exposed to the air for a while, they are put in a heap upon the field, covered with straw at the top, and on the sides, and with earth over the straw. By this means they stand the winter very well here, and do not become spungy. The Indians were very fond of turneps, and called them sometimes Hopniss, sometimes Katniss. The Swedes likewise cultivated carrots, in the old man's younger years. Among the fruit-trees were Apple-trees. They were not numerous, and only some of the Swedes had little orchards of them, whilst others had not a single tree. None of the Swedes made cyder, for it is come into use but lately. The Swedes brewed strong beer and small beer, and it was their common liquor. But at present there are very few who brew beer, for they commonly prepare cyder. Cherry-trees were abundant when Nils Gustafson was yet a boy. Peach-trees were at that time more numerous than at present, and the Swedes brewed beer of the fruit. . . .

The Indians had their little plantations of maize in many places; before the Swedes came into this country, the Indians had no other than their hatchets made of stone; in order to make maize plantations they cut out the trees and prepared the ground in the manner I have before mentioned. They planted but little maize, for they lived chiefly upon hunting; and throughout the greatest part of summer, their Hopniss or the roots of the Glycine Apios, their Katniss, or the roots of the Sagittaria Sagittifolia, their Taw-ho or the roots of the Arum Virginicum, their Tauskee or Orontium aquaticum, and whortleberries, were their chief food. They had no horses or other cattle which could be subservient, to them in their agriculture, and therefore did all the work with their own hands. After they had reaped the maize, they kept it in holes under ground, during winter; they dug these holes seldom deeper than a fathom, and often not so deep; at the bottom and on the sides they put broad pieces of bark.

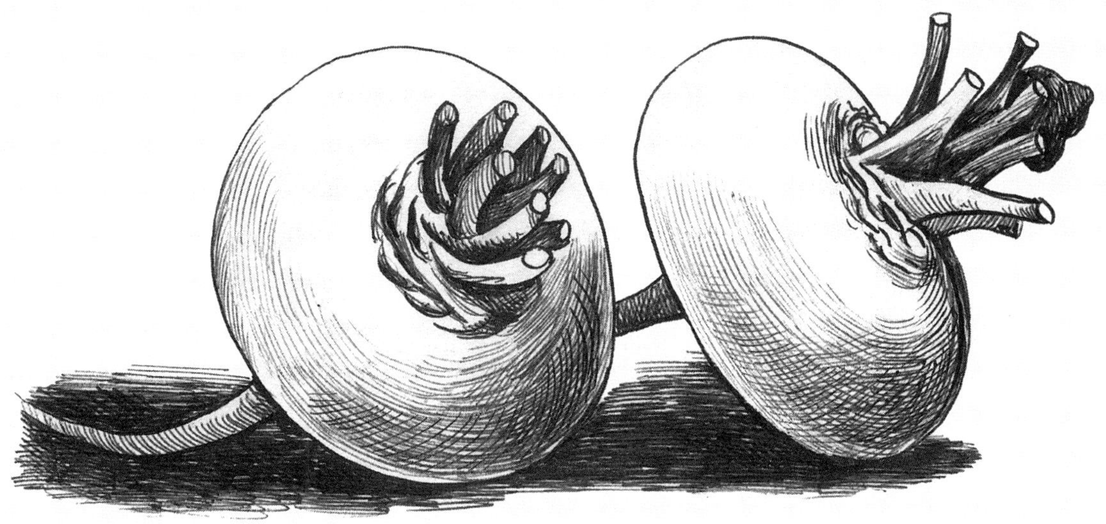

Peter Kalm visited America in the 1740s and wrote a detailed description of the flora (like turnips), fauna, and the social customs of Americans. (Denis Kozlenko/iStockphoto.com)

The Andropogon bicorne, a grass which grows in great plenty here, and which the English call Indian Grass, and the Swedes Wild Grass, supplies the want of bark; the ears of maize are then thrown into the hole and covered to a Considerable thickness with the same grass and the whole is again covered by a sufficient quantity of earth: the maize kept extremely well in those holes; and each Indian had several such subterraneous stores, where his corn lay safe, though he travelled far from it. After the Swedes had settled here and planted apple-trees and peach-trees, the Indians, and especially their women, sometimes stole the fruit in great quantity; but when the Swedes caught them, they gave them a severe drubbing, took the fruit from them, and often their clothes too. In the same manner happened sometimes that as the Swedes had a great increase of hogs, and they ran about in the woods, the Indians killed some of them privately and feasted upon them: but there were likewise some Indians who bought hogs of the Swedes and fed them; they taught them to run after them like dogs, and whenever they removed from one place to another, their hogs always followed them. Some of those Indians got such numbers of these animals, that they afterwards gave them to the Swedes for a mere trifle. When the Swedes arrived in America, the Indians had no domestic animals, except a species of little dogs. The Indians were extremely fond of milk, and ate it with pleasure when the Swedes gave it them. They likewise prepared a kind of liquor like milk in the following manner: they gathered a great number of hiccory nuts and walnuts from the black walnut-trees, dried and crushed them; then they took out the kernels, pounded them so fine as flour, and mixed this flour with water, which took a milky hue from them, and was as sweet as milk. They had tobacco-pipes of clay, manufactured by themselves, at the time that the Swedes arrived here; they did not always smoke true tobacco, but made use of another plant instead. . . .

Notes

1. *Apios americana.*
2. *Peltandra virginica.*
3. Iroquois.

Source: Pehr Kalm, *Travels into North America,* Vol. 2 (London: T. Lowndes, 1771), 95–117.

1750 • 14 • A Slave Song

Introduction: *In autumn, the harvest required a massive effort by enslaved people on plantations. To make the monotonous task of shucking corn slightly more enjoyable, slaves sang while they worked. On some southern plantations slaves were given a special meal, which was occasionally followed by a dance in the barn. In this song, slaves anticipated good food—and drink—at the meal.*

All dem puty gals will be dar,
Shuck dat corn before you eat,
Dey will fix it fer us rare,
Shuck dat corn before you eat,
I know dat supper will be big,
Shuck dat corn before you eat,
I think I smell a fine roast pig,
Shuck dat corn before you eat,
I hope dey'll have some whisky dar,
Shuck dat corn before you eat,
I think I'll fill my pockets full,
Shuck dat corn before *you* eat.

Source: William Wells Brown, *My Southern Home: or, The South and Its People* (Boston: A. G. Brown, 1880), 92–93.

1759 • 15 • Israel Acrelius, "Order of Meals" and "Drinks Used in North America"

Introduction: *Israel Acrelius (1714–1800) was a Swedish minister (Church of Sweden) who arrived in America in 1749. He served as pastor of the Swedish church in Wilmington, Delaware, until 1756, when he returned to Sweden. He published* History of New Sweden *in 1759. It dealt with both religious and secular matters, and Acrelius has many comments about food and beverages in America. The drinks that Acrelius took note of were only a small fraction of the mixed beverages served in*

America at the time. Below are two excerpts. The notes in the text are from the English translator of the work, William M. Reynolds.

5. Order of Meals

The meals are cleanly, and do not consist of a great variety of food. Ham, beef, tongue, roast beef, fowls, with cabbage set round about, make one meal. Roast mutton or veal, with potatoes or turnips, form another. Another, still, is formed by a pasty of chickens, or partridges, or lamb. Beef-steak, veal cutlets, mutton chops, or turkey, goose, or fowls, with potatoes set around, with stewed green pease, or Turkish beans, or some other beans, are another meal. Pies of apples, peaches, cherries or cranberries, etc., form another course. When cheese and butter are added, one has an ordinary meal.

The breakfast is tea or coffee. Along with these are eaten long and thin slices of smoked beef, in summer. In winter, bread roasted, soaked in milk and butter, and called toast; or pancakes of buckwheat, so light that one can scarcely hold them between his fingers, are also used. The afternoon meal ("four o'clock piece"), taken at four o'clock, is usually the same. Suppers are not much in use. Where one is so invited, chocolate is the most reliable. Whole pots of it are sometimes made, but little or no milk in it, chiefly of water.

Of these articles of food more or less is used in the country, according to the ability or the luxury of the people. Tea, coffee, and chocolate are so general as to be found in the most remote cabins, if not for daily use, yet for visitors, mixed with Muscovado, or raw sugar. Fresh fish for a meal is found nowhere either with high or low. Of soup they think in the same manner. It serves only for ordinary household fare. Salt and dried fish are seldom seen: as few have eaten them, they are almost unknown.

The arrangement of meals among country people is usually this: for breakfast, in summer, cold milk and bread, rice, milk-pudding, cheese, and butter, cold meat. In winter, mush[1] and milk, and milk-porridge, hominy[2] and milk. The same also serves for supper, if so desired.

For noon, in summer, soup (säppa),[3] fresh meat, dried beef, and bacon, with cabbage, apples, potatoes, Turkish beans, large beans, all kinds of roots, mashed turnips, pumpkins, cashaws[4] and squashes. One or more of these are distributed around the dish. Also boiled or baked pudding,[5] dumplings,[6] bacon and eggs,[7] pies[8] of apples, cherries, peaches, etc.

In winter hominy-soup is cooked with salt beef and bacon. Then also, pasties of lamb or chicken are used, and can keep cold a whole week; also pancakes of wheat flour or of buckwheat-meal.

Bread is baked once a week or oftener. It is in large loaves, mostly of wheat flour; seldom of rye. The wheat flour, which is used in the towns for bread or table use, is beautiful, like the finest powder. The flour in the country is dark and coarse.

Chapter 10. Drinks Used in North America

1. French wine.
2. Frontegnac.[9]
3. Pontac.[10]
4. Port a Port.

5. Lisbon wine.
6. Phial wine.[11]
7. Sherry.
8. Madeira wine, which is altogether the most used.[12]
9. Sangaree is made of wine, water, sugar, a dash of nutmeg, with some leaves of balm put in.
10. Hot wine, warmed wine, is drunk warm, with sugar, cardamoms, and cinnamon in it. Sometimes, also, it has in it the yolks of eggs beaten up together, and grains of allspice, and then it is called mulled wine.
11. Cherry wine. The berries are pressed, the juice strained from them, Muscavado or raw sugar is put in; then it ferments and, after some months, becomes clear.
12, 13. Currant wine, or black raspberry wine, is made in the same manner.
14. Apple-wine (cider). Apples are ground up in a wooden mill, which is worked by a horse. Then they are placed under a press until the juice is run off, which then put in a barrel, where it ferments, and after some time becomes clear.

    When apples are not of a good sort, decayed or fallen off too soon, the cider is boiled, and a few pounds of ground ginger is put into it, and it becomes more wholesome and better for cooking; it keeps longer and does not ferment so soon, but its taste is not so fresh as when it is unboiled.

    The fault with cider in that country is that, for the most part, the good and the bad are mixed together. The cider is drunk too fresh and too soon; thus it has come into great disesteem, so that many persons refuse to taste it. The strong acid[13] which it contains produces rust and verdigris, and frightens some from its use, by the fear that it may have the same effect in the body. This liquor is usually unwholesome, causes ague when it is fresh, and colic when it is too old. The common people damask the drink, mix ground ginger with it, or heat it with a red-hot iron.
15. Cider Royal is so called when some quarts of brandy are thrown into a barrel of cider along with several pounds of Muscavado sugar, whereby it becomes stronger and tastes better. If it is then left alone for a year or so, or taken over the sea, then drawn off into bottles, with some raisins put in it, it may deserve the name of apple-wine.
16. Cider Royal of another kind, in which one-half is cider and the other mead, both freshly fermented together.
17. Mulled cider is warmed, with sugar in it, with yolks of eggs and grains of allspice. Sometimes, also, some rum is put in to give it greater strength.
18. Rum, or sugar-brandy. This is made at the sugar plantations in the West India Islands. It is in quality like French brandy, but has no unpleasant odor. It makes up a large part of the English and French commerce with the West India Islands. The strongest comes from Jamaica, is called Jamaica spirits, and is the favorite article for punch. Next in quality to this is the rum from Barbadoes, then that from Antiguas, Montserrat, Nevis, St. Christopher's, etc. The heaviest consumption is in harvest-time, when the laborers most frequently take a sup, and then immediately a drink of water, from which the body performs its work more easily and perspires better than when rye whiskey or malt liquors are used.
19. Raw dram, raw rum, is a drink of rum unmixed with anything.
20. Egg dram, eggnog. The yolk of an egg is beaten up, and during the beating rum and sugar poured in.

21. Cherry bounce is a drink made of the cherry juice with a quantity of rum in it.
22. Bilberry dram is made in the same way.
23. Punch is made of fresh spring-water, sugar, lemon-juice, and Jamaica spirits. Instead of lemons, a West India fruit called limes, or its juice, which is imported in flasks, is used. Punch is always drunk cold; but sometimes a slice of bread is toasted and placed in it warm to moderate the cold in winter-time, or it is heated with a red-hot iron. Punch is mostly used just before dinner, and is called "a meridian."
24. *Mämm,* made of water, sugar, and rum, is the most common drink in the interior of the country, and it has set up many a tavern-keeper.
25. Manatham is made of small beer with rum and sugar.
26. Tiff, or flipp, is made of small beer with rum and sugar, with a slice of bread toasted and buttered.
27. Hot rum, warmed with sugar and grains of allspice; customary at funerals.
28. Mulled rum, warmed with egg-yolks and allspice.
29. Hotch pot, warmed beer with rum in it.
30. Sampson is warmed cider with rum in it.
31. Grog is water and rum.
32. Sling, or long sup, half water and half rum, with sugar in it.
33. Mintwater, distilled from mint, mixed in the rum, to make a drink for strengthening the stomach.
34. Egg punch, of yolks of eggs, rum, sugar, and warm water.
35. Milk punch, of yolks of eggs, rum, sugar, and grated nutmeg over it; is much used in the summer-time, and is considered good for dysentery and loose bowels.
36. Sillibub is made of milkwarm, wine, and sugar, not unlike our Oclost.[14] It is used in summer-time as a cooling beverage.
37. Milk and water is the common drink of the people.
38. Still liquor, brandy made of peaches or apples, without the addition of any grain, is not regarded as good as rum.
39. Whisky is brandy made of grain. It is used far up in the interior of the country, where rum is very dear on account of the transportation.
40. Beer is brewed in the towns, is brown, thick, and unpalatable. Is drunk by the common people.
41. Small beer from molasses. When the water is warmed, the molasses is poured in with a little malt or wheat-bran, and is well shaken together. Afterwards a lay of hops and yeast is added, and then it is put in a keg, where it ferments, and the next day is clear and ready for use. It is more wholesome, pleasanter to the taste, and milder to the stomach than any small beer of malt.
42. Spruce beer is a kind of small beer, which is called in Swedish "*lärda tidningarne*" (learned newspapers). The twigs of spruce-pine are boiled in the malt so as to give it a pleasant taste, and then molasses is used as in the preceding. The Swedish pine is thought to be serviceable in the same way.
43. Table beer made of persimmons. The persimmon is a fruit like our egg-plum.[15] When these have been well frosted, they are pounded along with their seeds, mixed up with wheat-bran made into large loaves, and baked in the oven. Then whenever desired, pieces of this are taken and moistened, and with these the drink is brewed.

44. Mead is made of honey and water boiled together, which ferments of itself in the cask. The stronger it is of honey, the longer it takes to ferment. Drunk in this country too soon, it causes sickness of the stomach and headache.
45. Besides these they also use the liqueurs called cordials, such as anise-water, cinnamon-water, applecin-water, and others scarcely to be enumerated, as also drops to pour into wine and brandy almost without end.
46. *Tea* is a drink very generally used. No one is so high as to despise it, nor any one so low as not to think himself worthy of it. It is not drunk oftener than twice a day. It is always drunk by the common people with raw sugar in it, Brandy in tea is called *lese.*
47. Coffee comes from Martinica, St. Domingo, and Surinam, is sold in large quantities, and used for breakfast.
48. Chocolate is in general use for breakfast and supper. It is drunk with a spoon. Sometimes prepared with a little milk, but mostly only with water.

Notes

1. Mush is made of corn-meal, boiled in water; it is of a bright-yellow color; eaten with milk, cider, or syrup.
2. Hominy . . . is the grain of maize; the grains are first laid in a steep to loosen the hull; then it is pounded in the section of a stock of a tree that has been dug out, and thus the hull comes off. Then the kernel is mixed with Turkish beans. From this is made sappa, mixed with flesh in winter time, and with milk in summer.
3. Säppa is a thin broth of meat, in which bread is crumbled; sometimes it is drunk, and sometimes it is eaten with a spoon of tin cups with handles, each person having one by himself.
4. The cashaw is a kind of pumpkin, reddish within, more firm and fleshy than the common sort; it makes a stiff pap when mixed with the fat taken off of meat broth. Squashes are a smaller kind, about as large as a man's fist, whitish within, sweetish, growing in various forms, and are prepared in the same manner. These are native American vegetables.
5. Boiled pudding is made of light dough mixed with fat; it is placed in a linen bag, and boiled in meat broth. When the dough is made of good flour, eggs, raisins, or dried peaches, it is called "a fine pudding." Baked puddings are the young peoples' pancakes, and are eaten with a sauce of butter and sugar, like the last one named.
6. Dumplings are lumps as big as a fist, made of dough in which fresh apples are inclosed; it is boiled in meat broth, and eaten with prepared sauces. Puddings and dumplings are called "Quakers' food."
7. The bacon is fried in a pan with the yolks of eggs whole—a common dish in poor places of entertainment.
8. A pie is a tart made of fruits named in the text. Apple-pie is used through the whole year, and when fresh apples are no longer to be had, dried ones are used. It is the evening meal of children. House-pie, in country places, is made of apples neither peeled nor freed from their cores, and its crust is not broken if a wagon-wheel goes over it!
9. A French wine.
10. A type of French claret.

11. A sweet wine from the Azores.
12. These are the common English wines, and show the predominance of English habits at this time.
13. It is rather remarkable that our author does not employ the term "vinegar"—*ättika*—in Swedish.
14. The Swedish *Oclost* is made by mixing warm milk with beer.
15. *Prunns institia* (Dalin).

Source: Israel Acrelius, *A History of New Sweden,* translated from the Swedish with an Introduction and Notes by William M. Reynolds (1759; reprint, Philadelphia: Historical Society of Pennsylvania, 1874), 157–164.

1773 • 16 • "An Impartial Observer," Account of the Boston Tea Party

Introduction: *On December 16, 1773, men with their faces smeared with grease or lamp black who were dressed in blankets and large woolen caps and were armed with tomahawks, hatchets, pistols, and rifles marched from Old South Church in Boston to the harbor. When they arrived at Griffin's Wharf, they boarded three ships. The raiders then staved the chests and threw them into the harbor. A crowd of about 1,000 people watched the proceedings and cheered them on. Three hours later all 342 tea chests—about 43 tons valued at £18,000—were destroyed, and the raiders and spectators departed. The day after the Boston Tea Party, as the event would inevitably be called, John Adams, the future second president of the United States, wrote in his diary that "This Destruction of the Tea is so bold, so daring, so firm, so intrepid and inflexible, and it must have so important Consequences, and so lasting, that I cannot but consider it as an epocha [sic] in history. The question is whether the destruction of the tea was necessary? I apprehend it was absolutely and indispensably so." This simple act of defiance set in motion events that culminated 16 months later in the beginning of the American Revolutionary War. The document presented here is one description of the Boston Tea Party that was written by a person who claimed to be "An Impartial Observer" and published four days after the event that would change American history. Although the identity of the "Impartial Observer" has not been uncovered, he is clearly not impartial, as he is sympathetic to those engaged in the Boston Tea Party.*

Having accidentally arrived at Boston upon a visit to a Friend the evening before the meeting of the Body of the People on the 29th of November, curiosity, and the pressing invitations of my most kind host, induced me to attend the Meeting. I must confess that I was most agreeably, and I hope that I shall be forgiven by the People if I say so unexpectedly, entertained and instructed by the regular, reasonable and sensible conduct and expression of the People there collected, that I should rather have entertained an idea of being transported to the British senate than to an adventurous and promiscuous assembly of People of a remote Colony, were I not convinced by the genuine and uncorrupted integrity and manly hardihood of the Rhetoricians of that assembly that they were not yet corrupted by venality or debauched by luxury.

The conduct of that wise and considerate body, in their several transactions, evidently tended to preserve the property of the East India Company. I must confess I was very disagreeably affected with the conduct of Mr. Hutchinson, their pensioned Governor, on the succeeding day, who very unseasonably, and, as I am informed, very arbitrarily (not having the sanction of law), framed and executed a mandate to disperse the People, which, in my opinion, with a people less prudent and temperate would have cost him his head. The Force of that body was directed to effect the return of the Teas to Great Britain; much argument was expended. Much entreaty was made use of to effect this desirable purpose. Mr. Rotch behaved, in my estimation, very unexceptionably; his disposition was seemingly to comport with the desires of the People to convey the Teas to the original proprietors. The Consignees have behaved like Scoundrels in refusing to take the consignment, or indemnify the owner of the ship which conveyed this detestable commodity to this port. Every possible step was taken to preserve this property. The People being exasperated with the conduct of the administration in this affair, great pains were taken and much policy exerted to procure a stated watch for this purpose.

The body of the People determined the Tea should not be landed; the determination was deliberate, was judicious; the sacrifice of their Rights, of the Union of all the Colonies, would have been the effect had they conducted with less resolution: On the Committee of Correspondence they devolved the care of seeing their resolutions seasonably executed; that body, as I have been informed by one of their members, had taken every step prudence and patriotism could suggest, to effect the desirable purpose, but were defeated. The Body once more assembled, I was again present; such a collection of the people was to me a novelty; near seven thousand persons from several towns, Gentlemen, Merchants, Yeomen, and others, respectable for their rank and abilities, and venerable for their age and character, constituted the assembly; they decently, unanimously and firmly adhered to their former resolution, that the baleful commodity which was to rivet and establish the duty should never be landed; to prevent the mischief they repeated the desires of the Committee of the Towns, that the owner of the ship should apply for a clearance; it appeared that Mr. Rotch had been managed and was still under the influence of the opposite party; he resisted the request of the people to apply for a clearance for his ship with an obstinacy which, in my opinion, bordered on stubbornness—subdued at length by the peremptory demand of the Body, he consented to apply, a committee of ten respectable gentlemen were appointed to attend him to the collector; the Body meeting the same morning by adjournment, Mr. Rotch was directed to protest in form, and then apply to the Governor for a Pass by the Castle; Mr. Rotch executed his commission with fidelity, but a pass could not be obtained, his Excellency excusing himself in his refusal that he should not make the precedent of granting a pass till a clearance was obtained, which was indeed a fallacy, as it had been usual with him in ordinary cases,—Mr. Rotch returning in the evening reported as above; the Body then voted his conduct to be satisfactory, and recommending order and regularity to the People, dissolved. Previous to the dissolution, a number of Persons, supposed to be the Aboriginal Natives from their complection, approaching near the door of the assembly, gave the War Whoop, which was answered by a few in the galleries of the house where the assembly was convened; silence was commanded, and prudent and peaceable deportment again enjoined. The Savages repaired to the ships which entertained the pestilential Teas, and had began their ravage previous to the dissolution of the meeting—they apply themselves to the destruction of the commodity in earnest, and in the space of about two hours broke up 342 chests and discharged their contents into the sea. A watch, as I am informed, was stationed to prevent embezzlement and not a single ounce of Teas was suffered to be purloined by the populace. One or two persons being detected in endeavouring to pocket a small quantity were stripped of their acquisitions and very roughly handled. It is worthy remark that, although a considerable quantity of goods of different kinds were still remaining on board the vessels, no injury was sustained; such attention to private property was observed that a small padlock belonging to the Captain of one of the ships being broke another was procured and sent to him. I cannot but express my admiration of the conduct of this People. Uninfluenced by party or any other attachment, I presume I shall not be suspected of misrepresentation. The East India Company must console themselves with this reflection, that if they have suffered, the prejudice they sustaine does not arise from enmity to them. A fatal necessity has rendered this catstrophe inevitable—the landing the tea would have been fatal, as it would have saddled the colonies with a duty imposed without their consent, and which no power on earth can effect. Their strength and numbers, spirit and illumination, render the experiment dangerous, the defeat certain: The Consignees must attribute to themselves the loss of the property of the East India Company: had they seasonably quieted the minds of the people by a resignation, all had been well; the customhouse, and the man who disgraces Majesty by representing him, acting in confederacy with the inveterate enemies of America, stupidly opposed every measure concerted to return the Teas.—That Americans may defeat every attempt to enslave them, is the warmest wish of my heart. I shall return home doubly fortified in my resolution to prevent that deprecated calamity, the landing the teas in Rhode Island, and console myself with the happiest assurance that my brethren have not less virtue, less resolution, than their neighbours.

An Impartial Observer

Source: *Boston Evening Post,* December 20, 1773.

1778 • 17 • George Washington, "To the Inhabitants of the States of Pennsylvania, New Jersey, and Delaware"

Introduction: *The Continental Army was almost always in need of food, especially during the winter of 1777–1778 when it was encamped at Valley Forge 25 miles west of Philadelphia, then occupied by the British. The army's commander, George Washington, was desperate to acquire food. Here is one of Washington's pleas that he sent out to the surrounding states trying to get food. Enough food came through for the army to survive and fight another day.*

To the Inhabitants of the States of Pennsylvania, New Jersey, and Delaware.

The good people of the State of Pennsylvania, and particularly those in the vicinity of this Camp, having expressed a desire of furnishing the Army with the produce of the country were Markets regularly established for that purpose: In order to encourage so laudable a design, I have thought fit to make known, that on the second Monday in February, at eight in the morning, the Market will be opened at the Stone chimney Picket, in front of the Camp, and that the same will be continued on every Monday and Thursday following at that place: That on every Tuesday and Friday the Market will be held on the east side of Schuylkill, near the New Bridge: And on every Wednesday and Saturday, in rear of the Camp, near the Adjutant General Office. That a Clerk of the Market, an inhabitant of this State, will attend on the respective days and at the places before mentioned, whose duty it shall be to protect the inhabitants from any kind of abuse or violence that may be offered to their persons or effects, and to see that they receive pay for their articles according to the prices hereafter mentioned, and for others not particularly enumerated in like proportion, viz.

Fresh Pork per lb 10
Roasting Pig do 16
Mutton do. 010
Veal do. 010
Fat Turkey do. 14
Fat Goose do. 10
Fat Ducks each 39
Fat Fowls do. 26
Fresh Butter per lb. 39
Firkin ditto do. 30
Hogs Lard do. 30
Cheese do. 30
Sausages do. 39
Eggs per dozen. 16
Rough skinned Potatoes per bushel. 100
Spanish ditto per do. 76
Turnips do. 50
Cabbages per head, 10
Onions per half peck, 26
Beans per quart, 13
Sour crout per half peck 39
Apples do. 16
Dried ditto do. 39
Indian Meal do. 20
Leaf Tobacco per lb. 40
Vinegar per quart, 26
New Milk do. 10
Soft Soap do. 10
Cyder per barrel, 400
Small Beer do. 1100

The Clerk of the Market is also to take effectual care that there be no fraud in weight or measure, and that whatsoever is offered to sale be of good quality.

All persons coming to the Markets aforesaid, for the purpose of supplying them, or returning from the same, may depend their carriages and cattle shall not be impressed or otherwise detained. The inhabitation are to take notice that they will not have liberty to receive from the Soldiery, any kind of cloathing or military stores in pay for their provision, or upon any pretence whatsoever.

It is hoped that all persons well affected to their country, both for their own advantage and from a regard to the accommodation of the Army, will manifest their zeal upon this occasion, and chearfully contribute to the success of a plan intended to answer the most valuable purposes.

G. WASHINGTON. Head Quarters, Valley Forge, January 30, 1778.

Source: *Pennsylvania Gazette,* February 7, 1778.

1789 • 18 • Benjamin Rush, *Enquiry into the Effects of Spirituous Liquors*

Introduction: *Dr. Benjamin Rush of Philadelphia was an American Renaissance man of the late 18th century. One of the nation's first medical professors, Rush also was a signer of the Declaration of Independence, a member of the Continental Congress, and the nation's first surgeon general. During the American Revolutionary War, Rush became concerned with alcoholism in the army. In 1782 he wrote a letter to the* Pennsylvania Journal *arguing against the common practice of providing workers with generous allotments of distilled beverages during harvest time. He suggested water, beer, and buttermilk as alternatives, but his advice was widely ignored. Rush believed that the best way to discourage people from drinking was to educate them. He launched an educational campaign against distilled spirits with the publication of a pamphlet,* An Enquiry into the Effects of Spirituous Liquors upon the Human Body *(1784). In it, he concluded that "a people corrupted by strong drink cannot long be free people" and that Americans should give up ardent spirits "suddenly and entirely." The pamphlet went through several editions and numerous reprintings during the next 50 years, and it would be cited thereafter as America's first temperance work. By the time he died in 1813 the temperance movement was well under way in America, and Rush has frequently been credited as its founding father.*

The effects of ardent sprits divide themselves into such as are of a prompt, such as of are of a chronic nature. The former discover themselves in drunkenness; the latter in a numerous train of diseases and vices of the body and mind.

I. I shall begin by briefly describing their prompt, or immediate effects, in a fit of drunkenness.

This odious disease (for by that name it should be called) appears with more or less of the following symptoms, and most commonly in the order in which I shall enumerate them.

1. Unusual garrulity.
2. Unusual silence.
3. Captiousness, and a disposition to quarrel.
4. Uncommon good humour, and an insipid simpering, or laugh.
5. Profane swearing, and cursing.

6. A disclosure of their own, or other people's secrets.
7. A rude disposition to tell those persons in company whom they know, their faults.
8. Certain immodest actions. I am sorry to say, this sign of the first stage of drunkenness, sometimes appears in women, who, when sober, are uniformly remarkable for chaste and decent manners.
9. A clipping of words.
10. Fighting; a black eye, or a swelled nose, often mark this grade of drunkenness.
11. Certain extravagant acts which indicate a temporary fit of madness. These are singing, hallooing, roaring, imitating the noises of brute animals, jumping, tearing off clothes, dancing naked, breaking glasses and china, and dashing other articles of household furniture upon the ground, or floor. After a while the paroxysm of drunkenness is completely formed. The face now becomes flushed, the eyes project and are somewhat watery, winking is less frequent than is natural; the upper lip is protruded;—the head inclines a little to one shoulder;—the jaw falls;—belchings, and hiccup take place;—the limbs totter;—the whole body staggers;—The unfortunate subject of this history next falls on his seat,—he looks around him with a vacant countenance, and mutters inarticulate sounds to himself;—he attempts to rise and walk. In this attempt he falls upon his side, from which he gradually turns upon his back. He now closes his eyes, and falls into a profound sleep, frequently attended by snoring, and profuse sweats, and sometimes with such a relaxation of the muscles which confine the bladder and the lower bowels, as to produce a symptom which delicacy forbids me to mention. In this condition, he often lies from ten, twelve, and twenty-four hours, to two, three, or four, and five days, an object of pity and disgust to his family and friends. . . .

II. Let us next attend to the chronic effects of ardent spirits upon the body and mind. In the body, they dispose to every form of acute disease; they moreover *excite* fevers in persons predisposed to them, from other causes. This has been remarked in all the yellow fevers which have visited the cities of the United States. Hard drinkers seldom escape, and rarely recover from them. The following diseases are the usual consequences of the habitual use of ardent spirits, viz.

1. A decay of appetite, sickness at stomach, and a puking of bile or a discharge of a frothy and viscid phlegm by hawking, in the morning.
2. Obstructions of the liver. . . .
3. Jaundice and dropsy of the belly and limbs, and finally of every cavity of the body. . . .
4. Hoarseness, and a husky cough. . . .
5. Diabetes. . . .
6. Redness, and eruptions on various parts of the body. . . .
7. A fetid breath, composed of every thing, that is offensive in putrid animal manner.
8. Frequent and disgusting belching. Dr. Haller relates the case of a notorious drunkard having been suddenly destroyed in consequence of the vapour discharged from his stomach by belching, accidentally taking fire by coming in contact with the flame of a candle.
9. Epilepsy.
10. Gout, in all its various forms of swelled limbs, colic, palsy, and apoplexy

Lastly, 11. Madness.

Source: Benjamin Rush, *An Enquiry into the Effects of Spirituous Liquors upon the Human Body* (Philadelphia: Thomas Bradford, 1784), 8.

1792 • 19 • Alexander Hamilton, Report on the Difficulties of Taxing Distilled Spirits

Introduction: *As a result of the American Revolution, the states that had borne the brunt of the conflict were left with heavy debts. Some states paid down their debts; others didn't. When the U.S. Constitution was ratified and Congress first met in 1789, one of the important questions for those attending was what to do with these debts. Alexander Hamilton, secretary of the treasury, and others wanted the federal government to assume responsibility. Virginians Thomas Jefferson, then the secretary of state, and James Madison, the leader in the U.S. House of Representatives, opposed this. They argued that since Virginia had already paid off half of its war debts, it was unfair that Virginians should now pick up part of the burden for other states that had not bothered to do so. But Jefferson and Madison wanted the nation's capital, then in Philadelphia, moved south, so they reached a compromise. The federal government would take care of the states' unpaid war debts, and the nation's capital would be moved to a spot along the Potomac River that ran between Virginia and Maryland. A serious problem remained, however. How could the federal government pay off the debts? Hamilton proposed taxing the production of alcohol in the United States. This Congress did, and it led to the Whiskey Rebellion.*

Spirits, Foreign and Domestic. Communicated to the House of Representatives, March 6, 1792.

The representation signed Edward Cook, chairman, as on behalf of the four most western counties of Pennsylvania, states, that the distance of that part of the country from a market for its produce, leads to a necessity of distilling the grain, which is raised, as a principal dependence of its inhabitants; which circumstance, and the scarcity of cash, combine to render the tax in question unequal, oppressive, and particularly distressing to them.

As to the circumstance of equality, it may safely be affirmed to be impracticable to devise a tax which shall operate with exact equality upon every part of the community. Local and other circumstances will inevitably create disparities, more or less great.

Taxes on consumable articles have, upon the whole, better pretensions to equality than any other. If some of them fall more heavily on particular parts of the community, others of them are chiefly borne by other parts. And the result is an equalization of the burthen as far as it is attainable. Of this class of taxes it is not easy to conceive one which can operate with greater equality than a tax on distilled spirits. There appears to be no article, as far as the information of the Secretary goes, which is an object of more equal consumption throughout the United States.

In particular districts, a greater use of cider may occasion a smaller consumption of spirits; but it will not be found, on a close examination, that it makes a material difference. A greater or less use of ardent spirits, as far as it exists, seems to depend more on relative habits of sobriety or intemperance than on any other cause.

Alexander Hamilton helped frame the U.S. Constitution and was a founding father of the new nation. (Library of Congress)

As far as habits of less moderation, in the use of distilled spirits, should produce inequality any where, it would certainly not be a reason with the Legislature either to repeal or lessen a tax, which, by rendering the article dearer, might tend to restrain too free an indulgence of such habits.

It is certainly not obvious how this tax can operate particularly unequally upon the part of the country in question. As a general rule it is a true one, that duties on articles of consumption fall on the consumers, by being added to the price of the commodity. This is illustrated, in the present instance, by facts. Previous to the law laying a duty on home-made spirits, the price of whiskey was about thirty-eight cents; it is now about fifty-six cents. Other causes may have contributed in some degree to this effect, but it is evidently to be ascribed chiefly to the duty.

Unless, therefore, the inhabitants of the counties which have been mentioned are greater consumers of spirits than those of other parts of the country, they cannot pay a greater proportion of the tax. If they are, it is their interest to become less so. It depends on themselves, by diminishing the consumption, to restore equality.

The argument, that they are obliged to convert their grain into spirits, in order to transportation to distant markets, does not prove the point alleged. The duty on all they send to those markets will be paid by the purchasers. They will still pay only upon their own consumption.

As far as an advance is laid upon the duty, or as far as the difference of duty, between whiskey and other spirits, tends to favor a greater consumption of the latter, they, as greater manufacturers of the article, supposing this fact to be as stated, will be proportionably benefited.

The duty on home-made spirits from domestic materials, if paid by the gallon, is nine cents. From the communications which have been received, since the passing of the act, it appears that, paying the rate annexed to the capacity of the still, and using great diligence, the duty may be, in fact, reduced to six cents per gallon. Let the average be taken at seven and a half cents, which is probably higher than is really paid.

Generally speaking, then, for every gallon of whiskey which is consumed, the consumer may be supposed to pay seven and a half cents; but for every gallon of spirits, distilled from foreign materials, the consumer pays, at least, eleven cents, and for every gallon of foreign spirits, at least twenty cents. The consumer, therefore, of foreign spirits, pays nearly three times the duty, and the consumer of homemade spirits, from foreign materials, nearly fifty per cent. more duty, on the same quantity, than the consumer of spirits from domestic materials, exclusive of the greater price, in both cases, which is an additional charge upon each of the two first mentioned classes of consumers.

When it is considered that 8/21 parts of the whole quantity of spirits consumed in the United States are foreign, and 7/21 are of foreign materials, and that the inhabitants of the Atlantic and midland counties are the principal consumers of these more highly taxed articles, it cannot be inferred that the tax under consideration bears particularly hard on the inhabitants of the Western country.

This may serve as an exemplification of a general proposition, of material consequence, namely, that, if the former descriptions of citizens are able, from situation, to obtain more for their produce than the latter, they contribute proportionally more to the revenue. Numerous other examples, in confirmation of this, might be adduced.

As to the circumstance of scarcity of money, as far as it can be supposed to have foundation, it is as much an objection to any other tax as the one in question. The weight of the tax is not certainly such as to involve any peculiar difficulty. It is impossible to conceive that nine cents per gallon on distilled spirits, which is stating it at the highest, can, from the magnitude of the tax, distress any part of the country, which has an ability to pay taxes at all—enjoying, too, the unexampled advantage of a total exemption from taxes on houses, lands, or stock.

The population of the United States being about four millions of persons, and the quantity of spirits annually consumed between ten and eleven millions of gallons, the yearly proportion to each family, if consisting of six persons, which is a full ratio, would be about sixteen gallons, the duty upon which would be less than one dollar and a half. The citizen who is able to maintain a family, and who is the owner or occupier of a farm, cannot feel any inconvenience from so light a contribution; and the industrious poor, whether artisans or laborers, are usually allowed spirits, or an equivalent, in addition to their wages.

The Secretary has no evidence to satisfy his mind that a real scarcity of money will be found, on experiment, a serious impediment to the payment of the tax any where. In the quarter where this complaint has particularly prevailed, the expenditures, for the defence of the frontier, would seem, alone, sufficient to obviate it. To this, it is answered, that the contractors for the supply of the army operate with goods, and not with money. But this still tends to keep at home whatever money finds its way there. Nor is it a fact, if the information of the Secretary be not materially erroneous, that the purchases of the contractors of flour, meat, &c., are wholly with goods. But, if they were, the Secretary can aver, that more money has, in the course of the last year, been sent into the Western country, from the treasury, in specie, and bank bills, which answer the same purpose, for the pay of the troops and militia, and for quartermaster's supplies, than the whole amount of the tax in the four western counties of Pennsylvania and the district of Kentucky, is likely to equal in four or five years. Similar remittances are likely to be made in future.

Hence, the Government itself furnishes, and, in all probability, will continue to furnish, the means of paying its own demands, with a surplus which will sensibly foster the industry of the parties concerned, if they avail themselves of it, under the guidance of a spirit of economy and exertion.

Whether there be no part of the United States in which the objection of want of money may truly exist, in a degree to render the payment of the duty seriously distressing to the inhabitants, the Secretary is not able to pronounce. He can only express his own doubt of the fact, and refer the matter to such information as the members of any district, so situated, may have it in their power to offer to the legislative body.

Should the case appear to exist, it would involve the necessity of a measure, in the abstract, very ineligible, that is, the receipt of the duty in the article itself.

If an alternative of this sort were to be allowed, it would be proper to make it the duty of the party paying, to deliver the article at the place in each county, where the office of inspection is kept, and to regulate the price according to such a standard as would induce a preference of paying in cash, except from a real impracticability of obtaining it.

In regard to the petition from the district of Kentucky, after what has been said with reference to other applications, it can only be necessary to observe, that the exemption which is sought by that petition is rendered impracticable by an express provision of the constitution, which declares that "all duties, imposts, and excises, shall be uniform throughout the United States."

In the course of the foregoing examination of the objections which have been made to the law, some alterations have been submitted for the purpose of removing a part of them. The Secretary will now proceed to submit such further alterations as appear to him advisable, arising either from the suggestions of the officers of the revenue or from his own reflections.

1. It appears expedient to alter the distinction respecting distilleries from domestic materials in cities, towns, and villages, so as to confine it to one or more stills worked at the same distillery, the capacity or capacities of which together do not fall short of four hundred gallons.

The effectual execution of the present provisions respecting distilleries from home materials in cities, towns, and villages, would occasion an inconvenient multiplication of officers, and would, in too great a degree, exhaust the product of the duty in the expense of collection. It is also probable that the alteration suggested would also conduce to public satisfaction.

2. The present provisions concerning the entering of stills are found, by experience, not to be adequate, and, in some instances, not convenient.

It appears advisable that there shall be one office of inspection for each county, with authority to the supervisor to establish more than one, if he shall judge it necessary for the accommodation of the inhabitants; and that every distiller, or person having or keeping a still, shall be required to make entry of the same at some office of inspection for the county, within a certain determinate period in each year. It will be proper, also, to enjoin upon every person, who, residing within the county, shall procure a still, or who, removing into a county, shall bring into it a still, within twenty days after such procuring or removal, and before he or she begins to use the still, to make entry at the office of inspection. Every entry, besides describing the still, should specify in whose possession it is, and the purpose for which it is intended, as, whether for sale or for use in distilling; and in the case of a removal of the person from another place into the county, shall specify the place from which the still shall have been brought. A forfeiture of the still ought, in every case in which an entry is required, to attend an omission to enter.

This regulation, by simplifying the business of entering stills, would render it easier to comprehend and comply with what is required, would furnish the officers with a better rule for ascertaining delinquencies, and, by avoiding to them a considerable degree of unnecessary trouble, will facilitate the retaining of proper characters in the offices of collectors.

3. It is represented that difficulties have, in some instances, arisen, concerning the persons responsible for the duty. The apparent not being always the real proprietor, an opportunity for collusion is afforded; and without collusion, the uncertainty is stated as a source of embarrassment.

It also, sometimes, happens, that certain itinerant persons, without property, complying with the preliminary requisitions of the law as to entry, &c., erect and work stills for a time, and before a half yearly period of payment arrives, remove and evade the duty.

It would tend to remedy these inconveniencies, if possessors and proprietors of stills were made jointly and severally liable, and if the duty were made a specific lien on the still itself; if, also, the proprietor of the land upon which any still may be worked should be made answerable for the duty, except where it is worked by a lawful and bona fide tenant of the land of an estate not less than for a term of one year, or unless such proprietor can make it appear, that the possessor of the still was, during the whole time, without his privity or connivance, an intruder or trespasser on the land; and if, in the last place, any distiller, about to remove from the division in which he is, should be required, previous to such removal, to pay the tax for the year, deducting any prior payments, or give bond, with approved surety, conditioned for the payment of the full sum for which he or she should be legally accountable to the end of the year, to the collector of the division to which the removal shall be, rendering proof thereof, under the hand of the said collector, within six months after the expiration of the year.

As well with a view to the forfeiture of the stills for non-entry, as to give effect to a specific lien of the duty (if either or both of these provisions should be deemed eligible), it will be necessary to enjoin it upon the officers of the revenue to identify, by proper marks, the several stills which shall have been entered with them.

4. The exemptions granted to stills of the capacity of fifty gallons and under, by the 36th section of the law, appear, from experience, to require revision.

Tending to produce inequality, as well as to frustrate the revenue, they have excited complaint. It appears, at least, advisable, that the obligation to enter, as connected with that of paying duty, should extend to stills of all dimensions, and that it should be enforced, in every case, by the same penalty.

5. The 28th section of the act makes provision for the seizure of spirits, unaccompanied with marks and certificates, in the cases in which they are required; but as they are required only in certain cases, and there is no method of distinguishing the spirits, in respect to which they are necessary, from those in respect to which they are not necessary, the provision becomes nugatory, because an attempt to enforce it would be oppressive. Hence, not only a great security for the due execution of the law is lost, but seizures very distressing to unoffending individuals must happen, notwithstanding great precaution to avoid them.

It would be, in the opinion of the Secretary, of great importance to provide, that all spirits whatsoever, in casks or vessels of the capacity of twenty gallons and upwards, should be marked and certified, on pain of seizure and forfeiture, making it the duty of the officers to furnish the requisite certificates gratis, to distillers and dealers, in all cases in which the law shall have been complied with.

In those cases in which an occasional recurrence to the officers for certificates might be inconvenient, blanks may be furnished, to be accounted for. And it may be left to the parties themselves, in the like cases, to mark their own casks or vessels in some simple manner, to be defined in the law. These cases may be designated generally. They will principally relate to dealers, who, in the course of their business, draw off spirits from larger to smaller casks, and to distillers, who pay according to the capacities of their stills.

As a part of a regulation of this sort, it will be necessary to require, that, within a certain period, sufficiently long to admit of time to know and comply with the provision, entry shall be made, by all dealers and distillers, of all spirits in their respective possessions, which shall not have been previously marked and certified, according to law, in order that they may be marked and certified as old stock.

The regulations here proposed, though productive of some trouble and inconvenience in the outset, will be, afterwards, a security both to individuals and to the revenue.

6. At present, spirits may not be imported from abroad in casks of less capacity than fifty gallons. The size of these casks is smaller than is desirable, so far as the security of the revenue is concerned, and there has not occurred any good objection to confining the importation to larger casks, that is to say, to casks of not less than ninety gallons. Certainly, as far as respects rum from the West Indies, it may be done without inconvenience, being conformable to the general course of business. The result of examination is, that the exception as to this particular, in favor of gin, may be abolished. Should any alteration on this subject take place, it ought not to begin to operate till after the expiration of the year.

7. There is ground to suppose, that the allowance of drawback, without any limitation as to quantity, has been abused. It is submitted that none be made on any less quantity than one hundred and fifty gallons.

8. There is danger that facility may be given to illicit importations, by making use of casks which have been once regularly marked, and the certificates which have been issued with them, to cover other spirits than those originally contained in such casks. Appearances which countenance suspicion, on this point, have been the subjects of representation from several quarters.

The danger may be obviated by prohibiting the importation in such marked casks, on pain of forfeiture both of the spirits and of any ship or vessel in which they may be brought. A prohibition of this sort does not appear liable to any good objection.

9. The duty of sixty cents per gallon of the capacity of a still was founded upon a computation that a still of any given dimensions, worked four months in the year, which is the usual period of country distillation, would yield a quantity of spirits, which, at the rate of nine cents per gallon, would correspond with sixty cents per gallon of the capacity of the still. It will deserve consideration, whether it will not be expedient to give an option to country distillers, at the annual entry of their stills, to take out a license for any portion of the year, which they may respectively think fit, and to pay at the rate of twelve and a half cents per gallon of the capacity, per month, during such period. This to stand in lieu of the alternative of paying by the gallon distilled; it would obviate in this case the necessity of accounting upon oath, and would leave it in the power of each distiller to cover the precise time he meant to work his still with a license, and to pay for that time only. A strict prohibition to distil at any other time than that for which

the license was given would be of course necessary to accompany the regulation as far as regarded any such licensed distiller.

The only remaining points which have occurred, as proper to be submitted to the consideration of the Legislature, respect the officers of the revenue.

It is represented that, in some instances, from the ill humor of individuals, the officers have experienced much embarrassment, in respect to the filling of stills with water, to ascertain their capacity, which, upon examination, is found the most simple and practicable mode. The proprietors have, in some instances, not only refused to aid the officers, but have even put out of their way the means by which the filling might be conveniently accomplished.

It would conduce to the easy execution of the law, and to the very important purpose of retaining and procuring respectable characters as collectors, if the proprietors and possessors of stills were required to aid them in the execution of this part of their duty, or to pay a certain sum as a compensation for the doing of it.

The limits assigned in the law, respecting compensations, are found in practice essentially inadequate to the object.

In the most productive divisions, the commissions of the collectors afford but a moderate compensation. In the greatest part of them, the compensation is glaringly disproportioned to the service; in many of them, it falls materially short of the expense of the officer.

It is believed that, in no country whatever, has the collection of a similar duty been effected within the limit assigned. Applying in the United States to a single article only, and yielding consequently a less total product than where many articles are comprehended, the expense of collection must of necessity be proportionally greater.

It appears to the Secretary, that seven and a half per cent. of the total product of the duties on distilled spirits, foreign as well as domestic, and not less, will suffice to defray the compensations to officers, and other expenses incidental to the collection of the duty. This is to be understood as supplemental to the present custom house expenses.

It is unnecessary to urge to the House of Representatives, how essential it must be to the execution of the law, in a manner effectual to the purposes of the Government, and satisfactory to the community, to secure, by competent, though moderate rewards, the diligent services of respectable and trustworthy characters.

All which is humbly submitted.

Alexander Hamilton.

Source: Alexander Hamilton, "Report on the Difficulties in the Execution of the Act Laying Duties on Distilled Spirits, [March 1792]," in *The Works of Alexander Hamilton,* Vol. 3, edited by John C. Hamilton (New York: John C. Trow, 1850), 297–325.

1794 • 20 • Jean Anthelme Brillat-Savarin, *Physiology of Taste*

Introduction: *The French gastronome Jean Anthelme Brillat-Savarin spent two years in exile in the United States during the French Revolution. In general he was not impressed with American food, but he was delighted with the wild turkey, which he* *proclaimed was "certainly one of the most delightful presents which the New World has made to the Old." He ate wild turkey as well as domesticated turkey and wrote that wild turkey flesh was "Darker and with a stronger flavor than that of the domestic bird." He recorded in his classic work* Physiology of Taste *that while visiting Hartford, Connecticut, he was invited to hunt on the land of a local farmer. Brillat-Savarin succeeded in bagging a turkey and roasted it. Unfortunately, he does not tell how he prepared it on this occasion, but he clearly loved truffled turkey. In his concluding essay, he imagines Adam and Eve and asks "what would you not have given for a truffled turkey hen?" As they didn't have one, his response was "I weep for you."*

One fine day in October, 1794, therefore, with a friend, I set out with the hope of reaching the farm of Mr. Bulow, five mortal leagues from Hartford, before night.

Though the road was hardly traced, we arrived there without accident, and were received with that cordial hospitality expressed by acts, for before we had been five minutes on the farm, dogs, horses and men were all suitably taken care of.

About two hours were consumed in the examination of the farm and its dependencies. I would describe all this if I did not prefer to display to the reader the four buxom daughters of Mr. Bulow, to whom our arrival was a great event.

Their ages were from sixteen to twenty-four, and there was so much simplicity in their persons, so much activity and abandon, that every motion seemed full of grace.

After our return from walking we sat around a well furnished table. A superb piece of corned beef, a stewed goose, and a magnificent leg of mutton, besides an abundance of vegetables and two large jugs of cider, one at each end of the table, made up our bill of fare.

When we had proven to our host, that in appetite at least, we were true huntsmen, we began to make arrangements for our sport. He told us where we would find game, and gave us land-marks to guide us on our return, not forgetting farm-houses where we could obtain refreshments.

During this conversation the ladies had prepared excellent tea, of which we drank several cups, and were then shown into a room with two beds, where exercise and fatigue procured us a sound sleep.

On the next day we set out rather late, and having come to the end of the clearings made by Mr. Bulow, I found myself in a virgin forest for the first time. The sound of the axe had never been heard there.

I walked about with delight, observing the blessings and ravages of time which creates and destroys, and I amused myself by tracing all the periods on the life of an oak since the moment when its two leaves start from the ground, until it leaves but a long black mark which is the dust of its heart.

My companion, Mr. King, reproached me for my moodiness, and we began the hunt. We killed first some of those pretty grey partridges which are so round and so tender. We then knocked down six or seven grey squirrels, highly esteemed in America, and at last were fortunate enough to find a flock of turkeys.

They rose one after the other, flying rapidly and crying loudly. Mr. King fired on the first and ran after it. The others were soon out of shot. The most sluggish of all arose at last, not ten paces from me. It flew through an opening, I fired and it fell dead.

One must be a sportsman to conceive the extreme pleasure this shot caused me. I seized on the superb bird and turned it over and over for a quarter of an hour. . . .

When we reached the farm supper was ready, but before we sat down to the table we drew near to a bright and brilliant fire which had been lighted for us, though the season did not indicate that such a precaution was necessary. We found it very comfortable, fatigued as we were, and were rested as if by enchantment. . . .

We ate as if we were famished; a large bowl of punch enabled us to finish the evening, and a conversation, which our host made perfectly free, led us far into the night. . . .

On the next day, in spite of Mr. Bulow's persuasions, we set out. I had duties to discharge; and while the horses were being prepared, Mr. Bulow took me aside and used these remarkable words.

"You see in me, sir, a happy man, if there be one under heaven; all that you see here is derived from my own property. My stockings were knit by my daughters, and my cloths were furnished by my flocks. They also, with my garden, furnish me with an abundance of healthy food. The greatest eulogium of our government is, that in the State of Connecticut there are a thousand farmers as well satisfied as I am, the doors of whom have no locks." . . .

On my way back I seemed absorbed by profound reflection. Perhaps the reader may think I mused on my host's parting words; I had very different thoughts, however, for I was studying how I should cook my turkey. I was in some trouble, for I feared I would not find all I needed at Hartford, and wished to make a trophy of my *spolia opima.*[1]

I make a painful sacrifice in suppressing the details of the profound science I exhibited in the preparation of an entertainment, to which I invited several friends. Suffice it to say that the partridge wings were served en papillote, and the grey squirrels stewed in madeira.

The turkey, which was our only roast dish, was charming to the sight, flattering to the sense of smell, and delicious to taste. Therefore, until the last fragment was eaten, there were heard around the table, "Very good"; "Exceedingly good"; "Dear sir; what a nice piece."

Note

1. Latin for a Roman trophy from a one-on-one battle with a foe.

Source: Jean Anthelme Brillat-Savarin, *The Physiology of Taste: Or, Transcendental Gastronomy* (Philadelphia: Lindsay and Blakston, 1853), 109–114.

1796 • 21 • AMELIA SIMMONS, *AMERICAN COOKERY*

Introduction: *Cookbooks had been published in America since 1742, but until 1796 they were all reprints of English cookbooks. Amelia Simmons's* American Cookery *(1796) was the first cookbook published in the United States by an American. Not much is known about her. According to the title page she was an orphan, and she likely lived in Hartford, Connecticut, where the first edition was published. She was also unable to read or write. Someone copied her recipes, and the publisher of the first edition wrote the preface below. Below are also recipes from the cookbook, including "How to Dress* *a Turtle," "Cookies," and "Pompkin." Turtles were a very important part of the American diet until they began to disappear in the early 19th century. The term "cookies" derived from America's Dutch heritage—the traditional English word was "cracker." Pumpkins were native to America and were commonly consumed in colonial times. The book went through at least 14 printings before 1831, and many of the recipes were pirated by other cookbook writers for years to come.*

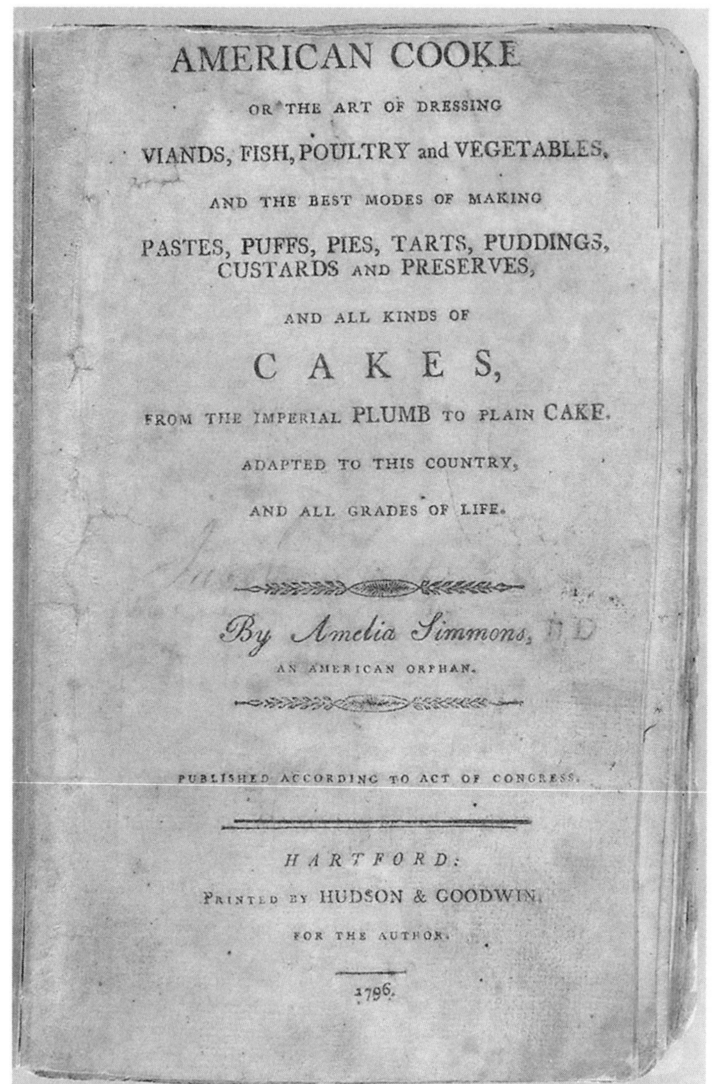

AMERICAN COOKE

OR THE ART OF DRESSING

VIANDS, FISH, POULTRY and VEGETABLES,

AND THE BEST MODES OF MAKING

PASTES, PUFFS, PIES, TARTS, PUDDINGS, CUSTARDS AND PRESERVES,

AND ALL KINDS OF

CAKES,

FROM THE IMPERIAL PLUMB TO PLAIN CAKE.

ADAPTED TO THIS COUNTRY,

AND ALL GRADES OF LIFE.

By Amelia Simmons,

AN AMERICAN ORPHAN.

PUBLISHED ACCORDING TO ACT OF CONGRESS.

HARTFORD:

PRINTED BY HUDSON & GOODWIN.

FOR THE AUTHOR.

1796.

Title page of the first edition of Amelia Simmons's *American Cookery* (1796), the first cookbook written by an American. (Library of Congress)

Preface.

As this treatise is calculated for the improvement of the rising generation of *Females* in America, the Lady of fashion and fortune will not be displeased, if many hints are suggested for the more general and universal knowledge of those females in this country, who by the loss of their parents, or other unfortunate circumstances, are reduced to the necessity of going into families in the line of domestics, or taking refuge with their friends or relations, and doing those things which are really essential to the perfecting them as good wives, and useful members of society. The orphan, tho' left to the care of virtuous guardians, will find it essentially necessary to have an opinion and determination of her own. The world, and the fashion thereof, is so variable, that old people cannot accommodate themselves to the various changes and fashions which daily occur; they will adhere to the fashion of their day, and will not surrender their attachments to the good old way—while the young and the gay, bend and conform readily to the taste of the times, and fancy of the hour.

By having an opinion and determination, I would not be understood to mean an obstinate perseverance in trifles, which borders on obstinacy—by no means, but only an adherence to those rules and maxims which have flood the test of ages, and will forever establish the female character, a virtuous character—altho' they conform to the ruling taste of the age in cookery, dress, language, manners, &c.

It must ever remain a check upon the poor solitary orphan, that while those females who have parents, or brothers, or riches, to defend their indiscretions, that the orphan must depend solely upon character. How immensely important, therefore, that every action, every word, every thought, be regulated by the strictest purity, and that every movement meet the approbation of the good and wise.

The candor of the American Ladies is solicitously intreated by the Authoress, as she is circumscribed in her knowledge, this being an original work in this country. Should any future editions appear, she hopes to render it more valuable. . . .

To Dress a Turtle.

Fill a boiler or kettle, with a quantity of water sufficient to scald the callapach and Callapee,[1] the fins, &c. and about 9 o'clock hang up your Turtle by the hind fins, cut of[f] the head and save the blood, take a sharp pointed knife and separate the callapach from the callapee, or the back from the belly part, down to the shoulders, so as to come at the entrails which take out, and clean them, as you would those of any other animal, and throw them into a tub of clean water, taking great care not to break the gall, but to cut it off from the liver and throw it away, then separate each distinctly and put the guts into another vessel, open them with a small pen-knife end to end, wash them clean, and draw them through a woolen cloth, in warm water, to clear away the slime and then put them in clean cold water till they are used with the other part of the entrails, which must be cut up small to be mixed in the baking dishes with the meat; this done, separate the back and belly pieces, entirely cutting away the fore fins by the upper joint, which scald; peal off the loose skin and cut them into small pieces, laying them by themselves, either in another vessel, or on the table, ready to be seasoned; then cut off the meat from the belly part, and clean the back from the lungs, kidneys, &c. and that meat cut into pieces as small as a walnut, laying it likewise by itself; after this you are to scald the back, and belly pieces, pulling off the shell from the back, and the yellow skin from the belly, when all will be white and clean, and with the kitchen cleaver cut those up likewise into pieces about the bigness or breadth of a card; put those pieces into clean cold water, wash them and place them in a heap on the table, so that each part may lay by itself; the meat being thus prepared and laid separate for seasoning; mix two third parts of salt or rather more, and one third part of cyanne pepper, black pepper, and a nutmeg, and mace pounded fine, and mixt all together; the quantity, to be proportioned to the size of the Turtle, so that in each dish there may be about three spoonfuls of seasoning to every twelve pound of meat; your meat being thus seasoned, get some sweet herbs, such as thyme, savory, &c. let them be dryed an rub'd fine, and having provided some deep dishes to bake it in, which should be of the common brown ware, put in the coarsest part of the meat, put a quarter pound of butter at the bottom of each dish, and then put some of each of the several parcels of meat, so that the dishes may be all alike and have equal portions of the different parts of the Turtle, and between each laying of meat strew a little of the mixture of sweet herbs, fill your dishes within an inch an half, or two inches of the top; boil the blood of the Turtle, and put into it, then lay on forcemeat balls made of veal, highly seasoned with the same seasoning as the Turtle; put in each dish a gill of Madeira Wine, and as much water as it will conveniently hold, then break over it five or six eggs to keep the meat from scorching at the top, and over that shake a handful of shread parsley, to make it look green, when done put your dishes into an oven made hot enough to bake bread, and in an hour and half, or two hours (according to the size of the dishes) it will be sufficiently done.

Pompkin.

No. 1. One quart stewed and strained, 3 pints cream, 9 beaten eggs, sugar, mace, nutmeg and ginger, laid into paste No. 7 or 3, and with a dough spur, cross and chequer[2] it, and baked in dishes three quarters of an hour.

No. 2. One quart of milk, 1 pint pompkin, 4 eggs, molasses, allspice and ginger in a crust, bake 1 hour.

Royal Paste.

No. 9. Rub half a pound of butter into one pound of flour, four whites beat to a foam, add two yolks, two ounces of fine sugar; roll often, rubbing one third, and rolling two thirds of the butter is best; excellent for tarts and apple cakes.

Cranberries [tart].

Stewed, strained and sweetened, put into paste No. 9, and baked gently.

Cookies.

One pound sugar boiled slowly in half pint water, scum well and cool, add two tea spoons pearl ash dissolved in milk, then two and half pounds flour, rub in 4 ounces butter, and two large spoons of finely powdered coriander seed, wet with above; make roles half an inch thick and cut to the shape you please; bake fifteen or twenty minutes in a slack oven—good three weeks.

Notes

1. Parts of the turtle adjoining the upper shell.
2. Cut it in squares.

Source: Amelia Simmons, *American Cookery* . . . (Hartford: Printed by Hudson and Goodwin, for the Author, 1796), 4, 21–22, 27, 30, 31, 35–36.

1796 • 22 • Joel Barlow, "The Hasty-Pudding"

Introduction: *One common way of eating corn in colonial times was through a dish called hasty pudding, borrowed from the British and Scottish dish of the same name. Its main ingredient depended on where one lived. In England hasty pudding was based on wheat, while in Scotland it was based on oats. In its simplest form, the grain was heated in water until it formed a thick paste. Frequently, sweeteners or other spices were added. More complex versions incorporated eggs and other additives. Following English custom, puddings might appear at any course or meal.*

Hasty pudding's fame derived from a poem written by Joel Barlow in 1793. Barlow was born in Connecticut in 1754 and grew up eating hasty pudding. He moved to France in 1788. When he stopped at an inn in Chambéry in January 1793, he was served polenta, and this dish reminded him of the hasty pudding. Barlow drafted a long poem titled "The Hasty-Pudding," which he sent to a Philadelphia publisher, reporting that it was "a little Poem on a little subject." The poem included a dedication to Martha Washington, who, said Barlow, was the proper model of "domestic virtues" for American women. One odd request was Barlow's insistence that his name be kept "a perfect secret." Barlow offered no reason for this, but he may have believed that a poem about hasty pudding might detract from his reputation as the serious poet who authored America's great epic. Yet some observers maintained that "The Hasty-Pudding" was a well-written poem of the U.S. Federalist era. The Hasty Pudding Club is a social club at Harvard University founded in 1795; hasty pudding was eaten at the first meeting.

The Hasty-Pudding

Canto I

. . . But here, tho' distant from our native shore,
With mutual glee we meet and laugh once more.
The same! I know thee by that yellow face,
That strong complexion of true Indian race,
Which time can never change, nor soil impair,
Nor Alpine snows, nor Turkey's morbid air;
For endless years, thro' every mild domain,
Where grows the maize, there thou art sure to reign.

But man, more fickle, the bold license claims,
In different realms to give thee different names.
Thee the soft nations round the warm Levant
Polanta call, the French, of course, Polente.
Ev'n in thy native regions, how I blush
To hear the Pennsylvanians call thee *Mush!*
On Hudson's banks, while men of Belgic-spawn
Insult and eat thee by the name *Suppawn.*
All spurious appellations, void of truth;
I've better known thee from my earliest youth:
Thy name is *Hasty-Pudding!* thus my sires
Were wont to greet thee fuming from their fire;
And while he argu'd in the just defence
With logic clear they thus explain'd the sense—
"In *haste* the boiling caldron, o'er the blaze,
Receives and cooks the ready-powder'd maize;
In *haste* 'tis served, and then in equal *haste,*
With cooling milk, we make the sweet repast.
No carving to be done, no knife to grate
The tender ear, and wound the stony plate;
But the smooth spoon, just fitted to the lip,
And taught with art the yielding mass to dip,
By frequent journeys to the bowl well stor'd,
Performs the hasty honors of the board."
Such is thy name, significant and clear,

A name, a sound to every Yankey dear,
But most to me, whose heart and palate chaste
Preserve my pure hereditary taste.

There are who strive to stamp with disrepute
The luscious food, because it feeds the brute;
In tropes of high-strain'd wit, while gaudy prigs
Compare thy nursling man to pamper'd pigs;
With sovereign scorn I treat the vulgar jest,
Not fear to share thy bounties with the beast.
What though the generous cow gives me to quaff
The milk nutritious: am I then a calf?
Or can the genius of the noisy swine,
Tho' nurs'd on pudding, thence lay claim to mine?
Sure the sweet song, I fashion to thy praise,
Runs more melodious than the notes they raise.

My song, resounding in its grateful glee,
No merit claims; I praise myself in thee.
My father lov'd thee thro' his length of days;
For thee his fields were shaded o'er with maize;
From thee what health, what vigor he possess't,
Ten sturdy freemen from his loins attest;
Thy constellation rul'd my natal morn,
And all my bones were made of Indian corn.
Delicious grain! whatever from it take,
To roast or boil, to smother or to bake,
In every dish 'tis welcome still to me,
But most, my Hasty-Pudding, most in thee.
Let the green Succotash with thee contend;
Let beans and corn their sweetest juices blend,
Let butter drench them in its yellow tide,
And a long slice of bacon grace their side;
Not all the plate, how famed soe'er it be,
Can please my plate like a bowl of thee.

Some talk of Hoe-cake, fair Virginia's pride,
Rich Johnny-cake this mouth has often tri'd;
Both please me well, their virtues much the same;
Alike their fabric, as allied their fame,
Except in dear New-England, where the last
Receives a dash of pumpkin in the paste,
To give it sweetness and improve the taste.
But place them all before me, smoaking hot,
The big round dumplin rolling from the pot;
The pudding of the bag, whose quivering breast,
With suet lin'd, leads on the Yankey feast;
The charlotte brown, within whose crusty sides

A belly soft the pulpy apple hides;
The yellow bread, whose face like amber glows,
And all of Indian that the bake-pan knows—
You tempt me not—my favorite greets my eyes,
To that lov'd bowl my spoon by instinct flies.

CANTO II

To mix the food by vicious rules of art,
To kill the stomach and to sink the heart,
To make mankind to social virtue sour,
Cram o'er each dish, and be what they devour;
For this the kitchen Muse first fram'd her book,
Commanding sweats to stream from every cook;
Children no more their antic gambols tri'd,
And friends to physic wonder'd why they died.

Not so the Yankey—his abundant feast,
With simples furnish'd and with plainness dres'd,
A numerous offspring gathers round the board,
And cheers alike the servant and the lord;
Whose well-bought hunger prompts the joyous taste,
And health attends them from the short repast.

While the full pail rewards the milk-maid's toil,
The mother sees the morning caldron boil;
To stir the pudding next demands their care;
To spread the table and the bowls prepare;
To feed the children as their portions cool,
And comb their heads, and send them all to labor or to school.

Yet may the simplest dish of some rules impart,
For nature scorns not all the aids of art.
Ev'n Hasty-Pudding, purest of all food,
May still be bad, indifferent, or good,
As sage experience the short process guides,
Or want of skill, or want of care presides,
Whoe'er would form it on the surest plan,
To rear the child and long sustain the man;
To shield the morals while it mends the size,
And all the powers of every food supplies,
Attend the lesson that the Muse shall bring.
Suspend your spoons, and listen while I sing. . . .

Meanwhile the house-wife urges all her care,
The well-earn'd feast to hasten and prepare.
The sifted meal already waits her hand,
The milk is strain'd, the bowls in order stand,
The fire flames high; and, as a pool (that takes

The headlong stream that o'er the mill-dam breaks)
Foams, roars, and rages with incessant toils,
So vext caldron rages, roars, and boils.

First with clean salt she seasons well the food,
Then strews the flour, and thickens all the flood.
Long o'er the simmering fire she lets it stand;
To stir it well demands a stronger hand;
The husband takes his turn; and round and round
The ladle flies; at last the toil is crown'd;
When to the board the thronging huskers pour,
And take their seats as at the corn before.

I leave them to their feast. There still belong
More copius matters to my faithful song.
For rules there are, tho' ne'er unfolded yet,
Nice rules and wise, how pudding should be ate.

Some with molasses line the luscious treat,
And mix, like Bards, the useful with the sweet.
A wholesome dish, and well deserving praise,
A great resource in those bleak wintry days,
When the chill'd earth lies buried deep in snow,
And raging Boreas dries the shivering cow.

Blest cow! thy praise shall still my notes employ,
Great source of health, the only source of joy;
Mother of Egypt's God—but sure, for me,
Were I to leave my God, I'd worship thee.
How oft thy teats these pious hands have presst!
How oft thy bounties proved my only feast!
How oft I've fed thee with my favourite grain!
And roar'd, like thee, to see thy children slain!

Ye swains who know her various worth to prize,
Ah! house her from Winter's angry skies.
Potatoes, pumpkins, should her sadness cheer,
Corn from your crib, and mashes from your beer;
When Spring returns she'll well acquit the loan,
And nurse at once your infants and her own.

Milk then your pudding I should always chuse;
To this in future I confine my Muse.
Till she in haste some further hints unfold,
Well for the young, nor useless to the old.
First in your bowl the milk abundant take,
Then drop with care along the silver lake
Your flakes of pudding; these at first will hide
Their little bulk beneath the swelling tide;

But when their growing mass no more can sink,
When the soft island looms above the brink,
Then check your hand; you've got the portion's due;
So taught our sires, and what they taught is true.

There is a choice in spoons. Though small appear
The nice distinction, yet to me 'tis clear.
The deep-bowl'd Gallic spoon, contriv'd to scoop
In ample draughts the thin diluted soup,
Performs not well in those substantial things,
Whose mass adhesive to the metal clings;
Where the strong labial muscles must embrace,
The gentle curve, and sweep the hollow space.
With ease to enter and discharge the freight,
A bowl less concave, but still more dilate,
Becomes the pudding best. The shape, the size,
A secret rests, unknown to the vulgar eyes.
Experienc'd feeders can alone impart
A rule so much above the lore of art.
These tuneful lips, that thousand spoons have tried,
With just precision could the point decide,
Though not in song; the Muse but poorly shines
In cones, and cubes, and geometric lines;
Yet the true form, as near as she can tell,
Is that small section of a goose-egg-shell,
Which in two equal portions shall divide
The distance from the center to the side.

Fear not to slaver; 'tis no sin.
Like the free Frenchman, from your joyous chin
Suspend the ready napkin; or, like me,
Poise with one hand your bowl upon your knee;
Just in the zenith your wise head project,
Your full spoon, rising in a line direct,
Bold as a bucket, heeds no drops that fall,
The wide mouth'd bowl will surely catch them all.

Source: Joel Barlow, "The Hasty-Pudding," *New York Magazine,* New Series, 1 (January 1796): 41–49.

1804 • 23 • Constantin-François de Volney, "The Most Radical Causes of All Their Diseases"

Introduction: *Constantin-François de Volney (1757–1820), a French historian and philosopher, lived in Philadelphia for three years beginning in 1795. President John Adams claimed that Volney was a French spy, and he was forced to return to France in*

1798. Volney wrote with disgust of American food in his work View of the Climate and Soil of the United States of America *(1804).*

. . . [T]he government, while it directs the attention of the inhabitants of the United States to these objects of domestic concern, should promote their being properly instructed with respect to one of the most essential and most radical causes of all their diseases, I mean their dietetic regimen which in consequence of their origin they have derived from the English and Germans. I will venture to say, that, if a prize were proposed for the scheme of a regimen most calculated to injure the stomach, the teeth, and the health in general, no better could be invented than that of the Americans. In the morning at breakfast, they deluge their stomach with a quart of hot water, impregnated with tea, or so slightly with coffee, that it is mere coloured water: and they swallow, almost without chewing, hot bread, half baked, toast soaked in butter, cheese of the fattest kind, slices of salt or hung beef, ham, &c., all which are nearly insoluble. At dinner they have boiled pastes under the name of puddings, and the fattest are esteemed the most delicious: all their sauces, even for roast beef, are melted butter: their turnips and potatoes swim in hog's lard, butter, or fat: under the name of pie, or pumkin, their pastry is nothing but a greasy paste, never sufficiently baked; to digest these viscous substances, they take tea almost instantly after dinner, making it so strong, that it is absolutely bitter to the taste; in which state it affects the nerves so powerfully, that even the English find it brings on a more obstinate restlessness than coffee. Supper again introduces salt meats, or oysters: as Chatelux says, the whole day passes in heaping indigestions on one another: and to give tone to the poor relaxed and wearied stomach, they drink Madeira, rum, French brandy, gin, or malt spirits, which complete the ruin of the nervous system.

Such a regimen might agree with the Tatars, the primitive stock of the Germans and Anglo-saxons, who used none of these dangerous stimuli. Their equestrian and erratic life rendered and still renders them capable of digesting any thing: but when nations change their climate, or by the progress of civilization become wealthy and idle, they experience as a whole the changes that take place in individuals. The ploughmen or mechanics of England and Germany may live on the diet of their ancestors without inconvenience: but it is not the same with the inhabitants of cities; still less with those, who, emigrating from their cold and damp climate, settle in hot countries like Georgia, the Carolinas, Virginia, &c. Even the power of native habit is incapable of naturalizing a system essentially repugnant to a climate. Accordingly, of all the people of Europe we see the English are least able to resist the effects of tropical climes: and if their descendants the Americans do not alter their old habits in this respect, they will experience the same inconveniencies.

It is so true, that their regimen is one of the grand predisposing causes of disease, and of the yellow fever, that in the height of the epidemics a single case never appeared within the confines of the prison at Philadelphia: and this evidently because the system of diet there is regulated by a scale of temperature, affording no opportunity for overloading the stomach, and consequently for a depravation of the fluids. The abuse of spirituous liquors in particular is totally banished from this admirable establishment; an abuse so general in the United States, that drunkenness is a vice as prevalent in them as among the savages.

Source: Constantin François de Chassebœuf Volney, *View of the Climate and Soil of the United States of America* (London: J. Johnson, 1804), 323–326.

1823 • 24 • James Fenimore Cooper, "Shooting the Christmas Turkey"

Introduction: *James Fenimore Cooper (1789–1851) was one of America's most prolific and distinguished writers of the early 19th century. His more popular novels included* The Last of the Mohicans *and* Leatherstocking Tales. *Below is an excerpt from* The Pioneers: Or, the Sources of the Susquehanna *(1823) about shooting the Christmas turkey. In Dutch New Amsterdam, Mary L. Booth, author of* History of the City of New York *(1860), reported that on Christmas day "the young men repaired to the 'commons' or to 'Beekman's swamp' to shoot at turkeys which were set up for a target. Each man paid a few stuyvers for a shot, and he who succeeded in hitting the bird took it off as a prize." Whether or not this accurately represents events in Dutch New Amsterdam, the turkey shoot was an important Christmas tradition in America during the 19th century. David Sturges Copeland described the event in Clarendon, New York. Turkeys were tied down in a meadow, and the shooters would "blaze away at the poor turkey's head." Samuel H. Hammond described a slightly different rendition. Shooters gave money to the proprietor, and "A plank was placed at some five and twenty rods distance, with a hole in it, through which was thrust the head of the turkey, while his body was secured behind it. At this mark the sportsmen fired. If blood was drawn, the marksman was entitled to the turkey." Below are two excerpts from James Fenimore Cooper's* The Pioneers. *The first deals with shooting the Christmas turkey, and the second is a description of the Christmas meal.*

The ancient amusement of shooting the Christmas turkey is one of the few sports that the settlers of a new country seldom or never neglect to observe. It was connected with the daily practices of a people who often laid aside the axe or the scythe to seize the rifle, as the deer glided through the forests they were felling, or the bear entered their rough meadows to scent the air of a clearing, and to scan, with a look of sagacity, the progress of the invader.

On the present occasion, the usual amusement of the day had been a little hastned, in order to allow a fair opportunity to Mr. Grant, whose exhibition was not less a treat to the young sportsmen than the one which engaged their present attention. The owner of the birds was a free black, who had prepared for the occasion a collection of game that was admirably qualified to inflame the appetite of an epicure, and was well adapted to the means and skill of the different competitors, who were of all ages. He had offered to the younger and more humble marks men divers birds of an inferior quality, and some shooting had already taken place, much to the pecuniary advantage of the sable owner of the game. The order of the sports was extremely simple, and well understood. The bird was fastened by a string to the stump of a large pine, the side of which, toward the point where the marksmen were placed, had been flattened with an axe, in order that it might serve the purpose of a target, by which the merit of each individual might be ascertained. The distance between the stump and shooting-stand was one hundred measured yards; a foot more or a foot less being thought an invasion of the right of one of the parties. The negro affixed his own price to every bird, and the terms of the chance; but, when these were once established, he was obliged, by the strict principles of public justice that prevailed in the country, to admit any adventurer who might offer.

Hunting scene from James Fenimore Cooper's novel *The Last of the Mohicans* (1826). (Library of Congress)

The throng consisted of some twenty or thirty young men, most of whom had rifles, and a collection of all the boys in the village. The little urchins, clad in coarse but warm garments, stood gathered around the more distinguished marksmen, with their hands stuck under their waistbands, listening eagerly to the boastful stories of skill that had been exhibited on former occasions, and were already emulating in their hearts these wonderful deeds in gunnery.

The chief speaker was the man who had been mentioned by Natty as Billy Kirby. This fellow, whose occupation, when he did labor, was that of clearing lands, or chopping jobs, was of great stature, and carried in his very air the index of his character. He was a noisy, boisterous, reckless lad, whose good-natured eye contradicted the bluntness and bullying tenor of his speech. For weeks he would lounge around the taverns of the county, in a state of perfect idleness, or doing small jobs for his liquor and his meals, and cavilling with applicants about the prices of his labor; frequently preferring idleness to an abatement of a little of his independence, or a cent in his wages. But, when these embarrassing points were satisfactorily arranged, he would shoulder his axe and his rifle, slip his arms through the straps of his pack, and enter the woods with the tread of a Hercules. His first object was to learn his limits, round which he would pace, occasionally freshening, with a blow of his axe, the marks on the boundary trees; and then he would proceed, with an air of great deliberation, to the centre of his premises, and, throwing aside his superfluous garments, measure, with a knowing eye, one or two of the nearest trees that were towering apparently into the very clouds as he gazed upward. Commonly selecting one of the most noble for the first trial of his power, he would approach it with a listless air, whistling a low tune; and wielding his axe with a certain flourish, not unlike the salutes of a fencing-master, he would strike a light blow into the bark, and measure his distance. The pause that followed was ominous of the fall of the forest which had flourished there for centuries. The heavy and brisk blows that he struck were soon succeeded by the thundering report of the tree, as it came, first cracking and threatening with the separation of its own last ligaments, then threshing and tearing with its branches the tops of its surrounding brethren, and finally meeting the ground with a shock but little inferior to an earthquake. From that moment the sounds of the axe were ceaseless, while the falling of the trees was like a distant cannonading; and the daylight broke into the depths of the woods with the suddenness of a winter morning.

For days, weeks, nay months, Billy Kirby would toil with an ardor that evinced his native spirit, and with an effect that seemed magical, until, his chopping being ended, his stentorian lungs could be heard emitting sounds, as he called to his patient oxen, which rang through the hills like the cries of an alarm. He had been often heard, on a mild summer' evening, a long mile across the vale of Templeton; when the echoes from the mountains would take up his cries, until they died away in the feeble sounds from the distant rocks that overhung the lake. His piles, or, to use the language of the country, his logging ended, with a dispatch that could only accompany his dexterity and herculean strength, the jobber would collect together his implements of labor, light the heaps of timber, and march away under the blaze of the prostrate forest, like the conqueror of some city who, having first prevailed over his adversary, applies the torch as the finishing blow to his conquest. For a long time Billy Kirby would then be seen sauntering around the taverns, the rider of scrub races, the bully of cock-fights, and not infrequently the hero of such sports as the one in hand.

Between him and the Leather-Stocking there had long existed a jealous rivalry on the point of skill with the rifle. Notwithstanding the long practice of Natty, it was commonly supposed that the steady nerves and the quick eye of the wood-chopper rendered him his equal. The competition had, however, been confined hitherto to boasting, and comparisons made from their success in various hunting excursions; but this was the first time they had ever come in open collision. A good deal of higgling about the price of the choicest bird had taken place between Billy Kirby and its owner before Natty and his companions rejoined the sportsmen. It had, however, been settled at one shilling[1] a shot, which was the highest sum ever exacted, the black taking care to protect himself from losses, as much as possible, by the conditions of the sport.

The turkey was already fastened at the "mark," but its body was entirely hid by the surrounding snow, nothing being visible but its red swelling head and its long neck. If the bird was injured by any bullet that struck below the snow, it was to continue the property of its present owner; but if a feather was touched in a visible part, the animal became the prize of the successful adventurer.

These terms were loudly proclaimed by the negro, who was seated in the snow, in a somewhat hazardous vicinity to his favorite bird, when Elizabeth and her cousin approached the noisy sportsmen. The sounds of mirth and contention sensibly lowered at this unexpected visit; but, after a moment's pause, the curious interest exhibited in the face of the young lady, together with her smiling air, restored the freedom of the morning; though it was somewhat chastened, both in language and vehemence, by the presence of such a spectator.

"Stand out of the way there, boys!" cried the wood-chopper, who was placing himself at the shooting-point—["]stand out of the way, you little rascals, or I will shoot through you. Now, Brom, take leave of your turkey."

"Stop!" cried the young hunter; "I am a candidate for a chance. Here is my shilling, Brom; I wish a shot too."

"You may wish it in welcome," cried Kirby, "but if I ruffle the gobbler's feathers, how are you to get it? Is money so plenty in your deer-skin pocket, that you pay for a chance that you may never have?"

"How know you, sir, how plenty money is in my pocket?" said the youth fiercely. "Here is my shilling, Brom, and I claim a right to shoot."

"Don't be crabbed, my boy," said the other, who was very coolly fixing his flint. "They say you have a hole in your left shoulder yourself, so I think Brom may give you a fire for half-price. It will take a keen one to hit that bird, I can tell you, my lad, even if I give you a chance, which is what I have no mind to do."

"Don't be boasting, Billy Kirby," said Natty, throwing the breech of his rifle into the snow, and leaning on its barrel; "you'll get but one shot at the creatur', for if the lad misses his aim, which wouldn't be a wonder if he did, with his arm so stiff and sore, you'll find a good piece and an old eye coming a'ter you. Maybe it's true that I can't shoot as I used to could, but a hundred yards is a short distance for a long rifle."

"What, old Leather-Stocking, are you out this morning?" cried his reckless opponent. "Well, fair play's a jewel. I've the lead of you, old fellow; so here goes for a dry throat or a good dinner."

The countenance of the negro evinced not only all the interest which his pecuniary adventure might occasion, but also the keen excitement that the sport produced in the others, though with a very different wish as to the result. While the wood-chopper was slowly and steadily raising his rifle, he bawled;

"Fair play, Billy Kirby—stand back—make 'em stand back, boys—gib a nigger fair play—poss-up,—gobbler; shake a head, fool; don't you see 'em taking aim?"

These cries, which were intended as much to distract the attention of the marksman as for anything else, were fruitless.

The nerves of the wood-chopper were not so easily shaken, and he took his aim with the utmost deliberation. Stillness prevailed for a moment, and he fired. The head of the turkey was seen to dash on one side, and its wings were spread in momentary fluttering; but it settled itself down calmly into its bed of snow, and glanced its eyes uneasily around. For a time long enough to draw a deep breath, not a sound was heard. The silence was then broken by the noise of the negro, who laughed, and shook his body with all kinds of antics, rolling over in the snow in the excess of delight.

"Well done, a gobbler," be cried, jumping up and affecting to embrace his bird; "I tell 'em to poss-up, and you see 'em dodge. Gib anoder shillin', Billy, and halb anoder shot."

"No—the shot is mine," said the young hunter; "you have my money already. Leave the mark, and let me try my luck."

"Ah! it's but money thrown away, lad," said Leather-Stocking. "A turkey's head and neck is but a small mark for a new hand and a lame shoulder. You'd best let me take the fire, and maybe we can make some settlement with the lady about the bird."

"The chance is mine," said the young hunter. "Clear the ground, that I may take it."

The discussions and disputes concerning the last shot were now abating, it having been determined that if the turkey's head had been anywhere but just where it was at that moment, the bird must certainly have been killed. There was not much excitement produced by the preparations of the youth, who proceeded in a hurried manner to take his aim, and was in the act of pulling the trigger, when he was stopped by Natty.

"Your hand shakes, lad," he said, "and you seem over eager. Bullet-wounds are apt to weaken flesh, and to my judgment you'll not shoot so well as in common. If you will fire, you should shoot quick, before there is time to shake off the aim."

"Fair play," again shouted the negro; "fair play—gib a nigger fair play. What right a Nat Bumppo advise a young man? Let 'em shoot—clear a ground."

The youth fired with great rapidity, but no motion was made by the turkey; and, when the examiners for the ball returned from the "mark," they declared that he had missed the stump.

Elizabeth observed the change in his countenance, and could not help feeling surprise that one so evidently superior to his companions should feel a trifling loss so sensibly. But her own champion was now preparing to enter the lists.

The mirth of Brom, which had been again excited, though in a much smaller degree than before, by the failure of the second adventurer, vanished the instant Natty took his stand. His skin became mottled with large brown spots, that fearfully sullied the lustre of his native ebony, while his enormous lips gradually compressed around two rows of ivory that had hitherto been shining in his visage like pearls set in jet. His nostrils, at all times the most conspicuous feature of his face, dilated until they covered the greater part of the diameter of his countenance; while his brown and bony hands unconsciously grasped the snow-crust near him, the excitement of the moment completely overcoming his native dread of cold.

While these indications of apprehension were exhibited in the sable owner of the turkey, the man who gave rise to this extraordinary emotion was as calm and collected as if there was not to be a single spectator of his skill.

"I was down in the Dutch settlements on the Schoharie," said Natty, carefully removing the leather guard from the lock of his rifle, "just before the breaking out of the last war, and there was a shooting-match among the boys; so I took a hand. I think I opened a good many Dutch eyes that day; for I won the powder-horn, three bars of lead, and a pound of as good powder as ever flashed in pan. Lord! how they did swear in Jarman! They did tell me of one drunken Dutchman who said he'd have the life of me before I got back to the lake agin. But if he had put his rifle to his shoulder with evil intent God would have punished him for it; and even if the Lord didn't, and he had missed his aim, I know one that would have given him as good as he sent, and better too, if good shooting could come into the 'count." By this time the old hunter was ready for his business, and throwing his right leg far behind him, and stretching his left arm along the barrel of his piece, he raised it toward the bird. Every eye glanced rapidly from the marks man to the mark; but at the moment when each ear was expecting the report of the rifle, they were disappointed by the ticking sound of the flint.

"A snap, a snap!" shouted the negro, springing from his crouching posture like a madman, before his bird. "A snap good as fire—Natty Bumppo gun he snap—Natty Bumppo miss a turkey!"

"Natty Bumppo hit a nigger," said the indignant old hunter, "if you don't get out of the way, Brom. It's contrary to the reason of the thing, boy, that a snap should count for a fire, when one is nothing more than a fire-stone striking a steel pan, and the other is sudden death; so get out of my way, boy, and let me show Billy Kirby how to shoot a Christmas turkey."

"Gib a nigger fair play!" cried the black, who continued resolutely to maintain his post, and making that appeal to the justice of his auditors which the degraded condition of his caste so naturally suggested. "Eberybody know dat snap as good as fire. Leab it to Massa Jone—leab it to lady."

"Sartain," said the wood-chopper; "it's the law of the game in this part of the country, Leather-Stocking. If you fire agin you must pay up the other shilling. I b'lieve I'll try luck once more myself; so, Brom, here's my money, and I take the next fire."

"It's likely you know the laws of the woods better than I do, Billy Kirby," returned Natty. "You come in with the settlers, with an ox-goad in your hand, and I come in with moccasins on my feet, and with a good rifle on my shoulders, so long back as afore the old war. Which is likely to know the best? I say no man need tell me that snapping is as good as firing when I pull the trigger."

"Leab it to Massa Jone," said the alarmed negro; "he know eberyting." This appeal to the knowledge of Richard was too flattering to be unheeded. He therefore advanced a little from the spot whither the delicacy of Elizabeth had induced her to withdraw, and gave the following opinion, with the gravity that the subject and his own rank demanded:

"There seems to be a difference in opinion," he said, "on the subject of Nathaniel Bumppo's right to shoot at Abraham Freeborn's turkey without the said Nathaniel paying one shilling for the privilege." The fact was too evident to be denied, and after pausing a moment, that the audience might digest his premises, Richard proceeded: "It seems proper that I should decide this question, as I am bound to preserve the peace of the county; and men with deadly weapons in their hands should not be heedlessly left to contention and their own malignant passions. It appears that there was no agreement, either in writing or in words, on the disputed point; therefore we must reason from analogy, which is, as it were, comparing one thing with another. Now, in duels, where both parties shoot, it is generally the rule that a snap is a fire; and if such is the rule where the party has a right to fire back again, it seems to me unreasonable to say that a man may stand snapping at a defenceless turkey all day. I therefore am of the opinion that Nathaniel Bumppo has lost his chance, and must pay another shilling before he renews his right."

As this opinion came from so high a quarter, and was delivered with effect, it silenced all murmurs—for the whole of the spectators had begun to take sides with great warmth—except from the Leather-Stocking himself.

"I think Miss Elizabeth's thoughts should be taken," said Natty. "I've known the squaws give very good counsel when the Indians had been dumfounded. If she says that I ought to lose, I agree to give it up."

"Then I adjudge you to be a loser for this time," said Miss Temple; "but pay your money and renew your chance; unless Brom will sell me the bird for a dollar. I will give him the money, and save the life of the poor victim."

This proposition was evidently but little relished by any of the listeners, even the negro feeling the evil excitement of the chances. In the mean while, as Billy Kirby was preparing himself for another shot, Natty left the stand, with an extremely dissatisfied manner, muttering:

"There hasn't been such a thing as a good flint sold at the foot of the lake since the Indian traders used to come into the country; and, if a body should go into the flats along the streams in the hills to hunt for such a thing, it's ten to one but they will be all covered up with the plough. Heigho! it seems to me that just as the game grows scarce, and a body wants the best ammunition to get a livelihood, everything that's bad falls on him like a judgment. But I'll change the stone, for Billy Kirby hasn't the eye for such a mark, I know."

The wood-chopper seemed now entirely sensible that his reputation depended on his care; nor did he neglect any means to insure success. He drew up his rifle, and renewed his aim again and again, still appearing reluctant to fire. No sound was heard from even Brom, during these portentous movements, until Kirby discharged his piece, with the same want of success as before. Then, indeed, the shouts of the negro rang through the bushes and sounded among the trees of the neighboring forest like the outcries of a tribe of Indians. He laughed, rolling his head first on one side, then on the other, until nature seemed exhausted with mirth. He danced until his legs were wearied with motion in the snow; and, in short, he exhibited all that violence of joy that characterizes the mirth of a thoughtless negro.

The wood-chopper had exerted all his art, and felt a proportionate degree of disappointment at the failure. He first examined the bird with the utmost attention, and more than once suggested that he had touched its feathers; but the voice of the multitude was against him, for it felt disposed to listen to the often-repeated cries of the black to "gib a nigger fair play."

Finding it impossible to make out a title to the bird, Kirby turned fiercely to the black and said:

"Shut your oven, you crow! Where is the man that can hit a turkey's head at a hundred yards? I was a fool for trying. You needn't make an uproar like a falling pine-tree about it. Show me the man who can do it."

"Look this a-way, Billy Kirby," said Leather-Stocking, and let them clear the mark, and "I'll show you a man who's made better shots afore now, and that when he's been hard pressed by the savages and wild beasts."

"Perhaps there is one whose rights come before ours, Leather-Stocking," said Miss Temple. "If so, we will waive our privilege."

"If it be me that you have reference to," said the young hunter, "I shall decline another chance. My shoulder is yet weak, I find."

Elizabeth regarded his manner, and thought that she could discern a tinge on his cheek that spoke the shame of conscious poverty. She said no more, but suffered her own champion to make a trial. Although Natty Bumppo had certainly made hundreds of more momentous shots at his enemies or his game, yet he never exerted himself more to excel. He raised his piece three several times: once to get his range; once to calculate his distance; and once because the bird, alarmed by the death-like stillness, turned its head quickly to examine its foes. But the fourth time he fired. The smoke, the report, and the momentary shock prevented most of the spectators from instantly knowing the result; but Elizabeth, when she saw her champion drop the end of his rifle in the snow and open his mouth in one of its silent laughs, and then proceed very coolly to recharge his piece, knew that he had been successful. The boys rushed to the mark, and lifted the turkey on high, lifeless, and with nothing but the remnant of a head. "Bring in the creatur'," said Leather-Stocking, "and put it at the feet of the lady. I was her deputy in the matter, and the bird is her property."

"And a good deputy you have proved yourself," returned Elizabeth—"so good, Cousin Richard, that I would advise you to remember his qualities." She paused, and the gayety that beamed on her face gave place to a more serious earnestness. She even blushed a little as she turned to the young hunter, and with the charm of a woman's manner added: "But it was only to see an exhibition of the far-famed skill of Leather-Stocking, that I tried my fortunes. Will you, sir, accept the bird as a small peace offering for the hurt that prevented your own success?"

The expression with which the youth received this present was indescribable. He appeared to yield to the blandishment of her air, in opposition to a strong inward impulse to the contrary. He bowed, and raised the victim silently from her feet, but continued silent.

Elizabeth handed the black a piece of silver as a remuneration for his loss, which had some effect in again unbending his muscles, and then expressed to her companion her readiness to return homeward.

"Wait a minute, Cousin Bess," cried Richard; "there is an uncertainty about the rules of this sport that it is proper I should remove. If you will appoint a committee, gentlemen, to wait on me this morning, I will draw up in writing a set of regulations—" He stopped, with some indignation, for at that instant a hand was laid familiarly on the shoulder of the High Sheriff of ——.

"A merry Christmas to you, Cousin Dickon," said Judge Temple, who had approached the party unperceived: "I must have a vigilant eye to my daughter, sir, if you are to be seized daily with these gallant fits. I admire the taste which would introduce a lady to such scenes!"

"It is her own perversity, 'Duke," cried the disappointed sheriff, who felt the loss of the first salutation as grievously as many a man would a much greater misfortune; "and I must say that she comes honestly by it. I led her out to show her the improvements, but away she scampered, through the snow, at the first sound of fire-arms, the same as if she had been brought up in a camp, instead of a first-rate boarding-school. I do think, Judge Temple, that such dangerous amusements should be suppressed, by statute; nay, I doubt whether they are not already indict able at common law."

"Well, sir, as you are sheriff of the county, it becomes your duty to examine into the matter," returned the smiling Marmaduke. "I perceive that Bess has executed her commission, and I hope it met with a favorable reception." Richard glanced his eye at the packet which he held in his hand, and the slight anger produced by disappointment vanished instantly.

"Ah! 'Duke, my dear cousin," he said, "step a little on one side; I have something I would say to you."

Marmaduke complied, and the sheriff led him to a little distance in the bushes, and continued: "First, 'Duke, let me thank you for your friendly interest with the Council and the Governor, without which I am confident that the greatest merit would avail but little. But we are sisters' children—we are sisters' children, and you may use me like one of your horses; ride me or drive me, 'Duke, I am wholly yours. But in my humble opinion, this young companion of Leather-Stocking requires looking after. He has a very dangerous propensity for turkey."

"Leave him to my management, Dickon," said the Judge, "and I will cure his appetite by indulgence. It is with him that I would speak. Let us rejoin the sportsmen."

. . . [T]he whole party were seated at the table. As the arrangements of this repast were much in the prevailing taste of that period and country, we shall endeavor to give a short description of the appearance of the banquet.

The table-linen was of the most beautiful damask, and the plates and dishes of real china, an article of great luxury at this early period of American commerce. The knives and forks were of exquisitely polished steel, and were set in unclouded ivory. So much, being furnished by the wealth of Marmaduke, was not only comfortable but even elegant. The contents of the several dishes, and their positions, however, were the result of the sole judgment of Remarkable. Before Elizabeth was placed an enormous roasted turkey, and before Richard one boiled, in the centre of the table stood a pair of heavy silver casters, surrounded by four dishes: one a fricassee that consisted of gray squirrels; another of fish fried; a third of fish boiled; the last was a venison steak. Between these dishes and the turkeys stood, on the one side, a prodigious chine of roasted bear's meat, and on the other a boiled leg of delicious mutton. Interspersed among this load of meats was every species of vegetables that the season and country afforded. The four corners were garnished with plates of cake. On one was piled certain curiously twisted and complicated figures, called "nut-cakes," On another were heaps of a black-looking substance, which, receiving its hue from molasses, was properly termed "sweet-cake;" a wonderful favorite in the coterie of Remarkable. A third was filled, to use the language of the housekeeper, with "cards of gingerbread"; and the last held a "plum-cake," so called from the number of large raisins that were showing their black heads in a substance of suspiciously similar color. At each corner of the table stood saucers, filled with a thick fluid of some what equivocal color and consistence, variegated with small dark lumps of a substance that resembled nothing but itself, which Remarkable termed her "sweetmeats." At the side of each plate, which was placed bottom upward, with its knife and fork most accurately crossed above it, stood another, of smaller size, containing a motley-looking pie, composed of triangular slices of apple, mince, pumpkin, cranberry, and custard so arranged as to form an entire whole. Decanters of brandy, rum, gin, and wine, with sundry pitchers of cider, beer, and one hissing vessel of "flip," were put wherever an opening would admit of their introduction. Notwithstanding the size of the tables, there was scarcely a spot where the rich damask could be seen, so crowded were the dishes, with their associated bottles, plates, and saucers. The object seemed to be profusion, and it was obtained entirely at the expense of order and elegance.

Note

1. Before the Revolution, each province had its own money of account though neither coined any but copper pieces. In New York the Spanish dollar was divided into eight shillings, each of the value of a fraction more than sixpence sterling. At present the Union has provided a decimal system, with coins to represent it.

Source: James Fenimore Cooper, *The Pioneers: Or, the Sources of the Susquehanna, a Descriptive Tale* (1823; reprint, New York: Charles Wiley, 1855), 113, 246–261.

1823 • 25 • Adam Hodgson, "The Profusion and Waste Usually Exhibited at Meals"

Introduction: *Adam Hodgson, a businessman from Liverpool, England, arrived in the United States in 1819 and left in 1821. During this time, he traveled 7,000 miles on horseback. Hodgson, like many other Europeans, was surprised at the quantity of food served on American tables and the speed with which Americans ate. Here are two selections from his book.*

Another thing which has displeased me, is the profusion and waste usually exhibited at meals. Except in the very best society, the plate is often loaded with a variety of viands, which are dismissed half-eaten. An Englishman is shocked at the liberal portions allotted to the young ladies, till he finds they afford no measure of the appetites of those to whom they are sent, who appear to be as abstemious as his own fair country-women. Still this exhibition of waste is always displeasing; and when viewed in connexion with the sufferings of so many of the population of our country, is also distressing. But the necessaries of life are here produced in abundance, and, with very few exceptions, are within the reach of every one. I only recollect seeing three beggars since I landed.

. . . I have already described the nature of the accommodations on the road; and as I do not intend to trouble you with an account of our meals, I will once for all give you a general idea of a tavern, or inn, in the *Southern* towns. These are sometimes quite as large, often nearly so, as the York-House at Bath. On arriving, your luggage is immediately carried to the baggage-room, that the lobby may not be crowded; and the passengers afterwards either send it to their bed-rooms at their leisure, or allow it to remain locked up. You are then shown into a large room, which communicates with the bar, or into a reading-room, filled with newspapers from almost every state in the Union. Usually about half past eight o'clock the bell rings for breakfast, and you sit down, with sixty or eighty persons, to tea and coffee, and every variety of flesh, fowl, and fish, wheat bread, Indian-corn bread, buck-wheat cakes, &c. &c. Every one rises as soon as he has finished his meal, and the busy scene is usually over in ten minutes. At two or three o'clock the bell rings, and the door unlocks, for dinner. The stream rushes in and dribbles out as at breakfast, and the room is clear in less than a quarter of an hour. At dinner, there are frequently four or five turkeys on the table, and the greatest possible variety and profusion of meat, poultry, and pastry. The waiters, who are numerous, civil, and attentive, carve; few persons appearing to have leisure to assist their neighbours. There are decanters of brandy in a row down the table, which appeared to me to be used with great moderation, and for which no extra charge is made. Tea is a repetition of breakfast, with the omission of beef-steaks, but in other respects with almost an equal profusion of meat, fowls, turkey-legs &c. While on the subject of eating, which I do not intend to resume, (I mean, the subject,) I will mention, that I do not recollect to have dined a single day, from my arrival in America till I left Virginia, without a turkey on the table; often two, in gentlemen's houses. On Christmas-Eve, in the little town of Norfolk, Virginia, it was said that 6000 turkeys were in the market. The picture which I have given you of the meals at taverns is not an inviting one: they more resemble a school-boy's scramble than a social repast.

Source: Adam Hodgson, *Remarks during a Journey through North America in the Years 1819, 1820, and 1821* (New York: Samuel Whiting, 1823), 92, 106.

1827 • 26 • Sarah Josepha Hale, "Our Thanksgiving Dinner"

Introduction: *Sarah Josepha Hale (1788–1879) was born in Newport, New Hampshire. After running a school for five years, she married David Hale, a lawyer, who died in 1822. To support her five children, Sarah Hale turned to writing. In 1823 she published her first book of poetry,* The Genius of Oblivion, *and five years later she published her first novel,* Northwood: Or, a Tale of New England, *which featured an entire chapter describing Thanksgiving dinner. Hale would later lead a campaign to make Thanksgiving a national holiday, which succeeded in 1863.*

A long table, formed by placing two of the ordinary size together, was set forth in the parlor. . . . The table was covered with a damask cloth, vieing in whiteness, and nearly equaling in texture, the finest imported, though spun, woven and bleached by. Mrs. Romillee's own hand, was now intended for the whole household, every child having a seat on this occasion; and the more the better, it being considered an honor for a man to sit down to his Thanksgiving supper surrounded by a large family. The provision is always sufficient for a multitude, every farmer in the country being, at this season of the year, plentifully supplied, and every one proud of displaying his abundance and prosperity.

The roasted turkey took precedence on this occasion, being placed at the head of the table; and well did it become its lordly station, sending forth the rich odour of its savoury stuffing, and finely covered with the froth of the basting. At the foot of the board a sirloin of beef, flanked on either side by a leg of pork and loin of mutton, seemed placed as a bastion to defend innumerable bowls of gravy and plates of vegetables disposed in that quarter. A goose and pair of ducklings occupied side stations on the table, the middle being graced, as always is on such occasions, by that rich burgomaster of the provisions, called a chicken pie. This pie, which is wholly formed of the choicest parts of fowls, enriched and seasoned with a profusion of butter and pepper, and covered with an excellent puff paste, is, like the celebrated pumpkin pie, an indispensable part of a good and true Yankee Thanksgiving; the size of the pie usually denoting the gratitude of the party who prepares the feast. . . .

Plates of pickles, preserves, and butter, and all the necessaries for increasing the seasoning of the viands to the demand of each palate, filled the interstices on the table, leaving hardly sufficient room for the plates of the company, a wine glass and two tumblers for each, with a slice of wheat bread lying on one of the inverted tumblers. A side table was literally loaded with the preparations for the second course, placed there to obviate the necessity of leaving the apartment during the repast. Mr. Romillee keeping no domestic, the family were to wait on themselves, or each other. There was a huge plum pudding, custards and pies of every name and description ever known in Yankee land; yet the pumpkin pie occupied the most distinguished niche. There were also several kinds of rick cake, and a variety of sweetmeats and fruits. On the sideboard was ranged a goodly number of decanters and bottles; the former filled with currant wine, and the latter with excellent cider and ginger beer—a beverage Mrs. Romillee prided herself on preparing in perfection. There were no foreign wines or ardent spirits, Squire Roomily being a *consistent* moralist; and while he deprecated the evils. . . .

It was the breathings of a good and grateful heart acknowledging the mercies received, and sincerely thanking the Giver of every good gift for the plenteous portion he had bestowed.

Source: Mrs. S. J. Hale, *Northwood: Or, Life North and South,* Vol. 1 (Boston: Bowles and Dearborn, 1827), 107–111.

1832 • 27 • Frances Trollope, *Domestic Manners of the Americans*

Introduction: *Frances Trollope (1779–1863) was an English woman who visited the United States in 1827. She lived for a time in a utopian community in Tennessee and then moved to Cincinnati. Trollope subsequently traveled about the United States. She*

Frances Trollope, an English author and mother of novelist Anthony Trollope, visited America and wrote about her experiences in *Domestic Manners of the Americans* (1832). (Trollope, Frances Eleanor. *Her Life and Literary Work,* 1895)

collected notes on her travels, and when she returned to England, she wrote her Domestic Manners of the Americans *(1832). Two of her seven children later became writers, the more famous of whom was Anthony Trollope. The excerpt below is a description of a food scene in Cincinnati.*

Had I passed as many evenings in company in any other town that I ever visited as I did in Cincinnati, I should have been able to give some little account of the conversation I had listened to; but, upon reading over my notes, and then taxing my memory to the utmost to supply the deficiency, I can scarcely find a trace of any thing that deserves the name. Such as I have shall be given in their place. But, whatever may be the talents of the persons who meet together in society, the very shape, form, and arrangement of the meeting is sufficient to paralyze conversation. The women invariably herd together at one part of the room, and the men at the other; but in justice to Cincinnati, I must acknowledge that this arrangement is by no means peculiar to that city, or to the western side of the Alleghanies. Sometimes a small attempt at music produces a partial reunion; a few of the most daring youths, animated by the consciousness of curled hair and smart waistcoats, approach the piano-forte, and begin to mutter a little to the half-grown pretty things, who are comparing with one another "how many quarters' music they have had." Where the mansion is of sufficient dignity to have two drawing-rooms, the piano, the little ladies, and the slender gentlemen are left to themselves, and on such occasions the sound of laughter is often heard to issue from among them. But the fate of the more dignified personages, who are left in the other room, is extremely dismal. The gentlemen spit, talk of elections and the price of produce, and spit again. The ladies look at each other's dresses till they know every pin by heart; talk of parson somebody's last sermon on the day of judgment, on Dr. t'otherbody's new pills for dyspepsia, till the "tea" is announced, when they all console themselves together for whatever they may have suffered in keeping awake, by taking more tea, coffee, hot cake and custard, hoe cake, johnny cake, waffle cake, and dodger cake, pickled peaches, and preserved cucumbers, ham, turkey, hung beef, apple sauce, and pickled oysters, than ever were prepared in any other country of the known world. After this massive meal is over, they return to the drawing-room, and it always appeared to me that they remained together as long as they could bear it, and then they rise en masse, cloak, bonnet, shawl, and exit. . . .

Perhaps the most advantageous feature in Cincinnati is its market, which, for excellence, abundance, and cheapness, can hardly, I should think, be surpassed in any part of the world, if I except the luxury of fruits, which are very inferior to any I have seen in Europe. There are no butchers, or indeed any shops for eatables, except bakeries, as they are called, in the town; every thing must be purchased at market; and to accomplish this, the busy housewife must be stirring betimes, or, 'spite of the abundant supply, she will find her hopes of breakfast, dinner, and supper for the day defeated, the market being pretty well over by eight o'clock.

The beef is excellent, and the highest price when we were there, four cents (about two-pence) the pound. The mutton was inferior, and so was the veal to the eye, but it ate well, though not very fat; the price was about the same. The poultry was excellent; fowls or full-sized chickens, ready for table, twelve cents, but much less if bought alive, and not quite fat; turkeys about fifty cents, and geese the same. The Ohio furnishes several sorts of fish, some of them very good, and always to be found cheap and abundant in the market. Eggs, butter, nearly all kinds of vegetables, excellent, and at moderate prices. From June till December tomatoes (the great luxury of the American table in the opinion of most Europeans) may be found in the highest perfection in the market for about sixpence the peck. They have a great variety of beans unknown in England, particularly the lima-bean, the seed of which is dressed like the French harrico;[1] it furnishes a very abundant crop, and is a most delicious vegetable: could it be naturalized with us it would be a valuable acquisition. The Windsor, or broad-bean, will not do well there: Mr. Bullock had them in his garden, where they were cultivated with much care; they grew about a foot high and blossomed, but the pod never ripened. All the fruit I saw exposed for sale in Cincinnati was most miserable. I passed two summers there, but never tasted a peach worth eating. Of apricots and nectarines I saw none; strawberries very small, raspberries much worse; gooseberries very few, and quite uneatable; currants about half the size of ours, and about double the price; grapes too sour for tarts; apples abundant, but very indifferent, none that would be thought good enough for an English table; pears, cherries, and plums most miserably bad. The flowers of these regions were at least equally inferior: whether this proceeds from want of cultivation or from peculiarity of soil I know not, but after leaving Cincinnati, I was told by a gentleman who seemed to understand the subject, that the state of Ohio had no indigenous flowers or fruits. The watermelons, which in that warm climate furnish a delightful refreshment, were abundant and cheap; but all other melons very inferior to those of France or even of England, when ripened in a common hot-bed.

From the almost total want of pasturage near the city, it is difficult for a stranger to divine how milk is furnished for its supply, but we soon learnt that there are more ways than one of keeping a cow. A large proportion of the families in the town, particularly of the poorer class, have one, though apparently no accommodation whatever for it. These animals are fed morning and evening at the door of the house, with a good mess of Indian corn, boiled with water; while they eat, they are milked, and when the operation is completed the milk-pail and the meal-tub retreat into the dwelling, leaving the republican cow to walk away, to take her pleasure on the hills, or in the gutters, as may suit her fancy best. They generally return very regularly to give and take the morning and evening meal; though it more than once happened to us, before we were supplied by a regular milk cart, to have our jug returned home empty, with the sad news that "The cow has not come home and it was too late to look for her to breakfast now." Once, I remember, the good woman told us that she had overslept herself, and that the cow had come and gone again, "not liking, to hanker about by herself for nothing, poor thing."

Note

1. Small white beans.

Source: Frances Trollope, *Domestic Manners of the Americans* (London: Whittaker, Treacher, & Co.; New York: Reprinted for the Bookseller, 1832), 64–68.

1833 • 28 • Thomas Hamilton, "Dinner at Niblo's," "Breakfast at the Hotel," and "New York Parties"

Introduction: *Thomas Hamilton (1789–1842), a British aristocrat and philosopher, offered a critical view of America and its manners associated with food. Below is his account of his first dinner in America—at Niblo's Garden, one of New York's best spots for entertainment and refreshments at the time—and his first breakfast at a New York hotel.*

The dinner at Niblo's,—which may be considered the London Tavern of New York,—was certainly more excellent in point of materiel, than of cookery or arrangement. It consisted of oyster soup, shad, venison, partridges, grouse, wild-ducks of different varieties, and several other dishes less notable. There was no attempt to serve this chaotic entertainment in courses, a fashion, indeed, but little prevalent in the United States. Soup, fish, flesh and fowl, simultaneously garnished the table; and the consequence was, that the greater part of the dishes were cold, before the guests were prepared to attack them. The venison was good, though certainly very inferior to that of the fallow-deer. The wines were excellent, the company agreeable in all respects, and altogether I do not remember to have passed a more pleasant evening, than that of my first arrival at New York.

I had nearly completed my toilet, on the morning after my arrival, when the tinkling of a large bell gave intimation that the hour of breakfast was come. I accordingly descended as speedily as possible to the mile a manger, and found a considerable party engaged in doing justice to a meal, which at first glance one could scarcely have guessed to be a breakfast. Solid viands of all descriptions loaded the table, while in the occasional intervals were distributed dishes of rolls, toast, and cakes of buckwheat and Indian corn. At the head of the table sat the landlady, who, with an air of complacent dignity, was busied in the distribution of tea and coffee. A large bevy of negroes was bustling about, ministering with all possible alacrity to the many wants which were somewhat vociferously obtruded on their attention. Towards the upper end of the table I observed about a dozen ladies, but by far the larger portion of the company were of the other sex.

The contrast of the whole scene with that of an English breakfast-table was striking enough; here was no loitering or lounging; no dipping into newspapers; no apparent lassitude of appetite; no intervals of repose in mastication; but all was hurry, bustle, clamour and voracity, and the business of repletion went forward with a rapidity altogether unexampled. The strenuous efforts of the company were, of course, soon rewarded with success. Departures, which had begun even before I took my place at the table, became every instant more numerous, and in a few minutes the apartment had become, what Moore beautifully describes in one of his songs, 'a banquet hall deserted.' The appearance of the table, under such circumstances, was by no means gracious either to the eye or the fancy. It was strewed thickly with the *disjecta membra*[1] of the entertainment: here lay fragments of fish, somewhat unpleasantly odoriferous; there the skeleton of a chicken; on the right, a mustard-pot, upset, and the cloth defiled with stains of eggs, coffee, gravy—but I will not go on with the picture. One nasty custom, however, I must notice. Eggs, instead of being eat from the shell, are poured into a wine-glass, and after being duly and disgustingly churned up with butter and condiment, the mixture, according to its degree of fluidity, is forthwith either spooned into the mouth, or drunk off like a liquid. The advantage gained by this unpleasant process, I do not profess to be qualified to appreciate, but I can speak from experience to its sedative effect on the appetite of an unpractised beholder. . . .

The formalities of a New York dinner do not differ much from those of an English one. Unfortunately, it is not here the fashion to invite the fairer part of creation to entertainments so gross and substantial; and it rarely happens that any ladies are present on such occasions, except those belonging to the family of the host. The party, however, is always enlivened by their presence at the tea-table; and then comes music, and, perhaps dancing; while those who, like myself, are disqualified for active participation in such festivities, talk, with an air of grave authority, of revolutions in Europe, the prospects of war or peace, Parliamentary Reform, and other high and interesting matters.

Before dinner, the conversation of the company assembled in the drawing-room is here, as elsewhere, generally languid enough; but a change suddenly comes over the spirit of their dream. The folding-doors which communicate with the dining-room are thrown open, and all paradise is at once let in on the soul of a gourmand. The table, instead of displaying, as with us, a mere beggarly account of fish and soup, exhibits an array of dishes wedged in close column, which it would require at least an acre of mahogany to deploy into line. Plate, it is true, does not contribute much to the splendour of the prospect, but there is quite enough for comfort, though not perhaps for display. The lady of the mansion is handed in form to her seat, and the entertainment begins. The domestics, black, white, snuff-coloured, and nankeen, are in motion; plates vanish and reappear as if by magic; turtle, cold-blooded by nature, has become hot as Sir Charles Wetherell, and certainly never moved so rapidly before. The flight of ham and turkey is incessant; venison bounds from one end of the table to the other, with a velocity scarcely exceeded in its native forest; and the energies of twenty human beings are all evidently concentrated in one common occupation.

During soup and fish, and perhaps the first slice of the haunch, conversation languishes, but a glass or two of Champagne soon operates as a corrective. The eyes of the young ladies become more brilliant, and those of elderly gentlemen acquire a certain benevolent twinkle, which indicates that for the time being they are in charity with themselves and all mankind. At length the first course is removed, and is succeeded by a whole wilderness of sweets. This, too, passes; for it is impossible, alas! to eat for ever. Then come cheese and the dessert; then the departure of the ladies; and Claret and Madeira for an hour or twain are unquestioned lords of the ascendant.

The latter is almost uniformly excellent. I have never drunk any Madeira in Europe at all equalling what I have frequently met in the United States. Gourmets attribute this superiority partly to climate, but in a great measure to management. Madeira, in this country, is never kept, as with us, in a subterranean vault, where the temperature throughout the year is nearly equal. It is placed in the attics, where it is exposed to the whole fervour of the summer's heat and the severity of winter's cold. The effect on the flavour of the wine is certainly remarkable.

The Claret is generally good, but not better than in England; Port is used by the natives only as a medicine, and is rarely produced at table except in compliment to some English stranger, it being a settled canon, here as elsewhere, that every Englishman drinks Port. I have never yet tasted fine Sherry, probably because that wine has not yet risen into esteem in the United States.

The gentlemen in America pique themselves on their discrimination in wine, in a degree which is not common in England. The ladies have no sooner risen from table than the business of wine-bibbing commences in good earnest. The servants still remain in the apartment, and supply fresh glasses to the guests as the successive bottles make their appearance. To each of these a history is attached, and the vintage, the date of importation, &c., are all duly detailed. Then come the criticisms of the company; and as each bottle produced contains wine of a different quality from its predecessor, there is no chance of the topic being exhausted. At length, having made the complete tour of the cellar, proceeding progressively from the commoner wines to those of finest flavour, the party adjourns to the drawing-room, and, after coffee, each guest takes his departure without ceremony of any kind.

It would be most ungrateful were I not to declare, that I have frequently found these dinner parties extremely pleasant.

Note

1. Disjecta membra are scattered parts.

Source: Thomas Hamilton, *Men and Manners in America* (Philadelphia: Carey, Lea and Blanchard, 1833), 20–25, 65–70.

1834 • 29 • Asa Greene, *The Perils of Pearl Street*

Introduction: *Asa Greene (1789–1838) was a writer of several books. This selection is about a traveling salesman, a drummer, whose job was to promote and sell the products of his employer. At the time hotels were expensive, and most travelers stayed in boardinghouses. The excerpt below is about the food served in a boardinghouse in New York. It is from a novel,* The Perils of Pearl Street *(1834), written about the period when the Erie Canal era (1825–1830) greatly increased New York City's commercial prominence.*

But apropos of my landlady. I must give a short account of her. As I have just hinted, she was a short woman. True, she was short in every sense of the word. Her person was short; her neck was short; her fingers were short; her provisions were short; and she was short and crusty. In speaking of her shortness, however, I should perhaps except her tongue, which upon certain occasions was quite long enough. She was a little, squat old woman, somewhat wrinkled in the face, somewhat sharp in the matter of a nose, and particularly sharp in the matter of money.

Such was Mrs. Conniption. She kept a four-dollar boarding house; and made money, not so much by the high price which she exacted of her guests, as by the low price of the conveniences with which she furnished them. Her charge for board and lodging was sufficiently moderate; but the rate, at which she purchase[d] provisions for bed and board, was quite too moderate.

And this was the secret of Mrs. Conniption's wealth. She made money by stinting her boarders. She purchased the cheapest articles in the market—the very refuse of more generous house-keepers. Whether it was meat, vegetables, or fruit, she took care to obtain such only as could be purchased at half price. Fifty per cent, said she to herself, is worth saving; and as for my boarders—la! they'll never know the difference. But my pocket will feel it most sensibly.

As for me, I might say my stomach felt it most sensibly. I shall never forget the impression of Mrs. Conniption's boarding house, the longest day I have to live. I seem at this moment to see every thing before me, as it happened at the time. I will give a picture—merely the picture of a day.

I must begin then with the breakfast table. There were some fifteen or twenty boarders, and at least two dishes—a salt shad, or mackerel, and a lean beef steak, which had been dried, not broiled, over the coals. Perhaps one or the other of these, for a rarity, was alternated with stale sausages, or salt leg of pork—salted almost beyond the possibility of being eaten. No fowls, no eggs, no oysters, ever made their way to the breakfast table. Along with the fish or flesh, the stale sausages or trebly-salted pork, might be seen a plate or two of bread, sometimes of rye, sometimes of wheat, baked by Mrs. Conniption herself, thoroughly soured, and as heavy as a grindstone; but no admittance was allowed to toast, buckwheat cakes, or hot rolls. There was a small quantity of butter, such as it was; but its color was nearly as various as the rainbow; and after having been doubly salted at home to make it weigh more, it had been salted again by Mrs. Conniption to make it go the further with her boarders.

So much for the morning eatables. At the head of the table sat the sweet lady herself, drawing from a coffee urn and distributing—oh heavens! I have not yet found a name for it. The basis of it, however, was water, drawn from the Manhattan hydrant or the pump, which in its purest state was scarcely drinkable. Added to this was a small quantity of damaged coffee, burnt crust, or roasted rye, well pulverised—which, having boiled awhile, was thoroughly incorporated with the water; and both drawn together into the cups, exhibited, when combined with a little milk, very much the appearance of ashes and water. The taste of this strange mixture, being indescribable, I leave to the reader's imagination. The lady presidentess never asked, Is your coffee—she certainly called it coffee!—I say, she never asked, Is your coffee agreeable, sir?—Do I make your coffee to suit you, madam? lest some one should have the impudence to ask for more sugar or milk, and she should be a loser by her ill-judged politeness.

At the dinner table, the picture was a shade or two brighter. But here there was nothing to boast of—for the meat, having been bought at a reduced price in the market, did not of course consist of the prime pieces; and, what was worse still, it was spoilt in the cooking. If roasted, it had never felt the softening and savory influence of the basting-spoon; but was as dry as a chip, and totally destitute of any inviting qualities. Add to this, it was accompanied by no gravy—or nothing deserving of that title—the contents of the attending butter-boat being neither more nor less than unmingled grease at the top, a watery mixture in the middle, and a variously compounded sediment of salt and other ingredients at the bottom. Such was the character of the roast, whether it were beef, mutton, veal, or swine's flesh. As for chickens, ducks, or poultry of any kind, they never winged their way so far as Mrs. Conniption's table. A boiled leg of mutton was rarely seen—and when seen, was never accompanied by its legitimate attendant, drawn-butter-and parsley. But roasted mutton, smelling strong of its sheepish qualities and reeking in its own grease, was seldom wanting to grace the board. For vegetables, there were round watery potatoes, sliced beats, boiled cabbage, and so forth; but for celery—crisp, well-bleached, delicious, appetite-inspiring celery—we had none of it.

Wait a minute, and you shall have the dessert—and a desert indeed it was, nearly as barren of attraction as the desert of Arabia. Behold an apple dumpling, with the crust so tough, that it needed not, like that which so puzzled old King George—as said and sung by Peter Pindar—to be sewed, to keep it together; but would rather require an axe or cleaver to cut it asunder—enclosing an apple so sour that, if you ate it, your children's teeth would be set on edge. A pudding made of rice and water, in which the latter ingredient most plentifully abounded; or a batch of boiled rice, concreted nearly into the hardness of a stone, to be eaten with W. I. molasses. An apple pie, with the crust as strong as sole-leather, enclosing here and there a bit of apple, as tart as the woman that made it; or sweetened, if at all, merely with that same W. I. molasses. Or perchance your eye might be feasted upon a dessert of fruits—but what fruits!—shrivelled peaches, purchased dearly at fifty cents a bushel, sour pears not worth twenty-five cents, or wormy apples not worth a shilling.

But all this was princely compared with the tea-table, which, in the first place, was nothing but a suite of bare boards—mahogany it might be, and faithfully polished—but no table can be considered as properly set without a cloth. However, it is not so much the table itself I would depict, as the articles upon it, and the mistress at the upper end of it. As at breakfast, so at tea, there sat Mrs. Conniption—heavens, what a countenance! If the milk had not been watered beyond the possibility of being soured, her face would certainly have turned it to bonny-clabber. The eatables consisted chiefly of dry bread and extra-salted butter; but the tea, or that liquid which was so called, is the object most deserving of particular admiration. How so large a quantity of beverage could be made from so small a quantity of the Chinese herb, would certainly have been matter of marvel to any one not acquainted with the economy of Mrs. Conniption's boarding house. Some might suppose it was owing to a peculiar virtue in the inside of the good lady's teapot, or to some superior quality of the herb employed. But I can assure them this was not the case; and no person, who had ever tasted the infusion, or rather decoction, could have much doubt as to the mode of its preparation. One thimbleful of tea was put into a quart, a gallon, or some other assignable quantity of water; and the leaves of the herb might be seen, like the wrecked Trojans, floating in a vast sea, few and far apart. Mrs. Conniption always measured her tea in a thimble. At first, the teapot was filled with water, and after a thorough decoction of the thimbleful, it was brought upon the table. As soon as it began to run low, it was again filled with water. A second pouring out took place, and it was again replenished with water. And so on, alternately pouring out and filling up, as long as there were any guests to be served. From this account of its preparation, it requires no Yankee to guess at the nature of the liquid prepared. On the same general principle of economy, the boarders were not allowed to sweeten their own tea, lest they should be too profuse of the sugar; nor to cream it, lest they should draw too largely on the precious milk and water, whereof a single gill was made to serve the whole table. The presiding goddess of the teapot—alias, Mrs. Conniption—put into each cup half a tea spoonful of brown Havana sugar, and five drops of milk. If any one was dissatisfied with this quantity, and had the impudence to send up his cup for more, she put in perhaps one fourth of a tea-spoonful of sugar, and three other drops of milk, at the same time glancing at him a look as if she would bite his head off. But though so sparing of the sugar and milk, it is but justice to Mrs. Conniption to say, she dealt bountifully with us in the article of tea, for pump-water was cheap, and the process of pouring in, very easily supplied the exhaustion of pouring out. In short, had it not been for the expense of sugar and milk, we might have had the tea, like a certain modern author's poetry,—

"In one weak, washy, everlasting flood."

Source: Asa Greene, *The Perils of Pearl Street* (New York: Betts and Anstice, 1834), 35–42.

1834 • 30 • Davy Crockett's First Political Speech

Introduction: *Davy Crockett (1786–1836) was an east Tennessee frontiersman who was elected to the U.S. House of Representatives in 1826. When he was defeated in 1834 he wrote his autobiography, in which he described a speech at a barbecue in Tennessee when he first ran for Congress. Political speeches were often accompanied by food and almost always by alcoholic beverages, especially hard cider. In 1835 Crockett went with a group of Tennessee volunteers to Texas, then a part of Mexico, to support the revolution organized by Sam Houston against Mexico. Crockett died when the Alamo fell to Mexican general Antonio Lopez Santa Anna in 1836. Crockett's life was subsequently immortalized by many writers and during the 1950s by Walt Disney in a very popular television series and movie.*

About this time there was a great squirrel hunt on Duck river, which was among my people. They were to hunt two days: then to meet and count the scalps, and have a big barbecue, and what might be called a tip-top country frolic. The dinner, and a general treat, was all to be paid for by the party having taken the fewest scalps. I joined one side, taking the place of one of the hunters, and got a gun ready for the hunt. I killed a great many squirrels, and when we counted scalps, my party was victorious.

The company had every thing to eat and drink that could be furnished in so new a country, and much fun and good humour prevailed. But before the regular frolic commenced, I mean the dancing, I was called on to make a speech as a candidate; which was a business I was as ignorant of as an outlandish negro.

David "Davy" Crockett was a frontiersman, soldier, and politician who became a mythic hero after he defended the Alamo in 1836. (Stephenson, Nathaniel W. *Texas and the Mexican War,* 1921)

A public document I had never seen, nor did I know there were such things; and how to begin I couldn't tell. I made many apologies, and tried to get off, for I know'd I had a man to run against who could speak prime, and I know'd, too, that I wa'n't able to shuffle and cut with him. He was there, and knowing my ignorance as well as I did myself, he also urged me to make a speech. The truth is, he thought my being a candidate was a mere matter of sport; and didn't think, for a moment, that he was in any danger from an ignorant back-woods bear hunter. But I found I couldn't get off, and so I determined just to go ahead, and leave it to chance what I should say. I got up and told the people, I reckoned they know'd what I come for, but if not, I could tell them. I had come for their votes, and if they didn't watch mighty close, I'd get them too. But the worst of all was, that I couldn't tell them any thing about government. I tried to speak about something, and I cared very little what, until I choaked up as bad as if my mouth had been jam'd and cram'd chock full of dry mush. There the people stood, listening all the while, with their eyes, mouths and ears all open, to catch every word I would speak.

At last I told them I was like a fellow I had heard of not long before. He was beating on the head of an empty barrel near the road-side, when a traveler, who was passing along, asked him what he was doing that for? The fellow replied, that there was some cider in that barrel a few days before, and he was trying to see if there was any then, but if there was he couldn't get at it. I told them that there had been a little bit of a speech in me a while ago, but I believed I couldn't get it out. They all roared out in a mighty laugh, and I told some other anecdotes, equally amusing to them, and believing I had them in a first-rate way, I quit and got down, thanking the people for their attention. But I took care to remark that I was as dry as a powder horn, and that I thought it was time for us all to wet our whistles a little; and so I put off to the liquor stand, and was followed by the greater part of the crowd.

I felt certain this was necessary, for I knowed my competitor could open government matters to them as easy as he pleased. He had, however, mighty few left to hear him, as I continued with the crowd, now and then taking a horn, and telling good humoured stories, till he was done speaking. I found I was good for the votes at the hunt, and when we broke up, I went on to the town of Vernon, which was the same they wanted me to move. Here they pressed me again on the subject, and I found I could get either party by agreeing with them. But I told them I didn't know whether it would be right or not, and so couldn't promise either way.

Their court commenced on the next Monday, as the barbacue was on a Saturday, and the candidates for governor and for Congress, as well as my competitor and myself, all attended.

The thought of having to make a speech made my knees feel mighty weak, and set my heart to fluttering almost as bad as my first love scrape with the Quaker's niece. But as good luck would have it, these big candidates spoke nearly all day, and when they quit, the people were worn out with fatigue, which afforded me a good apology for not discussing the government. But I listened mighty close to them, and was learning pretty fast about political matters. When they were all done, I got up and told some laughable story, and quit. I found I was safe in those parts, and so I went home, and didn't go back again till after the election was over. But to cut this matter short, I was elected, doubling my competitor, and nine votes over.

Source: Davy Crockett, *A Narrative of the Life of David Crockett, of the State of Tennessee . . . Written by Himself* (Philadelphia: E. L. Cary and A. Hart, 1834), 140–143.

1835 • 31 • William A. Alcott, "Tea Drinking a Waste and a Crime"

Introduction: *Tea was introduced into America late in the 17th century and quickly became a commonly served beverage that was consumed especially by women. British medical professionals questioned the benefits of tea drinking. A Dr. Smith of Edinburgh, Scotland, for instance, demonstrated in 1707 that green tea "had the same effect as henbane, tobacco, cicuta,*[1] *etc., on the living tissues of the animal body; in all cases first diminishing and finally destroying their vital properties." In 1730 a writer in the* New York Gazette *proclaimed that tea produced fatal effects on health and the mind. Beginning in the 1830s, a number of American health professionals opposed the consumption of tea. Dr. William A. Alcott (1798–1859), one of America's prominent medical professionals and the uncle of author Louisa May Alcott, maintained that tea was not only useless but was also a narcotic and therefore was poisonous.*

We may now put the question fairly before the tea drinker, what mighty gain is secured by being accessory to making this immense quantity of hot drink, at an expense of $100,000,000 yearly, or $3,000,000,000 in a single generation of 30 years. We will even set aside the question of injury, for a few moments; and ask what good is done, which will, compensate for this great sacrifice of property. We do not ask what pecuniary gain is secured; for there are other goods in this world than money. How many are made, on the whole, happier? Where is the healthy individual, who is a tea drinker, who enjoys a more complete immunity from pain, and a greater average share of strength, vigor, and elasticity of body and mind, than falls to the lot of the simple water drinker? We should be willing to institute, were it possible, a fair comparison. We should be willing to set individuals or nations side by side, and prosecute the inquiry. We should be willing to put Europe, as it was 200 years ago, when no tea was drank, by the side of Europe as it now is.

Who are they that complain most of nervousness; of irregular appetite and sleep; of unequal warmth and strength; and of their own health, and future moral and physical prospects? Who find most fault with those around them, and with the emptiness and sickliness of the world in which they live.

Now if nothing is gained—no, nothing at all—to the individual or to the nation that drinks tea, the next question is, How much is lost? We do not ask, just now, how much is lost of good and equable feeling,—but how much is lost in property? One thousand million of dollars to a generation in Europe and the United States, might be so applied as to accomplish much good. It is sufficient to feed, clothe, educate, and train to habits of intelligent industry—supposing we take them from the cradle, and carry them on to twenty years of age—the children of the whole slave population of the United States. Would not this be a good? And is not the use of a particular drink, which is on the whole productive of no happiness, individual or collective, but which involves so great an expense—so much means of doing good—a most amazing waste?

But there is another consideration. We maintain that tea is not only useless, but positively hurtful. In our last number, an attempt was made to show that it was a narcotic, and therefore poisonous. And if tea be a narcotic, and poisonous to all persons in health, then it is a legitimate object of inquiry, how poisonous it is. The inquiry is attended with difficulties, but will now be attempted.

From partial experiments which have been made, we are of opinion that 100 pounds of tea, of average strength, contain enough of the narcotic or poisonous principle, could it be extracted and taken in a form sufficiently concentrated, to destroy the life of any individual. If so, the 63,000,000 pounds consumed annually in Europe and America, would destroy outright 630,000 persons; and in Europe, America and China, not much less than seven millions.

But as China is a great way off, we will return to Europe and America. At 630,000 a year, the number of deaths which our tea would thus produce in thirty years, would be 18,000,000; a number nearly equal to the present population of Great Britain, and much larger than that of the United States. In 100 years it would be 63,000,000; or a number nearly five times as great as that of all the people now in the United States.

It is a principle which we have before advanced, and upon which we have long insisted, that poison does not become the less poisonous to the human system by being divided into minute doses, greatly diffused, or taken at long intervals. In all those circumstances it is either mixed with the chyle, and passes with it, unchanged, into the blood; or—what more generally happens—it gets into the circulation by a much shorter route, as soon almost as it touches the stomach. But in either case it gets into the circulation, and accomplishes its work;—we think, not only as surely and effectually as if several of these small doses were united in one, but more so. For it is a well known fact, that when we take a large dose—if not so large as to overwhelm the powers of life, and produce death at once—the system re-acts, in some measure, and prevents a part of the mischief that would otherwise ensue; whereas a small dose insinuates itself more cautiously, as it were, and rouses less opposition.

The inference we would make from this is, that the narcotic principle of tea, which would destroy the lives of 630,000 persons annually, if sufficiently concentrated, does not perform the less mischief by being widely diffused. If we estimate the average duration of human life at 30 years, the destruction of 630,000 persons is the destruction of 18,900,000 years of human life. Now, without saying that tea, as we drink it, does more harm than if the same quantity were taken in a more concentrated manner, we firmly maintain that it does at least as much; and that if 18,900,000 years of life are destroyed in the one case, they are so in the other. That is, the life of one is cut short by one year, or part of a year; another, perhaps, by several years; or, what is more often the case, the work of destruction is indirectly accomplished, by inducing some disease that wears out life slowly, or rendering a disease produced by a cause entirely different, more dangerous, and perhaps ultimately fatal. The amount of time, which, on the foregoing calculation, is 'clipped' off from the lives of each individual in the United States, upon an average, is a little less than eight weeks. Still these various 'clippings' form an aggregate of 2,100,000 years; or 70,000 whole lives; and either the above calculations are not well founded, or this is the loss of life sustained by the use of this narcotic drink.

It will still be doubted—for it always has been doubted by many—whether poisonous substances received into the human system, though they may not be the less poisonous from being minutely divided, may not produce less and less effect;—whether, in short, the system does not get accustomed to their presence, and hence less liable to disturbance from them.

Now we think this is the often result; but it only confirms the sentiments already advanced. The system probably does get accustomed to their presence; but how? Answer: By wearing out physical sensibility, or as some call it, vitality; and this is the very thing that shortens human life. Contrive to keep an individual, ever after birth, as highly stimulated as possible by means of alcoholic and narcotic drinks, and you might exhaust his vitality in fifteen or twenty years, and perhaps sooner; and he would sink, in despite of every human effort, into the grave. And this is what tea does, by its stimulus, only more slowly than in the case last mentioned.

If tea, then, does no permanent good to individuals or to communities; if it involves an amazing waste of property; if in addition to all this, it destroys happiness, and health, and life, at a most tremendous rate,—is it not high time for the christian world to cast it off?

Should it be said, that the disuse of tea would throw many persons, now concerned in its importation, out of employ, our reply is that the same might be said, and indeed has often been said, of the disuse of intoxicating liquors; and if the argument is good for anything in the one case, it must be valid in the other. Besides, we can never expect to remedy the evil by legislation; and christian influence will at best effect a change so slowly as to injure, materially, nobody's business. It should also be recollected that the commerce of Europe went on very well before the tea trade was introduced;—and it cannot be doubted that it could go on without it now.

But the strongest plea will be made in behalf of China. 'What is she to do, if she cannot sell her tea to Americans and Europeans?'—Why, just what she did before she sold them any. When the trade with us for this article commenced, tea was only cultivated in two of the larger provinces. It has since been extended to three more; but with what effects? Do their inhabitants live any better than before? Does the population increase any faster? There is not the smallest reason for believing that either of these results has followed.—The number of inhabitants is about the same; and they live just about as well as they did before. If they could not sell their tea, they would probably raise something else on the same soil. Perhaps it would be as easy for them to raise rice, corn and grain, and also make their own clothing, as to raise tea and sell it, and purchase their necessaries.

We are well aware that this is one of the strong holds of tea drinkers. They are so benevolent to the poor Chinese! They can, however, spend their money for this useless herb, while their very neighbors are freezing or starving before their eyes. Boston can spend $50,000 annually on tea, in spite of human want and wo.—We have no sympathy with that mawkish sensibility to the condition of others in a foreign land, which overlooks or forgets misery at its own doors.

If we could even prove that a discontinuance of the use of tea would subject the inhabitants of the Celestial Empire to a little inconvenience at first, it is no more than happens to our own distillers, and retailers, and brewers, and confectioners, in the progress of the cause of temperance;—and, as we have already said, an argument which would be good in the one case, would be equally so in the other. Continue tea for the sake of the Chinese, and we ought by the same rule to continue the use of fermented and distilled liquors, for the sake of our own countrymen who are concerned in their manufacture and sale.

We have hitherto gone on the supposition that tea was unadulterated, and contained no poison superadded by the manufacturers. But here comes another serious objection to tea drinking, if we may rely on the statements of the London Quarterly. This journal assures us that there is a manufactory near Canton, where the worst kinds of coarse black tea are converted into green, by means, principally, of that dangerous substance, white lead. The process is as follows:

'Stir it about on iron plates, moderately heated, mixing it up with a composition of turmeric, indigo, and white lead by which process it acquires a blooming blue color of plums, and that crispy appearance which is supposed to indicate the fine green teas.'

The Quarterly states, on good authority, that there were not long since, 50,000 chests of this spurious article prepared ready for shipping. On inquiry for what market it was intended, the reply was—'The American.'—As two-thirds of the tea used in America is green tea, nominally so, we see the bearing of this statement, and, if it can be relied on, our own danger.

Will the people of America expose themselves longer to costly foreign poisons, when the cheap, pure, wholesome, unadulterated, and only drink which the Author of nature ever made, is suffered to flow from millions of fountains untasted and unheeded; or at best rarely used as a drink, except to dilute that which had better never have crossed the ocean? Is here no need of reform? . . .

Tea Drinking, Again

The respectable editor of an eastern paper advises us—and we are fond of advice from any quarter—not to make war upon tea until we have banished all drinks of a more questionable character.

If the editor will look over both of our long articles on the subject of tea, he will probably find it there stated, and we think shown, that tea is seldom drunk for the sake of its adaptation to quench thirst, but rather for the Excitement which it affords to the nervous system; and that the excitement is substantially the same, whether produced by alcoholic drinks, by tea or coffee, or anything else. Now if this is so, what is the difference, really and intrinsically, between tea drinking and rum or wine drinking, except that we usually take a larger quantity of that which excites, in the one case, than in the other?

We are persuaded—most fully persuaded—that we must and shall all come ultimately to the point of using water as our only common drink. Without this we are even satisfied that the wheels of the temperance car will ere long roll backward. We began the temperance reformation—and perhaps in the horrid slavery to which our depraved appetites had reduced us, some may think that we could not have begun otherwise—by endeavoring to cleanse the flood of intemperance near its mouth, regardless of the numerous tributary streams that under milder and less suspicious names were continually pouring in their polluted mass to continue it. Nay, we even added to their power by encouraging the use of wine, tea, coffee, &c. as substitutes for alcoholic liquors.

But the great error of substituting wine for other fermented drinks, particularly ale, for those drinks which contain a little more alcohol, is now beginning to be seen in its true light, and the public mind, both in this country and in Europe, is speedily getting right. Our transatlantic brethren, especially in wine countries, are indeed in this respect in advance of us; for while we were talking of the mighty degree of temperance which prevailed in those countries, and proposing to introduce the vine among us as a temperance measure, they saw more clearly—for they had a better opportunity—that it was of no use to banish rum while we retained wine, and they told us so. Rev. Henry Ware, Jr. but the other day, at Woburn, told his audience that an eminent medical gentleman of France made this statement to him most distinctly.

Now then, since both alcoholic and fermented liquors are 'gone by the board,' to use a sailor phrase; since people are determined to have some excitement or other, either as food or drink, the public appetite seems to be directed at present to tea and coffee. We acknowledge that these are less injurious in themselves than spirits and wine, and ale and cider; but they are still injurious; besides they are among the fountains which have hitherto fed the same mighty stream, and are likely to continue to do so. As long as tea and coffee are used for the sake of the unnatural stimulus they contain—and for what other purpose were they ever used?—so long we are in danger as a people of going back to the pollutions from which we have but partially escaped. He who says that tea and coffee must be abandoned by the community is not now deemed half so heterodox, as was the man who dared five years ago to say that we must abandon fermented liquors. And if there were persons to be found then, who dared to stem the torrent of ridicule and censure, and breast the odium which was heaped upon those who touched the subject of fermented liquors, is it likely that there are none to be found at the present time who are willing to stand in the same position, with respect to the votaries of tea and coffee?

We know, at the least, of some such individuals. Convinced as we are of the immense evil which results to society from the use of these drinks, independently of their tendency to intemperance in other things, we shall never cease to pronounce them pernicious; and shall never hesitate to say that their use, except to those who are wholly ignorant of their questionable nature, or cannot get any thing better to drink, is decidedly wrong; and to endeavor to prove our assertion. When the fountains from the hills cease to flow, and the rain from heaven ceases to descend, we may perhaps alter our opinion, or pursue a different course of conduct.

Note

1. Highly poisonous plants in the *Apiaceaein* family.

Source: William Alcott, "Tea Drinking, Again," *Moral Reformer and Teacher on the Human Constitution* 1 (October 1835): 299–305; (November 1835): 349–351.

1836 • 32 • Charles Ball, *Slavery in the United States*

Introduction: *Charles Ball (1781?–?), most likely a pseudonym, was a slave for 40 years in Maryland, South Carolina, and Georgia. He escaped from slavery several times, only to be captured again. During the War of 1812 he fought with the Americans at the Battle of Bladensburg, where British forces routed the American militia. Ball married but was separated from his wife and children when he was sold to a plantation owner in Georgia. He escaped but was recaptured and sold to a cotton plantation in South Carolina. Around 1830 he escaped again to Pennsylvania, where with the assistance of a white lawyer Ball wrote* Slavery in the United States: A Narrative of the Life and Adventures of Charles Ball *in 1836; it was an instant success. The book was reprinted more than 20 times before the Civil War. Because Ball was a fugitive slave, he moved again after publication, and what became of him is unknown. The excerpts below are about the food that slaves ate. The story begins when Ball and 250 other enslaved men were forced to walk in chains from Maryland to be sold in Columbia, South Carolina.*

We here, again, received boiled rice for supper, without salt, or any kind of seasoning; a pint was allotted to each person, which we greedily devoured, having had no dinner to-day, save an allowance of corn-cakes, with the fat of about five pounds of bacon, extracted by frying, in which we dipped our bread. I slept soundly after this day's march, the fatigues of the body having, for once, overcome the agitations of the mind. The next day, which was, if my recollection is accurate, the ninth of June, was the last of our journey before our company separated; and we were on the road before the stars had disappeared from the sky. Our breakfast, this morning, consisted of bacon soup, a dish composed of corn-meal, boiled in water, with a small piece of bacon to give the soup a taste of meat. For dinner we had boiled Indian peas, with a small allowance of bacon. This was the first time that we had received two rations of meat in the same day, on the whole journey, and some of our party were much surprised at the kindness of our master; but I had no doubt that his object was to make us look fat and hearty, to enable him to obtain better prices for us at Columbia.

At supper this night, we had corn mush, in largo wooden trays, with melted lard to dip the mush in before eating it. We might have reached Columbia [South Carolina] this day if we had continued our march, but we stopped, at least an hour before sun-set, about three miles from town, at the house of a man who supported the double character of planter and keeper of a house of entertainment; for I learned from his slaves that their master considered it disreputable to be called a tavern-keeper, and would not put up a sign, although he received pay of such persons as lodged with him. His house was a frame building, weather-boarded with pine boards, but had no plastering within. . . .

About seven o'clock in the morning the overseer sounded his horn; and we all repaired to the shade of some persimmon trees, which grew in a corner of the field, to get our breakfast. I here saw a cart drawn by a yoke of oxen, driven by an old black man, nearly blind. The cart contained three barrels, filled with water, and several large baskets full of corn bread that had been baked in the ashes. The water was for us to drink, and the bread was our breakfast. The little son of the overseer was also in the cart, and had brought with him the breakfast of his father, in a small wooden bucket.

The overseer had bread, butter, cold ham, and coffee for his breakfast. Ours was composed of a corn cake, weighing about three-quarters of a pound, to each person, with as much water as was desired. I at first supposed that this bread was dealt out to the people as their allowance; but on further inquiry I found this not to be the case. Simon, by whose side I was now at work, and who seemed much pleased with my agility and diligence in my duty, told me that here, as well as every where in this country, each person received a peck of corn at the crib door, every Sunday evening, and that in ordinary times, every one had to grind this corn and bake it, for him or herself, making such use of it as the owner thought proper; but that for some time past, the overseer, for the purpose of saving the time which had been lost in baking the bread, had made it the duty of an old woman, who was not capable of doing much work in the field, to stay at the quarter, and bake the bread of the whole gang. When baked, it was brought to the field in a cart, as I saw, and dealt out in loaves.

They still had to grind their own corn, after night; and as there were only three hand-mills on the plantation, he said they experienced much difficulty in converting their corn into meal. We worked in this field all day; and at the end of every hour, or hour and a quarter, we had permission to go to the cart, which was moved about the field, so as to be near us, and get water.

Our dinner was the same, in all respects, as our breakfast, except that, in addition to the bread, we had a little salt, and a radish for each person. We were not allowed to rest at either breakfast or dinner, longer than while we were eating; and we worked in the evening as long as we could distinguish the weeds from the cotton plants.

Simon informed me, that formerly, when they baked their own bread, they had left their work soon after sundown, to go home and bake for the next day, but the overseer had adopted the new policy for the purpose of keeping them at work until dark. . . .

This beef was intended as a feast for the slaves, at the laying by of the corn and cotton; and when I had it hung up, and had taken the hide off, my young master, whom I had seen on the day of my arrival, came out to me, and ordered me to cut off the head, neck, legs, and tail, and lay them, together with the empty stomach and the harslet,[1] in a basket. This basket was sent home, to the kitchen of the great house, by a woman and a boy, who attended for that purpose. I think there was at least one hundred and twenty or thirty pounds of this offal. The residue of the carcass I cut into four quarters, and we carried it to the cellar of the great house. Here one of the hind quarters was salted in a tub, for the use of the family, and the other was sent, as a present, to a planter, who lived about four miles distant. The two fore-quarters were cut into very small pieces, and salted by themselves.—These, I was told, would be cooked for our dinner on the next day (Sunday) when there was to be a general rejoicing among all the slaves of the plantation.

After the beef was salted down, I received some bread and milk for my breakfast, and went to join the hands in the corn field, where they were now harrowing and hoeing the crop for the last time. The overseer had promised us that we should have holiday after the completion of this work, and by great exertion, we finished it about five o'clock in the afternoon.

On our return to the quarter, the overseer, at roll-call—which he performed this day before night—told us that every family must send a bowl to the great house, to get our dinners of meat. This intelligence diffused as much joy amongst us, as if each one had drawn a prize in a lottery. At the assurance of a meat dinner, the old people smiled and showed their teeth, and returned thanks to master overseer; but many of the younger ones shouted, clapped their hands, leaped, and ran about with delight.

Each family, or mess, now sent its deputy, with a large wooden bowl in his hand, to receive the dinner at the great kitchen. I went on the part of our family, and found that the meat dinner of this day was made up of the basket of tripe, and other offal, that I had prepared in the morning. The whole had been boiled in four great iron kettles, until the flesh had disappeared from the bones, which were broken in small pieces—a flitch of bacon, some green corn, squashes, tomatos, and onions had been added, together with other condiments, and the whole converted into about a hundred gallons of soup, of which I received in my bowl, for the use of our family, more than two gallons. We had plenty of bread, and a supply of black-eyed peas, gathered from our garden, some of which Dinah had boiled in our kettle, whilst I was gone for the soup, of which there was as much as we could consume, and I believe that every one in the quarter had enough.

I doubt if there was in the world a happier assemblage than ours, on this Saturday evening. We had finished one of the grand divisions of the labors of a cotton plantation, and were supplied with a dinner, which to the most of my fellow slaves appeared to be a great luxury, and most liberal donation on the part of our master, whom they regarded with sentiments of gratitude for this manifestation of his bounty. . . .

We had allowances of meat distributed to all the people twice this fall—once when we had finished the saving the fodder, and again soon after the murder of the young lady. The first time we had beef, such as I had driven from the woods when I went to the alligator pond; but now we had two hogs given to us, which weighed, one a hundred and thirty, and the other a hundred and fifty-six pounds. This was very good pork, and I received a pound and a quarter as my share of it. This was the first pork that I had tasted in Carolina, and it afforded a real feast. We had, in our family, full seven pounds of good fat meat; and as we now had plenty of sweet potatoes, both in our gardens and in our weekly allowance, we had on the Sunday following the funeral, as good a dinner of stewed pork and potatoes as could have been found in all Carolina. We did not eat all our meat on Sunday, but kept part of it until Tuesday, when we warmed it in a pot with an addition of parsley and other herbs, and had another very comfortable meal.

I had, by this time, become in some measure acquainted with the country, and began to lay and execute plans to procure supplies of such things as were not allowed me by my master. I understood various methods of entrapping rackoons, and other wild animals that abounded in the large swamps of this country; and besides the skins, which were worth something for their furs, I generally procured as many rackoons, opossums, and rabbits, as afforded us two or three meals in a week. The woman with whom I lived, understood the way of dressing an opossum, and I was careful to provide one for our Sunday dinner every week, so long as these animals continued fat and in good condition.

All the people on the plantation did not live as well as our family did, for many of the men did not understand trapping game, and others were too indolent to go far enough from home to find good places for setting their traps. My principal trapping ground was three miles from home, and I went three times a week, always after night, to bring home my game, and keep my traps in good order. Many of the families in the quarter caught no game, and had no meat, except that which we received from the overseer, which averaged about six or seven meals in the year.

Note

1. A piece of meat to be roasted.

Source: Charles Ball, *Slavery in the United States: A Narrative of the Life and Adventures of Charles Ball, a Black Man, Who Lived Forty Years in Maryland, South Carolina and Georgia, as a Slave* (Lewistown, PA: J. W. Shugert, 1836), 50–51, 120–121, 138–139, 196.

1837 • 33 • Harriet Martineau, Dinner in South Carolina

Introduction: *Harriet Martineau (1802–1876) was a British journalist who visited America for two years during the early 1830s. She was deeply concerned about the treatment of women and slaves. While in South Carolina in 1835, Martineau described southern food as served by plantation owners.*

It was now the middle of April. In the kitchen garden the peas were ripening, and the strawberries turning red, though the spring of 1835 was very backward. We had salads, young asparagus, and radishes.

The following may be considered a pretty fair account of the provision for a planter's table, at this season; and, except with regard to vegetables, I believe it does not vary much throughout the year. Breakfast at seven; hot wheat bread, generally sour; corn bread, biscuits, waffles, hominy, dozens of eggs, broiled ham, beef-steak or broiled fowl, tea and coffee. Lunch at eleven; cake and wine, or liqueur. Dinner at two; now and then soup (not good,) always roast turkey and ham; a boiled fowl here, a tongue there; a small piece of nondescript meat, which generally turns out to be pork disguised; hominy, rice, hot corn-bread, sweet potatoes; potatoes mashed with spice, very hot; salad and radishes, and an extraordinary variety of pickles. Of these, you are asked to eat everything with everything else. If you have turkey and ham on your plate, you are requested to add tongue, pork, hominy, and pickles. Then succeed pies of apple, squash, and pumpkin; custard, and a variety of preserves as extraordinary as the preceding pickles: pine-apple, peach, limes, ginger, guava jelly, cocoa-nut, and every sort of plums. These are almost all from the West-Indies. Dispersed about the table are shell almonds, raisins, hickory, and other nuts; arid, to crown the whole, large blocks of ice-cream. Champagne is abundant, and cider frequent. Ale and porter may now and then be seen; but claret is the most common drink. During dinner a slave stands at a corner of the table, keeping off the flies by waving a large bunch of peacock's feathers fastened into a handle,—an ampler fan than those of our grandmothers.

Supper takes place at six, or seven. Sometimes the family sits round the table; but more commonly the tray is handed round, with plates which must be held in the lap. Then follow tea and coffee, waffles, biscuits, sliced ham or hung-beef, and sweet cake. Last of all, is the offer of cake and wine at nine or ten.

Source: Harriet Martineau, *Society in America,* 3rd ed., Vol. 1 (London: Saunders and Otley, 1837), 227–228.

1838 • 34 • "Intoxicating Drinks Not Necessary to Men in Health"

Introduction: *By 1830, alcohol consumption by Americans over the age of 15 was estimated at seven gallons per capita, most of it in the form of whiskey. The temperance movement gained momentum during the early 19th century. In addition to opposition from the medical profession, many members of religious groups jumped on the temperance bandwagon. More than 5,000 temperance societies with a total of 1.25 million members were operating in America by 1833. Two years later there were 8,000 societies with 1.5 million members. In the early 1830s, temperance leaders embraced total abstinence. The Dutch Reformed Church supported this principle, as would many Quakers, Universalists, Presbyterians, Methodists, and Baptists. As a result, the focus of the movement shifted from serious medical issues to a moral crusade against all alcohol. Temperance advocates used sermons, books, tracts, hymns, mass meetings, and cartoons to make life uncomfortable for those who manufactured, sold, and drank alcohol. Temperance orators drew large crowds, and two temperance plays found wide audiences. As the temperance fervor increased, public drinking became less acceptable, and moderate drinkers found themselves in an especially uncomfortable position, despised by both teetotalers and hard drinkers. The excerpts below, from* The Temperance Textbook: A Collection of Facts and Interesting Anecdotes Illustrating the Evils of Intoxicating Drinks *(1837), reflect both medical opinion of the day against the consumption of alcohol and the statistics that demonstrated, at least to temperance advocates, the close connection between drinking and crime. Because of such efforts of the temperance societies, alcohol consumption dropped sharply such that by 1845, Americans drank an estimated 75 percent less alcohol than they did in 1830.*

Intoxicating Drinks Not Necessary to Men in Health. Opinions of Medical Men.

'On comparing my own observations,' says Dr. Willan, 'with the bills of mortality, I am convinced that considerably more than one eighth of all the deaths which take place in persons above twenty years old, happen prematurely through excess in drinking.'

Dr. Paris says that, 'The art of extracting alcoholic liquors by distillation, must be regarded as the greatest curse inflicted on human nature.'

Dr. Rush says,—'Since the introduction of spirituous liquors into such general use, physicians have remarked that a number of new diseases have appeared among us, and have described many new symptoms as common to all diseases.'

Dr. Trotter says,—'Amid all the evils of human life, no cause of disease has so wide a range, or so large a share, as the use of spirits.'

In 1834, according to the February No. of the American Quarterly Temperance Magazine, of that year, nearly two thousand physicians in Europe and America had expressed the opinion, that men in health are never benefited by the use of intoxicating drinks, and that their effect on the human system is to produce or aggravate disease.

Dr. Wilson gives it as his opinion, that the use of spirits, in large cities, causes more diseases than confined air, unwholesome exhalations, and the combined influence of all other evils.

Dr. Kirk, of Scotland, dissected a man who died in a fit of intoxication, a few hours after death. And from the lateral ventricles of the brain, he took a fluid distinctly visible to the smell, as whisky; and when he applied a candle to it in a spoon, it took fire, and burnt blue; 'The lambent blue flame,' he says, 'characteristic of the poison, playing on the surface of the spoon for some seconds.'

If any one is disposed to question the correctness of this statement, the following particulars of a case, which, as says Dr. Sewall, are attested by unquestionable authority, must remove all doubts:—

A man was taken up dead in the streets of London, soon after having drank a quart of gin, on a wager. He was carried to the Westminster hospital, and there dissected. 'In the ventricles of the brain was found a considerable quantity of limpid fluid, distinctly impregnated with gin, both to the sense of smell and taste, and even to the test of inflammability. The liquid appeared to the senses of the examining students, as strong as one third gin, and two-thirds water.'

Says Professor Mussey, 'I deny that alcoholic spirit is essential to the practice of either physic or surgery. All its medical virtues are found in other articles.'

Dr. Armstrong speaks of the chronic inflammation of the brain and its membranes, as frequently proceeding from the use of strong liquors.

'The art of procuring ardent spirits by distillation,' says Professor Waterhouse, 'was the discovery of the Arabian chymists, a century or two after the death of Mahomet, who died in 631. But so sensible were these Mahometans of the destructive effects of spirituous liquors, that the use of them was prohibited even by their own laws. Such, however, was their prejudice against Christianity, that they willingly suffered this infernal and fascinating spirit to be introduced among Christian nations. A more subtle plan, perhaps, could not have been devised to eradicate every religious principle from the human mind, and to disseminate those of an opposite nature.

Dr. Cheyne, of Dublin, Ireland, after thirty years practice and observation, gives it as his opinion, that should ten young men begin, at twenty-one years of age, to use but one glass of two ounces a day, and never increase the quantity, nine out of ten would shorten life more than ten years.'

Dr. Porter, of Portland, Me. after sixty years practice, says, 'I exceedingly regret the exception (in favour of ardent spirits as a medicine,) in the constitutions of Temperance Societies.'

Favourable Influence of Total Abstinence upon Health and Longevity.

Says Dr. Mussey, 'If ardent spirits be necessary to health and activity, how did the world get along without it for forty-eight hundred years? How could the Roman soldiery withstand the frightful onset of Hannibal, with nothing to drink stronger than vinegar and water? Take a soldier of the present day, clothe him with heavy Roman armour, and give him the pilum and short sword, weapons which "conquered the world," and it will soon appear what blessings we have derived from alcohol. The modern Achilles cripples under his load, unable to raise from the ground the instrument with which he is to meet his foe.'

It is said by Dr. Hosack, in his late address, that 'it appears from the society of Friends, that, in consequence of their habitual temperance, one-half of the members of that society live to the age of forty-seven: and that one in ten lives to be eighty; whereas the average of human life is thirty-three years, and not more than one in forty, of the general population, lives to be eighty years of age. The amount of human life, then, gained by temperance, is more than the difference between thirty-three and forty-seven,—or an average of fourteen years gained in every life, which is equal to forty-two per cent.'

'The early settlers of New England,' says the Rev. Dr. Beecher, 'endured more hardship, and performed more labour, and carried through life more health and vigour, than appertains to the existing generations of labouring men. And they did it without the use of ardent spirits.'

Says Dr. Hill, in his biography of the celebrated Blair, 'Though his bodily constitution was by no means robust, yet, by habitual temperance, and by attention to health, his life was happily prolonged beyond the usual period. During the summer before his death, he was occupied in preparing the last volume of his sermons for the press; and, for this purpose, he copied the whole with his own hand. It seemed to give him much pleasure that, at his advanced period of life, he was able to make this exertion.' Dr. Blair died December 27th, 1800, in the eighty-third year of his age.

Of more than one thousand deaths by cholera in Montreal, it is stated that only two were members of Temperance Societies; and that, as far as is known, no members of Temperance Societies in Ireland, Scotland, or England, have as yet fallen victims to that dreadful disease.

At a meeting of the British and Foreign Temperance Society, in London, great applause was elicited by the address of Thomas Shillitoe, an aged member of the society of Friends, (near ninety years old, we believe,) whose health had been ruined, and who was brought near to the grave, by a nervous affection in early life; but who, by practising total abstinence from intoxicating liquors, and by regulating his diet, had restored his constitution, and was enjoying a vigorous and happy old age. A gentleman present said, 'Mr. Shillitoe had walked from Tottenham, (six miles,) to attend the meeting, and would probably walk home again.'

Died, in the Maury County (Tenn.) Almshouse, Abraham Bogard, aged one hundred and eighteen. He never drank spirits, nor was sick, nor took medicine of any kind. He was once bled, out of curiosity. He retained the faculties of seeing, hearing, and memory, until his death.

By the aid of temperance St. Anthony, St. Jerome, and James the Hermit, lived to more than a century.

The rail roads from Boston to Providence, Lowell, and Worcester, have been completed without the use of spirituous liquors. The men employed on the road, to manage the engines and cars, are cold water men.

The City Hall at Albany stands as a monument to mark a new era in the erection of public edifices. From first to last, not a single accident has occurred; and, in the opinion of good judges, the workmanship will not suffer, when compared with that of any similar building in the state. The expense to the public, it is believed, has been ten thousand dollars less than it would have been, had ardent spirits been used.

Dr. Benjamin Rush says that, 'There is no nourishment in ardent spirits. The strength they produce in labour is of a transient nature, and is always followed by a sense of weakness and fatigue.'

Mr. E. Whipple, the enterprising manufacturer of stoves, in Cincinnati, has one hundred men in his employ, not one of whom is known to use strong drink.

The stupendous bridge now being erected over the Susquehanna river, is emphatically a cold water bridge; ardent spirits not being used by any one of the hands employed on the work.

In the erection of the Massachusetts' Lunatic Asylum, the state commissioners say that more than eleven hundred thousand brick have been laid during the past year; that not an accident has happened; that not an hour's time has been lost by the indisposition of any of the workmen; and that not a drop of ardent spirit has been consumed in the performance.

From the commencement of the erection of an extensive block of buildings on the corner of Beaver and Greene streets, Albany, about sixty men were constantly employed. The superintendent says that not a drop of ardent spirit was allowed on the premises, and no man was permitted to leave his work to procure any, under penalty of immediate dismission. Among the men employed, there was but one death by cholera, and in that case, the man would drink spirit after his hours of labour.

Advantages of total abstinence to mechanics and labouring men.

1. They have a better appetite, and partake of their food with a keener relish, and it is more nourishing to them than when they drink rum.
2. They possess much greater vigour and activity, both of body and mind.
3. They perform the same labour with much greater ease, and are, in a great measure, free from the lassitude and fatigue common to rum-drinkers.
4. They have greater wages, and lay up a much larger portion of what they earn.
5. Their example will be useful to those around them.

Advantages of total abstinence to him whose farm is conducted upon strict temperance principles.

1. The men do their work in a satisfactory manner, and at a small expense of tools.
2. He can, with much greater ease, have a place for every thing, and every thing in its place.
3. When a stone has fallen from the wall, it is laid up, as the men are passing by, without his mentioning it. The gates are locked, and the bars put up; so that the cattle do not get in and destroy the crops.
4. His summer work is done in such season, that earth, loam, &c. are carted into the yard in the fall. The consequence is, when carried out, they are richer, and render the farm more productive.
5. His barns, in winter, are kept clean, and less fodder is wasted. The cattle and horses are daily curried, and appear in good order.
6. When his men go into the forests, instead of cutting down the nearest, thriftiest, and largest trees, they cut those that are decayed, crooked, and not likely to grow any better; pick up those that are blown down, and thus leave the forest in a better state.
7. The men are uniform, still, and peaceable; are less troublesome in the house, and more contented with their manner of living.
8. On the Sabbath, instead of wishing to stay at home, or spend the day in roving about the fields, rivers, and forests, they choose statedly and punctually to attend public worship. . . .

Folly and Danger of Moderate Drinking.

We knew a beautiful young woman, an only daughter, the pride and joy of her feeble and declining parents. There came into her father's employ a benevolent, industrious, pleasant young man, of some natural talent, who very prudently had resolved not to drink but two glasses a day, one in the forenoon, and one in the afternoon. He paid his

Advertisement for Robbertson's Genuine Bourbon Cordial, from the Harrison Company in Kentucky, 1847. (Buyenlarge/Getty Images)

addresses to her, and she received them. In about a year they were married. He had at this time doubled his dose, and very prudently resolved that he would never drink more than four glasses a day. Rum, however, soon had more power over him than prudence. His face began to swell, his breath grew foetid, he lost his good nature, his industrious habits left him at a time when a growing family called for his exertions,—he was thrown out of employment; and there he was, a poor, miserable, profane, idle, beggarly drunkard. This came gradually, but it came certainly. His poor wife was an object of distress, and of universal pity. She bore up under her sufferings as well as so frail a thing was able to; and in a short time death came and gave her release. It broke down the whole family, father, mother and brothers, for all their hopes were placed on her.

We were once very much surprised to hear a gentleman of good sense say, 'I had rather my daughter should marry an old drunkard, than a cautious drinker.' On our expressing our surprise, he added, 'if she were to marry a drunkard, he would soon die, and she would be released; but if she marry a temperate drinker, she must witness his degradation, she must follow him in his downward course, she may be connected with him many years, and her trouble would kill her about as soon as his intemperance would kill him.' Reader, do not be a cautious drinker.

Dr. Harris states that, the moderate use of spirituous liquors has destroyed many who were never drunk.

Dr. Kirk gives it as his opinion, that men who were never considered intemperate, have often shortened life, by daily drinking, more than twenty years.

Says Dr. Benj. Rush,—'Ardent spirits often bring on fatal diseases without producing drunkenness. I have known many persons destroyed by them, who were never completely intoxicated during the whole course of their lives.'

'A respectable and influential man,' says the Rev. Dr. Edwards, [']early in life adopted the habit of using a little ardent spirit daily. He and his six children are now in the drunkard's grave; and the only surviving child is rapidly following, in the same way, to the same dismal end.[']

Of the twelve hundred persons who were attacked with the cholera at Montreal, all were either confirmed drunkards, or moderate drinkers.

Says the Rev. Wilbur Fisk, President of the Wesleyan university:—'It cannot be denied that all the drunkenness in the land is produced by what is called the temperate use of ardent spirits.'

'It is by the temperate use of ardent spirits,' says an intelligent writer, 'that intemperate appetites are formed. And the temperate use of it cannot be continued, without, in many cases, forming intemperate appetites.'

Says a writer in the American Quarterly Temperance Magazine, 'We have all seen the drunkard, in youth a temperate drinker, in manhood a tippler, and in old age a sot.'

Says E. Taylor, Esq. of Schenectady, in his letter to the Rev. Dr. Edwards, 'All drunkards began to drink temperately, and not one designed to be a drunkard. What desolations, for time and eternity, have been induced by temperate drinking!'

Temperate Drinking.

''Tis but a drop,' the father said,
And gave it to his son;
But little did he think a work
Of death was then begun.
The 'drop' that lured him when the babe
Scarce lisp'd his father's name,
Planted a fatal appetite
Deep in his infant frame.
''Tis but a drop,' the comrades cried,
In truant school-boy tone;
'It did not hurt us in our robes,
It will not now we're grown.'
And so they drank the mixture up,
That reeling, youthful band;
For each had learn'd to love the taste,

From his own father's hand.
''Tis but a drop,' the husband said,
While his poor wife stood by,
In famine, grief, and loneliness,
And raised th' imploring cry.
''Tis but a drop,—I'll drink it still—
'Twill never injure me;
I always drank—so, madam, hush!
We never can agree.'
''Tis but a drop,—I need it now.'
The staggering drunkard said;
'It was my food in infancy—
My meat, and drink, and bread.
A drop—a drop—O, let me have,
'Twill so refresh my soul!'
He took it—trembled—drank—and died,
Grasping the fatal bowl.

Abstinence is said to be of easier practice than temperance. We can, by a moderate effort, forbear entirely from an indulgence; but, to partake of it in moderation, is a task of infinite difficulty.

Intoxicating Drinks a Cause of Crime.

A Man had the choice of committing the least of three offences—murder, robbery, or drunkenness. He chose the latter, got drunk and then committed the other two.

Agreeably to a memorandum kept by the Rev. Dr. Cathcart, of York, Pa., it appears that one hundred and nine murders were committed in the United States, within the year 1831. A large proportion of them are regarded as the consequence of an intemperate use of ardent spirit.

Wm. H. Boulton, of Augusta, was committed to jail to take his trial for stabbing Wm. Brett, his brother-in-law, while under the influence of strong drink. They were both drunkards.

Israel Douglass, of Hallowell, another drunkard, has also been committed for an attempt to murder his wife and children, while in a drunken frenzy.

Of 119 commitments in a year, to the state prison at Charlestown, Mass., it is stated by an officer of the prison, that one hundred at least appear to have been occasioned by intemperance.

Says the Fifth Annual Report of the inspectors of the Eastern Penitentiary of Pennsylvania,—

The number of prisoners received into the Penitentiary in 1834, was 118; of which number the habitual drunkards were, 5; Frequently intoxicated, 16; Occasionally drunk, 73.

Nearly seven-eighths of the whole number addicted to the use of spirituous liquors.

He could not do it until he had taken some brandy! Fieschi, the constructor of the 'infernal machine,' acknowledged that his heart failed him a short time before the king arrived, but he went to a shop, drank some brandy, and thus wound his courage up for the hellish attempt.

'Intoxicating liquor,' says the Fifth Report of the American Temperance Society, 'exposes the children of those who use it, in an eminent degree, to dissipation and crime. Of six hundred and ninety children prosecuted and imprisoned for crimes, more than four hundred were from intemperate families.'

'Of seventeen hundred and sixty-four criminals in different prisons in the United States,' says the Fifth Report of the American Temperance Society, 'more than thirteen hundred were either intemperate men, or were under the power of intoxicating liquor, when the crimes, for which they were imprisoned, were committed. And of forty-four murders, according to the testimony of those who prosecuted or conducted the defence of the murderers, or witnessed their trials, forty-three were committed by intemperate men, or upon intemperate men, or those who at the time of the murder were under the power of strong drink.'

Russell and Crockett were executed at Boston, on the 16th of March last, for setting fire to a house containing several families, chiefly Irish. Crockett was a young man, and nothing appeared unfavourable to his past good character, during his trial, except that it was distinctly stated 'he was sometimes intemperate.' The following extract from a letter written by him, the night previous to his execution, speaks in forcible language of the evil consequences of dram-drinking.

Boston Jail, March 15, 1836.

Under a deep sense of my situation, I write a few lines, which I leave in the hands of the Rev. E. T. Taylor. I would leave them to show how I came here. I never was inclined to lie, cheat, or steal for a living, but designed to get it honestly, by labour. And it would have been so to this day, if I had not fallen into bad company. I never was accustomed to crime. My mind has always been far from it; and I never should have been engaged in this, if they had not caught me intoxicated. I knew not what I was about, nor where they were getting me to.

Now I feel the effect of falling into bad company. I would warn my young friends to keep out of it, and Never to drink ardent spirit! I consider it the surest weapon a man can use to take his life with, and make him eternally miserable. I would warn you as a dying friend, in the name of God, to abstain from drinking, for 'when rum is in, wit is out'; and the devil is always ready to aid in doing mischief. He will lead a man into trouble, and then leave him to get out as he can.

Henry Ferguson and Ephraim Tally had jointly bought a quart of liquor, and received in change two cents. A dispute originated as to the distribution of the change. Ferguson demanded both cents; but Tally was willing to give him but one. A dispute, therefore, about a single cent, cost one of the parties his life, made the other a murderer, and sent him for twelve years to the penitentiary. But the liquor, the abominable whisky, was no doubt the real cause of all this wo.

In August, 1834, of eight hundred and thirty-four prisoners in the Sing Sing state prison, N. Y., four hundred and eighty-five had been habitual drunkards, and about one third of the number actually committed their respective crimes when intoxicated.

Of six hundred and seventy convicts in the Auburn state prison, N. Y., five hundred and three were intemperate, and one hundred and fifty-nine what have been called temperate drinkers; leaving but eight out of the whole number who were total abstinents.

The warden of the Connecticut state prison, Mr. Pilsbury, states the proportion of convicts who acknowledged themselves to be habitually intemperate, to be seventy-five in one hundred.

The Rev. Mr. Hecwelder relates the following fact of the influence of rum upon an Indian:—'An Indian, who had been brought up at Minisink, near the Delaware Water Gap, told me, near fifty years ago, that he had once, under the influence of strong liquor, killed the best Indian friend he had, fancying him to be his worst avowed enemy.'

A drunkard in Union county, Indiana, recently murdered his whole family, consisting of a wife and three children. His excuse was that they were likely to become a county charge.

Thomas Jones was sentenced to be hung at the Westmoreland Circuit, in Maryland, for the murder of his wife. It appears by the charge of Judge Lomax, that intemperance was the leading cause of this, as of seven-tenths of all the crimes that lead men to the prison house and the gallows.

Mr. Badlam, in a letter to a gentleman of Boston, Mass., says, 'There have not been ten persons committed to the house of correction, the past year, who were not in the habit of drinking ardent spirit to excess. It appears that intemperance is almost the sole cause of all the commitments. Those who are committed as pilferers, are almost all of them drunkards.'

A man who had displeased a number of others, was shortly after visited by them, and beaten till he was left for dead. He, however, recovered; and the magistrate, who came to take his deposition, asked him, 'Did you know any of the party?' 'No, sir.' 'Were they drunk?' 'No; they were able to do their business.' 'Had they drank any thing?' 'Well, I wonder,' said he, 'that your honour, a gentleman of your knowledge, should ask such a simple question; sure you do not think they would come without preparing themselves; I'll engage they had taken two or three glasses of whisky to a man.'

An atrocious crime was committed, in which an unfortunate man, by the name of Shaes, was burnt to death. A young man, not twenty years of age, was implicated in the crime, and he was asked how it was possible that he could commit such a crime. He answered, 'By the aid of whisky I could commit twenty others like it.'

According to the 'Documents relating to the State Prison,' addressed to Governor Lincoln and the Honourable Council of Massachusetts, the results of some inquiries made of 220 convicts, within a few weeks past, are as follows:

Addicted to habits of intemperance . . 156
Ascribed their imprisonment to the influence of intemperate drinking, . . . 122
State that their parents were in the habit of giving them ardent spirit when children, 116
Parents, one or both intemperate, . . . 54.

Judge Edwards, in passing sentence upon Catherine Cashiere, convicted of the murder of Susan Anthony, in the city of New York, said that, 'It is undeniably true, that a very large proportion of the crimes that are committed, are traceable, either directly or indirectly, to the influence of spirituous liquors. And I will add that the poverty and wretchedness which prevails in society, are to be ascribed more to this, than all other causes united.'

Cowen, who was recently executed at Cincinnati, for the murder of his wife, solemnly warned the multitude against the use of ardent spirit He said, 'Beware of the bowl! There is madness in it. Its accursed poison was my earthly ruin! Whatever of gentleness existed in my nature before I sought it, it was withered and banished when I found it. If I was a sinner when I first met the intoxicating cup, I certainly became a demon after I swallowed its venom. "Wine is a mocker; strong drink is raging!" How bitterly have I been mocked!'

An unlicensed grog-dealer, named Treadwell, keeping a shop at Bangor, Me., with the assistance of an under-strapper, named Woodward, undertook to furnish an Irishman with as much wine as he could drink for twenty-five cents[.] The Irishman drank a pint of stuff, which was drawn for him as port wine, and walked off. In about half an hour, he returned and drank two pints more. The result was death. Woodward was apprehended, on complaint of the coroner, who held an inquest over the body: he was examined, and required to recognise in, the sum of five hundred and fifty dollars, for his appearance at the next term of the Supreme Judicial Court, for trial, on the charge of manslaughter.

Source: *The Temperance Textbook: A Collection of Facts and Interesting Anecdotes Illustrating the Evils of Intoxicating Drinks* (Philadelphia: E. L. Carey and A. Hart, 1837), 10–19.

1838 • 35 • James Fenimore Cooper, *The American Democrat*

Introduction: *James Fenimore Cooper (1789–1851) was one of America's most prolific writers in the early 19th century. His most well-known works are* The Last of the Mohicans *and* Leatherstocking Tales. *Cooper's* The American Democrat: Or, Hints on the Social and Civic Relations of the United States of America *(1838) was an indictment of American political, civic, and, as the excerpt below shows, culinary life.*

There is a familiar and too much despised branch of civilization, of which the population of this country is singularly and unhappily ignorant; that of cookery. The art of eating and drinking, is one of those on which more depends, perhaps, than on any other, since health, activity of mind, constitutional enjoyments, even learning, refinement, and, to a certain degree, morals, are all, more or less, connected with our diet. The Americans are the grossest feeders of any civilized nation known. As a nation, their food is heavy, coarse, and indigestible, while it is taken in the least artificial forms that cookery will allow. The predominance of grease in the American kitchen, coupled with the habits of hearty eating, and the constant expectoration, are the causes of the diseases of the stomach which are so common in America. The science of the table extends far beyond the indulgence of our appetites, as the school of manners includes health and morals, as well as that which is agreeable. Vegetable diet is almost converted into an injury in America, from an ignorance of the best modes of preparation, while even animal food is much abused, and loses half its nutriment.

The same is true as respects liquors. The heating and exciting wines, the brandies, and the coarser drinks of the laboring classes, all conspire to injure the physical and the moral man, while they defeat their own ends.

These are points of civilization on which this country has yet much to learn, for while the tables of the polished and cultivated partake of the abundance of the country, and wealth has even found means to introduce some knowledge of the kitchen, there is not perhaps on the face of the globe, the same number of people among whom the good things of the earth are so much abused, or ignorantly wasted, as among the people of the United States. National character is, in some measure, affected by a knowledge of the art of preparing food, there being as good reason to suppose that man is as much affected by diet as any other animal, and it is certain that the connection between our moral and physical qualities is so intimate as to cause them to react on each other.

Source: James Fenimore Cooper, *The American Democrat: Or, Hints on the Social and Civic Relations of the United States of America* (Cooperstown, NY: H. and E. Phinney, 1838), 208–209.

1838 • 36 • Kentucky Barbecue on the Fourth of July

Introduction: *The only two national holidays in America until 1862 were George Washington's birthday and the Fourth of July. The Fourth of July holiday was celebrated throughout the nation, although regionalism was a major characteristic of the food served. In New England it was a salmon feast, while in the Midwest it might have been a chicken. But throughout the South, it was barbecue. Below is a description of a barbecue in Kentucky.*

Bearorass Creek, which is one of the many beautiful streams of the highly cultivated and happy state of Kentucky, meanders through a deeply shaded growth of majestick beech woods, in which are interspersed various species of walnut, oak, elm, ash, and other trees, extending on either side of its course. The spot on which I witnessed the celebration of an anniversary of the glorious Proclamation of our Independence is situated on its banks, near the city of Louisville. The woods spread their dense turfs toward the shores of the fair Ohio on the west, and over the gently rising grounds to the south and east. Every open spot forming a plantation was smiling in the luxuriance of a summer harvest. The farmer seemed to stand in admiration of the spectacle: the trees of his orchards bowed their branches, as if anxious to restore to their mother earth the fruit with which they were laden; the flocks leisurely ruminated as they lay on their grassy beds; and the genial warmth of the season seemed inclined to favour their repose.

The free, single hearted Kentuckian, bold, erect, and proud of his Virginian descent, had, as usual, made arrangements for celebrating the day of his country's Independence. The whole neighbourhood joined with one consent. No personal invitation was necessary where every one was welcomed by his neighbour, and from the governor to the guider of the plough all met with light hearts and merry faces.

It was indeed a beautiful day; the bright sun rode in the clear blue heavens; the gentle breezes wafted around the odours of the gorgeous flowers; the little birds sang their sweetest songs in the woods, and the fluttering insects danced in the sunbeams. Columbia's sons and daughters seemed to have grown younger that morning. For a whole week or more, many servants and some masters had been busily engaged in clearing an area. The undergrowth had been carefully cut down, the low boughs lopped off, and the grass alone, verdant and gay, remained to carpet the sylvan pavilion. Now the wagons were seen slowly moving along under their load of provisions, which had been prepared for the common benefit. Each denizen had freely given his ox, his ham, his venison, his turkeys, and other fowls. Here were to be seen flagons of every beverage used in the country; "La belle Riviere" had opened her finny stores; the melons of all sorts, peaches, plums, and pears, would have sufficed to stock a market. In a word, Kentucky, the land of abundance, had supplied a feast for her children.

A purling stream gave its waters freely, while the grateful breezes cooled the air. Columns of smoke from the newly kindled fires rose above the trees; fifty cooks or more moved to and fro as they plied their trade; waiters of all qualities were disposing the dishes, the glasses, and the punch-bowls, amid vases filled with rich wines. "Old Monongahela" filled many a barrel for the crowd. And now, the roasted viands perfume the air, and all appearances conspire to predict the speedy commencement of a banquet such as may suit the vigorous appetite of American woodsmen. Every steward is at his post, ready to receive the joyous groups that at this moment begin to emerge from the dark recesses of the woods.

Each comely fair one, clad in pure white, is seen advancing under the protection of her sturdy lover, the neighing of their prancing steeds proclaiming how proud they are of their burden. The youthful riders leap from their seats, and the horses are speedily secured by twisting their bridles round a branch. As the youth of Kentucky lightly and gaily advanced towards the Barbecue, they resembled a procession of nymphs and disguised divinities. Fathers and mothers smiled upon them, as they followed the brilliant cortege. In a short time the ground was alive with merriment. A great wooden cannon, bound with iron hoops, was now crammed with home-made powder; fire was conveyed to it by means of a train, and as the explosion burst forth, thousands of hearty huzzas mingled with its echoes. From the most learned, a good oration fell in proud and gladdening words on every ear, and although it probably did not equal the eloquence of a Clay, an Everett, a Webster, or a Preston, it served to remind every Kentuckian present of the glorious name of Washington. Fife and drums sounded the march which had ever led him to glory; and as they changed to our celebrated "Yankee Doodle," the air again rang with acclamations.

Now the stewards invited the assembled throng to the feast. The fair led the van, and were first placed around the tables, which groaned under the profusion of the best productions of the country that had been heaped upon them. On each lovely nymph attended her gay beau, who in her chance or sidelong glances ever watched an opportunity of reading his happiness. How the viands diminished under the action of so many agents of destruction I need not say, nor is it necessary that you should listen to the long recital. Many a national toast was offered and accepted, many speeches were delivered, and many essayed an amicable reply. The ladies then retired to booths that had been erected at a little distance, to which they were conducted by their partners, who returned to the table, and having thus cleared for action, recommenced a series of hearty rounds. However, as Kentuckians are neither slow nor long at their meals, all were in a few minutes replenished, and after a few more draughts from the bowl, they rejoined the ladies, and prepared for the dance.

Double lines of a hundred fair ones extended along the ground in the most shady part of the woods, while here and there smaller groups awaited the merry trills of reels and cotillions. A burst of musick from violins, clarionets, and bugles, gave the welcome notice, and presently the whole assemblage seemed to be gracefully moving through the air. The "hunting-shirts" now joined in the dance, their fringed skirts keeping time with the gowns of the ladies, and the married people of either sex stepped in and mixed with their children. Every countenance beamed with joy, every heart leaped with gladness;

no pride, no pomp, no affectation, were there; their spirits brightened as they continue their exhilarating exercise, and care and sorrow were flung to the winds. During each interval of rest, refreshments of all sorts were handed round, and while the fair one cooled her lips with the grateful juice of the melon, the hunter of Kentucky quenched his thirst with ample draughts of well tempered punch.

I know, reader, that had you been with me on that day, you would have richly enjoyed the sight of this national *fete champetre.* You would have listened with pleasure to the ingenious tale of the lover, the wise talk of the elder on the affairs of the state, the accounts of improvement in stock and utensils, and the hopes of continued prosperity to the country at large, and to Kentucky in particular You would have been pleased to see those who did not join the dance, shooting at distant marks with their heavy rifles, or watched how they shewed of the superiour speed of their high bred "old Virginia" horses, while others recounted their hunting exploits, and at intervals made the woods ring with their bursts of laughter. With me the time sped like an arrow in its flight, and although more than twenty year elapsed since I joined a Kentucky Barbecue, my spirit is refreshed every fourth of July by the recollection of that day's merriment.

But now the sun has declined, and the shades of evening creep over the scene. Large fires are lighted in the woods, casting the long shadows of the living columns far along the trodden ground, and flaring on the happy groups, loath to separate. In the still clear sky, began to sparkle the distant lamps of heaven. One might have thought that Nature herself smiled on the joy of her children. Supper now appeared on the tables, and after all had again refreshed themselves, preparations were made for departure. The lover hurried for the steed of his fair one, the hunter seized the arm of this friend, families gathered into loving groups, and all returned in peace to their happy home.

Source: "Kentucky Barbecue on the Fourth of July," *Family Magazine* 5 (1838): 117.

1838 • 37 • William A. Alcott, "Summary of Leading Principles"

Introduction: *William A. Alcott (1798–1859) was an educator and author. He was also one of America's early vegetarians. Alcott, one of America's prominent medical professionals and the uncle of author Louisa May Alcott, maintained that tea was not only useless but was also a narcotic and therefore poisonous.*

Summary of Leading Principles.

Simplicity in diet. Penalties of neglecting it. Importance of mastication. Temperature of food should be low. Why it should be so. Why purely nutritious substances should not be used. Why solid food is preferable to liquid. Drinks in general. Our meals should be regular. Proper hours of eating. Number of meals a day. Rules for the proper combination of several articles of food at a meal. Regard to the season of the year, hour of the day, and time of the week. Regard to our employment. Regard to age.

The preceding chapters, if carefully studied, contain, at least by inference, nearly if not quite all of what I deem the essential principles of rational and scientific dietetics, together with the more important rules of cookery. Still, it may not be amiss to present some of the most important of them in a more connected as well as a more condensed form.

1. The first rule in regard to food is, to observe simplicity. I have often heard people say, in relation to diet, Well, after all, the great error is in eating too much. And there is much truth in the remark. If error in quality slays its thousands, error in quantity slays its ten thousands. And though there may be a few who go to the extreme of eating too little—an evil of at least equal magnitude with the former, wherever it exists—yet cases of this sort are believed to be very few indeed. The great dietetic error, in this country at least, is excessive alimentation.

Multitudes, in this country of abundance, are trained from their veriest infancy to eat three or four times as much as they ought. Probably the estimate of many intelligent writers, that we eat upon an average, about twice as much as the general condition of the system demands, is a safe and correct one. People seem to go upon the principle of eating as much as they can and not immediately get sick, I say immediately; for as to the after consequences, few seem to care or inquire. Whereas the only safe rule for any individual in health is, to eat as little as he possibly can, and yet sustain, in the best condition, all the powers, functions and faculties of his system. Four or five pounds of solid food, such as bread, puddings, potatoes, beans, peas, &c., are consumed in a day by hundreds of hard-laboring individuals, besides a large amount of apples, and cider, and beer, and some tea, coffee, and fruits. Nay, we may find—without going to Siberian—many young men of sixteen, eighteen or twenty years of age, among our hills and mountains, who will consume their twelve or fifteen pounds of food daily, including milk, apples, &c., nor dream of danger till they chance, some five, ten or fifteen years afterwards, to be sick; and even then, neither their friends nor themselves—perhaps not the doctor himself—ever dream that the disease was produced or aggravated, as one leading cause, by excessive alimentation.

But although this is a common dietetic sin, it will never, in my view, be cured or prevented, till people come to habits of simplicity. It is in vain to tell of the evils, dreadful as they are to soul and body, from over-eating, so long as the custom prevails of placing in their way, to tempt them, three or four times a day, a dozen, or twenty, or thirty high-seasoned and highly stimulating dishes.

I grant indeed that some will eat to excess, even of a single article, as bread, or beans, or potatoes. But who are they that do this? Are they those who were brought up temperately and simply? Seldom, I believe, if ever. All the gormandizers on a single dish plainly cooked, I have ever met with, had been first trained to distend their stomachs enormously; and that, too, with stimulating food. When such persons first break off, in regard to quantity, especially if what they retain is of a mild, bland nature, they feel as if they had taken almost nothing at all. But train children to proper qualities of food, and they will not so often err as to quantity. I have seen the experiment so effectually made, that I speak on this point with certainty and decision.

Let our training be as favorable, however, as it may have been, and let the day of reformation be deferred to the latest possible period of life, still simplicity will be safest. If we are not safe at a simple table, we shall not surely be so elsewhere. Those who are on their guard will more readily perceive what a large amount they consume, when they eat wholly from one dish, than when they make their meal from half a dozen or a dozen different ones.

I do not undertake to say with precision what quantity of food, as the maximum, should be used by a healthy adult in a day; for so various are constitutions, conditions, employments, habits, &c., that it would be impossible. If, however, we place it as high as a pound and eight ounces of solid food—and I presume no intelligent dietetic writer will allow more—and if all above that quantity is in excess and is slowly producing disease, what a mass of error there is among us! By solid food, however, I here mean bread, rice, beans, peas, corn, &c.—substances which contain from eighty to one hundred per cent of pure nutriment. For if a pound and eight ounces of these be the standard, than we may eat some three or four pounds, in twenty-four hours, of apples, potatoes, turnips, beets, &c., and perhaps from three to four pounds of plainly cooked lean meat.

I would not set people to weighing their food with too much exactness, lest I should promote the very evils I wish to avoid and remove. Nor would it be so necessary, if each one would make a few experiments in weighing some of his more common articles of diet, and having found out what a very small quantity it takes to make a pound, learns to confine himself chiefly to a single dish at the same meal, and to measure out with his eye, the appropriate quantity—and withal never to violate the monitions of conscience.

2. Another great principle in dietetics is, to masticate our food well. This is indispensable, not only to the highest gustatory enjoyment, but to the most healthy digestion. Nay, it is indispensable to the well being of the teeth, the salivary glands, the gastric secretion, and the whole system. It is not enough insisted on by writers on this subject, and in the practical world almost wholly overlooked. It could scarcely be more neglected if the universal end and aim were to neglect it as much as possible. But the penalty is as universal as the disobedience; and is experienced in a bad state of the stomach, unhealthy sympathies of the system with the stomach, especially an unhealthy state of the skin and bowels, and foul and early decaying teeth.

3. Food should not be of a high temperature. I will not say, indeed, that it should be as cold as ice; but it should be cool. The system has the power of generating heat for itself; and it not only has this power, but its well being requires that our heat should be thus generated. All unnecessary heat, applied either externally or internally, diminishes the powers of the system to accomplish this work, and is hence injurious. What would be the effect of living constantly immersed in an atmosphere of the temperature of 90 or 100° of Fahrenheit? Who does not know that it weakens us to remain long in a temperature above 60 or 70°; and that in fact the lower the temperature, provided we are quite comfortable under it, the better for the lungs, the skin, and the whole system. Now the same remark would be applicable to the substances, whether liquid or fluid, received into the stomach. Above 60 or 70°, they are, as a general rule, more or less injurious; and they would probably be better at a much lower temperature still; for the stomach is not so well able to resist heat by evaporation as the skin, or even as the lungs. What, then, must be the effect of hot tea, hot coffee, hot soups, hot bread, &c?

4. Food ought not to be too nutritious. This doctrine might be inferred from analogy. Domestic animals, the horse for example, is known to suffer soon on a diet too nutritious—hence the necessity of mixing hay, potatoes, or even straw, with his grain. Nay, it is said, that when his health has been failing from confinement to grain, a mixture of thin shavings of wood has sometimes restored him to sound health.

But what is true of the horse and other domestic animals, is equally true of man. He will soon fall off, and finally sicken, on purely nutritious substances. His diet should always contain a proportion of innutritious matter. Thus wheat, rye, corn, &c., are best unbolted; and wheat meal, if bolted and used to the exclusion of everything else, soon produces injury. On the same principle, in part, should we use not only the farinaceous articles, but fruits and esculent roots; and the simpler they are prepared the better. I would also, both on this principle and those which precede it, avoid butter and oil of every description, cheese, eggs, and pastry. There are many doubts in regard to the long continued exclusive use of arrow-root, cassavi flour,[1] tapioca, sago, &c., and even rice. If these substances are used for an occasional meal, they should, all of them, except rice, be alternated with those of a contrary character.

5. Solid food is generally preferable to that which is liquid. If there be an exception, it is in favor of milk. But this, in any considerable quantity, except to children and to those older persons who are predisposed to certain forms of disease, is believed to be inferior in point of healthfulness to that which is more solid. Soups and porridge, however, are more decidedly objectionable; and so are gravies, jellies, toasts, &c. Puddings, rice, hommony, mush, &c., though less solid than bread, may be greatly improved by using them when they are several days old. In these circumstances they become much more solid than when hot.

This rule would seem also to prohibit the use of molasses, honey, sugar, &c. These, however, are not only liquid, but some of them are too concentrated. Eaten in any considerable quantity, they are quite objectionable; and most of them ought to be avoided in every quantity, by those who would enjoy the highest health.

The truth is, that our food should furnish a large proportion of the liquids our systems need; and if it is of a proper quality and in proper quantity, it will do so. Almost everything we eat—fruit and roots especially—abounds with water; and even the driest bread is not destitute of it. But what is not supplied in this way, should be made up in nature's own way, by the saliva, the gastric juice, the bile, and the pancreatic fluid.

But there is another important reason why solid substances are better, as food, than liquids. The latter—so much of them at least as is merely water—never undergo the process of digestion. They are absorbed, after their arrival in the stomach, instead of forming chyme, or chyle, or blood. The absorbent vessels take up the liquids of the stomach, whether received in the food or in the way of drink, until the mass is of a suitable consistence; after which, the work of digestion proceeds.

When we swallow bread and milk—I speak now of adults and not of infants—or broth, or gruel, or chocolate, or coffee, or tea, the first thing is for the absorbents of the stomach to take up the water which they contain; and as they are nearly all water, this requires a considerable time. When the process is over, what remains but a sediment, not only unmasticated and without being subjected to the action of the salivary glands, but consisting of too highly concentrated nutriment? The sediment of the broth, and the milk and sugar of the tea and coffee, are by no means in so good a condition to be digested properly, as if they were mixed with more innutrititus matter, and properly masticated and insalivated.

Hence may be seen some of the principal objections to coffee, tea, chocolate, &c., whether with our meals or without them. It is true, that the coffee and tea contain a poison, but it is in small quantity. They are also usually taken hot; but this is only one evil. They also add to the variety—almost always sufficiently large without them—of a single meal, which is a matter worth considering. But when to all these evils, we add those which were mentioned in a preceding paragraph, surely the evidence is sufficiently strong against them to lead to their rejection from the rational tables of all rational house-keepers.

Their use between meals involves another evil still. The stomach needs time for rest, as well as any other muscular organ. But if we swallow a drink between meals when the stomach is just ready for rest, which contains nutriment, it sets it to work again. No liquid should therefore be used between our meals but pure water; any more than in connection with them.

The remarks connected with our fifth rule supersede the necessity of a separate chapter on drinks. It at once sets them all aside, so far as our meals and the best purposes of health are concerned. Indeed, it seems to me a waste of time and strength, in this day of light and intelligence, to dwell on that subject. A few thoughts respecting them may naturally arise—indeed, seem almost unavoidable—in a future chapter.

6. Our meals should be as regular as possible. Children require food more frequently than adults. But both children and adults should have fixed hours for their meals as much as possible; and should as seldom as possible depart from them. If six, twelve and six are the hours for an adult, I would recommend that they be scrupulously adhered to; and if occasional and unforeseen circumstances sometimes prevent our taking a meal at the usual hours, it is better to omit taking anything at all till the next meal. The omission of one meal a day, living as we do in this land of abundance, would be beneficial rather than injurious;—I now mean one meal in three. This number I suppose to be the maximum; and if sedentary men prefer to use but two, I have no sort of objection. I ought to add, that if we omit a meal, it is an error to make up for our abstinence by eating the more freely at the next meal; for if there be any variation, it should be to eat less.

7. I have said that all our meals should be as simple as possible. If, however, there are departures from the strict letter of this rule, as I presume there will be—if we use several articles of food at the same meal, it is desirable that they should resemble each other as much as possible. The contrary doctrine has usually been taught, but it is believed to be untrue. If good mealy potatoes, for example, are to be eaten with something else, let it be with beans or peas cooked so as to be dry and mealy, rather than with apples or pears, or other juicy fruits, and rather than with meat. There are one or two exceptions, however, to the universality of this rule. If rice or pulse is to be a principal article at dinner, I would prefer the combination, with a substance so highly nutritious, of something which does not contain much nutriment, even if its general qualities are somewhat dissimilar; as turnips, or potatoes, or apples. Again, if one article is very soft, or is liquid, as pudding or milk, and we are determined to combine something or other with it, I would use a hard substance, requiring much mastication, as wafers made of unfermented meal, bread crusts, &c.

8. Some regard should be paid to the hour of the day, as well as to the season of the year. If we ever eat that which is comparatively difficult of digestion, it should be when our bodies and minds are most vigorous; as at breakfast or dinner. With most persons, perhaps, it should be in the morning. Thus if milk or gruel are taken, especially by adults, it should be either in the morning or at noon; and I prefer, for most persons, the morning. So also is the morning meal the best time for fruits, and for the more crude vegetables, the nuts, &c. In any event, the supper should be light, and should consist of substances easy of digestion—as a little rice, a piece of coarse wafer cake, or a little dry bread.

In the greatest heat of summer, as well as in the extremest cold of winter, particular pains should be taken to have our food light and easy of digestion. If we use anything less digestible, it should be either in the autumn, or late in the spring, when our labors are neither too violent, too exhausting, nor too frequently remitted. We also require less food towards the end of the week than at the beginning, as well as that which is milder.

The old custom of substituting on Saturday a little dried fish for a more full diet, which once prevailed in many parts of New England, was therefore quite philosophical, to say nothing of its favorable tendency in regard to the duties of the Sabbath.

9. In deciding on the quality and quantity of our food in general, regard should be had to the nature of our employment. Both he who uses too much and he who uses too little exercise of body and mind, should eat less, and of that which is milder in its nature. It is he who labors, thinks, recreates himself, and sleeps in the most just proportion, who can eat the most food, as well as that which is strongest. By the strongest food, I here mean bread, rice, beans, peas, potatoes, &c. It is these—and not animal food—that hold out longest with the laborer, especially when he has been trained to their use, or has duly reformed his habits, as the experience of hundreds of millions could testify. The mass of the hard laborers—the bone and sinew of the world—have in all ages to the present hour, been fed principally and often exclusively on this class of aliments. Females require food which is less stimulating than males.

10. Regard should also be paid to age. Children need food which is rather more active than that of adults. On this point, however, I would speak with diffidence. Nature seems to have provided for the tender infant a food, which, in the process of digestion, creates a good deal of heat; and yet the more intelligent of physicians recommend that it should be weaned to mild vegetable food. I am inclined to think this is the order of nature; and that the physicians are right. Many of them, however, recommend a mixture of animal with the vegetable food, sometime afterward—but without agreeing among themselves when the change shall commence. It seems to me that either the child should not be habituated to vegetable food after weaning, or else, if the habit is once formed, it should not be broken up.

Cookery, as it Is.

Present object of Cookery. What its object should be. Example of abuse. Error of eating hot food. Condiments and accompaniments of food. Another example of abuse in cookery. Another, still. Objections to cool food answered. A laughable sight. Gustatory pleasure perfectly lawful. Who best secure it. A great but common mistake. Losses sustained by those who have fashionable appetites. An anecdote of a country table. Usual views and feelings of house-keepers about plain meals. "Trimmings" of our meals. Woman too much a slave to fashion. Cooking not her main object. What she should glory in, if she glories at all.

The two great purposes of all cookery should be to improve the quality of food, and increase its quantity. Sometimes both these ends can be secured at the same time; but it too often happens, as the fashions of cookery now are, that we accomplish neither. Indeed, as a more general rule, the quality of substances submitted to the cook is deteriorated, and the quantity actually diminished.

In short, if it were the universal object of all house-keepers, so far at least as food and cookery are concerned—and this, now-a-days, forms a very considerable part of the business of the housewife, since it occupies, in one way or another, most of her time and thoughts—to defeat, at every step they take, and every process in which they engage, the real purposes for which food and cookery are designed, it is scarcely possible for me to conceive how they could better accomplish it, than by the course which is current among us.

Take the article of flour, for example, as it is received by the house-keeper; that is, in as fine a state as it can be—for if it were not so, it would scratch some delicate throat! If it is wheat flour, instead of making good, sweet, plain cakes or loaves of it, the house-keeper who has time enough for the purpose, immediately converts it into hot biscuits, or hot rolls, or waffles, or compound cakes, or dishes of some sort or other.

I do not say that wheat is improved in passing from a coarser state to that of superfine flour, quite the contrary. But we will suppose, for the present, that this is a matter beyond the housekeeper's control. We will suppose her duty is to increase the quantity or improve the quality of the article as it comes to her hands.

Two hundred pounds of superfine wheat flour will make about two hundred and seventy pounds of wheat bread. The increase of weight is chiefly by means of the water which is taken up, a part of which, as some think, is rendered solid in the loaf, as it is in the mass of lime to which it is applied in slacking. Let this be as it may, there is little doubt, in my own mind, that the changes are in favor, greatly so, of nutrition. I believe two hundred and seventy pounds of bread will go very much farther in sustaining human life—nay, and sustain it twice as well—than two hundred pounds of flour from which it is made would do, even if its taste, &c., were equally agreeable. The nature of the changes—so favorable—which take place in kneading and baking, I do not pretend to understand; but their existence is beyond all dispute.

I believe, moreover, that the change is nearly as great and as favorable in the formation of bread, plain puddings and unleavened cakes, from coarse meal as from fine flour; and from the meal of other grains as well as wheat. Thus far, then, cookery, whether modern or ancient, might seem to be a blessing and not a curse to mankind.

But when people will not eat these things, after the cook has prepared them, unless they are hot from the oven or stove, or full of pearlash,[2] saleratus,[3] or lime, or soaked in butter, or toasted and then buttered; and whenever the cook herself contributes all she can to promote such a belief, and thinks a plain raised loaf, or an unleavened cake, of wheat, rye or Indian, or a plain pudding, is unfit, after it is cooled to the temperature of the surrounding atmosphere, for anything but swine, who does not begin to doubt the usefulness of the art of cookery as it now is?

When, however, we go still farther, and to our meal, and yeast, and pearlash, and artificial heat, and butter, add molasses, or sugar, or eggs, or wine, or spices, or fruits—or all of these and many more things—and when it comes to pass that fashion will not admit of a plain rice cake, or the plainest dish of any sort, without its being tinctured with flour, butter and eggs, a most unnatural trio, what are we to say? Does female labor, thus expended, tend to increase the quantity and improve the quality of our nutriment?

Again, take milk. Now if the cook or the dairy woman can either improve its quality or increase its quantity by her labors on it, I have not a word to say. But is she doing this when she spends her days and weeks, and I might say months, in changing it into butter and cheese—which, to say the least, are less wholesome than the milk is—and in preparing which, instead of gaining in nutriment, we actually lose?

Let me not be told of the difficulty of preserving milk, especially in warm weather, without changing it into butter or cheese; or of the pleasant variety which these afford in our bills of fare. We are not obliged to keep so many cows; since, on my principles, the more we keep the more evil is produced by it. And as to the variety of food, we have variety enough of simple things, (as I trust has been already seen in the chapters on food,) without forming doubtful compounds.

Once more. To boil, steam, roast or bake a potato, is a useful process. If it does not increase the quantity of the nutriment, it certainly improves its quality. But how few house-keepers stop here! Salt must certainly be added, and probably butter. Nay, this is but common-place; and does not bring into view the skill of the cook at all. By no means. A simple boiled potato is surely unfit to be eaten; and to eat a cold potato—one I mean which is not smoking—would be horrid. How heavy it would lie on the stomach! And does not this prove it to be unwholesome? Yes, just as much as the fact that simple cool water is at first too heavy for the stomachs of those who have been accustomed twenty, thirty, or fifty years to hot tea or coffee, or to cider, beer, or spirits, proves that cool water is unwholesome. And when house-keepers can prove cold potatoes to be, in their nature, unwholesome, I will be ready to prove that cold water is so.

But who could eat things which are not smoking? say some. I have even heard sensible people say they preferred going without their dinner, to eating it cold, especially the vegetables. Now there is not one of the latter—the potato itself not excepted—which to an unperverted taste would not be preferred when cold. Remember, I say once more, I do not mean as cold as ice; that would be the other extreme;—but I mean the temperature of the surrounding atmosphere.

Is it asked again, what evidence there is that vegetables could ever be relished when cold? I answer by asking what evidence there is that they would not be? Besides, the farmer in the interior of New England often makes his supper chiefly of cold potatoes and turnips; and he eats heartily, and enjoys his meal, too. Is here no evidence?

But we cannot eat so freely when food is cold as when it is hot, it will be said. I know this, very well. People cannot eat so much of a thing which is cool, as of that which is smoking. They cannot eat so much bread, so much meat, so much pudding, so many potatoes, so many cakes! They must eat a pound of hot bread, a pound of pudding, a pound of johnny cake or buckwheat cakes, or two or three pounds of potatoes or hot baked apples, when half the quantity, or at most two thirds, if cool, would satisfy their appetites (at least if unperverted) far better, and be a thousand times better for their health, to say nothing, for the present, of other advantages which would result from a little self-denial and retrenchment.

It is enough to make one smile, to hear people say they are fond of bread, or potatoes, or rice, or boiled puddings, or Indian or buckwheat cakes, and yet if presented by the house-keeper with either of these, twelve hours after it is cooked, and without some accompaniment or other, to see them stare. Eat such fare as this? they seem to say. And yet they talk about being fond of the very things which are set before them!

But is not the taste to be gratified at all? I shall probably be asked. Certainly it is. I go for the greatest degree of palate gratification. But who has it? Is it he who cannot eat his meal—who finds himself thrown out of his element, and miserable—because one of a dozen of the articles on the table happens not to be hot, or happens not to be seasoned to his liking? Or is it he who finds all things sweet; who can make his meal and enjoy it with the highest zest whether cold or hot, and whether it consist of one article or a dozen, and whether or not there is a single accompaniment to his simple dishes—even common salt; who cannot, in one word, be "put out," but who can eat and relish all things?

It is a great mistake to suppose that those who eat simple things do not enjoy so much gustatory pleasure as those who eat compounds, and especially sweet and high-seasoned dishes. The reverse were far more true. The long use of compound and high-seasoned dishes, ruins our taste and our smell. I have seen people of fifty years of age, to whom almost everything was inodorous and insipid. And there is a tendency to this state of things in every eater of compound or high-seasoned dishes, as well as in every one who indulges in a large variety, even of simple things, at the same meal. How can it—how should it be otherwise? All things must have a salt taste—here is perpetual monotony. All things must be buttered or shortened—here again is monotony. All things must be hot with pepper—soaked or mashed—hot from the oven or pan—semi-liquid, &c—what is there in all this but monotony, taking the month or the year together, although there is variety at the same meal. But this monotony and this stimulus of high seasoning soon wear out the taste; and when once worn out, it cannot be restored.

I know, full well, that high-seasoned dishes give more gustatory pleasure than plain dishes, at first; but the keenness of our relish for them finally wears out. But then the great difficulty soon is, not only that we cannot enjoy what is not high-seasoned, but also that we cannot enjoy a thing which is not seasoned in the right manner. And as no housekeeper is perfect—-as every one is likely to fail occasionally of hitting right, especially in the preparation of some one dish at a given table of a dozen or twenty various articles, even where she knows beforehand the tastes of all her household—as this is much more likely to happen abroad than at home—and as whenever it does happen, the fashionable eater is at once miserable, can it be doubted who is the gainer in the end, in mere gustatory pleasure?

Nor is this all. To a person who eats of fashionable dishes and mixtures, there is only a small portion of each meal, even at fashionable tables, that really delights him. He eats almost everything in the way of doing penance. Bread he must eat, at least a little of it; but why? He does not relish it. It is a kind of penance to eat it. Because it is fashionable to make believe we eat bread, we therefore taste a little of it; but even when hot, it is insipid stuff to many. Besides, it sometimes comes to the table cold. Potatoes, too, even when mashed, buttered and peppered, go down with some difficulty. The same may, in fact, be said of almost all the dishes. A modern epicure is almost always eating the present dish as a kind of introduction to something else: or as a kind of purgatory he must pass through to the bliss beyond it. Whereas, the rational eater has high gustatory pleasure, in even the simplest dish; and hence is never doing penance or going through purgatory, eat what he will which he knows to be wholesome. Indeed, to him all things are wholesome, as I have already said, when they are the best he can get. He enjoys one thing or another. And if occasionally a dainty dish comes in his way, and it seems necessary for him to partake of it, he enjoys that too. He takes care, however, that such dishes do not come in his way often; for he knows that if they do, they would soon spoil his appetite for plain things.

The common belief, that those who eat simple things and only one thing at a time, have less of gustatory enjoyment than others, though utterly unfounded, is nevertheless the rock on which thousands and millions split. Many a house-keeper ruins her own health and the health of her family in this vain belief, and in the practice which naturally results from it. For though both the young and the old house-keeper often take very great delight in showing their skill in compounding and preparing dishes, and in furnishing the table, at each meal, with a great variety, yet it is not their pride in the matter which alone prompts them. They suppose that physical enjoyment is actually promoted by it; and if their own is, they expect that of their households will be. And many pass through life and go down to the grave in this deplorable error. Nay, the error gives them upon the average six months of disease during the progress of their whole lives, and deprives them of from five to twenty years of life.

I have been at a table provided for only about half a dozen persons, most of whom required plain food, and all of whom would have been contented with two or three sorts, and yet the following was the variety:—Bread of unbolted wheat meal, Indian bread, wheat flour bread, boiled rice, boiled Indian pudding, beans, potatoes, turnips and boiled corn. Of these nine sorts, seven were cooked for the occasion.

Now why all this? Partly from a desire on the part of the house-keeper to show her skill; much from mere habit; but more than all, that there might be variety, for variety's sake. The idea of sitting down to dinner with nothing on the table but an Indian pudding of suitable size for six persons, would seem to her monstrous. Or if to a large platter of rice, or potatoes, or beans, she should add bread also, still it would seem to her as if there was nothing at all on the table. And if, above all, the rice or the pudding had been boiled the day before, and was to be eaten without sauce, sugar, molasses or condiments, she would be unable to suppress her feelings. No, indeed! unless she had toiled a whole forenoon to get ready a dinner of seven, eight or ten separate and different articles, so that every one could taste a little bread, a little meat, a little rice or pudding, a potato, a turnip, and a few beans, with a little salt, vinegar, molasses, cream or sauce, and unless all were blazing hot, she would be miserable, and think those at her table so.

I know there are many things which consume the time of a house-keeper besides mere cookery; but I also know that, as things are, the latter comes in for a very large share of her efforts and strength. It is no light task to prepare hot water and make tea or coffee, twice or three times a day; to heat one's self over the fire, the stove or the oven, two or three times a day; to prepare several hot dishes for every meal; and to make ready the sauces, gravies, and other accompaniments for each meal. Nor is it a small matter to wash a host of plates, and platters, and tea cups, and coffee bowls, and tumblers, and knives, and forks, and spoons, three or four times a day.

I verily believe that it is the trimmings of our meals—the non-essentials rather than the essentials—that consume the great bulk of the time of our females. Cooking, there must indeed be; boiling, baking, stewing, roasting, &c.—but these processes, as I shall endeavor to show in another chapter, need not be so conducted as to absorb all our time. There is no more need of cooking everything new for each meal, than there is of washing clothes every day; not a whit. Nor is there any necessity for having half a dozen courses of food at the same meal. One course is enough, and one cooked dish is enough—for prince or peasant—at one meal. The preparation of meat, and potatoes, and turnips, and pudding, and pie, and fruits, to succeed each other as so many different courses, with their accompaniments—pickles, sauces, gravies, &c.—to say nothing of any hot drinks to accompany them, is a species of tyranny imposed by fashion, to which no house-keeper ought ever to be compelled to submit. It may be difficult for her to oppose the current; but it is for her life and the life of her husband and children to do so.

I tremble when I think how woman's time—one of the most precious of the gifts of God—is frittered away in pampering the wants and administering to the pleasures of the mere physical nature of man. She must toil twelve, fifteen or eighteen hours a day in attending to his apartments, his clothes, his stomach, &c., and wear herself out in this way, and leave the marks of this wear and tear in the constitutions of her children; and to her daughters the same legacy which she herself received from her mother—the permission to wear herself out prematurely in the same manner—while the immortal minds and hearts of her children, and husband, and domestics—if domestics she has—must be neglected!

Nobody doubts that the mind is of more value than the body—infinitely so; and few reject the proposition, in the abstract, that woman is the divinely appointed teacher of man; and yet where is the person to be found, who labors, in any considerable degree, to make her so? Where is the person, indeed, who does not, by indulging the demands of a pampered appetite, contribute daily and hourly to rivet the chains of her slavery?

And the worst of all is—I repeat the sentiment—woman neither knows nor feels her degradation. Nay, she often glories in it. This is, in fact, the worst feature of slavery; it obliterates the very relish of liberty, and makes the slave embrace her chains. Especially is this so with the slavery of our lusts, and passions, and propensities, and appetites. Woman not only toils on, the willing slave of an arbitrary fashion that demands of her to surrender her whole nature—bodily, mental and moral—to the din of plates, and pots, and kettles, but she is often proud of these employments, and seeks her reputation in them. She vainly seems to suppose that to prepare fashionable compounds in the most fashionable style, and to set an immense variety of her fashionable compounds on the same table, is to act up to the highest dignity of her nature. I do not mean that she ever asserts this, in so many words; but she does so in her actions—and actions, according to the old maxim, speak much louder than words. Whereas the truth is, that while the bodies of those whom she educates—for educate her household she does inevitably, whether it be well or ill—should not be neglected, their morals and souls should receive a large share of her attention; and in this, if in anything, should she principally glory. She should be infinitely prouder of eliciting a good, and enlarged, and noble thought, and a warm, and benevolent, and pious sentiment, than of making a mince pie with eighteen different ingredients in it, or of setting a table with forty-five various compound dishes upon it.

If this book should fall into the hands of one person who believes there is more of truth than declamation in the foregoing sentiments, let me prevail with her when I urge her to read, and consider, and study the chapters which follow.

On this subject, I may be thought tedious; especially as I have dwelt upon it, at considerable length in the first chapter. But it is, in my view, a matter of very great moment. If, says Mr. Flint, in the Western Review, this world is ever to be made better and happier, woman is to be a principal agent in the great work. But what can she do as things now are? Is she not completely enslaved—voluntary, though her slavery may be—to the never ending din of pots and kettles?

Notes

1. Flour made from cassava or yucca root.
2. *Potassium carbonate.*
3. *Sodium bicarbonate.*

Source: William A. Alcott, *The Young House-keeper: Or Thoughts on Food and Cookery* (Boston: George W. Light, 1838), 389–318.

1839 • 38 • "The Tomato"

Introduction: *Who first introduced the tomato into America is unknown. Spanish colonists introduced tomatoes in their settlements into what are today the states of Florida, New Mexico, Texas, and California. As English and American settlers occupied* *territories previously controlled by Spain, they were exposed to tomato cookery. From the South, tomato culture slowly spread up the Atlantic coast and the Mississippi River system. By the early 19th century, tomatoes were consumed in all regions of the country, and tomato recipes frequently appeared in American cookery manuscripts and cookbooks. During the 1830s, the medical profession concluded that tomatoes were a medicine that cured many medical problems, and patent medicine manufacturers began marketing tomato pills. By the 1840s, the tomato was the queen of the vegetable market. Below is an excerpt from the* Yankee Farmer *discussing the tomato as a medicine and as an article of diet.*

The Tomato.

We published some articles last year on the Tomato, showing that it was considered a good food, and that it possessed excellent medical qualities, particularly useful in diseases of the liver. A correspondent in the Maine Farmer under the signature "Candor" censured us for recommending the tomato; this was in July, but the number containing it was not received until this year, when it came with the missing numbers. We quote the following from "Candor:"

The Yankee Farmer says, "We know that the Tomato is considered by the profession generally highly useful both as medicine and as an article of diet. . ."

We now assert from the best authority, the experience of intelligent men, that the tomato is valuable both as medicine and food. We do not deny that food is one thing and medicine another, as "Candor" remarks, but it is highly important that they should be united in the same dish and in this way should medicine generally be taken, in order that health be preserved. Many diseases may be cured by abstinence and the use of wholesome food and drink, with proper attention to exercise, rest, air, business, recreation, protection from inclement weather, and cleanliness, by which last we include frequent bathing and occasionally a good steaming. By wholesome food and drink we mean such as possess medicinal qualities; not those unwholesome dishes that "Candor" would recommend, wholly free from medicine. By due attention to these things there would be but few cases of disease so violent as to require medicine alone.

The assertion of "Candor" that "just in proportion to the fitness of an article to be used as a medicine is its unfitness to be used as food" is, in our humble opinion, one of the most absurd statements that was ever made. In this we shall be supported by correct observation, experience, and common sense, and none who honor the profession of medicine will, we believe, advance a different opinion.

We have heard a number of intelligent persons who have used the tomato speak of it as an excellent article for food and medicine—One gentleman observed that he had been severely afflicted with dyspepsia for ten years—that he could not eat any boiled meat or vegetables, and often suffered much by this disorder; seeing the tomato recommended in the Yankee Farmer, last spring, as a good diet to correct this disorder, he cultivated the plant, and in the fall had a sauce made of the fruit. The first time he ate it, he did not like the taste, but after that he relished it well. He continued its use, and found it to be a pleasant food, and as a medicine it proved to be excellent, and afforded him relief from his complaint. He informed us a month or two ago, that since he used the tomato his health was better than it had been for ten years before. "Facts are stubborn things."

He used the sauce considerably, and then had a jelly made of the remainder of the tomatoes, which he has taken frequently. The sauce was made as follows: "Peel ripe tomatoes, stew them as apples for sauce, and season with a little salt and sugar or molasses." The jelly was made thus. "Peel the tomatoes and squeeze them through a fine cloth, add their weight in sugar, boil to a jelly and then bottle it."

Source: "The Tomato," *Yankee Farmer* 5 (April 20, 1839): 122–123.

1839 • 39 • SYLVESTER GRAHAM, *LECTURES ON THE SCIENCE OF HUMAN LIFE*

Introduction: *Sylvester Graham (1794–1851) was a minister who was a popular and energetic speaker. He was also an early temperance advocate. Graham had become interested in medicine and immersed himself in the foremost medical works of the day. He concluded that intemperance in food was an even greater evil than alcoholic intemperance and that overindulgence in food frequently led to alcoholism, particularly among men. Graham believed that gluttony, and not alcoholism or starvation, was "the greatest of all causes of evil" (Ronald L. Numbers,* Prophetess of Health: Ellen G. White and the Origins of Seventh-day Adventist Health Reform *[Knoxville: University of Tennessee Press, 1992], 52–53). Graham's concern with temperance led him to vegetarianism. Beginning in 1831, he argued in part that people were unable to survive the ravages of diseases because they did not eat the proper diet. But it wasn't until the following year that Graham presented his culinary views in a "Lecture on Chastity." Graham believed that uncooked food in its natural state was best, and he condemned the use of all "stimulating foods"—liquor, meat, tea, coffee, condiments, spices, salt, and pepper. Unlike many contemporary medical professionals who were leery of fresh fruits and vegetables because they purportedly caused a variety of summer diseases, Graham advocated eating fresh produce. Graham's ideas struck a responsive chord among many Americans, thousands of whom listened to his lectures, read his essays, and changed their diets and habits based on his ideas.* Lectures on the Science of Human Life, *first published in 1839, was his magnum opus. Below is one of his lectures on vegetarianism. The numbers in parentheses refer to other sections of Graham's work where that topic has been discussed.*

What Is the Natural Dietetic Character of Man?

799. The prevailing opinion on this subject, in our country and in many parts of Europe, is, that man is naturally an Omnivorous animal; that the highest and most permanent good of his nature requires that he should subsist on a mixed diet of vegetable and animal substances.

800. Custom is the only authority for this opinion with the mass of those who entertain it. But many naturalists and physiologists have endeavored to support it by what they have supposed to be the indications of man's alimentary organs. It is an important truth, however, that naturalists and physiologists, even when they claim to be strictly governed by the principles of inductive reasoning, are not unfrequently as erroneous in their apprehension and interpretation of facts (39), and as absurd in their conclusions as the unscientific multitude, who are governed entirely by tradition, custom, habit, and feeling. . . .

Were it not for the well known truth, that the depraved appetites and propensities of man continually exert such a perverting influence upon his intellectual and moral powers (620) as lead him, through the misapprehension of facts, and unfair estimation of evidence, and fallacious conclusions. As a specimen of Mr. Lawrence's contradictory statements, take the following paragraphs selected from different pages of his works.

'That animal food renders man strong and courageous, is fully disproved by the inhabitants of northern Europe and Asia, the Laplanders, Samoides, Ostiacs, Tungusees, Burats, and Kamtschadales, as well as by the Esquimaux in the northern, and the natives of Terra del Fuego in the southern extremity of America, which are the smallest, weakest, and least brave people on the globe, although they live almost entirely upon flesh, and that often raw.

'Vegetable diet is as little connected with weakness and cowardice as that of animal matter is with physical force and courage. That men can be perfectly nourished, and their bodily and mental capabilities fully developed, in any climate, by a diet purely vegetable, admits of abundant proof from experience. In the periods of their greatest simplicity, manliness, and bravery, the Greeks and Romans appear to have lived almost entirely on plain vegetable preparations.

'If the experience of every individual were not sufficient to convince him that the use of animal food is quite consistent with the greatest strength of body and mind, the truth of this point is proclaimed by the voice of all history. A few hundreds of Europeans hold in bondage the vegetable-eating millions of the East. We see the carnivorous Romans winning their way from a beginning so inconsiderable, that it is lost in the obscurity of fable, to the empire of the world,' etc.

Here we have it first stated and proved, that flesh-eating is not conducive to strength and courage; and secondly, stated and proved that a vegetable diet does not make men weak and cowardly, but that vegetable-eaters may be brave and powerful and heroic. And in the third place, it is asserted that a few hundreds of Europeans, because they are flesh-eaters, are able to hold in bondage the millions of the East, because they are vegetable eaters. And the Romans, who are exhibited as vegetable-eating heroes in the second paragraph, are made to figure as carnivorous conquerors in the third. But this is quite as consistent as the reasoning of any who attempt to prove the carnivorous character of man, from anatomy, physiology, or experimental fact into the most egregious errors and absurdities, for the sake of defending and supporting those favorite opinions which are founded in sensual gratification, it would be exceedingly difficult to account for the many erroneous notions and absurd speculations which have been entertained by very intelligent men in regard to the natural history of the human species.

851. Since the advocates for the omnivorous character of man have found themselves compelled to acknowledge that the evidence of comparative anatomy is wholly and powerfully against them, they have mainly planted themselves on two positions. The one is, the peculiar quality of the gastric secretion in man, or the solvent fluid of the human stomach; and the other is, the peculiar intellectual and voluntary powers of man.

852. It is said that the stomach of every animal secretes a solvent fluid possessing precisely the properties requisite for the digestion of the natural food of the animal, and wholly inefficient on other kinds of food. Thus we are told that 'the gastric juice of carnivorous animals readily digests flesh, but will not digest vegetable substances; while, on the other hand, the gastric juice of herbivorous animals readily digests grass and other vegetable substances, but will not digest flesh; and therefore the gastric secretion

or solvent fluid of the stomach, fully and unequivocally determines the natural dietetic character of the animal. But the solvent fluid of the human stomach readily digests both animal and vegetable food, therefore man is naturally an omnivorous animal.'

853. This position is so manifestly contrary to truth and fact that it would be unworthy of notice, had it not been advanced by men of considerable reputation in the scientific world, and reiterated by many who have much influence on the popular mind. Yet superficial and preposterous as it is, it is eagerly embraced by those who are determined, by any means and by all means possible, to defend those habits which they regard as necessary to their highest sensual enjoyment.

854. The truth is, that though everything in nature is constituted into fixed principles (140, 144) and with determinate relations, yet in the organic world every constitution has a considerable range or compass of physiological capabilities; and although every organ in every animal has its determinate physiological character and precise constitutional adaptation (687), yet every organ possesses a physiological adaptability by which it is capable, to a certain extent, of varying from its truly natural constitutional adaptation, and still not so far impair its functional power and results as to interrupt the general vital economy of the system, or suddenly to destroy the vital constitution. Hence, whenever the physiological habits of the system are disturbed, or its particular or general condition is affected, every vital organ always endeavors to adapt itself to the requisition of circumstances; and the power and extent of adaptability in each organ, and its efforts to adapt itself to the requisition of circumstances, always correspond with the functional character and relations of the organ. This being a wise and benevolent provision of the Creator for the preservation of life, and especially with reference to the alimentary wants of living bodies, while the digestive organs are constituted and endowed with the most perfect natural adaptation to certain kinds of aliment (724), yet, to secure life as far as possible against emergencies, these organs possess the physiological capability of adapting themselves to an extensive variety of alimentary substances, as circumstances and necessities require; and, therefore, the extent of the physiological adaptability of the digestive organs is probably much greater than that of any other organs in the system.

855. Possessing these physiological powers, the human stomach, if it be regularly supplied with an exclusively vegetable diet, will soon become adapted to a diet, and secrete a solvent fluid most perfectly qualified for the digestion of it; and if the diet be suddenly changed to one of flesh-meat exclusively, the stomach will not be prepared to receive it, and will not at first be able to digest it, but it will cause, vomiting and purging, and other symptoms of physiological disturbance. Yet if the flesh diet be commenced by degrees, and regularly continued, the stomach will soon become adapted to it, and secrete a solvent fluid most perfectly qualified to digest it; and if the diet be again suddenly changed to an exclusively vegetable one, similar disturbances will take place; but if vegetable food be gradually introduced with the flesh-meat, the stomach will soon become adapted to a mixed diet, and secrete a solvent fluid qualified to digest it.

856. Now if this physiological adaptability were peculiar to the human stomach, it would certainly go very far towards proving that man is naturally an omnivorous animal; but when we know that it is common to the horse, ox, sheep, lion, tiger, cat, dog, and indeed to all the higher classes of animals, and perhaps to the whole animal kingdom, we see that it proves nothing but the wonderful resources of animated nature, and the wisdom and benevolence of God. Both carnivorous and herbivorous, as well as frugivorous animals generally, in the higher classes at least, possess this scope and versatility

of digestive power, nearly or quite as extensively as man; and therefore if it proves man to be naturally omnivorous, it equally proves the lion and the ox, the vulture and the lamb, and other animals generally, to be naturally omnivorous. For, as we have seen, even the sheep may become so accustomed to a flesh diet, that it will refuse its natural food; and if it be suddenly put upon its natural food, it will at first be unable to digest it.

857. Let it be remembered, however, as a very important physiological truth, that although the stomach generally possesses the power of adapting itself to the alimentary substances with which it is regularly supplied, and can at one time secrete a solvent fluid best qualified to digest animal food, and at another time secrete a solvent fluid best qualified to digest vegetable food, according to the character of the diet, and can also be trained to secrete a solvent fluid which will digest food composed of both vegetable and animal substances, yet neither the human stomach nor that of any other animal is capable of secreting a solvent fluid which, at the same time, is equally well qualified to digest both vegetable and animal substances. That is, the solvent fluid of the stomach accustomed to a mixed diet of the two substances, cannot digest flesh so well as the fluid of a stomach accustomed only to a flesh diet, nor vegetable substances so well as the fluid of a stomach accustomed only to a vegetable diet. Not even the stomach of the bear nor of the hog, which are as truly omnivorous animals as any in nature, can digest both vegetable and animal substances together at the same time, so well as it can digest each of them separately and at different times.

858. It is also true as a general physiological law, that where the stomach is accustomed to a mixed diet of vegetable and animal food, in proportion as animal food abounds and predominates in the diet, the power of the stomach to digest vegetable substances is diminished. Hence, among those portions of the human family that subsist on a mixed diet, children, before they become much accustomed to flesh-meat, will eat almost every variety of fruits and vegetables, with the greatest freedom and with little sensible inconvenience; but as they advance in life, and become accustomed to a free use of flesh-meat, and gradually increase its proportion in their diet, they find themselves obliged to become more and more careful and circumscribed in their use of fruits and other vegetable substances, till they often become unable to partake of any vegetable matter except bread and perhaps boiled rice and potatoes, or some other simple farinaceous article. Yet after all this, these very individuals, by an abandonment of flesh-meat and the adoption of a correct general regimen, may again return to their youthful enjoyment of fruits and vegetable substances generally.

859. The position that man is rendered naturally omnivorous by the possession of peculiar intellectual and voluntary powers (851), is perhaps less obviously, but not less essentially, erroneous and absurd, than the one just considered (852). Man, we are told, is endowed with Reason, and therefore he is not, like other animals, a mere creature of instinct, but he is capable of thinking, reflecting, and judging, and of acting from the dictates of his judgment; and consequently, what he finds deficient in the adaptations of nature to his wants, he makes up in the rational exercise of his voluntary powers. Hence, though, 'judging from his structure (846), his *natural* food appears to consist *of fruits, roots, and other esculent parts of vegetables;* though neither the length nor the strength of his jaws fit him for subsisting on herbs, nor the character of his teeth for devouring flesh, were these aliments not previously prepared for cooking; yet being able, by the exercise of his rational and voluntary powers, to catch and kill animals, and to cook his food with fire, every living being is

rendered subservient to his nourishment, thereby giving him the means of an infinite multiplication of his species.'

860. If the meaning of this language were simply a predication of the physiological capability of man to adapt himself to a mixed diet of vegetable and animal food, or to derive nourishment from almost every vegetable and animal substances in nature, the living demonstration of its truth from the flood to the present day would render it unquestionable. But if it means to affirm that the rational and voluntary powers of man render him capable of adapting things to his physiological powers which are not naturally adapted to them, so as to make them as perfectly congenial to his nature as things naturally adapted, it is utterly erroneous, and discovers a very superficial and limited knowledge of animal physiology (763).

861. Let us test this principle in another application. The natural drink of man appears to be water, or the juice of fruits, as in a pure state of nature he has no other beverage prepared for him. But, once acquainted with the arts of brewing and distilling, he is enabled to manufacture as much intoxicating liquor as he wants, and can drink and be merry when he chooses. Now it is perfectly obvious that this is only a statement of what is true in regard to the mental and voluntary power of man to manufacture intoxicating liquors, and in regard to his physiological power so far to adapt himself to the use of them as a beverage, as to be able to drink them pretty freely without destroying life for many years. But to carry out the principle, we must go further and assert that, because man possesses these powers, he is set free from the law of instinct, which guides the lower animal to the pure fountain or stream of water to slake his thirst, and is made more godlike in the rational privilege of drinking a generous beverage which his own superior reason has enabled him to prepare for himself; and consequently, such a beverage is more congenial to his wants, and better fitted to develop the best powers of his nature; and therefore, while the lower animals, from birth to death, from generation to generation, are bound by the law of instinct to pure water as their natural drink, more godlike man is made free, by his reason, to regale himself with every beverage that he has the ingenuity and the ability to devise and prepare (598).

862. This reasoning would undoubtedly be received with high acclaim as soundest logic and philosophy, by multitudes of human beings whose rationality is perverted by the influence of depraved, sensual appetite (598). But is it the true logic of sound physiology? We know that it is not. And yet it is quite as much so as the logic of those who endeavor to show that the reason of man not only lifts him above the law of instinct, but enables him with impunity, and even with advantage to his whole nature, to transgress that law at pleasure. Such philosophers ought to know that human reason is not substituted for animal instinct, but superadded to it, and established on the same constitutional laws (597), not for contrary, but for the same and higher accordant purposes. And they may with as much truth deny the perfect harmony between the natural and moral attributes of the Deity himself (603), as to deny the perfect correspondence between sound reason and pure natural instinct (761, 763).

863. No physiologists, I presume, will deny that the instincts of the lower animals are founded on the physiological wants of the body, and established in perfect accordance with all the physiological powers and interests of the organized system to which they belong, and with the most determinate regard to the highest well-being of the individual and the species; and therefore, the law of instinct is not only a safe rule of action to the brute animal, but a strict conformity to it is essential to his highest welfare, and

all deviation from it must be in some measure detrimental to him. Hence, though the horse, ox, sheep, and other herbivorous animals (839), can, by the exercise of the mental and voluntary powers of man, be trained to eat flesh and chew tobacco and drink ardent spirit, till they learn to love them, and greatly prefer them to their own natural diet, and feel dissatisfied and depressed and wretched without them, and languish and droop if they are suddenly withheld, and become so accustomed to them, and feel so dependent on them for comfort and enjoyment, that if they possessed the mental and the voluntary power, they would most certainly continue the use of them through life, and teach their progeny to do the same, yet in all that these habits differ from the pure natural dietetic habits of those animals, and deviate from the law of undepraved instinct in them, they must be detrimental to the constitutional nature of those animals; and none the less so, because the reason of man has been employed in creating and cherishing these habits nor would they be any the less so, if the rational and voluntary powers of man were superadded to the natural instincts of the brute, and he should create and cherish them by the exercise of his own powers. But we have seen (761) that, as an animal, man is constituted with the same physiological powers and upon the same great physiological principles as those which pertain to the constitutional nature of the horse, the ox, and other animals; and that the faculties of instinct in man (762) are as determinate in their functional character, and established with as fixed and precise relations to the physiological wants and interest of his nature, as those of the lower animals are; and hence, in all that concerns the interests of organic life and animal existence, man is subject to the same general laws as those which govern the lower animals.

864. Suppose a man and a horse to be standing together by a barrel of ardent spirit. The two animal bodies are constituted upon the same organic principles, have the same general tissue (156), which are endowed with the same vital properties, and arranged into similar organs, which have the same elements of functional power (312), and the same physiological relation to the nature and qualities of the ardent spirit. The horse has not the reasoning power to devise, nor does he know that he possesses the voluntary power to execute, any plan by which he can draw a quantity of that spirit from the barrel, and drink it; but the man possesses both the rational and voluntary powers requisite for such a transaction. Now, can any truly rational being believe for a moment, that, in such a case, the possession of reason by the man, or rather the possession of rational faculties, can so nullify the physiological law of relation between his organic system and the nature and properties of the ardent spirit, as that, if he drinks it, it will be less detrimental to the functional powers of his organs, the vital properties of his tissues, and the general physiological interests of his system, than it would be to the horse? Yet this is a true illustration of the principle which they assume, who assert that man is naturally an omnivorous animal by virtue of his reason.

865. If man is not organized to eat flesh in its natural state (846), and if flesh-meat is not congenial to the highest physiological interests of his nature, then no power of reason by which he is enabled to prepare flesh-meat and get it into his stomach, can render it suitable food for him, or make him *naturally* an omnivorous animal; nor yet can it make him artificially an omnivorous animal, without detriment to all the physiological properties, powers, and interests of his nature. The question is not simply, what substances man can contrive to get into his stomach, and so adapt himself to them as to feel and believe they are very comfortable to him, but what substances are adapted to his stomach and other organs, and to all the vital interests of his system? There are many

substances in nature which man can, by artificial means, bring into such a condition as that he will be able to masticate and swallow them, but this is far from proving that all such substances may thereby be rendered subservient to the healthy nourishment and sustenance of his system. In everything that relates to the dietetic habits of man, therefore, his reason must strictly accord with the pure law of his natural and undepraved instincts, or it is not true reason, but an erroneous exercise of his rational faculties; unless his deviation from that law be a case of necessity from the force of circumstances. For, as we have seen (725), while man is created to be the lord of the earth, and to occupy all portions of it, and is constituted with a wide range of adaptability to meet the exigencies of the circumstances and conditions in which he may be placed, yet it is always of necessity under this great and immutable law, that, in proportion as he turns aside from the truth of his natural and perfect constitutional adaptation, and educates himself, by virtue of his constitutional adaptability, to habits, circumstances, and conditions less adapted to the truth of his constitutional nature, he impairs all the powers of that nature, diminishes the general sum of his enjoyment, and abbreviates the period of his earthly existence (763).

866. We see, therefore, 1. That the whole evidence of comparative anatomy goes to prove that man is naturally a frugivorous animal (842); 2. That the physiological capability of man to subsist on a mixed diet, and to derive nourishment from almost every substance in the vegetable and animal kingdoms, is not peculiar to man, but is common to all the higher classes of animals, and therefore affords no determinate evidence in relation to the natural dietetic character of man, and only proves the wonderful resources of animated nature, and the wisdom and benevolence of God (856); and, 3. That human reason is not a substitute for animal instinct, but superadded to it, not to nullify, but to sustain its laws, and to act in conformity with its pure dictates in supplying the alimentary wants of the body; and therefore the rationality of man neither lifts him above the physiological laws and relations of his animal nature, nor enables him to transgress those laws with impunity (763); and consequently, the rationality of man in no measure determines his natural dietetic character. . . .

869. It is however contended, that the fact of man's being so extensively, not to say universally, omnivorous, proves that he is instinctively led to eat flesh-meat whenever he can get it, and therefore it is as truly his natural aliment as fruit is. But this shows how carelessly and superficially men observe facts, and with what extreme looseness they reason on this important subject. Indeed they almost always feel their way to their conclusions, rather than arrive at them by rigorously inductive reasoning, and consult their appetites more than they examine evidences. Tobacco is quite as extensively used by human beings as flesh-meat is, and those who are accustomed to the use of it would a thousand times sooner relinquish their flesh-meat for ever, than to abandon their tobacco. Yet no one, I presume, will contend that this proves man to have a natural instinctive desire or appetite for tobacco, and that tobacco was made for the use to which man has appropriated it. We know that man has naturally a deep and utter loathing of tobacco, and that he is obliged to overcome the most powerful antipathy of his nature in adapting himself to the use of it but if every human being were trained to the use of tobacco so early in life and by such delicate and imperceptible degrees that we could not appreciate nor remember the first effects of it upon the system, it would be almost impossible for us to believe that man has not a natural instinctive desire and necessity for it.

870. It is precisely so in regard to flesh-eating. All who have perfectively sanctified themselves from animal food, and restored their instinctive faculties of smell and taste to something of their native purity, well know that flesh-meat is most loathsome to them. And if any number of human children were born of vegetable-eating parents, and nursed by vegetable eating mothers, and at a proper age accustomed to a purely vegetable diet, and never permitted to smell animal food when cooking, nor to see others eat it, every one of them—if there were millions—would at first discover strong loathing if flesh-meat were given them for food, and they would spit it from their mouth with as much disgust as they would tobacco. But when children are born of flesh-eating parents, and nursed by flesh-eating mothers, and are habituated from the hour of their birth to the savior and the odor of animal food, in the nourishment which they derive from the mother's breast, in the respiration and the perspiration of their parents and other around them, and in the fumes of the kitchen and the table, and are accustomed to be fed with animal substances in their infancy, and to see their parents and others devour flesh-meat at almost every meal, they, as a matter of necessity, become depraved in their natural instincts, and almost as a matter of necessity discover an early fondness for animal food. So in the East, where every human being smokes, it is nearly a universal custom for nursing mothers, every few minutes, to take the pipe from their own mouths and put it into the mouths of their sucking infants. The necessary consequence is that all those children early discover the greatest fondness for the pipe, and seize and suck it with excessive eagerness whenever it is presented to them; and they are exceedingly discontented and fretful and unhappy if it is withheld from them; and therefore, according to the logic of those who would prove man to be naturally omnivorous from his dietetic habits, it is natural and proper for those infants, and for all human beings, to smoke, chew, and snuff tobacco.

871. The truth is, as we have seen, all animal beings, including man, are constituted upon certain physiological principles, out of which grow certain physiological wants; and upon these wants are established certain faculties of instinct, with determinate relation to the nature and qualities of the appropriate supplies. These faculties, while preserved in their integrity, are a law of truth to all; but they are capable of being depraved and rendered totally blind guides, which lead to the most pernicious errors. The lower animals have neither the mental nor the voluntary powers to deprave their natural instincts to any considerable extent, and therefore they remain from birth to death, and from generation to generation, subject to the law of instinct, and with little deviation from their truly natural dietetic habits (598). But man, possessing the mental and voluntary power to deprave his natural instincts, has exercised that power so freely and so extensively, that he no longer seems to be able to discriminate between his truly natural and his depraved instincts and appetites, nor to distinguish his artificial from his natural wants. Let it be remembered, however, that the whole range of physiological adaptation in man and other animals, admits of little variation from the great law of relation in regard to the proportions of nutritious and in nutritious matter in the alimentary substances on which the animal subsists, or to which the animal becomes adapted.

872. As to the statement that the different portions of the human race appear to have enjoyed about an equal amount of health, vigor, and longevity, whether their food has been purely vegetable or purely animal, or a mixture of the two, let it be understood that, so far as we are informed, no considerable portion of the human family ever intelligently adopted any particular mode of living, upon clear and well ascertained physiological

principles, and consistently and perseveringly, from generation to generation, adhered to a course of diet and general regimen conformable to all the laws of life; but, on the contrary, nearly every thing in the nature, condition, and circumstances of man, from the first transgression to the present hour, has served to fix his attention continually on present enjoyment (32), with no further regard to future consequences than experience has taught him to be necessary, in order to avoid sudden destruction or intolerable distress; and hence, as we have seen (639), the grand experiment of the whole human family seems ever to have been to ascertain how far they can go in indulgence, how near they can approach the brink of death, and yet not die so suddenly and violently as to be compelled to know that they have destroyed themselves. Whether, therefore, men have subsisted wholly on vegetable or on animal food, or on a diet consisting of both, they have done so without any regard to correct physiological principles, either in relation to the quality, quantity, or condition of their food; or in relation to other physiological wants and habits of the body, which are nearly as important to the general welfare of the system as the quality and condition of the food. If their climate and circumstances have been less favorable than others to health, vigor, and longevity, they have learned from experience how far, as a general rule, they must restrain their indulgences, and in what manner they must regulate their habits and appetites, so as to secure life long enough for one generation to become the progenitors and nurturing protectors of another generation (643). And if their climate and circumstances have been more favorable than others to health, vigor, and longevity, they have also learned from experience how far they may go in indulgence, and still keep within the bounds necessary for the perpetuation of the race. So that, in all cases, as a general rule, what they have wanted in natural advantages, they have made up in correctness of habits, and what they have possessed in natural advantages, they have squandered in erroneousness of habits. If their climate has been salutary, they have indulged the more freely in dietetic and other excesses. If their food has been congenial to their nature, they have balanced or counteracted its good effects by other things unfavorable to health and vigor and longevity; and, in this way, the whole human family,—whether inhabiting frigid, torrid, or temperate zones, whether dwelling on high mountains or in low valleys, whether residing in ceiled houses, or living in tents or in the open air,—whether subsisting on animal or vegetable food, or on a mixed diet of the two,—whether eating their food in its simplest and most natural state, or cooked and prepared in the most complicated manner,—whether confined to simple food and water, or indulging in every variety of condiments and stimulating and intoxicating liquors and substances (768), whether moderate or excessive in quantities,—whether cleanly or filthy,—whether chaste or lewd,—whether gentle or truculent,—whether peaceful or warlike,—have, in the great experiment to ascertain how much indulgence the human constitution is capable of sustaining without sudden destruction, so balanced their good and evil as to preserve throughout the world and for many centuries, very nearly a general and uniform level in respect to health, vigor, and longevity. This statement, however, is general, and admits of many particular exceptions of individuals and sects and societies and perhaps tribes; but these exceptions in no case militate against its truth as a general statement, nor against any of the facts on which it is predicated; for these are all most indubitably true, and the general reasoning and induction from them are irrefragably correct; and the whole is of so much importance to a correct understanding of the phenomena of human history with reference to physiological principles, that it ought continually to be borne in mind as we proceed with our investigations on the subject before us, and especially in ascertaining and appreciating the physiological evidence of the natural dietetic character of man.

873. The fact, then, that a large portion of the human family actually have, for many centuries, and probably ever since the flood, subsisted to a greater or less extent on animal food, or on a mixed diet of vegetable and animal food, and apparently done as well as those who have subsisted wholly on a vegetable diet, does not in any degree invalidate the evidence of comparative anatomy that man is naturally and purely a frugivorous animal (842).

874. In entering upon the consideration of the purely physiological evidence in relation to the natural dietetic character of man (804), it is necessary that we should clearly understand and keep in view those nice physiological principles by which the character and force of the evidence are to be determined.

875. We have seen that the human body is formed from the common matter of the world (118), brought into organic arrangement and structure by vital forces acting in and by living organs (121), and that these organs are composed of several primary tissues which are endowed with certain vital properties, which constitute the elements of the functional power of the organs (312). These properties of the primary tissues have a certain range of increase and diminution consistent with the continuance of vital control. By some means they are exhausted, by others they are replenished. When these vital properties are healthfully increased, there is always a corresponding increase of function, power, and activity, in the organ or organs to which the tissue belong; and when they are diminished, there is always a corresponding debility and sluggishness and langor of function. The action of all extrinsic laws and agents upon us (126) tends to exhaust our vital properties; and all our intrinsic actions and operations, both voluntary and involuntary, have an exhausting effect upon the acting organs (376). Even in the performance of those very functions which belong to the economy of nutrition, and which co-operate to replenish and repair the exhaustions and injuries of the system, each organ necessarily suffers some exhaustion of its vital properties and waste of its organized substance from its own particular action (687). Hence all our organic operations from birth to death, simultaneously carry on the two great processes of vital exhaustion and repletion, of organic composition and decomposition, of destruction and renovation (314).

876. Were the constitutional principles upon which this renovating capability of the vital economy depends, in themselves inexhaustible, then were these bodies of ours, even in the present state of being, capable of immortality; and by strictly obeying the laws of life, we might live on for ever, in the eternal ebb and flow of vital energy, and the unceasing incorporation and elimination of matter! But this is not so. The vital constitution itself wears out! The ultimate powers of the living organs, on which their replenishing and renovating capabilities depend, are, under the most favorable circumstances, gradually expended and finally exhausted (133).

877. Though the vital energies and sensibilities, therefore, which we exhaust to-day, are replenished to-morrow, yet of necessity the process has taken something from the measured fund of life, and reduced our vital capital in proportion to the frugality or the profligacy of our expenditure. However proper the nature and condition of our aliment, however completely all our laws of external relation are fulfilled, however perfectly the functions of our organs are performed, and however salutary their results, yet every digestive process of the stomach, every respiratory action of the lungs, every contraction of the heart, drawn something from the ultimate and unreplenishable resources of

organic vitality (887); and consequently the more freely and prodigally we expend the vital properties of our organ, the more rapidly we wear out the constitutional powers of replenishment, and exhaust the limited stock of life (875). Nothing can therefore be more dangerously fallacious than the opinion which is too generally cherished and too fervently promulgated, that our daily trespasses upon the laws of life are as the dropping of water upon a rock wearing indeed, but so slowly and imperceptibly as scarcely to make a difference in the duration and in the comfort of our lives.

878. In explaining and illustrating the constitutional laws of external relation, I have stated (897) that every substance in nature from which the human body can derive nourishment, possesses specific and peculiar qualities which the human organs have vital powers to perceive and appreciate (726). Thus the visual properties of things are perceived by the special sense of sight (458); the auditory properties, by the special sense of hearing (252); the olfactory properties, by the special sense of smell (691); the gustatory properties, by the special sense of taste (693); and the tangible properties, by the special seine of touch (253). These external substances have also certain other properties, which are only perceived and appreciated by the special organic senses (296) residing in the organs belonging to the domain of organic life, or the ganglionic system of nerves (228). These properties, in all proper alimentary substances, are the natural and appropriate stimuli of those nerves of organic sensibility (230) which are adapted by the Creator to perceive and appreciate them, and to convey the impressions received from them to the special centre which presides over the functions of the particular organ or apparatus (219). But we have seen that some alimentary substances are much more stimulating than others, in proportion to the quantity of nourishment which they actually afford the system, and that some substances in nature are purely stimulating without affording any nourishment (735).

879. The stimulation produced by these various substances is always necessarily exhausting to the vital properties of the tissues on which they act, just in proportion to its degree and duration; and every stimulus impairs the vital susceptibilities and powers, just in proportion as it is unfitted for the real wants of the vital economy, and unfriendly to the vital interests.

880. But whatever may be the real character of the stimulus, every stimulation to which the system is accustomed increases, according to the power and extent of its influence, what is called the tone and the action of the parts on which it is exerted, and *while the stimulation lasts, it always increases the feeling of strength and vigor in the system,* whether any nourishment be imparted to the system or not.

881. Yet by so much as the stimulation exceeds in degree that which is necessary for the full and healthy performance of the function or functions of the organs stimulated, by so much the more does the expenditure of vital power and waste of organized substance exceed for the time the replenishing and renovating economy of the system (502); and, consequently, the exhaustion and indirect debility which succeed the stimulation are always necessarily commensurate with the excess.

882. Hence, though that food which contains the greatest proportion of stimulating power to its quantity of nourishment causes, while its stimulation continues, a *feeling* of the greatest strength and vigor, it also necessarily produces the greatest exhaustion in the end, which is commensurately importunate and vehement in its demands for relief, by the repetition of the accustomed stimulus; and as the same food, more readily than any other, affords the demanded relief, by supplying the requisite degree of stimulation, our feelings always lead us to believe that it is really the most strengthening.

883. Hence, whenever a *less* stimulating diet is substituted for a *more* stimulating one, a corresponding physiological depression, or want of tone and action, always necessarily succeeds, varying in degree and duration according to the general condition of the system, and the suddenness and greatness of the change; and this depression is always attended by a feeling of weakness and lassitude, which is immediately removed, and the feeling of strength and vigor restored, by the accustomed *degree* of stimulation, by whatever produced, whether any increase of nourishment is actually afforded to the system or not.

884. The pure stimulants, therefore (733), which of themselves afford no nourishment to the system, and only serve to increase the expenditure of vital properties and waste of organized substance, by increasing vital action (735), cause, while their stimulation lasts, a sense of increased strength and vigor; and thus we are led by our feelings to believe that the pure stimulants are really strengthening; and in the same manner we are deceived by even those pernicious stimulants which not only exhaust by stimulation, but irritate, debilitate, and impair, by their deleterious qualities (768).

885. The feeling of *strength* produced by stimulation, therefore, is no proof either that the stimulating substance is nourishing, or that it is salutary, nor even that it is not decidedly baneful.

886. But we have seen (735) that those proper alimentary substances whose stimulating power is barely sufficient to excite a full and healthy performance of the functions of the digestive organs, in the appropriation of their nourishment to the system, are most conducive to the vital welfare of the body in all respects, causing all the processes of assimilation and organization to be most perfectly performed, without any unnecessary expenditure of vital power (875), and thus contributing to the most permanent and uniform health and vigor of the body, and to the greatest longevity. For every degree of stimulating power beyond this, necessarily increases the vital exhaustion, without contributing in any measure to the welfare of the body.

887. With a true application of these well ascertained principles, the physiological evidence in relation to the natural dietetic character of man may be correctly apprehended and accurately estimated; yet the utmost caution (786) and perspicacity and circumspection are requisite at every step, to avoid deception and error in the mazy and delusive paths of human experience and history.

888. It is generally, and perhaps universally, believed by those portions of the human family which subsist on animal food, either wholly or in part, that man requires a more nourishing and invigorating aliment than can be derived from the vegetable kingdom, and therefore that without the use of animal food, his body cannot be properly nourished and sustained. 'An entire abstinence from flesh,' says Buffon (801), 'can have no effect but to enfeeble nature. If man were obliged to abstain totally from it, he would not, at least in our climates, either multiply or exist'; and this is but the declaration of the common sentiment of flesh-eaters. But a correct examination of the subject will show that this position is a mere assumption in the face of facts, and as utterly destitute of any foundation in truth as are the anatomical reasonings from the fancied resemblance of the human teeth and digestive organs to those of carnivorous animals.

889. It is indeed surprising, that observing and reflecting minds, even long before the experiments of science had afforded demonstrations of the truth, did not detect and proclaim the error of the common notion, that flesh-meat is a more nutritious aliment for man than the best vegetable food. A proper attention to the history of the human

race might long ago have convinced the world of the inaccuracy of such an opinion. But unfortunately for man, he learns but little from experience, either in his individual or aggregate capacity; and Wisdom, though she meets him in ten thousand forms, and seeks to win him in ten thousand ways, is left unheeded by him, because his attention is so continually and completely engrossed in the present feeling and impulse, and in the pursuit of the most immediate gratification.

890. From the careful investigations of some of the ablest and most accurate chemists of the present age, it appears that the various kinds of flesh-meat average about thirty-five per cent, of nutritious matter, while rice, wheat, and several kinds of pulse, such as lentils, peas, and beans, afford from eighty to ninety-five per cent. And even potatoes, which, by some writers on human diet, have been denounced as too crude and innutritious for the aliment of man, afford twenty-five percent, of nutritious matter. So that, according to these results, a single pound of rice absolutely contains more nutritious matter than two pounds and a half of the best butchers' meat; and three pounds of good wheat bread contain more than six pounds of flesh; and three pounds of potatoes more than two pounds of flesh.

891. Incredible as this may at first appear to those who have given but little attention to the subject, yet a reference to facts in the history of the human species will abundantly prove the correctness of what is here stated. According to the united testimony of all the ancient writers who have spoken of the primitive generations of mankind, the first of the species, as we have seen (769), subsisted entirely upon vegetable food, in the plainest, simplest, and most natural forms.

892. Farinaceous seeds contain a greater proportion of nutritious matter than any other kind of natural aliment; and it is more than probable that these and other farinaceous vegetables in some form or other, have in all ages of the world constituted 'the staff of life' to the greater part of the human race, and that this kind of food mainly constituted the healthful and invigorating diet, not only of the antediluvians, but also of those who have occupied that period in the history of every nation which all their earliest writers call the golden age (638).

893. Different opinions have been entertained in regard to the dietetic use of flesh in the latter part of the antediluvian period. The enormous wickedness and atrocious violence and outrages of mankind immediately preceding the flood, strongly indicate, if they do not prove, an excessive indulgence in animal food. The fact also seems to be implied in the Divine annunciation to Noah after the flood, that every living thing that moveth, as well as the green herb, is constituted to afford nourishment to the human body; and is strongly evinced by the great and somewhat sudden abridgement of the period of human existence after the deluge. It appears to be very certain, however, that if such was the fact, the custom was a very great innovation on the early habits of the antediluvians, and that it had not long prevailed before the terrible catastrophe of that period. Still it does not appear from the Mosaic record that Noah received any Divine 'permission' to eat flesh, before the deluge; for in the sixth chapter of Genesis we find him instructed to gather and take with him into the ark, of all food that was eaten, which should be for food for him and for all the animals with him. Nor is there any historical evidence that animal food came into general and common and frequent use, until many centuries after the flood.

894. During the days of Abraham, flesh seems to have been eaten only on special occasions; such as some of their religious and social feasts, and when strangers were

entertained as guests. The same general custom continued down even to the time of the bondage of the Hebrews in Egypt; and during their long and severe servitude there, it appears that they subsisted mostly on the products of the vegetable kingdom; as indeed the inhabitants of that country have ever done, even to the present day. Coarse bread with cucumbers, melons, leeks, garlic, onions, and other vegetables, constituted the principal part of their diet; and with these—more however as a condiment than as an aliment—they consumed perhaps occasionally a small quantity of fish, and on particular occasions they indulged in flesh-meat. During their extremely tedious and winding journey through the wilderness, in which they were forty years in setting into a place which lies but about three hundred miles from Egypt, they subsisted entirely on vegetable food, except that they were a very few times suffered to indulge in flesh. For their manna appears to have been, if not real vegetable structure, at least of the nature of vegetable substance; and it seems to have become dry and hard, for 'the people went out and gathered it and ground it in mills, and beat it in mortars, and baked it in pans, and made cakes of it.' And after the conquest and possession of the 'Promised Land,' and the full establishment of the nation in Palestine, excepting the more luxurious and voluptuous few, the Jews ate but little animal food, and that principally on the occasion of their religious and social feasts and special hospitalities. In the reign of Saul their first king, we find Jesse, who was the owner of probably extensive flocks and herds, sending his son David, not with beef and mutton, but 'with parched corn and loaves of bread to his sons in the army, and with cheeses to the captains of thousands.'

895. It has been supposed by some that the Jews and other nomadic or shepherd tribes, who possessed extensive flocks and herds, must have made a free use of the flesh of their sheep and other animals in their ordinary diet, because, say they, no other sufficient reason can be perceived why they should possess themselves of such property, and be so anxious to increase it. But it should be remembered, that besides the tendency of their religious institutions to lead them to cultivate such possessions, this species of property constituted their wealth, and gave them respectability and influence in their tribe or nation, the same as do many acres of land, or many slaves, or ships, or much merchandize or money, the husbandman, or planter, or merchant, or banker; and hence, the extensiveness of their flocks and herds was a source of ambition and pride and satisfaction to them.

896. This same state of things is found even at the present day, among the nomadic or shepherd tribes in Asia and Africa, and in fact in all parts of the world. The enterprizing Landers inform us that in their late expedition in Africa, they found tribes 'who possessed abundance of bullocks, pigs, goats, sheep, and poultry, but they preferred vegetable food to animal; notwithstanding which, their animals were always held exceedingly dear, because the owners took pride in displaying the number and quality of them' (1032).

897. It is well known that from the earliest period of their history, the people of India generally, and particularly the Hindoos, who constitute a considerable portion of the human family, have subsisted mainly on vegetable food, making rice the principal article of their diet. And indeed the greater part of the inhabitants of Asia and Africa have in all ages derived nearly all of their sustenance immediately from the vegetable kingdom. 'Children of the sun' said one of the ancient and distinguished priests of India, 'listen to the dying advice of your faithful and affectionate instructor, who hastens to the bosom of the great Allah, to give an account, and to enjoy the expected rewards of his services.

Your regimen ought to be simple and inartificial. Drink only the pure, simple water. It is the beverage of nature, and not by any means nor in any way to be improved by art. Eat only fruits and vegetables! Let the predaceous animals prey on carnage and blood! Stain not the divine gentleness of your natures by one spark of cruelty to the creatures beneath you! Heaven, to protect them, hath placed you at their head! Be not treacherous to the important trust you hold, by murdering those you ought to preserve! nor defile your bodies by filling them with putrefaction! There is enough of vegetables and fruits to supply your appetites, without oppressing them by carrion, or drenching them in blood!'

898. Many parts of Asia are far too densely populated to admit of any considerable indulgence in animal food; for it is a well ascertained truth, that the use of animal food diminishes the alimentary resources of the human family, in all densely populated countries. It has been estimated by some writers on political economy, that the soil which is necessary to raise animals enough to supply the alimentary wants of one man who subsists wholly on animal food, will produce vegetable substance enough to sustain sixteen men who subsist wholly on vegetable food. Hence in China, where the population is so dense as to form almost a crowded congregation of hundreds of millions of human beings (1029), the nourishment or the people is of necessity derived immediately from the soil, which is made to produce two crops of rice annually, to meet the alimentary wants of its cultivators, and the small portion of animal food which they derive from domesticated animals, such as hogs, cats, dogs, etc., fed on the offals of the house, is nothing more than a mere condiment to their rice and other vegetable substances. And then again, on the other hand, it is because the soil of China is capable of being made to produce two crops annually, of one of the most nutritious vegetables in the world, that it is able to sustain such a population. It is therefore only in those countries where the population is small in proportion to the extent of soil, that the inhabitants can indulge freely in the dietetic use of flesh; unless they are a commercial people, and derive their supplies of animal food from other countries.

899. The early inhabitants of Greece and Rome, and of Europe generally, subsisted almost entirely on vegetable food. The Spartan simplicity of diet was by no means peculiar to Sparta nor to Greece. 'The Romans encouraged the use of vegetable diet, not only by the private example and precepts of many of their great men, but also by their public laws concerning food, which allowed but very little flesh, but permitted without limitation all kinds of food gathered from the earth, from shrubs, and from trees.'

900. Plutarch, a man of great learning and extensive research, who flourished long after the stern simplicity of Roman virtue had passed away, long after the foundations of the Roman Empire had begun to crumble under the influence of luxury and excess, thus expresses himself on the subject of human diet: 'I think it were better to accustom ourselves from our youth to such temperance as not to require any flesh-meat at all. Does not the earth yield abundance, not only for nourishment, but for luxury? some of which may be eaten as nature has produced it, and some dressed and made palatable a thousand ways.'

901. The inhabitants of modern Europe, even at the present day, to a very great extent subsist on the immediate products of the vegetable kingdom. The peasantry of Norway, Sweden, Denmark, Poland, Germany, Turkey, Greece, Italy, Switzerland, Spain, France, Portugal, England, Scotland, Ireland, and a considerable portion of Russia, and most other parts of modern Europe, subsist mainly, and many of them entirely, on vegetable food. The peasantry and laboring people of modern Greece subsist on coarse brown bread made of unbolted meal, and on different kinds of fruits, which they eat with their

bread; and they are remarkably vigorous and active and cheerful. 'In all the world,' says a recent traveller in Italy, 'there is not to be found a more lively mercurial population than the lazzaroni and laborers of Naples, whose diet is of the simplest kind, consisting mainly of bread, macaroni (a vegetable dish), or potatoes, or the fruits of the season, including a large supply of water-melons for their greatest luxury, with water for their drink. They are generally tall, stout, well formed, robust, and active men.' The peasantry in many parts of Russia live on very coarse bread, with garlics and other vegetable aliment; and, like the same class in Greece, Italy, and other parts of Europe, they are obliged to be extremely frugal even in this kind of food; yet they are very healthy, vigorous, and active. Many of the inhabitants of Germany live mainly on rye and barley, and mostly in the form of coarse bread. The Swiss peasantry subsist in much the same manner; and a very similar diet sustains the same class of people in Sweden, Poland, Spain, Portugal, and many parts of France. In the last three named countries, however, fruit is more abundantly used than in the others; but in all these countries, the people who live in this manner, and refrain from the use of alcoholic and narcotic drinks and substances, are well nourished, healthy, robust, active, and cheerful.

902. The potato, as is well known, is the principal article in the diet of the Irish peasantry; and few portions of the human family are more healthy, robust, athletic, and active, than they are, when uncontaminated by intoxicating substances, both alcoholic and narcotic. But alcohol, either in the form of distilled or fermented liquors, and tobacco, opium, coffee, and tea, have extended their blighting influence, as we have seen (768), over the greater portion of the human world; and nowhere do these scourges of mankind more cruelly afflict the self-devoted race, than in the cottages and hovels of the poor. 'I would sooner live on two beans a-day than do without my snuff,' exclaimed an aged female mendicant, to a gentleman who expostulated with her for indulging in the vile practice of thrusting powdered tobacco up her nose, even when in the act of asking alms! 'O, it does me good! I could not live without it!' said she; and doubtless she sincerely felt that what she said was true. And this is but the miniature resemblance of a large portion of the human species. And when by these indulgences, and the consequent neglect of cleanliness (872), and other means of health, they generate a variety of chronic diseases, and sometimes extensive epidemics, we are told, even by professional men of character, that all these evils arise from their poor, meagre, low, vegetable diet. Yet whenever these different species of intoxicating substances are avoided, and a decent degree of cleanliness observed, the vegetable diet is not thus calumniated.

903. That portion of the peasantry of England and Scotland who subsist on their barley and oatmeal bread and porridge, and on potatoes and other vegetables, with temperate and cleanly habits, are healthy and robust and active, and able to endure more fatigue and exposure than any other class of people in the same countries.

904. In short, from two-thirds to three-fourths of the whole human family, in all periods of time, from the creation of the species to the present moment, have subsisted entirely, or nearly so, on vegetable food; and always, when their alimentary supplies of this kind have been abundant and of a good quality, and their habits have been in other respects correct, they have been well nourished and well sustained in all the physiological interests of their nature.

905. But if one pound of good bread absolutely contains more nutritious matter than two pounds of fleshmeat (890), why is it that those who are accustomed to animal food

immediately droop and feel weak and languid when flesh-meat is wholly withheld from them? and why is their usual vigor restored when they return to their customary diet?

906. It is now well ascertained and universally acknowledged by those who are properly informed on the subject, that flesh-meat is far more stimulating or exciting in proportion to the quantity of nourishment which it actually affords the human body, than proper vegetable food is; and we have seen (880) that whatever be the real character of the stimulating substance, every stimulation to which the system is accustomed increases, according to the power and extent of its influence, what is called the tone and action of the parts on which it is exerted, and the whole domain of organic life being intimately united by a common and universal sympathy (225), is correspondently affected; and hence, while the stimulation lasts, it always increases the feeling of strength and general vigor in the system, whether any nourishment be imparted or not. By so much, therefore, as flesh-meat is more stimulating than vegetable food, it gives to those who are accustomed to it a feeling of greater strength and vigor; and as it is a law of the vital economy (883), that whenever a less stimulating diet is substituted for a more stimulating one, a corresponding physiological depression, attended with a feeling of weakness and lassitude, always succeeds, and as this physiological depression is promptly removed, and a feeling of strength and vigor restored by a return to the customary stimulus (882), those who are accustomed to animal food, and have only made temporary experiments of abstinence from it, have always found that when they abstain wholly from flesh-meat, they feel weaker and less energetic, and when they return to it they feel stronger and more vigorous and active; and hence they have inferred that animal food is much more nourishing and strengthening than pure vegetable food is.

907. But if this kind of experience proves animal food to be more nourishing and strengthening than vegetable food, then it also proves that the pure stimulants which actually afford no nourishment to the system, are really invigorating to the body (884); for every one who is accustomed to the use of the pure stimulants, always experiences a physiological depression and feeling of debility and lassitude from the sudden disuse of them, commensurate with the degree to which the system had been affected by them, or made dependent on them for tone and action; and this depression is instantly removed and the feeling of strength restored by a return to the use of the accustomed stimulants. Hence all who habitually use the pure stimulants, and especially the diffusable stimulants, such as the alcoholic, fully and sincerely believe that their bodies are invigorated and rendered stronger, and capable of more effort and endurance, by the use of such stimulants.

908. It is true, however, that as the pure stimulants afford no nourishment to the system, and flesh-meat nourishes while it stimulates, the physiological depression and general emaciation and debility experienced from a sudden abandonment of the latter, though less violent and distressing at first, are generally of greater duration, and sometimes even more dangerous to life, than from a sudden abandonment of the former.

909. But as flesh-meat is more stimulating to the system in proportion to the nourishment which it affords, than pure vegetable aliment is (906), so all the processes of assimilation and nutrition in the use of the former are more rapid, and attended with a greater expenditure of vital power and waste of organized substance, than in the use of the latter (879). The flesh-meat in the stomach, the chyme formed from it in the alimentary cavity, the chyle in the lacteals, the blood in the heart, arteries, veins, and capillaries, and all the fluids and substances elaborated from the blood, are more exciting to

the parts on which they severally act, and cause a greater intensity and rapidity of vital action and expenditure in the whole system, than is affected by alimentation, digestion, and nutrition, in the use of pure and proper vegetable food (991). And hence the well-known fact, that in the most healthy and robust men who have been accustomed to a pure vegetable and water diet from infancy, the skin is uniformly much cooler, and the pulse is slower from ten to thirty beats in a minute, than in those who subsist on a mixed diet, in the ordinary manner of civic life (476).

910. As flesh-meat passes more rapidly through all the processes of assimilation than most kinds of vegetable food (909), it is generally supposed to be more easily digested, and consequently the most suitable food for the dyspeptic and those of feeble digestive powers; and hence it has been a prevailing practice among physicians to prescribe for such persons a diet consisting mostly of flesh-meat. But this is contemplating the assimilating functions of the living body as purely chemical, and the stomach and other organs as mere lifeless vessels which have no direct agency in the processes effected in the substances which they contain (425); and therefore, the digestibility of different alimentary substances is determined purely by the time required for their solution. Such a view of the subject, however, is very far from being correct. The assimilating processes of the living body are to be contemplated by the physiologist as purely vital, effected by the living organs, and attended with an expenditure of the vital properties of the tissues, and the functional powers of those organs (875); and consequently, in the true physiological sense of language, the ease or difficulty with which any alimentary substance is digested by the human stomach, is not determined by the time in which it undergoes the chymifying process of that organ, but exclusively by the amount of vital power required to digest it. The substance which causes the greatest expenditure of vital power in undergoing the functional process of the digestive organs, and leaves those organs most exhausted from the performance of their function, is the hardest or most difficult to digest, whether the time in which it is undergoing that process be longer or shorter.

911. But we have seen (906) that flesh-meat is more stimulating in proportion to the quantity of nourishment which it affords to the human body than pure vegetable aliment is, and that all processes of assimilation and nutrition in the use of the former, are more rapid and attended with greater expenditure of vital power and waste of organized substance than in the use of the latter. It is therefore a physiological truth of great importance, that while animal food, or flesh-meat, passes through the stomach in a shorter time than most kinds of vegetable aliment, and therefore has been supposed to be more easily digested, yet it actually draws upon that organ and upon the sources of innervation for a greater sum of vital energy, and consequently causes a greater abatement of the sensorial power (165) of the brain and nervous system during the process of digestion, and leaves the stomach much more exhausted from the performance of its function, than vegetable food does. And hence, they who subsist principally on animal food or fleshmeat, always feel more stupid and dull during gastric digestion, and feel a much greater degree of exhaustion in the epigastric region, when the food has passed from the stomach into the intestinal canal (328), and suffer much more distress from hunger when deprived of their accustomed meals (882), than they do who subsist entirely on a pure vegetable aliment. And this is one important reason why—all other things being equal, and the system being fully established in its habits they who subsist on a well-chosen vegetable diet can endure protracted labor, fatigue, and exposure, much longer without food, than they can who subsist mostly or entirely on flesh-meat.

Source: Sylvester Graham, *Lectures on the Science of Human Life* (1839; reprint, Boston: Marsh, Capen, Lyon and Webb, 1839), 143–160.

1839 • 40 • Sarah Josepha Hale, "Soups and Gravies"

Introduction: *Sarah Josepha Hale (1788–1879) became the editor of* American Ladies Magazine, *a small magazine published in Boston, in the 1820s. Louis A. Godey, who had launched* Godey's Book *in 1830, purchased the* American Ladies Magazine *in 1836 and asked Hale to edit the combined magazine, now renamed* Godey's Lady's Book. *Under Hale's management, the newly named magazine went from selling 10,000 copies annually in 1837 to selling 150,000 copies by 1860. For her position as editor of America's most popular women's magazine, Hale also wrote (or had others ghostwrite for her) dozens of books, including several cookbooks. The excerpt below is from one of her cookbooks and focuses on soups and gravies, which were and continue to be important parts of American cookery. In the 19th century, soups—especially broths—were considered medicinal.*

Soups and Gravies

One of the popular errors in regard to diet is considering soups and broths as light food, and therefore always proper for weak stomachs and feeble constitutions.

"O, this nice broth cannot hurt you!"—"The hot soup must do you good this cold day," is often said to the poor shivering dyspeptic, or drooping invalid. And if they take this food and are injured by it—why, their case must be desperate, indeed, not to bear a little soup!

In Dr. Beaumont's experiments on the effect of the gastric fluid on the different kinds of food usually taken into the stomach, soups were found to be among the most indigestible; and the reason is, that the water in the soup must be separated from the nourishment before the process of digestion can begin. This separation takes some time; then if the stomach be weak or diseased, the secrete (or form) but little gastric juice, this becomes diluted and the action of the stomach materially deranged by the effort of separating the water from the nutritive particles in the soup. Dyspeptics, therefore, should not take this kind of food; nor any kind that is very liquid. Bilious persons, and those troubled with heart-burn and indigestion, would be injured by eating soups often. For children, if a good share of rice and other vegetables be in the liquid, or considerable bread eaten with it, soup is a generally healthy and invigorating food; and for those who are in health and labor hard, and require large meals, it is a good plan to begin the dinner with soup of some kind, as otherwise they would be inclined to take too much solid food.

With these restrictions, then, the good housekeeper will know how to plan her soup days, and for whom to make this savory dish, one of the most delicious when well prepared.

I have before remarked, that the liquor in which meats of all kinds are boiled, (except smoked meats,) should be saved and used, either in soups or gravies. This liquor contains much of the essence of the meat, (if the pot was kept closely covered, which it always should be when meats are boiling,) and, if rightly prepared, will prove a great saving in the expense for animal food in a family. If the meats or poultry are boiled for the table, it is better not to use the liquor the first day. Pour it into a well-glazed earthen pot or pan, and let it stand till the next morning. Then skim off the fat, and strain the liquid into a clean soup-boiler. By this means you entirely *separate the blood from the meat,* which is the great object of cookery, and should be conscientiously attended to by the Christians as abstaining from pork is by the Jew.

Most of the particles of blood, when meat is boiled, rise in the form of scum; these should be carefully removed—but there are always stray particles left floating in the water, and when this liquor is strained through a sieve or cloth (a colander is not fine enough) there will be coagulated blood at the bottom in the form of sediment. After the liquor is thus purified, you can add whatever vegetables you choose—rice, carrots, cabbage, onions, and potatoes are all used. If the liquor is too much, boil it awhile uncovered and let it evaporate. If it require richness, you had better take some of the fat skimmed off—melt it in a saucepan with a spoonful of flour well stirred in—this unites with the fat, and prevents it from floating, like oil, on the top of the liquor. Then stir this mixture into the soup, add whatever flavors of seasoning you choose: pepper and sweet herbs are usually in favor.—Crackers, toasted or hard bread may be added a short time before the soup is wanted; but do not put those libels on civilized cookery, called *dumplings!* One might about as well eat, with the hope of digesting, a brick from the ruins of Babylon, as one of the hard, heavy masses of boiled dough which usually pass under this name.

Indeed, it is, on many accounts, preferable, that bread should be eaten *with,* rather than *in,* our soups. In the former case, the bread assists to cool the broth, which is otherwise almost always taken *too hot.* Here is one great cause of disease to the stomach from this article of diet. Besides, hot liquors greatly injure the teeth; and also by passing immediately into the blood and thus circulating through the whole system, cause an unnatural glow and perspiration which often predisposes to colds, and is weakening to delicate constitutions. When we are well, and wish to continue so, it is best never to take food or drinks warmer than milk. In sickness, hot drinks are sometimes needed as stimulants.

Source: Sarah Josepha Hale, *The Good Housekeeper,* 6th ed. (Boston: Otis, Broaders, 1839), 57–59.

1839 • 41 • Frederick Marryat, *A Diary in America*

Introduction: *Frederick Marryat (1792–1848) was an English naval officer who retired in 1830 to write full-time. He visited the United States and Canada in 1837, and upon his return to England he published his diaries in two volumes. The first part of the excerpt is about Americans celebrating the Fourth of July in New York City. Americans had been doing so ever since 1776. Celebrations often included fireworks, eating, and drinking.*

The 4th of July, the sixty-first anniversary of American Independence.

Pop—pop—bang—pop—pop—bang—bang bang! Mercy on us! how fortunate it is that anniversaries come only once a year. Well, the Americans may have great reason to be proud of this day, and of the deeds of their forefathers, but why do they get so confoundedly drunk! why, on this day of independence, should they become so dependent upon posts and rails for support!—The day is at last over; my head aches, but there will be many more aching heads to-morrow morning!

What a combination of vowels and consonants have been put together! what strings of tropes, metaphors, and allegories, have been used on this day! what varieties and gradations of eloquence! There are at least fifty thousand cities, towns, villages, and hamlets, spread over the surface of America—in each the Declaration of Independence has been read; in all one, and in some two or three, orations have been delivered, with as much gunpowder in them as in the squibs and crackers. But let me describe what I actually saw.

The commemoration commenced, if the day did not, on the evening of the 3d, by the municipal police going round and pasting up placards, informing the citizens of New York, that all persons letting off fireworks would be taken into custody, which notice was immediately followed up by the little boys proving their independence of the authorities, by letting off squibs, crackers, and bombs; and cannons, made out of shin bones, which flew in the face of every passenger in the exact ratio that the little boys flew in the face of the authorities. This continued the whole night, and thus was ushered in the great and glorious day, illumined by a bright and glaring sun, (as if bespoken on purpose by the mayor and corporation,) with the thermometer at 90° in the shade. The first sight which met the eye after sunrise, was the precipitate escape, from a city visited with the plague of gunpowder, of respectable or timorous people in coaches, carriages, wagons, and every variety of vehicle. "My kingdom for a horse I" was the general cry of all those who could not stand fire. In the mean while, the whole atmosphere was filled with independence. Such was the quantity of American flags which were hoisted on board of the vessels, hung out of windows, or carried about by little boys, that you saw more stars at noon-day than ever could be counted on the brightest night.

On each side of the whole length of Broadway, were ranged booths and stands, similar to those at an English fair, and on which were displayed small plates of oysters, with a fork stuck in the board opposite to each plate; clams sweltering in the hot sun; pineapples, boiled hams, pies, puddings, barley-sugar, and many other indescribables. But what was remarkable, Broadway being three miles long, and the booths lining each side of it, in every booth there was a roast pig, large or small, as the centre attraction. Six miles of roast pig! and that in New York City alone; and roast pig in every other city, town, hamlet, and village in the Union. What association can there be between roast pig and independence? Let it not be supposed that there was any deficiency in the very necessary articles of potation on this auspicious day: no! the booths were loaded with porter, ale, cider, mead, brandy, wine, ginger-beer, mint juleps, besides many other compounds, to name which nothing but the luxuriance of American-English could invent a word. . . .

I was invited to dine with the mayor and corporation at the City Hall. We sat down in the Hall of Justice, and certainly great justice was done to the dinner, which (as the wife says to her husband after a party, where the second coarse follows the first with remarkable celerity) "went off remarkably well." The crackers popped outside, and the champagne popped in. The celerity of the Americans at a public dinner is very commendable; they speak only now and then; and the toasts follow so fast, that you have just time to empty your glass before you are requested to fill again. Thus the arranged toasts went off rapidly, and after them, any one might withdraw. I waited till the thirteenth toast, the last on the paper, to wit, the ladies of America; and, baring previously, in a speech from the recorder, bolted Bunker's Hill and New Orleans, I thought I might as well bolt myself, as I wished to see the fireworks, which were to be very splendid.

As a set-off to this funning, we will subjoin a few serious facts.

America is a wonderful country, endowed by the Omnipotent with natural advantages which no other can boast of; and the mind can hardly calculate upon the degree of perfection and power to which, whether the States are eventually separated or not, it may in the course of two centuries arrive. At present all is energy and enterprise; everything is in a state of transition, but of rapid improvement—so rapid, indeed, that those who would describe America now would have to correct all in the short space of ten years; for ten years in America is almost equal to a century in the old continent. Now you may pass through a wild forest, where the elk browses and the panther howls. In ten years, that very forest, with its denizens, will, most likely, have disappeared, and in their place you will find towns with thousands of inhabitants; with arts, manufactures, and machinery, all in full activity.

In reviewing America, we must look upon it as showing the development of the English character under a new aspect, arising from a new state of things. If I were to draw a comparison between the English and the Americans, I should say that there is almost as much difference between the two nations at this present time, as there has long been between the English and the Dutch. The latter are considered by us as phlegmatic and slow: and we may be considered the same, compared with our energetic descendants. Time to an American is everything, and space he attempts to reduce to a mere nothing. By the steam-boats, railroads, and the wonderful facilities of water-carriage, a journey of five hundred miles is as little considered in America, as would be here a journey from London to Brighton. "Go a-head" is the real motto of the country; and every man does push on, to gain in advance of his neighbour. The American lives twice as long as others; for he does twice the work during the time that he lives. He begins life sooner: at fifteen he is considered a man, plunges into the stream of enterprize, floats and struggles with his fellows. In every trifle an American shows the value he puts upon time.

Source: Frederick Marryat, *A Diary in America, with Remarks on Its Institutions* (New York: Wm. H. Colyer, 1839), 101–103.

I must now enter into a very important question, which is that of eating and drinking. Mr. Cooper,[1] in his remarks upon his own countrymen, says, very ill-naturedly—"The Americans are the grossest feeders of any civilized nation known. As a nation, their food is heavy, coarse, and indigestible, while it is taken in the least artificial forms that cookery will allow. The predominance of grease in the American kitchen, coupled with the habits of hearty eating, and the constant expectoration, are the causes of the diseases of the stomach which are so common in America."

This is not correct. The cookery in the United States is exactly what it is and must be every where else—in a ration with the degree of refinement of the population. In the principal cities, you will meet with as good cookery in private houses as you will in London or even Paris; indeed, considering the great difficulty which Americans have to contend with, from the almost impossibility of obtaining good servants, I have often been surprised that it is so good as it is. At Delmonico's, and the Globe Hotel at New York, where you dine from the Carte, you have excellent French cookery; so you have at

Astor House, particularly at private parties; and, generally speaking, the cooking at all the large hotels may be said to be good; indeed, when it is considered that the American table-d'hôte has to provide for so many people, it is quite surprising how well it is done. The daily dinner, at these large hotels, is infinitely superior to any I have ever sat down to at *public* entertainments given at the Free-Masons' Tavern, and others in London, and the company is usually more numerous. The bill of fare of the table-d'hôte of the Astor House is *printed every day.* I have one with me which I shall here insert, to prove the eating is not so bad in America as described by Mr. Cooper.

Astor House, Wednesday, March 21, 1838.

Table-d' Hôtel.

Vermicelli Soup
Boiled Cod Fish and Oysters
Boiled Corn'd Beef
Boiled Ham
Boiled Tongue
Boiled Turkey and Oysters
Boiled Chickens and Pork
Boiled Leg of Mutton Oyster Pie
Cuisse de Poulet Sauce Tomate
Poitrine de Veau au Blanc
Salade de Volalle
Ballon de Mouton au Tomate
Téte de Veau au Marinade
Casserolle de Fomme de Terre garnie
Compote de Pigeon
Rolleau de Veau à la Jardiniere
Côtelettes de Veau Sauté Filet de Mounton Piqué aux Ognons
Filet de Mounton pigué aux Ognons
Ronde de Bœuf
Fricandeau de Veau aux Epinards
Côtelettes de Mouton Panée
Macaroni au Parmesan
Roast Beef
Roast Pig
Roast Veal
Roast Leg of Mutton Roast Goose
Roast Goose
Roast Turkey
Roast Chickens
Roast Wild Ducks
Roast Wild Goose
Roast Guinea Fowl
Roast Brandt
Queen Pudding
Mince Pie
Cream Puffs
Dessert.

There are some trifling points relative to eating which I shall not remark upon until I speak of society, as they will there be better placed. Of course, as you advance into the country, and population recedes, you run through all the scale of cookery until you come to the "*corn bread, and common doings,*" (i.e. bread made of Indian meal and fat pork,) in the far West. In a new country, pork is more easily raised than any other meat, and Americans eat a great deal of pork, which renders the cooking in farm taverns, where they fry chickens without grease in a way which would be admired by Ude[2] himself; but this is a State receipt, handed down from generation to generation, and called *chicken fixings*. The meat in America is equal to the best in England; Miss Martineau[3] does indeed say that she never ate good beef during the whole time she was in this country; but she also says that as American stage-coach is the most delightful of all conveyances and a great many other things, which I may hereafter quote, to prove the idiosyncracy of the lady's disposition; so we will let that pass, with the observation that there is no accounting for taste. The American markets in the cities are well supplied. I have been in a game market, at New York, and seen at one time nearly three hundred head of deer, with quantities of bear, rackoons, wild turkies, geese, ducks, and every variety of bird in countless profusion. Near I abominate; rackoon is pretty good. The wild turkey is excellent; but the great delicacies in America are the terrapin, and the canvas-back ducks. To like the first I consider as rather an acquired taste. I decidedly prefer the turtle, which are to be had in plenty, all the year round; but the canvas-back duck is certainly well worthy of its reputation. Fish is well supplied. They have sheep's head, shad, and one or two others, which we have not. Their salmon is not equal to ours, and they have no turbot. Pine-apples, and almost all the tropical fruits are hawked about in carts in the Eastern-cities; but I consider the fruit of the temperate zone, such as grapes, peaches, & c., inferior to the English. Oysters are very plentiful, very large, and, to an English palate, rather insipid. As the Americans assert that the English and French Oysters taste of cooper, and that therefore they cannot eat them, I presume they do; and that's the reason why we do not like American oysters, cooper being better than no flavor at all.

I think, after the statement, that the English will agree with me that there are plenty of good things for the table in America; but the old proverb says: 'God sends meat and the devil sends cooks;' and such is, and unfortunately must be the case for a long while, in most of the houses in America, owing to the difficulty of obtaining, or keeping servants. But I must quit the subject of eating, for one of much more importance in America, which is that of drinking.

I always did consider that the English and the Swiss were the two nations who most indulged in potations; but on my arrival in the United States, I found that our descendants, in this point most assuredly, as they fain would be thought to do in all others, surpassed us altogether.

Impartiality compels me to acknowledge the truth; we must, in this instance, submit to a national defeat. There are many causes for this: first, the heat of the climate, next the coldness of the climate, then the changeableness of the climate; add to these, the cheapness of liquor in general, the early disfranchisement of the youth from all parental control, the temptation arising from the bar and association, and, lastly, the pleasantness, amenity, and variety of the potations.

Reasons, therefore, are as plentiful as blackberries, and habit becomes second nature.

To run up the whole catalogue of the indigenous compounds in America, from "iced water" to a "stone fence," or "streak of lightning," would fill a volume; I shall first speak of foreign importations.

The Port in America is seldom good; the climate appears not to agree with the wine. The quantity of Champagne drunk is enormous, and would absorb all the vintage of France, were it not that many hundred thousand bottles are Consumed more than are imported.

The small state of New Jersey has the credit of supplying the American Champagne, which is said to be concocted out of turnip juice, mixed with brandy and honey. It is a pleasant and harmless drink, a very good imitation, and may be purchased at six or seven dollars a dozen. I do not know what we shall do when America fills up, if the demand for Champagne should increase in proportion to the population; we had bettor drink all we can now.

Claret, and the other French wines, do very well in America, but, where the Americans beat us out of the field is in their Madeira, which certainly is of a quality which we cannot procure in England. This is owing to the extreme heat and cold of the climate, which ripens this wine; indeed, I may almost say, that I never tasted good Madeira, until I arrived in the United States. The price of wines, generally speaking, is very high, considering what a trifling duty is paid, but the price of good Madeira is surprising. There are certain brands, which if exposed to public auction, will be certain to fetch from twelve to twenty, and I have been told even forty dollars a bottle. I insert a list of the wines at Astor House, to prove that there is no exaggeration in what I have asserted. Even in this list of a tavern, the reader will find that the best Madeira is as high as twelve dollars a bottle, and the list is curious from the variety which it offers. . . .

But the Americans do not confine themselves to foreign wines or liquors; they have every variety at home, in the shape of compounds, such as mint-julep and its varieties; slings in all their varieties; cock-tails,—but I really cannot remember, or if I could, it would occupy too much time to mention the whole battle array against one's brains. I must, however, descant a little upon the mint-julep; as it is, with the thermometer at 100°, one of the most delightful and insinuating potations that ever was invented, and may be drank with equal satisfaction when the thermometer is as low as 70°. There are many varieties, such as those composed of Claret, Madeira, &c.; but the ingredients of the real mint-julep are as follows. I learnt how to make them, and succeeded pretty well. Put into a tumbler about a dozen sprigs of the tender shoots of mint, upon them put a spoonful of white sugar, and equal proportions of peach and common brandy, so as to fill it up one third, or perhaps a little less. Then take rasped or pounded ice, and fill up the tumbler. Epicures rub the lips of the tumbler with a piece of fresh pine-apple, and the tumbler itself is very often incrusted outside with stalactites of ice. As the ice melts, you drink. I once overheard two ladies talking in the next room to me, and one of them said, "Well, if I have a weakness for any one thing, it is for a mint-julep—" a very amiable weakness, and proving her good sense and good taste. They are, in fact, like the American ladies, irresistible. . . .

I have mentioned the principal causes to which must be assigned the propensity to drink, so universal in America. This is an undeniable fact, asserted by every other writer, acknowledged by the Americans themselves in print, and proved by the labours of their Temperance Societies. It is not confined to the lower classes, but pervades the whole mass: of course, where there is most refinement, there is less intoxication, and in the Southern and Western States, it is that the custom of drinking is most prevalent.

I have said that in the American hotels there is a parlour for the ladies to retire to: there is not one for the gentlemen, who have only the reading-room, where they stand and read the papers, which are laid out on desks, or the bar.

The bar of an American hotel is generally a very large room on the basement, fitted up very much like our gin palaces in London, not so elegant in its decorations indeed, but on the same system. A long counter runs across it, behind which stand two or three barkeepers to wait upon the customers, and distribute the various potations, compounded from the contents of several rows of bottles behind them. Here the eye reposes on masses of pure crystal ice, large bunches of mint, decanters of every sort of wine every variety of spirits, lemons, sugar, bitters, segars and tobacco; it really makes one feel thirsty, even the going into a bar. Here you meet every body and every body meets you. Here the senator, the member of Congress, the merchant, the store-keeper, travellers from the Far West, and every other part of the country, who have come to purchase goods, all congregate.

Most of them have a segar in their mouth, some are transacting business, others conversing, some sitting down together whispering confidentially. Here you obtain all the news, all the scandal, all the politics, and all the fun; it is this dangerous propinquity, which occasions so much intemperance. Mr. Head has no bar at the Mansion-House in Philadelphia, and the consequence is, that there is no drinking, except wine at dinner; but in all the other hotels, it would appear as if they purposely allowed the frequenters no room to retire to, so that they must be driven to the bar, which is by for the most profitable part of the concern.

The consequence of the bar being the place of general resort, is, that there is an unceasing pouring out, and amalgamation of alcohol, and other compounds, from morning, to late at night. To drink with a friend when you meet him is good fellowship, to drink with a stranger is politeness, and a proof of wishing to be better acquainted.

Mr. A. is standing at the bar, enter B. "My dear B. how are you!"—"Quite well, and you?"—"Well, what shall it be?"—"Well, I don't care—a gin sling."—"Two gin slings, Bar-keeper." Touch glasses, and drink. Mr. A. has hardly swallowed his gin sling, and replaced his segar, when, in comes Mr. D. "A. how are you?"—"Ah! D. how goes it on with you?"—"Well, I thankey—what shall we have?"—"Well, I don't care; I say brandy cocktail."—"Give me another," both drink, and the shilling is thrown down on the counter.

Then B. comes up again. "A. you must allow me to introduce my friend C."—"Mr. A."—shake hands—"Most happy to make the acquaintance. I trust I shall have the pleasure of drinking something with you?"—"With great pleasure, Mr. A., I will take a julep. Two juleps, bar-keeper."—"Mr. C. your good health—Mr. A. yours; if you should come our way, most happy to see you,"—drink.

Now, I will appeal to the Americans themselves, if this is not a fair sample of a bar-room.

They say that the English cannot settle any thing properly, without a dinner. I am sure the Americans can fix nothing, without a drink. If you meet, you drink; if you part, you drink; if you make acquaintance, you drink; if you close a bargain you drink; they quarrel in their drink, and they make it up with a drink. They drink, because it is hot; they drink because it is cold. If successful in elections, they drink and rejoice; if not, they drink and swear;—they begin to drink, early in the morning, they leave off late at night; they commence it early in life, and they continue it, until they soon drop into the grave. To use their own expression, the way they drink, is "quite a caution." As for water, what the man said, when asked to belong to the Temperance Society, appears to be the general opinion, "it's very good for navigation."

So much has it become the habit to cement all friendship, and commence acquaintance by drinking, that it is a cause of serious offence to refuse, especially in a foreigner, as the Americans like to call, the English. I was always willing to accommodate the Americans in this particular, as far as I could; (there at least, they will do me justice;) that at times I drank much more than I wished is certain, yet still I gave most serious offence, especially in the West, because I would not drink early in the morning, or before dinner, which is a general custom in the States, although much more prevalent in the South and West, where it is literally, "Stranger, will you drink or fight?" This refusal on my part, or rather excusing myself from drinking with all those who were introduced to me, was eventually the occasion of much disturbance and of great animosity towards me—certainly, most unreasonably, as I was introduced to at least twenty every forenoon; and had I drunk with them all, I should have been in the same state as many of them were—that is, not really sober for three or four weeks at a time.

That the constitutions of the Americans must suffer from this habit is certain; they do not, however, appear to suffer so much as we should. They say that you may always know the grave of a Virginian; as from the quantity of juleps he has drunk, mint invariably springs up where he has been buried. But the Virginians are not the greatest drinkers, by any means. I was once looking for an American, and asked a friend of his, where I should, find him. "Why," replied he, pointing to an hotel opposite, "that is his *licking place,* (a term borrowed from deer resorting to lick the salt:) we will see if he is there." He was not; the bar-keeper said he had left about ten minutes. "Well, then, you had better remain here, he is certain to be back in ten more—if not sooner." The American judged his friend rightly; in five minutes he was back again, and we had a drink together, of course.

I did not see it myself, but I was told that somewhere in Missouri, or thereabouts, west of the Mississippi, all the bars have what they term a kicking-board, it being the custom with the people who live there, instead of touching glasses when they drink together, to kick sharply with the side of the foot against the board, and that after this ceremony you are sworn friends. I have had it mentioned to me by more than one person, therefore I presume it is the case. What the origin of it is I know not, unless it intends to imply, "I'm your's to the *last kick.*"

Notes

1. James Fenimore Cooper, Document 35.
2. A famous French chef and cookbook writer in England.
3. Harriet Martineau, Document 33.

Source: Frederick Marryat, *Second Series of a Diary in America, with Remarks on Its Institutions* (Philadelphia: T. K. and P. G. Collins, 1840), 35–41, 120–127.

1840 • 42 • Samuel Prescott Hildreth, Life in a Tavern

Introduction: *Taverns, also called public houses and ordinaries, were places where alcohol and usually food were served. Taverns played important social, political, and economic roles. They were places where men met to drink, socialize, discuss events of the day, engage in business transactions, and occasionally participate in political processes, all of which were ratified with drink. Taverns were centers for the transmission of information, as they commonly made newspapers available, and they were also places where travelers would bring news from other communities. In colonial times, few rural communities had large public buildings, so taverns frequently hosted civic functions, such as court sessions and official gatherings. Tavern owners played an important role as well; they were generally well informed about current happenings and shared what they knew. Some taverns also had rooms for lodgers, although these were usually called inns. Taverns were licensed and regulated, but historically illegal establishments were common in America. Samuel Prescott Hildreth (1783–1863) was a medical professional who moved to Marietta, Ohio, in 1805, along with his wife and parents. His father opened a tavern in Marietta and the selection below is a description of life in the tavern.*

. . . [M]y father opened a tavern and a small store of dry goods, which for many years was kept in the little bed room at the end of the kitchen, and was about twelve feet square. The location being a central one, and all the town and public meetings held at the meeting house, made it a very good spot for a tavern, and especially in as much as at that day the soberest part of the community partook freely of "Flip" in winter and "Punch" in summer without once being aware that they were doing wrong, or infringing the strictest rule of morality, so long as they drank, not to the verge of intoxication. Even the deacons and preachers of the gospel, thought not of evil when they partook of the cheerful bowl on public occasions when every body drank. The calling of the tavern-keeper and mingler of strong drinks was often a very profitable one.

On such occasion very little was drank simple or only mixed with water and a little sugar as in more modern times; but it was made into some palatable form, often into toddy, with a biscuit toasted and put into it and eaten as the toddy was exhausted, technically called "a toad". Flip was made mostly in winter, with small beer, heated with a red hot iron called a "loger-head" and constantly kept in every public house for this expressed purpose, and generally in the fire when not in the beer can.

This drink was sweetened and spiced and made a very palatable beverage. Switchel,[1] rum and molasses; Eggnog, made by beating up eggs and mixing them with rum, sugar and water, was also another New England drink, much in use at that day, especially in the spring of the year at elections. The habit of drinking strong liquors had greatly increased since the revolutionary war, and the dissolute manners of the soldiers too often followed by the citizens, amongst whom they had became amalgamated, after the close of the war.

At the head of the various kinds of choice drinks, stood the universal favorite, Punch. It was composed of Rum, water, sugar and the fresh juice of the lemon. It was drank from large china bowls, if they had them, and was often partaken by the females, especially on the day of their grand national jubilee, the 4th of July. Wine, was a drink comparatively but little used, the variety was mostly Malaga or some of the sweet wines and chiefly appropriated to the use of females, at dances, balls, quiltings and weddings.

Cider was a drink in constant use at the table, and especially with their dinner. So habitual was its employment by all classes, that a store of four up to twenty or more barrels, was regularly stowed away in the cellar, every autumn, as one of the real necessaries of house keeping; with the beef, pork and potatoes. Very little, if any was used by the distillers of rum, etc. in New England; although it had been so appropriated for several years, especially during the war, when foreign liquors were scarce, by the people of New Jersey, Maryland and North Carolina.

The national beverage, cider, was constantly drank by the laboring classes at their work in the fields instead of water; and any farmer who furnished water in place of cider for his work hands was accounted a close fisted, niggardly man. And although very few of the farmers became drunkards from this habitual gurling of stimulating drinks, yet their red noses, blotched cheeks and sore eyes betrayed the constitutional effect of their favorite beverage.

Mixed with a little molasses and water, cider, with bread crumbled into it, was eaten by the children with a spoon from a bowl, or pewter poringer,[2] for their supper at seasons when milk was scarce. Tea at this early period of the republic, was viewed with rather a jealous eye, by a large portion of the people, although the females began pretty soon to have a hankering after it and none the less so from its having been a prohibited article; like their progenitor Eve, whose appetite was greatly stimulated from the prohibition laid upon it in the garden of Eden.

However, the females from their influence on the hearts and minds of the men, soon overcame this reluctance, and tea became in a few years one of the most common drinks of the country. Chocolate or cocoa and shells, the husk of the cocoanut, was for many years after the war one of the most common of the foreign articles used as a dietetic beverage. It was both palatable and nourishing. Coffee came into more general use at a later day, not very generally before the year 1800.

Notes

1. A drink made with water and vinegar, often seasoned with ginger and sweetened.
2. A porridge dish.

Source: Samuel Prescott Hildreth, *Genealogical and Biographical Sketches of the Hildreth Family* (Marietta, OH: n.p., 1840), 46–47.

1845 • 43 • James Fenimore Cooper, "Starvation Is a Serious Matter at Any Time"

Introduction: *Unlike England, land was plentiful in America, and so was food. In the excerpt below, novelist James Fenimore Cooper (author of* The Leatherstocking Tales *and* The Last of the Mohicans, *among other works) wrote about the land problems in upstate New York shortly after the American Revolution. Starvation in America, as discussed below, was quite different than starvation in other countries, where people had nothing to eat.*

I found but few more signs of cultivation between the point where I left the great northern road and the bounds of the patent than had been found by my father, as he had described them to me in his first visit, which took place a quarter of a century earlier than this of mine. There was one log tavern, it is true, in the space mentioned, but it afforded nothing to drink but rum, and nothing to eat but salted pork and potatoes, the day I stopped there to dine. But there were times and seasons when, by means of venison, wild-fowl and fish, a luxurious board might have been spread. That this was not the opinion of my landlady, nevertheless, was apparent from the remarks she made while I was at table.

"You are lucky, Major Littlepage," she said, "in not having come among us in one of what I call our 'starving times'—and awful times they be, if a body may say what she thinks on 'em."

"Starvation is a serious matter at any time," I answered, "though I did not know you were ever reduced to such difficulties in a country as rich and abundant as this."

"Of what use is riches and abundance if a man will do nothing but fish and shoot? I've seen the day when there wasn't a mouthful to eat in this house but a dozen or two of squabs, a string of brook trout, and maybe a deer, or a salmon from one of the lakes."

"A little bread would have been a welcome addition to such a meal."

"Oh! as for bread, I count that for nothin'. We always have bread and potatoes enough; but I hold a family to be in a desperate way, when the mother can see the bottom of the pork barrel. Give me the children that's raised on good sound pork, afore all the game in the country. Game's good as a relish, and so's bread; but pork is the staff of life! To have good pork, a body must have good corn; and good corn needs hoeing; and a hoe isn't a fishpole or a gun. No, my children I calkerlate [sic] to bring up on pork, with just as much bread and butter as they may want!"

This was American poverty as it existed in 1784. Bread, butter, and potatoes, *ad libitum;* but, little pork, and no tea. Game in abundance in its season; but the poor man who lived on game was supposed to be keeping just as poor an establishment as the epicure in town who gives a dinner to his brethren and is compelled to apologize for there being no game in the market. Curious to learn more from this woman, I pursued the discourse.

"There are countries, I have read," I continued, "in which the poor do not taste meat of any sort, not even game, from the beginning of the year to its end; and sometimes not even bread."

"Well, I'm no great hand for bread, as I said afore, and should eat no great matter of it, so long as I could get pork," the woman answered, evidently interested in what I had said; "but I shouldn't like to be without it altogether; and the children, especially, do love to have it with their butter. Living on potatoes alone must be a wild animal sort of a life."

"Very tame animals do it, and that from dire necessity."

"Is there any law ag'in their using bread and meat?"

"No other law than the one which forbids their using that which is the property of another."

"Good land!" This is a very common American expression among the women—"Good land! Why don't they go to work and get in crops, so they might live a little?"

"Simply because they have no land to till. The land belongs to others, too."

"I should think they might hire, if they couldn't buy. It's about as good to hire as it is to buy—some folks (folk) think it's better. Why don't they take land on shares, and live?"

"Because land itself is not to be had. With us, land is abundant; we have more of it than is necessary, or than will be necessary, for ages to come: perhaps it would be better for our civilization were there less of it, but, in the countries of which I speak, there are more people than there is land."

Source: James Fenimore Cooper, *The Chainbearer: Or, the Littlepage Manuscripts* (New York: Burgess, Stringer, 1845), 186–190.

1846 • 44 • Richard Smith Elliott, "Life in New Mexico"

Introduction: *During the Mexican-American War (1846–1848), the American military occupied Santa Fe in August 1846. Richard Smith Elliott (1817–1890) was a newspaperman and was appointed an Indian agent in 1843. When the Mexican-American War broke out, Elliott volunteered to serve in Alexander W. Doniphan's militia unit, part of the Army of the West commanded by General Stephen W. Kearney. This army captured Santa Fe, then part of Mexico. While in the army, Elliott, under the pseudonym John Brown, regularly wrote articles for newspapers describing what he saw. He later became a real estate broker and engaged in a variety of other businesses. Below is Elliott's description of food in Santa Fe in 1846.*

Red peppers with plant growing in the background, watercolor, ca. 1860. (Library of Congress)

Life in New Mexico.

Some Account of Mexican Onions, Potatoes, "Pass Brandy," and *Other* Vegetables! Also, a Full Account of Molasses Making Mexican fare is neither so plentiful or so luxurious as ours in the States; nor do I see that the natives are very particular as to the regularity of their meals. In truth, their whole lives are what we would consider long courses of *low diet*—little else than bread and cakes of wheat or corn meal, a little meat, onions and red peppers. Their onions merit especial notice, as they seem to be the best production of the country. They are very large, and the flavor is much better than that of ours at home; so mild are they, that one can eat heartily of them when tired, and feel no unpleasant heaviness thereafter. I have even been told by some of the youngsters that they have eaten them for dinner, and spent the afternoon in the society of senoritas, without perceiving their presence under such circumstances were at all repulsive—as it would be, you know, without *onions* in the States. The difference may have been in the *ladies,* but the boys insist that it was in the "*vegetable.*"

On the march here, I saw a number of potato plants growing wildly in the hills; but this vegetable is not at all cultivated by the Mexicans.

Some of the Mexican families who can afford it, have, at times, sugar, coffee and chocolate; and I have seen some houses, *sassafras tea* made of the bark of sassafras roots brought form the States, but I have seen none of the celestial article—though it is perhaps used among them, in limited quantities.

Red pepper sauce, which is simply the peppers stewed—or another dish, red peppers preserved in corn-stalk molasses—do not go badly, when you get used to them; albeit, before you know exactly what they are, and dip a little too deeply into the dish, they prove somewhat calorific in the region of the thorax.

I have seen them making molasses, or rather preparing for it. I was at a house in a little valley on the 15th September, taking my dinner of tortillas, boiled mutton and pepper sauce, when I noticed on the opposite side of the valley some objects apparently floating in the wind, like clothes on a line; but as there absolutely was no wind, I concluded that my impression could not be correct. When I mounted again, I determined to solve the riddle. As I approached, I found the object to be four very pretty Mexican girls, and three grave cooking matrons, perched on the end of a long pine pole about the size of the steering oar used on a flat-boat holding to the rail put up for the purpose, and seeing sawing up and down, but with much more the air of persons at business of play.

John Brown, Santa Fe, October 30, 1846

Source: John Brown [pseudonym for Richard Smith Elliott], "Life in New Mexico: Some Account of Mexican Onions, Potatoes, 'Pass Brandy,' and *Other* Vegetables! Also, a Full Account of Molasses Making," *Lowell Daily Courier,* February 12, 1847, 1.

1847 • 45 • William W. Brown, Eating While Escaping Slavery

Introduction: *William W. Brown (1814–1884) was born into slavery in Lexington, Kentucky. He escaped from slavery in 1833 and lived in Cleveland, where he worked on a steamboat and helped other fugitive slaves escape to Canada. In 1847 Brown wrote a narrative about his life, and he included in it a description of acquiring food while he was trying to escape.*

. . . I . . . started for Canada. In four days I reached a public house, and went in to warm myself. I there learned that some fugitive slaves had just passed through the place. The men in the bar-room were talking about it, and I thought that it must have been myself they referred to, and I was therefore afraid to start, fearing they would seize me; but I finally mustered courage enough, and took my leave. As soon as I was out of sight, I went into the woods, and remained there until night, when I again regained the road, and travelled on until next day.

Not having had any food for nearly two days, I was faint with hunger, and was in a dilemma what to do, as the little cash supplied me by my adopted father, and which had contributed to my comfort, was now all gone. I however concluded to go to a farm-house, and ask for something to eat. On approaching the door of the first one presenting itself, I knocked, and was soon met by a man who asked me what I wanted. I told him that I would like something to eat. He asked me where I was from, and where I was going. I replied that I had come some way, and was going to Cleaveland.

After hesitating a moment or two, he told me that he could give me nothing to eat, adding, "that if I would work, I could get something to eat."

I felt bad, being thus refused something to sustain nature, but did not dare tell him that I was a slave.

Just as I was leaving the door, with a heavy heart, a woman, who proved to be the wife of this gentleman, came to the door, and asked her husband what I wanted. He did not seem inclined to inform her. She therefore asked me herself. I told her that I had asked for something to eat. After a few other questions, she told me to come in, and that she would give me something to eat.

I walked up to the door, but the husband remained in the passage, as if unwilling to let me enter.

She asked him two or three times to get out of the way, and let me in. But as he did not move, she pushed him on one side, bidding me walk in! I was never before so glad to see a woman push a man aside! Ever since that act, I have been in favor of "woman's rights!"

After giving me as much food as I could eat, she presented me with ten cents, all the money then at her disposal, accompanied with a note to a friend, a few miles further on the road. Thanking this angel of mercy from an overflowing heart, I pushed on my way, and in three days arrived at Cleaveland, Ohio.

Being an entire stranger in this place, it was difficult for me to find where to stop. I had no money, and the lake being frozen, I saw that I must remain until the opening of the navigation, or go to Canada by way of Buffalo. But believing myself to be somewhat out of danger, I secured an engagement at the Mansion House, as a table waiter, in payment for my board. The proprietor, however, whose name was E. M. Segur, in a short time, hired me for twelve dollars a month; on which terms I remained until spring, when I found good employment on board a lake steamboat.

Source: William Wells Brown, *Narrative of William W. Brown, an American Slave: Written by Himself* (Boston: Anti-Slavery Office, 1847), 106–108.

1847 • 46 • "The Ground Pea of the South"

Introduction: *The peanut originated in South America and came into what is today the United States through the slave trade. With the exception of slaves and children, few Americans ate peanuts until the early 19th century, when they were sold on the streets of large cities by vendors. The peanut had many virtues, one of which was making vegetable oil. In 1839 Congress passed a small appropriation to require the U.S.*

commissioner of patents to issue an annual report disseminating "agricultural statistics and for other agricultural purposes." Below is an excerpt from the 1848 report that encourages the use of peanuts (which are about 50 percent oil) to make vegetable oil, something common today but avant-garde at the time.

The *ground pea* of the south, or as it is sometimes called, the gouber or pindar pea, is highly recommended in the *Tallahassee Floridian* as an oil plant. The account of it as follows: "To a few only it appears to be known, that the product of this plant gives out an oil in some respects unequaled, as an accompaniment to the table: in its natural state this oil has no rival, clear and mild, with a peculiar taste extremely gratifying to the palate, rich and buttery; it is of that consistency so much admired in the preparation of salads, anchovies, & c., for table use." "Among plants the gouber ranks deservedly as one of the surest crops, not withholding a generous yield even on poor land, and amply acknowledging the superiority of rich land if light and friable. The pea is easily gathered and with less labor than any of the seeds or beans is ready for the press; but when submitted to the known modes of clarifying oil, it becomes liquid and pure, and when immediately bottled and sealed appears to remain in a state of freshness and retains the fine order so highly agreeable to the amateurs of vegetable oils in the prep ration of food. The refuse, after expression, is admirable for hogs, and the vine for stock, if not returned to the soil in gathering the pea; if saved and cured, which is effected with much ease, it mixes in the cutting box well with rye, barley oats and rice. The product of the foder is estimated at more than a ton to the acre; and of peas when cultivated alone and well, fifty and seventy-five bushels. The plant is cultivated much north of us, but from fair trail it is found that, like other producing plants, it delights in the rays of a warm southern sun and soil, and that the product is richer with a finer aroma, than the oil from the same plant produced in Virginia and Carolina. I have no hesitation in saying that if this oil was fairly introduced into the northern states, it would take a high rank at the table of the bon-vivants. This oil is more readily and with less labor and expense, procured from the pea than it is neither very powerful nor expensive. The production of this oil for commerce challenges the early attention of planters and small as well as large capitalists. Any quantity could be produced and prepared for market, a great part of the labor being of that kind that would suit all; the child, old age, and the cripple—all might be employed in the production of this new material. I feel confident that after a little use it would become a successful rival of the best table oil of Europe." If the above account be correct, it would seem that the article is well worth a thorough experiment, and the question may thus be easily decided.

Source: *Annual Report of the Commissioner of Patents for the Year 1847,* Part 2, *Agriculture* (Washington, DC: Wendell and Van Bentbuysen, 1848), 190–191.

1849 • 47 • "How You Feed Your Negroes"

Introduction: *Slavery began in America in 1619 and slowly expanded, particularly in southern colonies. While slavery existed in all colonies, it was only financially viable in the South, where large plantations grew cash crops such as tobacco, indigo, rice, and* *cotton. What slaves ate depended to a great extent on where they were. Southerners often claimed that slaves were well fed. Below is an excerpt from an article published in a magazine in New Orleans that claims that slaves were well fed. Slaves and nonsoutherners, however, reported very different conditions. (See especially Frederick Douglass's remarks in Document 58 about slave owners' beliefs that slaves were well fed in comparison with poor people elsewhere, and see also other accounts from enslaved people about their lack of food in Documents 32, 45, 48, 67, 101, 106, 110.)*

Having feasted upon the diet of English factory operatives, let me introduce you now to the bed and board of negro slaves, in cotton-planting, negro-oppressing Mississippi. Contrary to my practice heretofore, I will call a few witnesses by name—I am sure that they will excuse the liberty, if it should ever come to their ears, for my witnesses are gentlemen in every sense of the word. John T. Leigh, of Yallubusha county, I invoke you first; state, if you please, as you did to me, how you feed your negroes?

"The most of my negroes have families, and live as you see in very comfortable cabins, nearly as good as my own,—with good fire places, good floors and doors, comfortable beds, plenty of cooking utensils and dishes, tables and chairs. But I intend, in the course of another year, to build them a new set of cabins, of uniform size, so as to correspond in appearance with the overseers house. Those who have not families of their own,—mess together; I give each of them 3½ lbs. of bacon, clear of bone, per week, and of the same quality that I use myself, and which I make upon the place, and generally about a peck and a half of corn meal, not being particular about the measure of that, as I raise plenty of corn and grind it in my own mill, and wish them to have all they will eat without wasting it. I also give them sweet potatoes and plenty of vegetables in the season of them. Those who choose to do so, can commute apart of the meat rations for an equivalent in molasses. I also give them a liberal supply of fresh meat from time to time during the year.

"They also, as you see, all have their hen houses, and as 'master's corn crib is always open,' they raise an abundance of eggs and fat chickens to eat or exchange for any other luxuries they wish. Besides, my negroes raise a crop of cotton every year for their own use, and several of the most provident of them always have money, often to the amount of fifty to one hundred dollars. You will observe that the children are all taken care of and fed during the day at the nursery, upon corn bread and fat, and hominy and molasses.

"All the cotton clothing and part of the woolen is spun and wove by women kept employed at that business on the plantation. I give my negroes a feast and frolic every Christmas. I was born and bred among slaves in Virginia. In buying and selling, good masters are always careful not to separate families. Two of my men have wives on President Polk's plantation which adjoins mine, and whom they are free to visit every Saturday night and remain with till Monday morning."

Now this is the testimony of a most honorable living witness, whom if you wish to cross-examine, you can do so at any time. If you will visit him, you will find that no father is better loved or more respected by his children, than he is by his slaves; and I should not be surprised if some of you should acknowledge that, in every respect, they lived more comfortable than many of us do.

I will next ask you to call on Capt. Win. Eggleston, of Holmes county, whom you will find a fine specimen of an old Virginia gentleman, and whose hundred and fifty fine, healthy, hearty looking slaves, will be the best evidence that he feeds them in the same way of the last witness. There I saw the same paternal love and the same respect for "old massa"—the little negroes running after him, as we passed through the village of negro cabins, to shake hands and say "How de do, massa,"—"God bless massa,"—and receive a reply, notwithstanding it comes from a slaveholder, acceptable in the sight of Heaven, of "God bless you, my children."

I will introduce to you one more witness, only because the system of feeding and dealing out rations, differs from the others; it is that of Col. Joseph Dunbar, of Jefferson county, now upward of sixty years of age, a native born Mississippian, who has lived all his life in the vicinity of Natchez, the very hotbed of all that is awful, wicked, bloodthirsty and cruel, in connection with southern slavery; where slaves, if they are starved anywhere, are starved here, or fed upon cotton seed, as I have heard asserted by those who believed it to be a fact.

"Upon the 'home plantation,' Col. Dunbar has one hundred and fifty negroes, fifty of which are field hands. The reason of this is, that he keeps nearly all the aged and children that would naturally belong to another plantation, where he can look every day to their wants, and provide with his own hands for their comfort. His negro quarters look more like a neat, pleasant, New England village, than they do like what we have often been taught to believe was the residence of poor, oppressed and wretched slaves. I did not give them a mere passing view, but examined the interior, and in some of them saw what may be seen in some white people's houses—a great want of neatness and care—but, so far as the master was concerned, all were comfortable, roomy and provided with beds and bedding in abundance. In others there was a show of enviable neatness and luxury; high-post bedsteads, handsomely curtained round with musketo netting, clipboards of blue Liverpool ware, coffee mills, looking-glasses, tables, chairs, trunks and chests of as good clothes as I clothe myself or family with. Every house having the universal henhouse appendage. In the nursery were more than a dozen cradles, and on the neat, green, grassy village common, were sporting more than forty negro children, neatly clothed, fat and happy looking, lazy little slaves. At a certain signal upon the cook-house bell, the young gang came up in fine order to the yard for their dinner; this consisted of meat gravy, and small pieces of meat, thickened with broken corn bread and boiled hominy, seasoned with salt and lard, to which is occasionally added molasses. The cooking for all hands is done in one great kitchen or cook-house, by an experienced cook, and must be well done, as I have no doubt that the cook would be punished severer for any careless or willful neglect about his business, than would any other hand for neglect of work in the field; and I judge this from the fact, that I accidentally overheard the Col., while examining some bread that was not well baked, ask the cook 'if he sent such bread as that to the field, because if he did, and he should repeat the offense, he would order the overseer to give him a dozen lashes—for, mind I tell you, boy, that my negroes shall have good bread and plenty of it.' On being assured by the cook that that was the only loaf not well baked, and that there was plenty without it, he appeared well satisfied. I afterward examined the other bread and tasted it, and found it better than that which I have found upon many a master's own table. The bacon, too, was excellent and well cooked, and given at the rate of 34 lbs. per week to each hand. Fresh meat and vegetables are also given here in plenty. The breakfast and dinner is generally put up in tin pails for each family or mess, or for single hands, as they prefer, and sent to the field, which they will sit and eat in the hot sun, in preference to going into the shade. The supper they take in their own houses, to which they often add luxuries from the hen-houses, or such as they purchase with the sale of eggs and chickens, which they frequently do to their own masters. In the yard of the overseer's house is a large, airy building, neatly whitewashed, which is used when needed, for a hospital; and upon Christmas and other holidays and wedding festivals, as a ball-room. I witnessed here again that same kind of deep-seated love for 'old massa,' from the children and several old negroes who were full grown when he was born, and had lived to see 'young massa' grow up in prosperity to provide for them in decrepid old age. The gleam of joyous satisfaction, too, that beamed from the eyes of two or three sick women, when 'good old massa' called to see sick old Kitty, was enough to warm his Christian heart to thank God that he was placed in a situation where he could give so much happiness to his fellow creatures."

Source: "Negro Slavery at the South," *De Bow's Commercial Review of the South & West* 1 (November 1849): 380–381.

1849 • 48 • Slave Food

Introduction: *The view expressed by the slaveholder in the excerpt above, called "How You Feed Your Negroes," was very different from those who were enslaved. Former slaves talked about their treatment and about the food they received, as thousands of slave narratives, many of which were published before the Civil War, attested. Excerpts from some narratives are included in this collection. During the Great Depression, the Writers' Project hired unemployed writers to interview 2,200 former slaves to capture a written history of their lives before the opportunity was lost. These interviews have been used by scholars ever since.*

If their food gave out before the time for another issue they waited until night and then one or two of them would go to the mill-house where the flour and the meal was kept. After they had succeeded in getting in they would take an auger and bore a hole in the barrel containing the meal. One held the sack while the other took a stick and worked it around in the opening made by the auger so as to make the meal flow freely. After their bags were filled the hole was stopped up and a hasty departure was made. Sometimes when they wanted meat they either went to the smoke house and stole a ham or else they would go to the pen where the pigs were kept and take a small pig out. When they get to the woods with this animal they proceeded to skin and clean it (it had already has killed with a blow in the head before they left the pen). All the parts that they did not want were either buried or thrown in the nearby river. After going home all of this meat was cooked and hidden. As there was danger in being caught none of this stolen meat was ever fried because there was more danger of the odor of frying meat going farther away than that odor made by meat being boiled. (George Womble, Georgia)

All the slaves ate together. They had a cook special for them. This cook would cook in a long house more than thirty feet long. Two or three women would work there and a man, just like the cooks would in a hotel now. All the working hands ate there and got whatever the cook gave them. It was one thing one time and another. The cook gave the hands anything that was raised on the place. There was one woman in there cooking that was called 'Mammy' and she seed to all the chilen.

After the old folks among the slaves had had their breakfast, the cook would blow a horn. That would be about nine o'clock or eight. All the children that were big enough would come to the cook shack. Some of them would bring small children that had been weaned but couldn't look after themselves. The cook would serve them whatever the old folks had for breakfast. They ate out of the same kind of dishes as the old folks. (William L. Dunwoody)

The Cook, wood engraving of an African American woman in a kitchen, 1865. (Library of Congress)

They had a great big kitchen for the slaves. They had what you call pot racks they could push them big pots in and out on. They cooked hog slop there. They had trays and bowls to eat out of that were made cut of gum wood. It was a long house used as a kitchen for the hands to go in and eat. They et dinner there and for supper they would be there. But breakfast, they would have to eat in the field. The young niggers would bring it out to them. They would bring it about an hour after the sun rose and the slave hands would eat it right out in the field; that was the breakfast. You see the hands went to the field before sunup, and they didn't get to eat breakfast in the kitchen and it had to be et in the field. Little undergrowth of children—they had plenty of them on the place—had to carry their meals to them. (Thomas Ruffin, Arkansas)

Dat was sho' good stuff to eat, and it make you fat too! Roast de green corn on de ears in de ashes, and scrape off some and fry it! Grind de dry corn or pound it up and make ash cake. Den bile de greens—all kinds of greens from out in de woods—and chop up de pork and de deer meat, or de wild turkey meat; maybe all of dem, in de big pot at de same time! Fish too, and de big turtle dat lay out on de bank!

Dey always have a pot full of sofki settin right inside de house, and anybody eat when dey feel hungry. Anybody come on a visit, always give 'em some of de sofki. Ef dey don't take none de old man git mad, too!

When you make de sofki you pound up de corn real fine, den pour in de water an drain it off to git all de little skin from off'n de grain. Den you let de grits soak and den bile it and let it stand. Sometime you put in some pounded hickory nut meats. Dat make it real good. (Lucinda Davis, Oklahoma)

Source: Norman R. Yetman, "An Introduction to the WPA Slave Narratives." Born in Slavery: Slave Narratives from the Federal Writers' Project, 1936–1938, http://memory.loc.gov/ammem/snhtml/snhome.html.

1851 • 49 • Herman Melville, "Chowder"

Introduction: *Herman Melville (1819–1891) is one of America's best novelists, and his book* Moby-Dick: Or, the Whale *is a classic. In this excerpt from the book, Melville describes a chowder dinner on Nantucket in the mid-19th century. Whether chowders were introduced into New England by French, Nova Scotian, or British fishermen is undocumented, but chowders were important dishes by 1732 in America. The first-located American recipe for chowder was published in Boston in 1751. Chowders were quite distinct from broths and soups. Chowders, originally stews, consisted of fish, seafood, and vegetables of various proportions. The object was to prepare a thick, highly seasoned dish without reducing the ingredients to the consistency of a puree.*

Chapter 15—Chowder

It was quite late in the evening when the little Moss came snugly to anchor, and Queequeg and I went ashore; so we could attend to no business that day, at least none but a supper and a bed. The landlord of the Spouter-Inn had recommended us to his cousin Hosea Hussey of the Try Pots, whom he asserted to be the proprietor of one of the best kept hotels in all Nantucket, and moreover he had assured us that Cousin Hosea, as he called him, was famous for his chowders. In short, he plainly hinted that we could not possibly do better than try pot-luck at the Try Pots. But the directions he had given us about keeping a yellow warehouse on our starboard hand till we opened a white church to the larboard, and then keeping that on the larboard hand till we made a corner three points to the starboard, and that done, then ask the first man we met where the place was; these crooked directions of his very much puzzled us at first, especially as, at the outset, Queequeg insisted that the yellow warehouse—our first point of departure—must be left on the larboard hand, whereas I had understood Peter Coffin to say it was on the starboard. However, by dint of beating about a little in the dark, and now and then knocking up a peaceful inhabitant to inquire the way, we at last came to something which there was no mistaking.

Two enormous wooden pots painted black, and suspended by asses' ears, swung from the cross-trees of an old top-mast, planted in front of an old doorway. The horns of the cross-trees were sawed off on the other side, so that this old top-mast looked not a little like a gallows. Perhaps I was over sensitive to such impressions at the time, but I could not help staring at this gallows with a vague misgiving. A sort of crick was in my neck as I gazed up to the two remaining horns; yes, two of them, one for Queequeg, and one for me. It's ominous, thinks I. A Coffin my Innkeeper upon landing in my first whaling port; tombstones staring at me in the whalemen's chapel, and here a gallows! and a pair of prodigious black pots too! Are these last throwing out oblique hints touching Tophet?[1]

I was called from these reflections by the sight of a freckled woman with yellow hair and a yellow gown, standing in the porch of the inn, under a dull red lamp swinging there, that looked much like an injured eye, and carrying on a brisk scolding with a man in a purple woollen shirt.

"Get along with ye," said she to the man, "or I'll be combing ye!"

"Come on, Queequeg," said I, "all right. There's Mrs. Hussey."

And so it turned out; Mr. Hosea Hussey being from home, but leaving Mrs. Hussey entirely competent to attend to all his affairs. Upon making known our desires for a supper and a bed, Mrs. Hussey, postponing further scolding for the present, ushered us into a little room, and seating us at a table spread with the relics of a recently concluded repast, turned round to us and said—"Clam or Cod?"

"What's that about Cods, ma'am?" said I, with much politeness.

"Clam or Cod?" she repeated.

"A clam for supper? a cold clam; is that what you mean, Mrs. Hussey?" says I, "but that's a rather cold and clammy reception in the winter time, ain't it, Mrs. Hussey?"

Herman Melville wrote about chowder in his novel, *Moby-Dick; or The Whale* (1851). (National Archives)

But being in a great hurry to resume scolding the man in the purple shirt who was waiting for it in the entry, and seeming to hear nothing but the word "clam," Mrs. Hussey hurried towards an open door leading to the kitchen, and bawling out "clam for two," disappeared.

"Queequeg," said I, "do you think that we can make a supper for us both on one clam?"

However, a warm savory steam from the kitchen served to belie the apparently cheerless prospect before us. But when that smoking chowder came in, the mystery was delightfully explained. Oh! sweet friends, hearken to me. It was made of small juicy clams, scarcely bigger than hazel nuts, mixed with pounded ship biscuits, and salted pork cut up into little flakes! the whole enriched with butter, and plentifully seasoned with pepper and salt. Our appetites being sharpened by the frosty voyage, and in particular, Queequeg seeing his favourite fishing food before him, and the chowder being surpassingly excellent, we despatched it with great expedition: when leaning back a moment and bethinking me of Mrs. Hussey's clam and cod announcement, I thought I would try a little experiment. Stepping to the kitchen door, I uttered the word "cod" with great emphasis, and resumed my seat. In a few moments the savoury steam came forth again, but with a different flavor, and in good time a fine cod-chowder was placed before us.

We resumed business; and while plying our spoons in the bowl, thinks I to myself, I wonder now if this here has any effect on the head? What's that stultifying saying about chowder-headed people? "But look, Queequeg, ain't that a live eel in your bowl? Where's your harpoon?"

Fishiest of all fishy places was the Try Pots, which well deserved its name; for the pots there were always boiling chowders. Chowder for breakfast, and chowder for dinner, and chowder for supper, till you began to look for fish-bones coming through your clothes. The area before the house was paved with clam-shells. Mrs. Hussey wore a polished necklace of codfish vertebra; and Hosea Hussey had his account books bound in superior old shark-skin. There was a fishy flavor to the milk, too, which I could not at all account for, till one morning happening to take a stroll along the beach among some fishermen's boats, I saw Hosea's brindled cow feeding on fish remnants, and marching along the sand with each foot in a cod's decapitated head, looking very slipshod, I assure ye.

Supper concluded, we received a lamp, and directions from Mrs. Hussey concerning the nearest way to bed; but, as Queequeg was about to precede me up the stairs, the lady reached forth her arm, and demanded his harpoon; she allowed no harpoon in her chambers. "Why not?["] said I; "every true whaleman sleeps with his harpoon—but why not?" "Because it's dangerous," says she. "Ever since young Stiggs coming from that unfort'nt v'y'ge of his, when he was gone four years and a half, with only three barrels of *ile,*[2] was found dead in my first floor back, with his harpoon in his side; ever since then I allow no boarders to take sich dangerous weepons in their rooms at night. So, Mr. Queequeg" (for she had learned his name), "I will just take this here iron, and keep it for you till morning. But the chowder; clam or cod tomorrow for breakfast, men?"

"Both," says I; "and let's have a couple of smoked herring by way of variety."

Notes

1. Tophet is believed to be the place where Canaanites sacrificed children.
2. Oil.

Source: Herman Melville, *Moby-Dick: Or, the Whale* (1851; reprint, New York: Harper and Brothers, 1899), 121–124.

1851 • 50 • Nathaniel Hawthorne, *The House of the Seven Gables*

Introduction: *Nathaniel Hawthorne (1804–1864), a popular American novelist, often included descriptions of American food in his works, such as* The House of the Seven Gables *(1851), excerpted below.*

It is within ten minutes of the dinner-hour! It surely cannot have slipped your memory that the dinner of to-day is to be the most important, in its consequences, of all the dinners you ever ate. Yes, precisely the most important; although, in the course of your somewhat eminent career, you have been placed high towards the head of the table, at splendid banquets, and have poured out your festive eloquence to ears yet echoing with

Webster's mighty organ-tones. No public dinner this, however. It is merely a gathering of some dozen or so of friends from several districts of the state; men of distinguished character and influence, assembling, almost casually, at the house of a common friend, likewise distinguished, who will make them welcome to a little better than his ordinary fare. Nothing in the way of French cookery, but an excellent dinner, nevertheless! Real turtle, we understand, and salmon, tautog,[1] canvas-backs, pig, English mutton, good roast-beef or dainties of that serious kind, fit for substantial country gentlemen, as these honorable persons mostly are. The delicacies of the season, in short, and flavored by a brand of old Madeira which has been the pride of many seasons. It is the Juno brand[2]; a glorious wine, fragrant, and full of gentle might; a bottled-up happiness, put by for use; a golden liquid, worth more than liquid gold; so rare and admirable, that veteran wine-bibbers count it among their epochs to have tasted it! It drives away the heart-ache, and substitutes no head-ache! Could the judge but quaff a glass, it might enable him to shake off the unaccountable lethargy which—(for the ten intervening minutes, and five to boot, are already past)—has made him such a laggard at this momentous dinner. It would all but revive a dead man! Would you like to sip it now, Judge Pyncheon?[3] Alas, this dinner!

Notes

1. *Tautoga onitis,* a fish common in saltwater along the East Coat of America.
2. A type of wine made on Madeira, an island in the Azores.
3. Judge Pyncheon is a character in the novel who is presented as austere and moral, but the community holds him in contempt.

Source: Nathaniel Hawthorne, *The House of the Seven Gables: A Romance* (Boston: Ticknor, Reed, and Fields, 1851), 292–293.

1852 • 51 • "McCormick's Celebrated Grain-Reaper and Grass-Cutter"

Introduction: *Cyrus McCormick began working on developing a horse- or ox-drawn mechanical reaper in 1831. Within a few years he had a working device, but it wasn't until 1847 that he had a reliable machine that farmers would accept. McCormick guaranteed that his enhanced reaper could harvest 10 acres a day—five times more than a large crew could harvest by hand—using far fewer workers. Mechanical reaper sales expanded, and in 1848 McCormick sold 1,500 of them. He moved his operation to Chicago, where he began mass-producing reapers to capitalize on the expansion of grain farming in the Midwest. The McCormick reaper soon became the gold standard in farming equipment, and mechanization took command of American agriculture. In addition to being an inspired inventor, McCormick was a smart businessman. He guaranteed farmers that his reapers would cut between 1 and 2 acres of small grains per hour. He also offered his customers credit to pay for machines. Farmers thus had little to lose by buying a McCormick*

Cyrus McCormick invented the first practical grain reaper and went into large-scale production of the farm machines in the 1840s. His invention enabled a huge increase in grain production. (Parsons, J. Russell, et al. *Memorial of Robert McCormick,*1885)

reaper. McCormick was also a good promoter. He displayed and competitively demonstrated his reaper at agricultural exhibitions and fairs throughout America, and it won many prizes. In 1851 McCormick displayed his reaper at London's Great Exhibition at the Crystal Palace, where it won a gold medal, leading to international visibility and substantial sales. In 1852 McCormick sold 5,000 reapers, and during the next seven years he sold 100,000 more. During the American Civil War, an astounding 250,000 reapers were operating on American farms. After the Civil War, McCormick's company continued to thrive. In 1884, the year McCormick died, his company sold 54,841 reapers. For his contributions, McCormick has been called the "Father of Modern Agriculture."

McCormick's Celebrated Grain-reaper and Grass-cutter, to Which Was Awarded, by the Great Exhibition of All Nations, a Great Medal.

There have been 5,000 of them, or more, sold; more than four-fifths of them from the Chicago manufactory, and all within a very few years, though it was first invented in 1831, and patented in 1834 and patented, afterwards, (for improvements made on it,) in the years of 1845 and 1847 such has been the time required to perfect the machine, in fact, in consequence of the short time in each year for making and testing experiments, in making required improvements from time to time. But, for a few years past, the demand for the Reaper has been steadily increasing, until it has become very considerable, and which is always the best evidence of the merits and value of such an improvement. And, as is perhaps the case with all really valuable improvements, as its great value has become more known and established, piracies upon it have been increased. A noted instance of this is found in the case of "Seymour Morgan," of the western part of New York, who, after having manufactured for several successive years for the Patentee, manufactured a considerable number on their own hook, with but colorable evasions of the patents, and against whom a verdict of $17,306 was rendered by a New York jury, in favor of the Patentee, in October last, for the infringement. Other manufacturing concerns in the West have been prosecuted for similar infringements, but which will probably be admonished, by the result of the New York case, to desist as will probably be the farmers of the country, not to purchase the spurious article, when they are as liable for using, as are the manufacturers for making and selling them. THIS world-renowned machine is manufactured by its inventor, Mr. C. H. McCormick, of Chicago, Illinois.

The most important difference between M'Cormick's and Hussey's Reapers are the following:

The cutting blade of M'Cormick's has a sickle or serrated edge

Hussey's a smooth one, which is of course more liable to become dull, and (then) to become clogged, especially in cutting damp grain.

M'Cormick's has "a reel" for gathering the grain to the machine, and laying it straight on the platform, and for want of which it is often necessary to drive Hussey's very fast sometimes at a trot of the horses to enable the attender, with a rake, to gather the grain on the platform; and this greater speed is oppressive on man, horses, and machine which has been spoken of by the inexperienced English only as not injuring the cutting not knowing that it was necessary! With the reel, too, the grain is deposited at the side of the machine, thereby enabling its operators to cut down a whole field, (more or less,) without waiting for, or regard to the binding; whereas, without it, as with Hussey's, the grain is deposited behind the machine, making it necessary to have it bound up or removed before passing with it a second time. This alone is an insuperable objection to Hussey's machine.

As a complete confirmation of the justice of the decision of the Committees of the Great Exhibition of all Nations, in awarding the great medal to M'Cormick's Reaper, the following Societies have during the last fall awarded their first premiums to the same, viz:

The State Agricultural Societies of Pa., New York, Michigan and Wisconsin, and the Phil. Franklin, and Chicago Mechanics' Institutes the latter, a gold medal, for the best Grain Reaper and Grass Cutter, tested by a committee in cutting prairie grass, in competition with two others. The addition to the Reaper, with another sickle, and all necessary extras, to make it a complete mowing machine, warranted, as is the Reaper, costs $25 to $30 additional.

The price of this Reaper alone is $115 cash, on delivery at the manufactory (at Chicago,) or the city of New York; or $30 on delivery, and $90, with interest, on the 1st of November thereafter. Warranted to give full satisfaction in all respects, as well as to cut 1 to 2 acres of all kinds of small grain per hour. The demand this year for this machine, promising to be much greater than in any previous year, it may be necessary to order early to secure a Reaper.

Source: D. Eldon Hall, *A Condensed History of the Origination, Rise, Progress and Completion of the "Great Exhibition of the Industry of All Nations," Held in the Crystal Palace, London, during the Summer of the Year 1851* (New York: Redfield, 1852), 77.

1852 • 52 • Harriet Beecher Stowe's *Uncle Tom's Cabin*

Introduction: *Harriet Beecher Stowe (1811–1896) was born in Litchfield, Connecticut. She was the daughter of Lyman Beecher, a Presbyterian minister who was also a temperance advocate and an abolitionist. Her husband, Calvin Ellis Stowe, was a theologian who taught at a seminary. The Stowes were strongly opposed to slavery and helped runaway slaves find their way to Canada through the Underground Railroad. In 1850 Harriet Beecher Stowe began writing fictional articles for the magazine* National Era *about the life of a slave, Uncle Tom, and his family. The story begins with a Kentucky plantation owner, Arthur Shelby, having to sell a slave, Uncle Tom, to pay debts. Below is a small selection from the novel focused on Aunt Chloe, an excellent cook who is Uncle Tom's wife. Aunt Chloe proposes to the Shelbys that she be rented out to raise money so she can buy back Uncle Tom, who has been sold to a barbarous man, Simon Legree. Aunt Chloe will earn enough money to buy back Uncle Tom, but by then he is dying. These articles were collected into a two-volume novel,* Uncle Tom's Cabin, *that was published in 1852. A play based on the book was released the following year. The book sold more copies than did any book other than the Bible.* Uncle Tom's Cabin *galvanized the North in opposition to slavery and angered many in the South. Some observers have claimed that* Uncle Tom's Cabin *was a contributing factor in causing the Civil War.*

Here the conversation was interrupted by the appearance of Aunt Chloe, at the end of the veranda.

"If you please, Missis," said she.

"Well, Chloe, what is it?" said her mistress, rising, and going to the end of the balcony.

"If Missis would come and look at dis yer lot o' poetry."

Chloe had a particular fancy for calling poultry poetry,—an application of language in which she always persisted, notwithstanding frequent corrections and advisings from the young members of the family.

"La sakes!" she would say, "I can't see; one jis good as turry,—poetry suthin good, any how;" and so poetry Chloe continued to call it.

Mrs. Shelby smiled as she saw a prostrate lot of chickens and ducks, over which Chloe stood, with a very grave face of consideration.

"I'm athinkin' whether Missis would be a havin' a chicken pie o' dese yer."

"Really, Aunt Chloe, I don't much care;—serve them any way you like."

Chloe stood handling them over abstractedly; it was quite evident that the chickens were not what she was thinking of. At last, with the short laugh with which her tribe often introduce a doubtful proposal, she said,—

"Laws me, Missis! what should Mas'r and Missis be a troublin' theirselves 'bout de money, and not a usin' what's right in der hands?" and Chloe laughed.

"I don't understand you, Chloe," said Mrs. Shelby, nothing doubting, from her knowledge of Chloe's manner, that she had heard every word of the conversation that had passed between her and her husband.

"Why, laws me, Missis!" said Chloe, laughing again, "other folks hires out der niggers and makes money on 'em. Don't keep sich a tribe eatin' 'em out of house and home."

"Well, Chloe, whom do you propose that we should hire out?"

"Laws! I an't a proposin' nothin'; only Sam he said der was one of dese yer perfectioners, dey calls 'em, in Louisville, said he wanted a good hand at cake and pastry; and said he'd give four dollars a week to one, he did."

"Well, Chloe."

"Well, laws, I's a thinkin, Missis, it's time Sally was put along to be doin' something. Sally's been under my care, now, dis some time, and she does most as well as me, considerin'; and if Missis would only let me go, I would help fetch up de money. I an't afraid to put my cake, nor pies nother, 'long side no perfectioner's."

"Confectioner's, Chloe."

"Law sakes, Missis! 't an't no odds;—words is so curis, can't never get 'em right!"

"But, Chloe, do you want to leave your children?"

"Laws, Missis! de boys is big enough to do day's works, dey does well enough; and Sally, she'll take de baby,—she's such a peart young un, she won't take no lookin' after."

"Louisville is a good way off."

"Law sakes! who's afeared?—it's down river, somer near my old man, perhaps?" said Chloe, speaking the last in the tone of a question, and looking at Mrs. Shelby.

Illustration titled "An evening in Uncle Tom's Cabin," from an early 20th century edition of *Uncle Tom's Cabin* by Harriet Beecher Stowe. (Lebrecht Music & Arts/Corbis)

"No, Chloe, it's many a hundred miles off," said Mrs. Shelby.

Chloe's countenance fell.

"Never mind; your going there shall bring you nearer, Chloe. Yes, you may go; and your wages shall every cent of them be laid aside for your husband's redemption."

As when a bright sunbeam turns a dark cloud to silver, so Chloe's dark face brightened immediately,—it really shone.

"Laws! if Missis isn't too good! I was thinking of dat ar very thing; 'cause I shouldn't need no clothes, nor shoes, nor nothin',—I could save every cent. How many weeks is der in a year, Missis?"

"Fifty-two," said Mrs. Shelby.

"Laws! now, dere is? and four dollars for each on 'em. Why, how much 'd dat ar be?"

"Two hundred and eight dollars," said Mrs. Shelby.

"Why-e!" said Chloe, with an accent of surprise and delight; "and how long would it take me to work it out, Missis?"

"Some four or five years, Chloe; but, then, you needn't do it all,—I shall add something to it."

"I wouldn't hear to Missis' givin' lessons nor nothin'. Mas'r 's quite right in dat ar;—'t wouldn't do, no ways. I hope none our family ever be brought to dat ar, while I's got hands."

"Don't fear, Chloe; I 'll take care of the honor of the family," said Mrs. Shelby, smiling. "But when do you expect to go?"

"Well, I warn't 'spectin' nothin'; only Sam, he's a gwine to de river with some colts, and he said I could go 'long with him; so I jes put my things together. If Missis was willin', I 'd go with Sam to-morrow morning, if Missis would write my pass, and write me a commendation."

"Well, Chloe, I 'll attend to it, if Mr. Shelby has no objections. I must speak to him."

Mrs. Shelby went up stairs, and Aunt Chloe, delighted, went out to her cabin, to make her preparation.

"Law sakes, Mas'r George! ye didn't know I's a gwine to Louisville to-morrow!" she said to George, as, entering her cabin, he found her busy in sorting over her baby's clothes. "I thought I'd jis look over siss' things, and get 'em straightened up. But I'm gwine, Mas'r George,—gwine to have four dollars a week; and Missis is gwine to lay it all up, to buy back my old man agin!"

"Whew!" said George, "here's a stroke of business, to be sure! How are you going?"

"To-morrow, wid Sam. And now, Mas'r George, I knows you 'll jis sit down and write to my old man, and tell him about it, won't ye?"

"To be sure," said George; "Uncle Tom'll be right glad to hear from us. I'll go right in the house, for paper and ink; and then, you know, Aunt Chloe, I can tell about the new colts and all."

"Sartin, sartin, Mas'r George; you go 'long, and I 'll get ye up a bit o' chicken, or some sich; ye won't have many more suppers wid yer poor old aunty."

Source: Harriet Beecher Stowe, *Uncle Tom's Cabin: Or, Life among the Lowly,* Vol. 2 (Boston: John P. Jewett, 1852), 278–280.

1853 • 53 • William Gilmore Simms, "Maize in Milk: A Christmas Story of the South"

Introduction: *Christmas was not observed in New England where Puritans opposed its celebration, a tradition that lasted well into the 19th century. It was celebrated in southern colonies, which had been mainly settled by Episcopalians and some Catholics in Maryland. William Gilmore Simms (1806–1870), a poet, novelist, and historian from South Carolina, describes an antebellum Christmas celebration in his novel* Marie de Berniere: A Tale of the Crescent City *(1853).*

Maize in Milk: A Christmas Story of the South

Old Colonel Openheart was one of those to whom the every-day world would give the title, sneeringly, of a man of affectations. He was certainly no humdrum personage.

His Christmas dinner, for example, was not a good dinner merely. It was a Christmas dinner. He did not summon his guests to eat, simply, and to drink. The mere swill was not his object. The intellectual tastes were to be consulted, the fancies, the very superstitions, which, in the progress of the ages would naturally accumulate about the practices of a people on peculiar occasions. His Christmas was a season of equal thanksgiving and enjoyment. There was to be a natural ebullition of the feelings at such a time. There should be exultation. High and humble should equally show gratitude; and the natural expression of gratitude is good-humor and cheerfulness. The high was to be high only in the exercise of an ability to make the lowly glad and happy; the humble was to exult in gratifications which showed them consciously in possession of bounties bestowed, in the first instance, by the Lord of all, and intermediately by those whose only boast was in being able in some degree to follow his example in its bounties and its sympathies.

Colonel Openheart strove for these objects. We have glimpsed at some of his household modes of doing this. His Christmas dinner, as it appealed somewhat to the superstitions and the fancies, was designed for this end also. And when the great hall was thrown open to his guests, dressed in a deep Gothic garment of green boughs and branches, sprinkled with red berries and blue, with candles distributed between, and a great oak wood fire blazing at the extremity—with a stately arch of green at each end of the table, and one of triumphal aspect and colossal size spanning its centre—the entering company felt themselves transported to the old baronial domains of our Anglo-Norman ancestry, and their minds were naturally elevated with the moral sentiments which grew out of their recollections of history. The quaint masking was not without its influence. The device was a homily; and when the head waiter made his appearance, bringing in, as the first dish, the "boar's head," done after the ancient Saxon method, dressed in rosemary, and with a huge lemon in its open mouth, they were all in the mood to join in chorus with the host, who, knife in hand, began chanting merrily the ancient carol:—

"Caput api defero
Reddens laudes Domino.
"The bore's head in hand bring we
With garlands gay and rosemarie,
I pray you all sing merrily,
Qui estes in convivio.

"This head you must understand,
Is chief service in this land,
Looke wherever it be scanned,
Servile cum cantico.

"Be glad, gentles, lord and lasse,
That to cheer you this Chrystmasse,
We do bid the bore's head passe,
Clad in rue and rosemarie."

Set in the centre of the table, this "armed head" was soon surrounded by the several solid meats for which John Bull has always been renowned, and the taste for which has been amply inherited in the South, with certain "graftings" of our own. Ham and turkey, for example, are certain as the day at our Christmas, and when venison is procurable it is never omitted from the board. But ours is no mere catalogue. The reader must imagine the variety. He must suppose the presence of roast and boiled—the beef and the venison pastry—the duck as well as the turkey, and much of these to have been stricken wild in the woods and waters, with all the provoking freshness of the game flavor upon them. Wines of ancient denomination—Madeira that had been walled up for thirty years, and sherry that had grown pale, indeed, from weight of years, was at hand; but our host confined himself, on this day, chiefly to his new supply of natty English ale—a potation which did honor to the British breweries. The dessert was composed of the fruits of Cuba and the North, nuts and figs, not forgetting pindars, groundnuts, or peanuts, as they call them north of the Delaware. Nor had the damsels of the household neglected the usual preparation of mince-pies and plum-puddings. In the latter article, in particular, our worthy colonel was resolute to do honor to his ancient English origin, and the plum-pudding was as certainly upon his Christmas table as was the soused head of the boar.

Source: W. Gilmore Simms, "Maize in Milk: A Christmas Story of the South," in *Marie de Berniere: A Tale of the Crescent City* (Philadelphia: Lippincott, Grambo, 1853), 379–382.

1853 • 54 • "Pop, Pop"

Introduction: *Popcorn, a variety of maize with a small hard kernel, appeared on the American culinary scene during the early 19th century. Unlike flint corn, which popped up to double the size of the kernel, popcorn popped up 20 to 50 times the size of the original kernel. This surprised everyone, and beginning in the 1820s, numerous reports of popcorn appeared in a wide variety of sources, such as the poem below in* Harper's Magazine. *Popcorn would not become popular until after the invention of the wire-over-the-fire popper, which made it possible to contain the popped corn in an enclosed space. Popcorn then moved from a novelty into the culinary mainstream.*

Here is a charmingly simple little *Home-Picture,* whose truthfulness will be admitted by thousands among the country readers of "The Drawer."

One autumn night, when the wind was high,
And rain fell in heavy plashes,
A little boy sat by the kitchen-fire,
A-popping corn in the ashes:
And his sister, a curly-haired child of three,
Sat looking on just close to his knee.

The blast went howling round the house,
As if to get in 'twas trying;
It rattled the latch of the outer door,
Then it seemed a baby crying:

Now and then a drop down the chimney came
And sputtered and hissed in the bright, red flame.

Pop, pop! and the kernels, one by one,
Come out of the embers flying;
The boy held a long pine-stick in his hand,
And kept it busily plying;
He stirred the corn, and it snapped the more,
And faster jumped to the clean-swept floor.

Part of the kernels hopped out one way,
And a part hopped out the other;
Some flew plump to the sister's lap,
Some under the stool of the brother:
The little girl gathered them into a hap,
And called them 'a flock of milk-white sheep,'

All at once the boy sat still as a mouse,
And into the fire kept gazing;
He quite forgot he was popping corn,
For he looked where the wood was blazing;
He looked, and he fancied that he could see
A house and a barn, a bird and a tree.

Still steadily gazed the boy at these,
And pussy's back kept stroking,
Till sister cried out, "Why, George,
Only see how the corn is smoking."
And, sure enough, when the boy looked back,
The corn in the ashes was burnt quite black.

"Never mind," said he, "we shall have enough,
So now let's sit back and eat it;
I'll carry the stool, and you the corn—
It's good—nobody can beat it."
She took up the corn in her pinafore,
And they ate it all, nor wished for more.

Source: "Pop, Pop," *Harper's Magazine* 6 (May 1853): 853.

1854 • 55 • "History of Beer"

Introduction: *English colonists brought their love of beer with them, but there were difficulties brewing beer in America, and beer drinking was eclipsed by other beverages, including cider, rum, and whiskey. Lager beer made with bottom fermenting yeast was introduced into the United States by German immigrants who began arriving in the*

1830s. Virtually every city in America that had a large German population also had breweries, and by the 1850s beer was the most popular beverage in America.

In almost every city and town of the United States, where a large German population resides, one or more breweries are to be found. We believe we do not make an exaggerated estimate when we rate the number of German breweries in the United States at upwards of five hundred, and the capital invested at seven to eight millions of dollars. The city of New York has twenty-seven breweries, and many of them, such as Turtle Bay, Gilley's, and Schaefer's, brew more than ten thousand barrels, of thirty gallons each, of lager beer in the course of the year. Williamsburg has thirteen breweries; Brooklyn three; Bedford 1; Morrisania one; Staten Island three; Albany three; Rochester one; Syracuse one; Utica one; Buffalo seven; Philadelphia twenty-eight; Pittsburg eleven; Pottsvilie, Harrisburg, Reading, Cincinnati, ten; Columbus, Cleveland, Chillicothe, Dayton, Toledo, Sandusky, Detroit, Chicago, Milwaukie, eleven; Madison, Guttenberg, Dubuque,

Men holding mugs of beer stand outside Petryl's Saloon in Chicago, Illinois, ca. 1883. (Chicago History Museum/Getty Images)

St. Louis, nineteen; Louisville, Madison, Indianapolis, Evansville, New Orleans, Hermann, (Mo.) Baltimore, Charleston, Savannah, Newark, seventeen.

The New York breweries produce annually about 85,000 barrels of lager beer—thirty gallons per barrel. From Philadelphia are imported about 8,000; from Newark, 5,000; from Bedford, 3,000; from Reading, 1,500. This shows the amount of consumption in the city of New York to be 102,500 barrels of thirty gallons each, or 3,075,000 gallons. The cost of production of a barrel of lager beer, varies—$3,50 to $4, all investments included. The winter beer is sold at $6 to 6,50; the summer or lager beer at $8 to $9 per barrel. The price of the beer, of course, depends on the price of grain and hops, which are at present very high. A bushel of malted barley stands now at eleven to twelve shillings, while in 1852, it was eight to nine shillings only. Hops are sold now at forty-five to fifty cents the pound; at twenty-one cents in 1852. Forty barrels of lager beer require fifty bushels of malt, sixty pounds of hops, three gallons of yeast, and the necessary water. A single brewing requires a half tun of coals. The hands in a German brewery are paid monthly from $10 to $25, besides their full board and free use of as much beer as they can drink. The season for brewing begins late in October and closes early in April.

The beer is sold at retail from four to six and a quarter cents a glass, a sixpence being paid in the better houses, and four and five cents in cellars and small shops. Brewers and retail sellers thus gain from 80 to 100 per cent. each.

According to our account, the beer-drinking public of the city of New York spend, by paying for a glass of beer with five cents, or forty-five cents by the gallon, the enormous sum of $1,383,750! There are about two thousand places in the city where lager beer is sold, and the more thriving hotels and restaurants consume about $5,000 to $6,000 worth of beer in the course of the year.

Lager Beer Retailing in New York.

We have shown how enormous the consumption of lager beer is. It remains now to answer the question: Who drinks these thirty millions, seven hundred and fifty thousand gallons of lager beer annually sold in New York? By far the greater portion is consumed by Germans. It is quite probable that the Germans consume the thirty millions of gallons, and leave to all other nationalities here residing only the 750,000.

As we have already said, there are about two thousand places where lager beer is retailed. Let us take a survey of some of these localities. But before we begin we ought to say a word about the people who keep and those who frequent them. The number of *ci-devant* professors, military officers, students, delegates to legislative assemblies, lawyers, judges and noblemen, who, compelled by the unfortunate issues of the years 1848–9 to leave their fatherland, now try to get a livelihood in this city by keeping lager beer saloons and hotels, is almost incredible. It may appear strange that gentlemen, who in their country occupied a distinguished position, should condescend to embrace a mode of living so many grades lower than that to which they had been accustomed. But want is omnipotent; and nearly all of those who left their country to escape a dungeon, or perhaps an imperial bullet or a royal rope, have left their property in the rapacious claws of their late rulers. Most of them are ignorant of the English language; they are skilled in no craft by which they could make their living; and if a man has been unaccustomed to manual labor for half a life-time, he will hardly be able to earn his daily bread by it here; at least, not until he has served a considerable apprenticeship. But they have a large circle of acquaintances and friends, who will be glad to see them in any situation where they can make a living; and a beer-house is very easily established. It requires no knowledge of English, very little money or credit; and if the new shopkeeper has good paying acquaintances, keeps order in his affairs and makes himself agreeable to his customers, he will accumulate more than he could do by the severest manual or intellectual labor. We may add that without an iron stomach there is less chance for making money. The keeper of a beer-house must always be ready for any amount of drinking, and the more friends he has the stronger should be his stomach and his head.

Let us look into a well-known saloon in William street. We find a small, middle-aged man listening to the noisy declamation of a tall customer, who sports enormous whiskers and mustaches. The tall man appeals to the complaisant host to bear witness to some revolutionary feat which he asserts that he performed several years ago. The walls of the room are adorned with cheap pictures, the most of them being portraits of revolutionary celebrities, such as Kossuth, Mazzini, Hecker, Blum and others; the furniture is very simple, without a vestige of luxury. Seven or eight deal tables, covered with English, German and French papers, and the glasses of the customers present; a dozen chairs nearly all occupied; one or two smoke stained looking-glasses, and a bar with the ordinary fixtures, constitute the inventory. Behind the bar, or rather hanging upon it, is a sleepy looking bar-keeper, roused only by calls for beer or payments offered. A peculiarity of the people is developed in these arrangements. A German must have time for his libations. He cannot march up to the bar, pour out a drink, dash it down without the possibility of tasting it, toss the money over the counter, and rush out like an ignited sky-rocket, as the majority of Americans do. Tables, chairs, newspapers, cigars or pipes, and friends, are not merely comfortable additions, but actual essentials to his enjoyment. Instead of a quarter of a minute he wants at least a quarter of an hour for the proper enjoyment of a drink. Conversation is another essential. However taciturn the German may appear among others, let him sit down at one of these tables and get his glass of lager beer, and a listening friend, and if any one desires to know how much talk a human tongue can reel off in any given period, then is the time to listen. But to our host. If you observe him closely, you will note that be is not yet at ease in his new vocation. He who was but a short time ago the orator to whom hundreds and thousands were listening, is apt to forget what he is now, an humble publican, subject to the rude commands of any one who chooses to show six pence in money and any quantity of self-importance in his saloon. This landlord was one of the most influential leaders of the German democracy, and escaped death, or at least the dungeon for life, by fleeing from his birth-land. Without money and with precarious health, what could he do? He was a lawyer; but the knowledge of German and Roman law is hardly available here. Manual labor his health would not permit. Finally he joined with a partner, (who stays up nights and does the drinking,) and here is our classically educated and talented gentleman—the keeper of a beer saloon. Had any one prophesied this ten years ago, the victim would have laughed at him. Now, he laughs at himself, and bears his blushing honors more philosophically than could have been expected.

The saloons kept by political exiles are nearly all in the lower part of the city. William, North William, Pearl, and Chatham street. City Hall place and the Bowery contain a large number of lager beer saloons. There are a large number in Greenwich, Hudson, and Washington streets; but in these latter streets there are no political exiles selling beer. The emigrant houses are, in the main, respectable; but the cellars in the first and third wards are kept by a hard class and frequented by the lowest of rowdies and vagabonds.

Some of the better class of saloons have other liquors and eatables. There are a number of this sort in Broadway, frequented not only by Germans, but by a constantly increasing representation of Americans. One place in Broadway numbers its daily customers by thousands. We have frequently seen more than a hundred at the tables at once, of whom a sixth part, perhaps, were Americans. Bread and cheese, bread and butter, sardines, and lager beer are the staple articles of trade here. Very little of other drink is called for. One attraction of these places is their cool and retired character. Being generally in large basements or cellars, and in some instances in the adjoining vaults, quite under the street, they are out of the heat, and out of the crowd. This applies particularly to the down-town saloons. Up-town, where rents are lower, the first floor is the usual location. A few years ago, a German beer-house was a sort of sleepy volcano in appearance, because of the enormous amount of smoke sent up from pipes. But now the case is different. Pipe-smoking is getting rare, and the common, low-priced cigars are too villainously bad for any human consumption; so that one may venture into almost any beer-shop without immediate danger of suffocation. That man who has once used good tobacco, and is not entirely cured of any disposition to smoke after burning a hundred of the four-cent cigars of these days, may consider his case hopeless. He is past medication. We opine that the quality of the tobacco, and not a change of taste, has thus materially broken down the German smoking customs.

A well-patronized beer-house will sell from eight to ten kegs per day. One large establishment in Broadway sells fifteen to seventeen. A keg is seven and a half gallons, or quarter of a barrel. So we have for this Broadway establishment four barrels per day, or 1,460 in a year; being 43,800 gallons, or about 525,600 glasses at 6 1-4 cents each, making $32,850 a year for beer alone. Beside this, other drinks are sold, to some extent; and a great quantity of bread and butter, bread and cheese, sardines, etc., disposed of. The annual receipts cannot fall below $45,000. But this is a favorite place, frequented by the best class of Germans and a very large number of Americans, embracing gentlemen of distinguished literary and social position.

Considering the enormous amount of drinking done in them, the German beer-houses are singularly free from rowdyism and noisy disturbances. Lager beer is not strong enough for the class of porter-house ruffians who make night hideous in other places. They take the worst sort of American brandy, a poisonous infusion of alcoholic and fiery drugs, the free use of which almost invariably results in delirium tremens, unless the victim reaches the state prison or the gallows at a very early period. The German people, too, are generally submissive to the laws. Since the tailor riots, there has been no considerable breach of the peace by this class of citizens, nor any serious disturbance in which they have been the aggressors. Except to the law forbidding the sale of liquor on Sunday, they yield a readier obedience to the powers that rule over them than even Americans. We should like to be able to say as much for another large class of aliens and adopted citizens.

Political questions, American as well as foreign, are a leading topic of conversation in the beer-houses. The Germans are naturally inclined to political investigation, and, as a class, they are by no means so ignorant of such matters as has been widely thought.

It is but just to remark that there are a great many vile holes in the lower part of the city, with flaunting German signs, where thieves and prostitutes are harbored, and the vilest of sour beer and adulterated liquors are sold. It is only by chance that respectable people get into these dens, and they are not likely to go there a second time. Respectable Germans keep clear of them, and the only regular frequenters are of the worst class of idlers, thieves, runners, rowdies, and vagabonds of the "rising generation." Most of these places are intolerably filthy, and scarcely a week passes without the shutting up of one or more on account of its dangerous moral and physical character. They are no more like a decent German beer house, than a Five-Point rum rookery is like the Astor House.—*New York Tribune.*

Beer In St. Louis.—The St. Louis *Republican* says there are twenty-four breweries in that city, every one of which stored nearly twice the quantity of "Ale" for the past summer that has been made in any preceding one. Tire manufacture reached sixty thousand barrels—40,000 of "Lager," and 20,000 of ordinary beer; on an average count, one barrel of thirty gallons gives about three hundred glasses; thus we have about twelve millions of glasses of lager beer, and about six millions of common bear; in all eighteen million glasses of beer drank in St. Louis, from the 1st of March last up to the 7th of September, the time the lager beer gave out. Common beer is sold at five dollars per barrel, and lager beer at seven dollars; that is at wholesale; this will make the amount received by the brewers for lager beer $290,000, and for common $100,000—together, say $390,000. The retailers, at five cents a glass, took in $600,000 for lager beer; and $300,000 for the common article. Just think of it. Nearly a million of dollars ($900,000) spent in St. Louis, during one summer, for beer! And that chiefly among the Germans themselves.

Source: *New York Tribune* article, in "History of Beer," *United States Magazine* 1 (October 15, 1854): 179.

1854 • 56 • Henry David Thoreau, "The Bean-field"

Introduction: *Henry David Thoreau (1817–1862), a transcendentalist philosopher and writer, lived for 26 months in the early 1850s alone in the woods at Walden Pond in Massachusetts. He intended it as an experiment in self-reliance. Thoreau lived simply and grew his own food. He wrote about his experiences in his book* Walden: Or Life in the Woods *(1854). The book was an immediate hit and has been regularly read ever since. This excerpt from the book is his attempt to grow beans on two and a half acres of land.*

The Bean-field

. . . [My] beans, the length of whose rows, added together, was seven miles already planted, were impatient to be hoed, for the earliest had grown considerably before the latest were in the ground; indeed they were not easily to be put off. What was the meaning of this so steady and self-respecting, this small Herculean labor, I knew not. I came to love my rows, my beans, though so many more than I wanted. They attached me to the earth, and so I got strength like Antaeus. But why should I raise them? Only Heaven knows. This was my curious labor all summer,—to make this portion of the earth's surface, which had yielded only cinquefoil,[1] blackberries, johnswort,[2] and the like, before, sweet wild fruits and pleasant flowers, produce instead this pulse. What shall I learn of beans or beans of me? I cherish them, I hoe them, early and late I have an eye to them; and this is my day's work. It is a fine broad leaf to look on. My auxiliaries are the dews and rains which water this dry soil, and what fertility is in the soil itself, which for the most part is lean and effete. My enemies are worms, cool days, and most of all woodchucks. The last have nibbled for me a quarter of an acre clean. But what right had I to oust johnswort and the rest, and break up their ancient herb garden? Soon, however, the remaining beans will be too tough for them, and go forward to meet new foes.

When I was four years old, as I well remember, I was brought from Boston to this my native town, through these very woods and this field, to the pond. It is one of the oldest scenes stamped on my memory. And now to-night my flute has waked the echoes over that very water. The pines still stand here older than I; or, if some have fallen, I have cooked my supper with their stumps, and a new growth is rising all around, preparing another aspect for new infant eyes. Almost the same johnswort springs from the same perennial root in this pasture, and even I have at length helped to clothe that fabulous landscape of my infant dreams, and one of the results of my presence and influence is seen in these bean leaves, corn blades, and potato vines.

I planted about two acres and a half of upland; and as it was only about fifteen years since the land was cleared, and I myself had got out two or three cords of stumps, I did not give it any manure; but in the course of the summer it appeared by the arrowheads which I turned up in hoeing, that an extinct nation had anciently dwelt here and planted corn and beans ere white men came to clear the land, and so, to some extent, had exhausted the soil for this very crop.

Before yet any woodchuck or squirrel had run across the road, or the sun had got above the shrub-oaks, while all the dew was on, though the farmers warned me against it,—I would advise you to do all your work if possible while the dew is on,—I began to level the ranks of haughty weeds in my bean-field and throw dust upon their heads. Early in the morning I worked barefooted, dabbling like a plastic artist in the dewy and crumbling sand, but later in the day the sun blistered my feet. There the sun lighted me to hoe beans, pacing slowly backward and forward over that yellow gravelly upland, between the long green rows, fifteen rods, the one end terminating in a shrub oak copse where I could rest in the shade, the other in a blackberry field where the green berries deepened their tints by the time I had made another bout. Removing the weeds, putting fresh soil about the bean stems, and encouraging this weed which I had sown, making the yellow soil express its summer thought in bean leaves and blossoms rather than in wormwood and piper and millet grass, making the earth say beans instead of grass,—this was my daily work. As I had little aid from horses or cattle, or hired men or boys, or improved implements of husbandry, I was much slower, and became much more intimate with my beans than usual. But labor of the hands, even when pursued to the verge of drudgery, is perhaps never the worst form of idleness. It has a constant and imperishable moral, and to the scholar it yields a classic result. A very agricola laboriosus was I to travellers bound westward through Lincoln and Wayland to nobody knows where; they sitting at their ease in gigs, with elbows on knees, and reins loosely hanging in festoons; I the home-staying, laborious native of the soil. But soon my homestead was out of their sight and thought. It was the only open and cultivated field for a great distance on either side of the road, so they made the most of it; and sometimes the man in the field heard more of travellers' gossip and comment than was meant for his ear: "Beans so late! peas so late!"—for I continued to plant when others had begun to hoe,—the ministerial husbandman had not suspected it. "Corn, my boy, for fodder; corn for fodder." "Does he live there?" asks the black bonnet of the gray coat; and the hard-featured farmer reins up his grateful dobbin to inquire what you are doing where he sees no manure in the furrow, and recommends a little chip dirt, or any little waste stuff, or it may be ashes or plaster. But here were two acres and a half of furrows, and only a hoe for cart and two hands to draw it,—there being an aversion to other carts and horses,—and chip dirt far away. Fellow-travellers as they rattled by compared it aloud with the fields which they had passed, so that I came to know how I stood in the agricultural world. This was one field not in Mr. Coleman's report. And, by the way, who estimates the value of the crop which Nature yields in the still wilder fields unimproved by man? The crop of English hay is carefully weighed, the moisture calculated, the silicates and the potash; but in all dells and pond holes in the woods and pastures and swamps grows a rich and various crop only unreaped by man. Mine was, as it were, the connecting link between wild and cultivated fields; as some states are civilized, and others half-civilized, and others savage or barbarous, so my field was, though not in a bad sense, a half-cultivated field. They were beans cheerfully returning to their wild and primitive state that I cultivated, and my hoe played the Ranz des Vaches for them.

Near at hand, upon the topmost spray of a birch, sings the brown-thrasher—or red mavis, as some love to call him—all the morning, glad of your society, that would find out another farmer's field if yours were not here. While you are planting the seed, he cries,—"Drop it, drop it,—cover it up, cover it up,—pull it up, pull it up, pull it up." But this was not corn, and so it was safe from such enemies as he. You may wonder what his rigmarole, his amateur Paganini performances on one string or on twenty, have to do with your planting, and yet prefer it to leached ashes or plaster. It was a cheap sort of top dressing in which I had entire faith.

As I drew a still fresher soil about the rows with my hoe, I disturbed the ashes of unchronicled nations who in primeval years lived under these heavens, and their small implements of war and hunting were brought to the light of this modern day. They lay mingled with other natural stones, some of which bore the marks of having been burned by Indian fires, and some by the sun, and also bits of pottery and glass brought hither by the recent cultivators of the soil. When my hoe tinkled against the stones, that music echoed to the woods and the sky, and was an accompaniment to my labor which yielded an instant and immeasurable crop. It was no longer beans that I hoed, nor I that hoed beans; and I remembered with as much pity as pride, if I remembered at all, my acquaintances who had gone to the city to attend the oratorios. The night-hawk circled overhead in the sunny afternoons—for I sometimes made a day of it—like a mote in the eye, or in heaven's eye. . . .

It was a singular experience that long acquaintance which I cultivated with beans, what with planting, and hoeing, and harvesting, and threshing, and picking over and selling them,—the last was the hardest of all,—I might add eating, for I did taste. I was determined to know beans. When they were growing, I used to hoe from five o'clock in the morning till noon, and commonly spent the rest of the day about other affairs. Consider the intimate and curious acquaintance one makes with various kinds of weeds,—it will bear some iteration in the account, for there was no little iteration in the labor,—disturbing their delicate organizations so ruthlessly, and making such invidious distinctions with his hoe, levelling whole ranks of one species, and sedulously cultivating another. That's Roman wormwood,—that's pigweed,—that's sorrel,—that's piper-grass,—have at him, chop him up, turn his roots upward to the sun, don't let him have a fibre in the shade, if you do he'll turn himself t'other side up and be as green as a leek in two days. A long war, not with cranes, but with weeds, those Trojans who had sun and rain and dews on their side. Daily the beans saw me come to their rescue armed with a hoe, and thin the ranks of their enemies, filling up the trenches with weedy dead. Many a lusty crest-waving Hector, that towered a whole foot above his crowding comrades, fell before my weapon and rolled in the dust.

Those summer days which some of my contemporaries devoted to the fine arts in Boston or Rome, and others to contemplation in India, and others to trade in London or New York, I thus, with the other farmers of New England, devoted to husbandry. Not that I wanted beans to eat, for I am by nature a Pythagorean, so far as beans are concerned, whether they mean porridge or voting, and exchanged them for rice; but, perchance, as some must work in fields if only for the sake of tropes and expression, to serve a parable-maker one day. It was on the whole a rare amusement, which, continued too long, might have become a dissipation. Though I gave them no manure, and did not hoe them all once, I hoed them unusually well as far as I went, and was paid for it in the end, "there being in truth," as Evelyn says, "no compost or laetation[3] whatsoever comparable to this continual motion, repastination, and turning of the mould with the spade." "The earth," he adds elsewhere, "especially if fresh, has a certain magnetism in it, by which it attracts the salt, power, or virtue (call it either) which gives it life, and is the logic of all the labor and stir we keep about it, to sustain us; all dungings and other sordid temperings being but the vicars succedaneous to this improvement." Moreover, this being one of those "worn-out and exhausted lay fields which enjoy their sabbath," had perchance, as Sir Kenelm Digby thinks likely, attracted "vital spirits" from the air. I harvested twelve bushels of beans.

But to be more particular, for it is complained that Mr. Coleman has reported chiefly the expensive experiments of gentlemen farmers, my outgoes were,—

For a hoe,.........$0.54
Ploughing, harrowing, and furrowing, 7.50 Too much.
Beans for seed.........3.12
Potatoes.........1.33
Peas.........0.40
Turnip seed.........0.06
White line for crow fence.........0.02
Horse cultivator and boy three hours.........1.00
Horse and cart to get crop..........0.75

My income was . . . from
Nine bushels and twelve quarts of beans sold.........$16.94
Five large potatoes.........2.50
Nine small.........2.25
Grass.........1.00
Stalks.........0.75
In all.........$23.44
Leaving a pecuniary profit, as I have elsewhere said, of $8.71.

This is the result of my experience in raising beans. Plant the common small white bush bean about the first of June, in rows three feet by eighteen inches apart, being careful to select fresh round and unmixed seed. First look out for worms, and supply vacancies by planting anew. Then look out for woodchucks, if it is an exposed place, for they will nibble off the earliest tender leaves almost clean as they go; and again, when the young tendrils make their appearance, they have notice of it, and will shear them off with both buds and young pods, sitting erect like a squirrel. But above all harvest as early as possible, if you would escape frosts and have a fair and salable crop; you may save much loss by this means.

This further experience also I gained. I said to myself, I will not plant beans and corn with so much industry another summer, but such seeds, if the seed is not lost, as sincerity, truth, simplicity, faith, innocence, and the like, and see if they will not grow in this soil, even with less toil and manurance, and sustain me, for surely it has not been exhausted for these crops. Alas! I said this to myself; but now another summer is gone, and another, and another, and I am obliged to say to you, Reader, that the seeds which I planted, if indeed they were the seeds of those virtues, were worm-eaten or had lost their vitality, and so did not come up. Commonly men will only be brave as their fathers were brave, or timid. This generation is very sure to plant corn and beans each new year precisely as the Indians did centuries ago and taught the first settlers to do, as if there were a fate in it. I saw an old man the other day, to my astonishment, making the holes with a hoe for the seventieth time at least, and not for himself to lie down in! But why should not the New Englander try new adventures, and not lay so much stress on his grain, his potato and grass crop, and his orchards,—raise other crops than these? Why concern ourselves so much about our beans for seed, and not be concerned at all about a new generation of men? We should really be fed and cheered if when we met a man we were sure to see that some of the qualities which I have named, which we all prize more than those other productions, but which are for the most part broadcast and floating in the air, had taken root and grown in him. Here comes such a subtile and ineffable quality, for instance, as truth or justice, though the slightest amount or new variety of it, along the road. Our ambassadors should be instructed to send home such seeds as these, and Congress help to distribute them over all the land. We should never stand upon ceremony with sincerity. We should never cheat and insult and banish one another by our meanness, if there were present the kernel of worth and friendliness. We should not meet thus in haste. Most men I do not meet at all, for they seem not to have time; they are busy about their beans. We would not deal with a man thus plodding ever, leaning on a hoe or a spade as a staff between his work, not as a mushroom, but partially risen out of the earth, something more than erect, like swallows alighted and walking on the ground:—

"And as he spake, his wings would now and then Spread, as he meant to fly, then close again," so that we should suspect that we might be conversing with an angel. Bread may not always nourish us; but it always does us good, it even takes stiffness out of our joints, and makes us supple and buoyant, when we knew not what ailed us, to recognize any generosity in man or Nature, to share any unmixed and heroic joy.

Ancient poetry and mythology suggest, at least, that husbandry was once a sacred art; but it is pursued with irreverent haste and heedlessness by us, our object being to have large farms and large crops merely. We have no festival, nor procession, nor ceremony, not excepting our Cattle-shows and so called Thanksgivings, by which the farmer expresses a sense of the sacredness of his calling, or is reminded of its sacred origin. It is the premium and the feast which tempt him. He sacrifices not to Ceres and the Terrestrial Jove, but to the infernal Plutus rather. By avarice and selfishness, and a grovelling habit, from which none of us is free, of regarding the soil as property, or the means of acquiring property chiefly, the landscape is deformed, husbandry is degraded with us, and the farmer leads the meanest of lives. He knows Nature but as a robber. Cato says that the profits of agriculture are particularly pious or just, (*maximeque plus qucestus*) and according to Varro the old Romans "called the same earth Mother and Ceres, and thought that they who cultivated it led a pious and useful life, and that they alone were left of the race of King Saturn." We are wont to forget that the sun looks on our cultivated fields and on the prairies and forests without distinction. They all reflect and absorb his rays alike, and the former make but a small part of the glorious picture which he beholds in his daily course. In his view the earth is all equally cultivated like a garden. Therefore we should receive the benefit of his light and heat with a corresponding trust and magnanimity. What though I value the seed of these beans, and harvest that in the fall of the year? This broad field which I have looked at so long looks not to me as the principal cultivator, but away from me to influences more genial to it, which water and make it green. These beans have results which are not harvested by me. Do they not grow for woodchucks partly? The ear of wheat, (in Latin spica, obsoletely speca, from spe, hope,) should not be the only hope of the husbandman; its kernel or grain (gramim, from gerendo, bearing,) is not all that it bears. How, then, can our harvest fail? Shall I not rejoice also at the abundance of the weeds whose seeds are the granary of the birds? It matters little comparatively whether the fields fill the farmer's barns. The true husbandman will cease from anxiety, as the squirrels manifest no concern whether the woods will bear chestnuts this year or not, and finish his labor with every day, relinquishing all claim to the produce of his fields, and sacrificing in his mind not only his first but his last fruits also.

Notes

1. A shrub, *Dasiphora fruticosa ssp. floribunda,* common in the northern United States and Canada.
2. St. John's wort (*Hypericum perforatum*).
3. Manure.

Source: Henry David Thoreau, *Walden: Or Life in the Woods,* Vol. 1 (Boston: Houghton, Mifflin, 1854), 241–259.

1855 • 57 • The Hasty Pudding Club, "Pudding Song"

Introduction: *The Hasty Pudding Club is a social club at Harvard University. It was founded in 1770 by students. Hasty pudding, a porridge typically made of ground corn with water or milk, was a common dish served in colonial America. By tradition, it was the first food served at the club's first function and continues to be consumed in honor of that tradition. "Pudding Song" was composed by Theodore Lyman (1833–1897) when he was chorister of the Hasty Pudding Club in 1855 and describes the mystical origin of the club. The club and the song have survived, and at least one president, George W. Bush, was a member of the club while at Harvard.*

Pudding Song

Long since, when our forefathers landed
On barren rock bleak and forlorn
They left their little boat stranded
To search through the wild woods for corn.
Soon some hillocks of earth met their gaze,
Like altars of mystical spell;
But within finding Indian maize
Arrangement in all of them fall

Quoth Standish: "Right hard have we toiled,
A dinner we'll have before long;
A pudding shall quickly be boiled
By help of the Lord and the corn."
At that moment the warhoop resounded.
O'er mountain and valley and glen,
And a Choctaw Chief savagely bounded
To slaughter those corn-steeling men.

"Ha! vile Pagan!" The Captain quoth he.
"'Tis true that we've taken a horn,
But though gained we all of us be,
Then, a wooden spoon held in his hand,
He seized the red foe by the nose,
And with pudding his belly he crammed
In spite of his struggles and throes.

The victor triumphantly grasped
The hair of his foe closely shorn
While the savage he struggled and gasped
O'erpowered by heat and by corn.

"Be converted!" the good Standish said,
"Or surely by fire you'll die,
Through an boiled this for you have fed,
We quickly will give you a fry."

Then straight was the savage baptized
In pudding all smoking and warm
While the Parson he him chatecized
Concerning the cooking of corn.
Then the Puritans chanted a psalm
with a chorus of, "Hey-ruba-dub,"
And amid gentle music's soft chorus
They founded the great Pudding Club.

Source: Theodore Lyman, "The Hasty Pudding Club: Address Delivered on the Club's Centennial, November 24, 1895," in *American Addresses,* edited by Joseph H. Choate (New York: Century, 1911), 144–145.

1855 • 58 • Frederick Douglass, *My Bondage and My Freedom*

Introduction: *Frederick Douglass (ca. 1818–1895) was born into slavery in Maryland. He learned to read from his aunt and from slave owners he worked for. In 1838 he escaped and moved to Massachusetts, where he became an advocate for abolition and a writer. He published several autobiographies of his life, the first in 1845. The excerpts below, detailing how little he had to eat when he was enslaved, are from his book* My Bondage and My Freedom *(1855).*

I had on that day offended "Aunt Katy," (called "Aunt" by way of respect,) the cook of old master's establishment. I do not now remember the nature of my offense in this instance, for my offenses were numerous in that quarter, greatly depending, however, upon the mood of Aunt Katy, as to their heinousness; but she had adopted, that day, her favorite mode of punishing me, namely, making me go without food all day—that is, from after breakfast. The first hour or two after dinner, I succeeded pretty well in keeping up my spirits; but though I made an excellent stand against the foe, and fought bravely during the afternoon, I knew I must be conquered at last, unless I got the accustomed reenforcement of a slice of corn bread, at sundown. Sundown came, but no bread, and, in its stead, their came the threat, with a scowl well suited to its terrible import, that she "meant to starve the life out of me!" Brandishing her knife, she chopped off the heavy slices for the other children, and put the loaf away, muttering, all the while, her savage designs upon myself. Against this disappointment, for I was expecting that her heart would relent at last, I made an extra effort to maintain my dignity; but when I saw all the other children around me with merry and satisfied faces, I could stand it no longer. I went out behind the house, and cried like a fine fellow! When tired of this, I returned to the kitchen, sat by the fire, and brooded over my hard lot. I was too hungry to sleep. While I sat in the corner, I caught sight of an ear of Indian corn on an upper shelf of the kitchen. I watched my chance, and got it, and, shelling off a few grains, I put it back again. The grains in my hand, I quickly put in some ashes, and covered them with embers, to roast them. All this I did at the risk of getting a brutal thumping, for Aunt Katy could beat, as well as starve me. My corn was not long in roasting, and, with my keen appetite, it did not matter even if the grains were not exactly done. I eagerly pulled them out, and placed them on my stool, in a clever little pile. Just as I began to help myself to my very dry meal, in came my dear mother. And now, dear reader, a scene occurred which was altogether worth beholding, and to me it was instructive as well as interesting. The friendless and hungry boy, in his extremest need—and when he did not dare to look for succor—found himself in the strong, protecting arms of a mother; a mother who was, at the moment (being endowed with high powers of manner as well as matter) more than a match for all his enemies. I shall never forget the indescribable expression of her countenance, when I told her that I had had no food since morning; and that Aunt Katy said she "meant to starve the life out of me." There was pity in her glance at me, and a fiery indignation at Aunt Katy at the same time; and, while she took the corn from me, and gave me a large ginger cake, in its stead, she read Aunt Katy a lecture which she never forgot. My mother threatened her with complaining to old master in my behalf; for the latter, though harsh and cruel himself, at times, did not sanction the meanness, injustice, partiality and oppressions enacted by Aunt Katy in the kitchen. That night I learned the fact, that I was not only a child, but somebody's child. The "sweet cake" my mother gave me was in the shape of a heart, with a rich, dark ring glazed upon the edge of it. I was victorious, and well off for the moment; prouder, on my mother's knee, than a king upon his throne.

Aunt Katy was a woman who never allowed herself to act greatly within the margin of power granted to her, no matter how broad that authority might be. Ambitious, ill-tempered and cruel, she found in her present position an ample field for the exercise of her ill-omened qualities. She had a strong hold on old master—she was considered a first rate cook, and she really was very industrious. She was, therefore, greatly favored by old master, and as one mark of his favor, she was the only mother who was permitted to retain her children around her. Even to these children she was often fiendish in her brutality. She pursued her son Phil, one day, in my presence, with a huge butcher knife, and dealt a blow with its edge which left a shocking gash on his arm, near the wrist. For this, old master did sharply rebuke her, and threatened that if she ever should do the like again, he would take the skin off her back. Cruel, however, as Aunt Katy was to her own children, at times she was not destitute of maternal feeling, as I often had occasion to know, in the bitter pinches of hunger I had to endure. Differing from the practice of Col. Lloyd, old master, instead of allowing so much for each slave, committed the allowance for all to the care of Aunt Katy, to be divided after cooking it, amongst us. The allowance, consisting of coarse corn-meal, was not very abundant—indeed, it was very slender; and in passing through Aunt Katy's hands, it was made more slender still, for some of us. William, Phil and Jerry were her children, and it is not to accuse her too severely, to allege that she was often guilty of starving myself and the other children, while she was literally cramming her own. Want of food was my chief trouble the first summer at my old master's. Oysters and clams would do very well, with an occasional supply of bread, but they soon failed in the absence of bread. I speak but the simple truth, when I say, I have often been so pinched with hunger, that I have fought with the dog—"Old Nep"—for the smallest crumbs that fell from the kitchen table, and have been glad when I won a single crumb in the combat. Many times have I followed, with eager step, the waitin' girl when she went out to shake the table cloth, to get the crumbs and small bones flung out for the cats. The water, in which meat had been boiled, was as eagerly sought for by me. It was a great thing to get the privilege of dipping a piece of bread in such water; and the skin taken from rusty bacon, was a positive luxury. Nevertheless, I sometimes got full meals and kind words from sympathizing old slaves, who knew my sufferings, and received the comforting assurance that I should be a man some day. "Never mind, honey—better day comin'," was even then a solace, a cheering consolation to me in my troubles. Nor were all the kind words I received from slaves. I had a friend in the parlor, as well, and one to whom I shall be glad to do justice, before I have finished this part of my story. . . .

It is the boast of slaveholders, that their slaves enjoy more of the physical comforts of life than the peasantry of any country in the world. My experience contradicts this. The men and the women slaves on Col. Lloyd's farm, received, as their monthly allowance of food, eight pounds of pickled pork, or their equivalent in fish. The pork was often tainted, and the fish was of the poorest quality—herrings, which would bring very little if offered for sale in any northern market. With their pork or fish, they had one bushel of

Indian meal—unbolted—of which quite fifteen per cent. was fit only to feed pigs. With this, one pint of salt was given; and this was the entire monthly allowance of a full grown slave, working constantly in the open field, from morning until night, every day in the month except Sunday, and living on a fraction more than a quarter of a pound of meat per day, and less than a peck of corn-meal per week. There is no kind of work that a man can do which requires a better supply of food to prevent physical exhaustion, than the field-work of a slave. So much for the slave's allowance of food; now for his raiment. The yearly allowance of clothing for the slaves on this plantation, consisted of two tow-linen shirts—such linen as the coarsest crash towels are made of; one pair of trowsers of the same material, for summer, and a pair of trowsers and a jacket of woolen, most slazily put together, for winter; one pair of yarn stockings, and one pair of shoes of the coarsest description. The slave's entire apparel could not have cost more than eight dollars per year. The allowance of food and clothing for the little children, was committed to their mothers, or to the older slave women having the care of them. Children who were unable to work in the field, had neither shoes, stockings, jackets nor trowsers given them. Their clothing consisted of two coarse tow-linen shirts—already described—per year; and when these failed them, as they often did, they went naked until the next allowance day. Flocks of little children from five to ten years old, might be seen on Col. Lloyd's plantation, as destitute of clothing as any little heathen on the west coast of Africa; and this, not merely during the summer months, but during the frosty weather of March. The little girls were no better off than the boys; all were nearly in a state of nudity. . . .

As a general rule, slaves do not come to the quarters for either breakfast or dinner, but take their "ash cake" with them, and eat it in the field. This was so on the home plantation; probably, because the distance from the quarter to the field, was sometimes two, and even three miles.

The dinner of the slaves consisted of a huge piece of ash cake, and a small piece of pork, or two salt herrings. Not having ovens, nor any suitable cooking utensils, the slaves mixed their meal with a little water, to such thickness that a spoon would stand erect in it; and, after the wood had burned away to coals and ashes, they would place the dough between oak leaves and lay it carefully in the ashes, completely covering it; hence, the bread is called ash cake. The surface of this peculiar bread is covered with ashes, to the depth of a sixteenth part of an inch, and the ashes, certainly, do not make it very grateful to the teeth, nor render it very palatable. The bran, or coarse part of the meal, is baked with the fine, and bright scales run through the bread. This bread, with its ashes and bran, would disgust and choke a northern man, but it is quite liked by the slaves. They eat it with avidity, and are more concerned about the quantity than about the quality. They are far too scantily provided for, and are worked too steadily, to be much concerned for the quality of their food. The few minutes allowed them at dinner time, after partaking of their coarse repast, are variously spent. . . .

. . . Here, appetite, not food, is the great desideratum. Fish, flesh and fowl, are here in profusion. Chickens, of all breeds; ducks, of all kinds, wild and tame, the common, and the huge Muscovite; Guinea fowls, turkeys, geese, and pea fowls, are in their several pens, fat and fatting for the destined vortex. The graceful swan, the mongrels, the black-necked wild goose; partridges, quails, pheasants and pigeons; choice water fowl, with all their strange varieties, are caught in this huge family net. Beef, veal, mutton and venison, of the most select kinds and quality, roll bounteously to this grand consumer. The teeming riches of the Chesapeake bay, its rock, perch, drums, crocus, trout, oysters, crabs, and terrapin, are drawn hither to adorn the glittering table of the great house. The dairy, too, probably the finest on the Eastern Shore of Maryland—supplied by cattle of the best English stock, imported for the purpose, pours its rich donations of fragrant cheese, golden butter, and delicious cream, to heighten the attraction of the gorgeous, unending round of feasting. Nor are the fruits of the earth forgotten or neglected. The fertile garden, many acres in size, constituting a separate establishment, distinct from the common farm—with its scientific gardener, imported from Scotland, (a Mr. McDermott,) with four men under his direction, was not behind, either in the abundance or in the delicacy of its contributions to the same full board. The tender asparagus, the succulent celery, and the delicate cauliflower; egg plants, beets, lettuce, parsnips, peas, and French beans, early and late; radishes, cantelopes, melons of all kinds; the fruits of all climes and of all descriptions, from the hardy apple of the north, to the lemon and orange of the south, culminated at this point. Baltimore gathered figs, raisins, almonds and juicy grapes from Spain. Wines and brandies from France; teas of various flavor, from China; and rich, aromatic coffee from Java, all conspired to swell the tide of high life, where pride and indolence rolled and lounged in magnificence and satiety. . . .

Let us now glance at the stables and the carriage house, and we shall find the same evidences of pride and luxurious extravagance. Here are three splendid coaches, soft within and lustrous without. Here, too, are gigs, phaetons, harouches, sulkeys and sleighs. Here are saddles and harnesses—beautifully wrought and silver mounted—kept with every care. In the stable you will find, kept only for pleasure, full thirty-five horses, of the most approved blood for speed and beauty. There are two men here constantly employed in taking care of these horses. One of these men must be always in the stable, to answer every call from the great house. Over the way from the stable, is a house built expressly for the hounds—a pack of twenty-five or thirty—whose fare would have made glad the heart of a dozen slaves. Horses and hounds are not the only consumers of the slave's toil. There was practiced, at the Lloyd's, a hospitality which would have astonished and charmed any health-seeking northern divine or merchant, who might have chanced to share it. Viewed from his own table, and not from the field, the colonel was a model of generous hospitality. His house was, literally, a hotel, for weeks during the summer months. At these times, especially, the air was freighted with the rich fumes of baking, boiling, roasting and broiling. The odors I shared with the winds; but the meats were under a more stringent monopoly—except that, occasionally, I got a cake from Mas' Daniel. In Mas' Daniel I had a friend at court, from whom I learned many things which my eager curiosity was excited to know. I always knew when company was expected, and who they were, although I was an outsider, being the property, not of Col. Lloyd, but of a servant of the wealthy colonel. On these occasions, all that pride, taste and money could do, to dazzle and charm, was done.

Who could say that the servants of Col. Lloyd were not well clad and cared for, after witnessing one of his magnificent entertainments? Who could say that they did not seem to glory in being the slaves of such a master? Who, but a fanatic, could get up any sympathy for persons whose every movement was agile, easy and graceful, and who evinced a consciousness of high superiority? And who would ever venture to suspect that Col. Lloyd was subject to the troubles of ordinary mortals? Master and slave seem alike in their glory here? Can it all be seeming? Alas! it may only be a sham at last! This immense wealth; this gilded splendor; this profusion of luxury; this exemption from toil; this life of ease; this sea of plenty; aye, what of it all? Are the pearly gates of happiness and sweet content flung open to such suitors? *far from it!* The poor slave, on his hard, pine plank, but scantily covered with his thin blanket, sleeps more soundly than the feverish voluptuary who reclines upon his feather bed and downy pillow. Food, to the indolent lounger, is poison, not sustenance. Lurking beneath all their dishes, are invisible spirits of evil, ready to feed the self-deluded gormandizers with aches, pains, fierce temper, uncontrolled passions, dyspepsia, rheumatism, lumbago and gout; and of these the Lloyds got their full share. To the pampered love of ease, there is no resting place. What is pleasant to-day, is repulsive to-morrow; what is soft now, is hard at another time; what is sweet in the morning, is bitter in the evening. Neither to the wicked, nor to the idler, is there any solid peace: "*Troubled, like the restless sea.*" . . .

But, to my story. It was now more than seven years since I had lived with Master Thomas Auld, in the family of my old master, on Col. Lloyd's plantation. We were almost entire strangers to each other; for, when I knew him at the house of my old master, it was not as a master, but simply as "Captain Auld," who had married old master's daughter. All my lessons concerning his temper and disposition, and the best methods of pleasing him, were yet to be learnt. Slaveholders, however, are not very ceremonious in approaching a slave; and my ignorance of the new material in the shape of a master was but transient. Nor was my new mistress long in making known her animus. She was not a "Miss Lucretia," traces of whom I yet remembered, and the more especially, as I saw them shining in the face of little Amanda, her daughter, now living under a step-mother's government. I had not forgotten the soft hand, guided by a tender heart, that bound up with healing balsam the gash made in my head by Ike, the son of Abel. Thomas and Rowena, I found to be a well-matched pair. He was stingy, and she was cruel; and—what was quite natural in such cases—she possessed the ability to make him as cruel as herself, while she could easily descend to the level of his meanness. In the house of Master Thomas, I was made—for the first time in seven years—to feel the pinchings of hunger, and this was not very easy to bear.

For, in all the changes of Master Hugh's family, there was no change in the bountifulness with which they supplied me with food. Not to give a slave enough to eat, is meanness intensified, and it is so recognized among slaveholders generally, in Maryland. The rule is, no matter how coarse the food, only let there be enough of it. This is the theory, and—in the part of Maryland I came from—the general practice accords with this theory. Lloyd's plantation was an exception, as was, also, the house of Master Thomas Auld.

All know the lightness of Indian corn-meal, as an article of food, and can easily judge from the following facts whether the statements I have made of the stinginess of Master Thomas, are borne out. There were four slaves of us in the kitchen, and four whites in the great house—Thomas Auld, Mrs. Auld, Hadaway Auld, (brother of Thomas Auld,) and little Amanda. The names of the slaves in the kitchen, were Eliza, my sister; Priscilla, my aunt; Henny, my cousin; and myself. There were eight persons in the family. There was, each week, one half bushel of corn-meal brought from the mill; and in the kitchen, corn-meal was almost our exclusive food, for very little else was allowed us. Out of this half bushel of corn-meal, the family in the great house had a small loaf every morning; thus leaving us, in the kitchen, with not quite a half a peck of meal per week, apiece. This allowance was less than half the allowance of food on Lloyd's plantation. It was not enough to subsist upon; and we were, therefore, reduced to the wretched necessity of living at the expense of our neighbors. We were compelled either to beg, or to steal, and we did both. I frankly confess, that while I hated everything like stealing, as such, I nevertheless did not hesitate to take food, when I was hungry, wherever I could find it. Nor was this practice the mere result of an unreasoning instinct; it was, in my case, the result of a clear apprehension of the claims of morality. I weighed and considered the matter closely, before I ventured to satisfy my hunger by such means. Considering that my labor and person were the property of Master Thomas, and that I was by him deprived of the necessaries of life—necessaries obtained by my own labor—it was easy to deduce the right to supply myself with what was my own. It was simply appropriating what was my own to the use of my master, since the health and strength derived from such food were exerted in his service. To be sure, this was stealing, according to the law and gospel I heard from St. Michael's pulpit; but I had already begun to attach less importance to what dropped from that quarter, on that point, while, as yet, I retained my reverence for religion. It was not always convenient to steal from master, and the same reason why I might, innocently, steal from him, did not seem to justify me in stealing from others. In the case of my master, it was only a question of *removal*—the taking his meat out of one tub, and putting it into another; the ownership of the meat was not affected by the transaction. At first, he owned it in the *tub,* and last, he owned it in *me.* His meat house was not always open. There was a strict watch kept on that point, and the key was on a large bunch in Rowena's pocket. A great many times have we, poor creatures, been severely pinched with hunger, when meat and bread have been moulding under the lock, while the key was in the pocket of our mistress. This had been so when she knew we were nearly half starved; and yet, that mistress, with saintly air, would kneel with her husband, and pray each morning that a merciful God would bless them in basket and in store, and save them, at last, in his kingdom. But I proceed with the argument.

It was necessary that the right to steal from others should be established; and this could only rest upon a wider range of generalization than that which supposed the right to steal from my master. . . .

Bad as my condition was when I lived with Master Thomas, I was soon to experience a life far more goading and bitter. The many differences springing up between myself and Master Thomas, owing to the clear perception I had of his character, and the boldness with which I defended myself against his capricious complaints, led him to declare that I was unsuited to his wants; that my city life had affected me perniciously; that, in fact, it had almost ruined me for every good purpose, and had fitted me for everything that was bad. One of my greatest faults, or offenses, was that of letting his horse get away, and go down to the farm belonging to his father-in-law. The animal had a liking for that farm, with which I fully sympathized. Whenever I let it out, it would go dashing down the road to Mr. Hamilton's, as if going on a grand frolic. My horse gone, of course I must go after it. The explanation of our mutual attachment to the place is the same; the horse found there good pasturage, and I found there plenty of bread. Mr. Hamilton had his faults, but starving his slaves was not among them. He gave food, in abundance, and that, too, of an excellent quality. In Mr. Hamilton's cook—Aunt Mary—I found a most generous and considerate friend. She never allowed me to go there without giving me bread enough to make good the deficiencies of a day or two. Master Thomas at last resolved to endure my behavior no longer; he could neither keep me, nor his horse, we liked so well to be at his father-in-law's farm. I had now lived with him nearly nine months, and he had given me a number of severe whippings, without any visible improvement in my character, or my conduct; and now he was resolved to put me out—as he said—"*to be broken.*"

There was, in the Bay Side, very near the camp ground, where my master got his religious impressions, a man named Edward Covey, who enjoyed the execrated reputation, of being a first rate hand at breaking young negroes. This Covey was a poor man, a farm renter; and this reputation, (hateful as it was to the slaves and to all good men,) was, at the same time, of immense advantage to him. It enabled him to get his farm tilled with very little expense, compared with what it would have cost him without this most extraordinary reputation. Some slave-holders thought it an advantage to let Mr. Covey have the government of their slaves a year or two, almost free of charge, for the sake of the excellent training such slaves got under his happy management! Like some horse breakers, noted for their skill, who ride the best horses in the country without expense, Mr. Covey could have under him, the most fiery bloods of the neighborhood, for the simple reward of returning them to their owners, well broken. Added to the natural fitness of Mr. Covey for the duties of his profession, he was said to "enjoy religion," and was as strict in the cultivation of piety, as he was in the cultivation of his farm. I was made aware of his character by some who had been under his hand; and while I could not look forward to going to him with any pleasure, I was glad to get away from St. Michael's. I was sure of getting enough to eat at Covey's, even if I suffered in other respects. This, to a hungry man, is not a prospect to be regarded with indifference.

Source: Frederick Douglass, *My Bondage and My Freedom* (New York and Auburn: Miller, Orton and Mulligan, 1855), 54–55, 75 100–101, 104, 117, 111–112, 187–189, 202–203.

1857 • 59 • Sarah J. Hale, "Cookery, As an Art"

Introduction: *Until the late 19th century, cookery was considered an art. Here is a good statement by Sarah J. Hale (1788–1879), a popular writer and the editor of* Godey's Magazine, *the most popular woman's magazine at the time. Notice how she defines roles of husbands and wives—"The husband earns, the wife dispenses"—and how important she views cookery when done properly: "it promotes health and happiness, moral and social improvement, and adds the charm of contentment to every-day life." Hale also opposes the advocates of vegetarianism.*

Cookery, as an Art, ranks in the highest department of useful knowledge, connected, as it is, with the welfare of every human being.

When understood in all its bearings and conducted on scientific principles, it promotes health and happiness, moral and social improvement, and adds the charm of contentment to every-day life.

Is not the Table, when wisely ordered with economy, skill, and taste, the central attraction of Home? And the lady who, with kindness, thoughtfulness, and dignity presides, does she not receive homage from the master of the house when he places at her disposal the wealth for which he toils?

The husband earns, the wife dispenses: are not her duties as important as his?

If these truths were acknowledged and acted upon, by giving to the Science of Domestic Economy a prominent place in the education of young ladies, we should soon see great improvement in household management.

Lithograph shows a woman in a kitchen with a cast-iron stove, from "Prang's Aids for Object Teaching: Tinsmith, Blacksmith, Baker and The Kitchen," 1874. (Library of Congress)

There are encouraging signs of reform. Some of the most esteemed among our lady writers have devoted their talents to the illustration of these home duties: the cookery books of Mrs. Child, Miss Leslie, Miss Beecher, and others, have done much for tho cause of Domestic Economy. Still it appeared to me that a "new book" on this science, combining features not hitherto included in any work of the kind, was needed. Some of these new features are the following:—

In this work the true relations of food to health are set forth, and the importance of good cookery to the latter clearly explained. . . .

"Preparations of Food for the Sick" have been carefully attended to, and many new and excellent receipts introduced.

"Cookery for Children" is an entirely new feature in a work of this kind, and of much importance.

A greater variety of receipts, for preparing Fish, Vegetables, and Soups, is given here, than can be found in any other book of the kind; these preparations, having reference to the large and increasing class of persons in our country who abstain from flesh meats during Lent, will be found excellent; and useful also to all families during the hot season.

As our Republic is made up from the people of all lands, so I have gathered the best receipts from the Domestic Economy of the different nations of the Old World.

Emigrants from each country will, in this "New Cook Book," find the method of preparing their favorite dishes.

The prominent features are, however, American. My own experience and studies gave some peculiar advantages in understanding "household good"; and then I have been favored by ladies, famed for their excellent housekeeping, with large collections of original receipts, which these ladies have tested in their own families. I feel, therefore, confident that this "New Cook Book" will be approved.

It has been my aim to give all directions in a concise, straightforward manner, and so vary the receipts and modes, that every American household may model its management, to advantage, from the instructions. . . .

Philosophy of Cookery

One of the first duties of woman in domestic life is to understand the quality of provisions and the preparation of wholesome food.

The powers of the mind, as well as those of the body, are greatly dependent on what we eat and drink. The stomach must be in health, or the brain cannot act with its utmost vigor and clearness, nor can there be strength of muscle to perform the purposes of the will.

But further, woman, to be qualified for the duty which Nature has assigned her, that of promoting the health, happiness and implement of her species, must understand the natural laws of the human constitution, and the causes which often render the efforts she makes to please the appetite of those she loves, the greatest injury which could be inflicted upon them. Often has the affectionate wife caused her husband a sleepless night and severe distress, which, had an enemy inflicted, she would scarcely have forgiven—because she has prepared for him food which did not agree with his constitution or habits.

And many a tender mother has, by pampering and inciting the appetites of her young sons, laid the foundation of their future course of selfishness and profligacy.

If the true principles of preparing food were understood, these errors would not be committed, for the housekeeper would then feel sure that the best food was that which best nourished and kept the whole System in healthy action; and that such food would be best relished, because, whenever the health is injured, the appetite is impaired or vitiated. She would no longer allow those kinds of food, which reason and experience show are bad for the constitution, to appear at her table.

We have, therefore, sought to embody, from reliable sources, the philosophy of Cookery, and here give to those who consult our "New Book" such prominent facts as will help them in their researches after the true way of living well and being well while we live.

Modern discovery has proved that the stomach can create nothing; that it can no more furnish us with flesh out of food, in which, when swallowed, the elements of flesh are wanting, than the cook can send us up roast beef without the beef to roast. There was no doubt as to the cook and the beef, but the puzzle about the stomach came of our not knowing what matters various sorts of food really did contain; from our not observing the effects of particular kinds of food when eaten without anything else for some time, and from our not knowing the entire uses of food. But within the last few years measures and scales have told us these things with just the same certainty as they set out the suet and raisins, currants, flour, spices, and sugar, of a plum-pudding, and in a quite popular explanation it may be said that we need food that as we breathe it may warm us, and to renew our bodies as they are wasted by labor. Each purpose needs a different kind of food. The best for the renewal of our strength is slow to furnish heat; the best to give us heat will produce no strength. But this does not tell the whole need for the two kinds of food. Out frames are wasted by labor and exercise; at every move some portion of our bodies is dissipated in the form either of gas or water; at every breath a portion of our blood is swallowed, it may be said, by one of the elements of the air, oxygen: and of strength-giving food alone it is scarce possible to eat enough to feed at once the waste of our bodies, and this hungry oxygen. With this oxygen our life is in wine sort a continual battle; we must either supply it with especial food, or it will prey upon ourselves;—a body wasted by starvation is simply eaten up by oxygen. It likes fat best, so the fat goes first; then the lean, then the brain; and if from so much waste, death did not result, the sinews and very bones would be lost in oxygen. . . .

It is an established truth in physiology, that man is omnivorous—that is, constituted to eat almost every kind of food which, separately, nourishes other animals. His teeth are formed to masticate and his stomach to digest flesh, fish, and all farinaceous and vegetable substances—he can eat and digest these even in a raw state; but it is necessary to perfect them for his nourishment in the most healthy manner, that they be prepared by cooking—that is, softened by the action of fire and water.

In strict accordance with this philosophy, which makes a portion of animal food necessary to develop and sustain the human constitution, in its most perfect state of physical, intellectual and moral strength and beauty, we know that now in every country, where a mixed diet is habitually used, as in the temperate climates. there the greatest improvement of the race is to be found, and the greatest energy of character. It is that portion of the human family, who have the means of obtaining this food at least once a day, who now hold dominion over the earth. Forty thousand of the beef-fed British govern and control ninety millions of the rice-eating natives of India.

In every nation on earth the rulers, the men of power, whether princes or priests, almost invariably use a portion of animal food. The people are often compelled, either from poverty or policy, to abstain.—Whenever the time shall arrive that every peasant in Europe is able to "put his pullet in the pot, of a Sunday," a great improvement will have taken place in his character and condition; when he can have a portion of animal food, properly cooked, once each day, he will soon become a man.

In our own country, the beneficial effects of a generous diet, in developing and sustaining the energies of a whole nation, are clearly evident. The severe and unremitting labors of every kind, which were requisite to subdue and obtain dominion of a wilderness world, could not have been done by a half-starved, suffering people. A larger quantity and better quality of food are necessary here than would have supplied men in the old countries, where less action of body and mind are permitted.

Still, there is great danger of excess in all indulgences of the appetite; even when a present benefit may be obtained, this danger should never be forgotten. The tendency in our country has been to excess in animal fond. The advocates of the vegetable diet system had good cause for denouncing this excess, and the indiscriminate use of flesh. It was, and now is, frequently given to young children—infants before they have teeth,—a sin against nature, which often costs the life of the poor little sufferer; it is eaten too freely by the sedentary and delicate; and to make it worse still, it is eaten, often in a half-cooked state, and swallowed without sufficient chewing. All these things are wrong, and ought to be reformed.

Source: Sarah J. Hale, *Mrs. Hale's New Cook Book* (Philadelphia: T. B. Peterson and Brothers, 1857), xix–xx, xxxvii–xliv.

1857 • 60 • Thomas Butler Gunn, "The Vegetarian Boarding-house (As It Was)"

Introduction: *In the mid-19th century, hotels were mainly for the well-to-do. For most Americans, the boardinghouse was the place to stay. As Walt Whitman proclaimed in 1842, the "universal Yankee nation" was "a boarding people." Boardinghouses were often people's homes, and they rented out rooms for lodgers. The vegetarian movement in the mid-19th century spawned vegetarian hotels and boardinghouses, such as the one that Thomas Butler Gunn (1826–1904) describes below.*

Our meals—at which we formed a snug family party—were served with uniform cleanliness, and excellently prepared. Every thing was of the herbaceous or farinaceous description, of course. We had no meats, no fish, no gravy-soups. Tea and coffee were also rejected, as stimulants. But every variety of vegetable appeared at our table, as also fruit and pastry. (No butter entered into the composition of the latter, that being a tabooed article.) Bananas, melons, peaches, grapes, oranges, cherries, pine-apples; all the daintier forms of Vegetarian fare were provided with a liberal hand. The display, indeed, exceeded our expectations. We saw Vegetarian diet under its most attractive (summer) aspect. Whether the fraternity were confined to turnips, etc., during the winter season, we can not determine. In spring they generally went out to graze at a country Establishment, located somewhere in Connecticut, and owned by a relative of the landlord's.

Source: Thomas Butler Gunn, *The Physiology of New York Boarding-Houses* (New York: Mason Brothers Publication, 1857), 184–185.

1858 • 61 • Henry Wadsworth Longfellow, "Catawba Wine"

Introduction: *French settlers in Cincinnati began growing Catawba grapes near Cincinnati in the late 18th century. Nicholas Longworth (1783–1863) arrived in Cincinnati in 1803 and acquired a vineyard. He slowly built up his business, which thrived during the next several decades. Longworth sent some Catawba wine to the American poet Henry Wadsworth Longfellow (1807–1882), who then wrote a poem in praise of Longworth's Catawba wine.*

Catawba Wine

This s.ong of mine
Is a Song of the Vine,
To be sung by the glowing embers

Of wayside inns,
When the rain begins
To darken the drear Novembers.

It is not a song
Of the Scuppernong,
From warm Carolinian valleys,
Nor the Isabel
And the Muscadel
That bask in our garden alleys.

Nor the red Mustang,
Whose clusters hang
O'er the waves of the Colorado,
And the fiery flood
Of whose purple blood
Has a dash of Spanish bravado.

For richest and best
Is the wine of the West,
That grows by the Beautiful River;
Whose sweet perfume
Fills all the room
With a benison on the giver.

And as hollow trees
Are the haunts of bees,
Forever going and coming;
So this crystal hive
Is all alive
With a swarming and buzzing and humming.

Very good in its way
Is the Verzenay,
Or the Sillery soft and creamy;
But Catawba wine
Has a taste more divine,
More dulcet, delicious, and dreamy.

There grows no vine
By the haunted Rhine,
By Danube or Guadalquivir,
Nor on island or cape,
That bears such a grape
As grows by the Beautiful River.

Drugged is their juice
For foreign use,
When shipped o'er the reeling Atlantic,
To rack our brains

With the fever pains,
That have driven the Old World frantic.

To the sewers and sinks
With all such drinks,
And after them tumble the mixer;
For a poison malign
Is such Borgia wine,
Or at best but a Devil's Elixir.

While pure as a spring
Is the wine I sing,
And to praise it, one needs but name it;
For Catawba wine
Has need of no sign,
No tavern-bush to proclaim it.

And this Song of the Vine,
This greeting of mine,
The winds and the birds shall deliver
To the Queen of the West,
In her garlands dressed,
On the banks of the Beautiful River.

Source: Henry Wadsworth Longfellow, "Catawba Wine," *Cozzen's Wine Press* 1 (January 20, 1858): 165.

1858 • 62 • Charles A. Goodrich, "Food"

Introduction: *Charles A. Goodrich (1790–1862) was a theologian who wrote books for adolescents. His History of the United States of America, first published in 1817, included considerable information about the food consumed in different regions of the United States before the Civil War.*

1. Food.—The people of no country on the globe are better, or so well fed, as the Americans. It is emphatically a land of plenty. In European countries, starvation is not uncommon: in the United States, it is a rare event.

2. With some nations the culinary art has attained to great perfection; and, in the United States, a marked advance has been made, within a few years. The employment of European cooks is not uncommon. The bills of fare on the tables of many of our principal hotels, in New York, Boston, Baltimore, Cincinnati,—especially on great occasions,—would compare well with those in London, Paris, and other trans-Atlantic cities. Our beef is said still to be inferior to the "roast beef of old England"; but it is a distinction, in some cases, it is believed, without a difference.

3. The Americans generally eat fast. They are too busy otherwise to enjoy their meals. Even the dinner, which is that great meal of the day, and altogether so with the English, and to which they give time, the Americans despatch often in a few minutes. Our breakfasts are

much richer and more substantial than theirs. Our suppers are various. With some classes, it is a light concern: with the laboring classes, it often consists of the most substantial food.

4. In New England, in the country towns, breakfast is usually at an early hour; often at sunrise, or before. In a farmer's family, it consists of ham, beef, sausages, pork, bread, butter, boiled or fried potatoes, pies, and coffee.

5. The use of coffee in the morning, and often at night, is almost universal. At hotels and boarding-houses, there is often a greater variety of dishes. In cities, the usual bread is made of wheat flour; on the other hand, in the country, until within a few years, the common bread was made of rye, or a mixture of rye and Indian corn. Wheat, however, has been substituted, to a great extent, especially in manufacturing districts. Hasty pudding was formerly a favorite dish, and most commonly prepared on Saturday evening. It was eaten with milk when warm, and fried when cooled. The Indian pudding, also, was once a very favorite dish throughout New England.

6. In the Middle States, the diet is much as in New England. More use, however, is made of the sweet potato, which is raised in New Jersey, and in states south of it. It is cooked variously, though it is generally preferred boiled or baked. Buckwheat is extensively used in the Middle States, though not peculiar to any one section. Hominy—coarse Indian meal-is much used.

7. In the Southern States, the food differs considerably from what it is at the North. Garden vegetables are not extensively cultivated; the Irish potato does not thrive; the sweet potato abounds. Rice, generally boiled, is a substitute for vegetables, and even for bread. Hominy is found at all tables. Hoe-cake,—the johnny-cake of New England,—and ash-pone,—a coarse cake, baked under the ashes,—are in as common use as bread. Ham is a general article, and often found on the table three times a day. In Virginia, it is commonly, in the season, accompanied by greens. In Louisiana, gumbo, a compound soup, is much used: in New Orleans, it is sold in the streets.

8. In the Western States, the two great articles of food are bacon and Indian corn. Fish abound in the rivers; but they are coarse. Game is plenty, rice is used: it is commonly boiled hard, and eaten with gravy. Coffee is very common, as are maple and other sugars. In the western cities and larger towns, however, within a few years, nearly all the varieties and delicacies of living are to be found which exist in any part of the country. The facilities for rapid transportation have so increased, that, in a few days, the finest fish, oysters, lobsters of the east, and other delicacies, can be furnished at Buffalo, Cleveland, and even Cincinnati, in the greatest perfection.

Source: Charles Augustus Goodrich, *A History of the United States of America* (Boston: Hickling, Swan and Brewer, 1858), 322–323.

1858 • 63 • John L. Mason, "Improvement in Screw-Neck Bottles"

Introduction: *On November 30, 1858, a 36-year old inventor, John L. Mason (1832–1902), patented the self-sealing zinc lid and glass jar. The screw-on lid greatly simplified the canning process and made the jars genuinely reusable. This revolutionized fruit and vegetable preservation in the home. The jars were easy to use and comparatively inexpensive to produce, and their popularity soared. By 1860, Mason jars*

John Landis Mason seated alongside stack of Mason jars, 1858. (Library of Congress)

were shipped throughout the United States. The Mason jar revolutionized home canning and commercial bottle production, such as mayonnaise jars and ketchup bottles, in the United States.

No. 22,186.—John L. Mason, of New York, N. Y.—Improvement in Screw-Neck Bottles.—Patent dated November 30,1858.—The engraving A represents the top or nozzle of the bottle. The screw thread terminates before reaching the top or bottom of the neck.

Be it known that I, John L. Mason, of the city, county, and State of New York, have invented new and useful Improvements in the Necks of Bottles, Jars, & especially such as are intended to be air and water tight, such as are used for sweetmeats, & of which the following is a specification. . . .

I claim a screw neck or nozzle of a jar or bottle in combination with a groove separating the head from the shoulder of the bottle or jar, as described.

I also claim a screw on the exterior of the neck of a bottle or jar in which the neck extends above the screw thread and the thread vanishes into the neck of the bottle or jar, substantially as described.

Source: Improvement in Screw-neck Bottles, Letters Patent No. 22,186, dated November 30, 1858.

1859 • 64 • Charles Mackay, "The Chief Wealth of Cincinnati Is Derived from the Hogs"

Introduction: *By far the most important meat for Americans until the late 19th century was pork. Cincinnati was an important hog-packing center and acquired the nickname "Porkopolis" by 1835. During the 1850s, German immigrants began flooding into the Midwest, bringing new techniques for salting meat, especially pork. German-owned packing facilities were established in such midwestern cities as Cincinnati, and pork production skyrocketed. The British writer Charles Mackay visited Cincinnati in 1857, and below is the description of the city that he published in his Life and Liberty in America (1859).*

. . . [T]he chief wealth of Cincinnati is derived from the hogs raised in the rich agricultural districts of Ohio, and slaughtered here, to the number of about 600,000 annually. The slaughter-houses are the great curiosities of the place; but, having a respect for hog as an article of diet, and relishing, at fitting seasons, both the ham and the rasher of bacon, I would not impair that respect, or diminish that relish, by witnessing the wholesale slaughter of the animal, however scientifically the slaughtering might be effected. I therefore left the slaughter-houses unvisited, contented to believe, upon hearsay, the marvellous tales which are related of the dexterity of the slaughterers, who, armed with heavy hammers, which they hold in both hands, are sometimes known to stun as many as sixty hogs in a minute, leaving them in that state to an assistant butcher, who with almost equal rapidity follows in the wake, and cuts their throats before they have time to recover from the stunning blow and vent their alarm by a single shriek. The 600,000 hogs slaughtered in the city are converted into packed merchandise with less noise than often attends the killing of one porker in the farmsteads of England. From the moment when the hog received the first hammer-stroke until it was singed, cleaned, cut up, placed in brine, and packed in a cask for exportation, not more than two hours were formerly suffered to elapse. But this celerity, being unnatural, led to mischief. The pork, drowned in brine before it had time to become cold, caused a fermentation in the pickle, and this fermentation in its turn caused a disease in the pork which was called measles, and which, whether deserving or not of this appellation, rendered it unwholesome. Much injury was thus done to the trade. The cause of the mischief was fully reported upon by the British Consul at New Orleans; and the men of Cincinnati, made wise by experience, now stay their hands and allow the pork to cool before they pickle it.

All Cincinnati is redolent of swine. Swine prowl about the streets and act the part of scavengers until they are ready to become merchandise and visit Europe. Swine are driven into it daily and hourly by every avenue; but not one of them ever goes out again alive. Barrels of them line all the quays; cartloads of their carcasses traverse the city at all seasons; and palaces and villas are built, and vineyards and orchards cultivated, out of the proceeds of their flesh, their bones, their lard, their bristles, and their feet.

In the early days of the pork trade, the feet and entrails of the swine were cast as rubbish on to the quays and streets, or swept into the waters of the Ohio, to be thence transferred, via the Mississippi, into the Gulf of Mexico. But the

Cincinnatians have learned more wisdom; and not the smallest portion of the animal is now allowed to be wasted. The entrails are boiled into lard; the feet are prepared as an article of food, or stowed into glue; and the blood carefully collected is used for various chemical purposes, besides being employed in the manufacture of black-puddings for home consumption. The average value of the hog before he is slaughtered is about ten dollars, or 21. sterling, so that from this source alone one million and a quarter sterling is annually brought into the purses of the farmers and people of Ohio and of its chief commercial city of Cincinnati. So plentiful are swine in Ohio, so much more plentiful and cheap in some parts than coals, that ere now pork has been burned instead of fuel to keep up the fires of steam-boats on the Ohio. Only three days ago I read a newspaper paragraph in reprobation of such cruel extravagance.

Source: Charles Mackay, *Life and Liberty in America: Or, Sketches of a Tour in the United States and Canada, in 1857–8* (New York: Harper and Brothers, 1859), 200–201.

1859 • 65 • "Clam-Bake"

Introduction: *Clams were plentiful along the New England coast and had been harvested by American Indians for hundreds of years. Clambakes were social gatherings in New England that began in the early 19th century. They could consist of a small family group or, as the report below indicates, thousands of people.*

Clam-bake. Clams, baked in the primitive style of the Indians, furnish one of the most popular dishes on those parts of the coast where they abound, and constitute a main feature in the bill of fare at pic-nics and other festive gatherings. The method of baking is as follows: A cavity is dug in the earth, about eighteen inches deep, which is lined with round stones. On this a fire is made; and, when the stones are sufficiently heated, a bushel or more of hard clams (according to the number of persons who are to partake of the feast) is thrown upon them. On this is put a layer of rock-weed gathered from the beach, and over this a second layer of sea-weed. Sometimes the clams are simply placed close together on the ground, with the hinges uppermost, and over them is made a fire of brush. This is called an *Indian bed* of clams. Clams baked in this manner are preferred to those cooked in the usual way in the kitchen.

Parties of ten or twenty persons, of both sexes, are the most common. Often they extend to a hundred, when other amusements are added; and on one occasion, that of a grand political mass-meeting in favor of Gen. Harrison on the 4th of July, 1840, nearly 10,000 persons assembled in Rhode Island, for whom a *clambake* and *chowder* were prepared. This was probably the greatest feast of the kind that ever took place in New England.

Clam-shell. The lips, or mouth. There is a common though vulgar expression in New England, of "Shut your clam-shell," that is, "Shut your mouth, hold your tongue." The padlock now used on the United States mail-bags is called the "Clam-shell padlock."

Source: John Russell Bartlett, *Bartlett's Dictionary of Americanisms,* 2nd ed. (Boston: Little, Brown, 1859), 84.

1859 • 66 • "An Eight Day's Trip in the Mountains"

Introduction: *Below is a newspaper article about a party that was headed into the mountains near Santa Rosa, California. The list is the amount of supplies the party will need for this eight-day trip. The article does not say how large the party was, but judging from the amount of food, it was not very big. What is striking about the list is the amount of alcohol compared with the amount of food.*

A party recently left Joe's store at Mormon Bar for the Valley, and a friend of the Star furnishes the following statistics—showing the amount of "the necessaries of life" which is required for an eight day's trip in the mountains:

8 lbs potatoes.
1 bottle whisky.
1 bottle pepper sauce.
1 bottle whisky.
1 box tea.
9 lbs onions.
2 bottles whisky.
1 ham.
11 lbs crackers.
1 bottle whisky.
1 doz. sardines.
2 bottles brandy, (4th proof.)
6 lbs sugar.
1 bottle brandy, (4th proof.)
7 lbs cheese.
2 bottles brandy, (4th proof)
1 bottle pepper.
5 gallons whisky.
4 bottles whisky (old Bourbon.)
1 small keg whisky.
1 bottle of cocktail, (designed for a "starter.")

The party proceeded as far as Sebastapol, (about two miles,) and halted to rest under a tree. They were there met by a teamster, who took the following message to the Bar. "Tell 'Sam' that we are all right—have got all the provisions we want—our pack animals are doing well—we will return in eight days. About the sixth we will be at the South Fork, on our way home. Tell him to try and meet us there with some whisky, say about two gallons, just enough to last us home. One of our kegs leaks."

Source: "An Eight Day's Trip in the Mountains," *Hutchings' California Magazine* 4 (October 1859): 185.

1861 • 67 • Harriet A. Jacobs, "The New Master and Mistress"

Introduction: *Harriet A. Jacobs (1813–1897) was born into slavery in Edenton, North Carolina. Her mistress taught her to read and write. When her mistress died, at the age of 12 Harriet was willed to the Norcom family, where she was sexually harassed by a "Dr. Flint," who was 35 years older. Jacobs ran away, eventually making it to New York in 1842, where she worked as a servant and was a strong supporter of the abolitionist movement. She published her book,* Incidents in the Life of a Slave Girl *(1861), under a pseudonym, as she could have been recaptured and returned to slavery. Her book was edited by Lydia Maria Child, a cookbook author and strong abolitionist. During the Civil War, Jacobs administered to African American soldiers. After the war, she worked with freed slaves in the South. In the excerpt below, she talks about some abuses and horrors of slavery connected with food.*

Mrs. Flint, like many southern women, was totally deficient in energy. She had not strength to superintend her household affairs; but her nerves were so strong, that she could sit in her easy chair and see a woman whipped, till the blood trickled from every stroke of the lash. She was a member of the church; but partaking of the Lord's supper did not seem to put her in a Christian frame of mind. If dinner was not served at the exact time on that particular Sunday, she would station herself in the kitchen, and wait till it was dished, and then spit in all the kettles and pans that had been used for cooking. She did this to prevent the cook and her children from eking out their meagre fare with the remains of the gravy and other scrapings. The slaves could get nothing to eat except what she chose to give them. Provisions were weighed out by the pound and ounce, three times a day. I can assure you she gave them no chance to eat wheat bread from her flour barrel. She knew how many biscuits a quart of flour would make, and exactly what size they ought to be.

Dr. Flint was an epicure. The cook never sent a dinner to his table without fear and trembling; for if there happened to be a dish not to his liking, he would either order her to be whipped, or compel her to eat every mouthful of it in his presence. The poor, hungry creature might not have objected to eating it; but she did object to having her master cram it down her throat till she choked.

They had a pet dog, that was a nuisance in the house. The cook was ordered to make some Indian mush for him. He refused to eat, and when his head was held over it, the froth flowed from his mouth into the basin. He died a few minutes after. When Dr. Mint came in, he said the mush had not been well cooked, and that was the reason the animal would not eat it. He sent for the cook, and compelled her to eat it. He thought that the woman's stomach was stronger than the dog's; but her sufferings afterwards proved that he was mistaken. This poor woman endured many cruelties from her master and mistress; sometimes she was locked up, away from her nursing baby, for a whole day and night.

Source: Harriet Jacobs, *Incidents in the Life of a Slave Girl* (Boston: Published for the Author, 1861), 22–23.

1862 • 68 • Lucius B. Northrop, "Confederate States of America, Subsistence Dept."

Introduction: *Lucius B. Northrop, commissary general of subsistence of the Confederate Army, accurately projected in 1862 that the Confederacy would face extremely severe shortages of food in the autumn of 1862. His predictions were accurate, and bread riots broke out in the spring of 1863. As food became scarce, desertions increased from the Confederate Army, and civilian morale sank. The lack of food was one reason why the South lost the Civil War.*

Confederate States of America, Subsistence Dept.,
Richmond, November 3, 1862. Hon. George W. Randolph,
Secretary of War:

Sir: In addition to the letters and telegrams already shown you in regard to the difficulty of transportation, particularly from Gordonsville to Richmond, I beg leave to inclose now a telegram from H. B. Hoomes, commissary agent, and also a letter from Mr. John S. Barbour, president Orange and Alexandria Railroad, to Major Ruffin, for your consideration and action. I feel it my duty to state in this connection that, notwithstanding the most strenuous efforts, wheat enough is not being received to furnish flour for General Lee's army alone. I am informed by reliable authority that in ordinary years, with an average crop of wheat, up to this time there would be received in Richmond 800,000 to 1,000,000 bushels of wheat, whereas, notwithstanding the high price that it commands, and notwithstanding the aid which has been extended to the farmers by commissary agents throughout the country, there has not been received more than 250,000 to 300,000 bushels. This proves that there is a great scarcity of wheat. This year's crop, it is believed, throughout the State is not more than one-fourth an average one, and a considerable portion of the State we cannot draw from at all. Unless, therefore, something is done to afford transportation for all the wheat that can be procured, I do not see anything but failure and ruin to our Army. As much grain as is needed cannot be procured, it is feared, even if this transportation is afforded, and without that transportation is obtained in some way we must break down. I feel it my duty to urge this matter upon your attention. It cannot be considered too deeply, nor the remedy applied with too much promptness. The chances of procuring sufficient supplies are becoming every hour more and more doubtful, and the area of country drawn from smaller and smaller. I am powerless—to remedy the evil, and can only lay before you the state of the case for your action. A sufficiency of bags is as great a necessity to secure a supply of flour as anything else. During the last summer the cotton mills throughout the country were written to with a view to secure an ample supply of bags, but this Bureau was requested not to purchase bags by Major Ferguson, of the Quartermaster's Department, who was engaged in the north and would procure them, it was said, for both the Commissary and Quartermaster's Bureaus. To avoid competition between two Government agents this was acquiesced in. Upon application now it seems that not one-tenth of the requisite quantity of bags can be obtained.

I have the honor to be, very respectfully, your obedient servant,
L. B. NORTHROP, Commissary-General C. S. Army

Source: L. B. Northrop to George W. Randolph, November 3, 1862, in *The War of the Rebellion: A Compilation of the Official Records of the Union and Confederate Armies,* Series 4, Vol. 2 (Washington, DC: U.S. Government Printing Office, 1902), 157–158.

1862 • 69 • The Pacific Railway Act

Introduction: *The construction of a railroad connecting the United States to the Pacific coast had been discussed since the 1830s. These proposals, however, snagged on disagreement as to what route such a railroad would take. Southerners wanted a route that connected the South with California, while legislators in the North lobbied for a central or northern route. When the Civil War began, Southern legislators withdrew from Congress, and opposition to a central route for the transcontinental railroad melted away. Legislators became convinced that the railroad was a necessary defense measure and also that it would strengthen trade with Asia via the West Coast. Congress passed the Pacific Railway Act on July 1, 1862. This legislation authorized two railroad companies to construct a transcontinental railroad along the 100th meridian. Construction on the railroad began in 1863 at opposite ends of the route. The Union Pacific, employing more than 8,000 immigrants, mainly Irish and Germans, built west from Omaha. The Central Pacific, employing 10,000 laborers, mainly Chinese, built eastward from Sacramento. When the construction crews met on May 10, 1869, the Pacific coast was connected with the rest of the nation. Railroads opened up local and regional markets to competition. Local producers had difficulty competing with large manufacturers, and many local companies went out of business or merged with other firms that produced similar foods.*

The Pacific Railway Act July 1, 1862

An Act to aid in the Construction of a Railroad and Telegraph Line from the Missouri River to the Pacific Ocean. . . .

Be it enacted, That . . . "The Union Pacific Railroad Company" . . . is hereby authorized and empowered to lay out, locate, construct, furnish, maintain and enjoy a continuous railroad and telegraph . . . from a point on the one hundredth meridian of longitude west from Greenwich, between the south margin of the valley of the Republican River and the north margin of the valley of the Platte River, to the western boundary of Nevada Territory, upon the route and terms hereinafter provided. . . .

Section 2. That the right of way through the public lands be . . . granted to said company for the construction of said railroad and telegraph line; and the right . . . is hereby given to said company to take from the public lands adjacent to the line of said road, earth, stone, timber, and other materials for the construction thereof; said right of way is granted to said railroad to the extent of two hundred feet in width on each side of said railroad when it may pass over the public lands, including all necessary grounds, for stations, buildings, workshops, and depots, machine shops, switches, side tracks, turn tables, and water stations. The United States shall extinguish as rapidly as may be the Indian titles to all lands falling under the operation of this act. . . .

Section 3. That there be . . . granted to the said company, for the purpose of aiding in the construction of said railroad and telegraph line, and to secure the safe and speedy transportation of mails, troops, munitions of war, and public stores thereon, every alternate section of public land, designated by odd numbers, to the amount of five alternate sections per mile on each side of said railroad, on the line thereof, and within the limits of ten miles on each side of said road . . . Provided That all mineral lands shall be excepted from the operation of this act; but where the same shall contain timber, the timber thereon is hereby granted to said company. . . .

Section 5. That for the purposes herein mentioned the Secretary of the Treasury shall . . . in accordance with the provisions of this act, issue to said company bonds of the United States of one thousand dollars each, payable in thirty years after date, paying six per centum per annum interest . . . to the amount of sixteen of said bonds per mile for each section of forty miles; and to secure the repayment to the United States . . . of the amount of said bonds . . . the issue of said bonds . . . shall ipso facto constitute a first mortgage on the whole line of the railroad and telegraph. . . .

Section 9. That the Leavenworth, Pawnee and Western Railroad Company of Kansas are hereby authorized to construct a railroad and telegraph line . . . upon the same terms and conditions in all respects as are provided [for construction of the Union Pacific Railroad]. . . . The Central Pacific Railroad Company of California are hereby authorized to construct a railroad and telegraph line from the Pacific coast . . . to the eastern boundaries of California, upon the same terms and conditions in all respects [as are provided for the Union Pacific Railroad].

Section 10. . . . And the Central Pacific Railroad Company of California after completing its road across said State, is authorized to continue the construction of said railroad and telegraph through the Territories of the United States to the Missouri River . . . upon the terms and conditions provided in this act in relation to the Union Pacific Railroad Company, until said roads shall meet and connect. . . .

Section 11. That for three hundred miles of said road most mountainous and difficult of construction, to wit: one hundred and fifty miles westerly from the eastern base of the Rocky Mountains, and one hundred and fifty miles eastwardly from the western base of the Sierra Nevada mountains . . . the bonds to be issued to aid in the construction thereof shall be treble the number per mile hereinbefore provided . . . and between the sections last named of one hundred and fifty miles each, the bonds to be issued to aid in the construction thereof shall be double the number per mile first mentioned. . . .

Source: *Statutes at Large,* 37th Congress, 2nd Session, Chapter 120, Section 11, 1862, p. 489.

1862 • 70 • "An Act to Establish a Department of Agriculture"

Introduction: *Discussion about the federal government's role in agriculture had been under way since 1790, when President George Washington proposed the creation of an* *agricultural board to disseminate scientific information to American farmers. Proposals continued to surface for decades, but none were ever accepted by Congress. In 1839, Congress did pass a small appropriation to require the U.S. commissioner of patents to issue an annual report disseminating "agricultural statistics and for other agricultural purposes." In 1852, prominent agriculturalists and congressmen organized the United States Agricultural Society, which lobbied regularly for the creation of a federal department solely focused on agriculture. But Southern legislators, concerned with states' rights, firmly opposed it. With Southern political leaders absent, Congress passed the bill that created the U.S. Department of Agriculture (USDA) on May 15, 1862. The USDA rapidly expanded its activities, and appropriations have accelerated ever since.*

An Act to Establish a Department of Agriculture Thirty-Seventh Congress of the United States

At the second session
Begun and Held at the City of Washington in the District of Columbia

Be It Enacted by the Senate and House of Representatives of the United States of America in Congress assembled, That there is hereby established at the seat of government of the United States a Department of Agriculture, the general designs and duties of which shall be to acquire and to diffuse among the people of the United States useful information on subjects connected with agriculture in the most general and comprehensive sense of that word, and to procure, propagate, and distribute among the people new and valuable seeds and plants.

Section 2. And be it further enacted, That there shall be appointed by the President, by and with the advice and consent of the Senate, a "Commissioner of Agriculture," who shall be the chief executive officer of the Department of Agriculture, who shall hold his office by a tenure similar to that of other civil officers appointed by the President, and who shall receive for his compensation a salary of three thousand dollars per annum.

Section 3. And be it further enacted, That it shall be the duty of the Commissioner of Agriculture to acquire and preserve in his Department all information concerning agriculture which he can obtain by means of books and correspondence, and by practical and scientific experiments, (accurate records of which experiments shall be kept in his office,) by the collection of statistics, and by any other appropriate means within his power; to collect, as he may be able, new and valuable seeds and plants; to test, by cultivation, the value of such of them as may require such tests; to propagate such as may be worthy of propagation, and to distribute them among agriculturists. He shall annually make a general report in writing of his acts to the President and to Congress, in which he may recommend the publication of papers forming parts of or accompanying his report, which report shall also contain an account of all moneys received and expended by him. He shall also make special reports on particular subjects whenever required to do so by the President or either House of Congress, or when he shall think the subject in his charge requires it. He shall receive and have charge of all the property of the agricultural division of the Patent Office in the Department of the Interior, including the fixtures and property of the propagating garden. He shall direct and superintend the expenditure of all money appropriated by Congress to the Department, and render accounts thereof, and also of all money heretofore appropriated for agriculture and remaining unexpended. And said Commissioner may send and receive through the mails, free of charge, all communications and other matter pertaining to the business of his Department, not exceeding in weight thirty-two ounces.

Section 4. And be it further enacted, That the Commissioner of Agriculture shall appoint a chief clerk, with a salary of two thousand dollars, who in all cases during the necessary absence of the Commissioner, or when the said principal office shall become vacant, shall perform the duties of Commissioner, and he shall appoint such other employees as Congress may from time to time provide, with salaries corresponding to the salaries of similar officers in other Departments of the Government; and he shall, as Congress may from time to time provide, employ other persons, for such time as their services may be needed, including chemists, botanists, entomologists, and other persons skilled in the natural sciences pertaining to agriculture. And the said Commissioner, and every other person to be appointed in the said Department, shall, before he enters upon the duties of his office or appointment, make oath or affirmation truly and faithfully to execute the trust committed to him. And the said Commissioner and the chief clerk shall also, before entering upon their duties, severally give bonds to the Treasurer of the United States, the former in the sum of ten thousand dollars, and the latter in the sum of five thousand dollars, conditional to render a true and faithful account to him or his successor in office, quarter yearly accounts of all moneys which shall be by them received by virtue of the said office, with sureties to be approved as sufficient by the Solicitor of the Treasury; which bonds shall be filed in the office of the First Comptroller of the Treasury, to be by him put in suit upon any breach of the conditions thereof.

Source: "An Act to Establish a Department of Agriculture," Thirty-seventh Congress, Session 2, May 15, 1862, Chap. 72, 12 Stat. 387.

1862 • 71 • Morrill Land-Grant College Act

Introduction: *The Morrill Land-Grant College Act of 1862 allotted states 30,000 acres of public land for every senator and representative a state had in Congress. The proceeds from the sale of this land were to be used to create agricultural colleges. This had been under discussion for 15 years, and as with other bills, this bill had been opposed by Southern legislators. The Morrill Land-Grant College Act passed with little dissent on July 2, 1862. During the next few years, most states established agricultural colleges. These institutions promoted agricultural education by offering courses in botany, chemistry, zoology, and other subjects related to farming. The colleges widely disseminated technology and scientific knowledge about agriculture, and their activities have greatly improved American agriculture.*

Morrill Land Grant College Act
Thirty-Seventh Congress of the United States

At the second session
Begun and Held at the City of Washington in the District of Columbia

An Act donating Public Lands to the several States and Territories which may provide Colleges for the Benefit of Agriculture and the Mechanic Arts.

Be it enacted by the Senate and House of Representatives of the United States of America in Congress as assembled, That there be granted to the several States, for the purposes hereinafter mentioned, an amount of public land, to be apportioned to each State a quantity equal to thirty thousand acres for each senator and representative in Congress to which the States are respectively entitled by the apportionment under the census of eighteen hundred and sixty: Provided, That no mineral lands shall be selected or purchased under the provisions of this act.

Section 2. And be it further enacted, That the land aforesaid, after being surveyed, shall be apportioned to the several States in sections or subdivisions of sections, not less than one quarter of a section; and whenever there are public lands in a State subject to sale at private entry at one dollar and twenty-five cents per acre, the quantity to which said State shall be entitled shall be selected from such lands within the limits of such State, and the Secretary of the Interior is hereby directed to issue to each of the States in which there is not the quantity of public lands subject to sale at private entry at one dollar and twenty-five cents per acre, to which said State may be entitled under the provisions of this act, land scrip to the amount in acres for the deficiency of its distributive share: said scrip to be sold by said States and the proceeds thereof applied to the uses and purposes prescribed in this act, and for no other use or purpose whatsoever: Provided, That in no case shall any State to which land scrip may thus be issued be allowed to locate the same within the limits of any other State, or of any Territory of the United States, but their assignees may thus locate said land scrip upon any of the unappropriated lands of the United States subject to sale at private entry at one dollar and twenty-five cents, or less, per acre: And provided, further, That not more than one million acres shall be located by such assignees in any one of the States: And provided, further, That no such location shall be made before one year from the passage of this act.

Section 3. And be it further enacted, That all the expenses of management, superintendence, and taxes from date of selection of said lands, previous to their sales, and all expenses incurred in the management and disbursement of the moneys which may be received therefrom, shall be paid by the States to which they may belong, out of the treasury of said States, so that the entire proceeds of the sale of said lands shall be applied without any diminution whatever to the purposes hereinafter mentioned.

Section 4. And be it further enacted, That all moneys derived from the sale of the lands aforesaid by the States to which the lands are apportioned, and from the sales of land scrip hereinbefore provided for, shall be invested in stocks of the United States, or of the States, or some other safe stocks, yielding not less than five per centum upon the par value of said stocks; and that the moneys so invested shall constitute a perpetual fund, the capital of which shall remain forever undiminished, (except so far as may be provided in section fifth of this act,) and the interest of which shall be inviolably appropriated, by each State which may take and claim the benefit of this act, to the endowment, support, and maintenance of at least one college where the leading object shall be, without excluding other scientific and classical studies, and including military tactics, to teach such branches of learning as are related to agriculture and the mechanic arts, in such manner as the legislatures of the States may respectively prescribe, in order to promote the liberal and practical education of the industrial classes in the several pursuits and professions in life.

Section 5. And be it further enacted, That the grant of land and land scrip hereby authorized shall be made on the following conditions, to which, as well as to the provisions hereinbefore contained, the previous assent of the several States shall be signified by legislative acts:

First. If any portion of the fund invested, as provided by the foregoing section, or any portion of the interest thereon, shall, by any action or contingency, be diminished or lost, it shall be replaced by the State to which it belongs, so that the capital of the fund shall remain forever undiminished; and the annual interest shall be regularly applied without diminution to the purposes mentioned in the fourth section of this act, except that a sum, not exceeding ten per centum upon the amount received by any State under the provisions of this act, may be expended for the purchase of lands for sites or experimental farms, whenever authorized by the respective legislatures of said States.

Second. No portion of said fund, nor the interest thereon, shall be applied, directly or indirectly, under any pretence whatever, to the purchase, erection, preservation, or repair of any building or buildings.

Third. Any State which may take and claim the benefit of the provisions of this act shall provide, within five years, at least not less than one college, as described in the fourth section of this act, or the grant to such State shall cease; and said State shall be bound to pay the United States the amount received of any lands previously sold, and that the title to purchasers under the State shall be valid.

Fourth. An annual report shall be made regarding the progress of each college, recording any improvements and experiments made, with their cost and results, and such other matters, including State industrial and economical statistics, as may be supposed useful; one copy of which shall be transmitted by mail free, by each, to all the other colleges which may be endowed under the provisions of this act, and also one copy to the Secretary of the Interior.

Fifth. When lands shall be selected from those which have been raised to double the minimum price, in consequence of railroad grants, they shall be computed to the States at the maximum price, and the number of acres proportionately diminished.

Sixth. No State while in a condition of rebellion or insurrection against the government of the United States shall be entitled to the benefit of this act.

Seventh. No State shall be entitled to the benefits of this act unless it shall express its acceptance thereof by its legislature within two years from the date of its approval by the President.

Section 6. And be it further enacted, That land scrip issued under the provisions of this act shall not be subject to location until after the first day of January, one thousand eight hundred and sixty-three.

Section 7. And be it further enacted, That the land officers shall receive the same fees for locating land scrip issued under the provisions of this act as is now allowed for the location of military bounty land warrants under existing laws; Provided, their maximum compensation shall not be thereby increased.

Section 8. And be it further enacted, That the Governors of the several States to which scrip shall be issued under this act shall be required to report annually to Congress all sales made of such scrip until the whole shall be disposed of, the amount received for the same, and what appropriation has been made of the proceeds.

Source: Public Law 37-108, July 2, 1862; Enrolled Acts and Resolutions of Congress, 1789–1996; Record Group 11; General Records of the United States Government; National Archives.

1863 • 72 • Edward Peron Hingston, The Art of Bartending

Introduction: *Edward Peron Hingston (1823–1876) was an Englishman who visited America during the Civil War. While in San Francisco in 1863, he ran into Gerry Thomas (1830–1885), who bartended at the Occidental Hotel.*

. . . From Folsom Street wharf we drive to the Occidental Hotel, where we at once find ourselves to be at home. No better hotel do we wish to stop at, in whatever part of the world we wander. We announce our relationship to the showman's fraternity, and are gladly welcomed. Our arrangements are soon made. A nice commodious room is assigned to us, and we are free of the house for the sum of two dollars and a half per day, payable in gold. Greenbacks are not current in California. There is a State law that payments shall be made in coin. . . .

For the English reader to understand what we get for two dollars and a half per day at the Occidental Hotel, it is necessary to take a cursory peep at the hotel itself. So very different is it in its arrangements from that which an untravelled man might expect to find far away out here on the extreme western edge of civilization.

There are five brothers of the name of Lei and who are engaged in hotel business in the United States. They have establishments in New York, at Saratoga, here in San Francisco, and elsewhere. In New York they conduct the great Metropolitan Hotel in Broadway, inside which, like a kernel in a nut, is the theatre known as Niblo's Garden. The Lelands have a special talent for hotel-keeping. It seems to have been born in their blood, and—viret acquirit eundo—to develope itself with more force the more hotels they build. The Occidental, San Francisco, is managed, at the time of which we are writing, by Mr. Louis Leland, who is at hand ready to receive his guests just arrived by the steamer. An air of sumptuous splendour and easeful comfort strikes us immediately we enter the doors, as being characteristics of the house. Newly built, only a portion of the intended edifice completed, and the grand staircase not yet opened, the Occidental is but an incomplete sample of that which it is intended to be. The interior fittings are those of a first-class hotel; the bedrooms are airy, the beds soft and large; the salle-a-manger is a spacious hall, with elaborate embellishments and columns of noble proportions. There are breakfast-rooms and supper-rooms, hot and cold baths for everybody, well-carpeted stairs, elegant drawing-rooms for the use of the ladies, pianos of the best manufacture, and lounges and rocking-chairs of the most luxurious construction. The attendance is far better than in most English hotels, with none of that bowing and scraping servility among the waiters which constitutes the most offensive form of attention. Our two dollars and a half per day includes attendance. The waiters do not expect to receive a gratuity for every little act of duty they may chance to perform; but if they know you to belong to a show and likely to give them a free pass, they will shower upon you every civility they can manifest.

Americans have a cuisine of their own; not always acceptable to Europeans. The dishes are not such as an Englishman is accustomed to at home, and to some of them he may very possibly object. If he is fastidious about having his joint roasted instead of baked he is likely to meet with disappointment in the course of his American travel. Should he like his beef underdone, he may feel annoyed at Americans liking theirs well done and at the cook sending up the meat brown instead of red. To compensate for these little drawbacks he will find more than a balance of advantage in the copiousness of the menu and the numerous luscious dishes peculiar to the Western continent. There is no roast turkey in Europe comparable with the roast turkey of the United States, and there is no vegetable so delicious as a cob of green corn served up hot on a white napkin with butter, pepper, and salt. Here, at the Occidental Hotel, the bill of fare comprises everything which the Pacific coast produces, and any number of luxurious dainties imported from Europe. The tables groan with good things—with beef from Contra Costa and potatoes from Bodega, with richly-tinted apples from Oregon and the juiciest of grapes from Sonoma, with strawberries from Oakland and peaches from Marysville. There is breakfast to be had at any hour of the morning, with any dainty or any number of dainties you may please to select to accompany it. The milk rich, the butter magnificent. There is luncheon at mid-day, the tables covered with tempting dishes and the best of fruits. At dinner the dishes are numerous, and the dessert one to which Apicius[1] might sit down and be happy, or Lucullus[2] himself feel that he had done the right thing in coming to California. When you express a desire for tea you are furnished with some of the rarest flavour and fragrance; and when you come in Into and seek your supper you will find it waiting for you, laid out in the very best style. All these we obtain for two dollars and a half per day.

But there is more to be had for your money yet. Pass downstairs and you will find a large reading-room furnished with newspapers from all parts of the United States, and with magazines of every description. Here too you will find the latest numbers of the Times, Punch, and the Illustrated News that have arrived from England. Do you want to know how they are getting on with the war in Virginia or Kentucky? Here are the latest telegrams posted on the wall, and here are abstracts of the state of the money-market in New York this morning, and of the discussions in Congress yesterday. Here too in the same reading-room is a telegraph office if you wish to send a message; here are desks for writing, and a library if you desire to read a book. More still beyond. Pass into this back apartment and you are in a museum of the mineral products of California. With most commendable care for the comfort of his guests, Mr. Leland has provided a collection of specimens of every variety of gold ore from the different diggings of California, and with properly labelled exemplifications of the various rocks and earths to be found throughout the State. There is more information to be obtained in this room in one hour, relative to the geology of the Pacific coast, than a week of reading would furnish. Then, the excellence of the idea—a museum in the hotel! and we get it all for two dollars and a half per day. We know that some people pay three, and some a little more, but we do not.

Fresh from our voyage, and about to part with pleasant acquaintances whom we have become familiar with during our ocean trip, we descend to the bar to partake of a social glass. Were we in England we should order it into our room, but being in California we do nothing of the kind. The bar is the right place at which to take it, and to the bar we go. Our host accompanies us; for no one better than he knows how to speed the parting guest, or welcome the coming one.

The bar is fitted up with great taste, and the good things with which it is stocked are numerous, consequently full a score of the gentlemen passengers by the Golden Age have already found their way there. It is a commodious apartment, luxuriously appointed, scrupulously clean, and radiant with white marble, gilt fixtures, and glittering crystal. Nothing to remind one of the garish glare of polished brass, the greasy mahogany, or the unpleasant odour of black beetles, occasionally to be met with in hotel bars of certain English towns.

Behind the counter is one of the most distinguished, if not the chief, of American "bar-tenders." His name is Jerry Thomas—a name as familiar in the Eastern States as it now is out here in California. Bar-tending, as it is called, is an art in the United States, and Mr. Jerry Thomas is an accomplished artist. In the manufacture of a "cocktail," a "julep," a "smash," or an "eye-opener," none can beat him, though he may have successful rivals. For instance, there is Mr. William Pitcher, of the Tremont House, Boston, who because he has obtained proficiency in the making of cocktails and is accustomed to make them for the students of Harvard, and for other learned imbibers, mingles Greek with his gin, and entitles himself on his card "Professor of Kratisalectronouratation." But Mr. Jerry Thomas is author as well as artist, and has written a work on the art of compounding drinks. He is clever also with his pencil as well as with his pen, and behind his bar are specimens of his skill as a draughtsman. He is a gentleman who is all ablaze with diamonds. There is a very large pin, formed of a cluster of diamonds, in the front of his magnificent shirt, he has diamond studs at his wrists, and gorgeous diamond rings on his fingers. Diamonds being "properties" essential to the calling of a bar-tender in the United States. Unless he already possesses them it is said that no member of the craft can expect to attain to a high-class position. Mr. Jerry Thomas we are told can command his hundred dollars, or twenty pounds weekly, for wages. It must be remembered however that he is in California, and that he is engaged as a "star." The interest on the value of his diamonds is worth the money.

Notes

1. Ancient Roman gourmet cook who is credited with writing the only surviving cookery manuscript to survive from the ancient Mediterranean.
2. A famous Roman gastronome. His name survives in the term "lucullan," often used as a adjective to mean a large, elaborate, and expensive feast.

Source: Edward Peron Hingston, *The Genial Showman: Reminiscences of the Life of Artemus Ward* (London: John Camden Hotten, n.d.), 240–246.

1863 • 73 • Bread Riots in Richmond

Introduction: *When Richmond became the capital of the Confederacy, politicians, civil servants, and military officials flocked to the city. On top of this, military operations in northern Virginia during the first two years of the Civil War sent a deluge of refugees into Richmond—many of them penniless, jobless, and occasionally homeless. By 1863, Richmond's population had grown to an estimated 120,000 people—three times its prewar size. Simultaneous with Richmond's* *swelling population was a shrinking regional food-supply base. This was caused by the wartime destruction of farmland in northern Virginia, declining agricultural production resulting from the loss of farm labor, an increasingly inefficient transportation system, and the military's impressment of food. In the early months of 1863, supplies dwindled further as heavy rains made many roads impassable. By February 1863, the price of available food skyrocketed. By the end of March, the food that was available in Richmond was so expensive that it was beyond the ability of many Richmonders to buy it. The result was a food riot in which an estimated 10,000 Richmonders participated.*

Bread Riots in Richmond, Va.

A refugee from Richmond, who left that city on Tuesday, gives an interesting account of the riot of the second instant. Considerable excitement had prevailed for some time in consequence of the exorbitant prices, and rumors of a popular movement had been in circulation for several days. Females had begged in the streets and at the stores until begging did no good, and many had been driven to robbery to sustain life. On the morning of the second instant, a large meeting, composed principally of the wives and daughters of the working classes, was held in the African church, and a committee appointed to wait upon the Governor to request that articles of food should be sold at government rates. After the passage of sundry resolutions the meeting adjourned, and the committee proceeded to wait upon Governor Letcher. That functionary declined to take any steps in the matter, and upon urging the case the ladies were peremptorily ordered to withdraw. The result of the interview was soon made public, when a body of females, numbering about three hundred, collected together and commenced helping themselves to bread, flour, meat, articles of clothing, etc. The entire city was at once thrown into consternation. Stores were closed, the windows barred, doors bolted, and every precaution taken against forcible entries; but hatchets and axes in the hands of women rendered desperate by hunger made quick work, and building after building was rapidly broken open. The destruction commenced on Carey street, above Fifteenth street, and was becoming general in that section of the city, when the City Guard, with fixed bayonets, arrived at the scene of

Richmond bread riots as depicted in *Frank Leslie's Illustrated Newspaper* on May 23, 1863. (Library of Congress)

operations. A few individuals attempted to resist the women, but without success. One man who struck a female was wounded in the shoulder by a shot from a revolver, and the threatening attitude of those armed with hatchets, etc., intimidated others from attempting force. The Mayor soon appeared, and, mounting a stool on the sidewalk, proceeded to read the riot act. During the reading of that document a portion of the crowd suspended operations, but no sooner had the Mayor concluded than the seizure of provisions commenced again more vigorously than before. At this juncture an attempt was made to arrest the more violent; but the party immediately scattered, and, entering Main street, resumed operations.

Governor Letcher then appeared, and, mounting a vehicle in the centre of the street, addressed the throng, characterizing the demonstration as a disgrace and a stigma upon the city, and announcing that but five minutes would be given them in which to disperse. If in that time the order was not complied with, the troops would be called upon to act. Again the crowd broke up, and in a few moments burst into the stores on Franklin street. But little damage was done here, however, and the riot finally subsided, but not until after the arrest of about forty of the women, and the promise of the Governor to relieve the wants of the destitute. A large amount of bread and bacon was carried off, and all engaged in the riot succeeded in getting a good supply of provisions. Steps have been taken to provide for the immediate wants of some of the families; but great suffering still prevails and is daily increasing. Another uprising is feared, and precautionary measures for its suppression have been instituted; but great uneasiness is felt throughout the city, and merchants are adding to the strength of doors and shutters in every possible manner. The effect of this riot upon the troops about Richmond was very demoralizing. The authorities are much exercised over it, and the greatest vigilance is enjoined upon the police force. The leading men of the city attempted to circulate the report that the women were "Irish and Yankee hags," endeavoring to mislead the public concerning the amount of loyal sentiment in the city, but miserably failed. The fact of their destitution and respectability was too palpable, and the authorities are forced to admit the conclusion that starvation alone incited the movement.

Troops are being hurried up from Richmond to Fredericksburgh. There is still a large force in the vicinity of Richmond; but these, it is believed, are about to leave for the Rappahannock. Fortifications are being thrown up on the Rapidan River, and the force in that section is being augmented. No work is going on upon the defences about Richmond. Two gunboats (iron-clads) are afloat in James River. The Virginia has been trying to get below the obstructions, and now lies near Drury's Bluff. The third is unfinished, but is rapidly approaching completion. The iron works are worked to their utmost in the manufacture of munitions of war; but the iron is of miserable quality, and many of their projectiles contain pieces of stone.

The railroads have almost entirely given out, and no material is to be had for their repair, great despondency prevails, and the events of the next three months are awaited with most absorbing anxiety.

Rebel Newspaper Account

Happily these daylight burglaries are undergoing judicial investigation. A great part of the stolen goods has been reclaimed. The ringleaders are being arrested; they will be tried and punished. A full account of the affair, from its obscure origin to its disgraceful culmination, will be made public, and the exaggerations that have one to the country will be counteracted.

That there was any just ground for the shameful disturbance of Thursday no one believes. The more it is looked into, the more causeless it appears. Doubtless there is much suffering in the city. But the fund voted the poor was by no means exhausted; the churches were willing and abundantly able to relieve distress; private Benevolence had not once been appealed to. No petition, no remonstrance had been made; yet, on a sudden, a hundred or a hundred and fifty well-dressed, plump-cheeked women, led by a virago who is known to have made a fortune by market-gardening, and cheered by a rabble of gamblers and ruffians, who are protected here by the special toleration of the confederate, State and municipal governments that misrule this unhappy city—all of a sudden this throng of courtesans and thieves assembles in the Capitol square, organizes, and proceeds to break open stores—to get what, forsooth? Not meat and bread, but boots, shoes, silk dresses, tobacco, jewelry, brooms and the like. These the Mayor in his investigation last Friday, suggests pertinently, are not articles of food. But there is a proof more convincing than any yet given of the absurdity and falsehood of the plea, that this row was occasioned by suffering for food or clothing, and that is the fact, substantiated by every housekeeper in the city, that notwithstanding high prices and scarcity of provisions, there have been fewer applications for charity than in any previous winter for many years. The entire absence of beggars at a time like this, and in a city so crowded by idlers as Richmond, is very notable. The writer of this article can testify, that during the whole winter he has encountered but two beggars, one of whom, an obvious impostor, wanted to fight because her veracity was doubted, while the other set upon him with the stunning petition for "a quarter to buy a catechism!" The truth is, this petticoated foray was political in its origin; as the simultaneous disturbances in other cities indicate, and as the evidences before the Mayor will yet prove.

If there be a soul of good in things evil, this ridiculous affair may be turned to account. It ought to put a stop to hoarding, to suppress speculation, to induce producers to bring in supplies, to make the government facilitate transportation, and to clean out the gamblers, loafers, and ruffians, stock, lock, and barrel. Let Congress at once pass a law requiring every man to show that he is engaged in some honest, useful calling or else go into the army forthwith. In this way the five and twenty gambling-houses that feed every day nearly as many thousand idlers, and thereby run up the price of provisions, will be swept away. And let our high officials display a little courage and a little reason. The people are not afraid of unpleasant truths; why should they be? Let them not attempt impossibilities. But the reports in the papers will go to the country and encourage other riots. Better a correct account in print than a thousand exaggerations from as many tongues and private letters. If the riots occur, put them down; it is easily enough done. But the Yankees will get hold of it. Certainly. What if they do? Let them make the most of it; they are going to do their worst, any way. Better a thousand fold that the Yankees should ply their lying arts with all the aid the disaffected here can give them, than that the people should see that the government of Jefferson Davis is timorous about any thing on earth. The people are manly; so should their government be, and put a bold, calm face on every thing. If any thing could be "kept back," the fate of Ananias should

warn us of the folly of attempting it. Have we gotten so deep in the mire of a sneaking, evasive, alternately truckling and bullying policy, as not to be able to turn round and face Yankees and females combined? Or shall it go to the country that the confederate government is scared out of its wits because a parcel of women broke open a store and stole a pair of shoes?
—*Richmond Whig,* April 6.

Source: Frank Moore, *The Rebellion Record,* Vol. 6, edited by Edward Everett (New York: Putnam, 1863), 522–524.

1863 • 74 • "A Rebel Bill of Fare"

Introduction: *On May 18, 1863, elements of the Union Army and the Union Navy closed in on the Confederate stronghold of Vicksburg on the Mississippi River. After assaulting the city's formidable fortifications and failing to break through, the Union army laid siege in hopes of starving the garrison inside into submission. Confederate provisions dwindled, and soldiers ate mule meat. When the supply of mule meat gave out, soldiers and civilians ate rats, and some allegedly consumed dogs and cats as well. After 47 days of siege, it became evident that there would be no last-minute intervention from outside the city and that famine would soon rage inside the city. On July 4, 1863, the starving city surrendered. Intended as a humorous joke, Union soldiers invented the menu below, which was widely reprinted in Northern newspapers.*

A Rebel Bill of Fare; An Eloquent Reminiscence of Vicksburg; Mule Meat Analyzed.

We are indebted to the courtesy of J. H. Early, surgeon, 17th Iowa regiment, for the following copy of a bill of fare found in the rebel camps at Vicksburg. While it is a capital specimen of burlesque, it is no less a melancholy burlesque upon the rations of mule flesh indulged in by them during the last days of the siege. We produce it entire for the satisfaction of our readers, making it as nearly *fac simile* as our engraver and typists are able:

Hotel De Vicksburg.
Bill of Fare for July, 1863.

Soup.
Mule Tail.
Boiled.

Mule Bacon, with poke greens.
Mule Ham, canvassed.

Roast.
Mule Sirloin.
Mule Bump, stuffed with rice.

Vegetables.
Peas and Rice.

Entrees.
Mule Head, stuffed a la mode.
Mule Ears, fricasseed a la gotch.
Mule Side, stewed, new style, hair on.
Mule Beef, jerked, a la Mexicana.
Mule Spare Ribs, plain.
Mule Salad.
Mule Tongue, cold, a la Bray.
Mule Liver, hashed.
Mule Brains, a la omelette.
Mule Hoof, soused.
Mule Kidneys, stuffed with peas.
Mule Tripe, fried in pea-meal batter.

Jellies.
Mule Foot.

Pastry.
Cottonwood Berry Pies.
Chinaberry Tarts.

Dessert.
White Oak Acorns.
Blackberry Leaf Tea.
Beech Nuts.
Genuine Confederate Coffee.

Liquors.
Mississippi Water, vintage of 1492. Superior, $3
Limestone Water, late importation. Very fine, $2.75.
Spring Water, Vicksburg brand, $1.50.

Meals at all hours. Gentlemen to wait upon themselves. Any inattention on the part of servants will be promptly reported at the office.

JEFF. DAVIS & Co., Proprietors.

CARD.—The proprietors of the justly celebrated Hotel de Vicksburg, having enlarged and refitted the same, are now prepared to accommodate all who favor them with a call. Parties arriving by the River or Grant's inland route, will find Grape, Cannister & Co.'s carriages at the landing, or any depot on the line of entrenchments. Buck, Ball & Co., take charge of all baggage. No effort will be spared to make the visit of all as interesting as possible.

Source: "A Rebel Bill of Fare," *Chicago Tribune,* July 25, 1863, 2.

1864 • 75 • E. N. Horsford, "The Army Ration"

Introduction: *By comparison with the malnutrition and some starvation among soldiers and civilians in large cities, the Union Army was well fed. Here is an excerpt from E. N. Horsford (1818–1893), formerly a professor at Harvard University. When this was written, he ran the Rumford Chemical Works, makers of baking powder. Below is his assessment of the proper rations for Union soldiers during the Civil War.*

The Army Ration

Our theatre of war is one of vast distances; of relatively sparse population, and indifferent wagon-roads. During a full third of the year, the roads of the South are rendered quite impassable to artillery and wagon-trains by a single heavy rain. They are without solid bed, narrow, and rapidly cut up by heavily pressed wheels. On the march, the army wagons containing the cooking utensils, and the sutlers' wagons, are usually at long distances in the rear. They are of course, liable to be cut off by the enemy's cavalry. For these and other reasons connected chiefly with the difficulties of transportation, the rations are not unfrequently reduced greatly in quantity and quality at most critical moments. Town bakeries are unknown in our southern villages. Even small collections of houses, scarcely

Union soldiers gather around a kitchen in 1864. (National Archives)

rising to the rank of villages, are widely separated from each other. Our supplies are of necessity sometimes drawn from points thousands of miles from the field of army operations. Our soldiers have not been accustomed at home to the simple and coarse fare of the peasantry of Europe, and not until they have been a year or more in the service do they become wholly suited to the plain, though in the main, nutritious fare of the active soldier.

What Is the Army Ration?

The present ration consists, substantially, of—
Bread,
Meat,
Coffee, and
Sugar.

The bread may be issued as flour, to be resolved at the soldiers' option into loaf bread baked in camp, biscuit, fritters, &c., as convenience or inclination may dictate; or as

Loaf Bread, baked at some of the bakeries of the Government or neighborhood, and transported as such to be distributed in camp; or as

Hard bread, which, baked without salt, in the form of crackers and kiln dried, is quite imperishable if kept from moisture.

The meat is beef, fresh or salt, and salt pork.

Coffee, without milk, is furnished roasted and ground.

Sugar is provided to be used with coffee, or as a condiment with other articles of diet.

Salt, pepper and vinegar are supplied in the needed quantities, and vegetables are furnished to the men in camp.

At first glance, the ration seems to fulfil every requisite. The organic and inorganic food are supplied in both the meat and bread. The nitrogenous and the respiratory food are present in the animal and vegetable fibrine and albumen, and in the oil, sugar, and starch of the meat and bread. The beverage of coffee is there; the salt, pepper and vinegar, as condiments or stimulants, are there; the sugar, more especially fulfilling the want of a saccharine or oleaginous constituent, is there. The ration has an apparent scientific as well as experimental foundation. It corresponds very nearly with the quantities and kinds established as essential by observation and experiment:

The supply found necessary to a man in full health consists of:

Meat 16 oz.
Bread 19 oz.
Butter or fat
Water 52 oz.

The army ration consists, substantially, of:
Meat 16 oz.
Bread 22 oz.
Coffee and Sugar

The extra bread and the sugar replace the butter or fat; and the coffee, besides affording an agreeable drink, exerts an antiseptic influence over the living tissues, retarding their decay.

Our ration is eminently flexible. The pork and beef may replace each other. When volunteers come first to the field, fresh from the variety of home and markets of comparatively easy access, they demand, of salt meats, beef rather than pork. But veterans prefer pork. The reason is obvious. The fat of the pork, cooked or uncooked, takes the place of butter, and fulfils the want of an oleaginous constituent in the food. It also enables the soldiers to cook mutton or poultry that fall in their way on the march or on foraging expeditions. There is another reason why they prefer pork; its fat retards the penetration of the gastric juice, and it continues longer the sense of fullness in the stomach.

Salt Meats.—Let us look a little further. Salt meats have this great advantage, when properly cured—that they do not decay, in the ordinary sense of the term, and become offensive to taste and smell; but they experience another kind of deterioration. Dr. Thompson, of Glasgow, observed many years ago that the brine of salt meats had parted with its saltpetre and become charged with phosphates and sulphates. The latter constituents had been withdrawn from the tissues in the very process of curing. This change takes place inevitably with the salt meats shipped with our navy and merchant marine, and supplied to our soldiers; and the effect of the protracted use of salt meats in the production of scurvy has long been observed. This effect, though more generally remarked as incident to long voyages, has appeared repeatedly in our armies, where for considerable periods the men have lived on salt pork and hard bread, as at Fair Oaks, Cumberland Gap, Lookout Valley, and before Charleston.

Fresh beef, as ordinarily served from the butcher's stall, is recognized as one of the most acceptable and healthful of all the forms of meat; but slaughtered and then immediately served up, as it uniformly is in camp, rarely, except in winter, having time to cool, it is proverbially less healthful than if slaughtered and kept till it has had experienced a sort of spontaneous curing. Butchers usually keep their dressed meats for days, and sometimes for weeks, before supplying them to customers.

This evil is, however, much less than that of the effects of transportation by railroad or on shipboard, where a condition of fright, and in the latter case of sea-sickness in addition, is maintained for days together. Cattle weighing 1,500 pounds on the hoof in Chicago are estimated to lose 200 pounds of dressed meat in transportation in the cars to Boston. They lose but little less in being brought to New York or Washington. The fine cattle sent by the subsistence department from New York to supply the troops at Hilton Head, also lost, on an average 200 pounds a head. It is not alone the loss in weight, but the great deterioration in quality, that is to be considered. It is shown by Medical Inspector Hamlin, in his notes on the "Alimentation of Armies," that "the flesh of mammalia undergoes a great change in its nutritive qualities by reason of fasting, disturbance of sleep, and long continued suffering, resulting in its becoming not only worthless but deleterious." This is also shown by the experiments of Claude Bernard, and is substantiated by history and every day life. Bull-baiting was once authorized by law to make the meat tender, and cattle and buffalo are run down for the same object. The meat of moose and deer, shot in the tracks, is known to be healthful; while if the animals are run down the meat rapidly perishes, and if eaten frequently produces sickness.

Raised bread, made from sound flour, with yeast before acetic or lactic fermentation has set in, carefully baked and served without long transportation or loss of its moisture, is beyond question one of the most agreeable preparations of farinaceous food. It is porous, and admits the saliva and juices of the stomach for ready digestion. But as it is bulky, and contains from thirty to fifty per cent. of water, its transportation any considerable distance, especially in the absence of railroads or where wagon-roads are bad, is attended with great expense and frequently with much difficulty and irregularity. A wagon that will carry fifteen barrels of flour will carry but one seventh of this quantity in the form of freshly baked bread. If heaped in wagons as it comes from the oven, it packs and becomes heavy, sodden, and unpalatable. Issued once in four days, it becomes dry and hard before it is all consumed.

Hard bread, or "hard tack," has the advantage, when kept dry, of not being liable to decay, and may therefore be trusted to stay hunger where more perishable food would fail. But it is exceedingly bulky. A barrel that will contain 196 pounds of flour will hold but 75 pounds of hard bread. The daily ration is a formidable pile of more than 60 cubic inches. If wet, it rapidly becomes unfit for food, and frequently becomes mouldy when kept in moist places. When made from some kinds of flour, in which the starch or gluten, or both, assume a gelatinous character, and show, when baked and kiln-dried, a glassy fracture, it is quite impenetrable to the fluids of the mouth and stomach and exceedingly difficult to masticate. Soldiers whose back teeth are defective have difficulty in reducing the hard bread to proper condition for digestion; and to the soldier benumbed by cold or fatigue, imperfect nutrition is not unfrequently followed by protracted and dangerous diarrhea.

The Marching Ration.

Whatever weight may be attached to these considerations, there is one duty of the Commissary Department for which the existing arrangements are altogether inadequate. This is the duty of supplying marching rations for movements independent of base, such as forced marches, reconnoisances, raids, &c. Pending such movements, the chief in command orders the preparation of three, five, or eight days' rations. These are given out, cooked, packed in the haversack and knapsack, and laid aside to await expected orders to march. Meanwhile the daily rations are issued, cooked and eaten. A few days pass; the necessity, real or fancied, for the movement, has gone by, and the marching rations are found to be spoiled, and are thrown away. Or, if the march is undertaken with the haversack and pack stuffed to unwieldy size and weight, the soldier soon feels obliged to abandon a part of his load; if he stops to rest, and leans back on his pack, his hard bread is crushed; if it rains, and the pack does not wholly shelter the rations, the powdered crackers, sugar, coffee, and meat become, together, an offensive mass and a total loss. Sometimes the salt beef and pork, though issued, are not taken by the men, and constitute a part of the aggregate loss. These losses in the army of the Potomac have been estimated by competent authority on the spot, from the organization of the army, to be little less than one third of the total cost of the commissary supplies.

Source: E. N. Horsford, *The Army Ration: How to Diminish Its Weight and Bulk, Secure Economy in Its Administration, Avoid Waste, and Increase the Comfort, Efficiency, and Mobility of Troops* (New York: D. Van Nostrand, 1864), 3–4.

1864 • 76 • "Dairy Farming and Cheese Making"

Introduction: *The American dairy industry began in New England in colonial times. After the completion of the Erie Canal, many farmers migrated westward where land was inexpensive and began dairy farming in central New York. During the 1850s, the factory system became the model for most successful dairy farms. In this system, farmers carried their own milk to a central factory, collectively paid a superintendent and also paid for other expenses, and received a percent of the profits. An early example of the factory system was the Cheese Manufacturing Association launched by Jesse Williams in Rome, New York. Williams was an experienced and skillful cheese maker. When his son married in 1851 and purchased his own farm, Williams contracted to make cheese from the milk of his son's cows. The son delivered the milk daily to his father's milk house. Williams then converted the milk into cheese. This worked admirably, and soon other neighbors joined in. By 1864, Williams manufactured cheese from the milk of about 1,000 cows and greatly lowered the cost of production. Williams had been engaged in cheese farming all of his life. He expanded his operation in order to take milk from others and erected buildings expressly for processing the milk. His success led to the creation of other factories. Below is a description of his farm in 1864.*

Dairy Farming and Cheese Making

The Factory System in Central New York.

Mr. Jesse Williams is the pioneer in the establishment of the present way of conducting the cheese factories in Central New York. Having been all his life engaged in cheese farming, and making an article which commanded always the best price, he was led by degrees into the way of taking milk from others to manufacture, until a few years ago he was receiving the milk from several hundred cows, and erected rough buildings expressly for the purpose. The success of the enterprise has led to the gradual erection of other factories, since 1860, and the number in operation or in progress in 1863 had become quite large, particularly in Oneida county, along the headwaters of the Mohawk, and to some extent in the counties of Herkimer, Oswego, Cortland, and perhaps also in the cheese region of Ohio.

System of Management.—There are two ways in which the business of the factories is conducted:

Under the first, a specified price, generally one cent per lb., is paid for the making of the cheese; an account is kept with those whose milk is sent to the factories; and the returns of sales are divided, after deducting the one cent per lb., together with the cost of bandages, annatto, or other material required, in proportion to the quantity of milk furnished. The contributors carry their own milk to the factory morning and night, or several of them in the same locality hire this done. In some instances, competition has led to the factory's collecting the milk without charge; but this is a tax it can hardly be asked to bear. The whey also goes to the factory, and is fed to pigs, "boarded" by the proprietors, at say 12½ cents per week. At the factory of Williams & Wright, Whitesboro, where milk has received from between 600 and 700 cows, 119 pigs were thus taken to board, at the price named.

Cows and a milkmaid on a dairy farm, 19th century. (Library of Congress)

Another system, of later introduction, approaches more nearly to the character of a "mutual benefit" arrangement than of a private enterprise. Instead of a charge of so much per lb. for making the cheese, the factory is erected by the parties who are to contribute milk; and, in the settlement of accounts, the salary of the superintendent, and other expenses, together with such a per centage on the capital invested as will pay for repairs, as well as interest to the shareholders, are deducted before a division of the returns, in proportion to the amount of milk contributed by each. The charge of 15 per cent. is thought to be sufficient to cover both interest and repairs. On this system the Rome cheese Manufacturing Association, of which Mr. Jesse Williams is the Superintendent, is conducted, and it is thought that with the business carried on upon a scale of sufficient extent—say in making up the milk of 800 or 1,000 cows—the net cost of the process will amount to not more than a small fraction above one-half cent per lb., thus effecting a considerable saving over the other system.

In factories of both kinds, the milk of small producers may be brought for manufacture, the proceeds of which would of course be divided in proportion to capital, if the milk is bought on account of all the stockholders.

Arrival of the Milk.—The milk is now brought to the factories mainly in a kind of can which we have nowhere else seen, or heard described, although it may be in use in other localities. The cans are of tin, of circular form, holding from 30 to 80 gallons; the covers have a flange six inches wide, which fits into the *inside* of the can as exactly as possible. An aperture is made in the top of the cover. With tin rim to contain a cork; this acts as a vent, to allow the escape of the air when the cover is put into the can; it goes to within half or three-quarters of an inch of the surface of the milk, when the vent is corked, and the milk is so closely confined that there is no splashing at all, and comparatively little agitation in hauling it to the factory. The cork must be removed, of course, to get the cover out; for the flange fits so closely to the inside of the can that the pressure of the atmosphere is exerted upon the top of the cover. These cans are driven long distances without a drop of the milk finding its way out on to the top of the cover. They are provided with a spigot to draw off the milk at the bottom, and are sometimes made, for the use of a particular factory, all of the same diameter, so that a single gage-rod will show the quantity contained in each, without other measurement.

On reaching the factory the milk is weighed out, however, and the number of pounds by this weight credited at once to the sender; it then runs off into the vats below. The accounts of the factories are properly kept by weight of the milk; and the system of wine and beer gallons *should be* wholly discarded. The beer gallon containing 282 cubic inches, has been introduced in the purchase of milk, in place of the common wine gallon of 231 cubic inches, because farmers who had milk for sale were found more ready to give a larger gallon than to receive a price nominally smaller. . . .

The *Vats,* used at the factories, are simple oblong tanks of wood, with an inner vat of tin, leaving a space between the two of one and a half inches . . . for admission and circulation of water and steam. They contain from 4,000 to 4,500 lbs. of milk. The thermometer may be conveniently suspended from a pulley over each vat, with weight at the other end of the cord, at the side of the room; it is thus plunged into the milk and withdrawn out of the way, without leaving the side of the vat.

Setting the Curd.—The morning's milk, as it comes in, is used to fill up the vats, (already half filled with that of the night before,) to their entire capacity; and if the temperature, after the two are intermingled, is found below 82°, steam is admitted around them—the space being partially filled with water, until this temperature, (or in some cases a degree or two higher,) is attained. A *slight* portion of annatto is added; the hue desired not being a deep one, but rather like that of rich cream, or, when the cheese is finished, a good butter color. The rennet is also put in—its amount being one of those things for which no specific rules can be given; the experience of the maker, and the relative strength of the rennet, determine how much will induce coagulation in from 40 to 45 minutes. During this time the vat may be covered with a cloth. When perhaps an hour has elapsed, and the curd has the right firmness of texture and clean fracture, it is cut perpendicularly with the curd knife shown in the annex figure, (1)—a knife with five two-edged blades, . . . sixteen inches long, seven-eighths of an inch wide, and one-fourth to one-half inch apart. This curd knife is generally considered a great improvement, although there are some who still use the old wooden cutter, with its ashen blades two inches wide and the same distance apart.

Soon after this first cutting, longitudinally and transversely, so that the curd stands in perpendicular columns, the whey separates sufficiently to stands over the top of the curd. Steam is then admitted, until the temperature of 86° or 88° is attained—the attendant meantime gently stirring with the hands, for some minutes. After this stirring, in about twenty minutes, the whey is quite completely separated, and may be partly drawn off by a syphon, into a trough, which carries it out into the whey tank.

Cooking and Salting the Curd.—The curd is now cut and re-cut with the knife, and steam admitted to the judgment of the operator. This cooking of the curd is continued from one to a half to four hours; and it is upon this part of the process, and the skill with which it is managed, both as to time and degree of heat, that success is mainly dependant. The cutting and stirring continue during the cooking, at least until the particles are subdivided to about the size of large grains of wheat, and all are equally subjected to the cooking process, which is a part of the preparation that should not be hurried. When the curd is judged to be sufficiently cooked—a point determined by the feeling under pressure, and by experience—the remainder of the whey is drawn off. A sink on rollers runs along the side of the room at the head of the vats, and out into the apartment containing the presses. It has a perforated bottom, over which a sheet is spread, and the curd being placed upon this, the whey drains off and is carried away by an outlet underneath. The curd is stirred continually as it is put into the sink, to facilitate the process of drainage, as well as to prevent the particles from caking together, and salt is added, which is carefully intermingled throughout. Mr. Williams' rule is, two and seven-tenths pounds of salt to 1,000 pounds of milk. The vat, which we have watched in the process of cooking and salting, at the Whitesboro factory of Messrs. Williams & Wight, we were told, had contained 3,900 lbs. milk, and that 10½ lbs. of salt were put with the curd, which would be nearly in accordance with the above figures.

The Whitesboro Factory, here referred to, we should add, is a model of its kind. It stands, as they generally do, on something of a side-hill, so that the milk is taken from the wagons on to a platform within, high enough to be out of the way of those passing below, and overlooking the whole room—on which platform the milk is weighed and credited, and the amount put into each vat computed, to regulate its subsequent treatment. A boiler set in brick-work stands somewhat to the left of this platform, with ten flues like those of a locomotive boiler, which makes the steam for heating purposes. That day, June 24, 14,915 lbs. of milk were received, and ten pounds of milk would make one of cheese. The press used is a simple screw press, or a series of them, side by side, to which the curd is taken as soon as salted, and the cheese hoops filled and placed under pressure. At night the cheese are turned in the press and bandaged; they are taken out the next day, after 24 hours are up. The labor of the factory is performed by three men and five women. It received the milk of 48 farms, or probably 650 cows, and had only been in operation since April 9th; its ultimate capacity is equal, we presume, to 1,000 cows.

The Cheese House, or curing building, is 30 by 100 feet in length, of two stories, lathed and plastered, ceiled and ventilated. It will contain about 200,000 lbs. of cheese, or 1,600 chesses of the average weight of 125 lbs. as then made. Each story has shelving in four rows for cheeses to stand upon, each cow containing two tiers, one above the other, and each tier two rows of cheeses side by side. An improvement has been adopted in the construction of this shelving, which renders the turning process much more easy. The *upper* shelf is not too high to be conveniently reached, not quite four feet; it is composed of two parallel pieces of scantling. . . .

The cheese are kept from 30 to 40 days before they are sold, daily turned, rubbed and greased. The whey butter used for grease is tinted with annato to about the same shade as the interior of the cheese, and the four or five hundred cheeses which we saw at this factory were as uniform in all respects as cheese well could be made.

The Cheese Boxes, for the use of the factories, are made with greater care, and of greater strength, than has been generally customary for private use. This is not only to give a better and more uniform appearance in selling, but in order to afford more secure protection in transportation. The cheeses are 21 inches in diameter, and average, at the factory of Messrs. Williams & Wight, about 125 lbs. weight. About 17,500 lbs. had already been sold, at the time of our visit, during the season, at 12 cents per lb.

The system of cheese making at the factories . . . differs mainly from that in private dairies for two reasons—first, owing to the greater hazard of souring to which the milk is liable in being Carried to them, and from any carelessness in contributors in not having their cans perfectly sweet; and, in the second place as regards the temperature at some stages in the process, owing to the larger quantity of milk together, so that a lower heat will often answer than is necessary where a smaller quantity would retain it for a shorter time. Each cheese . . . is marked neatly with the date at which it was made, and with its weight. There are slight variations in the system of manufacture at the different factories. Thus, there are some who, after adding the rennet to set the curd, *stir* the milk until the action of the rennet is perceptible, then covering the vat and letting it stand until sufficiently firm for the first cutting with the curd knife.

Source: *Illustrated Annual Register of Rural Affairs for the Year 1864* (Albany, NY: Luther Tucker and Son, 1864), 82–83, 87–91.

1864 • 77 • "Turkeys for the Sailors"

Introduction: *Unlike the South during the Civil War, Northern states were well stocked with food throughout the war. In early November 1864, citizens throughout the North decided to send a large amount of food—including cooked turkeys—to the Union sailors blockading Confederate ports and to troops fighting in Virginia. Below is a reporter's view of how the food was received.*

The steamer Kensington, having on board a large supply of turkeys for the navy, arrived in the Roads yesterday. The friends who so liberally contributed towards the purchase of this welcome gift will be pleased to know that their worthy effort has already been productive of the most cheering results. Both officers and men have repeatedly testified their appreciation of the generous motive which prompted this consideration of their comfort and happiness on Thanksgiving day, and look upon the act as one not to be forgotten. In a General Order, issued by Admiral Porter, it is directed that each man throughout the squadron shall receive at least a ration of two pounds. The vessels in the immediate vicinity of the Roads and Norfolk, are receiving their modicum to-day. A steamer was also at the steamer's side this morning taking on a supply of turkeys for the portion of the fleet up the James River. The Kensington will proceed up the blockading fleet off Wilmington in season to supply the vessels there. It isn't the Turkey but the Idea. Advices have been received from the turkeys sent to Sheridan's army for Thanksgiving. Forty-nine thousand eight hundred and fourteen pounds of poultry were distributed in that army exclusively to enlisted men. Gen. Sheridan, in a letter of thanks says "I am confident that as I write—now Thanksgiving day—many of our gallant soldiers are tacitly blessing those at home for the kind remembrances so substantially manifested." Seventy-five wagon loads of poultry reached Winchester. The agents accompanied the poultry report: T[h]anksgiving day we rode over part of our lines and made personal inquiries and inspection as to the practical result of our mission. The want of proper appliances compelled most men to broil or stew their turkeys, but every one seemed fully satisfied and appreciated the significance of this sympathetic thank-offering from the loyal North. One soldier said to me, "It isn't the turkey, but the idea that we care for," and he thus struck the key note of the whole festival. Could the donors of this Thanksgiving gift have been with us on this ride they would have felt satisfied that, whether as a token of grateful appreciation of past valor or as the inspiration of future effort in the good cause, it had not been made in vain.

Source: "Turkeys for the Sailors," *New York Times,* November 24, 1864, 1.

1864 • 78 • "The Late Destruction of Property in the Shenandoah Valley"

Introduction: *Throughout the Civil War, farms and plantations in the Shenandoah Valley in Virginia supplied food to Confederate armies and civilians in Richmond. In early 1864 General Ulysses Grant, commander of Union forces, made the decision to destroy all crops, agricultural equipment, storage facilities, and mills. Below is the description of what happened.*

The Late Destruction of Property in the Shenandoah Valley

Summary: Reviews the destruction resulting from General Grant's orders to turn the Shenandoah Valley into "barren waste." Criticizes this policy as "cold-blooded brutality."

The following account of the burning of barns and mills in the Shenandoah Valley [by] Gen. Sheridan, under the order of General Grant "to make the Shenandoah Valley a barren waste," the main facts of which are stated by Gen. Sheridan himself in his official report, is given by a correspondent of the New York World. If this is the way the war is to be carried on in the future. God save the people along the border! Here is the account:

The Shenandoah Valley Made A Barren Waste.

I have received two accounts of the manner in which Gen. Grant's orders "to make of the Valley a barren was[t]e," was executed. One of them is from an officer in the army. Both accounts agree in all essential particulars; and I think I may safely say that for real devilish malibnity and cool-blooded brutality, the execution of his order surpasses all the cruelty of Butler, and, in all save one particular, equals even the atrocity of Turchin. What do the readers of the World think of the wanton burning of twenty-seven hundred barns, filled with wheat, and more than eighty mills for grinding wheat and corn? This was done by soldiers of "The Union," with the Union flag waving over them. But they did more than that. The flames from the burning barns communicated, in many instances, to dwelling-houses contiguous, and houses and barns alike, in a few hours, with all their contents, were reduced to a mass of smouldering ruins. The kind-hearted soldiers, in some cases, wished to extinguish the flames of these burning houses, but there were other barns to be fired, and they were hurried away.

But the worst remains to be told. The burning of these houses was accidental, although the burning of the contiguous barns was intentional. But there is one district where three hundred and eighty seven dwelling houses were burned, with all their contents, by the express order of General Sheridan. This work was done with deliberation, and without any other than the briefest warning to the inmates. All appeals for mercy were vain. Tottering age and feeble infancy, delicate ladies, and women in that state which would find pity even in the eyes of a savage, were compelled to rush out of their houses, and then to witness their homes consumed before their eyes by devouring flames. Remember that the barns and granaries of these unfortunate people had been destroyed, and all their provisions carried away. They were now driven from their homes, their houses burned over their heads, their furniture, their clothing, all that they had in the world destroyed, and left to perish in these cold inclement nights. What pen can describe the horrors of these scenes? With a refinement of malignity worthy of the evil one himself, not only the seed for next year's crops, but even the very farming implements themselves were burned up.

General Sheridan says he burned all the houses within an area of five miles, because one of his officers was murdered there. I would like to see the murderer hung, and all of his accomplices. But to thus visit a crime, which at the worst was only one of the casualties of war, upon hundreds of innocent women and children, and to render homeless many innocent families, is an act that is not worthy of a general, and that will do the Union cause no good.

Citizens of Franklin county, what think you of the prospect before you? If the rebels should again invade our State, (which is not at all improbable) in what condition do you suppose they would leave our beautiful Valley with its fine farm-houses and magnificent barns and mills? Chambersburg in ashes is the fruit of Hunter's vandalism in Virginia last spring. The horrors that may accrue to our people through these unparalelled deeds of vandalism are happily, for the present, hid from our view. Would to God, they might forever remain hid!

It makes the blood run cold in our veins to contemplate the accumulation of sorrow that our misguided rulers are bringing upon this distracted land. May the hand of Omnipotence shield the people, and interpose between them and the blind fanaticism that rules the hour.

Source: "The Late Destruction in the Shenandoah Valley," *New York World,* reprinted in *Valley Spirit,* October 19, 1864, http://valley.lib.virginia.edu/news/vs1864/pa.fr.vs.1864.10.19.xml.

1865 • 79 • James H. W. Huckins, "Improved Tomato Soup"

Introduction: *Commercial canning began in America around 1820. James H. W. Huckins of Boston began canning soup in 1855 and was the first commercial soup company in America. The soups were sold in two-quart cans, and all the consumer needed to do was heat the contents and serve. The company patented its tomato soup recipe in 1865.*

Improved Tomato Soup

. . . I . . . have invented a new and useful or improved composition of matters, which may be termed "Tomato Soup," and I do hereby declare the same, or the materials of which it is composed and the mode of compounding them, to be described as follows, viz:

Take a stock-boiler that will hold about twenty gallons. Put into it fifty pounds of beef-shin to fourteen gallons of cold water. Boil it, partly uncovered, for fourteen hours. After the water has partly boiled away add a little hot water from time to time, as it may require. After it has boiled the required time take it from the fire and add to it one quart of cold water. Afterward let it stand for ten minutes. Next, skim off all of the fat and strain the liquor from the meat through a fine sieve, and we shall have very nearly seven gallons of the liquor. Should there be more than seven gallons of the liquor, boil it down to the required quantity, but should there be a less amount, add the difference in hot water. This is called "stock." Next, take one bushel and a half of tomatoes, put them into a boiler, mash them up a little, and let them boil in their own liquor for one hour and a half. Next, strain them through a fine sieve—fine enough to stop the seeds and the skins. All the rest of the tomato must go through the sieve, after which we shall have about six gallons of the tomato liquor. If more than six gallons, boil it down to such amount. If less, add more tomato. Next, mix the stock and the prepared tomato together, and keep the mixture somewhat under a boiling temperature until wanted for further action. Next, prepare the following vegetables: Peel and weigh one pound and a half of onions, the same amount of turnips, one pound and three-quarters of carrots, and one pound of beets. Chop them all together quite fine. Next, take a soup-boiler that will hold sixteen gallons. Put into it three and a half pounds of butter. Next, add the chopped vegetables. Put the boiler on a hot fire, and cook the vegetables well. Next, add to them three and one-quarter pounds of flour, and thoroughly mix the whole together while hot. Next, take the boiler from the fire and let it cool a little. Next, add one ounce of black pepper, one-half a pound of brown sugar. Mix the whole well together, and add the mixture of beef-stock and tomato. The composition must now be well stirred for about ten minutes, and afterward put on the fire and stirred until it may boil. Continue to let it boil and skim it for about five minutes, after which strain it through a fine sieve, but do not press the vegetables through the sieve. The composition will then be ready for the table, or for being hermetically sealed in cans. The amount of the preparation (which I term "tomato soup") so made will be about thirteen gallons. It is a composition containing preservative qualities, which will prevent it from decomposition for a great length of time.

I claim—

The composition made in manner and of materials substantially as hereinbefore specified.

James H. W. Huckins.

Source: U.S. Patent No. 47,545, issued May 2, 1865.

1867 • 80 • Thomas F. Devoe, "Going to Market"

Introduction: *There were no supermarkets in the 19th century. Most urbanites did their shopping at open-air markets, much like present-day farmers' and green markets.*

Thomas F. Devoe (1811–1892) was a butcher at a market in New York, and he wrote two books about markets. Below is an excerpt from The Market Assistant *(1867) that gives a brief introduction to those unfamiliar with city markets.*

Going to Market.

Some fifty years ago it was the common custom for the thrifty "old New Yorker," when going to market, to start with the break of day, and carry along with him the large "market-basket," then considered a very necessary appendage for this occasion. His early visit gave him the desired opportunity to select the cuts of meat wanted from the best animals; to meet the farmer's choice productions, either poultry, vegetables, or fruit, and catch the lively, jumping fish, which, ten minutes before, were swimming in the fish-cars.

Soon after followed the "good housewife," who would not trust anybody but herself to select a fine young turkey, or a pair of chickens or ducks, which she kept hold of until the bargain allowed her to place the coveted articles in her capacious basket, that was being carried by a stout servant, who also carried a bright tin, covered kettle, ready to receive several nice rolls of butter, so cleanly and neatly covered with white linen cloths.

The modern "marketer" will still occasionally observe some "relics of the past," who cling to the old custom taught them in their youth, perhaps, by an honored sire, who was not too proud to carry home a well-filled market-basket, containing his morning purchase, which his purse or taste prompted him to select. These old-fashioned ideas, alas! are all lived down, and we reluctantly turn from them, as we would from an interesting but worn-out book to peruse the pages of modern composition.

We now find many heads of families who never visit the public markets, who are either supplied through the butcher or other dealers in our markets, or by their stewards or other servants, or by some that may be termed go-between-speculators, who take orders for marketing, groceries, etc., on their own hook; and, of course, they purchase the various articles of those who will give them the largest percentages. I am sorry, however, to be compelled to state that there are but few of this species of help, or market assistants, who can lay claim to the title of trustworthy.

It is, therefore, as necessary for our health as it is to our interest to obtain the knowledge of what we desire to purchase, that the articles shall be what they are represented to be, and that they are furnished at the regular market price.

To market well, then, requires much experience, although many rules might be introduced, but they would be seldom successfully followed. Practice gives the looks, smell, feeling, and many signs that are almost indescribable, and which are formed from close observation.

Many dealers know too well how to disguise an inferior article, so as to deceive those who have but little knowledge of marketing; although a lower price may be demanded, such provisions are dear from the fact of their inferior quality, and when prepared are neither relished nor half consumed—perchance they are wholly wasted.

Another class of dealers, while they furnish good articles, they do not fail to obtain exorbitant prices, of such a character as to come under the name of extortion. To succeed in such extortions, different modes of misrepresentation are adopted, which, in our plain vernacular, might be termed absolute lying—"business lying," white or black lying, or any other lying the reader may choose to designate the system.

Their articles are represented as being—"The very best that were ever produced!"—"The finest and largest you ever saw!"—"Could not be better!"—"First-rate!"—"Excellent!"—"Beautiful!"—"Splendid!"—"Can't be beat!"—"As cheap as dirt!" and "Can't be got elsewhere!"

One day I heard a military hero say to a person who was extolling a good common goose, and enlarging on the numerous splendid accessories surrounding it—"Why, your geese are all swans—I do not want any of them. I merely want a good young goose, about that size."

The numerous falsehoods sometimes told, are expressed with such appearance of innocence, that many really feel that what they say must be "the truth, the whole truth, and nothing but the truth," and so accede to their extortionate demands. This class of dealers effect more business and succeed better than the honest, conscientious dealer, who, when asked, "Is this article the best I can get?" will answer, "I should not like to say it is, but I think it is as good." Such an answer is not always a satisfactory one to the questioner, as he would require one of certainty, or—"It is the very best that comes to the markets, and you cannot get it elsewhere so good, nor so cheap." This appears to be a great fault with many purchasers, that to induce them to buy the dealers must bespatter their articles with a dozen falsehoods, and sometimes fifteen or twenty per cent. above the market price, before the purchasers are fully satisfied with their bargains.

This wretched system or custom, we find, generally pervades everywhere, and in every business, where goods and other property are exposed to sale; both men and women, merchants and mechanics, tradesmen and salesmen, in fact all kinds, are afflicted with this prevailing tongue-disease of exaggeration.

This dishonest custom gives the honest salesman or purveyor but little satisfaction while doing business, as they are often subjected to many petty annoyances, which usually come from those whose education should teach them better. There are others who are deficient of this desideratum, who claim from the lack of educated honesty some charity and excuse for their acts. We occasionally find among purchasers some who are known as "shoppers" and "runners," who make no difference where they trade, so long as it shall be the best article at a low price; and to make a sale to such the market-price must generally be reduced; and when that is done, suspicion steps into the "shopper's" mind, who examines and re-examines, with question after question, whether "perfectly good, tender, and sweet;" and upon being answered in the affirmative, the "shopper" often turns from the dealer with a supercilious gesticulation, as if they placed no confidence in the recommendation. We recur to an instance where a lady had several times treated a butcher to this negative treatment to his recommended meat, when she was, by him, impressed with this well-merited retort: "My previous answers, in relation to the quality of meat which you several times before selected, have not received such attention as was expected from you; hereafter you will be obliged to judge for yourself." She was not a purchaser on that occasion, but afterwards she gave no further trouble in this respect.

There are other dealers, again, who use much of what may be termed outside deceit—that is, by placing some attractive mark or emblem, in the way of flags, ribbons, signs, etc., to represent the articles so dressed and decorated as being either premium or prize or superior, or some extraordinary quality about them, from the good or general average of what they should represent; and this is done for the purpose of procuring a higher price for an inferior article. In fact, I have heard it said: "I put ribbons and flags on my meat to make it sell for a good price, as I am bound to make money some way or another." This method this class adopt as a "legitimate manner of doing business."

The safest plan for the inexperienced is to select respectable dealers, on whom they can rely. They may charge higher prices for that which they furnish; in the end, however, more satisfaction is afforded, by less risk, and more saving and relish—in fact, cheaper in every way, because all good articles are with profit used—that, while the best articles may cost more money in the purchase thereof, they will be found to be the most economical in the end.

On the other view, unprincipled dealers are always ready for what they term chances, either by giving short weight, short measure, or short change; and, if they are detected, "Why, it's a mistake!" or, if he (or she) think that blustering, or loud and harsh words, will frighten the wronged purchaser, this mode of tactics is brought to bear.

Many respectable purchasers, not having the time to go to the public markets, will sometimes purchase of the "cheap shops," or street-pedlers, many of whom are still worse than those we have already spoken of, especially street-pedlers, who cannot be found when their fraud or deceit is too late discovered.

A few years ago, one of the city sealers of weights and measures, in one of the districts of our (New York) city, collected fifty-four measures, from grocers and wagon-pedlers, that fell short of the standard. A half-bushel fell short three and a half quarts; twenty-one half-peck measures fell short about one quart each; fifteen two-quart measures were short six quarts in the aggregate; and sixteen one-quart measures were short, in the aggregate, six quarts.

An old law, as well as a long-standing custom, makes it incumbent upon the seller that all articles subject to be sold by the measure—such as apples, peaches, potatoes, and others of a round, oval, or flat conformation—shall be heaped up above the even line of the measures, to make up for the interspaces between the irregularities of such articles of food, etc.

The fish, fruit, vegetables, etc., which are usually peddled about the streets in carts and wagons, are seldom found so good as those offered for sale in the public markets, they being either the refuse of the markets, unfit to be offered by the respectable dealer, or happens to be a glut, or very large quantities offered; and, even then, their selections are generally of those which sell at the lowest price; then, in their sales through the streets, their false-bottomed measures, short weights, or their stale or unfit articles, are detected by examination; they are off, and not to be found, until the frauds and their persons are forgotten.

When the purchaser desires to be served through orders by the butcher, or others, it is best that they should have such latitude or choice of sending the purchaser that which they may have in the best condition for immediate use. If it be for a roast, it should be either a rib, sirloin, or other piece of beef; or leg, loin, saddle, or shoulder of mutton; or fore or hind quarter of lamb; or fillet, loin, shoulder, or breast of veal; or turkey, capons, chickens, venison, partridges, or grouse, etc. If for a boil, a leg of mutton, rump or round, plate, navel, or brisket of corned beef; and the same, in fact, with all the various dishes.

Without particular joints, or other articles, are ordered for an arranged or "dinner-party," it is then best, as well as proper, to give notice a day or two before, that the butcher, or other, may prepare a particular, prime, or choice article, such as may not only please the purchaser, but will give the butcher, or other dealer, some

Vendors sell wares out of their pushcarts along Hester Street in New York City, ca. 1900. (Photo Collection Alexander Alland, Sr./Corbis)

satisfaction—as it is gratifying to the conscientious dealer to hear that his joints or other articles were praised, as it is to those who pay for that which is acceptable and pleasing to them.

Source: Thomas F. Devoe, *The Market Assistant* (New York: Hurd and Houghton, 1867), 22–26.

1868 • 81 • Louisa May Alcott, "The History of a Squash"

Introduction: *Louisa May Alcott (1832–1888) was an American writer and novelist. Her first literary success,* Little Women: Or, Meg, Jo, Beth, and Amy *(1868), was a semiautobiographical novel of her early life growing up with her sisters in Orchard House, the Alcott home in Concord, Massachusetts. In the book, the sisters create a make-believe story based on Charles Dickens's characters. They each wrote stories and poems to share with the others. Beth, nicknamed "Mr. Tupman," wrote up the recipe for squash, which was a common food consumed in prehistoric times by American Indians and was an important food adopted by European colonists.*

The History of a Squash.

Once upon a time a farmer planted a little seed in his garden, and after a while it sprouted and became a vine, and bore many squashes. One day to October, when they were ripe, he picked one and took it to market. A grocer man bought and put it in his shop. That same morning, a little girl, in a brown hat and blue dress, with a round face and snubby nose, went and bought It for her mother. She lugged it home, cut it up, and boiled it in the big pot; mashed some of it, with salt and butter, for dinner; and to the rest she added a pint of milk, two eggs, four spoons of sugar, nutmeg, and some crackers; put it in a deep dish, and baked it till it was brown and nice; and next day it was eaten by a family named March.

T. Tupman

Source: Louisa May Alcott, *Little Women: Or, Meg, Jo, Beth, and Amy* (Boston: Roberts Brothers, 1868), 123.

1868 • 82 • Gail Borden, "An Eminent Inventor"

Introduction: *Gail Borden (1801–1874) was an entrepreneur who had failed miserably at manufacturing dehydrated meat in the shape of biscuits and invented a method of preserving milk by adding sugar, heating it, and reducing it. Basically broke but with financial help from friends, Borden embarked on his condensed milk project. He felt that he had perfected the process in 1852, but his attempt to manufacture it on a commercial scale did not work out, and his faithful investors lost their money. Borden tried again in 1858 with yet another partner, opening a plant in Wolcottville, Connecticut. Just as Borden began shipping condensed milk to New York City,* Frank Leslie's Illustrated Newspaper *broke the shocking story of New York's "swill milk trade." In the wake of this nauseating exposé, which went on for months, Borden's canned and pasteurized milk found a ready market. Borden's advertising stressed the fact that his canned milk was safe, and panicked New Yorkers eagerly snapped it up. Encouraged by early sales figures, Borden optimistically began construction on several additional plants. These new factories came on line just as the Civil War began. Although Borden didn't know it, he had just taken a major step toward the industrialization of American food processing. Below is his biography, published in 1868.*

Gail Borden, of New York, formerly of Galveston, Texas, is an eminent inventor, who has extended his explorations into fields comparatively untrod by others. His name came prominently before the public by his invention, in 1850, of a Meat Biscuit, containing in the smallest possible bulk all the nutritive properties of the beef or other meat used in its manufacture. The means by which he accomplished this consisted in combining a concentrated extract of meat with the finest flour, and thoroughly desiccating the mixture. Beef, freshly slaughtered, was boiled for a protracted time in a quantity of water, and, after the careful removal of all fat, the broth, separated from the meat, was evaporated by steam heat to a uniform density. This extract, resembling syrup, was then kneaded with the best flour, cut into biscuits, which were subjected to moderate heat in an oven, and then ground into a powder for convenience in packing and use.

The Meat Biscuit received the careful study of many eminent scientific men in this country and in Europe. Professor Playfair, after a prolonged examination, pronounced it an excellent article, retaining unimpaired the nutritive properties of its constituents. Dr. Solly used even more laudatory language. The report, accompanying the award of a Council medal at the Great Exhibition in London in 1851, says: "A more simple, economical, and efficient form of portable concentrated food than the American Meat Biscuit has never been brought before the public."

Mr. Borden, however, entertained the idea that the extract might be perfectly preserved without the agency of the flour used in desiccation, and, after experiments for several years, in which he was assisted by Mr. J. H. Currie and Mr. S. L. Goodale, he perfected a process by which the pure broth, previously alluded to, is reduced to a solid form.

The extract, as at present made, is a nut-brown substance of the consistence of caoutchouc, readily dissolved in hot water, forming a broth possessing the flavor of delicately roasted meat. The points in the process, which the inventor considers of cardinal importance, are, 1st. Care in the selection of the beef. 2d. Great promptness in commencing the treatment after slaughter. 3d. Immediate and thorough exhaustion of the meat.

By the use of the vacuum pan the liquid extract is evaporated at a low degree of temperature. A product which is so useful wherever an easily portable aliment is desired, has met with marked favor. Physicians employ it in the sick-room, as a ready means of making beef tea of definite strength, so that they can now prescribe this supporting agent with as much certainty of having a good article made as they have in regard to their ordinary drug prescriptions. The value of this extract in long journeys, by land or sea, is obvious, and its general use by explorers and tourists is not a matter of conjecture. As a means of so perfectly preserving the beef of the great producing districts of the West and Southwest that the expense of transportation to the consuming cities is reduced to a minimum, this process becomes of national importance, and deservedly takes high rank among the valuable inventions of the century.

While prosecuting his investigations in regard to the preservation of Meat, Mr. Borden became convinced that milk could, by some process, be materially reduced in bulk, and preserved for any desirable length of time.

Several preparations of milk had already been presented by scientific men to the public of France, England, and America, but the disproportion between their price and that of new milk prevented their general introduction and use. Moreover, many of these preparations contained foreign substances, designed to resemble those solid constituents of milk of which they had been deprived in the process of manufacture, but these artificial substitutes fell far short of the caseine, oil, and salts of new milk in nutritive value. The successful method adopted by Mr. Borden, after a long series of experiments upon a large scale, was substantially as follows: The milk is brought by the dairyman immediately after milking to the factory, where it is subjected to a heating process preparatory to its evaporation in vacua. It is then strained and drawn into the vacuum pan, and reduced to its required density by the abstraction of about seventy-five per cent. of the water. That which is to be carried at once to the city is called plain condensed milk, and resembles a very tenacious syrup. That which is to be placed in cans is mixed intimately in the process with the best white sugar and hermetically sealed. This is known as Preserved Milk, and will keep in perfect order for a great length of time, readily dissolving in water after the lapse of years. This vacuum process, which had never before been carried out, obviates many practical difficulties that had discouraged those who had previously endeavored to condense or solidify milk. The high appreciation in which this article is held by physicians led to its immediate introduction into families in our large cities, and prepared the way for its very general use on voyages. During our late civil war, Mr. Borden's Milk was very extensively employed in the Army and Navy, and the concurrent testimony of soldiers and officers, of those who used it as a luxury and of those who used it in the hospitals, is of the most highly commendatory character.

Several manufactories of this Condensed Milk are now in operation in various parts of the country, the first having been located in Litchfield county, Connecticut. In 1860, more extensive works were erected on the Harlem Road, Dutchess Co., New York, where three vacuum pans are employed, capable of working five thousand gallons of milk per day. The next important factory is at Brewsters, Southeast, Putnam Co., with a large vacuum pan in which five thousand gallons of milk can be condensed in a day. Mr. Borden is also connected with a factory of a capacity of two thousand gallons, at Livermore Falls, Maine, and one of the same size at Elgin, Kane Co., on the Fox river, Illinois. Connected with the latter is a factory for the manufacture of the Extract of Beef.

Simultaneously with his experiments in the Condensation of Milk, Mr. Borden undertook the preparation of a decoction of Coffee in such a manner as to preserve the fine aroma of the roasted berry. The extract prepared by him contains condensed milk and pure sugar, and is easily soluble in hot water.

He also patented a process for the preservation of the juices of fruits, as apples, currants, and grapes, by which they may be reduced to one seventh of their original bulk, and are not then subjected to fermentation unless dissolved in water. The date of this patent is 22d of July, 1862.

The great success which has crowned the studies of Mr. Borden in the preservation of Food, may be attributed to the fact that he was one of the first to appreciate the importance of taking measures to prevent incipient decomposition or fermentation.

The full developments of the principles adopted by him in the manufacture of these new articles of commerce, has enabled him to preserve in their freshness and richness the most valuable nutritive liquids, and in such a perfect manner as to cause tourists and explorers to consider them among the indispensable necessaries of their journeys rather than mere luxuries.

Source: John Leander Bishop, *A History of American Manufactures from 1608 to 1860,* Vol. 2, 3rd ed. (Philadelphia: Edward Young and Co., 1868), 544–546.

1868 • 83 • Joseph G. McCoy, "Shipping Extra Choice Cattle"

Introduction: *Hollywood movies and fictional novels popularized the cattle drive, which drove cattle from Texas to the railroad junctions, such as Abilene, Dodge City, and Wichita in Kansas. From these railheads, the cattle were shipped to slaughterhouses in Chicago. Large-scale drives of longhorn cattle were conducted for only a 20-year period beginning after the Civil War. Outlaws and cattle rustlers made famous by Hollywood cowboy movies were of only minor concern to those engaged in the real cattle* *drives, as the following except from Joseph G. McCoy (1837–1915), author of* Historic Sketches of the Cattle Trade of the West and Southwest *(1874), demonstrates. McCoy was an entrepreneur who built a hotel and stockyard in the little village of Abilene. He told Texan cattle ranchers that if they drove their cattle to Abilene, he would guarantee them a good price for them. He kept his word, and cattle drives thrived until 1886, when railroads reached Texas, making long drives to Kansas unnecessary.*

Among the many fine herds of cattle that arrived at Abilene in the spring of 1868, there was one of 800 head, a very choice selection. Great pains had been taken in the best cattle regions of Texas in selecting choice fat cattle, and equally as great caution had been exercised in driving them to Kansas. After arriving at Abilene they were put on the best herd grounds in the county, where they added greatly to their already fine condition. The eye of a certain Illinoisan had been upon this herd for some time, fully determined when the opportune day arrived, to retrieve some of his severe losses sustained the previous year. When the proper time came he purchased two hundred and twenty-four head, his choice of the eight hundred head, and after selecting them carefully, one by one, drove them four miles to the shipping yards, and after standing them therein for twelve hours weighed them. They made the remarkable average of twelve hundred and thirty-eight pounds each, and amounted to seven thousand four hundred and sixty-eight dollars. They were placed upon the cars and sent forward to Chicago, thence forwarded to Buffalo, New York, where they were sold, and due account of sale made to shipper; but, alas, the net returns was only fourteen hundred and sixty-eight dollars, six thousand being lost, and not since found or heard of. The shipper has come to regard it as a permanent contribution, of a benevolent nature he hopes, toward feeding the oppressed laborers of New England's manufactories. So let it be, but not any more in the same way.

The charity of that cattle shipper is nearly exhausted, and bread for himself and family much in the same fix. This great loss was not because the cattle were not good and fat, for they were, but arose in part from the prejudice of people against Texas cattle, and the farther east the greater the prejudice, and the less they actually knew about the cattle. But the main cause of great sacrifice was the outbreak of the so-called "Spanish fever," which caused a tremendous excitement throughout the North. A disastrous panic occurred among holders of short-horn cattle, resulting in severe losses and often ruin to many northern cattle men. But before we go further into the discussion of the subject of the disease, its primal cause, preventives, etc., we will notice another enterprise that took practical shape in the spring of 1868. A certain firm of cattle-men in Chicago went to Texas and contracted with certain large cattle drovers to deliver about forty thousand head of cattle on the Mississippi river at the mouth of Red river where, upon delivery, the cattle were crowded in large numbers on the hot unventilated decks of large steamboats. After six to twelve days of perpetual standing upon the hard deck without room to lay down, or drink, or feed, suffering with heat and overcrowding, they were landed at Cairo, Illinois, in great poverty of flesh and famishing with hunger, and so near dead from exhaustion that in many instances they had to be helped up the levee to the shipping yards of the I. C. R. R.,[1] upon which road they were shipped to Tolono, ILL., and there unloaded and turned upon the prairies whereon all the domestic cattle of the county were grazing. Many of the Texas cattle were sold to feeders and grazers in that portion of Illinois, and some went into Indiana and were put in pastures, often mixed with the domestic cattle, no danger being apprehended. But before thirty days of hot weather had elapsed the domestic cattle on the prairies and in the pastures began to sicken and die at a frightful rate. Many grazers became alarmed and rushed their cattle off to market, fearing if they kept them that they would lose the entire herd by the dreaded disease. Several herds of domestic cattle which had been exposed were shipped east, and upon the way developed the disease, and speedily died, causing great losses to their owners and a feeling of indignant fear and excitement among all Eastern as well as Western cattle men, resulting, as before stated, in a crash and panic throughout the entire Northern cattle market, and a feeling of intense hostility toward southwestern cattle. Upon the prairie about Tolono, ILL., nearly every cow of domestic blood died. In one township every milk cow except one died. This was a great and serious loss to many poor farmers of that region and they became perfectly enraged at Texan cattle, and would have mobbed a man unto death who would have dared to talk in favor of Texan cattle, much less shipped a car-load of them. The trade via mouth of Red river was thoroughly broken up, with disaster to those engaged in it from the North. It was just at the outbreak of the excitement in the East that shipment of the two hundred and twenty-four head of fine Texan cattle from Abilene, arrived at Buffalo. Hence the great loss. About the same time that the disease appeared near Tolono, it also appeared in a much less fatal and less malignant form in other portions of Illinois, among domestic cattle which had been grazed with Texan cattle that had been introduced via Abilene Kas. But it is a fact well authenticated that but few cases of disease actually occurred after exposure to Texan cattle coming via Western Kansas, and those that did occur were of a milder type, and not sufficiently alarming to have created more than a local excitement, but coupled with the disaster that arose from the introduction of cattle, via mouth of Red river, it was sufficient to put an entire stop to the eastern demand, and consequent shipment of Texan cattle from all points to the east or anywhere into the northwest.

At the same time the disease appeared in Illinois, a few cattle died near Abiline, which were all or nearly all paid for by voluntary contributions of the cattle drovers and parties interested at Abilene; and thus the verbal pledges made to the farmers more than a year before—at a public meeting called to effect the dissolution of a hostile organization, the particulars of which have already been given—were made good to the letter.

The total loss of domestic cattle in Dickinson county was about forty-five hundred dollars in value. However, the prices at which the animals were appraised were often grossly exhorbitant, and in one or two cases fraudulent claims were made, a few of which were paid before detection. Of the fund necessary to liquidate these claims, about twelve hundred dollars was contributed by the drovers then at Abilene, the balance was paid by the parties who owned the shipping yards. The K. P.[2] Railway Company, by its general superintendent, agreed to contribute five hundred dollars, but after the claims were all settled and the Texan cattle shipped, the Railway Company repudiated its agreement and refused to pay anything. Such conduct became quite fashionable with the K. P. Railway Company in after days, indeed they soon became notorious for their bad faith in regard to contracts. It seemed to be their policy to repudiate every contract made. But we will speak of this more definitely in its proper place.

Throughout the entire Western states an unprecedented excitement arose about "Spanish fever," a name given by common consent to the malady or disease disseminated by Texan cattle. It was the subject of gossip by everybody and formed the topic of innumerable newspaper articles, as well as associated press dispatches. A panic seized upon owners of domestic herds everywhere and many rushed their cattle off to market only to meet panic-stricken operators from other sections and ruinously low prices for their stock.

The butchers, venders and consumers were alike alarmed and afraid to buy, sell or consume beef of any kind. The Agricultural Society of Illinois appointed of its members a committee of three to investigate the cause of the disease, the remedies, and the preventive, if any could be found. This investigation was conducted in all the districts in Illinois where the disease had made its appearance, also at Abilene, Kansas.

We believe it was as thorough in character and as conscientiously made as circumstances would admit. But no satisfactory cause of the disease was discovered, and of the various theories maintained none seemed to be entirely satisfactory or conclusive.

Soon after the outbreak of the disease the Governor of New York appointed inspectors and attempted to quarantine all cattle from the west or northwest. This soon began to work a hardship on the cattle shippers from Illinois and the Governor of that State appointed two commissioners to look after the interests of the Sucker State cattle boys. This diplomatic choir of ministers plenipotentiary in all matters pertaining to bulls of Suckerdom, were heavy weights, intellectually and otherwise.

We doubt not the State of New York was awed into respectfully considerate conduct by the magnetic presence of the mighty geniuses sent into her borders by the Governor of Illinois. Under the old Quaker rule they must have made splendid envoys.

This immortalizing act of the Governor of Illinois was followed by another, the calling of a convention of experts to assemble in the Sucker Capitol. This convention as a collection of quondam quacks, and impractical theorists, and imbecile ignoramuses, was without an equal.

There were in attendance delegates from most of the northern States; also two or more from the Canadas. A portion of the delegates were esculapians of the most deadly type—others mere political bummers—sent to that convention by their respective Governors to relieve the community, for a short time, at least, of a pestilential crew. Others were so prejudiced as to be utterly unfit to deliberate on, or investigate anything; a portion were of that class who will enjoy especial immunity on the final day, if it be true "That unto whom little is given, little will be required." There were a few earnest seekers after truth and information upon the vexed subject of "Spanish fever," and the importation of Texan cattle, and "What to do about it."

The convention as a body, was a prejudiced, impractical one, filled with a burning hatred of long-horned kine. The object of the convention was to determine upon a practical mode of protecting domestic cattle from disease, and to recommend a practical basis of legislation against the introduction of Texan cattle.

Upon the organization of the convention it was patent to the most casual observer that recommendations of absolute prohibition, for at least eight or ten months in the year, was the only policy that could or would be adopted, and such was the case.

There was but one man upon that floor, and he an honorary member from Kansas, that dare raise his voice in behalf of Texan cattle, and his speech brought forth a storm of indignation from the members of the convention, for it was exceedingly unpalatable to hear Texan cattle spoken of in any other terms than those of the strongest condemnation.

But it was idle for the speaker to point out that an attempt to prohibit absolutely the products of one State from passing through or into another State or to the common markets of the country, by the legislature enactment of a State, was clearly in violation of the Federal Constitution, wherein is delegated to Congress only, the power to regulate commerce between the States. It was futile to urge the equal rights of the owners of cattle, no matter whether the cattle's horns were long or short, although the owner of the former might be a citizen of Texas. It was useless to point out the utter failure of prohibitory legislation, as exemplified in the case of several of the western States, to accomplish the design sought, to-wit: To protect the short-horn cattle from disease. It were words spent in vain to point out legitimate and legal quarantine measures or methods of attaining the end desired. There were few who would heed whilst the arrangement of nature was pointed out, in that, that the west and southwest must produce, the northwest fatten, and the east consume the beef product of the United States; and that one section was dependent on the other for its ultimate prosperity.

All these and other weighty considerations were urged upon the attention of the convention; but their announcement fell as soft water upon the flinty stone, for it had predetermined on prohibition.

Of the various theories advanced concerning the primal cause of Spanish fever, three only had any considerable number of adherents. The first called the natural or "Sporule" theory, was advocated if not invented, by the scientists and doctors who composed in part at least nearly every commission sent out to investigate the disease and its causes. This theory is that the primal cause of the disease is found to be a small egg or sporule deposited upon the blades of grass in Texas, which being eaten by the animal finds its way into the blood and grows to be microscopic monsters. Disorganization of the blood, disease, the symptoms of which is fever, and death follows as a kind of natural result.

But it was worth enduring the evils of a perverse generation to have heard those sage theorists dilate upon the devilish character and proclivities of those horrible sporules. How their discovery had cost them so much profound scientific research—how they had dived in the carcass of the defunct bovine—searched his utmost intestine—torn to atoms and inspected his paunch, and subjected his stomach to the most rigid scrutiny—bursted asunder his liver, and looked into its innermost recess—pried into the secrets of his kidneys—subjected his bladder to the severest chemical tests—looked through powerful telescopes into his dying eye and discerned the anguish of his departing spirit. But it was in his gore that their indominitable energy and profound research was rewarded, by the discovery of the inexpressably horrible sporule. They well knew that in the very nature of things he must be somewhere, for it was plain to them that the symmetry and perfection of the universe would have been incomplete without him—the elements of material nature would have long since resolved themselves back into original chaos, if there had been such an omission in creation as the sporule. They justly felt that the discovery of him was the crowning glory and most momentous event of the nineteenth century—if not of all modern times. It was plain that none since the days of the ancient mathematician engulfed in his ablutions had so good a reason to cry out, "Eureka! Eureka!" But the advocaters of this theory failed to inform the waiting world what villain put those Sporules upon the grass blades in Texas, or from whence he got them, or why he wanted to make short-horned cattle sick unto death, or whether he had been told to desist, or warned that drawing "back pay" for services once paid for would not be tolerated; or that he was not "putting things where they would do him the most good." That fellow, whoever he is and whatever his malicious intent may be, must be a diabolical monster and worthy of immediate extermination. His body should be embalmed in carbolic acid and placed in the cabinet of those scientists; there to remain as a trophy of the most profound scientific research of the nineteenth century. But in this case it is questionable whether all the investigating conventions, commissions, doctors and scientists ever did the cause of truth one iota of practical good. Their learned and beautifully arranged theories were enunciated and elaborated with all manner of profound erudite detail. Although in practice and for all practical good, they were valueless unless it be as a curious specimen of what great profound thinkers can do for the relief of their country in distress. Indeed their bulky disquistitions clothed in high-sounding words when shorn of their verbiage and compressed into intrinsic truth and practical common sense, would remind matter of fact cattle men of the fabled mountain bringing forth the mouse. In fact the results of the various commissions for the investigation of Spanish fever reminds one of the ancient royal commission of sage scientists who spent many days and weeks investigating and profoundly debating the all absorbing question of natural history, to-wit: "Which is the butt end of a billy goat."

Aside from the honorary member from Kansas, who was the party in interest at Abilene, the convention was as eager to deal a death blow to the new opening stock trade of the southwest as are a pack of ravenous wolves to devour the powerless lamb. It was a noticeable fact that Texas as a State was without a single representative upon the floor of that convention, although the subject had been brought to the attention of a large number of drovers sojourning at Abilene, who did appoint a certain ex-Governor of their State to be a delegate, but failed as usual to provide funds for defraying necessary expenses, so he failed to put in an appearance. So Texas, the State above all others the most interested, was entirely unrepresented where her most valuable product was the subject of discussion, and measures adopted recommending a basis of legislation which effected her for weal or woe, to the amount of many millions of dollars in value; and all for the lack of public spirit and public enterprise of her citizens.

The recommendation of that convention formed the basis of legislation enacted by many of the northern States during the following winter. During the summer of 1868, the Federal Government employed to thoroughly investigate the subject of Spanish fever and its prime causes, manner of contraction, and prevention, Prof. John Gamgee, an English Veterinary Surgeon who had won distinction in England during the time when rinderpest made such sad havoc among the herds of England. This capable gentleman visited all portions of the United States where Spanish fever had raged, and also the State of Texas, and made a thorough and practical investigation of the disease, endeavoring to trace its primal cause, origin, and nature. But we have never seen his report in print, and we are not sure that the government had it printed, for the excitement soon abated and Texan cattle began to appear on market both east and west.

Indeed we have often thought that the outbreak of Spanish fever and the consequent excitement, really served to draw toward Texan cattle the attention of stock men from every quarter of the country, and eventuated in their becoming recognized as a staple commodity upon the markets.

It is the opinion of others that the doctors and scientists had caught up one of the effects or symptoms of the disease and manufactured a fine spun theory which looks plausible on paper, but has not one ounce of truth or fact in it. In Spanish fever like pneumonia in horses, the blood, we opine, becomes totally disorganized, in fact might be called rotten, and upon examining it with the microscope a very unnatural appearance is detected. But the actual cause of the disease can only be conjectured from this standpoint.

Another, the second theory, is that the disease is solely and entirely caused by the ticks peculiar to the climate and country of the southwest. It is argued that only ticky cattle will disseminate disease; that every native that dies of Spanish fever will always be found to have almost one tick for every hair on his hide; that his stomach will be found often to contain ticks although small yet numerous mingled with the food. It is held, truthfully too, that the large ticks seen in great numbers on almost all cattle fresh from Texas that have been shipped direct north, soon yield their hold on the animal and fall to the ground where they by a process peculiar to their nature, become as an egg, from each one of which a thousand or more little ticks will be hatched in a short space of time, and crawl upon the blades of grass wherefrom they get on the legs of the grazing animal, and when it lays down to rest get on to its body. Also the ticks whilst in this diminutive state are eaten by the domestic animal in great quantities. Whether on the outside of his body digging into his skin or within his stomach, they are to the domestic cattle rank poison, which, when a sufficient amount has been absorbed by the animal's system, acts in such a manner as to create fever and death. It is urged in support of the "Tick theory" that the advent of frost, as is well known to be the case, puts a stop to the spread of the disease by killing the young ticks. It is also a well known fact that in every case wherein a ticky herd of cattle came upon the pasture in contact with natives, that disease was sure to follow. The cattle that were introduced into Illinois via the Red river route was always very ticky, often having so many that the actual color of the animal would be hid by the large distended, greyish white bodies of the million of ticks which were clinging to his hide, and sticking blood from him.

Wherever on the pasture fields or prairies these cattle came in contact and grazed with the domestic stock, pestilential disease and death followed with infallible certainty.

The "Tick theory" had for its advocates some able practical cattle men, some of whom had lost heavily by Spanish fever, and had made close observations and tests to ascertain the real cause of the disease and its manner of contraction.

The third theory is that the Spanish fever is superinduced by much the same causes, as ship fever aboard emigrant steam ships, to-wit: by hard usage and privation of the usual and necessary rest, food, and water.

The cattle of Texas being wild and free, almost as much so as the buffalo of the plains in the west, are fretful and worried by restraint and handling much as is the full grown wild animal when caged.

It is not uncommon to over-drive and starve the Texan cattle en route for market. Often in dry seasons water being scarce herds do not get sufficient for a week at a time and often the haste of the drover or his indolence allows his cattle to be over-driven, and that too without sufficient food to prevent his stock from suffering.

We leave the reader to form his own opinion which of the theories stated is the correct one, only adding that a carefully driven herd of Texan cattle coming via Western Kansas into the northern States seldom if ever disseminate disease. If permitted to rest for thirty to sixty days on good range abounding with plenty of water and grass, they will not infect the domestic cattle. This we know to be correct. But whether during this rest from travel and hardship the fever becomes extinct by the recurperative power of the animals, or whether the losing of the ticks, as they invariably do, rids them of the seeds of disease, we leave the reader to form his own opinion, only adding that after the closest observation of many cases and often trying to seek out the real causes of Spanish fever, we are unable to say whether the "Tick theory" or the "Ship fever theory" is the correct one. For both theories have almost unanswerable arguments in their favor. Of one thing we feel certain, that is, that the cattle in Texas upon their accustomed range are as healthy as any cattle in the world.

There is one peculiar characteristic of Spanish fever among Texan cattle, that is, its presence is scarcely perceptible to the casual observer, for it never kills a Texan animal, and effects them so slightly that it requires an experienced eye to detect its presence in a herd of Texan cattle. Nevertheless, they do have the disease and occasionally one of them will be sick near unto death with it, especially is this the case with Texan cattle that have been wintered in the northern States.

It is a well settled fact, settled by every investigation yet instituted as well as by the unanimous testimony of the closest observing practical cattle men, that the disease is communicated to the domestic stock only by grazing and laying upon the same grounds or pasture lands which have been previously grazed over by Texan cattle.

That to travel upon the same road, to drink at the same pond of water, to pass through the same shipping yards or in the same cars, will not furnish the necessary conditions for contraction of the disease. But, we repeat, the domestic stock must eat of the same grass that has just previously been depastured by the Texan cattle. Whether the seeds of disease left on the grass are in the shape of ticks, or is a poison left in and with their saliva or slobbers, or in and with the urine or residuum deposited upon the grass, or whether they are the veritable "Sporules"of the scientists, is an undetermined question and one about which practical cattle men as well as doctors disagree.

We propose to deal with facts or practical effects, rather than with theories. One thing, there is little use to deny or gainsay, that there is such a malady as is commonly called Spanish fever; or that it is under certain circumstances disseminated by Texan cattle. It is in ninety-nine cases in one hundred, fatal in its effects upon the short-horn cattle. While it is an unsettled question just how the short-horn contracts, or the Texan disseminates, the disease, none other than an obdurate man, one who would not or could not, be convinced by evidence, will longer dispute or disbelieve the actual existence, at certain seasons of the year, of the disease among certain classes of cattle.

In about two to four weeks after the short-horn has been exposed to the necessary conditions; that is, grazed over and rested upon the same pastures upon which certain herds of Texan cattle have previously been pastured, he may be observed to become stupid, refuse to eat or drink, inclined to stand or lie in the fence corners, his head will droop below its natural position, his ears will lop down beside his head, his eyes will become nearly fixed, and a wild glaring stare, will be observed, whilst from his nostrils or mouth, will constantly drool a whitish ropey slobber resembling excessive salivary secretion. The animal's coat of hair will stand up on end or turn forward, presenting a rough unthrifty appearance, whilst his back will become arched. Frequent urinary discharges will occur presenting the appearance to the casual observer, of pure blood, but rare evacuations of the bowels will occur, and those will be very hard and dry. The animal will become intensely hot, and suffer great pain, and when near dissolution, will often bellow piercing shrieks, expressive of the racking pain endured. Sometimes they will plunge about wildly for a few moments and then suddenly fall down and expire instantly.

If the subject is milk stock, one of the first symptoms of approaching disease will be the diminution of the supply of milk, which in one or two days will cease altogether. Milk cows are more liable for some unknown reason to contract the disease, than are other cattle.

A sucking calf never takes Spanish fever, no matter if it sucks its dying or dead mother, as they have been seen do, without contracting the disease. One short-horn will not contract the fever from another short-horn, nor will a herd of short-horns contract Spanish fever from the worst infected herd of Texans, if they are separated by so much as a partition fence. Although the water the short-horns drink may have come first through the pasture whereon are grazing infected Texans; it will not convey the seeds of disease to the short-horns. We repeat, it is the necessary conditions for the native cattle to graze over, and lie upon pastures which have just previously been grazed over by Texans, in order to contract Spanish fever. No well authenticated instance of the contraction of the disease in any other manner or under other circumstances has yet been produced.

It is not difficult generally for an experienced western cattle man to detect the Spanish fever existing in a herd of Texan cattle, but it requires close scrutiny and experience, for the evidences of its presence are not discernable to the casual observer or inexperienced cattle man. No specific, infallible remedy has yet been found for Spanish fever, but enough is known or established as the result of experiments, to warrant the assertion, that if the animal is thoroughly drenched with any powerful purgatives, so as to relieve the system of all food while the animal is in the earlier stages of the disease, it is quite likely to recover. But inasmuch as the animal's stomach or manifold becomes as dry as a gunny sack, and the contents as dry and hard as a pine board, looking much like a hard sponge, in the latter stages of the disease, it is plain that physics or any other remedy can not afford relief. It has been found very beneficial as a preventive and cure to feed green corn, to exposed animals, or those taking the disease. It is found that corn will in this case as in "milk sickness," neutralize the poison, much as the essence of corn, familiarly called whisky, will neutralize the poison of the rattlesnake.

Many cattle men are fond of neutralizing snake bites. In fact, some of them neutralize so often, that they dream of snakes being in many disgustingly familiar attitudes, especially about their boots.

Perhaps no one man sustained greater losses, both direct and indirect, from Spanish fever, than John T. Alexander, of Morgan County, Illinois. Certainly no man in that State or any other has handled more Texan cattle on his own account than has he. Indeed, there are few, if any, who have handled more cattle of all classes than has Mr. Alexander. Beginning when he was a lad of thirteen years to assist his father, then an extensive drover from Ohio to the eastern markets he gradually grew to the business for which he had a natural taste, and great, good judgment—two indispensable qualifications for the successful cattle man. Although a Virginian by birth, he was reared in Ohio, spending his youthful days in aiding his father drive cattle from that State over the Alleghany Mountains to the Philadelphia, Baltimore, New York and Boston markets. At the age of twenty years, his father having met one of those severe reverses so common to the life of the drover or cattle shipper, young Alexander determined to try the West on his own account. Accordingly but a few short weeks elapsed before he might have been seen in St. Louis, looking for something to do in the line of his chosen business, without capital, other than his abilities and energy. He was not afraid of work, and gladly accepted a situation upon a moderate salary, to aid Christian Hays, then one of Louis' heaviest operators, in his live stock transactions. At that early day such a convenience at live Stock Scales for weighing animals alive was unknown, or if known, unused so far west as St. Louis. It was the custom to select an average bullock, slaughter him, weigh the carcass, and then from that compute the average weight of the entire herd. It was the custom then in vogue for the drover and the purchaser to select, or arrive at the average steer, by choosing alternately one the best and heaviest steer, the other the lightest and meanest steer, until all but one steer was chosen. This, of course, was taken for the average. It is easy to see that much depended upon the judgment of the parties who did the selecting. If the drover was a better judge than the buyer, he was sure to get the better of him, and vice versa. Young Alexander was soon detailed to average a drove for his employer, and the manner in which he did that duty, the mature judgment, the "cattle sense" which he evinced, was noticed by Mr. Hays, and he concluded that young Alexander possessed abilities fitting him for superior duties, and at once put him into commission and sent him to Central Illinois to buy fat cattle for the St. Louis market. Mr. Hays made no error in sending the young cattle man out with instructions to buy upon his own judgment, for it was more and more apparent from day to day that young Alexander well understood his business.

In a few months, after several trips to Central Illinois, he determined to feed a moderate sized drove on his own account. His friend Hays was quite willing to aid him to accomplish the undertaking by loaning any needed funds.

After spending two or three years in operating in live stock in connection with Mr. Hays, young Alexander determined to drive a herd of two hundred and thirty head of fat cattle of his own feeding to the eastern market. In those days there were no railroads extending into Illinois. Sending western cattle direct to the Atlantic coast markets was an experiment never before extensively tried, and it required a man of will and energy to undertake and execute the effort, for it was not only a great hazard, but required the entire summer to accomplish it. Great care had to be exercised, and the herd prudently managed and carefully driven, to prevent a ruinous shrinkage in flesh and condition. The cattle had been full fed during the previous six months, and were well fatted. Upon the skill of the drover in handling his herd depended the retaining or losing of this flesh or condition. No one understood how to handle a drove of fat cattle better than Mr. Alexander, and it is needless to add that he was successful. After driving over the broad prairies of Illinois and Western Indiana, feeding the cattle upon the natural grasses while upon the prairies—through the timbered portion of the remainder of his journey, turning them upon the fenced pastures of the farmers—he arrived in Albany, New York State, just in time to meet a purchaser, at thirty-one dollars per head, delivered in Boston, Mass. This price was considered very satisfactory, although it looks to a cattle man of the present day to be a very low figure. But everything was proportionately lower then, and one dollar would buy as much land or other valuables, as will ten dollars at this time. As a proof that Mr. Alexander made a good sale we add that his purchaser lost money on the cattle, not because they were not good, but because the Boston markets were too low.

After operating for three or four years longer as a trader, Mr. Alexander decided to purchase land, and embark in farming and cattle feeding exclusively. Accordingly in 1848 he made his first investment in real estate, selecting lands in Morgan County, Central Illinois, as being the best in the State. The first purchase was made at three dollars per acre for a large tract of land, still owned by Mr. Alexander, and now worth not less than seventy-five dollars per acre, and is located on the T. W. & W. Railway, near a station named after the extensive cattle shipper.

Indeed, there are few, if any, superior lands for agricultural or pastoral purposes within the limits of the United States, than are found in Central Illinois, and in that district there is no better lands than are those selected by Mr. Alexander.

Central Illinois has become universally wealthy by corn raising and hog and cattle feeding, or, in other words, making the live stock product of other regions fit for eastern markets and consumption.

The manner or corn feeding cattle is familiar to most northwestern men, but as it is a business of great importance and magnitude, one in which millions of dollars are annually invested; one that engages the attention and efforts of thousands of enterprising, energetic men; and one that doubles the value of every head of cattle fed, of which there are many thousands; it is deemed worthy of more than a passing notice. The best inland corn growing regions, where corn can be produced or bought cheaply are the cattle feeding centers. The farmer, who is often a feeder also, devotes his whole attention during the spring and summer months, to planting and cultivating a large crop of corn. When the fall season arrives, and the corn begins to mature, it is cut and shocked, which process consists in cutting and placing in the center, all the corn on a space of ground equal to fourteen or sixteen corn hills square. The corn stalks are cut off near the ground, and are set up snugly together, forming a compact shock, which is allowed to stand in the field until it is fed. A few weeks before the grass in the pasture fails, the feeder begins to give his cattle corn, at first but little, gradually increasing the amount until the cattle become thoroughly accustomed to it, without gorging or foundering. When the pasture becomes bare of grass, the cattle are brought into the feed yards, and there daily fed for from four to six months. The feeder's outfit is usually an ox team of one or more pairs of cattle, which are attached to a wagon upon which is placed a long, rude, strong rack, much like a hay frame, upon which the shock corn is thrown, then drawn from the field to the feed yard. Entering the yard with his team, the feeder mounts the load, and with a stake or standard from the rack, throws the corn to the ground, first upon one side then upon the other, while the team moves around a beaten circuit which they soon become accustomed to follow and which is soon marked by a high ridge of corn-stalks, which in muddy, rainy times, forms a dry spot or circle, as well as an excellent bed in cold weather.

The ground is literally floored or paved with corn stalks in the feed yard, and the cattle are allowed to eat as much as they desire, and that too of the best ears of corn. An average sized bullock will eat and waste, one-half bushel of corn each day, and will become, in time, very fat. The usual gain in four to six months feeding, is from two to three hundred pounds. Extra good feeding of extra good cattle, will often make greater gains. Many feeders prefer to feed husked or snapped corn, which is fed in boxes or troughs. There is less waste of corn, but this method requires feeding hay, or straw for roughness.

When shock corn is fed, two yards are provided, in which the cattle are fed alternate days. Whilst they are being fed in one, a herd of swine are eating up the waste and offal in the other. One to two hogs to each bullock are thus made fat. The profits on the hogs fatted, is no inconsiderable item in the feeding operation.

To secure the hogs to follow the feeding cattle, sometimes the whole country is scoured, and occasionally resort is had to distant counties. This branch of trade, like all others, developes characteristics peculiar to itself. In Central Illinois, a noted cattle feeding district, resort is sometimes had to southern counties for stock hogs to follow cattle. Those counties less adapted to corn production, but abounding in heavy forests of oak, hickory and walnut, which furnish mast, upon which the industrious long-nosed, cat-hamed porcines, indigenous to those regions, subsist. When the local trader becomes aware of their value, he will industriously seek them out, gather them into small squads, and ship them to central portions of the State, where, with a manner the most bland, he will seek to sell them to some cattle feeder. These itinerant pig-pedlers are of very doubtful morals, or virtue, and usually reside upon a State road, or public thoroughfare in a hilly district, where the yellow clay soil is uppermost; usually a few miles east of some pleasant plains. These pig venders are genuine heroes, and often hail from "Pinckneyville," or other mellifluous regions. Should the reader ever journey in those regions, he will not fail to hear of, or meet, one of those "heroes," and will know at once that he is in the presence of unappreciated greatness, of which he will be aware.

There is quite a diversity of opinion among feeders, as to the most profitable manner of feeding, as well as to kinds or classes of cattle to feed. Many hold, and practice a system of full feeding, and selling off of the grain feed. Whilst others feed less grain during the winter, and finish fatting on the pasture the following spring and summer. Others simply "rough through" and fatten exclusively on the grass.

Many feeders will not feed other than graded Durhams, or natives, whilst just as respectable and successful a class prefer the Texan, or southern cattle. Of course the whole matter hinges upon the question of profit.

The native to begin with cost fully twice as much as the southern bullock, and when fat sells for a better price per pound than Texan. But when both are fat, the difference in price per pound is not so great as the difference in first cost; but the native feeds better, eats corn to better advantage, takes on more fat on corn feed than does the Texan, but the southern bullock excels the native in fatting on grass—makes great gains in less time than the native.

It may be truthfully stated, that for fatting on corn, the native excels and is therefore preferable, whilst for "roughing through," and fatting on grass, the Texan is superior.

The feeder who reverses this order, in handling either class, rarely does it to his profit. Nevertheless a herd of Texan cattle which has been delivered in the north during the early part of summer, and has become thoroughly rested and climated before winter, can be made really fat on corn.

In various experiments made in feeding Texan cattle, it has been demonstrated that to shell the corn is of great advantage. It has been found that the cob, being hard and unnutritious, is unpalatable to them, and is a great obstacle to successfully feeding them. But as a rule, to "rough through" and fatten on the grass, is the most profitable manner to handle Texan cattle in the Northwestern States.

In Central Illinois many of the most successful dealers in Southern cattle, feed them upon the blue grass pastures, and never lot them up, but aim only to bring them to grass the following spring in strong thrifty condition, upon which they will soon become fit for the shambles of New York. This is the manner in which Mr. Alexander handles his large purchases of Texan cattle.

For many years, all the suitable cattle of the Missouri Valley region, were driven to Central Illinois, and there, by six months corn feeding, made fat, and doubled in value. Thus, by combining the products of those rich corn lands, as much money or value was created in six months, as the producer of the unfatted steer had made in three years handling or rearing the same animal. This fact soon became patent to the thinking agriculturists, and it was not long before the corn-growing portions of Illinois became either a cornfield or feed yard, annually sending to eastern markets thousands of fatted cattle. In this business Mr. Alexander saw and realized great profit and was fast becoming princely wealthy. But there occurred a year of severe drouth, something uncommon to that country, cutting off the corn crops upon the uplands, so that corn in sufficient quantities for cattle-feeding purposes could be found only on the river bottoms, and to those sections Mr. Alexander took his herds and full fed them during the winter of 1854 and 1855. When spring came no buyer offered him such prices as he thought he ought to have, so he determined to drive and ship on his own account. At that date the nearest railroad terminus, or shipping point, was at Logansport, Indiana, a distance of three or four hundred miles, and hither he turned his droves, carring them to Toledo, Ohio; thence to Dunkirk by lake steamer. Then recarring them to New York city, from whence a part was sent to Boston. In this transaction Mr. Alexander did not realize so much by several thousand dollars as he had had offered him for his cattle in the west.

Instead of discouraging him from future shipments it only excited his energy and determination to retrieve his losses in the same place and business wherein he had sustained them. Many readers would suppose that no man would leave a business in which he had in a few years acquired four thousand acres of fine, valuable land, and ten thousand dollars in cash, to engage in another; especially one that was uncertain, and had already lost the snug sum of five thousand dollars. But if they do so think they do not understand the peculiar turn of mind, and temperament necessary to constitute a cattle shipper. Nothing arouses his will and determination more surely and drives him to greater ventures than losses on the first shipments. Like the devotee of the card table, he determines to get even and more. This determination has ruined many good men and turned them out of house and home.

Mr. Alexander's loss only seemed to make him determined, and contrary to the advice of his financial friends, he engaged in shipping cattle via Chicago to the eastern markets during the year 1856, but without making or losing to speak of. But during the following year, in connection with his partner, he shipped via the T., W. & W. Railway, then just completed, ten thousand head of cattle, and at the end of the season divided the snug sum of sixty thousand dollars.

But success only stimulated him to greater undertakings, and the following year, his partner having been killed in a railroad accident, Mr. Alexander shipped eleven thousand head of cattle, but with more loss than profit. The succeeding year (that of 1859) fifteen thousand head of fat cattle went east as the contribution or business of Mr. Alexander. To say that this years's operation was a losing one, is putting it mild, it was "a ripper," as a cattle man would style it. Mr. Alexander's losses were equal to, or greater than the value of his entire estate, but the public did not know it, and still had the greatest confidence in his ability. During the two succeeding years but little money was made or lost, although an immense business was done.

Then the civil war broke out. There were many thousands of cattle and mules in the State of Missouri, one of the States deeply involved in the struggle, in fact was largely the battle ground. This turn of affairs made the tenure of personal property very insecure in that State, and most owners were willing to sell at any price, no matter how low. This offered a good opportunity to venturesome cattle men, and Mr. Alexander's financial condition was such that he was prepared to take any manner or kind of risks to retrieve his financial losses. Accordingly he put several energetic buyers in Missouri, with instructions to penetrate the disturbed districts, and, where war's dreaded cloud hung darkest and most threateningly, there buy every steer or mule they could (of course as cheap as possible) and send them to his farm in Illinois. Two years, affording such opportunities for good investments, were sufficient to make good all previous losses of Mr. Alexander. At the close of the war an inventory of his assets would have shown seventy-two hundred acres of land, worth seventy-five dollars per acre, one hundred thousand dollars in bank; his pastures full of cattle, and not one dollar of debt. One would think that such an exhibit would satisfy any one's greatest desires for wealth, so far at least, as to prevent him from engaging in any operations in which there was great hazard; but such was not the case with Mr. Alexander, he, like the ancient conqueror of the same name, looked and longed for other and greater conquests but, different to his ancient namesake, he soon found a "New World," which he essayed to conquer. It was the purchasing and improving of what was then called the "Sullivan," but afterwards the "Broad Lands" farm, a tract of twenty-six thousand acres of land, near the T., W. & W. Railway in Champaign County, Illinois. This purchase in connection with heavy losses by cattle shipping, also a loss of fully seventy-five thousand dollars by Spanish fever, to this may be added the repudiation of a contract by certain railroads whereby he was made to sustain a loss of near two hundred and fifty thousand dollars, produced a crisis in his affairs of the gravest nature. As is usual in such cases, every effort put forth to prevent impending disaster only brings additional distress. So in his case. Finally he took a survey of his affairs, and concluded to sell his Broad Lands farm, accordingly hunted up a purchaser in the person of the agent of a Canadian Company, and contracted to sell him the entire tract, for six hundred and seventy-five thousand dollars. Of this transaction he hastened to inform his most pressing creditors. But alas for him, when the time came to ratify the contract, the Canadian Company refused to abide the contract of its agent, and the land trade failed. This precipitated the impending crisis. In compliance with the advice of his friends, he turned his entire estates and immense personal property—in short all his assets—into the hands of three assignees for the benefit of his creditors.

This was perhaps the darkest, bitterest year of his existence—a year of crushing disappointment and pungent humiliation, such as a high ambitious sensitive soul could scarce endure. It was crushing and overwhelming to Mr. Alexander, for he had ever been a man of the keenest sensibilities; of the most exalted honor in all his business transactions; above petty spites or contemptible actions. The word "failed," which was bandied about from mouth to mouth, grated harshly upon his ears and wounded deeply his inmost soul and rendered life itself almost an undesirable burthen.

Such were the results of a few years of persistent cattle shipping in connection with incidental disastrous business transactions. A fortune of colossal proportions, riven to shreds, as is the oak by the lightning's hot bolt. Scattered as if by a cyclone, as are the fragments of a rock riven ocean steamer.

Notwithstanding the liabilities reached the enormous figures of twelve hundred thousand dollars, the estate was ample to pay every creditor, dollar for dollar, and leave Mr. Alexander about two thousand acres of the best of his Morgan county lands, without a single legitimate unsaid claim outstanding. With an energy peculiar only to men of real ability—but never found in the fungus brains of the maudlin goslings who flash like a meteor athwart the business horizon and die out never to be seen or heard of again, save as some abandoned loafer or drunken saloon ornament—Mr. Alexander set himself about retrieving his lost fortunes, and in his success during the last two years can be taken as a harbinger of the future, the time will be quite brief before his Morgan county estate will be as large as ever.

His greatest losses occurred in 1868, during the great excitement about Spanish fever, and were carried until 1870, in which a desperate effort was made to cover, and fully seventy thousand head of cattle were shipped to the eastern markets. This is the largest year, or season's business ever done by a single individual, in marketing cattle, in the United States, or perhaps in the world.

Mr. Alexander regards himself as taking his third start in the world—one at St. Louis, one at the beginning of the war, and one now.

His first financial friend was Christian Hays, of St. Louis; his second was Thomas Condell, for many years President of a strong banking institution of Springfield, Illinois, and a man who had almost unerring judgment in business matters, especially those pertaining to cattle transactions—one who stood by and aided with money and council, his friends and business patrons in the darkest hours as well as in the brightest. More than one cattle man remembers the name and fidelity of Thomas Condell with feelings of the deepest gratitude, if not of love and veneration. He has some years since retired from active business, greatly to the regret of many cattle men of Central Illinois. It seems strange that of the many bankers who in former years were more than willing to loan their money to Mr. Alexander, not one was willing, after he had met his great reverses, to aid him in his effort to recuperate his shattered fortune, although he had paid in full every legitimate claim against him. Yet, it is said, "where there is a will there is a way," and Mr. Alexander certainly had the will and a good vigorous one at that.

Finally to him came Geo. Wilson, a banker of Geneseo, Illinois, a man of considerable ready means and a shrewd operator; one who has made his money largely out of cattle, and with cattle men; one who is blessed with that rare quality called "Cattle sense"—an article quite rare among bankers—and proposed to furnish all cash needed to stock up Mr. Alexander's ends. This he did for two years, besides paying for three thousand fine cattle, at panic prices, during the fall of 1873, for the pastures and feed yards of Mr. Alexander. These cattle will be grazed on blue grass pastures until February, and then be fed corn on the pastures until spring. Then they will be grazed on the blue grass pastures and fatted which requires but few month's to accomplish.

But we can not close this imperfect sketch without offering a few thoughts upon the life and labors of such men as Mr. Alexander. No right thinking man can regard them other than public benefactors, and as such, are of much greater consequence and benefit in a substantial way than many think. They take from the feeder's yards his fatted stock, and four times out of five pay him more than it is worth, and that in cash without delay or serious inconvenience. By their perseverance and business tact they are able to get the lowest rate of freight possible, which the local feeder, nine times in ten, gets the benefit of, in the increased price obtained for his fat stock.

We do not hesitate to assert that the cattle men of the northwest, and especially those of Central Illinois, owe to John T. Alexander a debt of gratitude for many hundreds of thousands, yes, millions of dollars, distributed among them by his liberal hand. We confidently affirm that for more than ten years he added from three to ten dollars per head to the value of the cattle fatted in Central Illinois, which were and are many thousands of head, annually. Mr. Alexander is not above fifty-three years of age, is tall and of commanding appearance, looks hale, fresh and youthful, is of sanguine mental temperament, and naturally impulsive. He is very quiet and unassuming in manners, speaks but little, and never in a loud or boisterous tone, is affable, social, warm-hearted; appreciates true manhood, is upright, honorable, and high-minded in his business transactions. No superior has gone before him, and there are none to follow after him.

Notes

1. Illinois Central Railroad.
2. Kansas and Pacific Railroad, part of the transcontinental railroad.

Source: Joseph G. McCoy, *Historic Sketches of the Cattle Trade of the West and Southwest* (Kansas City, MO: Ramsey, Millett and Hudson, 1874), 147–178.

1876 • 84 • Estelle Wilcox, "Easter Sunday"

Introduction: *When the centennial of America rolled around in 1876, several cookbooks were published. The* Centennial Buckeye Cook Book, *published in Marysville, Ohio, was one. The compiler, Estelle Wilcox, was a resident of the community and a member of the unfinished Congregational church. The church needed money to complete its construction, so the churchwomen decided to compile, publish, and sell cookbooks, the profits of which would be used to complete the construction of the church. The cookbook went through many editions, and when its final edition was published in 1905, it had sold more than 1 million copies—more than any other cookbook at that time. Below is the cookbook's dedication and the preface to the 1876 edition. The "Easter Sunday" excerpt is from the 1883 edition.*

To the Plucky Housewives of 1876 who master their work instead of allowing it to master them, this book is dedicated.

The Women's Centennial Committees of the International Exhibition of 1876 respectfully offer this volume to their countrywomen and solicit their patronage.

Among the many enterprises planned by the committees to carry out the objects of their organization, was a National Cookery Book. It was thought proper in a department exclusively devoted to "women's work," that cookery—an art which has been consigned so largely to her—should not be forgotten. It was also believed that it would not be thought presumptuous to endeavor to afford the visitors from abroad, who might honor the Exhibition by their presence, an opportunity of judging of our progress in this art, and also of the resources of our country.

"Have any National Dishes?" is a question that has been asked by foreigners travelling in this country.

The Committees believe that the answer to this question may be found in their unpretending book.

Hotels, with their French cooks and gregarious customs, are not true exponents of the inner life of a people!

To carry out their plan in the most efficient manner, a printed circular was forwarded to all the corresponding committees in every State and Territory of the Union, asking for contributions to this object. The response has been gratifying, and the result is here given to the reader.

It would be impossible to thank individually each contributor who has kindly aided in this work. From the most remote as well as from the nearest States, the same desire to aid has been shown, the same lively sympathy exhibited. To each and all the cordial thanks of the Committees are tendered.

The size of the book has necessarily limited the number of receipts accepted; many were duplicates, and a large number came too late.

Source: Women's Centennial Executive Committee, *National Cookery Book Compiled from Original Receipts for the Women's Centennial Committees of the International Exhibition* (Philadelphia: Women's Centennial Executive Committee, 1876), xi–xii.

1880 • 85 • Mark Twain's Favorite American Foods

Introduction: *Mark Twain, the pen name of Samuel Clemens (1835–1910), was one of America's most famous and popular authors. His novels* The Adventures of Tom Sawyer *(1876) and* The Adventures of Huckleberry Finn *(1884) remain two of America's most cherished novels. Clemens traveled to Europe in the late 1870s and wrote a nonfiction book,* A Tramp Abroad *(1880), upon his return. While traveling in Europe he was not impressed with the food he was served, and he devised a list of the best American foods.*

. . . A man accustomed to American food and American domestic cookery would not starve to death suddenly in Europe, but I think he would gradually waste away, and eventually die.

He would have to do without his accustomed morning meal. That is too formidable a change altogether; he would necessarily suffer from it. He could get the shadow, the sham, the base counterfeit of that meal; but that would do him no good, and money could not buy the reality.

To particularize: the average American's simplest and commonest form of breakfast consists of coffee and beefsteak; well, in Europe, coffee is an unknown beverage. You can get what the European hotel-keeper thinks is coffee, but it resembles the real thing as hypocrisy resembles holiness. It is a feeble, characterless, uninspiring sort of stuff, and almost as undrinkable as if it had been made in an American hotel. The milk used for it is what the French call "Christian" milk—milk which has been baptized.

After a few months' acquaintance with European "coffee," one's mind weakens, and his faith with it, and he begins to wonder if the rich beverage of home, with its clotted layer of yellow cream on top of it is not a mere dream, after all, and a thing which never existed.

Next comes the European bread—fair enough, good enough, after a fashion, but cold; cold and tough, and unsympathetic; and never any change, never any variety—always the same tiresome thing.

Next, the butter—the sham and tasteless butter; no salt in it, and made of goodness knows what.

Then there is the beefsteak. They have it in Europe, but they don't know how to cook it. Neither will they cut it right. It comes on the table in a small, round, pewter platter. It lies in the centre of this platter, in a bordering bed of grease-soaked potatoes; it is the size, shape, and thickness of a man's hand with the thumb and fingers cut off. It is a little overdone, is rather dry, it tastes pretty insipid, it rouses no enthusiasm.

Imagine a poor exile contemplating that inert thing; and imagine an angel suddenly sweeping down out of a better land and setting before him a mighty porterhouse steak an inch and a half thick, hot and sputtering from the griddle; dusted with fragrant pepper; enriched with little melting bits of butter of the most unimpeachable freshness and genuineness; the precious juices of the meat trickling out and joining the gravy, archipelagoed with mushrooms; a township or two of tender, yellowish fat gracing an outlying district of this ample county of beefsteak; the long, white bone which divides the sirloin from the tenderloin still in its place; and imagine that the angel also adds a great cup of American home-made coffee, with the cream a-froth on top, some real butter, firm and yellow and fresh, some smoking hot biscuits, a plate of hot buckwheat cakes, with transparent syrup—could words describe the gratitude of this exile?

The European dinner is better than the European breakfast, but it has its faults and inferiorities; it does not satisfy. He comes to the table eager and hungry; he swallows his soup—there is an undefinable lack about it somewhere; thinks the fish is going to be the thing he wants—eats it and isn't sure; thinks the next dish is perhaps the one that will hit the hungry place—tries it, and is conscious that there was a something wanting about it also. And thus he goes on, from dish to dish, like a boy after a butterfly, which just misses getting caught, every time it alights, but somehow doesn't get caught after all; and at the end the exile and the boy have fared about alike: the one is full, but grievously unsatisfied, the other has had plenty of exercise, plenty of interest, and a fine lot of hopes, but he hasn't got any butterfly. There is here and there an American who will say he can remember rising from a European table d'hôte perfectly satisfied; but we must not overlook the fact that there is also here and there an American who will lie.

The number of dishes is sufficient; but, then, it is such a monotonous variety of unstriking dishes. It is an inane dead level of "fair-to-middling." There is nothing to accent it. Perhaps if the roast of mutton or of beef—a big, generous one—were brought on the table and carved in full view of the client, that might give the right sense of earnestness and reality to the thing, but they don't do that; they pass the sliced meat around on a dish, and, so you are perfectly calm, it does not stir you in the least. Now a vast roast turkey, stretched on the broad of his back, with his heels in the air and the rich juices oozing from his fat sides . . . but I may as well stop there, for they would not know how to cook him. They can't even cook a chicken respectably; and as for carving it, they do that with a hatchet.

This is about the customary table d'hote bill in summer:

Soup (characterless).

Fish—sole, salmon, or whiting—usually tolerably good.

Roast—mutton or beef—tasteless—and some last year's potatoes.

A pate, or some other made-dish—usually good—"considering."

One vegetable—brought on in state, and all alone—usually insipid lentils, or string beans, or indifferent asparagus.

Roast chicken, as tasteless as paper.

Lettuce-salad—tolerably good.

Decayed strawberries or cherries.

Sometimes the apricots and figs are fresh, but this is no advantage, as these fruits are of no account, anyway.

The grapes are generally good, and sometimes there is a tolerably good peach, by mistake.

The variations of the above bill are trifling. After a fortnight one discovers that the variations are only apparent, not real; in the third week you get what you had the first, and in the fourth week you get what you had the second. Three or four months of this weary sameness will kill the robustest appetite.

It has now been many months, at the present writing, since I have had a nourishing meal, but I shall soon have one—a modest, private affair, all to myself. I have selected a few dishes, and made out a little bill of fare—which will go home in the steamer that precedes me, and be hot when I arrive—as follows:

Radishes. Baked apples, with cream.
Fried oysters; stewed oysters.
Frogs.
American coffee, with real cream.
American butter.
Missouri partridges, broiled.
'Possum. Coon.
Boston bacon and beans.
Bacon and greens, Southern style.
Hominy. Boiled onions. Turnips.
Fried chicken, Southern style.
Porterhouse steak.
Saratoga potatoes.
Broiled chicken, American style.
Hot biscuits, Southern style.
Hot wheat-bread, Southern style.
Hot buckwheat cakes.
American toast. Clear maple syrup.
Virginia bacon, broiled.
Blue points, on the half-shell.
Cherry-stone clams.
San Francisco mussels, steamed.
Oyster soup. Clam soup.
Philadelphia terrapin soup.
Oysters roasted in shell, Northern style.
Soft-shell crabs. Connecticut shad.
Baltimore perch.
Brook trout, from Sierra Nevada.
Lake trout, from Tahoe.
Sheep's-head and croakers, from New Orleans.
Black bass from the Mississippi.
American roast-beef.
Roast turkey, Thanksgiving style.

Cranberry sauce. Celery.
Roast wild turkey. Woodcock.
Canvas-back duck, from Baltimore.
Prairie hens, from Illinois.
Pumpkin. Squash. Asparagus.
Butter beans. Sweet potatoes.
Lettuce. Succotash. String beans.
Mashed potatoes. Catsup.
Boiled potatoes, in their skins.
New potatoes, minus the skins.
Early Rose potatoes, roasted in the ashes, Southern style, served hot.
Sliced tomatoes, with sugar or vinegar. Stewed tomatoes.
Green corn, cut from the ear and served with butter and pepper.
Green corn, on the ear.
Hot corn-pone, with chitlings, Southern style.
Hot hoe-cake, Southern style.
Hot egg-bread, Southern style.
Hot light-bread, Southern style.
Buttermilk. Iced sweet milk.
Apple dumplings, with real cream.
Apple pie. Apple fritters.
Apple puffs, Southern style.
Peach cobbler, Southern style.
Peach pie. American mince pie.
Pumpkin pie. Squash pie.
All sorts of American pastry.

Fresh American fruits of all sorts, including strawberries, which are not to be doled out as if they were jewelry, but in a more liberal way.
Ice-water—not prepared in the ineffectual goblet, but in the sincere and capable refrigerator.

Americans intending to spend a year or so in European hotels will do well to copy this bill and carry it along. They will find it an excellent thing to get up an appetite with, in the dispiriting presence of the squalid table d'hote.

Source: Mark Twain [Samuel Langhorne Clemens], *A Tramp Abroad* (Hartford, CT: American Publishing Company, 1880), 220–226.

1882 • 86 • Abram C. Dayton, *Last Days of Knickerbocker Life in New York*

Introduction: *Abram C. Dayton (1818–1877) was a well-to-do New York writer who collaborated with Charles King, editor of the* New York American. *In the 1870s, Dayton began writing about the life he experienced in his youth. After his death, his manuscript was published under the title* Last Days of Knickerbocker Life in New York

(1882). According to reviews of the book published in the 1880s, Dayton gives an accurate picture of the times he was writing about. The excerpt below focuses on dining in New York in the 1830s.

The trade of the city was concentrated at the Southern end of the Island, and as a sequence the hotels were found in that section. They were not numerous, for their patronage in the main depended upon the then limited traveling public, and such bachelors as were forced from circumstances to avail themselves of this pretext for a home. To board was not considered exactly the thing by the matrons of the period, and the dame who voluntarily abandoned her house-keeping and adopted hotel or boarding-house life in its stead, soon found herself deliberately snubbed, while the one who was compelled by circumstances to submit to this curtailment of woman's rights, was heartily commiserated with by her friends at all their tea-party gatherings. Still, despite this positive drawback against hotel life, there was always to be found a fair sprinkling of human kind to enliven the parlor and prevent the dining-room from becoming a mere feeding trough. For man was not created to be alone when time began; left to himself even now he would soon degenerate and be contented with husks, if they satiated appetite. Miss Margaret Mann was the head and front of the noted boarding-house of New York, and as this was largely patronized by the ladies it deserves precedence. No. 61 Broadway was a celebrated locality; its capacity and reputation would perhaps entitle it to be styled a hotel. Aunt Margaret, as the hostess was familiarly styled, was an advanced specimen of her sex. She wore a plain frock, wholly unornamented, and scant as locomotion would permit; no laces, frills, ribbons, bows,—knicknacks of any description, did not find favor in her eyes; she mounted a scrimpy cap on extraordinary occasions, but in full business trim her lank hair was twisted in an unartistic lump at the back of her head, while the balance was forced to make shift with an occasional "lick and promise" hastily bestowed. Aunt Margaret was a driving woman. No one would have dreamed of such nonsense as addressing her in soft, soothing tones, for the result would have proved about as satisfactory should some fool attempt to pat and flatter a locomotive under a full head of steam. Compliment or suavity were not in her vocabulary. Brusque and bustling, she was never known to rest, and rumor says she gave but little to her hard-worked employees. She was thick-set and heavy in person, yet she seemed ubiquitous, and no detective, even old Hays himself, could surpass her prying qualities. She was rarely demonstrative, but was known to possess a tongue which when called into requisition was a most powerful weapon either for offense or defence as the case might be. Woe betide the unlucky wight who provoked her wrath, for when fully roused she respected neither person, time nor place.

But under Aunt Margaret's hard exterior there was hidden a well of human kindness which occasionally bubbled up and demonstrated that the fountain at her heart had not run dry. To her own she was gentle and kind. To an aged mother and three orphan children of a deceased sister, she was peculiarly attached, and her usually cold eye would light up with sympathetic pride when these were noticed by her guests; but to no one save these children, and a few of their young companions, did she ever betray the feelings which are generally attributed to woman. The house itself, beyond being eminently respectable, and so to speak, fashionable, had but little to recommend it. The parlors were plainly furnished and dimly lighted; the bedrooms scantily supplied with the commonest articles of necessity; the long dining-hall, lighted from either side by a row of naked, staring windows, unadorned with white walls; narrow tables furnished with a goodly variety of palatably prepared food, but set out with cheap crockery, cheap glass, cheap everything which tends to render a meal attractive; yet it was accepted by strangers of note, foreign and native. The guests of the house were, as a rule, sociable, perhaps from necessity, for the circle of amusements were limited, and so men were satisfied to enjoy themselves with a dance and an occasional song. It was in the parlor of 61 Broadway that Sinclair, the father of Mrs. Edwin Forrest, actually made his debut in America, for on the eve of his first appearance at the Park Theatre he delighted his listeners with the strains of the "Mistletoe Bough," a ballad which stamped his popularity with our lovers of music during his prolonged engagement. Tyrone Power, when here, was also a guest at this house, and enchanted all who met him with his rich, polished brogue, and rollicking fascination of manner. On the whole, Aunt Margaret had seldom cause to find fault with her patrons, but now and then, when some interloper would accidentally slip in, she soon discovered some summary method to dispense with the company of the objectionable inmate. The City Hotel occupied the entire front of the block on Broadway bounded by Thames and Cedar Streets. It was not only the most celebrated house of entertainment in the city but travelers asserted it had no equal in the United States. So far as architecture was concerned it was a plain, high structure, pierced with the usual number of square windows, unadorned by lace or damask hangings, with nothing, in fact, to exclude the rays of Old Sol or the impertinent glances of inquisitive neighbors but solid white inside shutters, most effectual bars against both light and air. The interior fittings of our Grand Hotel, whose register paraded the names of our most prominent citizens from every section, in addition to those of the limited number of travelers and tourists from abroad, who were sufficiently enterprising to brave the tedious passage across the boisterous Atlantic, were very plain when compared with the gilded, frescoed palaces, adorned by every article of vertu which the cunning artificers of the old and new world can devise to pander to an extravagant era. The furniture was the best of its kind, durable but unostentatious; in perfect keeping with the modest views which then ruled. Substantial comfort, so far as it could be had, was the ruling motive, and in no instance was that paramount essential ever lost sight of to make room for senseless display. The dining-room of the City Hotel was spacious, light and well ventilated, but its appointments could lay claim to little, save the most thorough neatness, and scrupulous cleanliness. The waiters, ample as to numbers, were well trained and obsequiously attentive to every want, and the guest would have been more than unreasonable who found fault with a feast abundant in quantity and selected with the greatest care by the most experienced caterer in the land. Our markets were not bare of delicacies, for our bay and rivers furnished fish in every variety and as delicate in flavor as they are conceded to be at present; wild duck and game of every sort abounded within limited distance; meats were plentiful and cheap, and, with the single exception of mutton, most excellent in quality. But, so far as fruits and vegetables were concerned, the supply beyond the commonest sorts was very limited, and that confined to the season when they could be raised out of doors in the immediate vicinity. The tomato, now so general an article of consumption, was unknown as an edible and grown merely as an ornamental plant in country gardens, where it was styled "love apple" by the agricultural dames.

Dinner has, however, always been a most important daily event with all classes and conditions of men, women and children. In the early days of our city the noon hour was devoted by the plodding burghers to the enjoy merit of the noontide feast. When the old Middle Dutch bell clanked twelve o'clock, work was suspended, as if "the affairs of men" had come to a full stop; master and man quit without compliment, each hastening to his abode to devote the prescribed respite to the positive refreshment of his important person. Lunch is a very modern word, so far as New York is concerned. Three meals per diem, and to be partaken of at home at specified periods, was the rule. Bites and nips were unknown in Knickerbocker parlance; what a man ate or drank, must be shared with his family. There were no convenient "dives," a word well understood at present; few eating houses, with "meals at all hours" displayed on flaming signs; free lunches not dreamed of; sandwiches only prepared at home, and only on such rare occasions when some protracted journey of several hours duration was necessarily undertaken. Breakfast, dinner and tea, at the specified hour, was prepared at home, and absence from either, or even a dilatory appearance, was deemed just cause for a domestic court martial, and if of frequent recurrence, worthy a sympathetic meeting of condolence by the watchful neighbors.

When the City Hotel was in its full prime, some glimmering rays of modem improvement were introduced by one and another, who after visiting England and France, had returned home inoculated with what was then contemptuously styled "foreign airs." Some of these hooted at the primitive noon-meal so hugely enjoyed in their unpolished youth, and by slow stages three o'clock became the extra fashionable limit for a meal called dinner, for it crowded so closely upon the old Knickerbocker tea, that the innovation was disputed inch by inch, as our Grandmother's prerogative of a long undisturbed afternoon was in a fair way of being wiped out by this newfangled change in domestic life.

The City Hotel was among the first to fall into line and three o'clock was announced as its dinner hour, though a noon table was spread for the accommodation of such thoroughbred sticklers as would not conform. As most of the guests were business men, the change, however, was of slight consequence, as these would not at any hour of the day have devoted the time to the discussion of a repast so essential to good digestion. Dyspepsia always has been an American weakness; all the Trollopes and Dickens of the world cannot eradicate this national trait. It may be said that New Yorkers, especially, love dyspepsia; at any rate they court it from their cradles to their graves. The choice viands of the City Hotel table were dealt with in the most summary manner, as the hungry partakers were compelled to hasten back to store, counting-house or office to resume the broken thread of traffic.

There were, however, a few choice spirits, bachelors or widowers, heaven only knows which, who had drifted, one by one, within the portals of the City Hotel, where, by similarity of tastes, they had formed a coterie of their own, and after passing the needful by-laws they had become a mutual admiration society. They clustered at a specified spot, of which they had formally taken possession, and each day settled themselves to enjoy to the lull of their bent the evening of their days. They were men who had lived beyond the time when drudgery was a prime necessity, and by common consent they lingered at the table after the heat of the battle for food was over, to crack their jokes, nibble their filberts, and sip their wine.

The wine cellar of the Old Hotel was a well known institution, and its memory is still cherished by not a few, who in youth had tasted its rare stores. Its shelves were loaded tier upon tier with the choicest vintages the nicest taste could call, and the selections were pronounced by connoisseurs as unsurpassed in purity or flavor. The judgment then expressed was in after years amply verified; for when the old stamping-ground was abandoned in consequence of the up-town movement, the remnants remaining of the favorite brands were secured at fabulous prices by the initiated. Light wines from the Rhine and clarets from France were not then in vogue, even the now indispensable Heidseck was but little affected, as the taste ran to the more generous, fruity and invigorating Madeira, port and sherry of a quality and perfume which gold cannot purchase now. In these rare juices of the grape, the bevy of old "bon vivants"[1] delighted to indulge, and it was rare sport to watch them as a bottle of some rare variety was carefully uncorked by Chester Jennings in person; it was a perfect study to note the genuine glow of expectation that mantled the ruddy faces of the group as each daintily raised his glass, that the eye might revel once more in the glorious tint ere the full fruition of taste should impart perfect earthly bliss. . . .

The café of the time was a very humble affair, still its existence was an evidence of growth and expansion. It affirmed that the European Continental element was becoming sufficiently important to demand its introduction, and by an unfailing law the supply was at hand. French and Italian citizens were few in number, so the consumption of "café noir" was very limited, and the enterprising men who had embarked in the business, were compelled to add the sale of candies and cakes to meet the moderate expenses thus incurred.

Delmonico and Guerin, so far as memory serves, were the pioneers in this peculiar branch of industry. Both were industrious, frugal, persevering men, professed cooks and confectioners, thus fully competent to meet any exigency and to profit by their skill.

The descendants and successors of Delmonico now occupy four costly and conspicuous buildings in the city; furnished with all the appliances that modern art can invent to pander to the luxurious taste of the time, and one of them, the corner of Fifth Avenue and Fourteenth Street, is, beyond all question, the most palatial café or restaurant on this continent. The stream of fashion which flows through its spacious apartments from morning until night, or rather, from morning until morning, amply demonstrates the source of the immense revenue required to move its intricate and expensive machinery. To lunch, dine or sup at Delmonico's is the crowning ambition of those who aspire at notoriety, and no better studio for character does the city afford than that expensive resort at almost any hour of the day. The indulgence of the whim may be depleting to a moderate purse, but the panorama once seen and carefully inspected in all its lights and shades will amply remunerate for the outlay of money, and the time will not be misspent. On entering from Fourteenth Street one cannot fail to be impressed by the absence of bustle and confusion, no boisterous commands are heard, and the waiters glide about as noiselessly as ghosts. An air of luxury surrounds you as the attentive "garcon" stands motionless before you, and respectfully awaits your wishes. The order once given, you have ample time to survey the scene. At the adjoining table is seated a grey-haired, soft treading "gourmand," who gloats over his "carte" as if "life and death were in the scroll," and everything depended upon the selection he was about to make; farther on is seen a fresh fledged millionaire, who furtively glances about him as if in dread lest some old acquaintance may see him, or that some new made friend should not, as he points to his order for the highest priced item on the list, having no remote idea what compound will be placed before him, only knowing that the figure in the margin is large, and he awaits, with all the "sang froid" he can summon, the result of his venture, but resolved to attack it no matter in what shape it may appear; opposite to this ambitious Gourtland

Street graduate lounges a puffy dowager, crowded into the nearest approach to shape by her dressmaker. The much dressed dame is perspiring at every pore, with the dread lest some stay prove ineffective to longer resistance; beside her sits what, by universal consent, is called the "Belle of the Period" and to describe one would be to describe the class, but the mere idea is ridiculous to use an inelegant but expressive Yankee phrase, "the thing can't be did," for man has failed in every attempt to compass the portraiture of the nondescript. A woman of raw talent might partially succeed, but the inference is that even Fanny Fern would be convinced that her experience and facile pen were both inadequate to the task, and would be driven to woman's "dernier resort," a postscript, i.e., for further particulars the reader is referred to a personal inspection of this unnatural curiosity. Nast can caricature men with tremendous effect, but all the shafts he has hurled at the modern city belle fall pointless; her make-up defies ridicule, it "out Herods Herod." In close proximity to the city belle are seated two fresh looking demoiselles, who evidently like yourself are strangers to the scene, and are so absorbed in scrutinizing what has so much puzzled your brain that they have apparently forgotten themselves, for their lunch remains untouched before them, while their eyes are riveted upon her as if counting each stitch in the innumerable array of frills, flounces and tucks prescribed by fashion. So there is no danger of detection by indulging in a somewhat minute comparison. These country girls, evidently of no mean pretensions, have chignons of considerable proportions, but they are mites when compared with the pillion of their city sister; their plentiful display of French jewelry pales before her varied assortment of flashing gems; air and exercise have tinted their cheeks with a delicate glow of health—high art has enameled her face with the choicest mineral shade; their eyes are sparkling with a natural lustre—restless dissipation has given her a cold, stolid stare, satiety and ennui in every outline and every movement; yet, strange to relate, when these country lassies had completed the critical analysis of this highly finished model of fashion, and their eyes fell upon their own neat but scanty embellishments, a half mortified expression of envious discontent spread over their innocent faces; they hurriedly applied themselves in silence to their lunch, and modestly withdrew as if dazzled by this unaccustomed glare. Woman is verily a puzzle.

Delmonico's Hotel at Fifth Avenue and Fourteenth Street, New York City, ca. 1900. (Schenectady Museum; Hall of Electrical History Foundation/Corbis)

At another table is a party of prinked-up young men, a collection of gaudy neckties, flash jewelry, and vapid pretense. These pride themselves on being fast, while in fact they are the dullest and slowest of mortals, and were it not for the amusement afforded by their ridiculous costumes, antics and grimaces, they would be hooted at by every true man and woman. This adjective *fast* has been taken up by Young America, female as well as male, and is used by them in lieu of the old-fashioned phrase "man of the world," which had and still has a deep, decided significance, and no upstart parvenu can for a single moment disguise himself so as to escape detection. The title, "man of the world," implies intellect, cultivation, grace of person, ease of manner, gentleness of tone, perfect self-control; in fine, a character so decided and so evenly balanced as never to be ruffled by petty crosses and annoyances. The dress of the man of the world is invariably suited to each occasion; he follows the style, but never leads it; it is perfect in its completeness, nothing striking in detail, everything "comme il faut."[2] His address, especially in the presence of ladies, although entirely free from awkward restraint, is characterized by modest repose; in conversation he eschews the personal pronoun, and perfectly understands when to lead, when to be led. How and in what respect, those noisy, fast society men, who are seated at that table, are entitled to the distinction they claim, they themselves must determine; that they are recklessly fast in squandering time, opportunity and means, no one will deny,—they certainly are very far from being Chesterfields or D'Orsays. The gambler's well-filled purse and politic lavish expenditure, insure his welcome here as elsewhere in the halls of fashion. His smiling face is known to all and his careless nods of recognition are returned from right and left as he leisurely saunters to his accustomed seat. His diamond is matchless for purity and size, his horses unequalled on the turf or drive, and so forsooth he is recognized by society. The lawyer seeks him for his client, the physician is prompt in attendance at his call, the tradesman bustles at his nod, and the politician courts his powerful influence,—in his ease all antecedents are ignored.

But it is needless to catalogue the scenes at Delmonico's in 1870, its frescoed ceilings, mirrored halls, and sumptuous appointments are too familiar to warrant description. The thousands who go there to see, and the tens of thousands who are straining every nerve to be seen there, may possibly be more interested by a brief outline of Delmonico's, as established during the last days, of Knickerbocker regime. In a small store on William Street, between Fulton and Ann, directly opposite the North Dutch Church the now metropolitan name first became known to New Yorkers. The little place contained some half-dozen pine tables with requisite wooden chairs to match, and on a board counter covered with white napkins was ranged the limited assortment of pastry. Two-tine forks and buck-handled knives were not considered vulgar then, neither were common earthenware cups and plates inadmissible. As a matter of course the first custom was derived from the foreign element, attracted by the "fillets," "maccaroni," "café," "chocolat" and "petit verre."[3] These were duly served by the "Chef" in person, who, with white paper cap and apron, was only too glad to officiate as his own "garcon." By slow stages the courteous manner of the host, coupled with his delicious dishes and moderate charges, attracted the attention, tickled the palate, and suited the pockets of some of the Knickerbocker youths who were on the lookout for something new, who at once acknowledged the superiority of the French and Italian cuisine as expounded and set forth by Delmonico. It must not, however, for a moment be thought, that the new converts from the plain roasted and boiled doctrine to the new rich gravy faith, plunged at once into the vortex of the elaborate and expensive spread, now every-day affairs at Fifth Avenue. By no means was such the case; their visits were at wide intervals and mostly confined to Saturday afternoons, when the good folks were almost certain to be at home laying out their Sunday clothes. Two or three would agree to meet at the Café for the purpose of indulging in a light French entertainment. On these occasions unusual secrecy was indispensable, for if detected, we were certain to incur the marked displeasure of our grandmother, and to be soundly berated in the first place for our foolish extravagance, and secondly, pitied for our lack of taste by giving preference to "such vile greasy compounds," which we were assured would destroy our stomachs; while if we dared to mention the cool, refreshing "vin ordinaire" that delightful beverage was denounced as a miserable substitute for vinegar. Still, in spite of the well-meant warnings we repeated our visits whenever we could do so with safety, and were warranted by our limited supply of "pocket money"; and yet farther, with what our old fogy ancestors would have pronounced unprincipled, we inducted others into the secret that good things to eat could be had at the little cook-shop on William Street. Gradually the little shop had not the requisite space to accommodate its increasing patronage, and Delmonico, instead of following the stream that pointed up-town, wisely removed his business still further down in the centre of the wholesale traffic before the disastrous conflagration of '35. When after a time that direful calamity was surmounted, he built the restaurant still standing on the corner of William and Beaver Streets, in which the brothers with their sons and nephews accumulated fortunes, and from which sprang the branches now so flourishing on the thoroughfares of New York.

Francis Guerin, a native of France and a cotemporary of the original Delmonico, opened his café on Broadway, between Pine and Cedar Streets, directly opposite the City Hotel, then the most busy portion of the leading thoroughfare. Keenly alive to the accumulation of dollars he ornamented his show windows to attract the attention of promenaders and stragglers who continually passed to and fro before his shop. His display consisted of imported and domestic confectionery, inviting specimens of pastry and cake, bottles of choice French cordials, fancy boxes filled with Parisian bon-bons interspersed with the fruits then in market. Inside, the shelves were lined with preserves in sugar and brandy while on a long counter, which reached from end to end, were spread the tarts and confections for which the place was noted until a very short time ago. From its location and limited dimensions this place was never, strictly speaking, a café or restaurant; sandwiches, sardines, and the sweets mentioned constituted the daily bill of fare, although at the rear of the store a small apartment was furnished with table and chairs, where coffee, chocolate, and, in Summer, ice cream, were served; but it was at best a dingy place, and as it had no entrance except through the store, it was but little frequented, and never by ladies. After a limited period the pie and cake counter was curtailed and the confectionary department became merely ornamental, except during the holiday season, to make space for the bar, which was lengthened and widened at the expense of the other branches,—for the retailing of liquors grew into the prominent feature of the business. Essentially it degenerated into a cosmopolitan drinking saloon, where Americans rushed for their hurried nip of brandy-and-water, Frenchmen sauntered about sipping absinthe and orgeat,[4] Italians smacked their lips over a thimble-full of maraschino,[5]—for all nationalities claimed to find at Père Guerin's their favorite beverage in perfection. From this trade a fortune was soon realized, but the proprietor had no ambition for display and very little love for even cleanliness; he spent nothing in repairs or renovation, and the old place became dingy through neglect, though it continued in the hands of a successor to drive a brisk trade until two or three years ago, when its site was required for more remunerative improvements, when the old crib was demolished "leaving no trace behind."

Delmonico and Guerin, though starting simultaneously in the same business, and though both were successful in amassing wealth, were, as proved by results, very different men in temperament and design. The former a generous, enterprising Italian, while he adhered strictly to his original plan, enlarged and improved when warranted by the demand and the growth of the city. A social host, his ambition was to please the public, and to outstrip competition by a lavish yet judicious expenditure. He rose from the obscurity of a petty shop and lived to have his name known everywhere, at home and abroad. The latter, a Frenchman of penurious tendencies, with no personal ambition, stuck to his shop, accumulated an immense estate, but so far as the public knows has left no record to tell when or how he had lived and died. The old sign "Francis Guerin, Confectioner," has been swept away.

Notes

1. A person of refined taste, especially when it comes to food and beverages.
2. French for following proper standards.
3. French for a sip, meaning in this case of alcohol.
4. A sweet syrup consisting of ground almonds and loaf sugar and served with flavored water.
5. A liqueur flavored with Marasca cherries.

Source: Abram C. Dayton, *Last Days of Knickerbocker Life in New York* (New York: G. W. Harlan, 1882), 38–49, 109–118.

1883 • 87 • George Augustus Sala, *America Revisited*

Introduction: *George Augustus Sala (1828–1895) was an English writer who visited American on two occasions. He wrote about his experiences, many of which were related to food and dining, in two books. Below are his views on American food when he visited the Continental Hotel on Walnut Street in Philadelphia on his second trip to the United States.*

During our sojourn at the Continental I did not, with the exception of a few fees to servants, who made no sign of expecting to be fee'd, pay a cent to anybody. For whatever the tariff at the Continental may be you are entitled to consume five ample meals in the course of every four-and-twenty hours—breakfast, luncheon, dinner, tea, and supper. The Continental would surely have tried the fortitude of Bernard Kavanagh, the Fasting Man; nor, without thinking twice, should I like to turn a Trappist, or even a vegetarian, loose in these halls, since all the meals, I am given to understand, include flesh meat.

I will speak, however, only of the repasts with which I became personally acquainted—breakfast and dinner. For the first-named collation, which is served from six in the morning—for the convenience of passengers by early trains—until ten or eleven, there is a bill of fare comprising such dishes as boiled, fried, poached, "dropped," and scrambled eggs, omelettes in every style, fried, stewed, and roasted oysters, hashed codfish with cream, fish-balls, dried and smoked salmon and herrings, salt mackerel, fresh fish in season, mutton chops, beefsteaks, pork cutlets, sausages, ham, bacon, cold meat, chicken, tea, coffee, and chocolate, a variety of fancy bread, including "waffles," muffins, and those buckwheat cakes so inexpressibly dear to those who are venturesome enough to eat them without thinking of the imminent perils of dissolution through indigestion, and, to crown all, a copious dessert—remember, we were in mid-December—of apples, Californian pears, oranges, fresh Malaga grapes, and bananas.

There is no limit whatsoever as to quantity. You may order as many dishes as you please. For dinner, which was served from two until five and from five until seven p.m., the menu is more varied. At least half a dozen varieties of soup, the same of fish, turkey with chestnut or with cranberry sauce, salmis[1] of chicken and game, beef, mutton, veal and pork, roasted or fried, three or four kinds of wild fowl, a wilderness of vegetables, including, in addition to our ordinary English esculents, sweet potatoes, fried bananas, "succotash," "squash," Lima beans, oyster plant, egg plant, preserved corn, and stewed celery, plenty of salad, and a dessert even more abundant than that which you enjoyed at breakfast. I noticed that the almost exclusive beverage partaken of at dinner was iced water. Symptoms of beer or of wine were almost altogether wanting; and, whatever may be the modes and whatever the times of the Americans sacrificing to Bacchus, it is certainly not at their meals that they seek to propitiate the rosy god.

The simultaneous feeding of hundreds of guests in an hotel so vast as the Continental is not altogether devoid of drawbacks; and, seeing that these drawbacks are complained of quite as bitterly by Americans as by foreigners, they may, I hope, without offence, be slightly glanced at here. Against the quality of the food, be it animal or vegetable, there is not one word to say. Touching the manner in which that food is cooked, I will not say that it equals the cuisine of Delmonico, of the Café Anglais, or of a London Pall-mall club; still, an American hotel dinner comprises an immensely greater variety of dishes than an English hotel dinner does, and in the way of sauces and seasoning the American chefs are a long way ahead of their British brethren; but the temperature of the dishes which are brought to you—not consecutively, but en masse—is uniformly tepid. The art of serving a dinner in courses seems to be utterly ignored, and dish covers to be utterly unknown. You order a heterogeneous assortment of viands, and the waiter brings them to you in a series of little oval dishes—which he carries, by means of some indiscriminate dexterity of muscle, on one arm—and he "dumps" down the dishes before you to pick your way through the wilderness of esculents as best you may.

This system would seem to afflict not only public but private dinner tables, and is beginning to be denounced by the Americans themselves—at least, so I am entitled to opine from the following significant passage in the *New York Tribune:* "The time is fast coming when the 'medley dinner,' will be a thing of the past. By the 'medley dinner' you are to understand a meal served in one course. It is all summed up in the remark which some people will no doubt remember having heard made by a kindly old-fashioned hostess, 'You see your dinner.' And a bountiful table it probably was, with a good dinner utterly ruined for lack of a little judgment in serving. Soup, a chicken pie, a dish of pork and beans, a roast, four or five vegetables, pickles, preserves, pastry, pies and fruit, are all crowded together, leaving little room for your own plate, and none for your appetite. It is a common saying of housekeepers that it is all very well for French people to serve their dinners in courses, their servants are used to it, know how to do it, and do not rebel; but that you cannot train a green Irish girl for instance—and most American housekeepers are subject to that kind of aid in their kitchens—to serve a dinner, nicely, in courses. Now the result of actual experience is that either a green Irish girl or a clever American girl can be taught to serve a dinner in the best style, and learn to appreciate the fact that it is on the whole the most convenient and least perplexing manner in which any meal can be served." Thus far that eminently serious and practical authority, the *New York Tribune;* and the reform which it advocates could probably be carried out without much difficulty at private and middle-class American dinner tables.[2]

The affluent and refined classes dine, it is almost needless to say, precisely as people dine in Europe, and in many particulars, notably as regards oysters, a great deal better than we do in Europe; but I gravely doubt the practicability of serving a great hotel dinner to two or three hundred guests at a time in duly following courses. The utmost that the waiters seem to be able to do is to bring your soup and your ice cream—I omitted the ice cream in my list of dishes—separately: and the soup is often as cold as the ice-cream is warm. In the first place, the distance, as Charles Dickens put it in the memorable case of "A Little Dinner in an Hour," is far too great between the kitchen and the tables. In the next place the bill of fare is, to my mind, far too varied. Be it generosity, or be it a desire to appear "splendiferous" and outshine all rival hotels, the Transatlantic caterer seems to offer his guests the choice of at least twenty more different preparations of food than they actually require. As it is, there is a superabundance of everything; and superabundance is apt to beget satiety. After all, the minds of mankind are more various than their appetites. There are certain edible things which some people like and others dislike; but strike an average all round, and the number of generally accepted eatables will not, I apprehend, be found to be very numerous.

The American bill of fare, as it at present stands, reads as though it were designed to meet the antagonistic tastes of a motley assemblage of Christians, Jews, Mohammedans, and Chinamen, and an infinite variety of Hindoo castes, all pertinaciously declining to eat what other castes eat. The result in my own case has sometimes been comparative starvation in the midst of plenty; for I have found so many good things offered to me in print that I have not known what to order, and have found myself at last dining on some lukewarm soup, a boiled onion, a couple of pig's feet fried, and a vanille ice. Surely in colossal hotels of the Continental calibre it would be feasible to provide what is known as a diner du jour—a bill of fare of moderate dimensions, comprising, say, a couple of soups, four or six entrees, a couple of roasts, with vegetables, sweets, and dessert in proportion.

Notes

1. A technique in classical French cookery where a roast or sauteed piece of meat is sliced and reheated in sauce.
2. While on the subject of dinners and dining, in the States, I may take the opportunity of mentioning that Schools of Cookery for young ladies are becoming prevalent in

the principal cities of the Union. At many of these establishments, the half-dozen members of the highest class, which includes married as well as unmarried ladies, enjoy the privilege on stated occasions, of each inviting a gentleman to partake with them of the dinner which they have previously prepared. The guests not unfrequently however, make their appearance long before the appointed time, and finding their way into the kitchen, occupy themselves in passing approving judgments on the soups and sauces beforehand.

Source: George Augustus Sala, *America Revisited: From the Bay of New York to the Gulf of Mexico* (London: Vizetelly and Co., 1883), 148–153.

1885 • 88 • Markets of New Orleans

Introduction: *New Orleans, a city settled by the French, has always been a culinary oasis. Its diverse population—American Indians, Cajuns, Creoles, French, Americans, African Americans, and Europeans—created a culinary mixture that rivaled or surpassed other American cities. Below is a description of the city's diverse markets and the foods they sold.*

Meat Market.

The first of the series of markets composing the French Market is the Meat Market, erected in 1813 at a cost of $30,000, on the spot where stood the first market, destroyed during the fearful hurricane of the year previous. The stalls are mostly occupied by Gascon butchers from France who monopolize the butcher business of the city. The meat sold is generally Texas beef and brings usually twelve and one-half cents per pound. The stalls are frequently ornamented with pictures of meadows on which graze most wonderful looking cattle in impossible attitudes; in the foreground the artist (?) often introduces what is supposed to be the portrait of the owner of the stall, but what may be taken for any butcher in the market. At the head of the market are the several coffee stands, much frequented by strangers. Before leaving this market, go over into the aisle nearest the street and examine the various kinds of potted meats, called in French "charcuterie[,]" some of which are excellent for cold lunches. Passing into the open space beyond, we come to the rendezvous of the Indians, a remnant of the once powerful tribe of Choctaws. These Indians live on the north side of Lake Pontchartrain, and belong to the tribe under the chief James Mahot-Aby, who, in 1879, was elected chief for life. Their principal occupation is gathering herbs and medicinal plants, which meet a ready sale in the market. Laurel and Bay leaves, used by Creole cooks to season soups and dishes, are sold by them as well as "File" (gumbo), a sort of green powder, used to make the celebrated gumbo soup. This is prepared by pounding up sassafras, bay leaves and some other herbs, previously dried in the shade. Plantain (deer tongue), used to perfume wardrobes and linen closets, by spreading the leaves among the clothes, is sold by them at certain seasons for a few cents a bunch; also pieces of *latannier* root or palmetto, used for scrubbing brushes. Among their medicinal stock, the Indian or wild turnip is found, which, boiled by the natives in syrup is considered a sure cure for

French Market, New Orleans, ca. 1906. (Library of Congress)

consumption. Blow guns and arrows made of wild cane are among their stock, and can be purchased for a trifle. Negro women station themselves at this spot offering for sale "pralines," sugar cake made of pecan or pea-nuts, "Callas," a species of soft doughnut made of rice and "pain patate," a kind of pie or cold pudding made of sweet potatoes.

Bazaar Market.

The next market is called the Bazaar Market, a structure of iron erected about ten years ago, and used for the sale of dry goods, boots, shoes, notions, china, and glass-ware. Its narrow aisles are festooned with bright-colored handkerchiefs, stockings, and other articles of wearing apparel, so that on a crowded day circulation is slow and difficult. Emerging from this city of miniature shops, like an Eastern Bazaar, we come into an open space occupied by vegetable, fruit and flower vendors. During the Louisiana orange season, October to January, bins full of fine oranges are seen on all sides. Bananas do not ripen in New Orleans and have to be brought from the neighboring islands of the Gulf of Mexico, but oranges and figs grow to perfection. During the height of the season oranges can be purchased at these bins as low as thirty cents a hundred.

Fruit Market.

Crossing the street, we reach a triangular market devoted to fruit and poultry. Here the fruits of the tropics are sold at reasonable rates.

Vegetable Market.

The next market is the great "Vegetable Market," a most interesting place, where vegetables, groceries, flowers and fruits are sold. Owing to the warm climate of the surrounding country, the seasons are very advanced and strawberries, green peas, and other early fruits and vegetables are sold here in December and January. Many of the vegetables sold in this market do not grow at the North and can be purchased here cheap. In the spring, the first fruit that makes its appearance in market is the "Japanese plum" or "Mespilus," a bright yellow and slightly tart fruit with a tender pulp and several large seeds. Pomegranates and figs appear in July. Of the latter the "figue celeste," a small brown fig, is much preferred to the large black or white fig, which is too coarse-grained and not sweet enough. Plantains, a large kind of banana, brought from the islands of the Gulf, are not sweet enough to eat raw, so the Creoles slice them and eat them fried or stewed, with butter and sugar. In this market bouquets made of vegetables artistically caned to represent flowers are offered for sale at moderate prices. At the lower end is the best coffee stand in the market—where good coffee and chocolate are kept steaming hot.

Fish Market.

After passing through the Vegetable Market, the Fish Market is reached. This building, a structure of iron and glass, is one of the most interesting on account of the great variety of fish offered for sale. On the white marble tables, are seen brilliant red-snappers with large coral fins, the red fish, much liked in "courtbouillon," the much appreciated sheephead, the famous Spanish Mackerel, and, last but not least, the pompano, considered by gourmets to be the finest and most delicate fish that swims in any waters, and which strangers should not fail to taste at some good restaurant. Crabs, hard and soft, and shrimp from the lake and river, the former being the largest, but not esteemed as much as the latter, are sold in quantities. Crayfish, a small lobster-like fish, are sold from large baskets and used to make the famous "bisque" soup. These little fish are caught principally in the river, where they do great damage to the levees, by boring holes in them. Sea-trout, mullet, catfish, croakers and many other varieties are always on sale. The fish business is carried on by a class of Spaniards and Italians who are usually called "Dagoes." They own their own boats, small sailing-vessels, called luggers, having one mast on which they hoist a lateen sail. These boats go through the various canals to the fishing grounds on the Gulf, and lay in their stock, pack it away in ice boxes, and hasten to the city. Some of the fish are brought from greater distances, for instance the pompano, which is only found in certain spots on the Florida coast. Green turtle comes also from Florida, and is always to be had in the market. The proximity of New Orleans to the sea and fresh water streams makes it the best fish and oyster market in the United States after that of Mobile; while in winter the bayous and woods are filled with game of all kinds. Fish is cheap here in comparison to other large cities. A fine red-snapper or red fish, enough for ten persons, can be bought for 50 cents; sheephead are little higher, and small pompano sell as low as 50 cents each and as high as $5. Shrimp, 10 cents a plate, and hard crabs 15 cents a dozen. Near the end of the Fish Market is the Game Market, which in winter is stocked with wild ducks, geese, turkeys, rabbits, woodcocks, and all varieties of game. Wild ducks are sometimes very abundant, and sell lower than 50 cents a pair. . . .

Poydras Market.

Corner of Baronne and Poydras streets. Market held every day, Sundays included, 5 A.M. to 11 A.M. Five blocks distant from Canal street. Take Baronne and St. Charles street cars.

The Poydras market, named after the street on which it stands, so called in honor of Julien Poydras, a benevolent citizen and founder of several orphan asylums, is the principal market of the American quarter, and resembles the French market on a much smaller scale. It is noted for the excellence of its meat and is well patronized. On week days, in the middle of the market, rows of negro women stand like soldiers, waiting for scrubbing or washing jobs and remind one of the time slaves stood in line for sale at the slave marts in the city.

Source: James S. Zacharie, *New Orleans Guide: With Descriptions of the Routes to New Orleans* (New Orleans: New Orleans News Co., 1885), 101–105.

1889 • 89 • Marion Harlan, "Soup-Making"

Introduction: *Mary Virginia Terhune (1830–1922), writing under the pseudonym Marion Harland, was one of America's most popular writers in the second half of the 19th century. She wrote 25 novels and a like number of books on domestic economy. It was during the late 19th century that home cooks lost the art of soup making as commercial manufacturers began canning food, such as soup. Below is Terhune's article "Soup Making" in which she reports that "The slovenly or indifferent housewife" produced "'wishy-washy stuff' that tantalizes a healthy appetite only to fill the gastronomic soul with worse than naught." Others produced soup with "no substance into it!" This article reflects the end of one era—that of the expert home cook—and the rise of the industrial food system.*

Soup-Making

Like dish-washing and tea-brewing, soup-making is classed by self-sufficient ignorance among the things which are too easy to be learned. The slovenly or indifferent housewife underrates to contempt a dish without which a dinner is not a dinner. In her opinion, soup is, at the best and most savory, "wishy-washy stuff" that tantalizes a healthy appetite only to fill the gastronomic soul with worse than naught.

The Jersey farmer's criticism upon the blanc-mange smothered in whipped cream, sent to his sick-room by a neighbor, embodies the estimate set by our ignoramus upon broth, bouillon, and clear consommé:

"It has no substance *into* it!" plained the bucolic invalid.

Much of the liquid that finds its way to better-advised people under the generic name of "Soup," deserves the stricture.

The average cook is usually imbibed with the heresy stated in our opening paragraph. She sets little "store by soup." If the family insist upon having it occasionally, she makes it under verbal or dumb protest, *with the grease on.* The oils she conceives to be "essential" to strengthen and nourishment, swim un flotillas of globules upon the muddy deeps within the tureen. The use of the strainer in the process is a refinement unknown or despised by her. If the twice-cooked bones and meat that yield up to the fast boil material for "stock," fail to produce more than a weak dish-water, our cook thickens lavishly, and gains converts to her disdainful judgment of the result from the unfortunates who feel that something, they know not what, is wanted to the disrelishful compound.

It is worth our little while to ask why this seemly head and front of the chief meal of the day gets the cold shoulder in perhaps one-half of the homes of what maybe called middle-class families. Why it is almost unknown except as sick-room broth among the really poor.

"I am tired of *acephalous* dinners!" said a boarder, while packing up for a return to the city from a snug and tidy farm-house. "There is a certain refinement in soup. The higher one rises in the social circle, the more nearly soup approximates the necessaries of life."

As I have elsewhere explained, omission arises partly from the disinclination to increase the care of the servantless mistress by adding a course to the family dinner that involves the need of changing and cleaning an extra set of plates. But the main course of the curious oversight of the claims of the tureen upon the appetite and respect is ignorant want of skill in soup-making. He who is accustomed to begin his dinner six days in the week with a plate of hot, nourishing, savory potage, or *purée,* or *consommé,* or broth, misses the cheer and sustenance it supplies, if deprived of it on the seventh. There is an odd sense of unseemly familiarity in the abrupt entrance upon the heavier business of the hour, like shaking hands with a man to whom you have not been introduced.

Our summer boarder was more shrewd than fanciful in extolling the refining influence of the soup-kettle.

To make good soup one must have patience and judgment, and take the time required for the various processes of manufacture. The hit-or-miss school of cookery is more disastrous in this department than in what are known as "fancy dishes."

"There must have been the grain, the grinding,
There must have been the slice of bread,"

says Mrs. Whitney of a crumb. The under-the-average housewife pleads the pressure of other duties, the throng of must-be-dones that cannot be crowded out.

"Soups will do well enough for rich people!" sighs the room-renter. "What have such as we to do with such finical ways?"

Conviction that the neglected and much-abused article herein treated of is almost necessary in the every-day bill-of-fare; that it is wholesome, economical, and, when properly made, delicious, sent me in search of methods by which even the spinster (or bachelor) occupant of a single room, and the over-wrought mother who "does her own work" may set a good nutritious soup on the table daily without serious increase of expense and labor.

In the course of my explorations, I was directed by a friend who had tested their products, to the building occupied by the Franco-American Food Company, of New York. I had seen some canning establishments; I had heard of others. I had promised my loathing inner self never to enter one again.

What I saw and learned of real soup-making—honest, clean, and appetizing—I propose, still in the interest of American housewives, to relate as frankly as I would expose the iniquities of conventional "canning," did diaphragm and taste allow me to undertake the task.

Beginning with the raw material—I, an unexpected visitor, found in the larder huge shins of beef; chickens, dressed and whole, fair, plump, and free from the suspicion of taint; calves' heads, white and firm; mutton and veal in prime order; barrels of healthy vegetables; parsley, celery, and other soup-herbs; all the appliances needful for the manufacture of divers kinds of soup in a private family, but on a gigantic scale.

Next we examined what the proprietor of the great kitchen aptly styles "the ABC of soup-making"—the stock-pot.

This is *not,* let us observe parenthetically and emphatically, an *omnium gatherum* in any well-ordered establishment. One cookery book gravely advises that frugal housekeeper to prepare stock for the week's soups, by setting a kettle with bones, cold meat, etc., at the side of the range, cover well with cold water, and adding from meal to meal, the scraps from dishes and plates, to "let all simmer slowly for three days!"

In one of the six sixty-gallon caldrons of *pot-au-feu* in the upper story of the Franco-American Company's building we found meat cut into small pieces, cracked bones, peeled carrots, onions, turnips, parsley, sweet herbs, a little salt, all covered with water. For eight hours the contents of the big pot are kept at a gentle bubbling boil, regulated by a thermometer. All the cooking is done by steam. The top of the kettle is propped open a little way to allow partial escape to the savory vapor. The eight-hour process obliges ingredients to give up all the good which is in them. The proprietor and his intelligent overlooker-son lay great stress upon the evils of fast boiling for soups. "Soup which has been boiled rapidly cannot be cleared," said the latter. "There should be no chance, no risk in such matters. Cookery can be reduced to an exact science. The effect of certain causes must be the same always. To suffer a hard boil—even for the minute when the cook's attention is diverted by other work—is to ruin a pot of soup."

The liquor drawn through a faucet from the *pot-au-feu* is clearer than much *consommé* I have seen ordered from expensive caterers and served at fashionable tables. The *débris* left in the caldron is strained and pressed into the liquor, then clarified.

For mock-turtle, the calves' heads are cleaned, soaked, blanched and boiled. The tongue, palate-fringe and brains are removed with all darkened pieces; the bones go back into the caldron, the gelatinous, almost translucent parts that remain are cut *by hand* into meat, uniform dice, and when the seasoned soup is ready for canning, are added to it.

Chicken broth is treated somewhat in the same manner. The bones and inferior portions are returned to the caldron, the best parts of the boiled cold fowls are cut into dice, mixed with boiled rice, and when the broth in which the chickens were boiled is ready, dice and rice are put with it into the can.

A plate of mutton broth was brought to us, hot and delicious, just as it was about to go into the cans. It is, like most French broths, unthickened by flour. To the meat and barley are added dice of vegetables—these cut by machinery.

The pea-soup put up by this firm is made from the best Cleveland split peas. After a night's soaking they are boiled in the stock to a pulp, rubbed through a sieve, returned to the caldron; more stock is added, a little butter and seasoning, a small quantity of flour to prevent separation of pulp and liquid, and a delightful *purée* is the result.

The clam broth made by the Franco-American Company has deservedly high reputation in hospital and sick-room. In albumen, it is far richer than meat. Little Neck clams are used. The soft clam is discarded as less nutritious. Green turtle soup is made of the gelatinous portions close to the upper and lower shells. The entrails, etc., of the turtle are thrown away as unfit for soup-making.

Bouillon, clam broth and all other soups are sealed in glass jars as well as in tin cans.

"Not," explains Mr. Biardot, the proprietor, "that there is danger from using our tin cans. But invalids and others who have a prejudice against 'canned goods' are quieted by the knowledge that their food comes to them in glass." The bouillon, served hot to a member of the party who was faint from weariness, was exquisite in color and flavor, and brought back strength and vivacity to the sufferer with surprising quickness.

None of the soups manufactured here or elsewhere exceed in rich toothsomeness the terrapin. But comparative enumeration is invidious, had we time to enter upon a list that contains nothing indifferent.

Pass we to a lower story to learn why nobody need fear injury from partaking of soups and *pâtés* preserved in the Biardot tins.

The material used is what is known as "charcoal tin." Charcoal is employed in the manufacture instead of mineral coal, the gasses from which enter into and permeate the fusing metal. "Charcoal tin" is exceedingly malleable, moreover, never cracking as cheaper qualities are apt to do, thereby suffering oxidation by exposure to air or acids. A breath upon the surface of the metal plate handed for our inspection passed rapidly and entirely as from a polished mirror. A can was made under our eyes in a marvelously short time. The square plate was fashioned into a cylinder, fitted with top and bottom, and soldered in as few minutes as suffice me to tell of it. *All the soldering is on the outside* of the utensil. It is, perhaps, not generally known that "American canned goods" must be soldered on the outside only for the foreign market. Solder, such as we often find inside of the can in which canned vegetables are preserved, contains absolutely poisonous matter. The circumstance challenges consideration even in a country where life is cheap and digestions are lightly esteemed.

After the cans are filled and soldered, they are steamed in a closed caldron until the contents are again at boiling heat, a process that tests the integrity of cases and solder. Next they are varnished to prevent rust on the outside; finally labeled and wrapped in paper.

"'Care and cleanliness' should be the motto of the cook," says Mr. Biardot, modestly oracular.

Passing from room to room of his enlarged edition of a model kitchen, one sees everywhere the practical illustration of the adage. There are no evil odors, no dirty corners, no repulsive sights, no hint of uncanny devices for bringing plausible results out of equivocal materials. All is honest and legitimate, corresponding so exactly with the methods and materials intelligent housewives employ for similar ends as to rob "canning" of disgustful terrors.

I have only room here for a few valuable hints gathered from observation of the methods in operation in Mr. Biardot's realm.

Soup should not form the whole meal, or a substantial part of it, but is, as I have said, the introduction to the ceremony of dining—the overture to the stately opera. The French never omit it. Their preliminary course is soup, light and varied in flavor and appearance. The lower classes of English know only broths or thick soups; eat these infrequently, and when they do, make a solid meal of them.

Many are ignorant of the value of *consommé* or French bouillon, for daily consumption. Boiled gently from paste, tapioca, sage, rice, barley, farina, or left clear and poured upon neatly-poached eggs in the tureen, it is nutritious, stimulating, and easily digested. The cook should be careful, however, not to make her soup into savory pudding by adding too much of the cereal. Let me add that the dexterity and neatness with which the excellent materials used in this establishment are handled, boned, cleaned, trimmed and cut up, refutes the saying: "Better not look into the kitchen if you would relish cooked food."

The visit—repeated at length—was full of interest and enjoyment. It is well for over-tasked housekeepers to know that soups at moderate prices—good and nutritious—can be had without the trouble of making them; for invalids in boarding-houses to be able to get bouillon and broths of the best quality that have not a suspicion of the "medicated taste" so abhorrent to the sensitive senses. For the country housekeeper—subject at all times to sudden irruptions of visitors, especially in the summer when the kitchen fire must burn low for part of the day, if workers in the room live through the heated term, there should be infinite comfort in the knowledge that her store-room shelves may be made equal to the fiercest midsummer emergency.

To such THE HOME-MAKER commends the perusal of this article, written with the frank sincerity of one who lauds nothing through custom or courtesy, and seeks, whenever it can be done conscientiously, to bring together the housewife's demand and the manufacturer's supply.

Source: Marion Harlan, "Soup Making," *Home-Maker Magazine* 2 (April 1889): 53–56.

1890 • 90 • Ward McAllister, "Giving Picnics at My Farm"

Introduction: *Ward McAllister (1827–1895) was a native of Savannah, Georgia. McAllister made a fortune in California during the Gold Rush and then moved to New York, where he married an heiress. He frolicked among the superrich of the eastern social establishment and created the list of 400 of New York's top social elite. McCallister published his memoirs,* Society as I Have Found It, *in 1890 and was ostracized by New York's superrich, who preferred their privacy. Before his downfall, McAllister delighted in giving picnics. Below is a description of an upper-class picnic in Rhode Island.*

Newport was now at its best. The most charming people of the country had formed a select little community there; the society was small, and all were included in the gaieties and festivities. Those were the days that made Newport what it was then and is now, the most enjoyable and luxurious little island in America. The farmers of the island even seemed to catch the infection, and they were as much interested in the success of our picnics and country dinners, as we were ourselves. They threw open their houses to us, and never heeded the invasion, on a bright sunshiny day, of a party of fifty people, who took possession of their dining-room, in fact of their whole house, and frolicked in it to their heart's content. To be sure, I had often to pacify a farmer when a liveried groom robbed his hen roost, but as he knew that this fashionable horde paid their way, he was easily soothed. I always then remarked that in Newport, at that time, you could have driven a four-in-hand of camels or giraffes, and the residents of the island would have smiled and found it quite the thing. The charm of the place then was the simple way of entertaining; there were no large balls; all the dancing and dining was done by daylight, and in the country. I did not hesitate to ask the very *créme de la créme* of New York society to lunch and dine at my farm, or to a fishing party on the rocks. My little farm dinners gained such a reputation that my friends would say to me: "Now, remember, leave me out of your ceremonious dinners as you choose, but always include me in those given at your farm, or I'll never forgive you." But to convey any idea of our country parties, one must in detail give the method of getting them up: Riding on the Avenue on a lovely summer's day, I would be stopped by a beautiful woman, in gorgeous array, looking so fascinating that if she were to ask you to attempt the impossible, you would at least make the effort. She would open on me as follows: "My dear friend, we are all dying for a picnic. Can't you get one up for us?"

"Why, my dear lady," I would answer, "you have dinners every day, and charming dinners too; what more do you want?"

"Oh, they're not picnics. Any one can give dinners," she would reply; "what we want is one of your picnics. Now, my dear friend, do get one up."

This was enough to fire me, and set me going. So I reply:

"I will do your bidding. Fix on the day at once, and tell me what is the best dish your cook makes."

Out comes my memorandum book, and I write: "Monday, 1 P.M., meet at Narragansett Avenue, bring *filet de bœuf piqué*" and with a bow am off in my little wagon, and dash on, to waylay the next cottager, stop every carriage known to contain friends, and ask them, one and all, to join our country party, and assign to each of them the providing of a certain dish and a bottle of champagne. Meeting young men, I charge them to take a bottle of champagne, and a pound of grapes, or order from the confectioner's a quart of ice cream to be sent to me. My pony is put on its mettle; I keep going the entire day getting recruits; I engage my music and servants, and a carpenter to put down a dancing platform, and the florist to adorn it, and that evening I go over in detail the whole affair, map it out as a general would a battle, omitting nothing, not even a salt spoon; see to it that I have men on the road to direct my party to the farm, and bid the farmer put himself and family, and the whole farm, in holiday attire.

On one occasion, as my farmer had just taken unto himself a bride, a young and pretty woman, I found that at mid-day, to receive my guests, she had dressed herself in bridal array; she was *décolleté*,[1] and seemed quite prepared to sing the old ballad of "Coming thro' the rye"; but as her husband was a stalwart young fellow, and extremely jealous, I advised the young men in the party to confine their attentions to their own little circle and let Priscilla, the Puritan, alone.

When I first began giving picnics at my farm, I literally had no stock of my own. I felt that it would never do to have a gathering of the brightest and cleverest people in the country at my place with the pastures empty, neither a cow nor a sheep; so my Yankee wit came to my assistance. I at once hired an entire flock of Southdown sheep, and two yoke of cattle, and several cows from the neighboring farm, for half a day, to be turned into my pasture lots, to give the place an animated look. I well remember some of my knowing guests, being amateur farmers, exclaiming:

"Well, it is astonishing! Mc has but fifty acres, and here he is, keeping a splendid flock of Southdowns, two yoke of cattle, to say nothing of his cows!"

I would smile and say:

"My friend I am not a fancy farmer, like yourself; I farm for profit."

At that time, I was out of pocket from three to four thousand dollars a year by my farm, but must here add, for my justification, that finding amateur farming an expensive luxury, I looked the matter squarely in the face, watched carefully the Yankee farmers around me, and satisfied myself that they knew more about the business than I did, and at once followed in their footsteps, placed my farm on shares, paying nothing out for labor, myself paying the running expenses, and dividing the profits with my farmer. Instead of losing three or four thousand dollars a year by my farm, it then paid me, and continues to pay me seven to eight hundred dollars a year clear of all expenses. We sell off of fifty acres of land, having seventeen additional acres of pasturage, over three thousand dollars of produce each year. I sell fifty Southdown lambs during the months of April and May, at the rate of eight to ten dollars each, to obtain which orders are sent to me in advance, and my winter turkeys have become as famous as my Southdown lambs. The farm is now a profit instead of a loss. I bought this place in 1853; if I had bought the same amount of land south of Newport, instead of north of the town, it would have been worth a fortune to-day.

To return to our picnic. The anxiety as to what the weather would be, was always my first annoyance, for of course these country parties hinge on the weather. After making all your preparations, everything ready for the start, then to look out of your window in the morning, as I have often done, and see the rain coming down in torrents, is far from making you feel cheerful. But, as a rule, I have been most fortunate in my weather. We would meet at Narragansett Avenue at 1 P.M., and all drive out together. On reaching the picnic grounds, I had an army of skirmishers, in the way of servants, thrown out, to take from each carriage its contribution to the country dinner. The band would strike up, and off the whole party would fly in the waltz, while I was directing the icing of the champagne, and arranging the tables; all done with marvelous celerity. Then came my hour of triumph, when, without giving the slightest signal (fearing some one might forestall me, and take off the prize), I would dash in among the dancers, secure our society queen, and lead with her the way to the banquet. Now began the fun in good earnest. The clever men of the party would assert their claims to the best dishes, proud of the efforts of their cook, loud in their praise of their own game pie, which most probably was brought out by some third party, too modest to assert and push his claim. Beauty was there to look upon, and wit to enliven the feast. The wittiest of men was then in his element, and I only wish I dared quote here his brilliant sallies. The beauty of the land was also there, and all feeling that they were on a frolic, they threw hauteur, ceremonial, and grand company manners aside, and, in place, assumed a spirit of simple enjoyment. Toasts were given and drunk, then a stroll in pairs, for a little interchange of sentiment, and then the whole party made for the dancing platform, and a cotillon of one hour and a half was danced, till sunset. As at a "Meet," the arrivals and departures were a feature of the day. Four-in-hands, tandems, and the swellest of Newport turnouts rolled by you. At these entertainments you formed lifetime intimacies with the most cultivated and charming men and women of this country.

These little parties were then, and are now, the stepping-stones to our best New York society. People who have been for years in mourning and thus lost sight of, or who having passed their lives abroad and were forgotten, were again seen, admired, and liked, and at once brought into society's fold. Now, do not for a moment imagine that all were indiscriminately asked to these little fetes. On the contrary, if you were not of the inner circle, and were a new-comer, it took the combined efforts of all your friends' backing and pushing to procure an invitation for you. For years, whole families sat on the stool of probation, awaiting trial and acceptance, and many were then rejected, but once received, you were put on an intimate footing with all. To acquire such intimacy in a great city like New York would have taken you a lifetime. A fashionable woman of title from England remarked to me that we were one hundred years behind London, for our best society was so small, every one in it had an individuality. This, to her, was charming, "for," said she, "one could have no such individuality in London." It was accorded only to the highest titled people in all England, while here any one in society would have every movement chronicled. Your "*personnel,*" she added, "is daily discussed, your equipage is the subject of talk, as well as your house and household." Another Londoner said to me, "This Newport is no place for a man without fortune." There is no spot in the world where people are more *en evidence.* It is worth while to do a thing well there, for you have people who appreciate your work, and it tells and pays. It is the place of all others to take social root in.

Note

1. Having a low neckline.

Source: Ward McAllister, *Society as I Have Found It* (New York: Cassell, 1890), 110–120.

1894 • 91 • John Harvey Kellogg, "What Are Foods?"

Introduction: *No single individual influenced American eating habits during the early 20th century more than John Harvey Kellogg (1852–1943). Kellogg studied medicine at Bellevue Hospital College in New York. In 1876 he was asked to manage the Western Reform Institute in Battle Creek, Michigan. Kellogg changed the institute's name to the Battle Creek Sanitarium, and under his guidance it thrived. America's rich and famous flocked to the sanitarium. Kellogg enforced a vegetarian regimen at the sanitarium and sought to develop new vegetarian products. He experimented with pressing grains and nuts between rollers. The resulting flakes became a staple at the sanitarium and launched the breakfast cereal industry in America. Here are his views on the physiology of food.*

What are Foods?—In the preceding chapter we have learned that the body is constantly sustaining losses in consequence of the vital work performed by its various organs. Foods are substances which, when introduced into the body, make good its natural wastes and losses, and furnish proper material for the repair of its tissues, or for carrying on its vital processes. As we have already learned, these requirements are met by organized matter, water, and oxygen, or what may be termed solid, liquid, and gaseous foods. Of these, the first only is commonly known as food. Liquid foods are called drinks, all of which have water for their essential element. In this chapter our attention will be confined to the consideration of organized foods.

A poison is the opposite of a food. It not only does not repair wastes and losses, but interferes with the vital processes, disturbing them in such a way as to occasion sickness and death.

33. Animal and Vegetable Foods.—Man employs both animal and vegetable substances as foods. Some nations, particularly the English people and Americans, use a large proportion of flesh, and some barbarous tribes live almost wholly upon the flesh of animals; but the larger portion of the human race live chiefly upon vegetable foods. Many millions of human beings in India and other parts of Asia never taste flesh, considering it a sin to do so.

34. Plants the only Food—producers.—Plants alone possess the power to construct living substance out of the elements of the earth and the air. Animals are able to subsist upon organized substances only, so that a lion, in dining upon an antelope, is only eating at second hand the grass and herbs which the latter has eaten; and a man, in eating roast beef, is taking at second hand the corn upon which the ox was fed.

35. Food Elements.—When a chemist examines a loaf of bread or a piece of meat, he finds it to be made up of various substances quite unlike each other, each possessing peculiar properties, and destined for different uses in the body when taken as food, called food elements.

36. Classification of Food Elements.—The various substances found in foods may be included in six classes: 1. Starch; 2. Sugars; 3. Albumen (all albuminous substances); 4. Fats; 5. Salts; 6. Indigestible Elements.

37. Starch.—This element is found only in vegetable foods. In a raw state, starch is found in small particles or granules, each enclosed in a woody envelope. Starch is the most abundant of all the food elements.

38. Sugar.—Sugar is very unlike starch in its general properties, although closely related to it. In the mysterious chemistry of plant life, the insoluble, tasteless starch is converted into this sweet and extremely soluble substance. Several different kinds of sugar occur in nature, the most important of which are cane-sugar, grape-sugar, and milk-sugar.

Cane-sugar is the sweetest of all the sugars, and is that commonly used as food. It is obtained from the sugarcane, the sorghum plant, the beet root, and the maple-tree. Grape-sugar is found in most fruits and in honey. Milk-sugar gives to milk its Sweetness. A sugar resembling grape-sugar, called glucose, is very extensively manufactured chemically, by boiling the starch of corn or potatoes with sulphuric acid. Glucose cannot be considered a perfect substitute for natural sugar.

39. Albumen.—The white of an egg is almost pure albumen. All true foods contain elements which in many respects resemble albumen and serve the same purposes in the body, and so are termed albuminous elements. For convenience, we shall apply the term albumen to any or all of them. The lean portion of flesh and the caseine of milk are forms of animal albumen. All vegetable foods also contain albumen. Caseine, for example, is found in peas and beans, as well as in milk. One of the most important of all the albumens is gluten, which is found in wheat, rye, and barley.

40. Fats.—Oil, or fat, is found in both animal and vegetable foods. The principal animal fats used as food are butter, lard, suet, and tallow. Vegetable oils are chiefly derived from oily fruits, as the olive, from nuts, and from various seeds. A very considerable quantity of fat is found in corn and oats.

41. Salts.—When a portion of animal or vegetable food is burned, there is left a residue of ashes, made up of inorganic or mineral elements. These are the so-called salts of the food. They do not exist in the food in the form in which they are found in its ashes, but in an organized form. The most important source of salts is the grains. Wheat, oats, barley, corn, and rye contain an abundant supply of this element, as do the potato and most other vegetables. The salts also exist in milk in good proportion.

42. Indigestible Elements.—All vegetable foods contain more or less of a woody substance, called cellulose. The bran of wheat belongs to this class of elements. Cellulose is not to any extent digestible, but it serves an important purpose in giving bulk to the food. The connective tissue elements of flesh foods—the ligaments, tendons, etc.—are hard to digest, and afford little or no nourishment.

In addition to the several elements mentioned, all food substances contain certain flavoring matters.

43. Condiments.—A condiment is an article which possesses little or no food value, but is added to food for the purpose of imparting to it a characteristic flavor. The condiments most commonly used in this country are mustard, pepper, ginger, spices, pepper-sauce, Worcestershire and other hot sauces, and vinegar. All condiments possess irritating or stimulating qualities. They stimulate the appetite, and act as whips to the stomach and other digestive organs, and are thus injurious.

44. Food Substances.—The several food elements which we have been considering are not, in any proper sense, to be regarded as food. An animal fed exclusively upon any one of them soon acquires such a disgust for its food that it will refuse to taste it, even though starving, and sooner or later dies. Gluten is the only exception to this rule. A true food contains various elements, which are combined in varying proportions in different foods. Let us now briefly notice some of the leading food substances.

45. Foods of Animal Origin.—Chief among animal foods is milk, the natural diet of most young animals. Milk contains the elements of nutrition in proper proportion, and will sustain life for an indefinite period. The chief albuminous element of milk is caseine. The white color of milk is due to the fact that it contains a considerable amount of fat or oil in a state of emulsion, or division into minute drops. When milk is allowed to stand for a few hours, the oily particles collect at the top, constituting the cream. By churning, the little drops are made to unite, producing butter. The ease with which it is digested renders milk a most suitable food for the young. It is, indeed, with rare exceptions, a most wholesome food for persons of all ages.

46. Cheese is made from milk by adding rennet, which separates the caseine and fat from the whey. Cheese undergoes partial decomposition in the process of "curing," and is on this account much less wholesome than fresh milk. It is difficult to digest, and likely to interfere with the digestion of other foods. Sometimes a peculiar fermentation takes place in cheese, which produces a very poisonous substance, known as tyrotoxicon. Very serious and sometimes fatal illness often results from the use of such cheese. This poison is destroyed by heat. On this account cheese is rendered less dangerous by cooking, while at the same time it is also made more digestible.

47. Flesh.—The flesh of the ox, sheep, or hog, is more largely used as food in this and most other civilized countries than any other kinds of flesh food. Mutton is not so well relished by some, but is nearly as nourishing as beef and equally easy to digest. Pork contains much fat, is difficult to digest, is likely to be diseased, and must be regarded as an inferior food. The Jews in ancient times were forbidden to eat the flesh of the hog,

and still abstain from the use of pork, doubtless for good reasons. The flesh of deer and other wild game, while usually less tender than that of stall-fattened animals, is more wholesome if eaten when fresh, on account of the healthier conditions of life which wild animals usually enjoy. Game is often allowed to become almost putrid before it is eaten. Such flesh is exceedingly unwholesome. Veal, like the flesh of all very young animals, is difficult to digest, and can not be recommended as food.

48. Fish and Fowl.—The nutritive value of fish and fowl is not quite equal to that of beef or mutton, but when properly cooked they are relished by most persons, and possess considerable value as foods.

49. Shell-fish contain very little nutriment, although some of them, oysters in particular, are in very great favor as table delicacies. All shell-fish are scavengers, however, and are sometimes poisonous. Frogs, lobsters, shrimps, sea-crabs, etc., are by many considered delicate eating, but can not be regarded as really first-class foods. The oyster is easily digested, though it does not possess the power to digest itself, nor to aid digestion when eaten raw, as many persons suppose. The oyster is a scavenger in its habits, and when the beds in which oysters grow are located in such a manner as to be reached by the impure matters carried into the sea by the sewers of a large city, they sometimes become diseased, and produce serious illness when eaten.

50. Eggs.—An egg contains within itself every element needed for the support of the body, and has the advantage, when properly cooked, of being one of the most easily digested of foods, and one of very high nutritive value.

51. Salted and Smoked Meats.—Most kinds of flesh foods are preserved by salting. The process of salting hardens the tissues and renders them difficult to digest. Smoked meats and fish are also hard to digest.

52. Vegetable Foods.—Vegetable foods are the original source of the nutritive elements contained in flesh foods; hence we should expect them to furnish all the elements of nutrition, and in good proportions. This is the case with the best vegetable foods.

53. Fruits, Grains, Vegetables.—Vegetable foods are usually divided into three classes—fruits, grains, and vegetables. Fruits comprise fleshy seeds and seed-bearing portions of plants, such as the apple, strawberry, and plum, each of which represents a different class of fruits. Melons and nuts are also fruits. The grains comprise those seeds used as foods which are produced by grass-like plants, as wheat, oats, rye, barley, corn, and rice. Allied to this class are the edible seeds of pod-bearing plants, the chief of which are peas, beans, and lentils. The grains are the most nourishing of all foods, and contain the elements of food in the best proportion. Fruits, grains, and milk constitute a perfect dietary, and one particularly suitable for young persons, and for students and other brain-workers.

Those parts of plants used as food, other than seeds or fruits, such as leaves, stems, roots, buds, and flowers, are called vegetables. The nutritive value of vegetables is much less than that of grains. The potato, one of the most valuable of all vegetables, is three-fourths water, and contains only about two per cent, of albuminous elements. The starch of vegetables is more difficult to digest than that of grains and fruits, and the large amount of woody matter contained in most vegetables adds to their indigestibility, so that they must be regarded, in general, as much inferior to fruits and grains as foods.

54. The Natural Diet of Man.—It is probable that the diet of the human family at first consisted almost wholly of fruits, grains, milk, and a few vegetables. History informs us that the dietary of the ancient Egyptians, Assyrians, and the early Greeks

and Romans was of this simple character, and the same primitive diet is still practically adhered to by fully two-thirds of the inhabitants of the globe. In densely populated countries, such as Japan and China, the dietary is necessarily almost exclusively vegetarian in character. The peasantry of France, Italy, and Spain, and other continental European countries, employ flesh so sparingly in their dietary that they may be said to use it as a luxury rather than as a food. Human life and health may be well maintained upon vegetable food.

55. Uses of the Several Food Elements.—The various food elements serve different purposes in the body. Sugar, starch, and fat form adipose tissue, and in the form of fat enter into the composition of nearly all the tissues of the body. They are of essential service to the body in the production of heat and force. The different forms of albumen nourish especially the brain, nerves, muscles, glands, and other highly active tissues of the body. The salts are largely used in nourishing the bones. They are also required by the brain and the nerves, as well as by other tissues. The indigestible elements give necessary bulk to the food.

Source: John Harvey Kellogg, *Second Book in Physiology and Hygiene* (New York: American Book Company, 1894), 23–31.

1894 • 92 • "The Steam Peanut and Pop Corn Industry"

> **Introduction:** *Peanuts and popcorn were America's first snack foods. Peanuts were sold on the streets by vendors in the late 18th century; popcorn followed by the mid-19th century. By the late 19th century, both peanuts and popcorn became big business. Companies began to manufacture mobile carts with a wide range of bells and whistles to attract customers. Here is a description from the* Scientific American *of one such machine.*

The Steam Peanut and Pop Corn Industry.

This machine, of which Charles Cretor, of Chicago, is inventor, was designed with the idea of moving it about to any location where the operator would be likely to do a good business. The apparatus, which is light and strong, and weighing but 400 or 500 pounds, can be drawn readily by a boy or by a small pony to any picnic ground, fair, political rally, etc., and to many other places where a good business could be done for a day or two. The wagon is about 5 feet in length and about 2 feet in width and made entirely of metal, with the exception of the popcorn case, which is made of hard wood and glass. The running gear is made light and strong. It has three springs on the rear end and a strong V spring in front. The hind and front wheels, which are made the same as bicycle wheels, with nickel plated spokes and rubber tires, are 30 and 20 inches in diameter. The peanut roaster and corn popper, which are attached to the ends of the wagon, are both run by steam power, the appliances for making the steam being all connected to the wagon bed. The water tank from which the boiler is supplied is made of sheet iron, about 2 feet square and about 5 inches in depth, and holds about four gallons. The water is drawn or forced into the boiler from the tank by means of a small steam pump connected to the machinery at the back of the wagon. The boiler is made of copper and is 2 feet in length and about 9 inches in diameter and holds about two gallons of water. The boiler is heated by gasoline which passes through a number of perforated pipes underneath, the pipes being supplied by means of a gasoline reservoir above, which also furnishes the gas for heating the peanut roaster and popcorn pan. This reservoir holds about one gallon and will burn about twelve hours. The peanut roaster is made of sheet iron and revolves inside of a stationary cylinder connected to the back end of the wagon. The roaster is about 2 feet in length and about 14 inches in diameter, and holds about fifteen pounds of peanuts. The popcorn pan is made of sheet iron, 12 inches in diameter and about inches in height. This pan rests on and over a conical shaped hollow piece of sheet iron containing a number of perforated pipes which connect with the gasoline reservoir. These perforated pipes heat the pan when in operation. Connected to the bottom of the pan are a number of flat movable iron rods, which connect to a circular shaft running down from the top of the popcorn case. This shaft is geared to another running horizontally across the top, connecting itself to the engine by means of a belt at the back of the wagon. The roaster shaft is also connected to the engine in the same manner. The engine, which is situated midway between the roaster and the corn popper, is about 22 inches in length and nickel plated, and runs with from ten to fifteen pounds of steam and makes a 4 inch stroke. The cylinder is about 4 inches in length and about 2 inches in diameter. The fly wheel is about 8 inches in diameter. Geared to this fly wheel is a horizontal shaft which passes out at the back of the wagon. Around the pulley at the end of the shaft the belts are placed, which, when the engine is in motion, causes the roaster and corn popper to revolve. The roaster revolves at a slow rate of speed, making about one revolution every twelve seconds. The peanuts, when roasted, which takes about from twenty to thirty minutes, are then tested by running along scoop-shaped instrument in a hole in the center of the roaster from the outside, the tester, when withdrawn, having a number of the roasted nuts in it. If the nuts are sufficiently roasted, a slide is removed from the cylinder and it is turned bottom up by the operator, and the nuts fall out and slide down into the 2 foot pan, which holds about fifty pounds, on the top of the water tank. This tank is heated by the waste steam which keeps the peanuts hot in the pan above. Two or three gallons of water will furnish enough steam to run the engine for one day. About one pint of rice corn is placed in the popper at a time. The shaft which connects with the flat rods in the bottom of the pan when in motion causes the rods to revolve, which stirs up and keeps the rice corn moving to prevent its burning. These rods revolve at the rate of about 250 revolutions per minute. The corn when popping is prevented from flying out of the pan by means of a circular piece of network about 2 inches in height resting over it, and of the same diameter as the pan. When the popping is completed, which takes about five minutes, the gas is turned off, the network raised up and the pan taken out and dumped and then replaced with another supply of corn, to go over the same operation. It takes about one half hour to get up steam to run the engine. The steam and gas pipes range in size from one half to one inch in diameter. Peanuts cost wholesale from 4½ to 6 cents per pound. A clean profit of 10 cents per pound can be made on roasted peanuts. Rice corn costs wholesale about 5 cents per pound, the corn after being popped bringing a profit of from 10 to 15 cents per pound. To sweeten pop corn about two and one half pounds of sugar dissolved into a sirup is rapidly stirred into about ten pounds of popped corn. The wagon costs $400[.]

Source: "The Steam Peanut and Pop Corn Industry," *Scientific American* 71 (December 29, 1894): 405.

1894 • 93 • Charles Ranhofer, *The Epicurean*

Introduction: *The Frenchman Charles Ranhofer (1836–1899) came to America in 1856, and six years later he was hired at Delmonico's, New York's haute cuisine restaurant. With the exception of three years, he remained at Delmonico's until he retired. Ranhofer produced his masterwork* The Epicurean *(1894), the most comprehensive French cookbook published in the United States up to that time. This imposing tome was extremely detailed and featured menus for every imaginable event and occasion. Leopold Rimmer, who was in charge of one of Delmonico's dining rooms, reported that there was "hardly one hotel in New-York to-day whose chef did not learn his cooking at Delmonico's, every one of them." When* The Epicurean *was published, Rimmer bitterly complained that Ranhofer had given "away all the secrets of the house." Rimmer believed that after the publication of* The Epicurean, *anyone could prepare French food. Below are some excerpts from* The Epicurean.

Table Service.

American, French, Russian—For Breakfast, Lunch, Dinner, Supper, Collation or Ambigu.

Dinner Service—American Style—And Bill of Fare (Dinner Service à l'Américaine et le Menu).

The success of a dinner depends upon good cooking, the manner in which it is served, and especially on entertaining congenial guests. The American service is copied more or less from the French and Russian, and remodeled to the tastes and customs of this country; as it varies somewhat from all others, a few instructions may be found useful to those desirous of learning the difference existing between them.

The Bill of Fare (Menu).

Menus are made for breakfasts, luncheons and suppers, but the most important one is for the dinner; these menus are generally composed a few days in advance to enable the necessary provisions to be purchased, so that on the day of the dinner, there has been ample time to prepare everything necessary, consequently much confusion is avoided and the work better done.

In carrying out the order the menu should be strictly followed, in fact, it must be an obligatory rule to do so.

Making out the bill of fare is the duty of the head cook, who composes and writes them according to the latitude he enjoys and the resources he has at hand.

Bills of Fare for Dinner.

Should the menu be intended for a dinner including ladies, it must be composed of light, fancy dishes with a pretty dessert; if, on the contrary, it is intended for gentlemen alone, then it must be shorter and more substantial. If the dinner be given in honor of any distinguished foreign guest, then a place must be allowed on the menu to include a dish or several dishes of his own nationality; avoid repeating the same names in the same menu. Let the gravies be of different colors, one following the other.

Also vary the color of the meats as far as possible, from one course to the other. Offer on the menus all foods in their respective seasons, and let the early products be of the finest quality (consult a general market list to find the seasonable produce), and only use preserved articles when no others can be obtained.

If the menus are hand written they must be very legible.

Menus are indispensable for service à l'Américaine; there should be one for each guest, for as no dish served from the kitchen appears on the table, every one must be informed beforehand of what the dinner is composed, and those dishes that are to follow each other.

Menus must be both simple and elegant, and of a size to allow them to be easily placed in the pocket without folding, as it is the general desire to keep the bill of fare of a dinner at which one has assisted.

A few important observations necessary to bills of fare and their classification are here given:

Oysters on the Half Shell.

Oysters appear on the menu the same as in the Russian service; on French bills of fare they do not mention them. Suppress oysters in every month not containing the letter R, such as: May, June, July and August, and serve Little Neck clams instead.

Soups.

Soups are served after the oysters. One clear and one thick soup should be selected but if only one is needed, give the preference to the clear soup.

Hors-d'œuvre, Side or Light Dishes.

Hot hors-d'œuvre are, generally, timbales, croustades, cromesquis, palmettes, mousselines, bouchées, cannelons, cassolettes, rissoles, etc. With the same course serve cold side dishes, such as olives, radishes, canapés, caviare, pickled tunny, anchovies, etc.

In the French service, the fish and the solid joints come under the head of relevés or removes. In the American and English service, first comes the fish, then the removes.

Fish.

If the fish be boiled or braized, add potatoes to the menu; if broiled or sautéd, some cucumber salad; and, if fried, serve plain or with a light sauce.

Removes or Relevés.

The relevés or solid joints are composed of saddles, either of veal, mutton, lamb, venison and antelope, or else beef tenderloins or middle short loins. Turkey, goose, capon, pullets, ducks, etc., may be served, accompanied by one or two vegetables.

Entrées.

Place on the bill of fare first the heaviest entrées, and conclude with the lightest; they must be previously cut up so as to avoid carving. No fish figures in the American service as an entrée, but terrapin or crabs may be allowed; also lobsters, shrimps, frogs, croquettes, etc.

Each entrée should be accompanied by a vegetable, served separately, except when it is one of those described above, such as terrapin, etc.

Punch or Sherbets.

A punch or sherbet is always served after the entrées and before the roast; do not make an extra heading on the menu for these, only placing them on a line by themselves, for instance: Roman punch or American sherbet.

Roasts.

Roasts are served after the sherbet; a game roast is usually preferred, but poultry, either truffled or not, may be substituted: such as turkey, capon, pullet, duck, guinea-fowl, squabs, etc.; also roasted butcher's meat; but game is usually considered to be more choice.

Cold Dishes.

Cold dishes come after the roast, and before the hot dessert; they are served with green salads; terrines of foies-gras and boned turkey are also served as a second roast. (In the French service these cold dishes are classified as the last entrée.)

Hot Sweet Dishes or Entremets.

These appear after the roast; they are composed of puddings, crusts, fried creams, fritters, pancakes, borders, omelets, and soufflées, and form a separate course by themselves.

Cold Sweet Dishes or Entremets.

The cold sweet entremets come after the hot and are composed of jellies, bavarois, creams, blanc-manges, macédoines, charlottes and large cakes, and form another course.

Dessert.

After the cold entremets come the dessert, composed of cheese, fresh fruits, preserved fruits, cakes, jams, dried fruits, candied fruits, bonbons, mottoes, papillotes, victorias, pyramids, frozen puddings, plombières, ices, ice cream and small fancy cakes, then the coffee and cordials.

Source: Charles Ranhofer, *The Epicurean* (New York: R. Ranhofer, 1894), 1–2.

1894 • 94 • Tamale de Carne

Introduction: *Tamales most often consist of beef, pork, or chicken encased in corn dough tied in corn husks and boiled or steamed. They were and still are a common food served in Mexico as well as in Texas, Arizona, New Mexico, and California. Harris Newmark, an early resident of southern California, claimed that tamales "took some time for the incoming epicure to appreciate all that was claimed for them and other* *masterpieces of Mexican cooking." Below is an early description of tamales that were sold on the streets of Los Angeles.*

Sixteen or seventeen years ago, when Los Angeles was still a dusty old adobe pueblo of 7000 or 8000 inhabitants, a good third of whom were paisanos, and the several saloons between Main street and Requena were all-night resorts with faro and stud-horse poker rooms attached, an old game-legged fellow did a great business in tamales, after the shades of evening had fallen and the sporty boys were out on their contract to drink up all the red liquor in town.

"Tamales calientes de gallina," was his rallying cry, and he always managed to unload his bucketful of red-hot peppery ware long before 2 in the morning. He had the monopoly of the business, too, and would have achieved a competency in the modest way of the paisano, had it not been that too much internal contact with chile colorado had produced in him a perpetual thirst of vast proportions, which nothing but the most potent alcoholic liquors could allay. This would lead him too often from the beaten path of commerce on Main street into smaller thoroughfares, where he had a better opportunity to imbibe forty-rod whiskey than to sell his husky fruit, and many a man who is now permanently settled in Evergreen Cemetery or in the now unused resting grounds on the hill, has heavily cussed old Don Pamfilo because he didn't show up late at night when his tired stomach craved some hot condiment to tone it up after too many glasses of Oh, be joyful!

Another reason why this tamalero failed to accumulate enough wealth to quit and take his otium cum dignitate et frijoles under his own fig tree was the persevering way in which the "cacos" or petty larceny thieves of several nationalities, who were fond of cheap tamales, pursued the old man when he was intoxicated beyond reason. Time and again was the poor devil inveigled into localities that were sparsely settled, and one did not have to go far for that, as Fourth street was then the ultima thule of the town, and, not content with adding insult to injury, the tamale guerrillas robbed him of his stock in trade, the money in his pocket and then stuck him, legs in the air, with his head in his own bucket and left him bewailing his unhappy lot in a smothered tone of voice.

Since those days the business of catering at night to the wants of belated or elated citizens has vastly increased, and the section of the city where itinerant merchants of spicy food can be found has greatly decreased. Against the old chap with the tamale bucket of a number of years ago who perambulated with a hop and a skip through Main street, there can now be found from the plaza up Main street as far as the Burbank, and from the corner of Temple and Spring streets away to Sixth, there can now be found scores of men with little wagons or portable stands who have a variety of edibles to offer for sale.

All of them make more or less of a good living, although their trade does not commence until after dark, and must of necessity soon cease after midnight because their customers are nearly always people who have patronized saloons too liberally, and those close punctually at midnight—at least "that's what the people say."

Down near the plaza, the "tamale de carne" still holds undisputed sway. The candy man and peanut vendor are visible for a couple of hours after supper, but their trade is dull. As one proceeds further toward the Temple Block, stands become more numerous and the bill of fare rises to ham-and-egg sandwiches, hamburger steak, pigs' feet, and a variety of comestibles, whose price never exceeds 10 cents and is often restricted to 5.

However, here tamales, both Texas and Spanish, trotters, ham, egg and hamburger steak sandwiches, and a bill of fare that includes a dozen different eatables, are offered for sale. An enterprising young man and the first to engage in the business, has specialty of oyster cocktails, and some evenings he does a land-office business. His cocktail as rather an artistic and inoffensive one, consisting of half a dozen California oysters, a liberal allowance of city water, a dash of pepper-sauce, another of tomato catsup, and a pinch of pepper and salt. But one can't be fastidious and exacting for the small sum of a dime.

The tamale men still form the majority of the fraternity of night purveyors, and from the appearance of things one would be inclined to believe that tamales are the exclusive regime upon which all night-hawks grow fat. But the tamale of today is a delusion and a snare. Some vendors have them better than others, but none are excellent, to paraphrase the expression of the Kentucky judge, who said that some whiskey was better than some other whiskey, but none was bad.

The tamale, as the Mexicans of the days of yore used to make it, was a thing fit for the gods, provided the gods had trained their inwards for the reception of chile colorado and chiltepines. Whether of beef meat or chicken, the further concomitants, olives, raisins and tortilla, were so nicely blended with it, and the whole wrapped up on "ojas de mais" in such a manner, as to make the picking of one a very pleasant job. But the tamale of today is too often a miserable parody of the Simon pure article. Whether made out of beef or chicken, or perchance the "perro vichi" or jackrabbit, it lacks the bouquet and the savor of the real thing. Too often the tortilla, which enwraps the meat is but a sloppy corn mush, too often are the olives absent, and too often, alas, is the meat so small in quantity that the buyer in despair feels like imitation the prodigal son in the parable and feeding on the husks which constitute the major part of his purchase. The cheapness of the various articles on the menu of these pushcart restaurants brings to them, apart from men whose stomach craves for something that will calm the fiery attacks made upon its coating by alcohol, the flotsam of the streets; men who, having but very little money, make shift with a few mouthfuls before seeking their hard couch. Some who have no money at all will, at times, order a tamale, sandwich or wiener wurst, and, having swallowed it, stand off the cook.

Indeed the open air restaurants and tamale men are but too often the prey of dead beats, who, not content at swindling them out of an 5-cent meal, insult them afterwards and run away. Not long ago a fellow of that kind, after getting his fill of tamales; refused to pay, and in the squabble over a settlement of the bill threw over the stand and ran away. The tamalero followed in hot pursuit and when he came back found his tamales in the gutter and his pushcart burned up by the benzoline of his open air lamp.

Source: "Tamales Calientes: Push-Cart Purveyors Who Flourish at Night," *Los Angeles Times,* September 23, 1894.

1895 • 95 • John G. Bourke, "The Folk-Foods of the Rio Grande Valley and Northern Mexico"

Introduction: *The United States acquired California and the American Southwest first by conquest and then by treaty with Mexico. Americans were unfamiliar with the people who lived in these areas and with the foods they ate. John G. Bourke (1843–1896) was a captain in the U.S. Army who was stationed along the border* *with Mexico. He collected a great deal of information about the people living in this area and recorded it in a diary. He used his diary to publish many articles, one of which was "The Folk-Foods of the Rio Grande Valley and Northern Mexico," published a year before his death. The article attempted to provide a comprehensive list of foods eaten by the Mexican population along the Rio Grande.*

In arranging a list of the aboriginal fruits and vegetables of Mexico and the Mexican portion of the United States, it seems to me to be proper to begin with those which have become cultivated, at least since the advent of the Castilian. Each of these will be described in its turn; and then the fruits which are still gathered in the wild state, and receive no attention from the hand of man, will be set down in as careful and complete a manner as I was able to obtain them.

The Piñon and Pecan, although indigenous to Mexico, may now be fairly classed among its cultivated foods. The pecan, which is said to be found in places from Wisconsin and Northern Virginia clear down to the Isthmus of Tehuantepec, is the best of all nuts, the almond not excepted. The Mexicans are very fond of a candy made from it with sugar caramel; this candy in appearance closely resembles our own ground-nut candy, which is also known to the Mexicans under the name of "Dulce de cacahuate." The Pecantree is one of the most beautiful of all that grow; it is tall, graceful, and umbrageous; some of the most graceful are to be seen in that part of San Antonio, Texas, called Maverick Park or Grove, in the lawns surrounding the residences of Hon. B. G. Duval and other prominent citizens. One of the most interesting, historically considered, is still in full vigor in the old city of Monclova, in the Mexican State of Coahuila; the people there call it "El arbol del Padre" (the Priest's or the Father's tree); because when the Spaniards had taken the patriot priest, Hidalgo, prisoner, and were carrying him off to Chihuahua to be executed, they passed through this old city with their prisoner, and remained here one day. Father Hidalgo wrapped himself in his cloak and went to sleep under the branches of the pecan which records this incident in its name.

Then come the Sapotes, Chirimoyas, Chilcoyotes, Guayavas, Tunas, or Cardones, the fruit of the Nopal, or Indian Fig Cactus, Bananas, Mangoes, Jicamas de agua, Chie, Chile, Chilchipin, Alicóchis, improperly called pitahaya, Coyotillo, Granjeno, Sunflowers, Squash, with its seeds, Watermelon, Chapote, Mame, Spanish Bayonet, Mango, Aguacates, Black Ebony beans, Acorns, Anacahuita nuts, Frijoles, another plant also called Frijol, Guadalupan, Mescal, Sotol, Tomato, Biznaga, Chicharrones, Mezquite, Guayacan, Lechuguilla, Amole, Onions, Sauco, Tejocote, Grapes, Socoyonostre, Pitahaya, Maguey, Corn, Strawberries, Mangostins, Ciruela, and also the true Plum (in certain districts), Cocoanuts (seen in Morelia only; all others were brought up from Tampico or Vera Cruz by rail, and need not be discussed).

There are several kinds of *Sapotes,* but they bear no resemblance to any northern fruits with which I am acquainted.

The *Chirimoya* is a large, dark green fruit, about as big as one of our Duchesse pears, and somewhat of the same shape, full of black seeds, with a pith the consistency of custard, which tastes like a mixture of pineapples, strawberries, and raspberries.

Chilcoyote looks much like the Chirimoya; if eaten by a person who is heated, will bring on chills and fever.

The *Guayava* or *Guava* is sufficiently well known to American readers through the palatable jelly made from it in Havana and imported into our country.

The *Tuna* or *Nopal* grows wild and is also cultivated; in the wild state it can be found, in an attenuated and shrivelled form, as far north almost as vegetation exists south of the Arctic Circle; in Mexico it seems to claim possession of the whole country, and is properly accepted as the principal figure of the present national coat-of-arms, as it was, we might say, in that of the Aztecs. It figures in the myths, traditions, and life of the country. The wild varieties bear fruit of different colors, generally red and purple and yellow. The cultivated variety bears a yellow fruit, very much larger and very much sweeter than the wild; it is piled up in the market-places and sold in quantities at all hours of the day and night. The Apaches say that the use of this fruit must be attended with some precautions, as it predisposes to fevers; their women collect it in great baskets carried on their backs, suspended from bands which pass around the forehead, and spread the split fruit out on rocks in the sun to dry. The outer skin being liberally supplied with acutely pointed thorns, the squaws have devised a brush of stiff hay, with which they knock off these spines before taking the fruit in the hand. Both wild and cultivated kinds are eaten raw, dried, baked, or boiled down into a stiff marmalade, which is sold in all the plazas under the name of "Queso de Tuna,"—Tuna Cheese. This is most agreeable to the taste, and might be mistaken by one ignorant of its true nature for a piece of preserved quince.

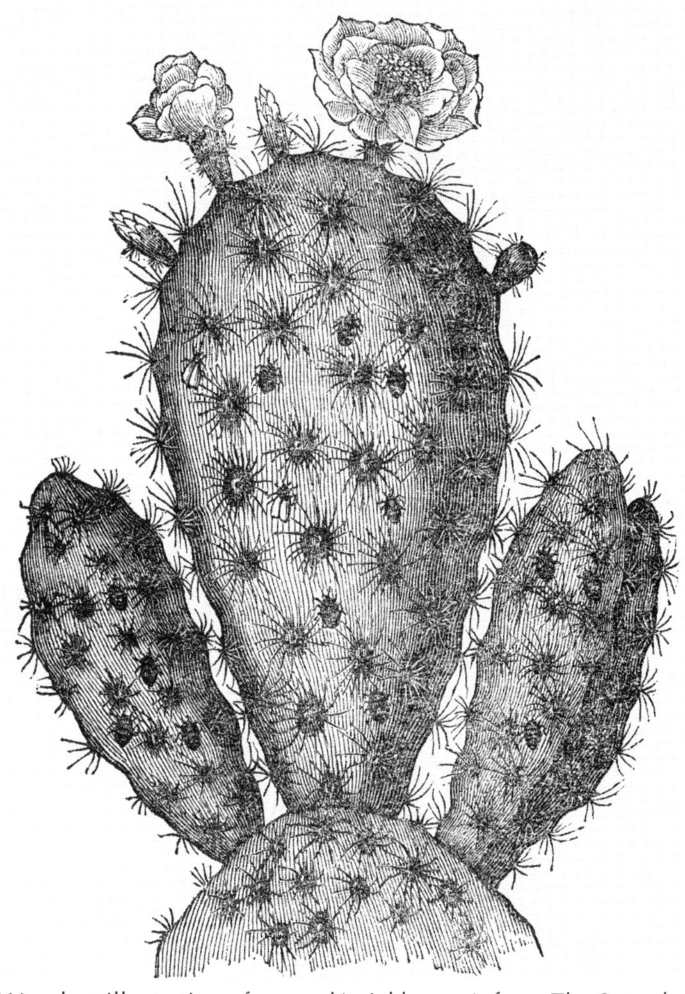

Woodcut illustration of a *nopal* (prickly pear), from *The Saturday Magazine,* 1833. (Linda Steward/iStockphoto.com)

Not only is the fruit eaten; the large plate-shaped leaf is brought into use for both man and beast. Grated down into a coarse powder, after having been skinned, the meat of this leaf is added to soups to give a mucilaginous thickening. Travellers through the southern portions of Texas, and almost all parts of Mexico, can see in the earliest hours of the morning fantastic figures dancing about in the smoke and flames of fires kindled for the sole purpose of burning off the spines of the nopal and letting draught oxen feed upon the leaves. Cattle, pigs, sheep, goats, and horses, running at large in the chaparral, do not wait for any such preparatory process, but take the plant as they find it. It is one of the sights of the Rio Grande to come suddenly upon a large, patriarchal, white goat with beard and breast dyed a blood red, from the juice of the tuna, and nostrils filled with the thorns of the fruit and leaf. Indeed, so well known is this peculiarity of all domestic animals in that region, especially during seasons of great drouth, that butchers will not accept orders to supply beef tongues, saying frankly that the meat is so full of ligneous fibre that it would be impossible to carve it upon the table.

Anti-scorbutic properties have been attributed to the nopal, and I have eaten the leaves fried, but am not able to express myself very warmly upon its merits, either as a medicine or an addition to the bill of fare.

Cut into strips, and thrown into a bucketful of turbid water, the nopal will cause the sedimentary matter in suspension to be precipitated to the bottom. This expedient was resorted to with success during our expedition to explore the Black Hills of Dakota in 1875. The juice of the nopal mixed with a small quantity of lime and a sufficiency of bullock's blood and river sand will form a cement finely adapted for flooring, as I have seen tried a number of times in Arizona and Texas.

Finally, the leaf, after being peeled of its thorny coat, is considered a valuable remedy as an embrocation in rheumatism, or as a plaster.

Whether or not bananas are indigenous to Mexico, I am unable to say, but I incline to the opinion that they were introduced by the Europeans; be that as it may, they grow wild in many parts, especially on the Rio Panuco, and do excellently in every place with a very slight amount of attention.

The same remarks apply to the sugar-cane; it becomes a reed, and one need not pay any attention to it; replanting is necessary only once in nine or ten years.

Mangoes might be mistaken for a small canteloupe; the fruit is rather insipid to my taste.

Chié is a peculiar seed, not unlike our linseed, but possessing properties worthy of commemoration. Several years since, I was paying a visit to the ruins of the grand old monastery of Atotonilco, and was received most cordially by the priest in charge, Padre Silva, who, seeing my heated and exhausted condition,—I had made a long ride over from San Miguel de Allende,—declined, to my great surprise, to let me have a drink of cool water from the "aljibe" (cistern).

"That is always the way with you Americanos," he said gently; "you come down here and rush all over the country in the hot sun and dust, and when you reach a house the first thing you do is to call for cold water, and drink a quantity of it; the stomach cannot stand such treatment and rebels against it, and the sick man blames our climate. Now let me show you how we Mexicans do; take it easy; take off your coat and collar and cool off, while I send Pepe here after some chi-é."

Pepe soon performed his errand, and brought back from one of the old Indian women a small package of the seeds, which the padre immersed in a cup filled with water; the seeds swelled up and the water became slightly mucilaginous.

"Now," said the padre, "you must not gulp down this mixture all at once; it would give you a chill if you did; take one third at this moment; another third in ten minutes, and the remainder in ten minutes more."

The results surprised me very much; not only were my feverish symptoms alleviated, but my voice became very clear and strong. What this chi-é was I never could ascertain. The Padre told me that the plant grew all over northern Mexico and, he thought, in southern Texas also, but I never had another opportunity to learn anything about it.

The Chiricahua Apaches, who have lived nearly always in Mexico, and pretty far down in the Sierra Madre, have a gens named the "Chi-é" a word which I never could get interpreted to my satisfaction; it has probably some connection with the plant which I am here attempting to describe.

Atotonilco is one of the out-of-the-way spots in America well worthy of a visit from the scholarly or the curious; it would be well to remember that one must go provided with food and blankets, as the padre may have other guests, and in that case a dependence upon the kind-hearted Indians of the adjacent village would be attended with most unsatisfactory consequences.

Chile, called "Aji" and "Quauhchilli" by the Aztecs, was the condiment used in all the feasts of the aborigines at the time of the landing of Cortez; there are several varieties,—the red, white, green, sweet, and bitter. No Mexican dish of meat or vegetables is deemed complete without it, and its supremacy as a table adjunct is conceded by both garlic and tomato, which also bob up serenely in nearly every effort of the culinary art.

The *Chilchipin* is the fiery berry forming the basis of Tabasco sauce; it can be found in a wild state just after you cross the Nueces, going south, and from that on no jungle is without it; the bush is of the same general size and shape as one of our rosebushes, with foliage light green in color. It is used both in the green and ripe, or red, state.

The *Alicóchis,* to which many people persist in giving the name of Pitahaya, is a cactus, resembling the Biznaga, or Turk's Head, but much smaller, and growing close to the ground; it yields, in the early days of summer, a fruit the size of a small plum, green in color, filled with fine black seeds; the skin is quite thin. This is generally regarded as the most delicious of all the wild fruits. It rivals the strawberry or the raspberry in delicacy of flavor and in the graciousness with which it submits to every mode of treatment. It seems to be equally good whether served raw, stewed, in pies and puddings, or in ice-cream; it makes an acceptable addition to juleps and lemonades.

The *Coyotillo* is a small bush, the sweet black berry of which is an agreeable food, but if the little seeds be swallowed, paralysis of the lower limbs results.

It is well known that the kernels of the delicious peach, plum, almond, and nectarine contain the deadly poison hydrocyanic acid, and something of the same nature may be the explanation of this peculiarity of the coyotillo. Mr. MacAllan, who was educated at Columbia College, New York, and at the University of Virginia, stated to me that he had made experiments at his father's ranch (Hidalgo County, on the Rio Grande, Texas), which proves the popular belief in regard to the Coyotillo, to be true; it paralyzed the hind extremities of goats, sheep, and pigs, upon which he experimented.

The *Coma* is a small, black, or deep blue berry, much like our own whortleberry, but dead sweet in taste; it grows on a stunted bush, and is ready for use from June to August.

The *Granjeno* is a parasitic bush, which entwines itself about a tree or larger bush, and grows, whenever possible, in the shape of a corkscrew; from the odd shapes often assumed under these conditions, it is a favorite wood for canes; the small, pinkish-red berries are not unpalatable, but the most that I feel at liberty to say in their favor is that they are not poisonous.

Sunflowers are not, to my knowledge, used as a food by any part of the Mexican population claiming an infiltration of Caucasian blood, but they are a favorite article of diet with many, if not all of the Indian tribes, in both Mexico and the United States. So much was this the case, that a quarter of a century ago, or less, the Moquis, Apaches, Navajoes, and Pueblos used to plant them; under cultivation, the seed-disk attained enormous dimensions; I have seen them in the fields of the Moquis and Ava-Supais at least a foot in diameter; the seeds, when mixed with corn and ground into a meal, make a cake which is believed to be highly nutritious.

Not only are squashes and watermelons eaten by the Mexicans, but the seeds also are utilized as a food in many districts, especially by the Indian element.

The *Chapote* is the Mexican persimmon; the tree is small, with a smooth, white bark; the fruit, dead sweet to the taste, the size of a cherry, black and pulpy.

Mami looks like a Nellis pear; has a smooth, russet skin, and an insipid pulp of firm, creamy, red matter, tasting much like a boiled sweet potato, and has a large black kernel.

The *Spanish Bayonet,* called *Datil,* or sometimes *Sotol.* The fruit, shaped like a banana, has a sweet, rather thick skin, and is filled with a mushy pulp, in which are imbedded a great number of black seeds, arranged symmetrically about the vertical axis. In Arizona, where it fills wide areas, it is much used by the Apaches, and the squaws dry it in the sun to keep for winter's use. It has a decidedly pleasant taste. The Rio Grande Mexicans do not make much use of the fruit, but take the young central shoot and bake it in live coals; it is not unlike a watery half-boiled sweet potato in flavor. From this same baked shoot they distil a variety of mescal, said by experts to be even more soul-destroying than the genuine.

Mango resembles a yellowish large cucumber.

Aguacate, or Alligator Pear. So much has been written about this that only a word seems to be necessary here. When the custard-like pulp is beaten up with egg, oil, vinegar, and spices, it makes a most delicious salad, and when sliced seems to be equally good. This fruit resembles a pear in shape; is purple in color; the pulp is sweetish and can be eaten raw.

The *Black Ebony* grows all over the country now under discussion; the beans, when in the milk, are highly considered as a vegetable when boiled with milk, pepper, and salt; after becoming hard and black a coffee is made of them, but I am in no humor to say much in its praise. It has a rather unpleasant, terebinthine[1] taste.

Acorns, which enter so largely into the dietary of the native tribes of the Pacific coast and the interior basin from Utah down to Texas, are used, to a slight extent, by the Mexicans of Caucasian derivation, and can occasionally be seen in the markets, but hardly in quantity sufficient to attract attention; allusion to them seems to be proper in an article of this kind.

The *Anacahuita,* a variety of the dogwood, bears a nut highly relished by pigs and goats, and used, to some extent, by the Mexicans; it is light-greenish in color, and grows in clusters.

The *Frijole,* or Mexican Bean, of both red and black varieties, is a plant indigenous to this continent, but all American readers are now so well acquainted with it, that reference only seems to be necessary; it is by far the most toothsome of all the pulse, and is cooked by the Mexicans in a half dozen different ways; stewed or boiled to a pulpy paste, it appears at almost every meal, and well deserves its title of "El plato nacional," the national dish.

There is another plant called "Frijol," which attains the dimensions of a tall bush; the long, thick pods are stewed in milk or water and eaten like the true bean. Some specimens which I sent to Professor Otis T. Mason, of the United States National Museum, Washington, D. C., were identified by Mr. George Vasey as the *Cahivalia obtusifolia.*

Guadalupan is a plant which I have never personally tried; I relate only what others have told me. In appearance, as I saw it first, growing at the Rancho "La Grulla," Starr County, Texas, in 1891, it is of the size of a rosebush, with a bright red, pulpy fruit.

Of the *Mescal,* I have written so much, at so many different times, that I may well be excused from adding another line upon the subject. Those who wish to learn more than is here related may consult the pages of the "Anthropologist" for the month of January, 1893, "On the Border with Crook," "An Apache Campaign," and other writings.

As a food, it has for centuries been in high repute among the nomadic tribes depreciating along the northern border of Mexico. Dr. Gustav Bruhl has identified the word "chichimec" as a compound of two words, meaning "mescal eaters," which would do something in the way of demonstrating that the wild tribes included under that designation, from whom the Aztecs, and after them the Spaniards, suffered so much, were of the same general type as our Apaches, Navajoes, and Comanches.

The Apaches used to make regular pits or ovens of heated stones, covered with earth, in which the stalk and leaves of the mescal were buried for three days, and when then taken out yielded a sweet, palatable, and nourishing but slightly laxative food. The laxative quality is accounted for readily, the Mescal, like its big brother, the Maguey, being a member of the Aloe family.

When these cooked leaves are bruised and allowed to ferment, a fiery liquor can be distilled from the mass, although the same result is obtained in another way by collecting the juice from the pit left after extracting the central shoot, allowing that "miel" or juice to ferment, and then distilling.

The whole process, as described by me among the Tarascoes of southwestern Mexico, was so crude that it opened my mind to the suggestion that distillation was a primitive art, and must have been known to the aborigines of Mexico prior to the coming of the Europeans. The grated root of this plant is also used as food.

A North American who has never traversed the vast areas covered by the Mescal and the Maguey in the wild state, cannot comprehend how valuable they were, and are, to the people as a source of food supply. Besides this, the central shoot was utilized as a lance-shaft, or was used to form the side walls of huts, while the leaves made a fair to middling good thatch, and the strong thorn at the end of a leaf, with the attached filament, served the Apache squaw, or warrior on the trail, with a substitute for needle and thread. Of the central shoot of the Mescal the Apaches made their fiddles.

The *Tomato,* in the wild state, is not very much bigger than a cherry, but in both green and red state is made to enter into salads and sauces of all kinds. It is also dried in the sun.

The *Biznaga,* or Turk's Head Cactus, cut in small, slender strips, and boiled for several hours in syrup, makes a candy of which the people are very fond and which is on sale at every street corner, in almost every town.

Chicharrones are a variety of peas, and need no description.

The *Mezquite* has been recognized as a food of the American aborigines ever since the Spaniard Alarcon ascended the Rio Colorado, in 1541; the form of the loaf of bread made from its meal remains the same among the Apaches to-day as it was when he wrote his notes. Some of the tribes, the Pimas, Opatas, Papagoes, and others, used to make a kind of effervescent beer from the beans, but this does not seem to be much in demand of late years.

There are two varieties of the Mezquite; that with the screw pod, which grows only in the valley of the Colorado, and that with the flat pod, of more extended distribution. Both are palatable, and are very fattening to horses and other live stock.

These are the American representatives of the Acacia family, and the gum exuded from the trunk equals the best gum arabic.

Guayacan (lignum vitae), lechuguilla, and amole are spoken of here, not as foods, but as important aids in the Mexican household economy; their powdered roots are detersive, and supply the place of soap, and possess the valuable peculiarity of not shrinking flannel; they make a good dentifrice and a fine hair wash. The use of the Guayacan root is avoided, when possible, because it burns the hands.

Onions grow wild in parts of Mexico, as they do everywhere in the great West of our country; they are, however, so far as my experience goes, much more plentiful in the extended plains near the Yellowstone than they are in the regions farther to the south. In size they are very diminutive, not much bigger than a cherry, and very pungent. When General George Crook made his celebrated "Starvation March" down from the Yellowstone to the Niobrara, in 1876, his officers and men were glad to discover patches of these onions, which furnished a most agreeable addition to the stews made of the horse meat captured from the hostile savages.

Of the *Sauco,* or elderberry, I have not much to say beyond the fact that it is edible.

The *Tejocote,* or bud of the wild rose, is eaten by Indians and Mexicans, and is on sale in the markets.

The *Grape* may be regarded either as a wild fruit or as one of the cultivated sort; when Spanish missionaries and explorers first penetrated into Northern Coahuila and Chihuahua, they were surprised by the luxuriant growth and fine flavor of the wild grape, and one locality, Parras, in Coahuila, derives its name from this fact. Here for more than two hundred years has been made a wine which is highly considered by the Mexicans, and has a taste intermediate between that of port and sherry, with a decided body.

This district, as well as its close neighbor, El Paso, or, as it is now styled, Ciudad Juarez, in Chihuahua, is noted for its crop of fruits of all kinds; the El Paso grapes and onions have no superior anywhere in the world, but of course I do not wish to be understood as saying that these are the wild varieties. In all likelihood, after it was learned that these two localities, Parras and El Paso, were naturally well adapted for viticulture, the Spaniards brought over cuttings from Xeres and the Madeira and Canary Islands.

The *Socoyonostre* is a variety of cactus much appreciated for its juice, which makes an especially good candy; the Mexicans, particularly those living well towards the centre of the republic, say that this is the best kind of cactus candy, but, so far as I could determine from the taste, it is no better than the biznaga, perhaps not quite so good.

In the beginning of this article, it was shown that the Mexicans of the Rio Grande Valley improperly applied the name Pitahaya to the cactus, which should be known as the Alicóchis, and which yields a fruit of surpassing sweetness and delicacy. The true Pitahaya is the Candelabrum, the Organ, the Giant, or the Saguara cactus of various writers; it has sometimes been called the umbrella cactus. There are two varieties: that growing in Arizona attains a height of from twenty-five to thirty-five feet, although, in extreme cases, the height has been put at as much as fifty-five feet, as determined by myself and other officers who measured one by its shadow near old Camp McDowell, Arizona, in 1870.

The difference between the two varieties is very slight; each shows in cross-section a number of ribs arranged at equal distances around the vertical axis of the stems or arms, the intermediate spaces being filled with a watery, stringy pith, the whole encased in a thick green skin, bristling with curvated spines.

From rib to rib, in the Arizona variety, the skin bulges outward, or assumes a convex surface, but in the variety found more to the south, in the Mexican States of Michoacan and Guadalajara, this same surface is concave.

The fruit, which grows at the very top of the high branches, is a big pear-shaped greenish pod, which, opening at the time of ripeness, discloses an interior filled with a ruby red pulp, in which are many tiny black seeds. The ripening of the pitahaya in Arizona used to be the signal for the arrival of great flocks of chattering birds, which fought for the rich spoil of the fruit, and of the downcoming from the mountains of bands of Apache Indians, who gathered the dainty feast and at the same time made war upon their hereditary enemies, the Pimas and Papagoes.

My first trip with Apache Indians was to assist them in a hunt for several jars of the preserve which their squaws knew how to make by boiling down this pulp of the pitahaya; in the present instance it had been necessary to hurry up matters and bury the jars containing the preserve, as a large war-party of Pimas had discovered the presence of the Apaches in the Pima country, and compelled them to take flight.

Maguey. All that has been said of mescal applies to its relative the maguey, excepting that when the central stock or shoot of the latter is cut out, the cavity made rapidly fills with a very sweet juice, which, under the name of "miel" (honey), is sold in all the market-places of Mexico.

Corn should be discussed under the title of cooked foods; the shucks carefully dried and rubbed smooth make the favorite wrapping for the Mexican cigarrittos. Corn-meal parched with a trifle of "pelonce," or coarse brown sugar, is one of the staple Mexican foods. Without the sugar, it was in use among the Aztecs. A similar preparation of parched wheat is called "atole." The nourishing properties of both these have been highly praised by writers who knew little about them. I had once to live on pinole for three days, and have never been able to arouse myself to enthusiasm over it.

Strawberries grow wild in the mountains, and are also carefully cultivated; in the neighborhood of Celaya and Queretaro they yield all the year round, or almost all the year, and a trade of some importance is springing up with the American cities to the north. The Mexican strawberry, as a rule, is of extremely delicious flavor, and growers have not fallen into our error of sacrificing taste and aroma to size and color.

Mangostins seem to be a variety of the mangoes.

Ciruela. Under the name of plum, one finds in the neighborhood of Toluca, Mexico, and in other places, a fruit which possesses very little merit, although not bad to the taste. It is yellow in color, of size of an egg, with a large stone inside.

Plums. The true plum, the same as that with which we are familiar in the United States, can be found in the vicinity of Linares and other small cities along "the Tampico Route," in Morelia and other places. The climate and soil of Mexico and Texas would seem to be very well adapted to the cultivation of the prune and the green gage, but no great amount of attention has thus far been paid to them.

Cocoanuts. Very few of these grow in the region which I am describing in this article; they do grow in Morelia, and in the country not far from Tampico, from which places they find their way on railroad trains and by wagon transportation to points farther inland and farther to the north, but without offering any peculiarities worth mentioning.

Sicamas. These are also called Xicamas de Agua; they look like a ruta baga; after being skinned they can be eaten raw, but should be followed by a drink of mescal to ward off chills and fever.

Having attempted to lay before my readers a list of the more prominent articles of food which attracted my attention while serving in this southern border country, it may not be amiss to venture upon a few references to the modes of preparing them which are peculiar to the people, beginning with those presented for sale at every street corner, and advancing from those to the supposedly more elaborate collations of the various "fondas," and the confessedly more cleanly and tempting refreshments offered in the hospitality of private houses.

The abominations of Mexican cookery have been for years a favorite theme with travelers rushing hastily through the republic, and pages have been filled with growls at the wretchedness and inadequacy of the accommodations offered in the hotels and restaurants,

I certainly have no desire to appear as the champion of the Mexican hotel, be its guise or its title what it may; not even when, as was the case with a small affair at which I was obliged to put up near Queretaro, it may be under the patronage of Our Lady of Guadaloupe, whose picture hung in the "zaguan" or main hall.

Neither shall I rush impetuously to the defence of Mexican cookery in the abstract, or in its entirety; as a general rule, there is an appalling liberality in the matter of garlic, a recklessness in the use of the chile colorado or chile verde, and an indifference to the existence of dirt and grease, which will find no apology in these pages.

These drawbacks are attributable directly to the illiteracy of the poorer classes, from which the cooks are drawn, and to some extent to depravity of taste due to long usage.

Once, when I had strongly urged upon a landlady in Camargo that the presence of garlic was inexpressibly repugnant to me at all times, she promised implicit obedience in the preparation of the dinner ordered for myself and friends, but when it appeared upon the table, "ajo" seemed to be the main feature of every dish.

Perhaps my temper got the better of my judgment, and led me to hasty expressions, which I would now gladly recall; but Señora Ornelas remained imperturbable. "Caramba!" she exclaimed, "one must have *some* garlic!"

But after all these disagreeable features have been conceded, there remain not a few excellences in Mexican cookery which occupy pleasant niches in the memory, and are deserving of preservation and imitation.

I will go farther than this, and say that the natural aptitude of the Mexicans in the culinary art is so pronounced, that I think it would be a wise policy for the general or state governments of that country to institute cooking-schools, and instruct classes in the chemistry and preservation of foods, with a view to aiding in the future establishment of factories for the canning of fruits, meats, and vegetables, or the making of the delicious "cajetes," "almibares," and "jaleatines," which will be referred to in other pages of this paper.

In justice to the cooks of Mexico, we should also remember that they are hampered by lack of proper utensils; as a general thing, food is prepared with a minimum of appliances, and the modest array of pots, pans, and kettles to be seen even in very well to do "fondas" and private houses throughout the republic would empty half the establishments of New York of their servants without a moment's warning.

A *caznela* (stew-pan) or two, an *asador* (spit), a *cucharron,* or ladle, a *tencdor,* or big fork, a bundle of twigs for stirring atole, one or two bricks upon which to support a pan, and perhaps, but only in the case of families of some social pretensions, a *hornito* or

Dutch oven, and you have the sum and substance of the paraphernalia of the Mexican kitchen.

Even in the most opulent houses in the City of Mexico itself, stoves and ranges are unheard of, their place being supplied by anarchitectural contrivance of brick, arranged for burning charcoal, the draught being regulated by an energetic use of a fan of feathers in the hands of a sweltering cook.

This was the cooking-stove of the Romans, although sheet iron boxes exhumed from Herculaneum and Pompeii are to be seen in the Museum of Naples.

The Mexican is tenacious of old usages; this because he is the descendant of five different races, each in its way conservative of all that had been handed down from its ancestors; these races, it needs no words to show, were the Roman, the Teuton, the Arab, the Celt, and the Aztec.

From no source did I receive greater help or encouragement in the preparation of this article than from the ladies of Mexico and southern Texas whom it was my great good fortune to meet; I found them eager to impart information, ready to concede deficiencies, anxious for the introduction of accessories of which they have heard more than most Americans would imagine, and possessed in an eminent degree of that true home spirit which impels every lady to the desire of becoming a "laf-dig," lady, or loaf-divider.

He who has "nosed around" Mexican towns, as I have, without guide-book, and generally without a companion, is sure to yield to the temptation of Indulging in historical retrospection and conjuring up in memory those centuries when the Spaniard was essentially the Roman, and the Roman had degenerated into a creature of "panem et circenses."

Bread and circuses are the mainstays of the Mexican population to-day, and no municipality is so poor that it does not attempt to provide open air concerts of some kind twice or thrice a week for all of its citizens.

The music is never really bad, and very frequently is as good as can be found anywhere, and no words of praise seem to me to be excessive for a policy which affords to the poor as well as the rich the most refining of all enjoyments, as well as an opportunity of coming in contact with one's neighbors. But to this policy we cannot give more than brief reference, and must pass on to describe the venders of street foods, who on such occasion throng the streets, and afford the traveler, the anthropologist, and the folklorist a never-ending source of interest and reflection in their wares, their usages, and their cries.

While there were many exceptions to the rule, yet the rule seemed to me to be that each street vender confined himself to some particular line of goods; there were those who dealt in candies only, while their neighbors hawked cakes of many kinds; some dispensed liquid hospitality, and others again had little portable ovens near their tables, and kept in readiness all sorts of savory compounds of meat, eggs, coffee, pastry, and vegetables.

It will be convenient for our purposes to consider this rule as absolute, and describe each in its turn.

Morelia may be selected as the typical Mexican town in this connection, but all such selections are matters of taste, and I should have no cause of complaint or dissent were some reader of these pages, experienced in Mexican matters, to take issue with me and defend the superior claims of Toluca, Patzcuaro, Chihuahua, Hermosillo, Queretaro, San Miguel de Allendo, Celaya, or San Luis Potosi.

In the streets of Morelia one finds no less than thirty kinds of candy carried about by the "dulceros"; this list includes all those to be seen in the cities farther to the north, such as San Antonio de Bexar in Texas, Laredo in the same state, Matamoros in Tamaulipas, Monterey, Monclova, and Chihuahua.

The number of cakes seems to go on *pari passu* with that of the candies. The reason for this preeminence in the matter of toothsome confections, as given to me by an intelligent Mexican gentleman whom I met, is that in Morelia and some other cities there were in olden days convents of Carmelite nuns, who devoted much attention to the making of cakes and candies, and instructed many of the young native women in the same art; the same rule would apply to the beautiful "drawn work," or "perfilada," for which many of these towns are famous; but in each case there is good reason for supposing that there was a substratum of native knowledge and aptitude upon which to build.

Included in the list of candies, we can fairly place candied fruits, and of these Morelia has to sell delicious candied bananas, apricots, figs, oranges, lemons, limes, pineapples, pears, apples, and almonds.

There are also candied slices of *Camotes* (sweet potatoes) and *Calabazas,* or pumpkins; and the favorite *biznaga* and *socoyonostre* candies are really nothing more or less than candied cactus.

Then come the candies of the pecan, *piñon,* and ground-nut, *cacahuate,* of which mention has already been made.

In the line of dried fruits sold by these peddlers of small wares, we find *tortas de higo,* a sort of fig paste, not at all bad, the *queso de tuna,* already fully described, *platanos pasados,* or dried bananas, but none of the dried Spanish bayonet fruit, so often seen among the Apaches, and none of the dried tuna itself; dried peaches, apples, and quinces are frequent, but rather among the street venders of groceries and the small *tendajones* than among the "dulceros" proper. The name *orejenes* (big ears) is commonly bestowed upon dried fruit of all kinds, from a supposed resemblance to the human ear.

Whether it be considered as a candied fruit or a cake by itself, I think I should here introduce the name of the *chaloupa* (sloop) or sweet potato hollowed out in shape of a small boat, fried in syrup and filled with a cargo of slices of the same material. It is very palatable and much relished by the Mexican *muchacho,* into whose good graces I have on several occasions forced my way by a diplomatic presentation of a mouthful.

With such an infinitude of material, I may be pardoned for selecting only those things which appear to me to be the most important. These are the *Carmancilla de leche,* a striated cream candy which will hold its own with any that can be found farther north. Next comes *Torreon de almendra,* a nougat of almond, and the *Charamusca,* a kind of sugar taffy, of all three of which, as of the pecan candy, my children sent me enthusiastic and appreciative praise from Omaha.

Charamusca is also applied to a cake much resembling our old fashioned horse-cakes or gingerbread.

Marcasotas are a variety of tea buns, quite good in their way. The anise-seeded little cakes of our own tables are known to the Mexicans.

Puches are identical with our doughnuts, and *marramos* and *ojarrosca* in general resemble our cakes, but I cannot recall exactly which ones.

In the larger cities and towns there are pretentious *dulcerias* and *neverias* for the sale of sweetmeats of all kinds and of ice-creams. In these can be found about the same class of goods to be seen in New York, Washington, Philadelphia, Chicago, or St. Louis. The prices are reasonable, and every attention is given to patrons; but for me these places possessed only slight attraction, as my desire was to watch the doings of the half-clad candy men of the street corners; so beyond acknowledging gratefully that the cream puffs which I found in Monterey, the City of Mexico, and other cities, were equal to the best anywhere, I will escort my reader back to the company of our friend, Don Procopio Ramirez, whom I should say we left dozing at the corner of the plaza soothed into a half slumber by the strains of the military band, which was rendering "En Suefio seductor" while the somnolent Procopio was trying to drive away the buzzing flies with a fly-flapper of paper.

Boys are boys the world over; those of Mexico are as mischievous as any, and a band of them, promenading restlessly around the plaza, listening to the music, soon espies the unfortunate Procopio, and is on him in a minute, flinging the greasy caps of unwary comrades in his face, and yelling in his ears the soul-disturbing epithet of *Cucaruchero!* or cockroach breeder, in allusion to the superstition prevalent among the boys of Mexico that all these street candies are made for the purpose of raising that domestic insect.

Don Procopio takes after them with an energy which does him great credit, but it is written in the annals of fate that rheumatic legs never shall catch the bad boy, and so poor old Procopio soon is back at his little table, under the flickering oil lamp, mechanically waving his "*flapper*" and droning out his monotonous song:—

"Charamusca! Charamusca! Carmencillo de leche! de leche!
Torreon de almendra! Almendra! Algo de Fruta! Algo de duke!"

When the sun is in the dog-star, when the days seem to be at their hottest, little tables are erected everywhere, and old men and women, and sometimes young ones too, engage in a lively trade in selling every conceivable kind of liquid refreshment. There is the inevitable *pulque,* smelling much like half-turned buttermilk, but cooling, palatable, refreshing, and nutritious. One penny will buy a big glassful. Alongside of it comes the pink *colonche* or cider of the tuna; this is an exceptionally good drink. Then you can buy lemonades, limeades, orangeades, pineappleades, and sometimes a pomegranateade, but all made with brown sugar or pelonce, white sugar not being any too plentiful in Mexico. The lemonade may be colored with rose, and is then called "limonada rosa," or it may, perchance, have a strawberry or two thrown in just for luck. More rarely, you may find fresh milk, of which I saw great quantities going by train from Lerma to the markets of the City of Mexico, or the acidulous *leche de mantequilla,* called *jocome* in the State of Michoacan, and known to us as buttermilk.

A fair to middling good ginger ale is made in Monterey, but it strikes upon the American palate with a peculiar taste, because it is nearly all flavored with rose or strawberry.

In the same city, and in Toluca and Patzcuaro, beer is made which as yet is only mediocre in quality; time will certainly improve it, and a great trade be developed, because the Mexicans are very fond of beer, and import quantities of it from Germany and Scandinavia; of late years, the American breweries of St. Louis and Milwaukee have had things all their own way, and send down train loads of their bottled product which commands a ready sale, despite the duty. Indeed, in the States of Sonora and Nuevo Leon I have seen Mexicans drinking beer for breakfast; but it is well to remember that the Mexican custom is much like that of the French in the matter of breakfast, and these people were travelling.

In the extravagant use of all these lemonade and other "ades," the Mexicans reveal the Moorish strain in their blood, and this is still further shown by the variety of *orclialas* (orgeats), which, of course, are not of American origin. Orchatas are made of the seeds of the melon, when those of the almond are not obtainable, and flavored with anything that suits the taste; they are pleasant and cooling and sold in great quantities, especially on such occasions as "La noche del Grito" (15th–16th of September), in the City of Mexico.

If one be not satisfied with these mild beverages, or with the honey water of the maguey, (*agna de miel*), he can enter the nearest *pulqueria* or *cantina,* and drink to his heart's content of pulque itself, or the more alcoholic mescal, of the brands "Legitimo Bacanora," "Legitimo San Carlos," "Legitimo Apam," all the while gazing upon the walls covered with highly colored representations of the Sacred Heart, the Good Shepherd, and other holy subjects, this being a perpetuation of the custom introduced by pious friars in the early days immediately succeeding the Conquest, the idea being that the sight of these sacred themes would distract the liquor-inflamed mind from thoughts of strife and blood.

Pulque and mescal are often "curado" or flavored with juice of the strawberry, pineapple, or orange, and with the peel of the last and of lemon; sometimes with the juice of pomegranate.

As I have shown in a paper on the Rio Grande, published in the "Anthropologist" of Washington, the mescal is adulterated with lime-water, a practice which was sternly prohibited by the Emperor Charles V. as far back as 1528.

The mescal "curado" with the orange peel and lemon is very palatable, and loses much of its fiery taste, which is also diminished by the curious Mexican custom of placing a pinch of salt upon the tongue before swallowing the draught of liquor. In all the *cantinas* in Sonora, Guadalajara, and Michoacan the proprietor of the *cantina* offers to each patron a scoopful of salt to use with his drink.

On the streets in the towns one can see conveyances passing from point to point loaded with pigskins filled with pulque or mescal; at times, bladders are used for the same purpose. A good-sized pigskin will hold from twenty-five to thirty gallons.

Very little American whiskey is to be found, and that nearly always of the poorest quality and heavily adulterated; but there are the heavy native wine of Parras, already mentioned, the "aguardiente de cafia," or sugar rum, and the "aguardiente de uva," or colorless grape brandy, also of Parras, and the fearful, fiery Catalan. The last had better be avoided.

French brandy, none too good, is on sale in many places, but it is not deserving of much attention, excepting in Matamoros, where it can always be found of excellent quality.

Mexicans of wealth are extremely fond of liqueurs, and many are in use among them which are unknown to Americans; among them may be mentioned "Crême de Rose," "Dessertine," "Crême de Menthe," "Crême de Nougat," and the Arabian liqueur prepared from wormwood, called "Byrrh."

In the centre of the plaza—that is to say of the principal plaza, if there be more than one, in a Mexican town—can always be seen rows of tables set out with some care, lighted with rather dingy oil lamps, and provided with hot coffee, hot chocolate, excellent bread, and many dishes, hot or cold, which are retailed in liberal portions at a moderate price; so moderate, indeed, that during the hotter months these tables serve all the purposes of the "trattoria" of Venice, and supply to families excellent food, already cooked, at prices which make it cheaper to patronize them than to depend upon servants.

Few tourists can have forgotten the "chile stands" of San Antonio, Texas, once a most interesting feature of the life of that charming city, but abolished within the past two or three years in deference to the "progressive" spirit of certain councilmen.

At these one was always tolerably sure of getting a cup of excellent hot coffee, or one of equally good chocolate, for the making of which the Mexicans are deservedly famous; tea, strange to relate, was never to be had, and milk only infrequently.

But "chile con carne," "tamales," "tortillas," "chile rellenos," "huevos revultos," "lengua lampreada," many other kinds of "pucheros" and "ollas," with leathery cheese, burning peppers, stewed tomatoes, and many other items too numerous to mention at this time, were always on sale.

The farther to the south one went, the more elaborate was the spread to be noted on these street tables, until at or near San Luis Potosi it might be called a banquet for the poor.

I may save time and space by condensing my remarks and referring to what my notebooks relate of the display upon the Grand Plaza of the City of Mexico, during the great national *fiesta* of September 15th and 16th, 1891.

It may be well to say that on this particular night of the year the fullest liberty is given to the boys and young men to make all the noise they wish, and a more conscientious discharge of a semi-constitutional privilege it has never been my fortune to witness. The walls of the public buildings seemed about to crack with the din of horns, the shrieks of *muchachos,* the howls of sandal-shod Indians saturated with pulque, and the cries of the men and women at the stands, imploring passers-by—I should not say passers-by, because no one could pass by, the jam being so fearful, but let us say standers-by—to walk right up and buy their wares.

"Do you not hear me? I am selling the best pulque in the republic of Mexico, and it is only a centavo a glass; come right up and taste it."

"This mescal comes from Apam; you 'll never drink any other if you once try this."

"Arroz con leche! Arroz con leche!"

"Nieve! Nieve! para regalarse!"

"Algo de Dulce! Algo de Fruta!"

"Charamusca! Charamusca! Carmencillo de leche!
Torreon de almendra!"

"Agua fresca!"

"Limonada rosa!"

And a thousand other yells, cat-calls, shrieks, whistles, snorts, blowing on horns, ringing of bells, and other diabolical noises which the small boy the world over can be relied upon to furnish if he be given half a chance.

To come to the tables or stands: they were loaded with chocolate, coffee, agua de miel, pulque, mescal, orchatas of several kinds, all the lemon and other "ades" already described, as well as all the cakes and candies, chile con carne, tamales, tortillas, fresh bread, rolls, cheese, fruits, sandwiches of all kinds, spare-ribs, stewed kidneys, stewed heart, fried liver, pork chops, hogs' head cheese, salad of the aguacate, and another salad made of boiled potatoes, sliced, with shredded ham, lettuce, beets, and sardines. There were enchiladas, chaloupas, fried chicken, cold turkey, and I dare not say what else; there were so many things on exhibition, the sight became bewildered.

Mexican women making tortillas, New Mexico, 1800s. (North Wind Picture Archive)

There was *arroz con leche,* or rice stewed to a pulp in rich milk, of which the Mexicans never seem to become tired; it is sold in little cups as custard, made into pies and cakes, and also without any addition at all; I found it very agreeable in all its forms, and I believe it to be a most nourishing food.

Sausages are very much in favor in Mexico; they are possibly the only "survival" now discernible of the Teutonic part of the lineage of the Mexican people. They bear names differing according to some peculiarity of shape or composition; the "longaniza" is the long thin variety most resembling our own "link" sausage; the "chorrizo" sells in largest quantity; it is made by boiling pork in strong vinegar, and then chopping it up with chile colorado and onions.

Chile con carne is meat prepared in a savory stew with chile colorado, tomato, grease, and generally, although not always, with garlic. Chile sauce is a sauce made of chile colorado, tomato, and lard. Chilchipin sauce is made on the same general principle.

Enchiladas are practically corn fritters allowed to simmer for a moment in chile sauce, and then served hot with a sprinkling of grated cheese and onion.

Tamales, a dish derived from the Aztecs, are croquettes of beef or chicken boiled in corn-husks.

Tortillas, as is well known, are corn cakes prepared by soaking maize in lime-water until the outer skin comes off, and then rubbing the softened kernels to a paste on a "metate" or stone mill.

Puchero is a stew of any kind; it resembles an "olla;" when made of tripe, it is called by the name "menudo."

Boiled squash is sold and eaten seeds and all, just as is the case among the Yumas and Cocopahs of Lower California.

Huevos revueltos are eggs fried on both sides, and served with chile sauce.

Cabra lamprcada and "lengua lampreada" are goat meat or tongue fried in egg.

Frijoles, it goes without saying, appear on every one of these tables.

The Mexicans have very excellent taste in the matter of preserves; several cities, notably Celaya and Morelia, make great quantities of the "cajetes," or wooden boxes of conserves of guavas, quinces, "leche quemado," and others which, in my opinion, will command a good market among the Americans as soon as they become acquainted with them.

In Monterey there are made three or four kinds of preserves such as were in vogue in the United States in our grandmothers' days: peaches, quinces, and pears, in glass jars; they are exceedingly good. The bread of Mexico is equal to any in the world; the "panaderias," or bakeries, are well patronized, very few families in the towns baking their own supply.

Coffee, in many sections, is made in the original Moorish or Arabic manner, as an "extracto," and in Michoacan, in the coffee districts, the servants do not ask you to take coffee, but to take "extracto." This "extracto" is kept in glass bottles, and a teaspoonful is enough, when mixed with hot milk, to make a cup of palatable coffee. The coffee of Mexico possesses both strength and fine flavor.

Chocolate is usually served with an egg foam on the top of the vessel; this is produced by rapidly revolving between the hands an instrument of wood made for that special purpose, and kept on sale in the market-places.

At Celaya and Morelia can be found a peculiar dish called *jaleatin,* or jelly, made by stewing pigs' feet in red wine; it is like our calves'-foot jelly, and is both cooling and refreshing.

In the early hours of morning, and especially of Sunday morning, a run through the markets of a Mexican town will always be found replete with interest and information.

The more prosperous tradesmen occupy large stalls or booths, but the poorer brethren are content with a mat or two upon which to spread piles of grapes, oranges, "cardones," "aguacates," "queso de tuna," and other fruits, vegetables, and table necessaries.

Each tries to drown the voice of his neighbor; but the Mexican men and women coming out to make purchases pass through the din apparently unmindful of the bawling of the vociferous costermongers who surround them on every side, or line the streets along which they are to pass.

"Will you look at me? Here I am throwing away the finest cardones in San Luis; six for five cents!"

"Perrones! Perrones! [big pears] here, only a medio for six; come up and carry them away!"

"Don't keep me here all day: I want to go home; I am throwing onions, fine, fine onions in the street; I am not selling them; I am giving them away!" and much more of like import.

But suddenly all this tumult was hushed, not a voice was raised, and every shouting street vender was kneeling on the stones of the street, and most of them with bent heads, devoutly crossing themselves.

"What is the matter?" I asked of the man nearest me.

"Señor, do you not see that carriage coming down the street; it contains a padre, who is bearing the last sacrament to a dying man."

"Is he a friend of yours?"

"Ah, no, señor, I don't even know where he lives; but it is some pobrecito[2] who is about to die."

I confess to having been deeply touched by this proof of the existence, in all this fierce struggle for bread, of a bond of common humanity, but I was not left much time for indulgence in such reflections; the carriage, with closed curtains, rolled slowly by, and the noise of traffic became worse than ever.

"Will you never listen to me? Sixteen great big pears for a shilling, and the finest cardones and tomatoes thrown in the street; I am not selling, I am giving things away," etc.

Before leaving these street venders, who always possessed a particular attraction for me, mention should be made of the "nevero," or ice-cream man who passes along the streets at certain hours of the day selling a palatable ice-cream, in those towns large enough to possess ice machines, or in communication by rail with their more fortunate neighbors.

They carry their wares on top of their heads in buckets, which are frequently painted in the national colors, green, white, and red. This cream is as good as one could expect from frozen milk, which is all it usually is; sometimes the maker seeks to enrich it by the addition of butter and cinnamon; it is then called "Amantequillado," and is a trial to both palate and stomach.

Once, in Monterey, a great *funcion* was in progress, and elaborate preparations had been made by all these dealers in street cakes, candies, fruits, and other refreshments, but a cold north wind coming up unexpectedly, with a shower or two of rain, proved a great disappointment. However, I was one of those who determined to make the effort of getting down to the Plaza Cinco de Mayo, where the most of the entertainment was to be held. At the entrance stood a "nevero," who manifested great distress on account of the heat of the weather; he was vigorously mopping his forehead with a red bandana, which might have been cleaner without hurting anybody's feelings, and at the same time calling out in a loud tone of voice:—

"Caliente! Caliente! Ah, que caliente hay! Pero aqui 'sta nieve tan dulce para resfrescarse, para regalarse!"

(Oh! how hot it is! Oh! how hot it is! But here you have sweet ice-cream with which to refresh yourself, with which to regale yourself!)

His language was so emphatic and vociferous, his acting so lifelike, that like numbers of others I was deluded into believing that the weather was indeed hot, and forgetting the "Norte," I bought cinco centavos' worth of his compound, and had nearly finished it before I realized that I had been duped.

In my contact with the street peddlers, and the keepers of the small stores or *tendajones,* I became impressed with the wonderful fact that the smaller and more insignificant the latter appeared to be to my unpracticed eye, the more consequential was the name borne upon its sign, because I wish to inform such of my readers as may never have had the opportunity to travel among Mexicans, that every store and magazine bears a title; it used to amuse me to see that the Store of the Two Hemispheres was probably not over two yards square of our measurement, and that the Magazine of the Globe was carrying a stock worth not a cent more than twenty-five dollars at the outside; but one must accept each country as he finds it, and I am compelled to say that in the larger cities of Mexico there are numbers of finely stocked emporia of different classes of goods.

The position of clerk in one of these great mercantile establishments is much in demand, for what reason it would be hard to say, excepting that the comparative seclusion of the young women makes it somewhat difficult to meet them often, unless one be a special attendant in a dry-goods store, in which case conversation is allowed to flow unreservedly.

If the clerk be young, handsome, well-mannered, bright, and of good family, it generally takes about four hours for a young lady to buy a paper of pins; an intelligent clerk may have a great amount of information to impart upon the subject of pins if the intending customer have dove-like eyes, a gentle voice, tiny, soft hands, and a rich old daddy. There are long pins, short pins, black pins, white pins, American pins, English pins, French pins, and many other varieties, all of which I have heard described at length, but I never found it in my heart to grumble at the delay, and always have murmured, "Bless you, my children, bless you," leaving the more earnest expressions of disapproval to the cross old "dueñas," for whom my antagonism dates back to the days when I was a lieutenant in Arizona, ever so many years ago.

Sometimes one will enter into a gorgeous establishment and feel a vague sensation of distrust at seeing some such firm name as that of "Patricio O'Dowd Hijos" (Patrick O'Dowd's Sons, Monterey).

The original Patrick has long since been gathered to his fathers, but his prosperous business is energetically carried on by descendants of decidedly Castilian appearance, whose only sign of a Celtic derivation lies in their name. And so with the banking firms of MacManus in Chihuahua, and Milmo in Monterey, or MacElroy in Tamaulipas, founded by enterprising, intelligent, quick-witted Irish and Scotch ancestors, who married among the natives and left influential families behind them.

In all these mercantile establishments there is the singular custom of *pelon,* which apparently counterbalances any attempt at overcharging on the part of the proprietors. When you become a regular customer, a tiny tin cylinder is provided and hung up in the store in full view of everybody, marked with your name and number. Every time that you make a purchase, a bean is dropped down into the cylinder, and at stated times these are all counted, and for every sixteen or eighteen, depending upon the commercial generosity of the firm, you are allowed six cents in money or goods.

This custom must be one of great antiquity; the word "pelon" means a stone, or other crude weight, with which in Spain it was in ancient days customary to balance the scales used in the markets.

Under the name of "l'agniappe," the very same thing exists among the Creole French in Louisiana. Perhaps the Romans had in their "bonus" a custom of similar import.

Once a week the beggars, the lame, blind, deaf and dumb, take possession of Mexican stores; there being very little, if any, organized charity in the republic, such a system is undoubtedly as good as any that could be devised. The merchants good-naturedly submit to the tax, and an employee doles out to each mendicant the "limosnita" determined upon in his case.

But I was astonished and amused one day, after listening to a beggar's whine:—

"Limosnita, señores, limosnita, por el amor de Dios, y de Nuestra Santa Madre, Maria Santissima, siempre Virgen, concebida sin pecado, madre de Dios, y de los santos Apostolos Pedro y Paulo, y Santo Tomas, San Buenaventura, San Antonio de Padua y

San Juan de Dios. Dios se lo pague, seflores," etc., and so on to the end of the recitation, which is always carefully committed to memory by the suppliant.

("Alms, just a trifle of alms, gentlemen, for the love of God, and of Our Blessed Mother, Mary, Most Holy, ever Virgin, conceived without sin, Mother of God, and of the Holy Apostles Peter and Paul, and Saint Thomas, Saint Buenaventura, Saint Anthony of Padua, and Saint John of God," etc.)

"Get out of here, you scoundrel," shouted the irate proprietor. "Get out of here, and go where you belong; you get your alms over at Samaniego's."

From the Mexican restaurant to the Mexican home is only a step, but a big step. There may not be such a great difference in the dishes served or in the manner of cooking, but a Mexican home presents a warm-hearted hospitality which he who has once been fortunate enough to encounter finds hard to forget. While much could be written upon this part of the subject, there are reasons why much must be left unsaid for fear of wounding the sensibilities of people whose homes have been visited. Then much that might properly be said here has been anticipated in the earlier paragraphs, such as those which treat of the stoves and kitchen furniture, as well as the character of the bread to be found on all Mexican tables.

The Mexican housewife does not copy the extravagant habits of her sister to the north of the Rio Grande; all nations belonging wholly or in part to the so-called Latin stock adhere to the one plan of food supply for domestic purposes. Only the amount needed for each day's use is purchased at one time, and very generally just the quantity required for the particular meal; in Teutonic or Northern nations, on the contrary, there is a more apparent tendency to purchase supplies in gross and lay them aside for a rainy day. But Italy, France, Spain, and Mexico never have a rainy day; theirs are the lands of perpetual sunshine; they have little, if any ice; and not being possessed of means of preserving food for more than a few hours, buy exactly what is needed for the occasion. With Northern nations, the reverse obtains: snow and ice and cold may be looked for at any time after winter has once begun. Food if bought can be preserved indefinitely, and unnecessary journeying to and fro avoided. So, our prudent little Mexican housewife sends her "Maria" or "Manuela" to buy in the plaza or from a passing vender a small bunch of fresh onions, tomatoes, and parsnips, with a diminutive slice of pumpkin and one of cabbage; all of which will cost her five centavos. This would be the duplicate of the package which I bought in Monterey, greatly to the surprise of the dealer, who could not altogether make out what a man wanted with such things. Or, she may do as I did in San Luis Potosi and buy for six cents a small-sized collection embracing juicy, sweet, scarlet tunas, with one or more each of chirimoyas, bananas, figs, apples, oranges, grapes, and mangoes, with a small slice of "queso de tuna." But when she sends out for meat, she will scarcely be so fortunate; it is true that she may be offered a choice of ham, goat, kid, sheep, beef, or hog meat, but it will be butchered in a way that will scarcely commend it even to an Apache Indian. The Mexican butcher is generally a fraud, a delusion, and a snare. He worries himself very little about questions of roasts, joints, and chops, but boldly cuts his meat in a manner to suit himself. "This piece you can have for a medio; that one will cost you a real, and that lomo will come to two reales." In the outlying districts beef is very frequently used as "carne seca," or jerked, a form which is far from agreeable to the American palate. Four and one half pounds of lean, fresh meat, free from bone, will make one pound of "carne seca," which has about as much taste as an equal bulk of shavings dipped in bullocks' blood.

Most of the dishes to be found on the tables of private families resemble our own sufficiently well to pass without special description; where there has been a difference, it has been indicated in the reference to foods on sale in the streets and plazas.

Some of the Mexicans have four meals daily, somewhat in the French style; there is a *desayuno* or early breakfast of strong coffee and rolls, or sweetened bread; the more elaborate *almuerzo,* which is a full meat breakfast at noon, after which follows the afternoon siesta; then *merienda* or *collacion* at about five in the evening, consisting of chocolate, sweet cakes, and milk, and the *cena* at 8.30 or 9 p.m., in which figure chile con carne, frijoles, tortillas, cabbage (soup made with onions and tomatoes), cheese, preserved peaches, guavas, quinces, or tunas, and black coffee.

At a fashionable wedding in Saltillo, Mexico, which I witnessed in company with my friend, Captain Francis Hardie, in 1891, there was a very unique procession of servants bearing to the house of the bride great platters upon which were chickens and ducks, roasted, but with the heads replaced and gilded, and decidedly barbaric and Oriental in their magnificence. At the wedding of the beautiful Miss Varrios and Mr. Yturri, in Laredo, the banquet, served in the open air, under canvas sheeting, was very much in the style of such things in the United States. There were cold dishes of turkey, chicken, ham, fried oysters and fish from the Gulf of Mexico, salads, fruits and vegetables of several kinds, cakes of a dozen kinds, rolls, bread, coffee, chocolate, sherry, claret, brandy, whiskey punch, champagne, and cigars. The bride very graciously sent for all the gentlemen who approached in single file and were made the recipients of rosebuds from the bridal bouquet. In the cathedral, the groom, at the words "With all my worldly goods I do thee endow," presented his bride with thirteen coins, in memory, so the local Solons assured us, of the twelve Apostles and their Master, but this is not so; the custom, called by a word of Arabic derivation the "jarras," came into Spain with the Moors, and is still known in Algeria and Morocco, as I find stated by an English writer in a late number of "All the Year Round."

The above will, no doubt, give a fairly clear idea of the foods and culinary methods of the Mexican people and the Americans living nearest to them; much more might be added, but it would be in the nature of surplusage. There remain to be described only two or three dishes which are peculiar to the country and somewhat different from those to be found in the United States. One is made of chicken, first parboiled and then roasted and stuffed with chopped onion, chile, tomatoes, and seeded raisins. Another is a salad of cucumbers sliced very thin and served with an Italian dressing to which are added hard boiled eggs, chile, a pinch of curry, and some chopped onion. This salad may have been introduced from the Creole portion of Louisiana. During the holy season of Christmas, the women on the Rio Grande make the "bufiuelos," a fritter or fried pancake, moulded into form on the cook's knee; in "The Medicine Men of the Apache," in volume ix. Annual Report of Bureau of Ethnology, Smithsonian Institution, I made an attempt to demonstrate the identity of this cake with the "Crispillae" of the Normans and Romans, as described by Ducange in his "Glossarium." Something of the same sort is still prepared among the Algerians, but without regard to seasons. . . .

Notes

1. Turpentine.
2. Poor person.

Source: John G. Bourke, "The Folk-Foods of the Rio Grande Valley and Northern Mexico," *Journal of American Folk-Lore* 8 (January 1895): 41–71.

1896 • 96 • Fannie Farmer, "How to Measure"

Introduction: *Fannie Farmer popularized the formulization of cookery in her* Boston Cooking-School Cook Book. *Farmer made significant stylistic changes in her cookbook. In many of her 1,849 recipes, she listed ingredients first and then offered simple step-by-step instructions so that virtually anyone could prepare a dish with a reasonable chance of success. This also helped the reader to be sure that all the ingredients were on hand before starting to cook. Scientific cookery remains a part of American cookbooks today, and most recipes in American cookbooks, magazines, and newspapers were subsequently organized in a manner consistent with Farmer's presentation. The idea that cookery was an art form disappeared from most American households. In the excerpt below, Farmer stresses level measurements.*

Correct measurements are absolutely necessary to insure the best results. Good judgment, with experience, has taught some to measure by sight; but the majority need definite guides.

Tin measuring-cups, divided in quarters or thirds, holding one half-pint, and tea and table spoons of regulation sizes,—which may be bought at any store where kitchen furnishings are sold,—and a case knife, are essentials for correct measurement. Mixing-spoons, which are little larger than tablespoons, should not be confounded with the latter.

Measuring Ingredients. Flour, meal, powdered and confectioners' sugar, and soda should be sifted before measuring. Mustard and baking-powder, from standing in boxes, settle, therefore should be stirred to lighten; salt frequently lumps, and these lumps should be broken. A cupful is measured level. To measure a cupful, put in the ingredient by spoonfuls or from a scoop, round slightly, and level with a case knife, care being taken not to shake the cup. A tablespoonful is measured level. A teaspoonful is measured level.

To measure tea or table spoonfuls, dip the spoon in the ingredient, fill, lift, and level with a knife, the sharp edge of knife being toward tip of spoon. Divide with knife lengthwise of spoon, for a half-spoonful; divide halves crosswise for quarters, and quarters crosswise for eighths. Less than one-eighth of a teaspoonful is considered a few grains.

Measuring Liquids. A cupful of liquid is all the cup will hold.

A tea or table spoonful is all the spoon will hold.

Measuring Butter, Lard, etc. To measure butter, lard, and other solid fats, pack solidly into cup or spoon, and level with a knife.

When dry ingredients, liquids, and fats are called for in the same recipe, measure in the order given, thereby using but one cup.

Source: Fannie Merritt Farmer, *The Boston Cooking-School Cook Book* (Boston: Little, Brown, 1896), 27–29.

1896 • 97 • "In a Sandwich Car"

Introduction: *In 1893 a manufacturer began selling a new type of lunch wagon that had gas grills. This made it possible for street vendors to serve hot food. Hamburger steak, a common food served on a plate in restaurants, could now be served on the streets provided that the patty was placed in a bun. Who invented the first hamburger sandwich is unknown, but it most likely occurred on the streets of a city in the Midwest, where America's meatpacking industry was situated. Below is an early citation to the sandwich wagons and the hamburger sandwich sold in Chicago.*

The piece de resistance is chicken sandwich, which consists of a quarter section of a small spring chicken, cold, placed between two slices of bread, with the accompaniment of a pickle, a green onion, or a dash of catsup. This costs 10 or 15 cents. Pork chops, ham, pig's feet (fresh or pickled), fried fish, codfish cakes, and eggs are also put in sandwich form, mostly at five cents each. A distinguished favorite, only five cents, is Hamburger steak sandwich, the meat for which is kept ready in small patties and 'cooked while you wait' on the gasoline ranges. Fried oysters, breaded, are also a popular sandwich ingredient.

The sandwich man takes in from $5 to $7 a night, perhaps $12 on Saturday or other special nights—this 'special' implying when many people are out late—and makes an average profit of 25 percent on his outlay, say $12 a week, besides much of the food required for himself and family. Many of them keep no horse, but hire one at 50 cents a day to haul the sandwich wagon to and from its nightly stand. It is a business principle of the class to sell out everything, if necessary even at startling reduction, before going home in the morning, so that supplies for next night may be all fresh cooked.

Source: "In a Sandwich Car," *Chicago Tribune,* July 5, 1896.

1896 • 98 • Cracker Jack, "Something New"

Introduction: *Popcorn vendors Louis and Frederick Rueckheim worked the streets of Chicago in the early 1880s, but they spent their spare time experimenting with new products to sell. One of their better efforts combined popcorn, molasses, and peanuts, and their customers liked it. The Rueckheims invested in new equipment, enabling them to boost their production capability. On February 17, 1896, they applied for a trademark on the name "Cracker Jack," and shortly thereafter they launched a promotional and marketing blitz in Chicago, followed closely by campaigns in New York and Philadelphia. They then began advertising Cracker Jack nationally. Cracker Jack was America's first national snack food. Below is an early advertisement that helped make Cracker Jack America's most popular confection in the early 20th century.*

Something New; The Craving for it is Contagious. Its Very appetizing.

There's something new in town. It is Cracker Jack. Or, as a dealer remarked to a customer:

"You dare not taste it for you'll be compelled to buy it. That sounds strange in this free country, but it's a fact. The more you taste Cracker Jack, the more Cracker Jack you'll want."

The taste of it is as catchy as the name. The longing for it becomes contagious. It won't harm you, because Cracker Jack is a healthful confection. It's the invention of a Chicago firm, F. W. Rueckheim & Brothers, the wholesale confectioners.

How do they make it? Ah, that's Rueckheim's secret. Their factory can't begin to supply Cracker Jack consumers. The people actually crave Cracker Jack as if they have been starved. They eat and eat and eat, and never seem to get enough of it. That's the beauty of Cracker Jack. It gives edge to the appetite. If you want personal experience, ask your confectioner, grocer, or your druggist about it.

Source: Advertisement, *Chicago Tribune* and *Times-Herald,* February 23, 1896.

1896 • 99 • Pecans

Introduction: *Many different nuts were consumed by American Indians in precolonial days. The only American nut that survived into the present day are pecans. Below is an excerpt from a U.S. Department of Agriculture bulletin that encouraged American farmers to grow pecans.*

Variations in Size of Tree and in Size and Quality of Fruit.

The largest trees are reported upon the northeastern area of its native growth. But the largest and thinnest shelled nuts have been received from Mississippi, Louisiana, and Texas. R. C. Koerber, a large dealer in pecans in New York City, who has personal knowledge of the tree and its habit in Texas, says: "The largest and best pecans come from Louisiana. They reach the market earlier than do those from Texas and are of large size, measuring from 1¾ to 2 inches in length by three-quarters of an inch in diameter, in the middle.["] The quantity marketed from this State, however, is very limited. "In Bee County and adjacent territory in Texas pecans are grown with very thin shells that may be crushed in the fingers; in Victoria County the more common pecan is large and round; in San Saba and Llano counties the pecan nut is large and the meat is plump, shell moderately thin."

The Texas pecan crop affords a large income for the inhabitants of some portions of the State, mainly in certain counties within the area named above. As early as 1871 it was reported from some of the cotton-growing sections of Texas that the pecan crop would be worth five times as much as the cotton crop of that year. Says Mr. Koerber: "But for this industry of nut gathering, the people of some localities must have starved for lack of remunerative labor. Hundreds of both white and colored people go out with horses and wagons to gather these nuts." Charles Mohr found that in 1880 there were marketed in San Antonio, Tex., the most important center of the pecan trade, over 1,250,000 pounds of nuts. The price paid by the wagonload varied from 5 to 6 cents per pound.

The best pecans of the State are produced in San Saba, Brown, and McCulloch counties and along the Concho and Guadalupe rivers and a few other streams. By the expression "best pecans" growers understand large nuts with thin shells. The Texas pecans vary greatly in size, but are generally egg-shaped, about 1 to 1½ inches long by one half to five-eighths inch in diameter. On the bottom lands of southern Illinois, though the trees usually ripen their fruit, the nuts are smaller and less rich in oil than those grown farther south. They are said to keep better, not becoming rancid as soon as the more oily nuts. Of all the hickory family the pecan seems most susceptible of improvement in the size and quality of its fruit, and marked improvements by selection have already been made by several planters. . . .

Cleansing and Polishing.

After the nuts are hulled or "shucked," they are placed by some harvesters in revolving churns where, by turning, they are cleaned and brightened. Others bleach the nuts with sulphur fumes, but this practice is objectionable and should be discouraged. An industry was established a few years since at Austin, Tex., by R. C. Koerber, for cleansing and polishing or "burnishing" pecans, a business which he has since transferred to New York City. Convenient establishments for cleansing the nuts in the neighborhood of the orchards will be the demand of the near future. A good assorting screen and dirt separator at every important center of gathering is a desirable adjunct to this business. Mr. Koerber's enterprise has added materially to the popularity of the pecan as a dessert nut, and indicates one direction for effort in broadening the market.

Marketing.

Between the grower and the consumer of pecans there are several handlings of the nut, and not a few intermediate dealers and merchants. The gathered nuts are of three classes, namely, those grown from selected stocks for planting, those for confectionery and dessert uses, and those suitable only for making oil. Pecans for seed are in good demand at the present time, owing to the general interest felt by planters within the probable area of its successful culture. With a confidence that amounts to enthusiasm on the part of propagators, it is a matter of no surprise that the price of choice pecans has been materially enhanced by the increased demands. For planting, the more popular-named varieties readily sold in the fall of 1891 and 1892 at from 50 cents to $1.50 per pound. The trade in these nuts is mainly done by orders through the mails, much the same as the retail trade in seeds and nursery business is carried on, and to a great extent by the same persons.

Dessert Pecans.

As a nut the pecan has for about a century been deservedly popular because of the thinness of its shell, from which the large, full kernel is easily removed, and because of the agreeable flavor and wholesome quality of its meat. A Frenchman named De Courset, who served with Washington in 1782, left the record that "that celebrated general always had his pockets full of these nuts, and that he was continually eating them."

For dessert and confectionery purposes the nuts commonly found in the markets are much smaller than those selected for seed. It is doubtful if many pecans of named varieties have yet been sold for other than seed purposes, owing to the scarcity of the choice varieties and the demand for them at high prices for planting. Of the proportion of pecans that are consumed for dessert purposes as compared with other nuts we have not been able to secure satisfactory data. The demand is believed to be steadily increasing, and the pecan seems to be supplanting other nuts for many uses.

Pecan Meats.

The industry of preparing the kernels, or meats, of pecans for market, though yet in its infancy, has assumed large proportions. It was begun by Mr. Koerber in 1884, and his books show that in 1887 he prepared 20,000 pounds, and in 1890 more than 100,000 pounds. Formerly very few confectioners used pecan meats, being unwilling to take the trouble to crack the nuts and pick them out. With a machine especially constructed for cracking these nuts Mr. Koerber finds that pecan meats are coming into general use. He thinks it will be but a short time before nut meats will replace the whole nuts on hotel tables. Three pounds of nuts contain about 1 pound of meats. Pecan meats in halves sell at 45 to 50 cents per pound. Smaller pieces of pecan meat sell at a lower price.

Nut Oil.

Louis Biediger writes: "As far as I know the small pecans have been sold every year at from 2 to 3 cents per pound and sometimes as low as three-fourths to 1 cent per pound. They are used for oil. I do not know the methods or the machinery used, but I believe the process is much the same as that used for peanuts. I think it would pay to establish mills to use up small pecans. I do not know the uses to which it could be put, but I believe it would be first-class oil for table use. It would probably be too expensive for illuminating, although for the latter purpose anyone can satisfy himself of its superior quality. A kernel when lighted will burn for some time and make a clear, brilliant light. Crushed with the shells on the mast will make acceptable hog feed, but the shells would be objectionable in the feed of neat cattle. If some means could be devised for removing the shells before expressing the oil, the mast would surpass either linseed or cotton-seed meal for feeding all animals. It would be more healthful to milch cows and its flavor would materially improve the butter."

Source: U.S. Department of Agriculture, *Nut Culture in the United States* (Washington, DC: U.S. Government Printing Office, 1896), 49–50, 60–61.

1896 • 100 • Horace Annesley Vachell, "Sea Fishing in Californian Waters"

Introduction: *Sportfishing began in England and arrived in America in colonial days. The main rule was that freshwater fish had to be caught by rods and reels, nit nets, and dynamite, the way many commercial fishermen did. Sportfishing was not applied to saltwater fishing until the Catalina Tuna Club was created in the late 1890s. The except below was written by Horace Annesley Vachell (1861–1955), a prolific British author who moved to California to ranch and fish.*

Sea Fishing in Californian Waters

The game fish to be described in this article are, the tuna, the king salmon, the albicore, the yellow tail, the black bass, or Jew fish, the halibut, the bonito, and the barracuda. These—taken, be it understood, with rod and reel—furnish the sportsman a maximum of entertainment. Other fish, smelt, mackerel, flounder, surf fish, rock cod, *et hoc genus omne,* present claims to the angler's consideration, but these claims will find due recognition at my hands elsewhere.

I am aware that a certain prejudice lurks in the hearts of fly-fishermen against those who go down to the sea with spoon, jig, and savory sardine. This prejudice I shall endeavor to remove. But I admit frankly that such fly-fishing as may be found in northern California and British Columbia, where the rivers, cool and pellucid, flow swiftly through primeval forests, where the pine and the hemlock sigh their lullabies above foaming rapids, where a stout trout puts to the proof the angler's utmost skill, where the fly must be cast with fairy-like delicacy and precision,—such fly-fishing, I emphatically declare, soars into the empyrean of sport, unrivaled, unapproachable. But the cream of fly-fishing can be skimmed but by few. And the art as practised upon most of the lukewarm streams of Southern California is bastard and degenerate, exacting neither ability nor strategy. To yank troutlets by the hundred into a barley sack, whether in season or out of season, may tickle the taste of a counter-jumper, but it is not sport.

Nor is it sport to hire a power launch and a boatman, to scour up and down amongst schools of yellow tail, bonito, and barracuda, with twenty hand lines out astern, to fill barrels with fish that are left to rot on the beach, or thrown back, dead, into the ocean, to stand in front of the camera with hecatombs of the slain behind you,—silent witnesses of your shame and cruelty—this is not sport, nor fun, nor folly, but wanton and inexcusable crime.

And this crime, beneath the aegis of sport, is committed daily, nay hourly, at Santa Catalina island!

A few gentlemen—the gods be praised!—insist upon and practise the rigor of the game. They use the finest lines, the lightest rods, and in short, give their quarry what is his lawful due—fair play. The strength of the tackle should depend upon the size of the fish. A sportsman will approve the golden rule of a "minute to the pound." For instance, in trolling for yellow tail the cuttyhunk line should be of fifteen ply; without putting undue strain upon this it is almost impossible to kill a fifteen pound fish in less than a quarter of an hour; a thirty pounder, in like manner, would keep one busy for thirty minutes. Some fish, of course, are more game than others, but the rule, in the majority of cases, holds good. In Florida, fishing for tarpon, the man who uses a line heavier than sixteen ply is voted a pariah; at Catalina, fishing for tuna, twenty-four ply line has alone withstood the terrific rushes and plunges of this prince of the Pacific. When he sounds and sulks he must be lifted, hence the necessity of stout tackle; but so far, only fifteen of these giants have been taken, further experience may modify our conclusions.

The first tuna killed with rod and reel was taken by my friend, Mr. Morehouse of Pasadena, last summer. This season, so far, fourteen have come to the gaff. Mr. W. Greer Campbell, an enthusiastic fisherman, has devoted six weeks to the tuna, and deservedly holds the record. Mr. Campbell assured me that the tuna is a gamer and stronger fish than the tarpon. The following excerpt from an article written by Professor Charles F. Holder for the Cosmopolitan magazine, and published less than eighteen months ago, is worth quoting:—

> The activity of the tuna is only comparable to the tarpon. I have seen them leap ten or fifteen feet into the air, while they have been known to jump over the boats in pursuit of them. Sportsmen from the East have devoted weeks to this fish, hoping to win fame and honor by taking one on the rod, but so far the tuna has harvested the rods, reels, and lines, and is still master of the situation.

My brother and I fished patiently for this high muck-a-muck of the mackerel tribe, and lost many sets of hooks, much line, and some solid flesh. Finally, using the same rod and reel that had done such effective work in Mr. Campbell's hands, and in the company of James Gardner, Mr. Campbell's boatman, I succeeded in bringing a tuna to the gaff that scaled one hundred and twenty-five pounds. The fish was on for one hour and five minutes. During that time he never rested once,—nor did I. He taxed all my powers of endurance; he rushed here and there with the speed and strength of a wild Texan steer; he sounded and sulked; he charged us again and again; he broke water; and he died like a true gladiator, when he was unable to strike another blow for freedom!

I watched an Homeric struggle between another titan and Mr. Morehouse, a fight that lasted four hours and a half. The fish had distinctly the best of it from first to last, and when the line parted left his opponent *hors de combat.* My brother Guy fought a tuna for three hours and a half, and lost him at the supreme moment of gaffing. This gallant fish towed the boat, at a conservative estimate, *at least eight or nine miles!* Jim, who is a member of the Ananias Club, says fifteen miles. He was hooked in Avalon harbor; he to wed the boat to Banning bay and back; thence to the farther point of Pebbly beach and back; then he put bravely to sea. When the line broke we hastened to our breakfast as fast as the launch could go, but we were fifty-five minutes in reaching our moorings!

You fish for tarpon at anchor, the bait resting upon the bottom; you troll for tuna at full speed, sitting in a boat towed by a launch. When the fish strikes, the boatman lets go of the painter and seizes the oars; upon his promptness and skill hang success and failure. If he can stop his boat and set her going in the wake of the tuna before your line has run out, if—this feat being successfully accomplished—he never once relaxes his vigilance, if, in a word, he does his part as boatman effectively and coolly, and if you, on the other hand, thoroughly understand your business and can estimate justly the strength of your tackle, then, even then, the chances of bringing the quarry to the steel are against you.

Tuna may be caught at Catalina (possibly elsewhere, but I can obtain no reliable information upon this point) from May to November, but Mr. Campbell considers June the best month. They feed voraciously upon flying fish, driving them, as do the seals, into small bays and inlets. And the authorities agree that it is prudent to fish for tuna as near the kelp as possible, in shallow water. Hooked in deep water, he may sound at once, and then nothing finer than a ship's cable would suffice to stop him. Unlike the monstrous Jew fish, he loves blue water, and as a rule puts to sea as soon as he feels the barb. If, unhappily, he should seek sanctuary in the kelp, the line must break. The bait used is a flying fish about fourteen inches long. A stout hook pierces the head, another, attached to the first with piano wire, is sewn to the belly; a trace of wire a yard long and a stout brass swivel complete the lure, which should be attached to the line by means of a clove hitch and a bowline. Piano wire rusts rapidly in salt water, the prudent sportsman, therefore, will buy vaseline and see personally that it is liberally used. By this means a catastrophe may be avoided. These hooks are provided by James Gardner.

The rods, reels, and lines, must be of superlative quality. A ten-ounce split bamboo rod should be bound with whipcord to within three feet of the tip, the reel—an Edwin Vom Hofe reel is the best—should hold three hundred yards of wet line, and the line must be reeled on wet. Dry line, moistened by the impact of wet line, is likely to expand at a critical moment, and thereby clog disastrously the reel's action.

The tuna feeds early and late, but so far nearly all the fish have been hooked between four and five A. M. The boatman's charges are reasonable. Four dollars will cover a single expedition: two dollars and a half to the owner of the launch, one dollar and a half to the boatman.

The illustration gives no idea of the tuna's superlative beauty. He belongs to the mackerel family—no handsomer fish can be found—and wears its blue and silver livery. Freshly killed, he gleams with an iridescence that may be compared to the sheen of mother of pearl, or abalone shell. The scales are beneath the outer skin, and the pectoral and dorsal fins are provided with wondrous sheaths. For speed, strength, and comeliness, he cannot be excelled.

Source: Horace Annesley Vachell, "Sea Fishing in Californian Waters," *Overland Monthly* 30 (December 1897): 483–485.

1897 • 101 • Louis Hughes, "Fourth of July Barbecue"

Introduction: *Louis Hughes (1830–1913) was a slave on a cotton plantation in Mississippi. He tried to escape five times but was returned to the plantation each time before he finally escaped to Union lines. After the war he became a successful businessman in Chicago and Milwaukee. He wrote his autobiography, which includes many descriptions about the food he consumed when he was a slave. Below Hughes describes a barbecue before the Civil War.*

Fourth of July Barbecue

Barbecue originally meant to dress and roast a hog whole, but has come to mean the cooking of a food animal in this manner for the feeding of a great company. A feast of this kind was always given to us, by Boss, on the 4th of July. The anticipation of it acted as a stimulant through the entire year. Each one looked forward to this great day of recreation with pleasure. Even the older slaves would join in the discussion of the coming event. It mattered not what trouble or hardship the year had brought, this feast and its attendant pleasure would dissipate all gloom. Some, probably, would be punished on the morning of the 4th, but this did not matter; the men thought of the good things in store for them, and that made them forget that they had been punished. All the week previous to the great day, the slaves were in high spirits, the young girls and boys, each evening, congregating, in front of the cabins, to talk of the feast, while others would sing and dance. The older slaves were not less happy, but would only say: "Ah! God has blessed us in permitting us to see another feast day." The day before the 4th was a busy one. The slaves worked with all their might. The children who were large enough were engaged in bringing wood and bark to the spot where the barbecue was to take place.

They worked eagerly, all day long; and, by the time the sun was setting, a huge pile of fuel was beside the trench, ready for use in the morning. At an early hour of the great day, the servants were up, and the men whom Boss had appointed to look after the killing of the hogs and sheep were quickly at their work, and, by the time they had the meat dressed and ready, most of the slaves had arrived at the center of attraction. They gathered in groups, talking, laughing, telling tales that they had from their grandfather, or relating practical jokes that they had played or seen played by others. These tales were received with peals of laughter. But however much they seemed to enjoy these stories and social interchanges, they never lost sight of the trench or the spot where the sweetmeats were to be cooked.

The method of cooking the meat was to dig a trench in the ground about six feet long and eighteen inches deep. This trench was filled with wood and bark which was set on fire, and, when it was burned to a great bed of coals, the hog was split through the back bone, and laid on poles which had been placed across the trench. The sheep were treated in the same way, and both were turned from side to side as they cooked. During the process of roasting the cooks basted the carcasses with a preparation furnished from the great house, consisting of butter, pepper, salt and vinegar, and this was continued until the meat was ready to serve. Not far from this trench were the iron ovens, where the sweetmeats were cooked. Three or four women were assigned to this work. Peach cobbler and apple dumpling were the two dishes that made old slaves smile for joy and the young fairly dance. The crust or pastry of the cobbler was prepared in large earthen bowls, then rolled out like any pie crust, only it was almost twice as thick. A layer of this crust was laid in the oven, then a half peck of peaches poured in, followed by a layer of sugar; then a covering of pastry was laid over all and smoothed around with a knife. The oven was then put over a bed of coals, the cover put on and coals thrown on it, and the process of baking began. Four of these ovens were usually in use at these feasts, so that enough of the pastry might be baked to supply all. The ovens were filled and refilled until there was no doubt about the quantity. The apple dumplings were made in the usual way, only larger, and served with sauce made from brown sugar. It lacked flavoring, such as cinnamon or lemon, yet it was a dish highly relished by all the slaves. I know that these feasts made me so excited, I could scarcely do my house duties, and I would never fail to stop and look out of the window from the dining room down into the quarters. I was eager to get through with my work and be with the feasters. About noon everything was ready to serve. The table was set in a grove near the quarters, a place set aside for these occasions. The tableware was not fine, being of tin, but it served the purpose, and did not detract from the slaves' relish for the feast. The drinks were strictly temperance drinks—buttermilk and water. Some of the nicest portions of the meat were sliced off and put on a platter to send to the great house for Boss and his family. It was a pleasure for the slaves to do this, for Boss always enjoyed it. It was said that the slaves could barbecue meats best, and when the whites had barbecues slaves always did the cooking. When dinner was all on the table, the invitation was given for all to come; and when all were in a good way eating, Boss and the madam would go out to witness the progress of the feast, and seemed pleased to see the servants so happy. Everything was in abundance, so all could have plenty. Boss always insisted on this. The slaves had the whole day off, and could do as they liked. After dinner some of the women would wash, sew or iron. It was a day of harmless riot for all the slaves, and I can not express the happiness it brought them. Old and young, for months, would rejoice in the memory of the day and its festivities, and "bless" Boss for this ray of sunlight in their darkened lives.

Source: Louis Hughes, *Thirty Years a Slave: From Bondage to Freedom* (Milwaukee: South Side Printing Company, 1897), 46–51.

1906 • 102 • Upton Sinclair, *The Jungle*

Introduction: *Upton Sinclair (1878–1868), a novelist, traveled to Chicago, where for seven weeks he toiled in the stockyards, interviewing workers, labor leaders, and journalists. Upon returning to his home near Princeton, New Jersey, Sinclair set to work on a novel about his adventure. On February 28, 1906,* The Jungle *was released, and overnight the book became an international cause célèbre. Magazines and newspapers throughout America reported its publication and its revelations. Within a matter of months, Congress passed the Pure Food and Drug Act and the Meat Inspection Act. Pure food became the law of the land, and the quality and safety of America's food supply improved as a result; however, the debate about what constitutes pure food and how the food industry should be regulated continues to shape what Americans eat today. (See also Documents 103 and 104.)*

Now Antanas Rudkus was the meekest man that God ever put on earth; and so Jurgis found it a striking confirmation of what the men all said, that his father had been at work only two days before he came home as bitter as any of them, and cursing Durham's with all the power of his soul. For they had set him to cleaning out the traps; and the family sat round and listened in wonder while he told them what that meant. It seemed that he was working in the room where the men prepared the beef for canning, and the beef had lain in vats full of chemicals, and men with great forks speared it out and dumped it into trucks to be taken to the cooking-room. When they had speared out all they could reach, they emptied the vat on the floor, and then with shovels scraped up the balance and dumped it into the truck. This floor was filthy, yet they set Antanas with his mop slopping the "pickle" into a hole that connected with a sink, where it was caught and used over again forever; and if that were not enough, there was a trap in the pipe, where all the scraps of meat and odds and ends of refuse were caught, and every few days it was the old man's task to clean these out, and shovel their contents into one of the trucks with the rest of the meat!

This was the experience of Antanas; and then there came also Jonas and Marija with tales to tell. Marija was working for one of the independent packers, and was quite beside herself and outrageous with triumph over the sums of money she was making as a painter of cans. But one day she walked home with a pale-faced little woman who worked opposite to her, Jadvyga Marcinkus by name, and Jadvyga told her how she, Marija, had chanced to get her job. She had taken the place of an Irish woman who had been working in that factory ever since any one could remember, for over fifteen years, so she declared. Mary Dennis was her name, and a long time ago she had been seduced, and had a little boy; he was a cripple, and an epileptic, but still he was all that she had in the world to love, and they had lived in a little room alone somewhere back of Halsted Street, where the Irish were. Mary had had consumption, and all day long you might hear her coughing as she worked; of late she had been going all to pieces, and when Marija came, the "forelady" had suddenly decided to turn her off. The forelady had to come up to a certain standard herself, and could not stop for sick people, Jadvyga explained. The fact that Mary had been there so long had not made any difference to her—it was doubtful if she even knew that, for both the forelady and the superintendent were new people, having only been there two or three years themselves. Jadvyga did not know what had become of the poor creature; she would have gone to see her, but had been sick herself. She had pains in her back all the time, Jadvyga explained, and feared that she had womb trouble. It was not fit work for a woman, handling fourteen-pound cans all day. It was a striking circumstance that Jonas, too, had gotten his job by the misfortune of some other person. Jonas pushed a truck loaded with hams from the smoke rooms on to an elevator, and thence to the packing-rooms. The trucks were all of iron, and heavy, and they put about threescore hams on each of them, a load of more than a quarter of a ton. On the uneven floor it was a task for a man to start one of these trucks, unless he was a giant; and when it was once started he naturally tried his best to keep it going. There was always the boss prowling about, and if there was a second's delay he would fall to cursing; Lithuanians and Slovaks and such, who could not understand what was said to them, the bosses were wont to kick about the place like so many dogs. Therefore these trucks went for the most part on the run; and the predecessor of Jones had been jammed against the wall by one and crushed in a horrible and nameless manner.

All of these were sinister incidents; but they were trifles compared to what Jurgis saw with his own eyes before long. One curious thing he had noticed, the very first day, in his profession of shoveller of guts; which was the sharp trick of the floor-bosses whenever there chanced to come a "slunk" calf. Any man who knows anything about butchering knows that the flesh of a cow that is about to calve, or has just calved, is not fit for food. A good many of these came every day to the packing-houses—and, of course, if they had chosen, it would have been an easy matter for the packers to keep them till they were fit for food. But for the saving of time and fodder, it was the law that cows of that sort came along with the others, and whoever noticed it would tell the boss, and the boss would start up a conversation with the government inspector, and the two would stroll away. So in a trice the carcass of the cow would be cleaned out, and the entrails would have vanished; it was Jurgis's task to slide them into the trap, calves and all, and on the floor below they took out these "slunk" calves, and butchered them for meat, and used even the skins of them.

One day a man slipped and hurt his leg; and that afternoon, when the last of the cattle had been disposed of, and the men were leaving, Jurgis was ordered to remain and do some special work which this injured man had usually done. It was late, almost dark, and the government inspectors had all gone, and there were only a dozen or two of men on the floor. That day they had killed about four thousand cattle, and these cattle had come in freight trains from far states, and some of them had got hurt. There were some with broken legs, and some with gored sides; there were some that had died, from what cause no one could say; and they were all to be disposed of, here in darkness and silence. "Downers," the men called them; and the packing-house had a special elevator upon which they were raised to the killing-beds, where the gang proceeded to handle them, with an air of businesslike nonchalance which said plainer than any words that it was a matter of everyday routine. It took a couple of hours to get them out of the way, and in the end Jurgis saw them go into the chilling-rooms with the rest of the meat, being carefully scattered here and there so that they could not be identified. When he came home that night he was in a very sombre mood, having begun to see at last how those might be right who had laughed at him for his faith in America. . . .

Then there was old Antanas. The winter came, and the place where he worked was a dark, unheated cellar, where you could see your breath all day, and where your fingers sometimes tried to freeze. So the old man's cough grew every day worse, until there came a time when it hardly ever stopped, and he had become a nuisance about the place. Then, too, a still more dreadful thing happened to him; he worked in a place where his feet were soaked in chemicals, and it was not long before they had eaten through his new boots. Then sores began to break out on his feet, and grow worse and worse. Whether it was that his blood was bad, or there had been a cut, he could not say; but he asked the men about it, and learned that it was a regular thing—it was the saltpetre. Every one felt it, sooner or later, and then it was all up with him, at least for that sort of work. The sores would never heal—in the end his toes would drop off, if he did not quit. Yet old Antanas would not quit; he saw the suffering of his family, and he remembered what it had cost him to get a job. So he tied up his feet, and went on limping about and coughing, until at last he fell to pieces, all at once and in a heap, like the One-Horse Shay. They carried him to a dry place and laid him on the floor, and that night two of the men helped him home. The poor old man was put to bed, and though he tried it every morning until the end, he never could get up again. He would lie there and cough and cough, day and night, wasting away to a mere skeleton. There came a time when there was so little flesh on him that the bones began to poke through—which was a horrible thing to see or even to think of. And one night he had a choking fit, and a little river of blood came out of his mouth. The family, wild with terror, sent for a doctor, and paid half a dollar to be told that there was nothing to be done. Mercifully the doctor did not say this so that the old man could hear, for he was still clinging to the faith that tomorrow or next day he would be better, and could go back to his job. The company had sent word to him that they would keep it for him—or rather Jurgis had bribed one of the men to come one Sunday afternoon and say they had. Dede Antanas continued to believe it, while three more hemorrhages came; and then at last one morning they found him stiff and cold. Things were not going well with them then, and though it nearly broke Teta Elzbieta's heart, they were forced to dispense with nearly all the decencies of a funeral; they had only a hearse, and one hack for the women and children; and Jurgis, who was learning things fast, spent all Sunday making a bargain for these, and he made it in the presence of witnesses, so that when the man tried to charge him for all sorts of incidentals, he did not have to pay. For twenty-five years old Antanas Rudkus and his son had dwelt in the forest together, and it was hard to part in this way; perhaps it was just as well that Jurgis had to give all his attention to the task of having a funeral without being bankrupted, and so had no time to indulge in memories and grief.

Now the dreadful winter was come upon them. In the forests, all summer long, the branches of the trees do battle for light, and some of them lose and die; and then come the raging blasts, and the storms of snow and hail, and strew the ground with these weaker branches. Just so it was in Packingtown; the whole district braced itself for the struggle that was an agony, and those whose time was come died off in hordes. All the year round they had been serving as cogs in the great packing machine; and now was the time for the renovating of it, and the replacing of damaged parts. There came pneumonia and grippe, stalking among them, seeking for weakened constitutions; there was the annual harvest of those whom tuberculosis had been dragging down. There came cruel, cold, and biting winds, and blizzards of snow, all testing relentlessly for failing muscles and impoverished blood. Sooner or later came the day when the unfit one did not report for work; and then, with no time lost in waiting, and no inquiries or regrets, there was a chance for a new hand.

The new hands were here by the thousands. All day long the gates of the packing-houses were besieged by starving and penniless men; they came, literally, by the thousands every single morning, fighting with each other for a chance for life. Blizzards and cold made no difference to them, they were always on hand; they were on hand two hours before the sun rose, an hour before the work began. Sometimes their faces froze, sometimes their feet and their hands; sometimes they froze all together—but still they came, for they had no other place to go. One day Durham advertised in the paper for two hundred men to cut ice; and all that day the homeless and starving of the city came trudging through the snow from all over its two hundred square miles. That night forty score of them crowded into the station-house of the stockyards district—they filled the rooms, sleeping in each other's laps, toboggan-fashion, and they piled on top of each other in the corridors, till the police shut the doors and left some to freeze outside. On the morrow, before daybreak, there were three thousand at Durham's, and the police-reserves had to be sent for to quell the riot. Then Durham's bosses picked out twenty of the biggest; the "two hundred" proved to have been a printer's error.

Four or five miles to the eastward lay the lake, and over this the bitter winds came raging. Sometimes the thermometer would fall to ten or twenty degrees below zero at night, and in the morning the streets would be piled with snowdrifts up to the first-floor windows. The streets through which our friends had to go to their work were all unpaved and full of deep holes and gullies; in summer, when it rained hard, a man might have to wade to his waist to get to his house; and now in winter it was no joke getting through these places, before light in the morning and after dark at night. They would wrap up in all they owned, but they could not wrap up against exhaustion; and many a man gave out in these battles with the snowdrifts, and lay down and fell asleep.

And if it was bad for the men, one may imagine how the women and children fared. Some would ride in the cars, if the cars were running; but when you are making only five cents an hour, as was little Stanislovas, you do not like to spend that much to ride two miles. The children would come to the yards with great shawls about their ears, and so tied up that you could hardly find them—and still there would be accidents. One bitter morning in February the little boy who worked at the lard machine with Stanislovas came about an hour late, and screaming with pain. They unwrapped him, and a man began vigorously rubbing his ears; and as they were frozen stiff, it took only two or three rubs to break them short off. As a result of this, little Stanislovas conceived a terror of the cold that was almost a mania. Every morning, when it came time to start for the yards, he would begin to cry and protest. Nobody knew quite how to manage him, for threats did no good—it seemed to be something that he could not control, and they feared sometimes that he would go into convulsions. In the end it had to be arranged that he always went with Jurgis, and came home with him again; and often, when the snow was deep, the man would carry him the whole way on his shoulders. Sometimes Jurgis would be working until late at night, and then it was pitiful, for there was no place for the little fellow to wait, save in the doorways or in a corner of the killing-beds, and he would all but fall asleep there, and freeze to death.

There was no heat upon the killing-beds; the men might exactly as well have worked out of doors all winter. For that matter, there was very little heat anywhere in the building, except in the cooking-rooms and fire places—and it was the men who worked in these who ran the most risk of all, because whenever they had to pass to another room they had to go through ice-cold corridors, and sometimes with nothing on above the waist except a sleeveless undershirt. On the killing beds you were apt to be covered with blood, and it would freeze solid; if you leaned against a pillar, you would freeze to that, and if you put your hand upon the blade of your knife, you would run a chance of leaving your skin on it. The men would tie up their feet in newspapers and old sacks, and these would be soaked in blood and frozen, and then soaked again, and so on, until by night-time a man would be walking on great lumps the size of the feet of an elephant. Now and then, when the bosses were not looking, you would see them plunging their feet and ankles into the steaming hot carcass of the steer, or darting across the room to the hot-water jets. The cruelest thing of all was that nearly all of them—all of those who used knives—were unable to wear gloves, and their arms would be white with frost and their hands would grow numb, and then of course there would be accidents. Also the air would be full of steam, from the hot water and the hot blood, so that you could not see five feet before you; and then, with men rushing about at the speed they kept up on the killing-beds, and all with butcher-knives, like razors, in their hands—well, it was to be counted as a wonder that there were not more men slaughtered than cattle.

And yet all this inconvenience they might have put up with, if only it had not been for one thing—if only there had been some place where they might eat. Jurgis had either to eat his dinner amid the stench in which he had worked, or else to rush, as did all his companions, to any one of the hundreds of liquor stores which stretched out their arms to him. To the west of the yards ran Ashland Avenue, and here was an unbroken line of saloons—"Whiskey Row," they called it; to the north was Forty-seventh Street, where there were half a dozen to the block, and at the angle of the two was "Whiskey Point," a space of fifteen or twenty acres, and containing one glue-factory and about two hundred saloons.

One might walk among these and take his choice: "Hot pea-soup and boiled cabbage to-day." "Sauerkraut and hot frankfurters. Walk in." "Bean-soup and stewed lamb. Welcome." All of these things were printed in many languages, as were also the names of the resorts, which were infinite in their variety and appeal. There was the "Home Circle" and the "Cosey Corner"; there were "Firesides" and "Hearthstones" and "Pleasure Palaces" and "Wonderlands" and "Dream Castles" and "Love's Delights." Whatever else they were called, they were sure to be called "Union Headquarters," and to hold out a welcome to workingmen; and there was always a warm stove, and a chair near it, and some friends to laugh and talk with. There was only one condition attached,—you must drink. If you went in not intending to drink, you would be put out in no time, and if you were slow about going, like as not you would get your head split open with a beer-bottle in the bargain. But all of the men understood the convention and drank; they believed that by it they were getting something for nothing—for they did not need to take more than one drink, and upon the strength of it they might fill themselves up with a good hot dinner. This did not always work out in practice, however, for there was pretty sure to be a friend who would treat you, and then you would have to treat him.

Then some one else would come in—and, anyhow, a few drinks were good for a man who worked hard. As he went back he did not shiver so, he had more courage for his task; the deadly brutalizing monotony of it did not afflict him so,—he had ideas while he worked, and took a more cheerful view of his circumstances. On the way home, however, the shivering was apt to come on him again; and so he would have to stop once or twice to warm up against the cruel cold. As there were hot things to eat in this saloon too, he might get home late to his supper, or he might not get home at all. And then his wife might set out to look for him, and she too would feel the cold; and perhaps she would have some of the children with her—and so a whole family would drift into drinking, as the current of a river drifts down-stream. As if to complete the chain, the packers all paid their men in checks, refusing all requests to pay in coin; and where in Packingtown could a man go to have his check cashed but to a saloon, where he could pay for the favor by spending a part of the money?

From all of these things Jurgis was saved because of Ona. He never would take but the one drink at noontime; and so he got the reputation of being a surly fellow, and was not quite welcome at the saloons, and had to drift about from one to another. Then at night he would go straight home, helping Ona and Stanislovas, or often putting the former on a car. And when he got home perhaps he would have to trudge several blocks, and come staggering back through the snowdrifts with a bag of coal upon his shoulder. Home was not a very attractive place—at least not this winter. They had only been able to buy one stove, and this was a small one, and proved not big enough to warm even the kitchen in the bitterest weather. This made it hard for Teta Elzbieta all day, and for the children when they could not get to school. At night they would sit huddled round this stove, while they ate their supper off their laps; and then Jurgis and Jonas would smoke a pipe, after which they would all crawl into their beds to get warm, after putting out the fire to save the coal. Then they would have some frightful experiences with the cold. They would sleep with all their clothes on, including their overcoats, and put over them all the bedding and spare clothing they owned; the children would sleep all crowded into one bed, and yet even so they could not keep warm. The outside ones would be shivering and sobbing, crawling over the others and trying to get down into the centre, and causing a fight. This old house with the leaky weather-boards was a very different thing from their cabins at home, with great thick walls plastered inside and outside with mud; and the cold which came upon them was a living thing, a demon-presence in the room. They would waken in the midnight hours, when everything was black; perhaps they would hear it yelling outside, or perhaps there would be deathlike stillness—and that would be worse yet. They could feel the cold as it crept in through the cracks, reaching out for them with its icy, death-dealing fingers; and they would crouch and cower, and try to hide from it, all in vain. It would come, and it would come; a grisly thing, a spectre born in the black caverns of terror; a power primeval, cosmic, shadowing the tortures of the lost souls flung out to chaos and destruction. It was cruel, iron-hard; and hour after hour they would cringe in its grasp, alone, alone. There would be no one to hear them if they cried out; there would be no help, no mercy. And so on until morning—when they would go out to another day of toil, a little weaker, a little nearer to the time when it would be their turn to be shaken from the tree.

Source: Upton Sinclair, *The Jungle* (New York: Doubleday, Page, 1906), 72–86.

1906 • 103 • Pure Food and Drug Act

Introduction: *Since the Civil War, magazine writers and citizen groups expressed concern about food safety in America. State legislatures, such as those in Illinois, New York, and New Jersey, passed pure food laws beginning in 1874, but the laws were difficult to enforce. Pure food bills were introduced into Congress every year beginning in 1879, but they failed to pass. Opposition came from agricultural interests, food processors, and political conservatives opposed to governmental interference in the marketplace. Upton Sinclair's book* The Jungle *(1906) (see Document 102) raised such a public outcry about food safety that Congress passed the Pure Food and Drug Act. The act established a regulatory body to set and enforce safety standards for thousands of different foods to prevent their adulteration or mislabeling and also mandated truth in labeling. Despite flaws, this law did establish that the federal government was responsible for abuses perpetrated by businesses. This legislation improved the safety of the nation's food supply, and Americans became more confident that processed foods were safe. These legislative acts boosted sales of processed food and the profitability of large food companies, which could more easily comply with the legislation's requirements, and many small companies went out of business.*

An Act for preventing the manufacture, sale, or transportation of adulterated or misbranded or poisonous or deleterious foods, drugs, medicines, and liquors, and for regulating traffic therein, and for other purposes.

Be it enacted by the Senate and House of Representatives of the United States of America in Congress assembled, That it shall be unlawful for any person to manufacture within any Territory or the District of Columbia any article of food or drug which is adulterated or misbranded, within the meaning of this Act; and any person who shall violate any of the provisions of this section shall be guilty of a misdemeanor, and for each offense shall, upon conviction thereof, be fined not to exceed five hundred dollars, or shall be sentenced to one year's imprisonment, for each subsequent offense and conviction thereof shall be fined not less than one thousand dollars or sentenced to one year's imprisonment, or both such fine and imprisonment, in the discretion of the court.

Section 2. That the introduction into any State or Territory or the District of Columbia from any other State or Territory or the District of Columbia, from any other State or Territory or the District of Columbia, or form any foreign country, or shipment to any foreign country of any article of food or drugs which is adulterated or misbranded, within the meaning of this Act, is hereby prohibited; and any person who shall ship or deliver for shipment from any State or Territory or the District of Columbia to any other State or Territory or the District of Columbia, or to a foreign country, or who shall receive in any State or Territory or the District of Columbia, or foreign country, and having so received, shall deliver, in original unbroken packages, for pay or otherwise, or offer to deliver to any other person, any such article so adulterated or misbranded within the meaning of this Act, or any person who shall sell or offer for sale in the District of Columbia or the Territories of the United States any such adulterated or misbranded foods or drugs, or export or offer to export the same to any foreign country, shall be guilty of a misdemeanor, and for such offense be fined not exceeding two hundred dollars for the first offense, and upon conviction for each subsequent offense not exceeding three hundred dollars or be imprisoned not exceeding one year, or both, in the discretion of the court: Provided, That no article shall be deemed misbranded or adulterated within the provisions of this Act when intended for export to any foreign country and prepared or packed according to the specifications or directions of the foreign purchaser when no substance is used in the preparation or packing thereof in conflict with the laws of the foreign country to which said article is intended to be shipped; but if said article shall be in fact sold or offered for sale for domestic use or consumption, then this proviso shall not exempt said article from the operation of any of the other provisions of this Act.

Section 3. That the Secretary of the Treasury, the Secretary of Agriculture, and the Secretary of Commerce and Labor shall make uniform rules and regulations for carrying out the provisions of this Act, including the collection and examination of specimens of foods and drugs manufactured or offered for sale in the District of Columbia, or in any Territory of the United States, or which shall be offered for sale in unbroken packages in any State other than that in which they shall have been respectively manufactured or produced, or which shall be received from any foreign country, or intended for shipment to any foreign country, which may be submitted for examination by the chief health, food, or drug officer of any State, Territory, or the District of Columbia, or at any domestic or foreign port through which such product is offered for interstate commerce, or for export or import between the United States and any foreign port or country.

Section 4. That the examinations of specimens of foods and drugs shall be made in the Bureau of chemistry of the Department of Agriculture, or under the direction and supervision of such Bureau, for the purpose of determining from such examinations whether such articles are adulterated or misbranded within the meaning of this Act; and if it shall appear from any such examination that any of such specimens is adulterated or misbranded within the meaning of this act, the Secretary of Agriculture shall cause notice thereof to be given to the party from whom such sample was obtained. Any party so notified shall be given an opportunity to be heard, under such rules and regulations as may be prescribed as aforesaid, and if it appears that any of the provisions of this act have been violated by such party, then the Secretary of Agriculture shall at once certify the facts to the proper United States district attorney, with a copy of the results of the analysis or the examination of such article duly authenticated by the analyst or officer making such examination, under the oath of such officer. After judgment of the court, notice shall be given by publication in such manner as may be prescribed by the rules and regulations aforesaid.

Section 5. That it shall be the duty of each district attorney to whom the Secretary of Agriculture shall report any violation of this Act, or to whom any health or food or drug officer or agent of any State, Territory, or the District of Columbia shall present satisfactory evidence of any such violation, to cause appropriate proceedings to be commenced and prosecuted in the proper courts of the United States, without delay, for the enforcement of the penalties as in such case herein provided.

Section 6. That the term "drug," as used in this Act, shall include all medicines and preparations recognized in the United States Pharmacopoeia or National Formulary for internal or external use, and any substance or mixture of substances intended to be used for the cure, mitigation, or prevention of disease of either man or other animals. The term "food," as used herein, shall include all articles used for food, drink, confectionery, or condiment by man or other animals, whether simple, mixed, or compound.

Section 7. That for the purposes of this Act an article shall be deemed to be adulterated: . . .

In the case of confectionery:

If it contains terra alba, barites, talc, chrome yellow, or other mineral substance or poisonous color or flavor, or other ingredient deleterious or detrimental to health, or any vinous, malt or spirituous liquor or compound or narcotic drug.

In the case of food:

First. If any substance has been mixed and packed with it so as to reduce or lower or injuriously affect its quality or strength.

Second. If any substance has been substituted wholly or in part for the article.

Third. If any valuable constituent of the article has been wholly or in part abstracted.

Fourth. If it be mixed, colored powdered, coated, or stained in a manner whereby damage or inferiority is concealed.

Fifth. If it contain any added poisonous or other added deleterious ingredient which may render such article injurious to health: Provided, That when in the preparation of food products for shipment they are preserved by any external application applied in such manner that the preservative is necessarily removed mechanically, or by maceration in water, or otherwise, and directions for the removal of said preservative shall be printed on the covering or the package, the provisions of this act shall be construed as applying only when said products are ready for consumption.

Sixth. If it consists in whole or in part of a filthy, decomposed, or putrid animal or vegetable substance, or any portion of an animal unfit for food, whether manufactured or not, or if it is the product of a diseased animal, or one that has died otherwise than by slaughter.

Section 8. That the term "misbranded," as used herein, shall apply to all drugs, or articles of food, or articles which enter into the composition of food, the package or label of which shall bear any statement, design, or device regarding such article, or the ingredients or substances contained therein which shall be false or misleading in any particular, and to any food or drug product which is falsely branded as the State, territory, or country in which it is manufactured or produced.

That for the purposes of this Act an article shall also be deemed to be misbranded:

Provided, That an article of food which does not contain any added poisonous or deleterious ingredients shall not be deemed to be adulterated or misbranded in the following cases:

First. In the case of mixtures or compounds which may be now or from time to time hereafter known as articles of food, under their own distinctive names, and not an imitation of or offered for sale under the distinctive name of another article, if the name be accompanied on the same label or brand with a statement of the place where said article has been manufactured or produced.

Second. In the case of articles labeled, branded, or tagged so as to plainly indicate that they are compounds, imitations, or blends, and the word "compound," "imitation," or "blend," as the case may be is plainly stated on the package in which it is offered for sale: Provided, That the term blend as used herein shall be construed to mean a mixture of like substances, not excluding harmless coloring or flavoring ingredients used for the purpose of coloring and flavoring only: And provided further, That nothing in this Act shall be construed as requiring or compelling proprietors or manufacturers of proprietary foods which contain no unwholesome added ingredients to disclose their trade formulas, except in so far as the provisions of this Act may require to secure freedom from adulteration or misbranding.

Section 9. That no dealer shall be prosecuted under the provisions of this Act when he can establish a guaranty signed by the wholesaler, jobber, manufacturer, or other party residing in the united States, from whom he purchases such articles to the effect that the same is not adulterated or misbranded within the meaning of this Act, designating it.

Said guaranty, to afford protection, shall contain the name and address of the party or parties making the sale of such articles to such dealer, and such case said party or parties shall be amenable to the prosecutions, fines, and other penalties which would attach, in due course, to the dealer under the provisions of this Act.

Section 10. That any article of food, drug, or liquor that is adulterated or misbranded within the meaning of this Act, and is being transported from one State, Territory, District, or insular possession to another for sale, or, having been transported, remains unloaded, unsold, or in original unbroken packages, or if it be sold or offered for sale in the District of Columbia or the Territories, or insular possessions of the United States, or if it be imported from a foreign country for sale, or if it is intended for export to a foreign country shall be liable to be proceeded against in any district court of the United States within the district where the same is found, and seized for confiscation by a process of libel for condemnation. And if such article is condemned as being adulterated or misbranded, or of a poisonous or deleterious character, within the meaning of this Act, the same shall be disposed of by destruction or sale, as the said court may direct, and the proceeds thereof, if sold, less the legal costs and charges shall be paid into the Treasury of the United States, but such goods shall not be sold in any jurisdiction contrary to the provisions of this Act or the laws of that jurisdiction: Provided, however, That upon the payment of the costs of such libel proceedings and the execution and delivery of a good and sufficient bond to the effect that such articles shall not be sold or otherwise disposed of contrary to the provisions of this Act, or the laws of any State, Territory, District, or insular possession, the court may by order direct that such articles be delivered to the owner thereof. The proceedings of such libel cases shall conform, as near as may be, to the proceedings in admiralty, except that either party may demand trial by jury of any issue of fact joined in any such case, and all such proceedings shall be at the suit of and in the name of the United States.

Section 11. The Secretary of the Treasury shall deliver to the Secretary of Agriculture, upon his request from time to time, samples of foods and drugs which are being imported into the United States or offered for import, giving notice thereof to the owner or consignee, who may appear before the Secretary of Agriculture, and have the right to introduce testimony, and if it appear from the examination of such samples that any article of food or drug offered to be imported into the United States is adulterated or misbranded within the meaning of this Act, or is otherwise dangerous to the health of the people of the United States, or is of a kind forbidden entry into, or forbidden to be sold or restricted in sale in the country in which it is made or from which it is exported, or is otherwise falsely labeled in any respect, the said article shall be refused admission, and the Secretary of the Treasury shall refuse delivery to the consignee and shall cause the destruction of any goods refused delivery which shall not be exported by the consignee within three months from the date of notice of such refusal under such regulations as the Secretary of the Treasury may prescribe: Provided, That the Secretary of the

Treasury may deliver to the consignee such goods pending examination and decision in the matter on execution of a penal bond for the amount of the full invoice value of such goods, together with the duty thereon, and on refusal to return such goods for any cause to the custody of the Secretary of the Treasury, when demanded, for the purpose of excluding them from the country, or for any other purpose, said consignee shall forfeit the full amount of the bond: And provided further, That all charges for storage, cartage, and labor on goods which are refused admission or delivery shall be paid by the owner or consignee, and in default of such payment shall constitute a lien against any future importation made by such owner or consignee.

Section 12. That the term "Territory" as used in this Act shall include the insular possessions of the United States. The word "person" as used in this Act shall be construed to import both the plural and the singular, as the case demands, and shall include corporations, companies, societies and associations. When construing and enforcing the provisions of this Act, the act, omission, or failure of any officer, agent, or other person acting for or employed by any corporation, company, society, or association, within the scope of his employment or office, shall in every case be also deemed to be the act, omission, or failure of such corporation, company, society, or association as well as that of the person.

Section 13. That this Act shall be in force and effect from and after the first day of January, nineteen hundred and seven. Approved, June 30, 1906

Source: "Federal Food and Drugs Act of 1906," *U.S. Statutes at Large* 34 (1906): 768.

1906 • 104 • Meat Inspection Act

Introduction: *The Meat Inspection Act empowered the U.S. Department of Agriculture (USDA) to inspect animals before and after slaughter, to be present when diseased animals were destroyed, and to inspect processed products for dangerous chemicals, preservatives, and dyes. In addition, no meat that had not been inspected could be shipped across state lines. The USDA was responsible for setting sanitation standards. The Meat Inspection Act benefitted meatpackers, who could more easily meet the standards set down, and the law convinced many Americans that commercial meat was safe. The act was a direct result of public outcry about the horrifying conditions that Upton Sinclair's novel* The Jungle *described in the meatpacking industry in Chicago (see Document 102).*

That for the purpose of preventing the use in interstate or foreign commerce, as hereinafter provided, of meat and meat food products which are unsound, unhealthful, unwholesome, or otherwise unfit for human food, the Secretary of Agriculture, at his discretion, may cause to be made, by inspectors appointed for that purpose, an examination and inspection of all cattle, sheep, swine, and goats before they shall be allowed to enter into any slaughtering, packing, meat-canning, rendering, or similar establishment, in which they are to be slaughtered and the meat and meat food products thereof are to be used in interstate or foreign commerce; and all cattle, swine, sheep, and goats found on such inspection to show symptoms of disease shall be set apart and slaughtered

Meat inspectors at the Swift & Company packing house in Chicago, ca. 1906. (Library of Congress)

separately from all other cattle, sheep, swine, or goats, and when so slaughtered the carcasses of said cattle, sheep, swine, or goats shall be subject to a careful examination and inspection, all as provided by the rules and regulations to be prescribed by the Secretary of Agriculture as herein provided for.

That for the purposes hereinbefore set forth the Secretary of Agriculture shall cause to be made by inspectors appointed for that purpose, as hereinafter provided, a post-mortem examination and inspection of the carcasses and parts thereof of all cattle, sheep, swine, and goats to be prepared for human consumption at any slaughtering, meat-canning, salting, packing, rendering, or similar establishment in any State, Territory, or the District of Columbia for transportation or sale as articles of interstate or foreign commerce; and the carcasses parts thereof of all such animals found to be sound, healthful, wholesome, and fit for human food shall be marked, stamped, tagged, or labeled as "Inspected and passed;" and said inspectors shall label, mark, stamp, or tag as "Inspected and condemned", all carcasses and parts thereof of animals found to be unsound, unhealthful, unwholesome, or otherwise unfit for human food; and all carcasses and parts there of thus inspected and condemned shall be destroyed for food purposes by the said establishment in the presence of an inspector, and the Secretary of Agriculture may remove inspectors from any such establishment which fails to so destroy any such condemned carcass or part thereof, and said inspectors, after said first inspection shall, when they deem it necessary, reinspect said carcasses or parts thereof to determine whether since the first inspection the same have become unsound, unhealthful, unwholesome, or in any way unfit for human food, and if any carcass or any part thereof shall, upon examination and inspection subsequent to the first examination and inspection, be found to be unsound, unhealthful, unwholesome, or otherwise unfit for human food, it shall be destroyed for food purposes by the said establishment in the presence of an inspector, and the Secretary of Agriculture may remove inspectors from any establishment which fails to so destroy any such condemned carcass or part thereof.

The foregoing provisions shall apply to all carcasses or parts of carcasses of cattle, sheep, swine, and goats, or the meat or meat products thereof which may be brought into any slaughtering, meat-canning, salting, packing, rendering, or similar establishment, and such examination and inspection shall be had before the said carcasses or parts thereof shall be allowed to enter into any department wherein the same are to be treated and prepared for meat food products; and the foregoing provisions shall also apply to all such products which, having been issued from any slaughtering, meat-canning, salting, packing, rendering, or similar establishment, shall be returned to the same or to any similar establishment where such inspection is maintained.

That for the purposes hereinbefore set forth the Secretary of Agriculture shall cause to be made by inspectors appointed for that purpose an examination and inspection of all meat food products prepared for interstate or foreign commerce in any slaughtering, meat-canning, salting, packing, rendering, or similar establishment, and for the purposes of any examination and inspection said inspectors shall have access at all times, by day or night, whether the establishment be operated or not, to every part of said establishment; and said inspectors shall mark, stamp, tag, or label as "Inspected and passed" all such products found to be sound, healthful, and wholesome, and which contain no dyes, chemicals, preservatives, or ingredients which render such meat or meat food products unsound, unhealthful, unwholesome, or unfit for human food; and said inspectors shall label, mark, stamp, or tag as "Inspected and condemned" all such products found unsound, unhealthful, and unwholesome, or which contain dyes, chemicals, preservatives, or ingredients which render such meat or meat food products unsound, unhealthful, unwholesome, or unfit for human food, and all such condemned meat food products shall be destroyed for food purposes, as hereinbefore provided, and the Secretary of Agriculture may remove inspectors from any establishment which fails to so destroy such condemned meat food products: Provided, That, subject to the rules and regulations of the Secretary of Agriculture, the provisions hereof in regard to preservatives shall not apply to meat food products for export to any foreign country and which are prepared or packed according to the specifications or directions of the foreign purchaser, when no substance is used in the preparation or packing thereof in conflict with the laws of the foreign country to which said article is to be exported; but if said article shall be in fact sold or offered for sale for domestic use or consumption then this proviso shall not exempt said article from the operation of all the other provisions of this Act.

That when any meat or meat food product prepared for interstate foreign commerce which has been inspected as hereinbefore provided and marked "Inspected and passed" shall be placed or packed in any can, pot, tin, canvas, or other receptacle or covering in any establishment where inspection under the provisions of this Act is maintained, the person, firm, or corporation preparing said product shall cause a label to be attached to said can, pot, tin, canvas, or other receptacle or covering, under the supervision of an inspector, which label shall state that the contents thereof have been "inspected and passed" under the provisions of this Act; and no inspection and examination of meat or meat food products deposited or inclosed in cans, tins, pots, canvas, or other receptacle or covering in any establishment where inspection under the provisions of this Act is maintained shall be deemed to be complete until such meat or meat food products have been sealed or inclosed in said can, tin, pot, canvas, or other receptacle or covering under the supervision of an inspector, and no such meat or meat food products shall be sold or offered for sale by any person, firm, or corporation in interstate or foreign commerce under any false or deceptive name; but established trade name or names which are usual to such products and which are not false and deceptive and which shall be approved by the Secretary of Agriculture are permitted.

The Secretary of Agriculture shall cause to be made, by experts in sanitation or by other competent inspectors, such inspection of all slaughtering, meat canning, salting, packing, rendering, or similar establishments in which cattle, sheep, swine, and goats are slaughtered and the meat ands meat food products thereof are prepared for interstate or foreign commerce as may be necessary to inform himself concerning the sanitary conditions of the same, and to prescribe the rules and regulations of sanitation under which such establishments shall be maintained; and where the sanitary conditions of any such establishment are such that the meat or meat food products are rendered sanitary unclean, unsound, unhealthful, unwholesome, or otherwise unfit for human food, he shall refuse to allow said meat or meat food products to be labeled, marked, stamped, or tagged as "inspected and passed."

That the Secretary of Agriculture shall cause an examination and inspection of all cattle, sheep, swine, and goats, and the food products thereof, slaughtered and prepared in the establishments hereinbefore described for the purposes of interstate or foreign commerce to be made during the nighttime as well as during the daytime when the slaughtering of said cattle, sheep, swine, and goats, or the preparation of said food products is conducted during the nighttime.

That on and after October first, nineteen hundred and six, no person, firm, or corporation shall transport or offer for transportation, and no carrier of interstate or foreign commerce shall transport or receive for transportation from one State or Territory or the District of Columbia to any other State or Territory or the District of Columbia, or to any place under the jurisdiction of the United States, or to any foreign country, any carcasses or parts thereof, meat, or meat food products thereof which have not been inspected, examined, and marked as "inspected and passed," in accordance with the terms of this Act and with the rules and regulations prescribed by the Secretary of Agriculture: Provided, That all meat and meat food products on hand on October first, nineteen hundred and six, at establishments where inspection has not been maintained, or which have been inspected under existing law, shall be examined and labeled under such rules and regulations as the Secretary of Agriculture shall prescribe, and then shall be allowed to be sold in interstate or foreign commerce.

That no person, firm, or corporation, or officer, agent, or employee thereof, shall forge, counterfeit, simulate, or falsely represent, or shall without proper authority use, fail to use, or detach, or shall knowingly or wrongfully alter, deface, or destroy, or fail to deface or destroy, any of the marks, stamps, tags, labels, or other identification devices provided for in this Act, or in and as directed by the rules and regulations prescribed hereunder by the Secretary of Agriculture, on any carcasses, parts of carcasses, or the food product, or containers thereof, subject to the provisions of this Act, or any certificate in relation thereto, authorized or required by this Act or by the said rules and regulations of the Secretary of Agriculture.

That the Secretary of Agriculture shall cause to be made a careful inspection of all cattle, sheep, swine, and goats intended and offered for export to foreign countries at such times and places, and in such manner as he may deem proper, to ascertain whether such cattle, sheep, swine, and goats are free from disease.

And for this purpose he may appoint inspectors who shall be authorized to give an official certificate clearly stating the condition in which such cattle, sheep, swine, and goats are found.

And no clearance shall be given to any vessel having on board cattle, sheep, swine, or goats for export to a foreign country until the owner or shipper of such cattle, sheep, swine, or goats has a certificate from the inspector herein authorized to be appointed, stating that the said cattle, sheep, swine, or goats are sound and healthy, or unless the Secretary of Agriculture shall have waived the requirement of such certificate for export to the particular country to which such cattle, sheep, swine, or goats are to be exported.

That the Secretary of Agriculture shall also cause to be made a careful inspection of the carcasses and parts thereof of all cattle, sheep, swine, and goats, the meat of which, fresh, salted, canned, corned, packed, cured, or otherwise prepared, is intended and offered for export to any foreign country, at such times and places and in such manner as he may deem proper.

And for this purpose he may appoint inspectors who shall be authorized to give an official certificate stating the condition in which said cattle, sheep, swine, or goats, and the meat thereof, are found.

And no clearance shall be given to any vessel having on board any fresh, salted, canned, corned, or packed beef, mutton, pork, or goat meat, being the meat of animals killed after the passage of this Act, or except as hereinbefore provided for export to and sale in a foreign country from any port in the United States, until the owner or shipper thereof shall obtain from an inspector appointed under the provisions of this Act a certificate that the said cattle, sheep, swine, and goats were sound and healthy at the time of inspection, and that their meat is sound and wholesome, unless the Secretary of Agriculture shall have waived the requirements of such certificate for the country to which said cattle, sheep, swine, and goats or meats are to be exported.

That the inspectors provided for herein shall be authorized to give official certificates of the sound and wholesome condition of the cattle, sheep, swine, and goats, their carcasses and products as herein described, and one copy of every certificate granted under the provisions of this Act shall be filed in the Department of Agriculture, another copy shall be delivered to the owner or shipper, and when the cattle, sheep, swine, and goats or their carcasses and products are sent abroad, a third copy shall be delivered to the chief officer of the vessel on which the shipment shall be made.

That no person, firm, or corporation engaged in the interstate commerce of meat or meat food products shall transport or offer for transportation, sell or offer to sell any such meat or meat food products in any State or Territory or in the District of Columbia or any place under the jurisdiction of the United States, other than in the State or Territory or in the District of Columbia or any place under the jurisdiction of the United States in which the slaughtering, packing, canning, rendering, or other similar establishment owned, leased, operated by said firm, person, or corporation is located unless and until said person, firm, or corporation shall have complied with all of the provisions of this Act.

That any person, firm, or corporation, or any officer or agent of any such person, firm, or corporation, who shall violate any of the provisions of this Act shall be deemed guilty of a misdemeanor and shall be punished on conviction thereof by a fine of not exceeding ten thousand dollars or imprisonment for a period not more than two years, or by both such fine and imprisonment, in the discretion of the court.

That the Secretary of Agriculture shall appoint from time to time inspectors to make examination and inspection of all cattle, sheep, swine, and goats, the inspection of which is hereby provided for, and of all carcasses and parts thereof, and of all meats and meat food products thereof, and of the sanitary conditions of all establishments in which such meat and meat food products hereinbefore described are prepared; and said inspectors shall refuse to stamp, mark, tag, or label any carcass or any part thereof, or meat food product therefrom, prepared in any establishment hereinbefore mentioned, until the same shall have actually been inspected and found to be sound, healthful, wholesome, and fit for human food, and to contain no dyes, chemicals, preservatives, or ingredients which render such meat food product unsound, unhealthful, unwholesome, or unfit for human food; and to have been prepared under proper sanitary conditions, hereinbefore provided for; and shall perform such other duties as are provided by this Act and by the rules and regulations to be prescribed by said Secretary of Agriculture; and said Secretary of Agriculture shall, from time to time, make such rules and regulations as are necessary for the efficient execution of the provisions of this Act, and all inspections and examinations made under this Act shall be such and made in such manner as described in the rules and regulations prescribed by said Secretary of Agriculture not inconsistent with the provisions of this Act.

That any person, firm, or corporation, or any agent or employee of any person, firm or corporation who shall give, pay, or offer, directly or indirectly, to any inspector, deputy inspector, chief inspector, or any other officer or employee of the United States authorized to perform any of the duties prescribed by this Act or by the rules and regulations of the Secretary of Agriculture any money or other thing of value, with intent to influence said inspector, deputy inspector, chief inspector, or other officer or employee of the United States in the discharge of any duty herein provided for, shall be deemed guilty of a felony and, upon conviction thereof, shall be punished by a fine not less than five thousand dollars nor more than ten thousand dollars and by imprisonment not less than one year nor more than three years; and any inspector, deputy inspector, chief inspector, or other employee of the United States authorized to perform any of the duties prescribed by this Act who shall accept any money, gift, or other thing of value from any person, firm, or corporation, or officers, agents, or employees thereof, given with intent to influence his official action, or who shall receive or accept from any person, firm, or corporation engaged in interstate or foreign commerce any gift, money, or other thing of value given with any purpose or intent whatsoever, shall be deemed guilty of a felony and shall, upon conviction thereof, be summarily discharged from office and shall be punished by a fine not less than one thousand dollars nor more than ten thousand dollars and by imprisonment not less than one year nor more than three years.

That the provisions of this Act requiring inspection to be made by the Secretary of Agriculture shall not apply to animals slaughtered by any farmer on the farm and sold and transported as interstate or foreign commerce, nor to retail butchers and retail dealers in meat and meat food products, supplying their customers: Provided, That if any person shall sell or offer for sale or transportation for interstate or foreign commerce any meat or meat food products which are diseased, unsound, unhealthful, unwholesome, or otherwise unfit for human food, knowing that such meat food products are intended for human consumption, he shall be guilty of a misdemeanor, and on conviction thereof shall be punished by a fine not exceeding one thousand dollars or by imprisonment for a period of not exceeding one year, or by both such fine and imprisonment: Provided also, That the Secretary of Agriculture is authorized to maintain the inspection in this Act provided for at any slaughtering, meat canning, salting, packing, rendering, or similar establishment notwithstanding this exception, and that the persons operating the same may be retail butchers and retail dealers or farmers; and where the Secretary of Agriculture shall establish such inspection then the provisions of this Act shall apply notwithstanding this exception.

That there is permanently appropriated, out of any money in the Treasury not otherwise appropriated, the sum of three million dollars, for the expenses of the inspection of cattle, sheep, swine, and goats and the meat and meat food products thereof which enter into interstate or foreign commerce and for all expenses necessary to carry into effect the provisions of this Act relating to meat inspection, including rent and the employment of labor in Washington and elsewhere, for each year. And the Secretary of Agriculture shall, in his annual estimates made to Congress, submit a statement in detail, showing the number of persons employed in such inspections and the salary or per diem paid to each, together with the contingent expenses of such inspectors and where they have been and are employed.

Source: Meat Inspection Act, *United States Statutes at Large,* 59th Cong., Sess. 1, Chap. 3913, pp. 674–679.

1910 • 105 • "C. W. Post, Faker"

Introduction: *In January 1898 Charles W. Post, a former patient at John Harvey Kellogg's Battle Creek Sanitarium, began marketing Grape-Nuts, made from wheat and malted barley, which served to sweeten the cereal. Grape-Nuts was a variation on James Caleb Jackson's Granula and Kellogg's Granola, made by the same method. Post's advertisements touted Grape-Nuts as a "scientific health food" containing "vitalizing" elements, and health food advocates promptly endorsed it. Specifically, advertisements avowed that Grape-Nuts cured a wide range of illnesses—rickets, malaria, rheumatism, brain problems, heart disease, consumption, and appendicitis, to name but a few. In 1905* Collier's *magazine refused to advertise Grape-Nuts and launched a series of articles and op-ed pieces about the medical claims made by Post for his cereal. Post retaliated by claiming that the magazine published "mendacious falsehoods" and many other such statements.* Collier's *sued Post for libel. After extensive testimony, the court sided with* Collier's *and awarded the magazine $50,000. Below is an article published in* Collier's *that described the trial and the verdict.*

C. W. Post, Faker

The libel suit of Robert J. Collier against the Postum Company, Ltd., of Battle Creek, Michigan, resulted, after a long and thorough trial, in a verdict for *Collier's* and an award of damages in the unprecedented sum of $50,000. The offense was the publication, in forty-four newspapers and periodicals of New York State, of an advertisement charging us with soliciting advertising by methods akin to blackmail. This important victory over the forces of fraud, this exceptional award—the heaviest ever given for libel in New York and probably in the United States—will be news to many. For notwithstanding the importance of the case, the newspapers were generally silent or very taciturn. The Postum Company spends about a million dollars a year in advertising. Moreover, on the day after the trial closed, C. W. Post, head faker of the company, began a series of advertisements which garbled the testimony of *Collier's* medical experts to make it appear that they had endorsed the virtues of Grape-Nuts, and said nothing about the outcome of the trial—nay, gave the impression that Post had won.

Libel suits always wander from the strict cause at issue, involving the past reputations of both parties. This one exposed the career of C. W. Post, and it showed the real character of his widely advertised products. But before we go into that, it will be necessary, in order to correct the impression produced by the latest Post advertisements, to review the vital facts of the case.

In 1905 *Collier's* began the publication of Samuel Hopkins Adams's articles, "The Great American Fraud," that startling expose of patent medicines, quackery, and quack methods of advertising which bore fruit in the Pure Food and Drugs Act of 1906. *Collier's,* like every other periodical in the United States, had published in its early years advertising open to criticism on modern standards. When the Adams data began to come in, we saw the light. We announced a new business policy—exclusion of all misleading and unfair advertising. That was merely the new policy which nearly all the magazines have now adopted, and to which all reputable newspapers must come in the end.

On November 4, 1905, the announcement of this policy was printed in *Collier's* in the following words:

"Collier's will accept no advertisements of beer, whiskey, or alcoholic liquors; no advertisements of patent medicines; no medical advertisements or advertisements making claims to medicinal effect; no investment advertising promising extraordinary returns, such as stocks in mining, oil, and rubber companies. The editor reserves the right to exclude any advertisement which he considers extravagant in claim, or offensive to good taste." By a freak of the demon who torments printing offices, the announcement appeared next to a testimonial advertisement for Postum. This was very mild and harmless compared with matter which Post has printed since, but it did "lay claim to medicinal effect." A correspondent called our attention to this inconsistency.

Post's Advertising Refused

Forthwith, that advertising was ruled out of *Collier's.* Conde Nast, then advertising manager, wrote to the Grandin Company of Battle Creek, the advertising agency which had placed this copy, advising them of the fact. The Grandin Company was really only an annex to the Postum Cereal Company, formed to secure the agent's commission on all of their advertising. But at this time it was posing as an independent agency. In its advertisements it announced that "among other clients" it had the Postum Cereal Company. Mr. Nast made his refusal tactful. Such matter did not harmonize with *Collier's* editorial policy regarding patent medicines. If the Postum Company would replace this testimonial matter by its regular display advertising (which made at that time no medicinal claims), *Collier's* would be glad to accept it. Post, in an indignant letter, refused to make the change. "I do not state that your present advertising makes claims of medicinal ingredients," responded Mr. Nast, "but what conflicts with our advertising policy is that the advertising makes claims of medical effects." Thereupon, *Collier's* and the Postum Company broke off all business relations.

Note carefully the next stage in the proceedings. It constitutes the only shred of an answer which the Postum Company could offer in the subsequent libel proceedings. From time to time, *Collier's,* like most other publications, sends circulars to the great advertisers and the great advertising agencies. On the mailing list of five thousand names *Collier's* retained the Grandin Agency, though it struck off Postum. For the Grandin Company was still posing as a general agency, and announcing by implication that it had other clients than the Postum Company. In the next year or so, the Grandin Agency received from *Collier's* two circulars, calling attention to special numbers of *Collier's.*

After the publication of his articles on medical frauds, Samuel Hopkins Adams wrote for *Collier's* a series of editorials on the same subject. The Postum Company, in the mean time, had grown bolder and bolder in its published insinuations that Postum, a coffee substitute, had medicinal virtues; and it had begun to state that a diet of Grape-Nuts would ward off impending attacks of appendicitis. Adams noticed this; in the issue of July 27, 1907, *Collier's* published one of his editorials, written without consultation with any employee of *Collier's*—written solely on his own judgment and initiative—which contained this passage: "Take certain recent exploitations of 'Grape-Nuts' and its fellow article 'Postum,' put out by the same concern. One widely circulated paragraph labors to produce the impression that 'Grape-Nuts' will obviate the necessity of an operation in appendicitis. This is lying, and, potentially, deadly lying. Similarly, 'Postum' continually makes reference to the endorsements of 'a distinguished physician' or 'a prominent health official,' persons as mythical, doubtless, as they are mysterious." True, all of it, and rather mild, considering the facts.

C. W. Post, founder, dictator, and advertising expert of the Postum Company, was in Europe at the time. It was five weeks before he replied. Then appeared an advertisement signed by the company. It was headed: "The 'Yell-Oh' Man and One of His Ways." There is not room to publish all his abuse. We merely cull from it the phrases "mendacious falsehoods," "poor clown," "venom behind it." The damaging thing was the charge that *Collier's* had attacked him because he refused to advertise—in short, that we had attempted blackmail. "When a journal wilfully prostitutes its columns," he wrote, "to try and harm a reputable manufacturer in an effort to force him to advertise, it is time the public knew the facts. The owner or editor of *Collier's* Weekly cannot force money from us by such methods." Incidentally, he repeated the dangerous statement which justified the Adams editorial:

"It is a practical certainty that when a man has approaching symptoms of appendicitis, the attack can be avoided by discontinuing all food except Grape-Nuts and by properly washing out the intestines."

He published this advertisement as widely as the American press circulates. In New York State alone it appeared in forty-four city and small city newspapers. Robert J. Collier immediately sued him in the sum of $250,000 for libel. Post responded by publishing another advertisement, entitled "'Boo-Hoo'—Shouts a Spanked Baby." This reiterated his charge that the attitude of *Collier's* constituted a "systematic, mercenary hounding." "That great jury, the public," said Post, "will hardly blame us for not waiting until we get a petit jury in a court-room before denouncing this prodigal detractor." For that advertisement, also, Robert J. Collier has since entered suit.

An Unprecedented Verdict

The trial of the original case, founded on the charge of blackmail in the "'Yell-Oh' Man" advertisement, began in November. It lasted ten days; and the jury, after deliberating an hour and a half, found for the plaintiff and awarded damages in the sum of $50,000.

Above is our case. The Postum case had only one real support, and that so flimsy as to prove Post's desperation. The circulars sent by *Collier's* since 1907 to the Grandin Agency, and signed in rubber stamp with the name of the advertising manager, were interpreted by Mr. Post's counsel as attempts to make the Postum Company advertise, and the request for display matter instead of testimonial reading notices in Mr. Nast's polite letter of cancelation, as a veiled insinuation that *Collier's* expected the Postum Company to increase its advertising, since display generally takes up more space, and is therefore more costly, than reading notices.

This is a bare review of the bare issue. But the case went further. The attorney for *Collier's* stated in opening that he would rest not only on the claim of libel, but on the truth of Mr. Adams's statement. So, from the testimony taken at the trial, very slightly supplemented by other facts which will help make it intelligible, we are able to tell the reader of *Collier's* what Postum and Grape-Nuts are, by what means they are advertised, what is the real source and motive of their elaborate testimonials, a sample of which the reader can doubtless find by referring to this morning's newspapers, and, finally, who and what is C. W. Post.

Mr. Post first; for he is probably more interesting than his wares. Post, it appears, came into public notice as a mental healer near the city of Battle Creek, Michigan. He has testified in another trial that he was cured of "chronic ills" by a mental-science healer named Mrs. Agnes Chester—just as he was later cured of appendicitis by his own Grape-Nuts. In spite of his prosperity, he has been a heavily afflicted man, it appears. And in 1893 he was running at Battle Creek a sanitarium or boarding-house, called La Vita Inn, for persons under mental treatment. His particular brand of mental healing was known as Scientia Vitae. To spread the sect and fill the inn he published in 1893 his first book, a treatise on Mental Healing, entitled, "I Am Well." Really, this book was only a more intelligible copy of ideas presented in other more popular and better-known works on healing by the mind. There are the same pretentious claims to divine guidance—"it produces a feeling of great quiet and comfort within, to be the pen by which Our Father conveys to you his great truths which will make you free from pain and disease," says Post in beginning—the same generalities concerning the perfect man and the denial of pain, the same stories of marvelous cures. Concerning these tales, let us return to the late trial. By *Collier's* counsel, and by one of the jurors, Post, a squirming witness, was pinned down to the successive admissions that he had charge of mental healing at La Vita Inn, that he practised it himself, that he told, in his book, how he had "healed" a case of erysipelas by Scientia Vitae. Later, warming up, Mr. Post spoke quite readily of that cure, testifying as follows:

"A.—That case of erysipelas was a man who came to me . . . one morning when I was out in the carriage house of my stable doing a little work, sorting some pears, in fact, and I remember the case very well, indeed, because when I turned to look at the individual, there was a face swollen half beyond its ordinary size, with evidence of erysipelas. . . . He was in great pain, as he stated, and said that he had been treated by some physicians downtown, and had heard that there was some remedy out at the inn, so-called. . . . I am unable to say any more exactly, or to analyze exactly what it is that conveys or carries the healing impulse; it is sufficient to say that when the man told me his trouble I told him to go into the house, and that I would be in there shortly. . . . I went toward the house and at the back corner found the man standing. I said: 'Didn't I tell you to go around to the front and go into the house?' He said: 'Yes, but I have no reason to go in there.' I said: 'Why?' He said: 'Because my pain has left me, I have none.' I said: 'Do you mean to say that you have no pain, no trouble?' He said: 'None at all.' . . . I said: 'Go downtown and don't dig it up again, and in the course of two or three days Nature will set up a change in your face in a natural sort of a way. If your pain is gone, don't bring it up again.' . . . One morning he appeared about breakfast-time with his mother in a carriage . . . and he brought her up to see if she could be relieved. . . ." As one learns from the review of this case in "I Am Well," the mother had a very painful ulcerated tooth. Post looked at her and told her she was well. Guess what happened? The pain and swelling went away.

"I Am Well" contains accounts of about a dozen cures, all performed by Post through Scientia Vits. The complaints included dyspepsia (of twenty-five years' standing), insomnia (cured in five minutes), nervous trouble complicated by taste for tobacco and whisky (for which the patient lost all desire), a complex disease involving the stomach, liver, bowels, spinal cord, and the right ankle and heel (the patient was "one of the living skeletons"), inflammation of the neck of the bladder, and a complaint only vaguely described—"a person lifted from a death-bed through Scientia Vitae, and who became round, fat, and rosy quickly."

The Stomach and the Soul

But the passages in "I Am Well" which relate to the subject in hand are those touching on diet. No special kind of food, it appears, will make you well. What is necessary is to put yourself in tune with the infinite—"Read carefully, thoughtfully, not more than twenty pages daily. Afterward seek an easy position where you will not be disturbed, relax every muscle, close your eyes, and go into the silence where mind is plastic to the breathings of Spirit and where God talks to the Son. The thoughts from Divine Universal Mind come as winged angels and endow you with their healing power. If you go into the silence, humble and trusting, you will come out enriched and greatly strengthened in body, by contact, even for a short time, with the Father of all Life and all power. You will feel refreshed in every way, and food taken will digest readily, as stomach works smoothly when under the influence of Higher Power." Again: "Let it be known, once for all, that all causes of disease in man, whether of so-called stomach trouble, bowel trouble, consumption, cancer, heart disease, rheumatism, or what not, are the result of mental conditions of inharmony. The dead material of which the body is made can originate and produce nothing." This in 1893. By the end of the century, Post had changed his doctrine, as many great teachers do. He was then manufacturing Postum and Grape-Nuts; and, as the advertisement in your daily newspaper will show you, every package contains a pamphlet entitled: "The Road to Wellville." This includes a great many sentences, and a great many ideas, lifted bodily from his earlier work, "I Am Well"; but with an important addition. Divine Harmony alone will not make you well, according to "The Road to Wellville." It must be Divine Harmony plus a diet of Postum and Grape-Nuts. Listen to one passage. The author has been describing Positive and Negative currents of thought, showing how hate, anger, and the like disturb the body, and how thoughts of health, happiness, peace, harmony, beauty, restore it. But: "You can not get well by exercise alone, or by thinking positive thoughts alone. You absolutely must give up the food and drink that disagree with you. . . . Postum Food Coffee and Grape-Nuts will prove their solid worth and inestimable value in rebuilding the body, if steadily used, and the improvement can generally be noticed in a week's time."

Post Enlarges His "Mission"

That is ahead of the story, however. What started Post in the cereal food business is uncertain. He says himself that he needed a food to ward off attacks of appendicitis, and that his experiments led him to the Grape-Nuts "formula," and, further, that he worked out Postum as a coffee substitute at La Vita Inn. More likely, he proceeded on the lines of the advertising agent who telegraphed once to a wholesale drug, firm in St. Louis: "What is your bottom price for a million dozen sweet cathartic pills? I have a name." At any rate, he began the manufacture of Postum, a plain coffee substitute, only a dilute copy of the roasted-wheat-and-molasses substitute coffee which our grandmothers made for our grandfathers, and Grape-Nuts, just a plain breakfast food. The era of heavily advertised breakfast foods was just dawning. Post, who used the newspapers liberally from the first, was the one important producer of these commodities who lied persistently in his advertising. At first he claimed almost impossible powers of nutrition for Grape-Nuts. "The system will absorb a greater amount of nourishment from one pound of Grape-Nuts than from ten pounds of Meat, Wheat, Oats, or Bread," he used to say on his packages. The Pure Food Law of 1906 made that method of labeling illegal. It did not, unfortunately, prevent such claims in advertising. And more and more Post exploited the "remedial" virtues of both Postum and Grape-Nuts. The latter was "the food for brain and nerves," the "stuff brain is made of," "predigested," "almost wholly composed of pure grape-sugar," "predigested food." Finally, he advertised that a diet of "predigested Grape-Nuts alone" would ward off appendicitis. As for Postum, from a plain coffee substitute it became a food drink; and from praising it negatively by exploiting the real or alleged dangers of the "coffee habit," Post came to praise it positively as a "builder" which "nourishes and strengthens without depressing." And his business flourished until he covered the old site of La Vita Inn with a dozen factories, and until he reckoned his net profits at a million a year.

He began his testimonial advertising early; this was a paying line, it would seem, for he used it more and more. If you wish a sample, refer again to your newspaper. It must be there. These testimonials are anonymous. Sometimes a mother of many children is stricken with heart failure or palpitation. After trying all remedies, she gives up coffee and uses Postum. It always works a cure—when well boiled. Sometimes it is a wise physician who has recommended it. Sometimes the physician himself writes in praise of Postum. As for Grape-Nuts, there are "endorsements" without number of its effects in cases of impending appendicitis and chronic indigestion. These testimonials are never signed, but they always conclude: "Name given by Postum Co., Ltd., Battle Creek, Mich. There's a Reason." And, finally, the Post advertising proclaimed the endorsement of "prominent physicians" and "health officers." Let us mention here that no physician of standing would give public endorsement to a patent food any more than he would perform a criminal operation or refuse aid to a sick pauper. It is against the ethics of the most highly honorable of all professions.

Post got those testimonials by advertising for them. In New York he used for that purpose the "New York Magazine of Mysteries," whose editor is now in the Federal penitentiary for fraudulent use of the mails. For example, Post announced in that magazine in 1907: "More Boxes of Gold and Many Greenbacks—325 boxes of gold and greenbacks will be sent to persons who write the most interesting and truthful letters on the following topics: 1. How have you been affected by coffee drinking and by changing from coffee to Postum? 2. Give name and account of one or more coffee drinkers who have been hurt by it and who have been induced to quit and use Postum, etc., etc."

For each of the five best answers the Postum Company offered a prize of a $10 gold piece in a box, to the next twenty $5 each, to the next one hundred $2, and to the next two hundred $1. He varied that copy with another headed "Y I O—Grape-Nuts." Prizes were offered to the persons forming the greatest number of words from the above combination of letters. One read far into the conditions before he learned that each answer must be accompanied by a testimonial to Grape-Nuts.

Post admitted on the stand that he got "10,000, 20,000, 100,000" testimonial letters a year by this method. And by his own admission these letters were "rewritten" before publication. Post, in fact, declared under oath that not one of them had ever been printed just as it was written by the author. Further, the Postum Company never made any attempt to investigate the truth of the testimonials. Still further, the company sent stamps to the authors of popular letters, that they might answer inquiries. The originals of these testimonials never reached the jury. Mr. Collier's attorneys demanded them during a preliminary examination held at Battle Creek. "They are in the hands of our New York attorney," said Post; "I promise to produce them at the trial." When, at the trial, James W. Osborne, of counsel for Mr. Collier, demanded them, Mr. Philbin, representing Post, said: "I have never seen them. Why didn't you serve the customary five days' notice?" Probably the world is poorer in laughter for the suppression of these valuable human documents.

Post's "Prominent Physician"

In the crucible of law, the testimonials from "prominent physicians" and "health officers" melted down to one item—the endorsement of Dr. B. F. Underwood. Mr. Post, it is true, had promised to put a health officer on the stand; but the man telegraphed at the last moment that he could not come. Dr. Underwood, however, was there. He was the only author of a Postum Cereal Company testimonial who appeared in court, and *Collier's* produced him. And this is his story—the essential facts from his testimony, the rest from private conversation.

He is no longer a physician. He is a printer. Once, however, he practised in small Pennsylvania and New Jersey towns as a homeopathist. He held the belief that coffee is a common cause of common ills. Knowing of the Post anti-coffee campaign, he tried to patch out his income by writing him an anticoffee article. Post looked over the article and amended it by adding two sentences which mentioned Postum. He sent it back to Underwood, saying in effect: "If you get this published, including the name of Postum, in some medical journal, I will pay you for it." Underwood had it printed in the "American Physician," lately born and now dead. And Post made good. He sent Underwood $10. That article, whose form and wording gave Postum a kind of medical seal and approval, Post published over the country in half-page advertisements. This was the "endorsements of prominent physicians" of which we hear so much in Postum advertising.

Now, just what is Postum, and what is Grape-Nuts?

Our grandmothers and our mothers used to make for members of their families suffering from too much coffee a homely substitute. They poured molasses over wheat grains, dried and ground the mixture, and got the liquid by the usual process of boiling. Postum would be just that but for the bran mixture. To those who have never fed the cattle on the farm, be it explained that bran is the shell of wheat. It contains nutritive elements, as sawdust does, but, as with sawdust, they are not in such form that the human stomach can assimilate them. Cattle, with their four stomachs, can get nourishment from bran. We can not.

And Postum is made from roasted and ground bran, wheat, and molasses—mostly bran. The exact proportion of bran can not be wormed out of the reluctant Post employees, even on the witness stand. It is certainly more than fifty per cent; it may be much more. Eight million pounds of bran are delivered every year to the Postum works in Battle Creek. As a harmless, nontoxic substitute for coffee, it is all right if you like it. As a "food drink" it has no more value than the coffee which it supplants, and little more than hot water. It is not true, as some believe, that Postum is "doped" with coffee extract. It would be harmless were it not so advertised that it leads the sick to attempt treatment by Postum instead of by a physician.

A Plain Breakfast Food

Grape-Nuts is a breakfast food, very like brown bread in composition, but prepared by a special process which involves, so Mr. Post says, twenty-seven hours of baking and drying. It is just a breakfast food, nothing more. It is a little more nourishing, ounce for ounce, than some, less nourishing than others, and far less nourishing than many simple foods which never bore a trade-mark. The Michigan State Agricultural College published in 1904 their results on a series of experiments to determine the value of breakfast foods, patent and plain. Pound for pound, the fuel value of Grape-Nuts proved a little higher than that of whole wheat bread or graham bread; but that is because it contains less water. But the table headed "Total Amount of Nutrients and Their Fuel Values in the different foods for ten cents" told a different story. Ten cents' worth of entire wheat bread or graham bread, it appears from that table, has one and a half times the fuel value of ten cents' worth of Grape-Nuts.

However, Post has almost ceased to claim that Grape-Nuts "contains more nourishment than any other known food." His main hold now is the assertion that it is "predigested," that it is "dextrose and grape-sugar, made by special process of entire wheat and barley." From this grows the absurd, the murderous, claim that a person attacked by the swift and deadly appendicitis may get well through eating Grape-Nuts, without any other food, and "washing out the intestines." On that point—the alleged predigestion of Grape-Nuts—the court took several days of testimony. The reader must bear with a little scientific terminology; we will keep it as brief as possible.

Grape-Nuts is made of wheat, barley, salt, and yeast. The barley, in the process of making, is malted or allowed to sprout. It is ground and mixed with whole wheat flour in the proportion of one part to two; the mixture is then treated like ordinary bread, being mixed with yeast, raised, and baked. The brown bread, after baking, goes through a grinding and drying process, lasting several hours. It comes out, ready for packing, in brown grains.

Now the food constituents of Grape-Nuts, like those of other cereal foods, are proteins and carbohydrates. Of the former, this food has ten per cent; of the latter, seventy-five. Let us dismiss the proteins. The long baking hardens and toughens them; it is pretty certain that this decreases their digestibility. The white of an egg, which is a typical protein, is less digestible hard-boiled than soft-boiled. And the same is probably true of the proteins of Grape-Nuts.

The carbohydrates of wheat and barley are starch. Grape-Nuts, therefore, is seventy-five per cent starch. And the process of starch-digestion is as follows: In the mouth the saliva starts the transformation. A little of the starch is changed to dextrin. As soon as the starch strikes the stomach the process of digestion ceases, not to be resumed until the starch reaches the duodenum. There, through several intermediate processes, the whole mass finally becomes dextrose. In that form it is ready to be taken up by the blood, and the process of digestion is complete. Grape-sugar is a common name of dextrose.

Now as to Grape-Nuts, which Post at various times has advertised as "pure grape-sugar" and "dextrose": The process of malting the barley, and perhaps to a very slight degree the long baking, changes part of the barley into maltose, one of the intermediary substances between dextrin and dextrose. This maltose comprises about ten per cent of the whole substance of Grape-Nuts. Only a trace of it becomes dextrose or grape-sugar. Weigh the ten per cent of proteins, rendered tougher and less digestible by long baking, against the ten per cent of carbohydrates modified into one of the preliminary substances of starch-digestion, and the balance between increased digestibility and retarded digestibility is about even. If anything, it favors Grape-Nuts. But this relates only to the starch in the barley; it does not reckon with the starch in the wheat. None of that is changed into maltose or into any other substances progressing toward dextrose. The starch granule is surrounded by a little envelope of fiber which must be broken before the digestive process can begin. That is why we cook wheat flour. And experiment has shown that fewer of these envelopes are broken in Grape-Nuts than in wheat bread, for example. Of the starch remaining in Grape-Nuts after ten per cent has been converted into maltose, thirty-six per cent is in an insoluble state—the envelope of fiber is not broken. And this tips the scale slightly against Grape-Nuts. As a matter of fact, in digestibility there is practically very little difference between Grape-Nuts and the brown bread which it resembles. One would suit one man a little better, and the other another, according to individual idiosyncrasy. Neither is an invalid food. And on the basis of Post's own claims, Grape-Nuts would probably be a little more likely to cause appendicitis than bread—if either ever causes appendicitis. For Post declared in the hectic advertisement which cost him a $50,000 verdict: "Let it be understood that appendicitis results from long-continued disturbance in the intestines, caused primarily by undigested food, and chiefly by undigested starchy food. . . . These lie in the warmth and moisture of the bowels in an undigested state, and decay, generating gases and irritating the mucous surfaces until, under such conditions, the lower part of the colon and the appendix become involved." Now as our brief analysis shows, Grape-Nuts has a greater proportion of "undigested starchy" matter than bread. And yet we would not go so far as to charge that Grape-Nuts causes appendicitis.

Post's attorneys tried to drag from this expert or that facts about appendicitis, facts about the chemical constituents of food, which would cloud the issue. But on one thing the experts of the plaintiff and the experts for the defendant were all agreed, namely:

The first thing to do in an attack of appendicitis is to make the patient discontinue all food. Acute, subacute, septic—it is the same thing. Food, even the lightest and most easily digested food, is almost inevitably fatal, owing to its action on the bowels.

Dr. Paul Outerbridge, called as an expert by the Postum Company, was on the stand, under cross-examination by Mr. Osborne. This passage occurred:

Q.—You would not undertake to give advice for the whole world that in a case of approaching appendicitis a man could go on eating food, would you?

A.—I should want to see my case.

Q.—That advice might prove extremely hazardous, might it not?

A.—It might.

Q.—And perhaps fatal? I think you said that. Is not that right?

A.—Yes, that is right.

Here we have it, the kernel of the whole matter. To sell his food products, to make his million a year in profits, his million a year in advertising, C. W. Post bargains and compounds with death exactly as do the patent-medicine fakers. If any one, feeling the first pains of acute appendicitis, ever took the advice of C. W. Post and "ate only Grape-Nuts," he doubtless added his epitaph to the "unsolicited testimonials" which Post would not produce in court.

Further, the expert testimony proved that Grape-Nuts is not a brain food. There is no such thing as a "brain food." Any food nourishes the little toe as well as the brain; and the only way to build up a depleted brain by food is to build up the whole system. "The stuff brains are made of—Grape-Nuts"; "We say again the food for brain is Grape-Nuts"—these assertions, although less dangerous, are as ridiculous as the assertion that a diet of Grape-Nuts will ward off appendicitis.

Now, concerning C. W. Post and the kind of man he is. To the picture of his mind and morals which appears in this sober statement of facts, let us add two incidents from the trial, as a kind of summing up.

Post was on the stand—a dodging, squirming witness. There was in evidence a piece of his own testimony in his bankruptcy suit. "Did you testify to this?" Mr. Osborne asked again and again. "I don't remember," was Post's stereotyped reply. In the end Mr. Philbin, his counsel, stepped forward and said: "We admit that this is his testimony."

They came to examine him as to his qualifications to write of appendicitis in 1905—the period when *Collier's* threw out his advertising.

He was asked what authorities on the subject he had consulted. He named six or eight. He pointed out a pile of books in possession of his attorney as the very ones he had read.

"Did you consult the books from these editions here?" asked Mr. Osborne.

"From those and various editions," answered Post, overlooking the bait.

Mr. Osborne picked up book after book from the pile and showed the title-pages to the jury. All, except two, had been published since 1905.

One short word, the pet of ante-bellum journalism, has gone a little out of fashion in these mild later days. It should be revived occasionally, because none other fits so well. We should use it now, but we won't. We'll merely state:

C. W. Post is a faker.

Source: "C. W. Post, Faker," *Collier's* 46 (December 24, 1910): 13–15.

1911 • 106 • BROOKER T. WASHINGTON, "ALL-DAY MEETING"

Introduction: *Brooker T. Washington (1856–1915) was an African American educator who was born into slavery. He founded Tuskegee Institute in Alabama. Below is his description of the foods served at an "all-day meeting" taken from* My Larger Education, Being Chapters from My Experience *(1911), one of his three autobiographies.*

In Macon County, Ala., where I live, the coloured people have a kind of church-service that is called an "all-day meeting." The ideal season for such meetings is about the middle of May. The church-house that I have in mind is located about ten miles from town. To get the most out of the "all-day meeting" one should make an early start, say eight o'clock. During the drive one drinks in the fresh fragrance of forests and wild flowers. The church building is located near a stream of water, not far from a large, cool spring, and in the midst of a grove or primitive forest. Here the coloured people begin to come together by nine or ten o'clock in the morning. Some of them walk; most of them drive. A large number come in buggies, but many use the more primitive wagons or carts, drawn by mules, horses, or oxen. In these conveyances a whole family, from the youngest to the eldest, make the journey together. All bring baskets of food, for the "all-day meeting" is a kind of Sunday picnic or festival. Preaching, preceded by much singing, begins at about eleven o'clock. If the building is not large enough, the services are held out under the trees. Sometimes there is but one sermon; sometimes there are two or three sermons, if visiting ministers are present. The sermon over, there is more plantation singing. A collection is taken—sometimes two collections—then comes recess for dinner and recreation.

Sometimes I have seen at these "all-day meetings" as many as three thousand people present. No one goes away hungry. Large baskets, filled with the most tempting spring chicken or fresh pork, fresh vegetables, and all kinds of pies and cakes, are then opened. The people scatter in groups. Sheets or table-cloths are spread on the grass under a tree near the stream. Here old acquaintances are renewed; relatives meet members of the family whom they have not seen for months. Strangers, visitors, every one must be invited by some one else to dinner. Kneeling on the fresh grass or on broken branches of trees surrounding the food, dinner is eaten. The animals are fed and watered, and then at about three o'clock there is another sermon or two, with plenty of singing thrown in; then another collection, or perhaps two. In between these sermons I am invited to speak, and am very glad to accept the invitation. At about five o'clock the benediction is pronounced and the thousands quietly scatter to their homes with many good-bys and well-wishes. This, as I have said, is the kind of church-service that I like best. In the opportunities which I have to speak to such gatherings I feel that I have done some of my best work.

Source: Booker T. Washington, *My Larger Education, Being Chapters from My Experience* (Garden City, NY: Doubleday, Page, 1911), 32–34.

1912 • 107 • MENUS FROM THE *TITANIC*, APRIL 1912

Introduction: *Prior to the establishment of passenger jet service to Europe, ships transported passengers across the Atlantic. By the early 20th century, luxury liners plied the* *oceans, moving hundreds—and in some cases thousands—of passengers from one place to another. RMS* Titanic, *the largest ship in the world at that time, was on its maiden voyage when it collided with an iceberg on the evening of April 14, 1912, and sank a few hours later in the mid-Atlantic. Of the 2,224 people on board, 1,541 died. The ship had three types of passengers on board—first class, second class, and third class. Each class was offered different menus each day for each meal. The White Star Line that operated the ship prided itself on the meals that it served passengers. Below are menus that have survived from each class during the last few days before the ship sank.*

Menus from the *Titanic*

First Class Luncheon Menu, April 14, 1912

LUNCHEON
Consomme Fermier
Cockie Leekie
Fillets of Brill
Egg a L'Argenteuil
Chicken a la Maryland
Corned Beef
Vegetables
Dumplings

FROM THE GRILL
Grilled Mutton Chops
Mashed, Fried & Baked Jacket Potatoes
Custard Pudding
Apple Merinque
Pastry

BUFFET
Salmon Mayonnaise
Potted Shrimps
Norwegian Anchovies
Soused Herrings
Plain & Smoked Sardines
Roast Beef
Round or Spiced Beef
Veal & Ham Pie
Virginia & Cumberland Ham
Bologna Sausage
Brawn
Galantine of Chicken
Corned Ox Tounge
Lettuce
Beetroot
Tomatoes

CHEESE
Cheshire

Stilton
Gorgonzola
Edam
Camembert
Roquefort
St. Ivel
Cheddar

—Iced draught Munich Lager 3d. & 6d. a Tankard.—

First Class Dinner Menu, April 14, 1912

Hors D'Oeuvre Varies
Oysters
Consomme Olga
Cream of Barley
Salmon
Mousseline Sauce
Cucumber
Filet Mignons Lili
Saute of Chicken Lyonnaise
Vegetable Marrow Farcie
Lamb Mint Sauce
Roast Duckling
Apple Sauce
Sirlon of Beef
Chateau Potatoes
Green Peas
Creamed Carrots
Boiled Rice
Parmentier & Boiled New Potatoes
Punch Romaine
Roast Squab & Cress
Cold Asparagus Vinagrette
Pate du Foie Gras
Celery
Waldorf Pudding
Peaches in Chartreuse Jelly
Chocolate & Vanilla Eclairs
French Ice Cream

Second Class Breakfast Menu, April 11, 1912

Rolled Oats
Boiled Hominy
Fresh Fish
Yarmouth Blothers
Grilled Ox Kidneys and Bacon
American Dry Hash au Gratin

Grilled Sausage
Mashed Potatoes
Grilled Ham & Fried Eggs
Fried Potatoes
Vienna & Graham Rolls
Soda Scones
Buckwheat Cakes
Maple Syrup
Conserve
Marmalade
Tea
Coffee
Watercress

Second Class Luncheon Menu, April 12, 1912

LUNCHEON
Pea Soup
Spaghetti au Gratin
Corned Beef
Vegetable Dumplings
Roast Mutton
Baken Jacket Potatoes

COLD
Roast Mutton
Roast Beef
Sausage
Ox Tounge
Pickles
Salad
Tapioca Pudding
Apple Tart
Fresh Fruit
Cheese
Biscuits
Coffee

Second Class Dinner Menu, April 14, 1912

FIRST COURSE—SOUP
Consomme with Tapioca

SECOND COURSE—MAIN DISHES
Baked Haddock with Sharp Sauce
Curried Chicken with Rice
Lamb with Mint Sauce
Roast Turkey with Savory Cranberry Sauce
Turnip Sauce

Green Peas
Boiled Rice
Boiled and Roast Potatoes

THIRD COURSE—DESSERTS
Plum Pudding with Sweet Sauce
Wine Jelly
Coconut Sandwich
American Ice Cream
Assorted Nuts
Fresh Fruit
Cheese
Biscuits

AFTER DINNER
Coffee

Third Class Bill of Fare, April 14, 1912

BREAKFAST
Oatmeal Porridge & Milk
Smoked Herrings & Jacketed Potatoes
Fried Trips & Onions
Fresh Bread & Butter
Marmalade & Sweedish Bread
Tea & Coffee

DINNER
Vegetable Soup
Roasted Pork with Sage & Pearl Onions
Green Peas
Boiled Potatoes
Plum Pudding with Sweet Sauce
Cabin Biscuits
Oranges

TEA
Ragout of Beef with Potaotes & Onions
Currant Buns
Fresh Bread & Butter
Apricots
Tea

SUPPER
Cabin Biscuits & Cheese
Gruel
Coffee

WHITE STAR LINE.

R M.S. "TITANIC." APRIL 14, 1912.

THIRD CLASS.

BREAKFAST.
OATMEAL PORRIDGE & MILK
SMOKED HERRINGS, JACKET POTATOES
HAM & EGGS
FRESH BREAD & BUTTER
MARMALADE SWEDISH BREAD
TEA COFFEE

DINNER.
RICE SOUP
FRESH BREAD CABIN BISCUITS
ROAST BEEF, BROWN GRAVY
SWEET CORN BOILED POTATOES
PLUM PUDDING, SWEET SAUCE
FRUIT

TEA.
COLD MEAT
CHEESE PICKLES
FRESH BREAD & BUTTER
STEWED FIGS & RICE
TEA

SUPPER.
GRUEL CABIN BISCUITS CHEESE

Any complaint respecting the Food supplied, want of attention or incivility, should be at once reported to the Purser or Chief Steward. For purposes of identification, each Steward wears a numbered badge on the arm.

An original *Titanic* third class menu postcard details the meals available on April 14, 1912. The *Titanic* sank the following day. (AP Photo/Chitose Suzuki)

Source: "Titanic Menus," WebTitanic, http://www.webtitanic.net/framemenu.html.

1913 • 108 • Henry T. Finck, "Gastronomic America"

Introduction: *Henry T. Finck (1854–1926) was a Missouri-born music critic who wrote extensively for newspapers. In 1913 he published* Food and Flavor: A Gastronomic Guide to Health and Good Living. *He reviews the food of many European countries and in a long chapter examines the gastronomic and nongastronomic qualities of American food and flavor.*

It is now time to raise our flag and do a little patriotic boasting. There is a gastronomic America as well as an ungastronomic America; we have unequaled opportunities for producing the best of nearly everything, and if we utilize those opportunities, recognizing the all-importance of Flavor in food, in its various stages from the field to the grill and the table, we can easily become, within a few decades, a leading—perhaps even the leading—gastronomic nation. In the present chapter and the following one I purpose to dwell on some of the delicacies for the enjoyment of which at their best Europeans must come to America.

Sweet Corn and Corn Bread.

Probably the most characteristically American thing a summer visitor from Europe will see in our dining-rooms is the eating of green corn off the cob. To be sure, he might see the same thing in visiting the Hindoos or South Africans; but they are imitators, we the originators of this delectable habit. In saying "we" I mean Americans in the broadest sense of the word, including the red Indians. It was they who first cultivated corn, in the central part of our hemisphere. From there it came north, and Columbus took it to Europe, whence it reached the other continents. They call it maize in Europe, mealies in South Africa. In England "corn" means wheat, in Scotland oats, those being their principal crops respectively. In America the main crop still is, as it was twenty centuries ago, Indian corn, which therefore is of all things edible the most thoroughly American. Three cheers for corn!

In Italy, two-thirds of the rural population subsist mainly on corn, which is, however, eaten nearly always as polenta (mush), alone or with cheese, fish, or meat; whereas we have on our tables an almost endless variety of corn and corn products. The red man set the example. He ate green corn. He made a mush of ripe corn, pounding it, either parched or unparched, into a coarse meal. He mixed it diversely with pumpkins, nuts, berries, and other foods. Succotash is an Indian name which we borrowed from him, together with the dish it denotes—beans and unripe corn cooked together. The site of Montreal was once an Indian cornfield. In the "dreadful winter" of 1620–21 the colonists in Plymouth bought "eight hogsheads of corne and beanes" from the Indians, who taught them "bothe ye manner how to set it and after how to dress and tend it."

Yet the most imaginative Indian could never have dreamt of how amazingly their successors on the soil would multiply the uses of corn, for the table and for countless industrial uses. We now have cook books concerned solely with corn foods.

Mark Twain's appetizing list of the American dishes he missed in Europe, to which reference was made in the first chapter of this book, includes five made of cornpone, hoecake, green corn on the ear, green corn cut from the ear and served with butter and pepper, and hominy. Among those he surely would have mentioned also, had he happened

A family gathers to eat corn-on-the-cob, Lanesboro, Minnesota, ca. 1919. (Minnesota Historical Society/ Corbis)

to recall their merits at the moment, are samp, gruel, hulled corn, or lye hominy, Indian pudding, hasty pudding, pop-corn, succotash, Boston brown bread, griddle cakes, johnnycake, mock oysters, cream of corn, Kentucky corn dodgers, and cornmeal gems.

Welcome as all these specialties and many others are on American tables—fried mush and hominy are particularly to be commended to those who know not how tasty they are for breakfast, or as a dinner course, occasionally, in place of the everlasting potatoes—none of them—not even genuine pone—is quite so luscious as green corn.

It may not be "elegant" to eat sweet corn off the cob, but that is the only way to get its full Flavor. There is delicious fragrance in the juicy cob, too, and in the bosom of your family it is permissible (and decidedly advisable) to suck it. Sugar cane and oranges are not the only things that are best when sucked. American horticultural ingenuity has achieved wonders in developing varieties of sweet corn with new refinements of Flavor. A few years ago C. D. Keller, of Toledo, Ohio, originated a new kind which he called the "Howling Mob," which "peculiar but apt name," in the words of Mr. Burpee, "refers to the vociferous demand for the ears when Mr. Keller takes them to market."

Great, indeed, is the demand in Amer0ican markets, homes, and hotels for green corn, and much ingenuity has further been expended in rearing early and late varieties so as to make the season as long as possible. Between the early Malakoff, from Siberia, and the late Country Gentleman, there are dozens of desirable varieties the characteristics of which are described in the catalogues of our seedsmen. The last-named has long been considered the sweetest of all kinds, but the new Golden Bantam is a formidable rival.

Its color, which makes it look like ordinary field corn, is against it, but those who have once tasted it, sing its praises forevermore.

It is related that the Rev. Sidney Smith's parishioners did not want him to visit America for fear that the allurements of canvasback duck might tempt him to remain. Sweet corn, also, might have alienated his patriotic affections. Covent Garden, to be sure, sometimes offers so-called green corn, but England has too cool nights and not enough sunshine to develop the Flavor of this vegetable.

Even in America, where it grows to perfection, pains must be taken if one wants to get that Flavor at its best. All who have lived in the country agree with Dr. Wiley's dictum that "there is only one way to eat Indian corn. That is to go out just before sun-up and harvest the ears, and have them boiled for early breakfast. To people in cities who have never eaten freshly harvested Indian corn, such an experience would be a revelation."

Not only do corn cobs that are kept a day or two before eating lose much of their precious fragrance, but, as the same eminent chemist informs us, "corn which is perfectly sweet and delicious at the moment of harvest, has been found to lose half of its sugar within twenty-four hours."

Those who find sweet corn indigestible do not know how to eat it. If a sharp knife is pressed on each row of kernels the skin—which is the indigestible part—is cut and remains on the cob.

While the demand for sweet corn is ever on the increase and fortunes are made by those who grow or handle the best—that is, the most agreeably flavored—sorts, the foods made of ripe dried corn are not eaten so generally as they ought to be, at least in the Northern States.

It is desirable that everybody should know the interesting reason for the fact, known to all, that the South is more addicted than the North to the eating of dishes made of corn.

That reason is very simple: corn bread in the South is made of meal which has more Flavor than the meal sold in the Northern States, and is therefore more appetizing and wholesome.

Why is its Flavor better? Because it is made of ground corn from which only the indigestible hulls have been removed by bolting, whereas in the making of meal for Northern markets, the millers remove also the germ which contains the fat and most of the Flavor of corn, besides its most important mineral contents. They have contrived a diabolical machine known as the "degerminator" for the special purpose of bolting out the germs, that is, the very heart and soul, of the corn.

If I add that, in the words of Dr. Charles D. Woods, Director of the Maine Agricultural Experiment Station "from the manufacturer's standpoint the removal of the germ does not represent a loss, as it is used for the manufacture of gluten feeds—so important for live stock—and corn oil, which has many industrial uses and is used to some extent as a salad oil and as a culinary fat"—the reader will begin to suspect one reason why the millers market cornmeal from which its most valuable constituent has been removed.

But there is another reason for this dastardly crime and that is that "the germ lowers the keeping quality of the meal because its abundant fat easily becomes rancid."

In other words cornmeal made for sale in the North is denatured deliberately in order that the miller and the grocer may not run the risk of having a few sacks of it spoil on their hands occasionally! The consumer is not considered at all.

Ungastronomic America has meekly submitted to this outrage, largely because the facts of the case are not generally known. Gastronomic Americans, whose numbers are increasing rapidly, will insist on their rights, refusing to buy cornmeal from which most of the Flavor has been eliminated, and the North will in time eat as much corn bread as the South.

Personally, I agree with those who think it even more tasty than wheat bread. The only advantage wheat has is that, with yeast or baking powder, it can be made into a lighter and more porous loaf; but this advantage can be neutralized by baking the corn bread in thin cakes; and corn bread thus made is far more digestible than loaves of wheat bread as ordinarily made in America. A good quality of it is also much more easily and more quickly made at home. Soldiers and campers prefer it, partly for this reason. "It has been said," writes Dr. Woods, "that johnny cake is a corruption of journey cake, and that corn bread was so called because it could be so easily prepared on the road."[1]

Griddle Cakes and Maple Syrup.

Our breakfasts, more than other meals, are made delectable by diverse corn dishes. Corn flakes, properly made are more flavorful than any others, and of all the varieties of griddle cakes, so dear to the American palate, none quite equals those made of corn. If these are at present seen less frequently on bills of fare than are wheat, rice, or buckwheat cakes, it is because of the way in which cornmeal is usually deprived of what most appeals to the palate.

Griddle cakes made of wheat are widely known as flannel cakes. I have never eaten any woolen stuff, but I imagine it might taste a good deal like the average "flannel" cake, though it would be much lighter. The French and German pancakes are far superior to our wheat cakes; but even to these I prefer the American corn griddle cakes, for which the whites of egg have been beaten stiff and added gradually; and I bask in the proud consciousness that my preference is thoroughly patriotic.

The liking for buckwheat cakes is to me a mystery and always has been, although as a boy I used to eat them with rich sausage gravy, which made them palatable. Buckwheat cakes are not eaten so much as they used to be, so maybe I am not alone in disliking them. For the gratification of those who do like them I quote from the New York "Sun" a characteristically American communication from "Middle Aged":

> I saw in a store window to-day a sign "New Buckwheat," so I know people still eat buckwheat; but I doubt if it is as much eaten as it was in years back, say in the days when I was a youngster.

We always had buckwheat cakes for breakfast. Mother, sometimes father, used to stir the batter the night before in a curious tall, round, straight sided, brown earthenware pot with a handle on it, which was sacredly reserved for that purpose. I have never seen anywhere at any time another pot just like that one; and then it was set in just the right spot by the kitchen stove, for the batter to rise through the night.

In the morning they thinned this batter out just a little with water and then they fried the cakes; in our house on a long double griddle that covered two stove holes and on which you could cook two or three cakes at a time.

Every morning in winter we had those buckwheat cakes, light as a feather, and with them we always had sausages or pork chops; and such sausages and pork chops I have never seen since. Sausages, not as you see them nowadays as big around as a cigar and filled with some sort of pasty material, but big sausages stuffed with meat chopped coarse and that burst open when you fried them as if anxious to reveal to you their delightful, savory richness—I hope it is given to you to be able to recall such sausages; and pork chops from pigs country raised on nearby farms, a delight to the taste and always tender.

Whichever we had that morning, whether sausages or pork chops, we ate the sausage or the pork chop gravy on the cakes. Really the recollection moves me. My smiling mother—Heaven bless her!—never stinted me on the cakes; she gave me all I could eat. My father when I asked him for another sausage would sometimes ask me good-naturedly if I didn't think I had had enough; but he always handed over the sausage. And now, if you won't think I am quite a pig, I would like to say that I used to eat the last plate not with gravy but with butter and molasses on them; later we came to have syrup. And this sort of breakfast never did me any harm. There is a popular delusion that the ostrich has the hardiest of all stomachs, but really his would not for a moment bear comparison with that of the growing, outdoors boy.

The serving of sausages and pork chops with griddle cakes is not so customary as it used to be; usually the cakes, whether wheat, buckwheat, rice, or corn, are now eaten with some kind of syrup.

The syrup served with our griddle cakes is as characteristically American as the cakes themselves, or as the endless variety of cereal breakfast foods, one or the other of which nearly every American eats daily, with cream and sugar, and which foreigners know nothing about.[2]

Strictly speaking, a syrup is "the direct product of the evaporation of the juice of a sugar-yielding plant or tree without the removal of any of the sugar," whereas molasses is "the saccharine product which is separated from sugar in the process of manufacture." Commercial "syrup" is usually a mixture of syrup, molasses (of which there are many grades) and other things. Much of it is injurious to health, and housewives who wish to see nothing unwholesome on their breakfast tables should read what Dr. Wiley has to say on this subject, on pp. 472–482 of his "Foods and Their Adulteration."

The sap of sugar cane and sorghum is usually good and safe, besides being American. Even more so is the sap of the maple.

George Washington and Bret Harte were not more thoroughly and exclusively American than is the Acer saccharinum, or sugar maple tree. Europe nor any other continent has aught to match it. The sugar made from its sap is one of the delicacies discovered by the American Indian. The early white settlers learned from him how to make it, and for many years it was the only sugar they had. It was "dark and ill-tasting" compared with the best modern product.

In their appeal to the sense of taste all sweet syrups are alike. It is their fragrance, their Flavor, that makes us prefer some kinds to others. The Flavor of maple syrup has been much improved, and is still being improved, by perfecting the methods of tapping the tree, gathering the sap, boiling it, and storing the sweet product.

Uncle Sam has not neglected this important branch of national gastronomic industry. His chemists have been at work to ascertain the causes of the souring of the sap under certain conditions, and to explain why the later runs do not have so pleasant a Flavor as the earlier ones. They have found it in the action of micro-organisms.

While I was writing this chapter I received from Washington Farmers' Bulletin 516, a brochure of 46 pages in which the making of maple syrup and sugar is fully discussed, with detailed directions for securing the best-flavored product.[3] As in the making of butter, many things have to be done and many avoided to get the best results, but they are worth the trouble.

The demand for genuine maple sugar is great, and would be much greater still if adulteration were not so much practised. In 1910, according to the U.S. Census Reports, the maple syrup production of the country was 4,106,418 gallons, and in addition to this there were made over 14,000,000 pounds of maple sugar.

In that year Ohio led all the States in the production of maple syrup, followed by New York, Vermont, Pennsylvania, Indiana, Michigan, Wisconsin, and New Hampshire. In many other States it can be made in paying quantities. Farmers are advised to attend to this industry as a source of extra income. In the Bulletin just referred to, attention is called to two important economic considerations: "The season of production comes at a time of the year when little or no other work can be done on the farm, thus allowing the aid of the family and farm help for the boiling and manufacture. Moreover, since the sugar bushes as a general rule are situated on hilly country that would not be suitable for any other crop, these two items could hardly be placed at a high value in a table of costs."

Every farmer who lives in a State and region where the sugar maple prospers should secure Bulletin 516 through his representative in Washington. By attending strictly to the matter of delicate Flavor, not only can the industry be enormously increased at home but foreign markets can easily be won. Adulteration must, however, be severely curbed. Under present conditions American epicures do not put their faith in grocers but get their annual supplies early every year direct from the producer. It is best when freshly made, and unless put in cans and sealed while still hot it gradually loses its Flavor. Syrup made of dissolved maple sugar is often used, but it is less delicately flavored than that which is made at once from the sap. Many a time have I thanked Heaven that I was brought up in the country. How I pity those persons who, in the days of their youth, had no chance to kneel before an Acer saccharinum, as I did in my Missouri days (only a few miles from Mark Twain's birthplace, by the way) and drink in the nectar as it trickled through the spout into my mouth. It was more glorious even than it was some years later to suck fresh Oregon cider from a barrel through a straw.

Apple Pie and Cranberries.

Is pie as thoroughly American as maple syrup, griddle cakes, and corn bread?

An American is likely to answer "Yes," while an Englishman might say "No."

In the English "Who's Who" the "recreations" of most of the eminent men and women of the time in Europe and America are referred to. Had Theophile Gautier lived to be included in that volume, he would have probably named among his favorite recreations "reading the dictionary," to which he is said to have been much addicted. I could never quite see the fun of this diversion till I made the acquaintance of Murray's wonderful Oxford dictionary, which traces the meaning and history of every word back through the centuries.

Nothing, surely, could be more interesting, for instance, than to read in this work that the first reference to apple pie, so far as known, was as far back as 1590, when Greene, in his "Arcadia," wrote the line: "Thy breath is like the steame of apple-pyes"—thus proving himself, as I may add, an epicure as well as a poet and a lover.

On another page we read: "The pie appears to have been at first of meat or fish; doubtful or undefined uses appear in 16th century; fruit pies (also called, especially in the north of England and Ireland, in Scotland, and often in the United States, tarts) appear before 1600, the earliest being Apple-Pie." Were these apple pyes the same as the American apple pie of our day? I doubt it. If they had been, the Britons of our time certainly would make the same kind, but they don't. Their substitute for our fruit pie is the tart, which has only one crust and is otherwise different.

Even if it could be proved that we got our fruit pie from England, shape, contents, and all, I still would claim it as a national American dish—American by right of conquest, improvement, and country wide use. Millions of American families eat it daily, at lunch or at dinner. The poet Emerson even ate it at breakfast, and when a guest refused it, he was surprised and exclaimed: "What is pie for?" You can make a fruit pie in the American style in Great Britain or on the Continent, but you cannot duplicate its excellence, for the simple reason that European fruit is rarely as tasty as American fruit. It must be admitted that in the making of a light, digestible crust most American cooks could learn a lesson from foreign pastry cooks, who would advise them, among other things, to partly bake the lower crust or glaze it with white of egg before the fruit is put in. But, after all, the Flavor of the fruit is the all important thing, and in that the American pie is supreme.

The Rev. Henry Ward Beecher, in his eloquent sermon on apple pie, exclaimed: "But, oh! be careful of the paste! Let it be not like putty, nor rush to the other extreme and make it so flaky that one holds his breath while eating, for fear of blowing it away. Let it not be plain as bread, yet not rich like cake."

Has ever an English divine paid such attention to pie? No; the apple pie is ours, as much as our flag.

But alack and alas, the apple pie is often insulted and maltreated in its own bailiwick by being overseasoned. Beecher called attention to the fact that "it will accept almost every flavor of every spice," and he mentioned nutmeg, cinnamon, and lemon as among those which it is permissible to use.

"Permissible," yes, but most inadvisable. You may say it is a matter of taste, and that you have a right to put as much nutmeg, cinnamon, or lemon extract into your pie or your apple sauce as you please. If you make it for yourself and your family, yes; but not if you make it for a restaurant. The spices named are penetrating and monopolistic; even in small quantities they obliterate the natural Flavor of the apple, or at least modify it in a way obnoxious to those true epicures who like their fruit dishes au naturel, just as they like prime cuts of butcher's meats without obtrusive sauces, and sausage mild-flavored, without the screaming sage or too much pepper.

Nutmeg is the spice with which our apple pie is most frequently alloyed. An alloy is defined as "anything that reduces purity or excellence." If you put nutmeg into apple pie or sauce, you make it taste always the same, be it made of European or American fruit or of this or that variety of apples. Now, to an epicure the best thing about apple pie or sauce is that when served without spice it retains the peculiar Flavor of the kind of apple it is made from.

To go to your grocer and buy "cooking apples" is almost as bad as to ask for "cooking butter." The best butter and the best apples should always be used in the kitchen—if you can afford to buy them. If you cannot, eat oatmeal and prunes. To those who have refined palates it makes a world of difference whether their apple pie and sauce are made of "cooking apples" or of Gravensteins, Red Astrachans, Newtown Pippins, or Spitzenbergs. Each variety—and dozens of others might be named—has its own special charm; and the same is true of pies and sauces made of other fruits.

In the baking of pumpkin pie, which, next to that made of apples, is perhaps the most characteristically American pie, mace (which is derived from the covering of the nutmeg seed) or some other spice, is not only permissible but commendable; while mince pie, which we borrowed from the English but eat probably oftener than they do, is such a jumble of condiments—sugar, raisins, currants, almonds, apples, lemon and orange juice and peel, molasses, suet, quince jelly, and other things ad libitum—that it makes little difference what you add in the way of mace, cloves, cinnamon, ginger, or other spices within reason. Time was when caraway seeds, saffron, rosewater, ambergris, and other impossible things were added. As made now, mince pie is as agreeable to most palates as it is indigestible. I am told it can be made so as to be easily digestible, but I "hae ma doots."

Some years ago mince pie was dignified by being made the subject of a political squabble in Washington. Dr. Wiley wanted a definition of "normal mincemeat," and thirty manufacturers were summoned to testify. Evidently some of these manufacturers were making mincemeat without the chopped meat which is an essential ingredient of the best home-made article, for they engaged a trained lexicographer, Prof. C. D. Childs, of the University of Pennsylvania, to prepare a treatise on mince pie, in which it was demonstrated that mincemeat does not necessarily contain meat.

The definition in Murray's Oxford Dictionary is "a mixture made of currants, raisins, sugar, suet, apples, almonds, candied peel, etc., and sometimes meat chopped small; used in mince pies"; which shows that in England, also, meat is not always an ingredient. It is only fair to consumers, however, that the law should compel the manufacturers to print the ingredients in each case on the label. Mince pie with meat is certainly better than mince pie without.

Perhaps I erred in saying that pumpkin pie is, next to apple pie, the most characteristic American pastry dish. It certainly is not more so than cranberry pie. The cranberry is not exclusively American, like maple syrup, terrapin, and canvasback duck, for it grows in some parts of Europe; but it remained for American epicures to discover its rare gastronomic merits. It took genius to do this, for in its natural wild state the berry is excessively astringent and acid. But it had a Flavor that made an irresistible appeal and invited further cultivation. Particularly agreeable is the Oxycoccus erythrocarpus, a variety which grows in the mountains of Virginia and Georgia. The European berries, though they used to be abundant in England, were neglected because of their inferior Flavor, and England now imports cranberries in large quantities from the United States, as do France, Italy, and Germany, chiefly for tarts.

Cape Cod is now the chief camping ground of the cranberry. It has been doubled in size by cultivation, and its Flavor improved by enriching and draining the soil, and in other ways. The annual production is about three million bushels. Thanks to the growing demand for them, bog lands which were worth $5 an acre now sell at $300 to $700 per acre.

The darker the berry the richer the flavor. Once upon a time I wrote a book on Romantic Love and Personal Beauty in which I tried to prove that brunettes are more beautiful than blondes. I am not sure that I succeeded—there are certainly some ravishing exceptions!—but in the matter of foods there can be no doubt that as a rule the dark are finer than the light colored.

Does not Boston, the center of American culture, give its name to brown bread, and does not Boston prefer dark eggs to the anemic white ones favored in New York?

Does any one who has had the good sense to buy "rusty" oranges and grapefruit deny that they are sweeter and more fragrant than the light yellow ones? Ask any epicure if he does not think the second joint of a fowl is more savory than the white meat. Bread which has a deep brown crust is more tasty than pale crumb. Crackers toasted brown are more appetizing than crackers untoasted. English rusks, German zwieback, Italian breadsticks, are they not all brunettes? Do not all vegetables, fruits, and berries darken as they ripen and develop their flavor?

The darkest cranberries therefore are the ones you want to buy. And be sure that your cook in preparing cranberry sauce or jelly presses the pulp through a sieve to remove the indigestible skins. It is only when they are cooked whole and candied with an equal weight of sugar that the skins may be left on them.

Turkeys, Guinea Fowl, and Game.

Cranberry sauce is in America associated inseparably with turkey, and the turkey is another of our gastronomic specialties.

Benjamin Franklin argued that the turkey—which is surely a finer bird than the eagle, less vicious, and infinitely more useful—should have been adopted as the emblem of the United States, for it is a truly indigenous and national bird. In Franklin's day "the log cabin of the pioneer was surrounded by these birds, saluting each other in the early morning from the treetops."

Those were gala times for hunters and epicures, when wild turkeys used to fly in flocks of hundreds! They owe their name to the notion, once current, that they came to Europe from Asia. But it is now established beyond doubt that they are aboriginal Americans. It did not take the Spaniards long to find out their value, for, little more than a quarter of a century after Columbus discovered this Continent, they took some of the birds across the sea to their own country and thence the turkey soon made its way to other parts of Europe. Records show that in England, in 1541, the turkey was enumerated among the dainties, while in 1573 it had become the customary fare of the farmer.

"The turkey is beyond doubt one of the finest presents the New World has made the Old," wrote the best-known of French epicures, Brillat-Savarin; and in his "Physiologie du Gout" he has a chapter in which he proudly relates how he shot one of these birds. It was in 1794; he was visiting a friend at Hartford, Connecticut, who took him out hunting one day, after having treated him on the previous evening to a dinner one course of which consisted of the entirely American corned beef, which the eminent epicure found "splendid."

They shot some fat tender partridges and seven gray squirrels, "which are highly esteemed in this country"; then he had his chance at the turkey, bagged it, took it back to Hartford and had it cooked for some guests who kept exclaiming: "Very good! Exceedingly good! Oh, dear sir, what a glorious bit."

Though he had a high opinion of his own judgment in matters gastronomic, Brillat-Savarin was much pleased when a friend of his, M. Bose, who lived in Carolina, contributed to the "Annates d'Agriculture" of Feb. 28, 1821, an article which confirmed his own judgment as to the superiority of the American turkey to the bird as reared in France, attributing this superiority to the fact that the American turkey roamed the woods freely and thus gained a finer Flavor than the domesticated bird has.

Unfortunately, it took American poultry raisers several generations to realize the full significance of this fact. All was well so long as there were plenty of wild turkeys, the flesh of which was of perfect savor, especially during the autumn, when they lived largely on pecan nuts. All was well, too, so long as the farms were few and scattered, and there was interbreeding of wild and domesticated birds. Rut the time came when the turkeys degenerated, owing to excessive inbreeding and too close confinement. It is only within a few years that farmers have begun to heed the advice that "it is better to send a thousand mites for a new male than to risk the chances of inbreeding," and to restore to the turkey his forest freedom.

"While our present-day turkeys are classed as 'domestic fowls.' they are rather semi-domestic when compared with other poultry," writes T. F. McGrew.[4]

It is this semi-game quality of the best turkeys that make them so dear to the epicure. Brillat-Savarin's verdict is that the turkey, "though not the most tender, is the most tasty of all the farm fowls,"—and few will disagree with him.

For the benefit of the rapidly growing number of farmers who increase their income by raising turkeys, I will cite the words of an expert which sum up the philosophy of the subject:

> The flavor of all turkeys raised by careful farmers within five or six years is much finer than in the run down stock raised by old fogy farmers. The improvement in flavor has also been accompanied by an increase in size and tenderness. This is due to the admixture of the strain from wild turkeys from Canada and the South and the Southwest and to the modern system of keeping the birds out of doors as much as possible and giving them opportunities for getting plenty of mast and the seeds of wild and cultivated plants and pure water from brooks and streams kept clear from noxious plants and sewage.

Birds thus reared bring fancy prices—a point to which I shall recur in the next chapter under "Feeding Flavor Into Food."

It has been customary for a long time for patriotic persons to send to the President of the United States choice turkeys for the Thanksgiving and Christmas dinners. Woodrow Wilson received one in December, 1912, from Kentucky which weighed forty-three pounds and had been nurtured "as befits a King Gobbler," on sweet chestnuts, with celery and pepper to improve its Flavor.

The Guinea fowl is another bird which must roam wild to do well, and which consequently has a gamy Flavor, like the semi-domestic turkey. Though not an aboriginal American, it has become acclimated. It is an African cousin of the turkey.

In his useful treatise on "The Guinea Fowl and Its Use as Food" (Farmers' Bulletin No. 234), Dr. Langworthy states that in Jamaica and some other regions the Guinea birds "have gone back to their wild state and are hunted in their season as game birds. They are also well known as game birds in England, where large flocks are sometimes kept in game preserves."

On the continent they are more domesticated and are raised in large numbers for the markets of France, Austria, and Germany. What we want in our markets, however, is not the domesticated Guinea fowl so much as the half-wild. We have plenty of other good barnyard birds, including the savory squab, but we are woefully short of game, and the Guinea fowl, more than the turkey, comes to the rescue. While the mature bird has its own gamy Flavor, the chicks resemble young quail, and the eggs are a good deal like the highly valued plover eggs. Even the domesticated birds retain a surprising number of their wild traits and on this bird, therefore, we may have to depend largely for our game of the future.

To the deplorable condition of our present game market I referred briefly in the chapter on Germany, where they do things so much better. In New York, quail (so abundant until a few years ago) are now imported from far-away Egypt, and grouse from Scotland, while prices have gone up like rockets. In Louisiana alone it was computed that over 4,265,000 game birds were killed in the season 1909–1910. Mrs. Russell Sage's generous gift of $150,000 secured Marsh Island as a refuge for the wild fowl. Others have helped the cause, and the Government's efforts are thus summed up in Circular No. 87 of the Bureau of Biological Survey:

> For purposes of administration the bird reservations are grouped in six districts: (1) The Gulf district, including 10 reservations in Florida, 4 in Louisiana, and 1 in Porto Rico; (2) the Lake district, including 2 in Michigan, 2 in North Dakota, and 1 in Wisconsin; (3) the Mountain district, including 12 in the Rocky Mountain States, South Dakota, and Nebraska; (4) the Pacific district, including 3 in California, 4 in Oregon, and 8 in Washington; (5) the Alaska district, including 8 reservations; and (6) the Hawaiian district, including 1 reservation. Wardens are stationed on the more important reservations and the National Association of Audubon Societies . . . cooperates actively with the Department of Agriculture in protecting the birds.

There is a special periodical, the "Gamebreeders' Magazine," devoted to the task of replenishing our stock of wild animals, which was for so many generations one of the chief assets of Gastronomic America. There are also Breeders' Associations which are planning to make American game, feathered and unfeathered, abundant once more. No one can ever bring back the large flocks of wild turkeys, the pigeons that darkened the skies, the herds of countless buffaloes; but we can at least bring back in part our former abundance of some kinds of game by following European methods.

The Government is also ready to help by supplying, without charge, birds to be liberated and allowed to multiply in various places. Our native birds are, of course, best adapted for this purpose, but what can be done with imported birds is shown in Farmers' Bulletin No. 390, in which Henry Oldys of the Biological Survey tells the interesting story of how the Chinese and English pheasants have been made to feel at home in Oregon and in other States, where they have become permanent additions to the game list. "Deer Farming in the United States" is another valuable Farmers' Bulletin (No. 330), by D. E. Lantz. Its object is thus summed up:

> As a result of the growing scarcity of game animals in this country the supply of venison is wholly inadequate to the demand, and the time seems opportune for developing the industry of deer farming, which may be made profitable alike to the State and the individuals engaged therein. The raising of venison for market is as legitimate a business as the growing of beef and mutton, and State laws, when prohibitory, as many of them are, should be so modified as to encourage the industry. Furthermore, deer and elk may be raised to advantage in forests and on rough, brushy ground unfitted for either agriculture or stock raising, thus utilizing for profit much land that is now waste. An added advantage is that the business is well adapted to landowners of small means.

Mr. Lantz is convinced that, with favorable legislation, "this excellent and nutritious meat, instead of being denied to 99 per cent, of the population of the country, may become as common and as cheap in our markets as mutton."

Lobsters, Scallops, Crabs, and Fishes.

Every inch an American is the Homarus Americanus. There are not so many inches of him as there used to be, but that makes him none the less precious. The Pilgrim lobsters "five or six feet long," ascribed to New York Bay in the days of Olaus Magnus, are now classed as a myth, but four-foot lobsters (measured from the tip of the claws to the end of the tail) have been caught. Such a giant weighs about thirty-four pounds.

The American lobster was originally found only on the eastern coast of North America. These lobster grounds some seven thousand miles, including the curves of the shore, were the finest the world has ever seen. In Canada alone a hundred million lobsters have been captured in a year.

In one respect the lobster differs strangely from other creatures of sea and land. Like the eel, he is a scavenger of the deep, but while the eel is often offensive to the taste because of this feeding habit, the lobster is always sweet. "Nothing could be more offensive to the human nostril," writes Dr. Francis Hobart Herrick,[5] "than the netted balls of slack-salted, semi-decomposing herring, which are commonly used as bait on the coast and islands of Maine, but by the wonderful chemical processes which are continually going on in the laboratory of its body, the lobster is able to transmute such products of organic decay into the most delicate and palatable flesh."

Were it not for this alchemistic marvel the most plutocratic restaurants in the United States, especially those which cater to the persons who sup after the theater, would never have become known as Lobster Palaces. The lobster served in these places, plain boiled, broiled, à la Newburg, and in other ways, is one of those characteristic American foods which foreign epicures not only envy but enjoy, though they cannot have our crustaceans as fresh as we do.

It has been well said that "the story of the lobster in its progress from the fisherman's pots on the Maine coast to the grills and silver chafing-dishes on Broadway is the whole story in miniature of the high cost of living under an artificial economic condition." The lobsterman gets a little over ten cents a pound. "The wholesaler doubles the price, the retailer trebles it, and in the end the restaurant-keeper marks it up 1,000 per cent, above the first cost, charging patrons $1.50 a portion for what the lobsterman was paid a tenth of that sum."

To this extortion I, for one, refuse to submit. In the market you can buy a lobster for one quarter to one-third the price charged in most restaurants. You can make sure he is alive—never buy a dead lobster, though they say he is safe to eat if his tail is curled and springs back when pulled. To kill him by plunging him in boiling water may seem cruel, but is no more so than other ways, and is certainly infinitely less so than the usual way—which should be forbidden—of letting him perish slowly in a barrel, or on ice.

Canned lobster is a food a wise man avoids, though, to be sure, he runs perhaps no greater risk in eating it than in consuming many other things, tinned or untinned. Millions of dollars' worth of canned lobsters, crabs, and salmon are eaten every year.

A new American delicacy hails from Canada: lobster rarebit, a compound of certain parts of the lobster which had previously been thrown away as waste by the canners. The annual output of canned lobster by the Eastern Provinces of Canada now amounts to about ten million cans, worth about $3,000,000. Lobster rarebit, which is said to be a highly appetizing delicacy, easily digested and nourishing may, it is believed, in time equal the money value of canned lobsters. Consul Frank Deedmeyer, of Charlottetown, gave these details at the time when lobster rarebit was first introduced:

> Canned lobster, as known to the trade, consists of the meat taken from the claws and the tail. The whole of the body proper is now rejected by the packers, and it has heretofore been used in the maritime Provinces of Canada as a fertilizer. In the rejected portion is found a crescent-shaped meaty layer to which the tail is attached and the liver. Lobster

> rarebit is a compound of this meaty layer, of the liver, and of the roe, to which some spice is added. The first named of the components used is the fattest part of the crustacean; the liver, glandular, is large and retains a high percentage of bile. The number of eggs found in a lobster is estimated from 5,000 to 40,000, according to size. The three ingredients are mixed in these proportions: Six-tenths meat, three-tenths liver, and one-tenth roe.

While the efforts to propagate the Atlantic lobster have met with scant success on the Pacific Coast there are other marine delicacies to console those who dwell on the shore from Southern California to Washington and British Columbia; among them the abalone of Catalina, which makes delicious soup, the razor clam and monster specimens of other clams in Washington waters, oysters, huge crabs, and above all, crawfish.

In Oregon, the crawfish abounds in creeks and rivers, varying in size with the volume of the river. One of my favorite amusements as a boy used to be to sit on the bank of a creek taking care of several lines, to the ends of which were tied pieces of meat. No net was needed; the crustaceans were so abundant and so hungry that they refused to let go when lifted out of the water, and often I landed six or more fastened to the same piece of meat. Our favorite picnics were those for which we took along no food—only a kettle and a handful of salt. The crawfish did the rest. They are more tender and succulent than lobsters, and even more delicate in flavor.

St. Louis disputes with Portland the honor of being the greatest crawfish-eating center in the United States. The Mississippi River crawfish has made St. Louis famous among epicures. Until a few years ago, the "Republic" of that city informs us, "the waters around St. Louis on every side fairly swarmed with this freshwater relation of the lobster. Every pond, slough, and back water was full of them. All the creeks and pools were their homes. Their little mud 'chimneys' dotted the creek bottoms and lined the banks of the ponds and sloughs. Hundreds of joyous St. Louisans struck out for the open on every holiday, armed with a pole, a few pieces of liver, and a dip net, bent on their capture. They caught so many that they brought them in by the sackful. Thousands of the little crustaceans were eaten every day of the season. From April until after the snowfalls of November every real St. Louisan ate a few crawfish every week."

In 1910 this abundance had diminished to such an extent that a mandate was issued by the State Fish and Game officials which put a stop to angling in the city's waters. The crawfish multiplies so rapidly, however, that it will doubtless soon replenish the waters, and once more there will be parts of St. Louis and other cities where the evening air will be "laden with the unmistakable odor of boiling crawfish."

Of the great variety of crabs peculiar to our waters the one which most appeals to epicures is the "soft shell," which, when very soft, is eaten skin, bones, and all. But wait—there is another kind, still more delicate and toothsome—the oyster crab. It dwells within the mantle chamber and feeds on the juices of the oyster. No wonder it tastes good. Fortunately, it is not one of the many enemies of the bivalve, being quite harmless. Its scarcity, combined with its diminutive size, makes it a luxury comparable to the old Roman millionaire's dish of nightingale tongues.

A foreigner looking at an American bill of fare is struck first of all by the number of ways in which oysters are listed: raw, stewed, fried, steamed, baked in the shell, scalloped, creamed, and so on; and by the fact that the locality from which the oysters that are served raw are supposed to come is named—Blue Point, Shrewsbury, Rockaway, Buzzard's Bay, Cape Cod, Norfolk, Saddle Rock, etc. In this matter there is, to be sure, much deception. It has become customary, in particular, to give the name of Blue Point to any small oyster, and to call any kind of large size a Saddle Rock; while many a worthless floated oyster masquerades under the name of the juicy and delicious Lynnhaven. The oyster cracker, and the soda cracker in general, is an American specialty which Europeans will doubtless adopt some day as tasty, nutritious and easily digested additions to the dietary. As sold now, in dust and moisture-proof packages, they will easily find their way to foreign stomachs.

Clam chowder, steamed soft clams, and raw Littlenecks are among the delicacies an American misses in Europe.

As for our scallop, Paderewski thinks it is the best edible thing America produces. Many other epicures doubtless agree with him.

As seen in our markets the scallop is simply the abductor muscle of the bivalve. The remainder of the body is thrown away or used as fertilizer, though much of it is tender and of fine Flavor. Nor is this wasteful[n]ess the only cause for complaint. The best scallops are small; they are expensive, and the dealers, knowing that by soaking them they can bloat a pint of them till they fill a quart, subject them to this "freshening," which as thoroughly takes all the marine Flavor out of them as "floating" takes it out of the oyster. In this condition, too, they spoil sooner and become dangerous to eat. I agree with F. Powers that "a man who soaks scallops and then offers them for sale should be imprisoned." The scallop dredgers were among the first to take advantage of the new parcel post, which enables them to send the unspoiled mollusc to any one within a reasonable distance.

Concerning our fishes it is easy to say that the finest flavored are the shad, the whitefish, the Chinook salmon, the rainbow trout; but when you happen to be eating a baby bluefish or a Spanish mackerel just out of the water, you may change your mind for the time being; you are sure to do this, also, if you happen to be in New Orleans and eat fresh pompano as prepared by a Creole cook. The sheepshead, the smelt, the catfish, the sturgeon, the halibut, are excellent; and so is the swordfish, which is far too little known among gourmets. Its flesh might be more tender, but it has a fine Flavor, suggesting a combination of salmon and halibut.

It is for the cod, however, that I wish to plead most earnestly. Some persons (usually persistent smokers, or individuals whose sense of smell is not well developed) maintain that the cod is "tasteless." As a matter of fact it has a subtle but most delicious Flavor which, when the fish is fresh, reminds me of the flesh of crawfish.

At present (1913) the cod enjoys the advantage of being the only fish, with the exception of trout, that can be bought alive in the markets of New York. "Live cod," when listed on restaurant menus, is in great demand. It is not always equally good, however, because much of the "live cod" is really live hake, which is far inferior in Flavor. The substitution of haddock for cod is less objectionable. Much of the salted and dried fish which goes into the typically American codfish balls, is also cod in name only. Dealers who use benzoate of soda or other chemicals to preserve it, give elaborate directions for soaking them out. It is needless to say that this soaking process also takes out all the Flavor.

Vegetables Steadily Gaining Ground.

Historians are usually so deeply interested in all the petty details of politics that such trifles as the food which keeps us alive gets no attention at all. Macaulay was a laudable exception. Another is Macmaster. In the first volume of his "History of the People of the United States" he remarks that a century ago tomatoes, cauliflower, and eggplants were not to be found at the corner grocery; oranges and bananas were a luxury of the rich; and there were no cultivated varieties of strawberries or raspberries. Of apples and pears there were plenty, but "none of those exquisite varieties, the result of long and assiduous nursing, grafting, and transplanting, which are now to be had of every greengrocer."

In Boston, at that time, "beef and pork, salt fish, dried apples and vegetables, made up the daily fare from one year's end to another." "The wretched fox grape was the only kind that found its way to the market, and was the luxury of the rich." "Among the fruits and vegetables of which no one had then even heard are cantaloupes, many varieties of peaches and pears, tomatoes and rhubarb, sweet corn, the cauliflower, the eggplant, head lettuce and okra."

To-day, how different the situation! In the catalogues of the seedsmen more than fifty kinds of vegetables are listed, and of each kind a dozen, or several dozen, distinct varieties are offered for sale. Yet these varieties represent only a very small proportion of the vast number that have been created.

In his instructive book on Plant Breeding, L. H. Bailey has a chapter on one of the most deserving of American originators of new varieties of vegetables, N. B. Keeney, of Leroy, New York. Mr. Keeney was at one time raising sixty-five varieties of garden peas and sixty-nine of beans, thirteen of the latter of his own originating, including the stringless kinds which have been introduced throughout the country by Mr. Burpee, and which are one of America's greatest achievements in plant development. The Professor was told by Mr. Keeney that fully three thousand varieties and forms of beans had been discarded by him as profitless!

In the same volume Professor Bailey informs us that the date of the first fruit book is 1817. "In 1845, nearly two hundred varieties of apples were described as having been fruited in this country, of which over half were of American origin." In 1872 the number of varieties described was 1823, and in 1892 American nurserymen offered for sale 878 varieties of apples.

Among the vegetables which have been varied and improved by American breeders are the squashes, pumpkins, sweet potatoes, rhubarb, celery, corn, lettuce, tomatoes, watermelons, cantaloupes, cucumbers, potatoes, and eggplants.

One vegetable, Brussels sprouts, has not been improved but greatly impaired by some man (whether an American or a European I do not know) who crossed it with cabbage, making the sprouts larger but less finely flavored and also less digestible.

As I wrote of tomatoes, which are of American origin, in the chapters on France and Italy I have only a few words to add.

It is an odd fact that although we can claim this succulent vegetable as one of the New World blessings, it was in the Old World, in the Mediterranean countries that its gastronomic value was first fully realized. In the United States, as in England and Germany, there seems to have been a prejudice against it because of its belonging to the same family as the deadly nightshade.

Much ingenuity has been expended in creating new varieties and prolonging the season. It is a most unfortunate circumstance that some of our most important vegetables are killed by the slightest frost. This is true of squashes, pumpkins, potatoes, beans, cucumbers, melons, and tomatoes. Knowing that Luther Burbank had succeeded in making apple-blossoms frost-proof, I once asked him to please do the same for tomatoes. He shook his head and replied that that was beyond his powers, because of their semi-tropic origin and habits. Yellow tomatoes are not so much used (except for preserves) as they deserve to be. They have a very fine Flavor of their own. In regard to red varieties, it may be well to warn the breeders not to go too far in their efforts to create "beefsteak" varieties by reducing the seed pulp to a minimum. It is in that pulp that the richest Flavor is found, and the seeds do not appear to be indigestible.

Like the tomatoes, celery belongs to a family of poisonous plants and was also for a long time considered poisonous, which is doubtless the reason why it is only within comparatively recent years that it has come so much into demand. To-day it is raised all the way from Florida to Michigan, where it flourishes, particularly in the muck-bed area.

Celery is not indigenous to our soil. It has been used in Europe for centuries, but in the kitchen rather than as an ornament of the dining-room. In Italy, France, Germany, it is treated as a pot-herb, for flavoring stews and soups, the unbleached plant being preferred because of its more powerful Flavor; but all celery tops and leaves are useful for this purpose; they certainly do much to give zest to soups and stews. So far as known England was the first country to appreciate the charm of blanched celery. In a book called "The New World of Words," published by a nephew of Milton in 1678, we read that "Sellerie is an herb which, nursed up in a hot-bed and afterwards transplanted into rich ground, is usually whited for an excellent winter sallad."

We also use it to some extent as a salad, but it needs no vinegar for pungency, and most of us prefer to eat the stalks plain, cum grano salts. Few who eat it this way know that it is much more digestible if the stalk is broken in pieces and the fiber stripped off. Stewing softens the fibers. Cooked au jus, celery is almost better even than raw. If I had the choice of a dozen vegetables at dinner, I would more often than any other choose celery au jus.

Raw celery is seen so much more frequently on the table in this country than in any other that it may be virtually considered an American specialty. Nowhere else is it so crisp and tender, or so eagerly craved. It is a nerve tonic, and we need nerve tonics. While melons are not indigenous to America, many of the choicest varieties of cantaloupes and watermelons are creations of our growers. Nowhere in the world will you find anything to surpass in sweetness and fragrance the Emerald Gem, the New Spicy, or the Rocky Ford, most luscious of all.

The New World's most important contribution to other countries, so far as nutritive value is concerned, is the potato. How Ireland and Germany, in particular, could have ever got on without this vegetable, it is difficult to imagine.

Sweet potatoes also are of American origin. They have been slow in making headway in Europe because they do not, like the white potato, grow in almost any soil and climate. Farmers' Bulletin No. 324 is devoted to sweet potatoes. Its author, W. R. Beattie, of the Bureau of Plant Industry, remarks that "as a commercial truck crop the sweet potato would be included among the five of greatest importance, ranking perhaps about third in the list. As a food for the great mass of the people living in the warmer portions of our country the use of this crop is exceeded by hominy and rice only." In the Philippine Islands it is at certain seasons almost the only food available for the lower classes. There are many varieties, the soft, moist kinds being richer in Flavor than the others. These are preferred in the South where a mealy sweet potato would not be eaten.

The Fruit Eaters' Paradise.

Many a time, in contemplating the conditions described under the heading of "Ungastronomic America," have I wished I lived in Europe; yet, every time, my gastronomic allegiance to the Stars and Stripes is cemented again by the contemplation of the glorious fruits we produce. This feeling is the stronger because I had the rare good fortune to grow up in an Oregon apple orchard. Oregon apples gave me my college education, and my sturdy health, too, for nothing is more wholesome than apples, and from my eighth to my eighteenth year I ate more apples than anything else. In our orchard of many hundreds of trees there were scores of varieties, some of which I would no more have thought of eating than a raw potato. Not that they would not have found a ready sale in any market; but at home they were rejected because of their inferiority in Flavor to the Gravenstein, the Red Astrachan, the Baldwins, the Northern Spy, Yellow Newtown and Green Newtown Pippins, Winesap, Roxbury Russet, White Winter Pearmain, Swaar, Seek-No-Further, and the Rambo, juiciest of cider apples and good to eat out of hand.

We also used to peel and cut up apples for drying. Very few people know the most delicious way to eat apples. We knew it. Turn the wheel of the peeler round two or three times; that removes the skin; then keep on turning till all the pulp has peeled off into your left hand. Raise your head, drop into your mouth the pulp of the apple and you will know the meaning of the word Flavor. And the best of it is that if eaten that way, raw apples are not indigestible for anybody.

Thirty-two years after these glorious feasts had come to an end I was pleased to get for review E. P. Powell's delightful book, "The Country Home,"[6] and to find that that eminent connoisseur's ideas regarding the best American apples coincided in the main with my youthful convictions. I cannot too strongly urge my readers to get that volume and enjoy Mr. Powell's remarks—written con amore as well as with the knowledge of an expert—on the kinds of apples, pears, peaches, plums, cherries, and other fruits which it is most advisable to raise on American farms, and what is the best way to do it. Strawberries, gooseberries, currants and blackberries have a chapter to themselves, for of all these there are distinct American varieties—and under the heading, "Tons of Grapes," the author gives pages of appetizing information about the fruit which, next to apples, is a prime article of diet. He shows how you can manage to have grapes six or seven months every year, and tells what are the best varieties to grow. Every farmer and owner of a country home should raise grapes. "It is cheaper and better food than meat and vegetables, and they never tire of it. I recommend that you go out before breakfast and sample a half-dozen sorts; repeat the experiment before dinner, and if the digestion is poor, take nothing else for supper."

Grapes are nothing if not American—that is, some grapes are. They are indigenous to the soil, growing wild nearly everywhere, from the extreme south to the banks of the Androscoggin in Maine, where I have often picked them.

A curious and important difference between grapes in America and in Europe is noted by Professor Bailey in his "Sketch of the Evolution of Our Native Fruits." The American grape—that is, the ameliorated offspring of the native species, "is much unlike the European fruit. It is essentially a table fruit, whereas the other is a wine fruit. European writings treat of the vine, but American writings speak of grapes." Yet it was not till the middle of the nineteenth century that "the modern table use of the native grape began to be appreciated and understood."

That grapes were not brought from Europe to America is absolutely certain. Long before Columbus, there came across the sea Leif, who, in the words of Justin Winsor, "found vines hung with their fruit, which induced Leif to call the country Vineland." In New England, Edward Winslow wrote in 1621 that "here are grapes, white and red, and very sweet and strong also."

Professor Bailey's book is largely devoted to the men who improved American fruits—men who, as he justly intimates, deserve commemoration quite as much as persons who are distinguished in military operations. But while we, as a nation, have reason to feel proud of the achievements of these men, a great deal more remains to be done. Professor Bailey does not say which of our Eastern grapes he considers the best, but I am sure he would agree with me that the Delaware has a finer Flavor than any other kind, and of the four chief American grapes the Delaware is the only one "which gives any very strong evidence of foreign blood." This point has been disputed; but it is certainly true that "the types we grow are yet much inferior to the Old World types." Our Concords, Niagaras, and Catawbas, in particular, are capable of great improvement in the matter of Flavor. Fortunes are in store for growers who will take the hint.

It is well to bear in mind that there are varieties, such as the Iona, Eldorado, Brighton, Worden, Hayes, and Lindley, which, though not to be found in our wretched markets, are delicious. They are enjoyed by owners of country residences and their guests, even though city folk are unaware of their existence.

Altogether, the American grapes have given rise to some eight hundred domestic varieties, about one hundred of which may be found listed in catalogues. Flavors cannot be transplanted. European grapes grown in America get a different "taste," and the wines made of them have not the same bouquet. A few exceptions there are, notably the muscatel grape, which is almost as delicious in California as it is in Spain. But as a rule it is a waste of money to attempt to duplicate European fruits. Many millions have been spent in vain efforts to do this. To succeed, we must be American.

Long ago we learned to enjoy our game and our many varieties of distinctive sea foods of unique Flavor. Our native vegetables, wild nuts, fruits, and berries, we also appreciated, but these still offer limitless opportunities for improvement of their qualities—a proceeding which pays better than importing things European. Our nuts, among them the hickory, pine, and black walnut, are delightfully racy of the soil. They, too, are as American as the Indians, and wherever possible their intermarriage with our domesticated fruits and berries is a consummation devoutly to be wished.

Our wild crab-apples, for instance, of which there are five types, while excessively sour, have a superabundance of flavor. By transfusing their blood into the domesticated apples we can eliminate the excess of acid and give to many of our big apples a richer aroma.

The persimmon is one of our native fruits of unlimited possibilities. Heretofore, our markets have been supplied chiefly with the Japanese khaki, raised in California or Florida. It is a delicious fruit, but there are native varieties which in the opinion of some are even finer than the Japanese. Ordinarily the wild American persimmon is as sour and astringent as a crabapple, fit only for the 'coon and the 'possum. But there have been enthusiasts whose belief in the future of our persimmon amounted to a passion. One of these was Bryant, "whose zeal as a cultivator and whose interest in fruit-growing were almost as great as his poetic enthusiasm." To Professor Bailey he expressed his belief that the finest persimmons of the future would be grown in the alluvial meadows of southern Indiana.

While the persimmon is as delicious as the banana, the demand for it has not been so great as it will be when the public learns that this fruit has the finest Flavor and is most wholesome when it looks like an overripe tomato which no one would buy. An Italian pushcart man used to smile when he saw me approaching. He knew I would pick out those which were so soft that they could be taken home only in a paper box. "Ah, you know, you know!" he used to say, pleased that his best things were not left on his hands by the uninformed multitude.

As a boy I used to enjoy hugely the May apple—a plum-shaped fruit growing on a low plant. What was my indignation when, some years later, I began to study botany and found in Professor Asa Gray's text book a description of that fruit, ending with the words: "Eaten by pigs and boys." I promptly made up my mind that if adults do not relish this luscious fruit they have something to learn from pigs and boys.

Another Southern fruit, abundant in Missouri, which greatly pleased my boyish palate, was the pawpaw. Professor Bailey says that most people do not relish its flavor, nor does he believe that it will be possible to awaken much interest in this fruit. Mr. Powell, on the other hand, pays it a high tribute. He sees "no reason why this delicious fruit, a sort of hardy banana, should not be grown everywhere in our gardens."

Those are the words of an epicure. I am sure the pawpaw has a great future. To many it may be an acquired taste, but so are olives, and the most appetizing of all table delicacies, Russian caviare. I thank my stars that I always took naturally to such things; it has added much to the pleasures of life. So far as pawpaws are concerned, it will be easier to persuade skeptics to try to learn to like them if they are told that their juice is considered by medical men a great aid to digestion. Papain is much used as a substitute for soda mints.

Notes

1. "Food Value of Corn and Corn Products." Farmers' Bulletin No. 298, Washington, 1907.
2. "Cereal Breakfast Foods" is the title of Farmers' Bulletin No. 249, which tells about their composition, variety, digestibility, cost, adulteration, etc. American magazines thrive on the advertisements of breakfast cereals.
3. "The Production of Maple Syrup and Sugar." By A. Hugh Bryan, Chief Sugar Laboratory, Bureau of Chemistry, and William F. Hubbard, Forest Assistant, Forest Service, 1912.
4. "Turkeys: Their Standard Varieties and Management." Farmers' Bulletin, No. 200.
5. In his beautifully and illustrated "Natural History of the American Lobster." From Bulletin of the Bureau of Fisheries, 1909.
6. New York: McClure, Phillips & Co., 1904.

Source: Henry T. Finck, *Food and Flavor: A Gastronomic Guide to Health and Good Living* (New York: Century, 1913), 432–502.

1913 • 109 • Martha McCulloch-Williams, "There Was Barbecue, and Again There Were Barbecues"

Introduction: *Barbecue has been an American institution since the earliest days. American Indians barbecued game, and colonists barbecued game and domesticated animals. Below is one description on a barbecue that was prepared in one Southern* *family. The author, Martha McCulloch-Williams, was born in Tennessee but moved to New York, where she became a writer who contributed articles, short stories and poetry to national magazines such as* Harper's Monthly, Harper's Bazaar, *and* McClure's. *The excerpt below is from* Dishes & Beverages of the Old South *(1913), which was more than just a cookbook, as the excerpts about Southern barbecue demonstrate.*

There was barbecue, and again there were barbecues. The viand is said to get its name from the French phrase *a barbe d' ecu,* from tail to head, signifying that the carcass was cooked whole. The derivation may be an early example of making the punishment fit the crime. As to that I do not know. What I do know is that lambs, pigs, and kids, when barbecued, are split in half along the backbone. The animals, butchered at sundown, and cooled of animal heat, after washing down well, are laid upon clean, split sticks of green wood over a trench two feet deep, and a little wider, and as long as need be, in which green wood has previously been burned to coals. There the meat stays twelve hours—from midnight to noon next day, usually. It is basted steadily with salt water, applied with a clean mop, and turned over once only. Live coals are added as needed from the log fire kept burning a little way off. All this sounds simple, dead-easy. Try it—it is really an art. The plantation barbecuer was a person of consequence—moreover, few plantations could show a master of the art. Such an one could give himself lordly airs—the loan of him was an act of special friendship—profitable always to the personage lent. Then as now there were free barbecuers, mostly white—but somehow their handiwork lacked a little of perfection. For one thing, they never found out the exact secret of "dipney," the sauce that savored the meat when it was crisply tender, brown all over, but free from the least scorching.

Daddy made it thus: Two pounds sweet lard, melted in a brass kettle, with one pound beaten, not ground, black pepper, a pint of small fiery red peppers, nubbed and stewed soft in water to barely cover, a spoonful of herbs in powder—he would never tell what they were,—and a quart and pint of the strongest apple vinegar, with a little salt. These were simmered together for half an hour, as the barbecue was getting done. Then a fresh, clean mop was dabbed lightly in the mixture, and as lightly smeared over the upper sides of the carcasses. Not a drop was permitted to fall on the coals—it would have sent up smoke, and films of light ashes. Then, tables being set, the meat was laid, hissing hot, within clean, tight wooden trays, deeply gashed upon the side that had been next the fire, and deluged with the sauce, which the mop-man smeared fully over it.

Hot! After eating it one wanted to lie down at the spring-side and let the water of it flow down the mouth. But of a flavor, a savor, a tastiness, nothing else earthly approaches. Not food for the gods, perhaps, but certainly meat for *men.* Women loved it no less—witness the way they begged for a quarter of lamb or shoat or kid to take home. The proper accompaniments to barbecue are sliced cucumbers in strong vinegar, sliced tomatoes, a great plenty of salt-rising light bread—and a greater plenty of cool ripe watermelons, by way of dessert.

So much for barbecue edible. Barbecue, the occasion, has yet to be set forth. Its First Cause was commonly political—the old south loved oratory even better than the new. Newspapers were none so plenty—withal of scant circulation. Besides, reading them was work—also tedious and tasteless. So the great and the would-be great, rode up and down, and roundabout, mixing with the sovereigns, and enlightening the world. Each party felt honor bound to gather the sovereigns so they might listen in comfort. Besides—they wanted amusement—a real big barbecue was a sort of social exchange, drawing together half of three counties, and letting you hear and tell, things new, strange, and startling. Furthermore, it was no trouble to get carcasses—fifty to a hundred was not uncommon. Men, women, children, everybody, indeed, came. The women brought bread and tablecloths, and commonly much beside. There was a speaker's stand, flag draped—my infant eyes first saw the Stars and Stripes floating above portraits—alleged—of Filmore and Buchanan, in the campaign of '56. That meant the barbecue was a joint affair—Whigs and Democrats getting it up, and both eagerly ready to whoop it up for their own speakers. Naturally in that latitude, Fremont was not even named. No court costume with a tail three yards long, could to-day make me feel one-half so fine as the white jaconet, and green sash then sported.

It was said there were a thousand at the barbecue. The cheering, at its loudest, was heard two miles away. To me it seemed as though all the folk in the world had gathered in that shady grove—I remember wondering if there could possibly be so many watermelons, some would be left for the children. Four big wagon loads lay bobbing in the coolth of the spring branch. It was a very cold spring with mint growing beside it, as is common with springs thereabout. Early settlers planted it thus hard by the water—they built their houses high, and water got warm in carrying it up hill. Lacking ice houses, to have cool juleps, they had to be mixed right at the well-head. Sugar, spoons, goblets, and the jug, were easily carried down there.

Juleps were not mixed openly that day—but the speakers had pitchers full of something that seemed to refresh their eloquence, no less than themselves. They hammered each other lustily, cheered to the echo by uproarious partisans, from nine in the morning until six in the afternoon. Luckily for them, there were four of them, thus they could "spell" each other—and the audience. I did not mind them—not in the least. How should I—when right in front of me sat a lady with the most gorgeous flowers upon her white chip bonnet, and one beside me, who insisted upon my wearing, until time to go home, her watch and chain!

The watermelons held out—we took two big ones home to Mother, also a lot of splendid Indian peaches, and a fore-quarter of lamb. Mother rarely went out, being an invalid—so folk vied with each other in sending her things. I mention it, only by way of showing there were things to be sent, even after feeding the multitude. The black people went away full fed, and full handed—nobody who carried a basket had much relish for taking home again any part of its contents.

Source: Martha McCulloch-Williams, *Dishes & Beverages of the Old South* (New York: McBride, Nast, 1913), 273–278.

1914 • 110 • Gaillard Hunt, "The National Cookery"

Introduction: *Gaillard Hunt (1862–1924) was an American historian and civil servant. His book* Life in America One Hundred Years Ago *(1914) includes a chapter on American food in which he attributes good cookery to African Americans.*

The professional cooks of the country were negroes, and the national cookery came from them. They were taught the art by their white mistresses, but they had a natural aptitude for it and made it their own. They liked the heat of the kitchen, and preferred the desultory labor of cooking to any other form of work. They were proud of the praise they received from their masters and mistresses when they performed it well. It gave them a position of importance in the house and flattered their self-esteem. Their own pleasures were sensual, and they were very fond of eating, so they cooked with appreciation. While their cooking varied in the different sections of the country, in its general characteristics it was the same, and it was marked with the tropical origin of the cooks. The trained palate could tell if the food was cooked by a negro in New York as well as in Savannah. Probably the best cooking was in New Orleans, where the negroes had been taught by the French or creole settlers; but traces of creole cooking penetrated to the North. The race of good negro cooks lasted until the rise of the second generation of negroes after the Civil War. It has now almost disappeared, because the free-born negroes take no pride in domestic service and refuse to learn the art which their mothers in bondage practiced with so much success.

But it must not be supposed that the people who were rich enough to own or hire negro cooks were the only ones who lived well. On the farms in the well-settled portions of the country the prosperous and thrifty housewives were too intelligent to live uncomfortably, and epicures who had catholic tastes testified that their gastronomical experiences were agreeable when they enjoyed the hospitality of American farm-houses. The most interesting tribute came from the greatest authority, Anthelme Brillat Saverin, a French statesman who fled from France at the time of the revolution and spent several years of his exile in the United States. . . . He died in 1826, and his classic work, the *Physiologie du Gout,* was published after his death. It contains many pleasing allusions to the good eating he enjoyed when he lived in the United States. He described the abundant dinner he had at a farm-house in Connecticut—the superb piece of corned beef, the stewed goose, the magnificent leg of mutton, vegetables in plenty, and at each end of the table an enormous jug of excellent cider; and after dinner the daughters of the house prepared excellent tea.

In a primeval forest near Hartford Brillat Savarin shot a large wild turkey, and the feast which followed the next day he set down as a noteworthy event in a life of gastronomical adventures. He declared that the turkey was "one of the most beautiful presents that the New World had made to the Old," and he called attention to the fact that while it had been domesticated in all the countries of Europe, in America alone was it found in a state of nature. It was, he said, the favorite food of all classes, and they were united by this preference. When the farmers wished to make a feast they chose for the principal dish a turkey; so did the artisans and the workmen; so did the politicians and financiers. Dr. Johnson, writing his dictionary in 1755, defined a turkey as "a large domestick fowl supposed to come from Turkey," but the American origin of the fowl was generally known at a later day. It was plentiful enough in 1815 to be accessible to all but the poorest people.

Equally accessible to everybody and equally prized by all classes of the population were the oysters, which existed in the greatest profusion in the bays and rivers along the whole coast, but were thought to reach their perfection in Chesapeake Bay. Oyster-houses were common in the cities, where they were eaten raw on the shell. At Le Count's United States Refectory, at the corner of Fifth and Chestnut Streets, in Philadelphia, was a famous oyster-bar, presided over for many years by John Gardener, who opened so many oysters that he became an authority on their habits and printed the result of his observations in an amusing and instructive pamphlet.

But the people were fond of other and less wholesome food than turkeys and oysters. There is an account of Mrs. Madison at breakfast at Monticello buttering her muffin carelessly and being told how she ought to do it by one of the young children at the table. Thus from childhood to old age the Southerners were eaters of hot bread; but the evil existed in all parts of the country. Buckwheat-cakes and flapjacks were eaten immoderately in the East, and hot rolls, muffins, and biscuits were on every breakfast-table in the South. There was a cheerful interchange of products between the sections, and buckwheat-cakes were in the South and hot rolls in the North. Foreigners generally commented unfavorably upon the habit of eating hot bread, and declared it was the cause of much of the ill health of the people. American physicians also advised against it; but admonition was in vain, and it has continued without appreciable diminution to the present day.

The custom of eating salted meat, especially pork, was not confined to America, but was more prevalent here than it was elsewhere. Nearly everybody in the country districts and many in the city regarded salt pork as the staff of life. The hogs were killed late in the autumn and their meat eaten every day in the year. Even to this day in certain sections of the country the word "meat" is commonly understood to mean pork. Probably the constant use of salted meat was another reason for the thirst of the people. Pork in the shape of hams was eaten by everybody, and a well-furnished dinner-table was considered to be incomplete without it.

The custom of serving dinner in courses was not practised as we now practise it. Ordinarily, the whole dinner was on the table at the same time, but for a special feast there might be two courses of the same character and each a dinner in itself. The attractiveness of the table depended upon the symmetrical arrangement of the dishes and upon their garnishment. There would be nine or ten large dishes upon the table, besides a number of smaller ones. The tablecloth would hardly be visible. An opulent man giving a dinner-party would serve something like the following: for the first course, "cod's head," being the head and shoulders of a fresh codfish, a dish much esteemed at the time; pea-soup, venison, chickens roasted, boiled ham, beef collops, which corresponded with beefsteak; potatoes, celery, parsnips, jelly, pies, and marrow pudding. For the second course, turkey poults (young turkeys), scolloped oysters, roasted rabbits, wild ducks, lamb, smelts, haricot (usually written "harrico," being a mutton ragout), several vegetables, cherry tarts, and stewed pippins. Then there would be brought in some ice-cream by itself. It was considered to be a great luxury, and it was eaten on rare occasions. The decanters of wine were distributed about the table. The servants placed the dishes on the table and changed the plates and knives and forks from time to time. The largest dishes of meat were carved by the host and hostess, and the person nearest a dish was expected to help his neighbors to it. Thus they all fed one another, and everybody was busy. The wine-drinking began early in the feast, and the people drank one another's health individually and collectively. After the second course the cloth was removed, the wine was replaced, fresh glasses were put on, and probably a fresh vintage, with nuts and fruit. The hostess then withdrew with the other ladies, if there were any; but the dinner-party was a pleasure generally reserved for men. Around the bare mahogany they drank lightly or heavily, as the case might be. At these dinners discussions of importance often took place as the madeira or claret circulated, agreements for political action were reached, the fate of ambitious aspirants for public office was determined, financial projects were arranged. How many acts done in the cold light of day were the result of suggestion or encouragement coming from men who were warmed with wine and good feeding sitting at the dinner-table is beyond power of calculation. One illustration can be given, but similar instances could be multiplied. It was at a dinner-party given by Thomas Jefferson to Alexander Hamilton in 1789 that an agreement was made by which the Capital of the United States was located upon the banks of the Potomac and the general government assumed the debts of the states. It may be that those communities where dinner-giving was common exerted greater influence upon national affairs than communities where the men seldom ate and drank together enjoyed.

After the wine-drinking at a dinner-party the surviving guests went to the drawing-room and drank tea with their hostess. Coffee did not figure on these occasions, and it was not as generally drunk as it was at a later period. In fact, the consumption in the next thirty years increased by more than twelve-fold. The tea-drinking or the uninterrupted wine-drinking might run into supper, in which case the party would not break up till eleven o'clock at night. The dinner having begun at three o'clock, which was a late hour even in the cities, there would have been about eight hours of continuous eating and drinking. At some tables an innovation in the courses was being adopted by serving the fish and soup as a first course by themselves, but nobody had yet thought of a dinner of eight or ten courses. Silver forks were used at the dinner-party, but for every-day purposes steel three-pronged forks were universal. As they did not hold some kinds of food very well, it was not considered inelegant to convey food from the plate to the mouth with the knife.

Naturally, it was only a small proportion of the people who went to private dinner-parties, but the public had opportunities of accomplishing something of the same result by attending the public dinners which were given in the towns and villages and attended by people from the surrounding country. The reason, or the excuse, for holding them was to celebrate notable anniversaries or events or to do honor to public men. A great many were given on the 4th of July and the 22d of February, and there were a number in honor of the Treaty of Ghent. Often they were political gatherings designed to influence public opinion. A local committee managed the feast and sold the tickets to any one who cared to pay for them. They cost about a dollar each, or perhaps more, some dinners being more expensive than others. The shopkeepers, proprietors, people of all classes except the laborers, attended them. It was easy enough to load the long tables with substantial food and with liquor, punch, and wine. If a band of music was obtainable it played before and during the dinner. Usually it could not play afterward. The local militia escorted the lion of the occasion in procession through the streets to the dinner. If there was a cannon available it thundered salutes to persons and sentiments. The committee drew up a long list of toasts, to which were added by various guests what were called "volunteers." Most of the toasts were printed in the newspaper after the dinner, and they were supposed to show the trend of public sentiment. They aimed to be epigrammatical expressions of that sentiment. A few will serve to illustrate their general character. At the dinner given early in 1815 to Commodore McDonough at Trap, New Castle County, Delaware, near the place of his birth, one toast was: "The American character, as much caressed since, as it was despised before our late struggle—Honor to the brave men, both on the sea and land, who, at imminent risk of their lives, brought their country into notice and established its national character."

At one given June 15, 1815, at Fairfield, Vermont, to General Wooster: "The Constitution of the United States—the basis of our independence, the cement of our Union—may it be kept sacred and inviolable as the tables of stone in the Ark of the Covenant."

At a dinner given to General William Henry Harrison at Petersburg, Virginia, in March, 1817: "The people—brave, patriotic, virtuous; free, sovereign, and independent. Four guns."

"The American navy—the ocean and the lakes, the grand theaters of its glory. Two guns."

"The Spanish patriots—contending for liberty. Whilst we sigh for their misfortunes we glory in their triumph. Two guns."

There might be twenty toasts or more at a dinner, and a man who drank them all must have got very tipsy, but many of the diners did so independently of the toasts. In a former chapter we saw that the members of the first temperance society excepted public dinners from their agreement not to drink; and in another place, that the doctors said there was always an increase in the amount of sickness in a town after a public dinner. They were demoralizing assemblages. What with the music, the speech-making, the hurrahing, the cannon-firing, and the drinking, there was excitement enough to tear the nerves of the participants asunder. The only thing that can be said in their favor is that they brought men of different classes together on a plane of common interest and enabled them to know one another at their worst. The whisky-bottle is a rough promoter of democracy.

Source: Gaillard Hunt, *Life in America One Hundred Years Ago* (New York: Harper and Brothers, 1914), 219–227.

1914 • 111 • Smith-Lever Act

Introduction: *The Smith-Lever Act of 1914 established the Cooperative Extension Service and provided federal funds for cooperative extension activities through a partnership of the U.S. Department of Agriculture and the land-grant universities. The intent was to enhance the sharing of practical information with homemakers and farmers. The act required states to match federal funding and is considered one of the most successful pieces of agricultural legislation ever adopted by the U.S. Congress.*

Smith-Lever Act

Be it enacted by the Senate and House of Representatives of the United States of America in Congress assembled, That in order to aid in diffusing among the people of the United States useful and practical information on subjects relating to agriculture and home economics, and to encourage the application of the same, there may be inaugurated in connection with the college or colleges in each State now receiving, or which may here-after receive, the benefits of the Act of Congress approved July second, eighteen hundred and sixty-two, entitled "An Act donating public lands to the several States and Territories which may provide colleges for the benefit of agriculture and the mechanic arts" (Twelfth Statues at Large, page five hundred and three), and of the Act of

Congress approved August thirtieth, eighteen hundred and ninety (Twenty-sixth Statutes Large, page four hundred and seventeen and chapter eight hundred and forty-one), agricultural extension work which shall be carried on in cooperation with the United States Department of Agriculture: Provided, That in any State in which two or more such colleges have been or hereafter may be established, the appropriations hereinafter made to such State shall be administered by such college or colleges as the legislature of such State may direct: Provided further, That, pending the inauguration and development of the cooperative extension work herein authorized, nothing in this Act shall be construed to discontinue either the farm management work or the farmers' cooperative demonstration work as now conducted by the Bureau of Plant Industry of the Department of Agriculture.

Section 2. That cooperative agricultural extension work shall consist of the giving of instruction and practical demonstrations in agriculture and home economics to persons not attending or resident in said colleges in the several communities, and imparting to such persons information on said subjects through field demonstrations, publications, and otherwise; and this work shall be carried on in such manner as may be mutually agreed upon by the Secretary of Agriculture and the State agricultural college or colleges receiving the benefits of this Act.

Section 3. That for the purpose of paying the expenses of said cooperative agricultural extension work and the necessary printing and distributing of information in connection with the same, there is permanently appropriated, out of any money in the Treasury not otherwise appropriated, the sum of $480,000 for each year, $10,000 of which shall be paid annually, in the manner hereinafter provided, to each State which shall by action of its legislature assent to the provisions of this Act: Provided, That payment of such installments of the appropriation herein before made as shall become due to any State before the adjournment of the regular session of the legislature meeting next after the passage of this Act may, in the absence of prior legislative assent, be made upon the assent of the governor thereof, duly certified to the Secretary of the Treasury: Provided further, That there is also appropriated an additional sum of $600,000 for the fiscal year following that in which the foregoing appropriation first becomes available, and for each year thereafter for seven years a sum exceeding by $500,000 the sum appropriated for each preceding year, and for each year thereafter there is permanently appropriated for each year the sum of $4,100,000 in addition to the sum of $480,000 hereinbefore provided: Provided further, That before the funds herein appropriated shall become available to any college for any fiscal year plans for the work to be carried on under this Act shall be submitted by the proper officials of each college and approved by the Secretary of Agriculture. Such additional sums shall be used only for the purposes hereinbefore stated, and shall be allotted annually to each State by the Secretary of Agriculture and paid in the manner hereinbefore provided, in the proportion which the rural population of each State bears to the total rural population of all the States as determined by the next preceding Federal census: Provided further, That no payment out of the additional appropriations herein provided shall be made in any year to any State until an equal sum has been appropriated for that year by the legislature of such State, or provided by State, county, college, local authority, or individual contributions from within the State, for the maintenance of the cooperative agricultural extension work provided for in this Act.

Section 4. That the sums hereby appropriated for extension work shall be paid in equal semiannual payments on the first day of January and July of each year by the Secretary of the Treasury upon the warrant of the Secretary of Agriculture, out of the Treasury of the United States, to the treasurer or other officer of the State duly authorized by the laws of the State to receive the same; and such officer shall be required to report to the Secretary of Agriculture, on or before the first day of September of each year, a detailed statement of the amount so received during the previous fiscal year, and of its disbursement, on forms prescribed by the Secretary of Agriculture.

Section 5. That if any portion of the moneys received by the designated officer of any State for the support and maintenance of cooperative agricultural extension work, as provided in this Act, shall by any action or contingency be diminished or lost, or be misapplied, it shall be replaced by said State to which it belongs, and until so replaced no subsequent appropriation shall be apportioned or paid to said State, and no portion of said moneys shall be applied, directly or indirectly, to the purchase, erection, preservation, or repair of any building or buildings, or the purchase or rental of land, or in college-course teaching, lectures in colleges, promoting agricultural trains, or any other purpose not specified in this Act, and not more than five per centum of each annual appropriation shall be applied to the printing and distribution of publications. It shall be the duty of each of said colleges annually, on or before the first day of January, to make to the governor of the State in which it is located a full and detailed report of its operations in the direction of extension work as defined in this Act, including a detailed statement of receipts and expenditures from all sources for this purpose, a copy of which report shall be sent to the Secretary of Agriculture and to the Secretary of the Treasury of the United States.

Section 6. That on or before the first day of July in each year after the passage of this Act the Secretary of Agriculture shall ascertain and certify to the Secretary of the Treasury as to each State whether it is entitled to receive its share of the annual appropriation for cooperative agricultural extension work under this Act, and the amount which it is entitled to receive. If the Secretary of Agriculture shall withhold a certificate from any State of its appropriation, the facts and reasons therefor shall be reported to the President, and the amount involved shall be kept separate in the Treasury until the expiration of the Congress next succeeding a session of the legislature of any State from which a certificate has been withheld, in order that the State may, if it should so desire, appeal to Congress from the determination of the Secretary of Agriculture. If the next Congress shall not direct such sum to be paid, it shall be covered into the Treasury.

Section 7. That the Secretary of Agriculture shall make an annual report to Congress of the receipts, expenditures, and results of the cooperative agricultural extension work in all of the States receiving the benefits of this Act, and also whether the appropriation of any State has been withheld; and if so, the reasons therefor.

Section 8. That Congress may at any time alter, amend, or repeal any or all of the provisions of this Act.

Source: Smith-Lever Act, May 8, 1914, 7 USC §343.

1918 • 112 • Pauline Dunwell Partridge and Hester Martha Conklin, *Wheatless and Meatless Days*

Introduction: *When the United States entered World War I, food was an important matter. More than 1 million Americans served in the U.S. Army and the U.S. Navy during the war, and many had been farm laborers before the war. With less labor, American farmers had to feed the army and navy and the American population. Because most of our new allies, particularly the United Kingdom and France, were in desperate need of food, President Woodrow Wilson created the U.S. Food Administration and appointed Herbert Hoover to lead the agency. To support the war effort, Hoover asked American civilians to eat less wheat and meat and consume more fruit and vegetables. This is one of many cookbooklets published during World War I that encouraged civilians to eat wheatless and meatless meals in the expectation that food would win the war.*

This Is What the Food Administrator Urges. Is this Little Too Much?

The wise and careful use of butter, fat, and milk.
The substitution of other fats for butter in cooking.

FDA poster promoting its Meatless and Wheatless Days conservation campaign, ca. World War I. (Library of Congress)

The substitution, wherever possible, of other cereals for wheat.
The use of fish, eggs, and cheese to reduce the demand for beef, pork, and mutton.
The more extensive use of vegetables and fruits.
Waste must be eliminated.
Perishable foods locally grown must be consumed more freely.

Foreword

Our object in the preparation of this little book at this critical time in our nation's history, when the conservation of food by the women of the country is a part of our battle array, is to put before the housewives of America, at low cost, recipes for dishes so simple, nourishing, and attractive that the matter of reducing the household expenditure and the preserving of the food supply will be an interesting pastime rather than a disagreeable experiment.

We have not gone into the matter of food values as we feel that the average housewife from her own experience will realize from the recipes themselves their substantial qualities.

Once introduced into the family circle they are certain to make many friends who will cling to them long after the war is over.

The practical self-denial of our meatless and wheatless days is strengthening the arms and the hearts of all Americans at home in a peaceful land or abroad in the turmoil of war, as well as sending food to thousands stripped of the very necessities of existence.

We offer you this little volume with the hope that it may prove a helpful guide in your daily efforts to do your bit in your household, and in a larger way assist our Nation and our Allies by pointing the way toward a reasonable self-sacrifice possible to every man, woman, and child whose heart "follows the flag."

Source: Pauline Dunwell Partridge and Hester Martha Conklin, *Wheatless and Meatless Days* (New York: D. Appleton, 1918), v–vii.

1919 • 113 • "Is This the Biggest Farm in the World?"

Introduction: *During World War I, the U.S. government called on farmers to maximize production, especially of wheat that was needed for the war effort. Mechanization of farms accelerated due to the loss of farm labor to the military and the massive profits generated for farmers as a result of the increased demand for farm goods. The result was the beginning of a very different type of farm. Thomas Campbell, owner of a large Montana wheat farm, proclaimed that the farm is a factory. Such farms were operated on mass production, cost accounting, specialized machinery, and skilled labor. Below is a description of that farm in 1919. Campbell's farm thrived (see Document 119).*

Is This the Biggest Farm in the World?

One result of the Government's efforts to increase the production of wheat during the last two years has been the creation of the largest wheat farm in the world, some 200,000 acres of Indian lands in Montana and Wyoming. If this farm yields only

20 bushels per acre it will mean 4,000,000 bushels of wheat added to the 1919 crop, which at the government price of $2.26 per bushel, would be worth $9,040,000.

There are two other remarkable things about this farm: in the first place, it was conceived and is being managed by one man, Thomas D. Campbell, formerly a North Dakota farmer; in the second place, not a single horse will be in use on the property. Instead, huge tractors, the largest ever built, will do all the work of plowing, seeding, and harvesting. They will also do it more quickly than has ever been done by the use of horses. As a matter of fact, without tractors it would be impossible to run this big farm at all. The number of horses, or other animals, required would be prohibitive, to say nothing of the expense of feeding them and extra farm laborers to handle them.

The farm has been divided into units of 5,000 acres and to each unit has been assigned one giant tractor, with a dozen held in general reserve in case of accident. Each unit also has its own group of permanent buildings, modernly equipped, and is under the direct charge of a competent farm manager. Under this manager is a general foreman, who will see to hiring the help and getting the work done. But over all stands Mr. Campbell, who is constantly on the go from unit to unit, supervising the more important features of the entire job.

In the beginning Mr. Campbell figured out the whole thing: how much machinery would be required, and how much time should be allowed for plowing, seeding, harvesting and so on. Everything is done on a schedule and as this is dry farming land, no allowance has to be made for bad weather. The greater part of the plowing was done last fall. Some idea of the capacity of the huge tractors may be gained from the fact that fourteen of them plowed more than 350 acres in a day, none of which had ever before been broken by the plow.

Before he could lease the Indian lands Mr. Campbell had to make arrangements with Secretary of the Interior Lane. He was actuated purely by patriotic motives—to help the Government in its efforts to stimulate the food production. He stated frankly to Secretary Lane that he was willing to enroll with the dollar-a-year man if the Government financed the project, and if he financed himself he only wanted a chance to break even. The latter plan was accepted by Secretary Lane.

Source: Robert H. Moulton, "Is This the Biggest Farm in the World?," *Scientific American* 121 (August 23, 1919): 183.

1919 • 114 • Harvey V. Wiley, "Soft Drinks"

Introduction: *Soft drinks—beverages that contained little or no alcohol—emerged in the mid-19th century. In general, they were considered alternatives to hard (or alcoholic) drinks. Thousands of different types of sodas emerged as the temperance movement picked up steam in the early 20th century. Not everyone was happy with the ingredients in many soft drinks. Harvey W. Wiley (1844–1930), for instance, was a crusader for pure food who was instrumental in exposing adulterated foods, and his work contributed to the passage of the Pure Food and Drug Act in 1906. He was also concerned about adulterations in beverages, including soft drinks. Below is an excerpt from his book,* Beverages and Their Adulteration *(1919).*

Pop.—The term "pop" is applied to a carbonated beverage, and doubtless the name has been derived from the slight explosion which takes place when the stopper is removed. There is no rule nor regulation followed by the manufacturers of so-called pops. Generally the water which is used is colored, usually with caramel, and also flavored with different flavoring substances, either of a natural or synthetic character. If the flavoring substances are of natural origin they can hardly be objected to. The use of synthetic flavors, that is, ethereal compounds derived from alcohols, is not to be commended in any case. While many of these flavors are practically harmless in small quantities, they belong to a class of bodies which must be used with great discrimination, and it is best to have them eliminated altogether. There is one component of these waters which the consumer should be aware of, namely, that they are generally sweetened. Pops are sold largely in hot weather, and especially at great outdoor gatherings, like baseball games. A sweetened water has very little, if any, value as a remedy for thirst. In fact, one of the best ways to induce thirst is to eat large quantities of sugar or drink large quantities of sweetened water. Nature requires a lot of dilution in order to make this excess of sweets tolerable. Therefore, there is little if any benefit, as far as quenching thirst is concerned, derived from the consumption of these articles.

Lemonade.—Lemonade is a beverage almost as widely consumed as soda water throughout all parts of the United States. Lemonade is a beverage made from the expressed juice of lemons, sweetened to suit the taste with sugar. The water which is employed may be either plain, potable water or sometimes water impregnated with carbon dioxid. The lemon juice which is used in lemonade contains not only the acid citrate of potash as its acidifying agent, but also the aromatic flavors, consisting of oil, ethers, etc., characteristic of the lemon itself. The rinds are frequently added and give an additional bitter taste due to a glucoside of some kind, probably of a tannic nature, residing particularly in the skins.

Orangeade.—Orangeade is a beverage similar to that described under lemonade, in which the orange juice is employed instead of lemon juice. The same descriptive matter is applied to it as to lemonade. Inasmuch as orange juice is less acid than lemon juice, a smaller quantity of sugar is employed in the manufacture of this beverage.

Limeade.—The term "limeade" is applied to a beverage made from the juice of limes and in the same manner as described for lemonade. As lime juice is considerably more acid than lemon juice, a larger quantity of sugar is employed than for lemonade. All of these beverages are usually served very cold, in fact, colder than is required for health and flavor. Instead of having them near the temperature of ice, they would be much better in every respect if drunk at a temperature of about 50°.

Soft Drinks Containing Caffein.—The laws controlling the traffic in cocain and its sales have become so strict that the use of this body in so-called soft drinks is practically prohibited. The only alkaloid which is employed at the present time in the preparation of these beverages is caffein. Caffein is an alkaloid of somewhat restricted occurrence, being found chiefly in coffee, tea, cola nuts, yerba mate, and guarana. In the cylindrical sticks of the plant guarana prepared for the market, as high as 5 percent of caffein is sometimes found.

The caffein which is used commercially is extracted chiefly from tea sweepings, although it may be obtained from coffee which is used in making Kaffee Hag and similar preparations. It is a white crystalline powder, colorless when pure, and at high temperatures is sublimed unchanged. It has a somewhat bitter taste and is soluble in water. It is a substance known in chemistry as a base, that is, it unites with acids to form salts.

The effects of caffein are well known, and in large quantities it produces sleeplessness and other injurious effects. Even in small quantities it acts strongly on certain individuals who are more or less idiosyncratic to its effects. It is consumed in large quantities by the tea and coffee drinkers of the world. Chocolate and cocoa also contain small quantities of caffein, but the principal alkaloid in cocoa is theobromin.

The chief soft drink which contains caffein is coca cola. In addition to the content of caffein, coca cola also contains the extract from coca leaves from which the cocain has been previously obtained. In addition to this, also, a very small quantity of cola nut is employed, together with sugar, caramel and acid and aromatic substances. The composition of coca cola syrup as disclosed before the federal court in Chattanooga is as follows:

Caffein (grains per fluid ounce).........0.92–1.30
Phosphoric acid (H_3PO_4) (percent).........0.26–0.30
Sugar, total (percent).........48.86–58.00
Alcohol (percent by volume).........0.90–1.27
Caramel, glycerin, lime juice, essential oils, and plant extractive.........Present
Water (percent).........34.00–41.00

From the above composition it is seen that coca cola, that is, the syrup from which the drink is made, consists of about half sugar, one-third water, and the remainder the substances mentioned in the analysis above. In preparing the beverage about one ounce of the syrup, as indicted above, is used per glass. The active principle on which its vogue mainly depends is the caffein. When caffein is taken in from one- to two-grain doses, as is the case with those who drink tea, coffee and coca cola, the effects are prompt and, as a rule, agreeable. There is a sense of gentle exhilaration, a relief from the oppression of fatigue, and a decided wakefulness or stimulation of the nerve centers. This condition continues for several hours, so that the effect produced is never by any means transitory.

Authorities competent to judge of the effects of caffein from a scientific point of view, differ widely in their estimates of its effect upon the human system. All admit that in excessive quantities it is harmful. Some maintain that even in small quantities, when its use is continued, harm is done the organism. Others maintain that in small quantities in most persons, that is, in quantities not exceeding from 5 to 10 grains of caffein per day, no evil effects are produced, and even beneficial effects may be expected. The layman is of necessity somewhat confused in this multitude of conflicting opinions. The safe attitude to take on a question of this kind, it seems to me, is that which should be assumed in reference to alcoholic beverages and tobacco, namely, that inasmuch as there is a difference of opinion among experts, the layman will do well to follow the rule of avoiding in his diet anything which is not necessary and which may possibly produce injury. These various opinions are well illustrated by the testimony of experts before the federal court. Dr. John Witherspoon, former President of the American Medical Association, testified that he had treated twenty or thirty patients afflicted with coca cola habit in four or five years. When they gave up the habit their health improved. He said:

A driver in New Orleans stands in front of his Coca-Cola delivery truck full of cases of the bottled soft drink, 1929. (Bettmann/Corbis)

> I regard coca cola as habit-forming. One glass creates a demand for another, because it stimulates the user and makes him feel better. Then when the effect wears off the feeling is one of depression, and he gets very nervous and seemingly cannot do without it very well.

The above may be regarded as a type of the testimony given by physicians who believe that coca cola is harmful.

Dr. Victor C. Vaughn, former President of the American Medical Association, testified:

> I am of the opinion that coca cola syrup, taken in the form of a beverage in proportion of one ounce of syrup to 6 or 7 ounces of carbonated water, taken five or six times in the course of a day, would not produce injurious effects. I have no doubt it would be stimulating to the brain and muscles and to some extent possibly to the kidneys slightly, but such stimulation would be normal. . . . I should say that caffein should not be given to children under 7 years of age. . . . Because a certain drug does not produce an observably harmful effect, does not at all prove that it is not deleterious. Even one or one and a half grains of caffein may prove harmful to many persons, and I have no doubt there are many people who should not take caffein at all. I would prohibit caffein altogether to children under 7 years of age, and even above that age there may be some, and no doubt there are many, to whom it should not be given.

The above-contrasted opinions of two eminent medical men, each of whom has been President of the American Medical Association, show the wide variance of view of competent experts in the case, and yet a quite agreeing opinion that at times and in some individuals caffein is harmful.

When coca cola was first made the unextracted leaves of the coca were employed, and thus a small amount of cocain was found in the beverage. Subsequently the use of the fresh leaves of coca was abandoned and the exhausted leaves employed in their place. Many attempts have been made to introduce other caffeinated beverages to the people of the country, at first by giving them a name similar in some respects to coca cola. The courts have uniformly decided that such imitations are a violation of the copyrights of the Coca Cola Company. These imitations of coca cola, both in name and composition, have therefore not secured any lasting vogue. It is of importance that the people of the country should understand the nature of a beverage of this kind, in order that they may intelligently assume a proper position in respect of its use.

The Cola or Ola Drinks.—The remarkable success of the Coca Cola Company of Atlanta, Georgia, in building up a very great and lucrative business in the sale of coca cola has induced many other manufacturers to imitate, as nearly as possible, the name adopted by the Coca Cola Company. Aside from the unethical principle involved, it is gratifying to know that the public is not slow to distinguish the genuine from the imitation. In other words, if anyone wishes to drink a cola or an ola he prefers to take the original article rather than its substitutes. Whether or not all the various beverages which use "cola" or "ola" in some form in their names are also imitations of coca cola in composition, I am unable to say. At least, however, an informed person, knowing the nature of coca cola, would reasonably expect that any "cola" or "ola" drink of any kind would not be content with imitating only the name of the original article, but also to some extent its composition. It is fair to presume, therefore, that the "colas" or "olas" as a class contain caffein as the active and valuable ingredient.

The family of colas or olas is increasingly great. The Report of the President's Homes Commission, appointed by President Roosevelt to study the condition existing in the homes of the country, contained a list of cola or ola drinks, so-called, which is found on pages 268 and following of the Report. The names of these beverages, as printed in this Report, are as follows:

Afri Cola, The Afri Cola Co., Atlanta, Ga.
Ala Cola, Ala Bottling Works, Bessemer, Ala.
Carre Cola, E. Carre Co., Mobile, Ala.
Celery Cola, The Celery Cola Co., Birmingham, Ala.; Dallas, Texas; Nashville, Tenn., and St. Louis, Mo.
Chan Ola, L. M. Channell, New Orleans, La.
Chera Cola, Union Bottling Works, Columbus, Ga.
Coca Cola, Coca Cola Co., Atlanta, Ga.
Cola Coke, Lehman-Rosenfeld Co., Cincinnati, Ohio. (This preparation was formerly sold under the name of Rocco Cola.)
Cream Cola, Jebeles & Calias Co., Birmingham, Ala.
Four Kola, Big Four Bottling Works, Waco, Texas.
Hayo Kola, Hayo Kola Co., Norfolk, Va.
Heck's Cola, Heck & Co., Nashville, Tenn.
Kaye Ola, A. W. Kaye, Meridian, Miss.

Kola Ade, Wiley Manufacturing Co., Atlanta, Ga.
Kola Kola, W. J. Stange Co., Chicago, Ill.
Kola Phos, John Wyeth and Bro., Philadelphia, Pa.
Kos Kola, Sethness Co., Chicago, Ill.
Lime Cola, Alabama Grocery Co., Birmingham, Ala.
Lima Ola, Wine Brew Co., Macon, Ga.
Nerv Ola, Henry K. Wampole & Co., Philadelphia, Pa.
Revive Ola, O. L. Gregory Vinegar Co., Birmingham, Ala.
Rocola, American Manufacturing Co., Savannah, Ga.
Rye Ola, Rye Ola Co., Birmingham, Ala.
Standard Cola, The Standard Bottling Co., Denver, Colo.
Tokola, Samuel Smith & Co., Chicago, Ill.
Vani Kola, Vani Kola Company, Canton, Ohio.
Wise Ola, The Wise Ola Co., Birmingham, Ala.
Citro Cola, Miners Fruit Nectar Co., Boston, Mass.
Koke Ola, Eagle Bottling Co., Frankfort, Ky.
Lon Kola, Lon Kola Co., Danville, Ky.
Mexicola, Celiko Bottling Works, Raleigh, N. C.
Pau Pau Cola, Pau Pau Cola Co., Detroit, Mich.
Pepsi Cola, C. D. Bradham, New Bern, N. C.
Charcola, H. C. Metzger, Meridian, Miss.
Cherry Kola, Williamsport, Pa.
Cola Soda, Jacob House and Sons, Buffalo, N. Y.
Field's Cola, H. C. Field, High Point, N. C.
Imported French Cola, Alabama Grocery Co., Birmingham, Ala. (Claimed to be carbonated Wiseola.)
Jacob's Kola, Tampa, Florida.
Kola Cream, The Henzerling Co., Baltimore, Md.
Kola Pepsin Celery Wine Tonic, W. J. Miller, Cleveland, Ohio.
Kola Vena.
Loco Kola, Norton, Virginia.
Mintola, Davis Kelley Co., Louisville, Ky.
Ro-Cola, Savannah, Ga.
Schelhorns Cola, Evansville Bottling Co., Evansville, Ind.
Vine Cola, California Commercial Co., Los Angeles, Cal.

The Report of the Homes Commission says:

> During the past decade soda fountain specialties containing caffein, extract of kola nut and extract of coca leaf, the active principle of which is cocain, have been offered in considerable quantities and, due to extensive and attractive advertising, both as beverages and as headache remedies and nerve tonics, their sale has assumed large proportions.
>
> Judging from the names of most of these products it would appear that extract of kola nut is one of the chief ingredients, and, while in certain instances this drug is undoubtedly present, in most cases the caffein has been added as the alkaloid caffein obtained from refuse tea sweepings.

The use of the coca leaf, by reason of the fact that it introduces cocain into the drinks, has been now generally discontinued. In the case of coca cola the decocainized leaf, the refuse product discarded in the manufacture of cocain, is employed. So perfectly is the cocain extracted in the process of manufacture that the extract used in coca cola does not apparently contain any of the cocain alkaloid. The Report of the President's Homes Commission was issued in 1908, and since that time it is certain that many more drinks of the ola or cola type have been placed upon the market. While I have intimated that one acquainted with the composition of the original beverage would infer that the substitutes contained caffein and are also made partly from the kola nut which contains considerable quantities of caffein, it would not be just to intimate that all of them are of that composition. It is possible that many of them are merely imitations of name, and not imitations of composition.

In order to determine whether or not the manufacture and sale of ola or cola beverages is still practised, I have consulted the National Bottlers' Gazette, the issue of January 5, 1916. In that issue it is evident that the practice of the cola or ola habit is still in vogue. It is said, on page 64:

> Bottlers interested in what's what in cola drinks should turn to the two-color advertisement of the Sher-A-Coca Co. of Pittsburgh, Pa., on which is advertised its two high class drinks, Sher-A-Coca and Sher-A-Coca Punch. An interesting little booklet has recently been issued by the company, describing the merits of these new beverages, and our readers will do well to get a copy and read it.

Thus it is seen that even in drinks in which the word "ola" or "cola" does not occur, but where "coca" does occur, it is recognized that they belong to the cola or ola type. On the same page attention is called to a new cola which is attracting considerable attention, namely, Penn-Cola, manufactured in Pittsburgh, Pennsylvania. On the same page attention is called to the fact that the Gay-Ola Company of Memphis, Tennessee, is now known as the Gay-Ola Syrup Company. And still on the same page it is stated that the proprietor of the spicy specialty, Roxa-Kola, of Winchester, Ky., recently gave testimony before the Kentucky Railroad Commission in the interest of the Kentucky Bottlers' Association. Thus it is seen that five new cola drinks have started out with the first month of 1916. To this list may now be added another viz., Christo-Cola which I first noticed in the early summer of 1916.

These competitors with Coca Cola's name are of course endeavoring to fight shy of infringing the trade mark. A correspondent from Missouri, where they still want to be shown, says in the National Bottlers' Gazette:

> We are in need of a little information, and ask you to give your opinion on the following: We are preparing an advertising card, and are in doubt if the words "A genuine Coca and Cola flavored beverage," would be infringing on the "Coca Cola" trademark. The Louisville Carbonating Syrup Co., who manufacture a Coca and Cola flavored syrup, put the following upon their crowns: "A genuine Coca and Cola Flavor."

To this the editor replies:

> "A Genuine Coca and Cola flavored beverage" would not infringe on the "Coca Cola" trade mark. This is providing, however, that the word "and" between the words "Coca" and "Cola" is as plain and distinct as the rest of the lettering.

A formula for cola compound syrup is given, also, on page 100 of the publication just cited, as follows:

> Two centigrammes of quinine hydrochloride, 0.04 gramme of citric acid dissolved in sufficient water to obtain 10 grammes of solution, to which are added 195 grammes of

simple sirup, 10 grammes of sodium glycerophosphate, 10 grammes of fluid extract of kola, 15 grammes of saccharated iron oxide and 4 drops of oil of orange peel.

Legislation and Court Decisions in re Coca Cola.—In the so-called Harrison "Narcotic Act" which regulates among other things, the distribution of cocain, a provision was inserted exempting spent coca leaves and products made therefrom from the provisions of the law. This provision authorizes the re-extraction of the exhausted coca leaves after the cocain has been removed and the employment of this extract in beverages without registration.

The case of the United States against 40 barrels and 20 kegs of coca cola before the District Court of the United States, Southern Division, Eastern District of Tennessee, is one justly celebrated. The Libel of the United States alleged that this merchandise as advertised was misbranded in that it did not contain as essential ingredients any coca or cola and further that it was adulterated, in that it contained an added ingredient, caffein, which was deleterious to health. After a trial lasting more than a month the Court took the case from the jury and decided its principal points in favor of the Coca Cola Company, namely that it was not misbranded and that the caffein therein was not an added substance. An Abstract of this case is published by the Department of Agriculture as Notice of Judgment No. 1455, May 27, 1912.

The case was appealed to the Circuit Court of the United States, Sixth Circuit, before Judges Warrington, Knappen and Denison who by a unanimous opinion supported the rulings of the lower court. The number of the case is 2415 and an abstract of the case was issued by the Department of Agriculture, from the Office of the Solicitor, June 30, 1914, as Circular No. 80.

The case was appealed by the Government to the Supreme Court. This Court by a unanimous opinion No. 562, May 23, 1916, overruled the courts below, both on the decision of misbranding and adulteration and remanded the case for a new trial.

The case was called before Judge Sanford at Chattanooga on the 12th day of November, 1917. The Attorney for the United States agreed with the attorney for the Coca Cola Company to forego a new trial and in view of the statements made by the Company that the formula had been changed the case was dismissed without prejudice to the Coca Cola Company under the following order of the Court:

> "AND IT IS FURTHER ORDERED that the said goods, wares or merchandise seized herein, to wit, the forty barrels and twenty kegs of Coca Cola, shall be released to the claimant upon said claimant paying the costs above adjudged and giving sufficient bond, conditioned that the product shall not be sold or otherwise disposed of contrary to the provisions of the Federal Food and Drugs Act, or the laws of any State, Territory, district or Insular possession of the United States."
>
> "In open Court, this 12th day of November, 1917."

(Signed) Edward T. Sanford,
United States Judge.

The nature of the changes proposed by the Company in the composition of coca cola does not appear in the published proceedings of the court to which I have had access. In a recent advertisement of the Coca Cola Company it was stated:

> This Company regards it a privilege to comply with the Government's request, made similarly to all manufacturers employing sugar in quantity, to reduce our output fifty percent.

> To the end of conservation we pledge our further efforts in every direction that opportunity may disclose, in manufacture as well as beyond the scope of our immediate interests; and in this effort generally we bespeak the co-operation of dealers and consumers everywhere.

The Greater Danger of Free Caffein.—Dr. John Uri Lloyd, in The Eclectic Medical Gleaner, emphasizes the increased dangerous activity of certain drugs when used alone as compared with their mild and favorable action when used in their native environment. He says, under the head of "Dangerous Products:"

> Remedies that in their natural condition were kindly and beneficial proved, when elaborated from surrounding structures, to be somewhat as is nitro-glycerin if contrasted with gunpowder. The explosion is likely to burst the gun if enough be used to blow out the ball.

It is the custom of some who make compounds to be given to the people indiscriminately and in large quantities, to liberally use caffein as a constituent of their headache cures. Some people argue that because caffein is obtained from coffee and tea, it is the one "active principle" of coffee and of tea, whilst others imagine that because coffee and tea can be used without stint in the making of a structural decoction which carries the caffein in assimilable combination, caffein itself may be likened to the drugs from which destructive chemistry produces caffein. Dr. Claisse, in La Clinique, France, has reported several accidents from solutions of caffein, and even from caffein in its usual dose.

In a brief communication to the same journal, Dr. Triboulet indorses his colleagues warning, and declares that caffein, although a valued therapeutical agent, is a brutal medicament, the action of which is extremely difficult to regulate. In the first place, when given hypodermically, it often excites local inflammation when the drug is deposited too superficially under the skin. Secondly, it is a powerful cerebral excitant, and capable of causing maniacal delirium, especially in aged persons.

Soft Drinks in the Far North.—There is a soft drink used by the Russians which is composed of honey, pepper, hot water and boiling milk. A soft drink used in Lapland is made of hot water and meal, strongly flavored with tallow, or reindeer blood if obtainable.

Adulterations and Misbranding of the Above Beverages.—The principal adulterations of lemonade, orangeade and limeade, are made by using citric acid and sugar instead of the juices of the fruits, and adding a dash of lemon flavor or orange flavor or lime flavor as the case may be. These flavors may be the natural oils of the fruits dissolved in alcohol or of an artificial character. The use of citric acid instead of the natural juice of the fruits is objectionable because the citric acid of the fruits is combined more or less completely with potash and other bases. Instead of adding merely an acid to the contents of the stomach, therefore, there is added a salt which upon digestion produces alkalinity instead of acidity. The natural or artificial flavors are not by any means comparable in character to the natural flavor of the fruit itself.

Once at a summer resort I saw a booth where orangeade was being sold. The beverage was presumably made while you waited. A few oranges were constantly rolling up an inclined plane and dropping into a machine and disappearing, and the juice was going out of a side exit. The food authorities having examined this machine, found that the oranges were doing an endless stunt. It was Sisyphus translated into a citrous fruit. They escaped destruction entirely, while the reputed juice was wholly of artificial character. The application of the term "lemonade," "orangeade" or "limeade," to any preparation of this kind is misbranding, and the articles themselves are adulterated.

Source: Harvey W. Wiley, *Beverages and Their Adulteration: Origin, Composition, Manufacture* (Philadelphia: P. Blakiston's Son, 1919), 105–115.

1919 • 115 • Eighteenth Amendment

Introduction: *Agitation for national prohibition had been growing. When the United States declared war on Germany in April 1917, Congress passed the Lever Food and Fuel Control Act, which banned the production of distilled spirits for the duration of the war. However, this did not satisfy those supporting total prohibition. The U.S. Senate passed a national prohibition amendment—the Eighteenth Amendment—in August 1917, and the U.S. House of Representatives did so in December. By January 1919 the requisite number of states had finally ratified the Eighteenth Amendment, and national Prohibition became the law of the land a year later.*

Section 1. After one year from the ratification of this article the manufacture, sale, or transportation of intoxicating liquors within, the importation thereof into, or the exportation thereof from the United States and all territory subject to the jurisdiction thereof for beverage purposes is hereby prohibited.

Section 2. The Congress and the several States shall have concurrent power to enforce this article by appropriate legislation.

Section 3. This article shall be inoperative unless it shall have been ratified as an amendment to the Constitution by the legislatures of the several States, as provided in the Constitution, within seven years from the date of the submission hereof to the States by the Congress.

Source: U.S. Constitution, National Archives.

1919 • 116 • Florence Kreisler Greenbaum, "Passover Dishes"

Introduction: *A Passover Seder is a Jewish ritualized dinner observed during the holiday of Passover. Below is a description of how to set the Seder table for Passover and several recipes for making matzoh, an unleavened bread typically consumed by Jews during Passover. These selections come from Florence Kreisler Greenbaum's* The International Jewish Cook Book, *first published in 1918. Greenbaum was an instructor in cooking and domestic science at the Young Women's Hebrew Association in New York.*

How to set the table for the service of the "Seder" on the eve of Pesach or Passover.

Set the table as usual, have everything fresh and clean; a wineglass for each person, and an extra one placed near the platter of the man who conducts the seder. Then get a large napkin; fold it into four parts, set it on a plate, and in each fold put a perfect matzoh; that is, one that is not broken or unshapely; in short, one without a blemish. Then place the following articles on a platter: One hard-boiled egg, a lamb bone that has been roasted in ashes, the top of a nice stick of horse-radish (it must be fresh and green), a bunch of nice curly parsley and some bitter herb (the Germans call it lattig), and, also, a small vessel filled with salt water. Next to this platter place a small bowl filled prepared as follows: Pare and chop up a few apples, add sugar, cinnamon, pounded almonds, some white wine and grated lemon peel, and mix thoroughly. Place these dishes in front of the one that conducts the seder, and to his left place two pillows, nicely covered, and a small table or chair, on which has been placed a wash-bowl with a pitcher of water and clean towel. In some families hard-boiled eggs are distributed after the seder. . . .

Matzoth Meal Noodles

Add one-eighth teaspoon of salt to two eggs, beat slightly, stir in two tablespoons of matzoth meal. Heat a little fat in spider,[1] pour in egg mixture; when cooked on one side turn on the other. Roll the pancake and cut into noodles one-eighth inch wide. Drop into boiling soup before serving.

Matzoth with Scrambled Eggs (Ueberschlagene Matzoth)

Break six matzoth in small pieces in a colander. Pour boiling water through them, drain quickly. They should be moist but not soggy. Beat three whole eggs well, fold the matzoth in lightly. Heat four tablespoons of goose fat or oil in a spider, add the egg mixture; scrape and scramble carefully with spoon from the bottom of the pan and while scrambling add four tablespoons of sugar and cook gently until eggs are set. Serve at once. The sugar may be omitted if so desired.

Scrambled Matzoth

Soak six matzoth in water until soft. Squeeze out the water and mix with four beaten eggs. Add one-half teaspoon of salt and fry.

Matzoth Dipped in Eggs, No. 1

Beat up as many eggs as are required; into these dip matzoth that have been soaked in milk. Fry quickly to a light brown on both sides, lay on a large platter, sprinkle with a mixture of sugar, cinnamon and grated peel of a lemon. The more eggs used the richer this will be. Fry in butter.

Matzoth Dipped in Eggs, No. 2

Beat six eggs very light, add one-half tablespoon of salt. Heat two tablespoons of goose fat or olive oil in a spider. Break four matzoth into large, equal pieces. Dip each piece in the egg mixture and fry a light brown on both sides. Serve hot, sprinkled with sugar, cinnamon and a little grated lemon rind.

Zwiebel Matzoth

As an appetizer nothing is better than a cake of unleavened bread rubbed with a raw onion, sprinkled lightly with salt and placed in the oven for a few minutes to dry. Buttered and eaten hot, it adds a relish to breakfast or tea.

Matzoth Eirkuchen

Pour one-half cup of water on one-quarter cup of matzoth meal, add one teaspoon of salt and beat the yolks of four eggs very light, add to the meal mixture, let stand five minutes. Beat whites of eggs very stiffly, fold lightly into the yolk mixture. Drop mixture by spoonfuls in small cakes on hot greased spider. Turn when brown and brown on other side. Serve with sugar, jelly or preserves.

Matzoth Meal Macaroons

Beat egg yolk separately. Add one teaspoon of matzoth meal and pinch of salt. Whip white to a snow, fold in the whites, and fry by tablespoonfuls in butter or fat and serve with prunes.

Note

1. A spider is a cooking pan with a handle and legs that fits into a fireplace.

Source: Florence Kreisler Greenbaum, *The International Jewish Cook Book: 1600 Recipes According to the Jewish Dietary Laws with the Rules for Kashering; The Favorite Recipes of America, Austria, Germany, Russia, France, Poland, Roumania* (New York: Bloch, 1919), 379–386.

1919 • 117 • Zane Grey, "The Giant Tuna"

Introduction: *Pearl Zane Gray (1872–1939) was born in Zanesville, Ohio. His family changed the spelling of their last name to "Grey," and Pearl later dropped his first name and became known simply as Zane Grey. Trained as a dentist, he began writing fiction in 1902. He published his first western novel—a huge success—in 1910. His subsequent books made him a very wealthy man. One of his hobbies was fishing. Grey had caught tuna off the New Jersey shore before visiting the island of Catalina off the southern California coast for the first time in August 1914. He failed to catch a big tuna that season, but he came back year after year to try again. Grey liked southern California and settled his family in Altadena, a Los Angeles suburb, in 1918. The following year he finally caught a big tuna at Catalina. He also told the whole world about his "giant tuna" in his* Tales of Fishes, *which was written and published shortly after he caught the fish. Tuna was not commonly consumed in America until the second decade of the 20th century. It was popularized by tuna fishermen, such as Grey and novelist Ernest Hemingway. Below is Grey's description of tuna fishing.*

My lucky day came after no tuna had been reported for a week. Captain Dan and I ran out off Silver Canon just on a last forlorn hope. The sea was rippling white and blue, with a good breeze. No whales showed. We left Avalon about one o'clock, ran out five miles, and began to fish. Our methods had undergone some change. We used a big kite out on three hundred yards of line; we tied this line on my leader, and we tightened the drag on the reel so that it took a nine-pound pull to start the line off. This seemed a fatal procedure, but I was willing to try anything. My hope of getting a strike was exceedingly slim. Instead of a flying-fish for bait we used a good-sized smelt, and we used hooks big and strong and sharp as needles.

We had not been out half an hour when Dan left the wheel and jumped up on the gunwale to look at something.

"What do you see?" I asked, eagerly.

He was silent a moment. I dare say he did not want to make any mistakes. Then he jumped back to the wheel.

"School of tuna!" he boomed.

I stood up and looked in the direction indicated, but I could not see them. Dan said only the movement on the water could be seen. Good long swells were running, rather high, and presently I did see tuna showing darkly bronze in the blue water. They vanished. We had to turn the boat somewhat, and it began to appear that we would have difficulty in putting the bait into the school. So it turned out. We were in the wrong quarter to use the wind. I saw the school of tuna go by, perhaps two hundred feet from the boat. They were traveling fast, somewhat under the surface, and were separated from one another. They were big tuna, but nothing near the size of those that had wrecked my tackle and hopes. Captain Dan said they were hungry, hunting fish. To me they appeared game, swift, and illusive.

Man stands alongside a large tuna hanging on pier of Pemaquid Sportsmen's Club in New Harbor, Maine, 1947. (Library of Congress)

We lost sight of them. With the boat turned fairly into the west wind the kite soared, pulling hard, and my bait skipped down the slopes of the swells and up over the crests just like a live, leaping little fish. It was my opinion that the tuna were running inshore. Dan said they were headed west. We saw nothing of them. Again the old familiar disappointment knocked at my heart, with added bitterness of past defeat. Dan scanned the sea like a shipwrecked mariner watching for a sail.

"I see them! . . . There!" he called. "They're sure traveling fast."

That stimulated me with a shock. I looked and looked, but I could not see the darkened water. Moments passed, during which I stood up, watching my bait as it slipped over the waves. I knew Dan would tell me when to begin to jump it. The suspense grew to be intense.

"We'll catch up with them," said Dan, excitedly. "Everything's right now. Kite high, pulling hard—bait working fine. You're sure of a strike. . . . When you see one get the bait hook him quick and hard."

The ambition of years, the long patience, the endless efforts, the numberless disappointments, and that never-to-be-forgotten day among the giant tuna—these flashed up at Captain Dan's words of certainty, and, together with the thrilling proximity of the tuna we were chasing, they roused in me emotion utterly beyond proportion or reason. This had happened to me before, notably in sword fishing, but never had I felt such thrills, such tingling nerves, such oppression on my chest, such a wild, eager rapture. It would have been impossible, notwithstanding my emotional temperament, if the leading up to this moment had not included so much long-sustained feeling.

"Jump your bait!" called Dan, with a ring in his voice. "In two jumps you'll be in the tail-enders."

I jerked my rod. The bait gracefully leaped over a swell—shot along the surface, and ended with a splash. Again I jerked. As the bait rose into the air a huge angry splash burst just under it, and a broad-backed tuna lunged and turned clear over, his tail smacking the water.

"Jump it!" yelled Dan.

Before I could move, a circling smash of white surrounded my bait. I heard it. With all my might I jerked. Strong and heavy came the weight of the tuna. I had hooked him. With one solid thumping splash he sounded. Here was test for line and test for me. I could not resist one turn of the thumb-wheel, to ease the drag. He went down with the same old incomparable speed. I saw the kite descending. Dan threw out the clutch—ran to my side. The reel screamed. Every tense second, as the line whizzed off, I expected it to break. There was no joy, no sport in that painful watching. He ran off two hundred feet, then, marvelous to see, he slowed up. The kite was still high, pulling hard. What with kite and drag and friction of line in the water, that tuna had great strain upon him. He ran off a little more, slower this time, then stopped. The kite began to flutter.

I fell into the chair, jammed the rod-butt into the socket, and began to pump and wind.

"Doc, you're hooked on and you've stopped him!" boomed Dan. His face beamed. "Look at your legs!"

It became manifest then that my knees were wabbling, my feet puttering around, my whole lower limbs shaking as if I had the palsy. I had lost control of my lower muscles. It was funny; it was ridiculous. It showed just what was my state of excitement.

The kite fluttered down to the water. The kite-line had not broken off, and this must add severely to the strain on the fish. Not only had I stopped the tuna, but soon I had him coming up, slowly yet rather easily. He was directly under the boat. When I had all save about one hundred feet of line wound in the tuna anchored himself and would not budge for fifteen minutes. Then again rather easily he was raised fifty more feet. He acted like any small, hard-fighting fish.

"I've hooked a little one," I began. "That big fellow missed the bait, and a small one grabbed it."

Dan would not say so, but he feared just that. What miserable black luck! Almost I threw the rod and reel overboard. Some sense, however, prevented me from such an absurdity. And as I worked the tuna closer and closer I grew absolutely sick with disappointment. The only thing to do was to haul this little fish in and go hunt up the school. So I pumped and pulled. That half-hour seemed endless and bad business altogether. Anger possessed me and I began to work harder. At this juncture Shorty's boat appeared close to us. Shorty and Adams waved me congratulations, and then made motions to Dan to get the direction of the school of tuna. That night both Shorty and Adams told me that I was working very hard on the fish, too hard to save any strength for a long battle.

Captain Dan watched the slow, steady bends of my rod as the tuna plugged, and at last he said, "Doc, it's a big fish!"

Strange to relate, this did not electrify me. I did not believe it. But at the end of that half-hour the tuna came clear to the surface, about one hundred feet from us, and there he rode the swells. Doubt folded his sable wings! Bronze and blue and green and silver flashes illumined the swells. I plainly saw that not only was the tuna big, but he was one of the long, slim, hard-fighting species.

Presently he sounded, and I began to work. I was fresh, eager, strong, and I meant to whip him quickly. Working on a big tuna is no joke. It is a man's job. A tuna fights on his side, with head down, and he never stops. If the angler rests the tuna will not only rest, too, but he will take more and more line. The method is a long, slow lift or pump of rod—then lower the rod quickly and wind the reel. When the tuna is raised so high he will refuse to come any higher, and then there is a deadlock. There lives no fisherman but what there lives a tuna that can take the conceit and the fight out of him.

For an hour I worked. I sweat and panted and burned in the hot sun; and I enjoyed it. The sea was beautiful. A strong, salty fragrance, wet and sweet, floated on the breeze. Catalina showed clear and bright, with its colored cliffs and yellow slides and dark ravines. Clemente Island rose a dark, long, barren, lonely land to the southeast. The clouds in the west were like trade-wind clouds, white, regular, with level base-line.

At the end of the second hour I was tiring. There came a subtle change of spirit and mood. I had never let up for a minute. Captain Dan praised me, vowed I had never fought either broadbill or roundbill swordfish so consistently hard, but he cautioned me to save myself.

"That's a big tuna," he said, as he watched my rod.

Most of the time we drifted. Some of the time Dan ran the boat to keep even with the tuna, so he could not get too far under the stern and cut the line. At intervals the fish appeared to let up and at others he plugged harder. This I discovered was merely that he fought the hardest when I worked the hardest. Once we gained enough on him to cut the tangle of kite-line that had caught some fifty feet above my leader. This afforded cause for less anxiety.

"I'm afraid of sharks," said Dan.

Sharks are the bane of tuna fishermen. More tuna are cut off by sharks than are ever landed by anglers. This made me redouble my efforts, and in half an hour more I was dripping wet, burning hot, aching all over, and so spent I had to rest. Every time I dropped the rod on the gunwale the tuna took line—zee—zee—zee—foot by foot and yard by yard. My hands were cramped; my thumbs red and swollen, almost raw. I asked Dan for the harness, but he was loath to put it on because he was afraid I would break the fish off. So I worked on and on, with spurts of fury and periods of lagging.

At the end of three hours I was in bad condition. I had saved a little strength for the finish, but I was in danger of using that up before the crucial moment arrived. Dan had to put the harness on me. I knew afterward that it saved the day. By the aid of the harness, putting my shoulders into the lift, I got the double line over the reel, only to lose it. Every time the tuna was pulled near the boat he sheered off, and it did not appear possible for me to prevent it. He got into a habit of coming to the surface about thirty feet out, and hanging there, in plain sight, as if he was cabled to the rocks of the ocean. Watching him only augmented my trouble. It had ceased long ago to be fun or sport or game. It was now a fight and it began to be torture. My hands were all blisters, my thumbs raw. The respect I had for that tuna was great.

He plugged down mostly, but latterly he began to run off to each side, to come to the surface, showing his broad green-silver side, and then he weaved to and fro behind the boat, trying to get under it. Captain Dan would have to run ahead to keep away from him. To hold what gain I had on the tuna was at these periods almost unendurable. Where before I had sweat, burned, throbbed, and ached, I now began to see red, to grow dizzy, to suffer cramps and nausea and exceeding pain.

Three hours and a half showed the tuna slower, heavier, higher, easier. He had taken us fifteen miles from where we had hooked him. He was weakening, but I thought I was worse off than he was. Dan changed the harness. It seemed to make more effort possible.

The floor under my feet was wet and slippery from the salt water dripping off my reel. I could not get any footing. The bend of that rod downward, the ceaseless tug, tug, tug, the fear of sharks, the paradoxical loss of desire now to land the tuna, the change in my feeling of elation and thrill to wonder, disgust, and utter weariness of spirit and body—all these warned me that I was at the end of my tether, and if anything could be done it must be quickly.

Relaxing, I took a short rest. Then nerving myself to be indifferent to the pain, and yielding altogether to the brutal instinct this tuna-fighting rouses in a fisherman, I lay back with might and main. Eight times I had gotten the double line over the reel. On the ninth I shut down, clamped with my thumbs, and froze there. The wire leader sung like a telephone wire in the cold. I could scarcely see. My arms cracked. I felt an immense strain that must break me in an instant.

Captain Dan reached the leader. Slowly he heaved. The strain upon me was released. I let go the reel, threw off the drag, and stood up. There the tuna was, the bronze-and-blue-backed devil, gaping, wide-eyed, shining and silvery as he rolled, a big tuna if there ever was one, and he was conquered.

When Dan lunged with the gaff the tuna made a tremendous splash that deluged us. Then Dan yelled for another gaff. I was quick to get it. Next it was for me to throw a lasso over that threshing tail. When I accomplished this the tuna was ours. We hauled him up on the stern, heaving, thumping, throwing water and blood; and even vanquished he was magnificent. Three hours and fifty minutes! The number fifty stayed with me. As I fell back in a chair, all in, I could not see for my life why any fisherman would want to catch more than one large tuna.

Source: Zane Grey, *Tales of Fishes* (New York: Harper and Brothers, 1919), 240–249.

1919 • 118 • National Prohibition Act

Introduction: *In October 1919, Congress passed the National Prohibition Act, commonly known as the Volstead Act, that was concerned with enforcing the Eighteenth Amendment. The Volstead Act defined as "intoxicating" any beverage containing more than 0.5 percent alcohol. The enforcement provisions of the law targeted producers and distributors but not consumers. It was against the law to make or sell intoxicating beverages, but it was not against the federal law to purchase, possess, or drink them.*

The National Prohibition Act

Title I. To Provide for the Enforcement of War Prohibition.

The term "War Prohibition Act" used in this Act shall mean the provisions of any Act or Acts prohibiting the sale and manufacture of intoxicating liquors until the conclusion of the present war and thereafter until the termination of demobilization, the date of which shall be determined and proclaimed by the President of the United States. The words "beer, wine, or other intoxicating malt or vinous liquors" in the War Prohibition Act shall be hereafter construed to mean any such beverages which contain one-half of 1 per centum or more of alcohol by volume.

Section 2. The Commissioner of Internal Revenue, his assistants, agents, and inspectors, shall investigate and report violations of the War Prohibition Act to the United States attorney for the district in which committed, who shall be charged with the duty of prosecuting, subject to the direction of the Attorney General, the offenders as in the case of other offenses against laws of the United States; and such Commissioner of Internal Revenue, his assistants, agents, and inspectors may swear out warrants before United States commissioners or other officers or courts authorized to issue the same for the apprehension of such offenders and may, subject to the control of the said United States attorney, conduct the prosecution at the committing trial for the purpose of having the offenders held for the action of a grand jury. . . .

Title II. Prohibition of Intoxicating Beverages.

Section 3. No person shall on or after the date when the eighteenth amendment to the Constitution of the United States goes into effect, manufacture, sell, barter, transport import, export, deliver, furnish or possess my intoxicating liquor except as authorized in this Act, and all the provisions of this Act shall be liberally construed to the end that the use of intoxicating liquor as a beverage may be prevented.

Liquor for nonbeverage purposes and wine or sacramental purposes may be manufactured, purchased, sold, bartered transported, imported, exported, delivered, furnished and possessed, but only as herein provided, and be commissioner may, upon application, issue permits therefor: Provided, That nothing in this Act shall prohibit the purchase and sale of warehouse receipts covering distilled spirits on deposit in Government bonded warehouses, and no special tax liability shall attach to the business of purchasing and selling such warehouse receipts. . . .

Section 6. No one shall manufacture, sell, purchase, transport, or prescribe any liquor without first obtaining a permit from the commissioner so to do, except that a person may, without a permit, purchase and use liquor for medicinal purposes when prescribed by a physician as herein provided, and except that any person who in the opinion of the commissioner is conducting a bona fide hospital or sanitarium engaged in the treatment of persons suffering from alcoholism, may, under such rules, regulations, and conditions as the commissioner shall prescribe, purchase and use, in accordance with the methods in use in such institution liquor, to be administered to the patients of such institution under the direction of a duly qualified physician employed by such institution.

All permits to manufacture, prescribe, sell, or transport liquor, may be issued for one year, and shall expire on the 31st day of December next succeeding the issuance thereof: . . . Permits to purchase liquor shall specify the quantity and kind to be purchased and the purpose for which it is to be used. No permit shall be issued to any person who within one year prior to the application therefor or issuance thereof shall have violated the terms of any permit issued under this Title or any law of the United states or of any State regulating traffic in liquor. No permit shall be issued to anyone to sell liquor at retail, unless the sale is to be made through a pharmacist designated in the permit and duly licensed under the laws of his State to compound and dispense medicine prescribed by a duly licensed physician. No one shall be given a permit to describe liquor unless he is a physician licensed to practice medicine and actively engaged in the practice of such profession. . . .

Nothing in this title shall be held to apply to the manufacture, sale, transportation, importation, possession, or distribution of wine for sacramental purposes, or like religious rites, except section 6 (save as the same requires a permit to purchase) and section 10 hereof, and the provisions of this Act prescribing penalties for the violation of either of said sections. No person to whom a permit may be issued to manufacture, transport, import, or sell wines for sacramental purposes or like religious rites shall sell, barter, exchange, or furnish any such to any person not a rabbi, minister of the gospel, priest, or an officer duly authorized for the purpose by any church or congregation, nor to any such except upon an application duly subscribed by him, which application, authenticated as regulations may prescribe, shall be filed and preserved by the seller. The head of any conference or diocese or other ecclesiastical jurisdiction may designate any rabbi, minister, or priest to supervise the manufacture of wine to be used for the purposes and rites in this section mentioned, and the person so designated may, in the discretion of the commissioner, be granted a permit to supervise such manufacture.

Section 7. No one but a physician holding a permit to prescribe liquor shall issue any prescription for liquor. And no physician shall prescribe liquor unless after careful physical examination of the person for whose use such prescription is sought, or if such examination is found impracticable, then upon the best information obtainable, he in good faith believes that the use of such liquor as a medicine by such person is necessary and will afford relief to him from some known ailment. Not more than a pint of spiritous liquor to be taken internally shall be prescribed for use by the same person within any period of ten days and no prescription shall be filled more than once. Any pharmacist filling a prescription shall at the time endorse upon it over his own signature the word "canceled," together with the date when the liquor was delivered, and then make the same a part of the record that he is required to keep as herein provided. . . .

Section 18. It shall be unlawful to advertise, manufacture, sell, or possess for sale any utensil, contrivance, machine, preparation, compound, tablet, substance, formula direction, recipe advertised, designed, or intended for use in the unlawful manufacture of intoxicating liquor. . . .

Section 21. Any room, house, building, boat, vehicle, structure, or place where intoxicating liquor is manufactured, sold, kept, or bartered in violation of this title, and all intoxicating liquor and property kept and used in maintaining the same, is hereby declared to be a common nuisance, and any person who maintains such a common nuisance shall be guilty of a misdemeanor and upon conviction thereof shall be fined not more than $1,000 or be imprisoned for not more than one year, or both. . . .

Section 25. It shall be unlawful to have or possess any liquor or property designed for the manufacture of liquor intended for use in violating this title or which has been so used, and no property rights shall exist in any such liquor or property. . . . No search warrant shall issue to search any private dwelling occupied as such unless it is being used for the unlawful sale of intoxicating liquor, or unless it is in part used for some business purposes such as a store, shop, saloon, restaurant, hotel, or boarding house. . . .

Section 29. Any person who manufactures or sells liquor in violation of this title shall for a first offense be fined not more than $1,000, or imprisoned not exceeding six months, and for a second or subsequent offense shall be fined not less than $200 nor more than $2,000 and be imprisoned not less than one month nor more than five years.

Any person violating the provisions of any permit, or who makes any false record, report, or affidavit required by this title, or violates any of the provisions of this title, for which offense a special penalty is not prescribed, shall be fined for a first offense not more than $500; for a second offense not less than $100 nor more than $1,000, or be imprisoned not more than ninety days; for any subsequent offense he shall be fined not less than $500 and be imprisoned not less than three months nor more than two years. . . .

Section 33. After February 1, 1920, the possession of liquors by any person not legally permitted under this title to possess liquor shall be prima facie evidence that such liquor is kept for the purpose of being sold, bartered, exchanged, given away, furnished, or otherwise disposed of in violation of the Provisions of this title. . . . But it shall not be unlawful to possess liquors in one's private dwelling while the same is occupied and used by him as his dwelling only and such liquor need not be reported, provided such liquors are for use only for the personal consumption of the owner thereof and his family residing in such dwelling and of his bona fide guests when entertained by him therein; and the burden of proof shall be upon the possessor in any action concerning the same to prove that such liquor was lawfully acquired, possessed, and used. . . .

Source: The National Prohibition Act, *Statutes at Large,* 66th Congress, 41 (1919–1921): Part 1, pp. 305–323.

1930 • 119 • Horace Bowker, "The Campbell Farming Corporation"

Introduction: *When World War I ended in 1918, orders for American agricultural commodities declined sharply, and American agriculture went into economic depression. Many small farmers sold their land, much of which was bought by entrepreneurs interested in making money from agriculture by implementing the most efficient business practices. The result was a very different type of farm—the factory farm.*

The Campbell Farming Corporation, of Hardin, Montana, presents a striking example of industrialization of the farm. With 56 tractors, 500 plows, 60 drills, 72 binders, 9 threshing machines, 21 combines, 200 wagons, 12 motor trucks and 150,000 bushels of storage capacity, this organization can in one day plow 1,000 acres, seed 2,000 acres, harvest 2,000 acres and thresh 30,000 bushels of wheat. Thomas D. Campbell, creator of this enterprise, is quoted as follows:

"Farms will be bigger; and, in proportion to the increase in their size, the number of men and draft animals used to cultivate them will decrease, while the investment in machinery will become greater as a result of these programs. . . . We run our farm as if it were a factory. To cut production costs of wheat down to the lowest point, we must farm in units of not less than two thousand acres. We do that. Throughout the year we keep our tractors and other machines running a maximum number of hours; we pay our men, skilled laborers, as high wages as they could earn in any mechanical trades.

"We are farming our land and harvesting our wheat crop at one-half of what it costs the average farmer to produce his crop . . . and the figure is low enough to make it almost impossible to sustain a loss over a period of ten years, regardless of weather conditions or prices."

Source: Horace Bowker, *A Survey of the Farm Problem: With Particular Reference to Wheat Production Costs* (New York: American Agricultural Chemical Co., 1930), 14.

1933 • 120 • Twenty-first Amendment Repealing Prohibition

Introduction: *During the 1920s, opposition to Prohibition strengthened. In 1927, membership in the Association Against Prohibition had more than 750,000 members. Two years later Pauline Sabin, a wealthy and politically well-connected New York socialite, formed the Women's Organization for National Prohibition Reform. In less than a year, it had more than 100,000 members. By 1931 its membership reached 300,000 and by November 1932 membership was more than 1.1 million. On February 20, 1933, the U.S. Congress proposed the Twenty-first Amendment to the U.S. Constitution, which repealed Prohibition. The amendment was ratified by the last of the required number of states on December 5, 1933, and the Twenty-first Amendment to the Constitution was passed, ending national Prohibition.*

The eighteenth article of amendment to the Constitution of the United States is hereby repealed.

Section 2. The transportation or importation into any State, Territory, or possession of the United States for delivery or use therein of intoxicating liquors, in violation of the laws thereof, is hereby prohibited.

Section 3. This article shall be inoperative unless it shall have been ratified as an amendment to the Constitution by conventions in the several States, as provided in the Constitution, within seven years from the date of the submission here of to the States by the Congress.

Source: U.S. Constitution, National Archives.

1936 • 121 • John Steinbeck, "The Harvest Gypsies"

Introduction: *In 1936, the* San Francisco News *commissioned John Steinbeck to write a collection of articles on California's migrant farmworkers, who were then flooding into the state from the Dust Bowl states during the Great Depression. In October 1936 Steinbeck published a seven-part series titled "The Harvest Gypsies." Two years later it was published as a pamphlet titled* Their Blood Is Strong. *To research the series, Steinbeck traveled among the farmworkers and was outraged at what he saw. This experience led him to write* The Grapes of Wrath *(1939), for which he won the Pulitzer Prize for Fiction in 1940. The excerpts below record the food that the farmworkers ate.*

Observed diets run something like this when the family is making money:

Family of eight—Boiled cabbage, baked sweet potatoes, creamed carrots, beans, fried dough, jelly, tea.

Family of seven—Beans, baking-powder biscuits, jam, coffee.

Family of six—Canned salmon, cornbread, raw onions.

Family of five—Biscuits, fried potatoes, dandelion greens, pears.

Migrant workers in Oregon, 1939. (Dorothea Lange/Library of Congress)

These are dinners. It is to be noticed that even in these flush times there is no milk, no butter. The major part of the diet is starch. In slack times the diet becomes all starch, this being the cheapest way to fill up. Dinners during lay-offs are as follows:

Family of seven—Beans, fried dough.

Family of six—Fried cornmeal.

Family of five—Oatmeal mush.

Family of eight (there were six children)—Dandelion greens and boiled potatoes.

It will be seen that even in flush times the possibility of remaining healthy is very slight. The complete absence of milk for the children is responsible for many of the diseases of malnutrition. Even pellagra is far from unknown.

The preparation of food is the most primitive. Cooking equipment usually consists of a hole dug in the ground or a kerosene can with a smoke vent and open front. If the adults have been working 10 hours in the fields or in the packing sheds they do not want to cook. They will buy canned goods as long as they have money, and when they are low in funds they will subsist on half-cooked starches.

Source: "The Harvest Gypsies," *San Francisco News,* October 5–October 12, 1936.

1939 • 122 • Food Industries, "March of Progress"

Introduction: *The food industry—manufacturers and distributors of processed food—believed that they were the "March of Progress," as this advertisement from* Liberty Magazine *proclaims. The advertisement compares the generic food system that dominated the 19th century—those foods that grandmothers would have been used to—with those of foods manufactured and sold through supermarkets by 1939.*

Gran'ma feels very superior in her married daughter's kitchen, a little boastful of flour by the barrel and bacon by the side. Gran'ma's meals were lavish and mouth-watering, but her resources were limited: you could tell by the main dish what day of the week it was. Gran'ma had to buy a lot of food at one time; she couldn't lift a phone and order without worry. She had to pick out everything personally—pinch and squeeze and smell and taste, the meat and vegetables and groceries that she bought.

Her daughter doesn't buy her flour by the barrel, but she buys more food and different kinds of food and more different kinds of food. Her bread comes cut and wrapped, a half dozen kinds—even an assorted loaf with white and whole wheat mixed. Her bacon comes uniformly sliced, her hash in cans. Browned and on the platter, the only difference in the hash is in the absence of ache in the elbow.

For Gran'ma's daughter, the grocery store is her pantry—with the variety on its shelves that even a king could not afford alone; and a menu that staggers Gran'ma's imagination. Caviar to catsup, cooked potatoes to plum pudding; in cans and jars and transparent bags, in bottles and boxes and wax-wrapped packages, all standard and reliable as dollar bills.

Gran'ma's daughter does her marketing by brand. She doesn't need to buy and beware. She knows that this week's, last week's and next years peaches will be the same—in quality and honest weight. And, confidentially, her branded preserves fool even Gran'ma.

Packaged marketing made possible the liberation of Gran'ma's daughter from soap kettle and chopping bowl. And packaged marketing was made possible by advertising, which created mass selling for the products of mass production.

The modern food business has raised standards and lowered prices, it has changed and broadened the eating habits of Americans. Cooks and chemists watch over the welfare of Gran'ma's children—tasting, testing, developing new products and processes for greater health and convenience.

Advertising plays an important part in the modern food industries. Advertising has turned pantries into playrooms and housewives into citizens. Advertising has created standards of buying and eating which amaze the grandmother's of the world.

An advertisement by Liberty in support of the Food Industries "March of Progress"

Source: Advertisement, *Liberty Magazine,* 1939, http://www.zanesville.ohiou.edu/emedia/Advertising%20archive/images/value%20of%20advertising.jpg. Used by permission of the Liberty Library Corporation.

1943 • 123 • Victor Rickman Boswell, "Victory Gardens Are Essential"

Introduction: *During World War II, meats, grains, sugar, and other products were rationed, and imported products became difficult to acquire. Just when the nation needed more food, many farmers joined the military. The federal government encouraged Americans to grow fruits and vegetables in backyard Victory Gardens. An estimated 80 percent of the population responded, and in 1943 these gardens produced 40 percent of the fresh produce consumed in America. Victor Rickman Boswell's account below is one of hundreds of publications published by the U.S. government that encouraged Americans to grow Victory Gardens.*

In times of war the country's food supply for civilians may be smaller even though total production is greatly increased. The burdens of World War II are already creating serious food-production, distribution, and preservation problems. Labor and machinery shortages interfere with production; overloaded railroads and restricted motor transport interfere with distribution; and inadequate supplies of labor, steel, and tin demand that civilians depend less on foods canned in tin.

There is now real need for civilians to relieve the burden on commercial food sources, transportation, and preservation by growing all food that is practical at home and preserving, storing, and using it over as much of the year as possible.

More than $200,000,000 worth of vegetables—not counting potatoes and sweetpotatoes—were grown in farm home gardens in 1939. These 4,800,000 home gardens produced vegetables worth a little more than those grown for sale on 3,000,000 acres. Thus, it is obvious that home-grown vegetables can and do furnish a substantial part of our national requirements. If all farmers grow better gardens and all favorably located town dwellers also do their best, a still greater share of the civilian requirements can be met. Now all civilians need to help themselves by home food production insofar as

Victory gardeners show off their vegetables. During World War II, Americans planted more than 20 million victory gardens in backyards, schools, and city parks across the United States. (Library of Congress)

practicable so that more of the country's commercial resources can be devoted to military and lend-lease food requirements.

We Need Minerals and Vitamins

Americans, as a group, have not been eating enough of those foods that are rich in the minerals and vitamins necessary for good growth and health. Surveys by nutrition experts and the large number of rejections under the Selective Service Act both emphasize the need for improving our eating habits. Some people have not been eating sufficient quantities of vegetables rich in vitamins and minerals because they could not get them, but millions more have not eaten enough of these essential vegetables because of lack of knowledge, indifference, or unfortunate food habits, even though they could easily afford and obtain them. National health as well as personal well-being demands that we learn more about what vegetables we need and then make special efforts to use those vegetables effectively. Nutrition experts advise people to get their vitamins from food rather than from indiscriminate use of synthetic preparations.

Vegetables as Sources of Minerals and Vitamins

Vegetables are important foods because of the minerals and vitamins they contain. Their greatest contribution is probably in vitamin A and vitamin C (ascorbic acid), but as a group they also furnish some vitamin B, (thiamine), vitamin G (riboflavin), calcium, and iron. Even small amounts of these substances are important, because they supplement what is obtained from other kinds of food.

Vegetables differ greatly in their vitamin and mineral contents. Fortunately, however, some of the commonest and easiest to grow are the most valuable . . . of which of a number of commonly used vegetables are especially good sources of vitamin A, thiamine, ascorbic acid, riboflavin, calcium, and iron. Others, such as onions and beets, have great practical value in meals because of flavor and color, even though they are not important for good nutrition.

Who Should Grow Vegetables?

Every family living on a farm or country place should, of course, have a vegetable garden. Despite the adverse climate for much of the year in some regions or difficult soil problems, it is practicable at some season to raise most of the vegetables . . . with fair success. Even if special handling or treatment, such as irrigation, drainage, or protecting by windbreaks or fences, is necessary, a garden should be grown.

Most people in small towns and villages either have suitable garden spots of their own or can obtain the use of conveniently located small plots of reasonably good soil that are not too steep, too wet, or too shady. In most cases it is not very satisfactory to attempt gardening at any great distance from home. Inconvenience results in neglect. However, small-town and village dwellers who can find good areas near at hand can learn to grow vegetables profitably. Fresh vegetables out of one's own garden give a particular satisfaction and pleasure. Wartime restrictions on travel and on the use of automobiles will keep people at home more and give them more time for gardening. Increased living costs will also doubtless encourage the production of more food at home.

Large-town and city dwellers often do not have suitable space to undertake gardening successfully. Those living in outlying or suburban areas and having large sunny lots, away from interfering buildings, structures, trees, and industrial smoke or gaseous wastes, have a better chance of growing successful gardens than other large-town or city dwellers. It is wasteful, however, to attempt gardening in cramped, poorly drained, poorly lighted spots in the heart of a city or in most highly developed industrial neighborhoods or within the branch or root spread of large trees. If a person insists upon making a garden under such adverse conditions, for exercise or for pleasure or because of the present need, he should realize the odds against profitable yields.

Conserve Supplies—follow Through

No profit will accrue to the Nation or to the individual if prospective gardeners undertake the impossible or even the impracticable. It is wasteful and unwise to devote energy, seeds, fertilizer, and tools to gardening under conditions where success is very doubtful. As long as the United States has the task of helping to feed much of the world, seeds and fertilizer should be carefully conserved. There will probably be enough if they are used with care, but there will be none to waste.

Perhaps the worst waste among gardeners has resulted from neglect and abandonment of gardens planted in a flush of enthusiasm but without adequate means or will to carry each crop through to harvest. The Nation cannot afford such waste of labor and materials when it is at war. Every crop planted should be properly sown at the right time, tended to harvest, then harvested at the proper stage of development, and utilized without waste. Unless the product is actually consumed by those who need it, there is no point in spending seeds, fertilizer, and energy in growing it.

Source: Victor Rickman Boswell, *Victory Gardens,* Miscellaneous Publication No. 483 (Washington, DC: U.S. Department of Agriculture, 1943), 1–6.

1956 • 124 • NATIONAL INTERSTATE AND DEFENSE HIGHWAYS ACT

Introduction: *The advent of long-haul trucks with roof-mounted refrigeration systems in 1948 made it possible for refrigerated and frozen foods to be easily distributed to even the most isolated communities The construction of the interstate highway system beginning in 1956 decentralized food processing, enabling processing plants to be constructed where labor costs were lowest and local and state zoning and taxing policies favored business. Also, the fast-food industry expanded alongside the interstate highway system, with outlets clustering around off-ramps. Below are excerpts from the federal legislation passed in 1956 that would eventually create the interstate highway system.*

Federal-Aid Highway Act of 1956

Section 102. Federal-Aid Highways.

(A) (1) Authorization of Appropriations.—For the purpose of carrying out the provisions of the Federal-Aid Road Act approved July 11, 1916 (39 Stat. 355), and all Acts amendatory thereof and supplementary thereto, there is hereby authorized to be appropriated for the fiscal year ending June 30, 1957, $125,000,000 in addition to any sums heretofore authorized for such fiscal year; the sum of $850,000,000 for the fiscal year ending June 30, 1958; and the sum of $875,000,000 for the fiscal year ending June 30, 1959. The sums herein authorized for each fiscal year shall be available for expenditure as follows:

(A) 45 per centum for projects on the Federal-aid primary high-way system.

(B) 30 per centum for projects on the Federal-aid secondary high-way system.

(C) 25 per centum for projects on extensions of these systems within urban areas.

(2) Apportionments.—The sums authorized by this section shall be apportioned among the several States in the manner now provided by law and in accordance with the formulas set forth in section 4 of the Federal-Aid Highway Act of 1944; approved December 20, 1944 (58 Stat. 838): Provided, That the additional amount herein authorized for the

fiscal year ending June 30, 1957, shall be apportioned immediately upon enactment of this Act.

(b) Availability for Expenditure.—Any sums apportioned to any State under this section shall be available for expenditure in that State for two years after the close of the fiscal year for which such sums are authorized, and any amounts so apportioned remaining unexpended at the end of such period shall lapse: Provided, That such funds shall be deemed to have been expended if a sum equal to the total of the sums herein and heretofore apportioned to the State is covered by formal agreements with the Secretary of Commerce for construction, reconstruction, or improvement of specific projects as provided in this title and prior Acts: Provided further, That in the case of those sums heretofore, herein, or hereafter apportioned to any State for projects on the Federal-aid secondary highway system, the Secretary of Commerce may, upon the request of any State, discharge his responsibility relative to the plans, specifications, estimates, surveys, contract awards, design, inspection, and construction of such secondary road projects by his receiving and approving a certified statement by the State highway department setting forth that the plans, design, and construction for such projects are in accord with the standards and procedures of such State applicable. . . .

Section 108. National System of Interstate and Defense Highways.

(a) Interstate System.—It is hereby declared to be essential to the national interest to provide for the early completion of the "National System of Interstate Highways", as authorized and designated in accordance with section 7 of the Federal-Aid Highway Act of 1944 (58 Stat. 838). It is the intent of the Congress that the Interstate System be completed as nearly as practicable over a thirteen-year period and that the entire System in all the States be brought to simultaneous completion. Because of its primary importance to the national defense, the name of such system is hereby changed to the "National System of Interstate and Defense Highways". Such National System of Interstate and Defense Highways is hereinafter in this Act referred to as the "Interstate System".

Source: The Federal Highway Act of 1956 (PL 627, June 29, 1956), 70 *United States Statutes at Large,* pp. 374–402.

1964 • 125 • Food Stamp Act of 1964

Introduction: *The Food Stamp Act passed in 1964 was a federal-assistance program that was administered by states to provide assistance to low- and no-income people and families living in America. The program was funded through the U.S. Department of Agriculture. Individuals and families who qualified for the program could redeem the stamps in grocery stores and supermarkets. The program was subsequently renamed the Supplemental Nutrition Assistance Program (SNAP). The system has shifted from stamps to electronic benefits transfer (EBT) cards that operate like credit cards and debit cards. Users are restricted in what they can acquire. For instance, liquor and tobacco are excluded, and participants cannot purchase hot food, such as rotisserie* *chicken. Attempts have been made to disallow certain junk food purchases through the program (such as sugary sodas and candy) but have not been successful.*

The Food Stamp Act of 1964, P.L. 88-525, 78 Stat. 703–709, Aug. 31, 1964

Authorized a food stamp program to permit low income households to receive "a greater share of the Nation's food abundance".

Defined the following terms as follows:

—"Secretary" to mean the Secretary of Agriculture
—"food" to mean any food or food product for human consumption except alcoholic beverages, tobacco, those foods which are identified on the package as being imported, and meat and meat products which are imported.
—"coupon" to mean any coupon, stamp, or type of certificate issued pursuant to the provisions of the FSA
—"coupon allotment" to mean the total value of coupons to be issued to a household during each month or other time period
—"household" to mean a group of related or non-related individuals, who are not residents of an institution or boarding house, but are living as one economic unit sharing common cooking facilities and for whom food is customarily purchased in common. Term also to mean a single individual living alone who has cooking facilities and who purchases and prepares food for home consumption.
—"retail food store" to mean an establishment, including a recognized department thereof, or a house-to-house trade route which sells food to households for home consumption.
—"wholesale food concern" to mean an establishment which sells food to retail food stores for resale to households
—"State agency" to mean the agency of the State government which has responsibility for the administration of the federally aided public assistance programs
—"bank" to mean member or nonmember banks of the Federal Reserve System
—"State" to mean the fifty States and the District of Columbia
—"food stamp program" to mean any program promulgated pursuant to the provisions of the FSA.

Authorized the Secretary to formulate and administer a FSP under which, at the request of an appropriate State agency, eligible households within the State shall be provided with an opportunity more nearly to obtain a nutritionally adequate diet through the issuance to them of a coupon allotment which shall have a greater monetary value than their normal expenditures for food.

Coupons to be used only to purchase food from retail food stores which have been approved for participation in the FSP.

Coupons issued and used to be redeemable at face value by the Secretary through the facilities of the Treasury of the U.S.

Prohibited distribution of federally owned foods to households under the authority of any other law except during emergency situations caused by a national or other disaster as determined by the Secretary.

Secretary to issue regulations, not inconsistent with the FSA, as he deems necessary or appropriate for the effective and efficient administration of the FSP.

FSP participation limited to those households whose income is determined to be a substantial limiting factor in the attainment of a nutritionally adequate diet.

Each State agency to establish standards to determine the eligibility of applicant households. Standards to include maximum income limitations consistent with the income standards used by the State agency in administration of its federally aided public assistance programs. Standards to also place a limitation on the resources to be allowed eligible households. Eligibility standards to be approved by the Secretary.

Coupons to be printed in such denominations as may be necessary, and issued only to eligible households.

Coupons issued to eligible households to be used only to purchase food in retail food stores which have been approved for participation in the FSP at prices prevailing in such stores.

Secretary prohibited from specifying prices at which food may be sold by wholesale food concerns or retail food stores.

Coupons to be simple in design. The name of any public official not to appear on coupons.

Face value of coupon allotment to be in such amount as will provide households with an opportunity more nearly to obtain a low-cost nutritionally adequate diet.

Households charged such portion of the face value of the coupon allotment issued to them as is determined to be equivalent to their normal expenditures for food.

Bonus value not to be considered income or resources for any purpose under any Federal or State laws including, but not limited to, laws relating to taxation, welfare, and public assistance programs.

Funds derived from the charges made for the coupon allotment to be promptly deposited in a manner prescribed in regulations, in a separate account maintained in the Treasury of the U.S. for such purpose.

Regulations to provide for the submission of applications for approval by retail food stores and wholesale food concerns which desire to be authorized to accept and redeem coupons under the FSP and for the approval of applicants whose participation will effectuate the purposes of the FSP.

Regulations to require an applicant retail food store or wholesale food concern to submit information which will permit a determination to be made as to whether such applicant qualifies, or continues to qualify, for approval under the FSA or regulations. Regulations to provide for safeguards which restrict the use or disclosure of such information to purposes directly connected with administration and enforcement of the provisions of the FSA or regulations.

Retail food store or wholesale food concern which has failed to receive approval to participate in the FSP may obtain a hearing on such refusal.

Regulations to provide for the redemption of coupons accepted by retail food stores through approved wholesale food concerns or through banks, with the cooperation of the Treasury Dept.

State agency of each participating State to assume responsibility for the certification of applicant households and for the issuance of coupons. Records to be kept as necessary to ascertain whether the program is being conducted in compliance with the provisions of the FSA and regulations. Records to be available for inspection and audit and to be preserved for such period of time, not in excess of three years, as may be specified in regulations.

Discrimination against any household by reason of race, religious creed, national origin, or political beliefs prohibited in the certification of applicant households.

Participating States or political subdivisions prohibited from decreasing welfare grants or other similar aid extended to any person or persons as a consequence of such person's or persons' participation in benefits made available under the FSA or regulations.

State agencies desiring to participate in the FSP required to submit a plan of operation specifying the manner in which the program will be conducted within the State. Plan to include standards to be used in determining the eligibility of applicant households; that certification of applicant households are to be undertaken in accordance with the general procedures and personnel standards used by them in the certification of applicants under the federally aided public assistance programs; safeguards which restrict the use or disclosure of information obtained from applicant households to persons directly connected with the administration or enforcement of the FSA or regulations; and for the submission of such reports and other information as may be required. Secretary to provide for an equitable and orderly expansion among the several States in accordance with their relative need and readiness to meet their requested effective dates of participation.

Secretary to direct that there be no further issuance of coupons in the political subdivisions where there is a failure by a State agency to comply substantially with the provisions of the FSA, or with the State plan of operation, following a reasonable period of time for the correction of such failure, until such time as satisfactory corrective action has been taken.

States are liable to the Federal Government for the cost of gross negligence or fraud in the certification of applicant households.

Any approved retail food store or wholesale food concern may be disqualified from further participation on a finding that it has violated any of the provisions of the FSA or regulations. Disqualification period to be determined in accordance with regulations and subject to review.

Secretary has the power to determine the amount of and settle and adjust any claim and to compromise or deny all or part of any such claim or claims arising under the provisions of the FSA or regulations.

Notice of administrative action to be issued to retail food store or wholesale food concern whenever:

an application to participate is denied
a retail food store or a wholesale food concern in disqualified, or
all or part of any claim of a retail food store or wholesale food concern is denied.

If store or concern is aggrieved by such action, it may, within 10 days of the date of delivery of such notice, file a written request for an opportunity to submit information in support of its position to such person or persons as the regulations may designate. If such a request is made, such information as may be submitted, as well as such other information as may be available, shall be reviewed by the person or persons designated, who shall make a final determination which shall take effect fifteen days after the date of the delivery of the final determination. If the store or concern feels aggrieved by such final determination he may obtain judicial review by filing a complaint in the U.S. district court or in any court of record of the State having competent jurisdiction, within

30 days after the date of delivery or service of the final notice of determination upon him.

Secretary may provide for the issuance or presentment for redemption of coupons to such person or persons, and at such times and in such manner, as he deems necessary.

$10,000 fine or five year imprisonment for anyone who knowingly uses, transfers, acquires, or possesses coupons in any manner not authorized by the FSP or regulations, or whoever presents, or causes to be presented, coupons for payment or redemption of the value of $100 or more, knowing the same to have been received, transferred, or used in any manner in violation of the provisions of the FSA or regulations if such coupons are of the value of $100 or more. $5,000 fine or one year imprisonment if such coupons are of the value of less than $100.

Coupons issued pursuant to the FSA to be deemed to be obligations of the U.S.

Each State responsible for financing, the costs of carrying out the administrative responsibilities assigned to it under the FSA including, but not limited to, the certification of households; the acceptance, storage, and protection of coupons after their delivery to receiving points within the States; and the issuance of such coupons to eligible households and the control and accounting therefor.

Secretary authorized to cooperate with State agencies in the certification of households which are not receiving any type of public assistance. Cooperation to include payments to State agencies for part of the cost they incur in the certification of such households. The amount of such payment to be 50% of the sum of: (1) the direct salary costs (including the cost of such fringe benefits as are normally paid to its personnel by the State agency) of the personnel necessary to certify the eligibility of such households, and of the immediate supervisor of such personnel, for such periods of time as they are employed in certifying the eligibility of such households; (2) travel and related costs incurred by such personnel in post interview field investigations of such households; and (3) an amount not to exceed 25% of the costs computed under (1) and (2) above.

Appropriated $75 million for FY 1965, $100 million for FY 1966, $200 million for FY 1967, and not in excess of such sum as may hereafter be authorized by Congress for any subsequent FY. Bonus amounts of such appropriation to be transferred to a separate Treasury account.

Secretary to limit the value of bonus coupons, to an amount which is not in excess of the portion of the appropriation for such FY which is transferred to the separate account. If the Secretary finds that the requirements of participating States will exceed this limitation, the Secretary must direct State agencies to reduce the amount of such coupons to be issued to participating households to the extent necessary to comply with the provisions of this section.

If Secretary determines that any of the funds in the separate account are no longer required to carry out the provisions of the FSA, such portion of such funds were to be paid into the miscellaneous receipts of the Treasury.

Amounts expended under this act not to be considered amounts expended for the purpose of carrying out the agricultural price-support program and appropriations for the purposes of this Act shall be considered, for the purpose of budget presentations, to relate to the functions of the Government concerned with welfare.

Source: Food Stamp Act of 1964, U.S. Code 7, §§ 2011 et seq.

1990 • 126 • NUTRITION LABELING AND EDUCATION ACT OF 1990

Introduction: *The Nutrition Labeling and Education Act of 1990 requires nutrition labeling of most foods regulated by the Food and Drug Administration (FDA). The FDA requires that processed food include on its label the number of total calories, calories from fat, total fat, cholesterol, sodium, dietary fiber, sugars, etc.*

Nutrition Labeling and Education Act of 1990

Section 2. Nutrition Labeling.

(A) Nutrition Information—Section 403 (21 U.S.C. 343) is amended by adding at the end the following new paragraph:

(q)(1) Except as provided in subparagraphs (3), (4), and (5), if it is a food intended for human consumption and is offered for sale, unless its label or labeling bears nutrition information that provides—

(A)(i) the serving size which is an amount customarily consumed and which is expressed in a common household measure that is appropriate to the food, or
(ii) if the use of the food is not typically expressed in a serving size, the common household unit of measure that expresses the serving size of the food,
(B) the number of servings or other units of measure per container,
(C) the total number of calories—
(i) derived from any source, and
(ii) derived from the total fat, in each serving size or other unit of measure of the food,
(D) the amount of the following nutrients: Total fat, saturated fat, cholesterol, sodium, total carbohydrates, complex carbohydrates, sugars, dietary fiber, and total protein contained in each serving size or other unit of measure,
(E) any vitamin, mineral, or other nutrient required to be placed on the label and labeling of food under this Act before October 1, 1990, if the Secretary determines that such information will assist consumers in maintaining healthy dietary practices.

The Secretary may by regulation require any information required to be placed on the label or labeling by this subparagraph or subparagraph (2)(A) to be highlighted on the label or labeling by larger type, bold type, or contrasting color if the Secretary determines that such highlighting will assist consumers in maintaining healthy dietary practices.

(2)(A) If the Secretary determines that a nutrient other than a nutrient required by subparagraph (1)(C), (1)(D), or (1)(E) should be included in the label or labeling of food subject to subparagraph (1) for purposes of providing information regarding the nutritional value of such food that will assist consumers in maintaining healthy dietary practices, the Secretary may by regulation require that information relating to such additional nutrient be included in the label or labeling of such food.

(B) If the Secretary determines that the information relating to a nutrient required by subparagraph (1)(C), (1)(D), or (1)(E) or clause (A) of this subparagraph to be included in the label or labeling of food is not necessary to assist consumers in maintaining healthy dietary practices, the Secretary may by regulation remove information relating to such nutrient from such requirement.

(3) For food that is received in bulk containers at a retail establishment, the Secretary may, by regulation, provide that the nutrition information required by subparagraphs (1) and (2) be displayed at the location in the retail establishment at which the food is offered for sale.

(4)(A) The Secretary shall provide for furnishing the nutrition information required by subparagraphs (1) and (2) with respect to raw agricultural commodities and raw fish by issuing voluntary nutrition guidelines, as provided by clause (B) or by issuing regulations that are mandatory as provided by clause (C).

(B)(i) Upon the expiration of 12 months after the date of the enactment of the Nutrition Labeling and Education Act of 1990, the Secretary, after providing an opportunity for comment, shall issue guidelines for food retailers offering raw agricultural commodities or raw fish to provide nutrition information specified in subparagraphs (1) and (2). Such guidelines shall take into account the actions taken by food retailers during such 12-month period to provide to consumers nutrition information on raw agricultural commodities and raw fish. Such guidelines shall only apply—

(I) in the case of raw agricultural commodities, to the 20 varieties of vegetables most frequently consumed during a year and the 20 varieties of fruit most frequently consumed during a year, and

(II) to the 20 varieties of raw fish most frequently consumed during a year.

The vegetables, fruits, and raw fish to which such guidelines apply shall be determined by the Secretary by regulation and the Secretary may apply such guidelines regionally.

(ii) Upon the expiration of 12 months after the date of the enactment of the Nutrition Labeling and Education Act of 1990, the Secretary shall issue a final regulation defining the circumstances that constitute substantial compliance by food retailers with the guidelines issued under subclause (I). The regulation shall provide that there is not substantial compliance if a significant number of retailers have failed to comply with the guidelines. The size of the retailers and the portion of the market served by retailers in compliance with the guidelines shall be considered in determining whether the substantial-compliance standard has been met.

(C)(i) Upon the expiration of 30 months after the date of the enactment of the Nutrition Labeling and Education Act of 1990, the Secretary shall issue a report on actions taken by food retailers to provide consumers with nutrition information for raw agricultural commodities and raw fish under the guidelines issued under clause (A). Such report shall include a determination of whether there is substantial compliance with the guidelines.

(ii) If the Secretary finds that there is substantial compliance with the guidelines, the Secretary shall issue a report and make a determination of the type required in subclause (I) every two years.

(D)(i) If the Secretary determines that there is not substantial compliance with the guidelines issued under clause (A), the Secretary shall at the time such determination is made issue proposed regulations requiring that any person who offers raw agricultural commodities or raw fish to consumers to provide, in a manner prescribed by regulations, the nutrition information required by subparagraphs (1) and (2). The Secretary shall issue final regulations imposing such requirements 6 months after issuing the proposed regulations. The final regulations shall become effective 6 months after the date of their promulgation.

(ii) Regulations issued under subclause (I) may require that the nutrition information required by subparagraphs (1) and (2) be provided for more than 20 varieties of vegetables, 20 varieties of fruit, and 20 varieties of fish most frequently consumed during a year if the Secretary finds that a larger number of such products are frequently consumed. Such regulations shall permit such information to be provided in a single location in each area in which raw agricultural commodities and raw fish are offered for sale. Such regulations may provide that information shall be expressed as an average or range per serving of the same type of raw agricultural commodity or raw fish. The Secretary shall develop and make available to the persons who offer such food to consumers the information required by subparagraphs (1) and (2).

(iii) Regulations issued under subclause (I) shall permit the required information to be provided in each area of an establishment in which raw agricultural commodities and raw fish are offered for sale. The regulations shall permit food retailers to display the required information by supplying copies of the information provided by the Secretary, by making the information available in brochure, notebook or leaflet form, or by posting a sign disclosing the information. Such regulations shall also permit presentation of the required information to be supplemented by a video, live demonstration, or other media which the Secretary approves.

(E) For purposes of this subparagraph, the term 'fish' includes freshwater or marine fin fish, crustaceans, and mollusks, including shellfish, amphibians, and other forms of aquatic animal life.

(F) No person who offers raw agricultural commodities or raw fish to consumers may be prosecuted for minor violations of this subparagraph if there has been substantial compliance with the requirements of this paragraph.

(5)(A) Subparagraphs (1), (2), (3), and (4) shall not apply to food—

- (i) which is served in restaurants or other establishments in which food is served for immediate human consumption or which is sold for sale or use in such establishments,
- (ii) which is processed and prepared primarily in a retail establishment, which is ready for human consumption, which is of the type described in subclause (I), and which is offered for sale to consumers but not for immediate human consumption in such establishment and which is not offered for sale outside such establishment,
- (iii) which is an infant formula subject to section 412,
- (iv) which is a medical food as defined in section 5(b) of the Orphan Drug Act (21 U.S.C. 360ee(b)), or
- (v) which is described in section 405(2).

(B) Subparagraphs (1) and (2) shall not apply to the label of a food if the Secretary determines by regulations that compliance with such subparagraphs is impracticable because the package of such food is too small to comply with the requirements of such subparagraphs and if the label of such food does not contain any nutrition information.

(C) If a food contains insignificant amounts, as determined by the Secretary, of all the nutrients required by subparagraphs (1) and (2) to be listed in the label or labeling of food, the requirements of such subparagraphs shall not apply to such food if the label, labeling, or advertising of such food does not make any claim with respect to the nutritional value of such food. If a food contains insignificant amounts, as determined by the Secretary, of more than one-half the nutrients required by subparagraphs (1) and (2) to be in the label or labeling of the food, the Secretary shall require the amounts of such nutrients to be stated in a simplified form prescribed by the Secretary.

(D) If a person offers food for sale and has annual gross sales made or business done in sales to consumers which is not more than $500,000 or has annual gross sales made or business done in sales of food to consumers which is not more than $50,000, the requirements of subparagraphs (1), (2), (3), and (4) shall not apply with respect to food sold by such person to consumers unless the label or labeling of food offered by such person provides nutrition information or makes a nutrition claim.

(E) If a food to which section 411 applies (as defined in section 411(C)) contains one or more of the nutrients required by subparagraph (1) or (2) to be in the label or labeling of the food, the label or labeling of such food shall comply with the requirements of subparagraphs (1) and (2) in a manner which is appropriate for such food and which is specified in regulations of the Secretary.

(F) Subparagraphs (1), (2), (3), and (4) shall not apply to food which is sold by a food distributor if the food distributor principally sells food to restaurants or other establishments in which food is served for immediate human consumption and does not manufacture, process, or repackage the food it sells.

(b) REGULATIONS—

(1) The Secretary of Health and Human Services shall issue proposed regulations to implement section 403(q) of the Federal Food, Drug, and Cosmetic Act within 12 months after the date of the enactment of this Act. Not later than 24 months after the date of the enactment of this Act, the Secretary shall issue final regulations to implement the requirements of such section. Such regulations shall—

(A) require the required information to be conveyed to the public in a manner which enables the public to readily observe and comprehend such information and to understand its relative significance in the context of a total daily diet,

(B) include regulations which establish standards, in accordance with paragraph (1)(A), to define serving size or other unit of measure for food,

(C) permit the label or labeling of food to include nutrition information which is in addition to the information required by such section 403(q) and which is of the type described in subparagraph (1) or (2) of such section, and

(D) permit the nutrition information on the label or labeling of a food to remain the same or permit the information to be stated as a range even though (i) there are minor variations in the nutritional value of the food which occur in the normal course of the production or processing of the food, or (ii) the food is comprised of an assortment of similar foods which have variations in nutritional value.

(2) If the Secretary of Health and Human Services does not promulgate final regulations under paragraph (1) upon the expiration of 24 months after the date of the enactment of this Act, the proposed regulations issued in accordance with paragraph (1) shall be considered as the final regulations upon the expiration of such 24 months. There shall be promptly published in the Federal Register notice of new status of the proposed regulations.

(3) If the Secretary of Health and Human Services does not promulgate final regulations under section 403(q)(4) of the Federal Food, Drug, and Cosmetic Act upon the expiration of 6 months after the date on which the Secretary makes a finding that there has been no substantial compliance with section 403(q)(4)(C) of such Act, the proposed regulations issued in accordance with such section shall be considered as the final regulations upon the expiration of such 6 months. There shall be promptly published in the Federal Register notice of new status of the proposed regulations.

(C) Consumer Education—The Secretary of Health and Human Services shall carry out activities which educate consumers about—

(1) the availability of nutrition information in the label or labeling of food, and
(2) the importance of that information in maintaining healthy dietary practices.

Source: Nutrition Labeling and Education Act of 1990; Public Law 101-535.

2000 • 127 • National Organic Program

Introduction: *The 1990 Farm Bill passed by the U.S. Congress contained the Organic Foods Production Act, which set national standards for how organic food must be produced, handled, and labeled. Organic foods could not include synthetic fertilizers or pesticides. The bill also established the National Organic Standards Board, which issues a list of prohibited substances, such as synthetic fertilizer and antibiotics, that cannot be used in organic food. After 12 years of work by the National Organic Standards Board, the National Organic Program (NOP) was issued in 2000 and took effect in October 2002; it is administered by the U.S. Department of Agriculture (USDA). The NOP covers in detail all aspects of organic food production, processing, delivery, and retail sale. Under the NOP, farmers and food processors who wish to use the word "organic" in reference to their businesses and products must be certified organic by the USDA. Producers with annual sales not exceeding $5,000 are exempt from the rule and do not require certification. However, they must still follow NOP standards, keep proper records, and submit to a production audit if requested, but they cannot use the term "certified organic."*

Use of the term, "organic."

(a) The term, "organic," may only be used on labels and in labeling of raw or processed agricultural products, including ingredients, that have been produced and handled in

Consumers choose organic apples at a farmers' market in San Francisco, California. (John Sigler/iStock-Photo.com)

accordance with the regulations in this part. The term, "organic," may not be used in a product name to modify a nonorganic ingredient in the product.

(b) Products for export, produced and certified to foreign national organic standards or foreign contract buyer requirements, may be labeled in accordance with the organic labeling requirements of the receiving country or contract buyer: *Provided,* That, the shipping containers and shipping documents meet the labeling requirements specified in §205.307(C).

(c) Products produced in a foreign country and exported for sale in the United States must be certified pursuant to subpart E of this part and labeled pursuant to this subpart D.

(d) Livestock feeds produced in accordance with the requirements of this part must be labeled in accordance with the requirements of §205.306.

§ 205.301 Product composition.

(a) *Products sold, labeled, or represented as "100 percent organic."* A raw or processed agricultural product sold, labeled, or represented as "100 percent organic" must contain (by weight or fluid volume, excluding water and salt) 100 percent organically produced ingredients. If labeled as organically produced, such product must be labeled pursuant to §205.303.

(b) *Products sold, labeled, or represented as "organic."* A raw or processed agricultural product sold, labeled, or represented as "organic" must contain (by weight or fluid volume, excluding water and salt) not less than 95 percent organically produced raw or processed agricultural products. Any remaining product ingredients must be organically produced, unless not commercially available in organic form, or must be nonagricultural substances or nonorganically produced agricultural products produced consistent with the National List in subpart G of this part. If labeled as organically produced, such product must be labeled pursuant to §205.303.

(c) *Products sold, labeled, or represented as "made with organic (specified ingredients or food group(s))."* Multiingredient agricultural product sold, labeled, or represented as "made with organic (specified ingredients or food group(s))" must contain (by weight or fluid volume, excluding water and salt) at least 70 percent organically produced ingredients which are produced and handled pursuant to requirements in subpart C of this part. No ingredients may be produced using prohibited practices specified in paragraphs (f)(1), (2), and (3) of §205.301. Nonorganic ingredients may be produced without regard to paragraphs (f)(4), (5), (6), and (7) of §205.301. If labeled as containing organically produced ingredients or food groups, such product must be labeled pursuant to §205.304.

(d) *Products with less than 70 percent organically produced ingredients.* The organic ingredients in multiingredient agricultural product containing less than 70 percent organically produced ingredients (by weight or fluid volume, excluding water and salt) must be produced and handled pursuant to requirements in subpart C of this part. The nonorganic ingredients may be produced and handled without regard to the requirements of this part. Multiingredient agricultural product containing less than 70 percent organically produced ingredients may represent the organic nature of the product only as provided in §205.305.

(e) *Livestock feed.* (1) A raw or processed livestock feed product sold, labeled, or represented as "100 percent organic" must contain (by weight or fluid volume, excluding water and salt) not less than 100 percent organically produced raw or processed agricultural product.

(2) A raw or processed livestock feed product sold, labeled, or represented as "organic" must be produced in conformance with §205.237.

(f) All products labeled as "100 percent organic" or "organic" and all ingredients identified as "organic" in the ingredient statement of any product must not:

(1) Be produced using excluded methods, pursuant to §201.105(e) of this chapter;

(2) Be produced using sewage sludge, pursuant to §201.105(f) of this chapter;

(3) Be processed using ionizing radiation, pursuant to §201.105(g) of this chapter;

(4) Be processed using processing aids not approved on the National List of Allowed and Prohibited Substances in subpart G of this part: Except, That, products labeled as "100 percent organic," if processed, must be processed using organically produced processing aids;

(5) Contain sulfites, nitrates, or nitrites added during the production or handling process, Except, that, wine containing added sulfites may be labeled "made with organic grapes";

(6) Be produced using nonorganic ingredients when organic ingredients are available; or

(7) Include organic and nonorganic forms of the same ingredient.

§ 205.302 Calculating the percentage of organically produced ingredients.

(a) The percentage of all organically produced ingredients in an agricultural product sold, labeled, or represented as "100 percent organic," "organic," or "made with organic (specified ingredients or food group(s))," or that include organic ingredients must be calculated by:

(1) Dividing the total net weight (excluding water and salt) of combined organic ingredients at formulation by the total weight (excluding water and salt) of the finished product.

(2) Dividing the fluid volume of all organic ingredients (excluding water and salt) by the fluid volume of the finished product (excluding water and salt) if the product and ingredients are liquid. If the liquid product is identified on the principal display panel or information panel as being reconstituted from concentrates, the calculation should be made on the basis of single-strength concentrations of the ingredients and finished product.

(3) For products containing organically produced ingredients in both solid and liquid form, dividing the combined weight of the solid ingredients and the weight of the liquid ingredients (excluding water and salt) by the total weight (excluding water and salt) of the finished product.

(b) The percentage of all organically produced ingredients in an agricultural product must be rounded down to the nearest whole number.

(c) The percentage must be determined by the handler who affixes the label on the consumer package and verified by the certifying agent of the handler. The handler may use information provided by the certified operation in determining the percentage.

§ 205.303 Packaged products labeled "100 percent organic" or "organic."

(a) Agricultural products in packages described in §205.301(a) and (b) may display, on the principal display panel, information panel, and any other panel of the package and on any labeling or market information concerning the product, the following:

(1) The term, "100 percent organic" or "organic," as applicable, to modify the name of the product;

(2) For products labeled "organic," the percentage of organic ingredients in the product; (The size of the percentage statement must not exceed one-half the size of the largest type size on the panel on which the statement is displayed and must appear in its entirety in the same type size, style, and color without highlighting.)

(3) The term, "organic," to identify the organic ingredients in multiingredient products labeled "100 percent organic";

(4) The USDA seal; and/or

(5) The seal, logo, or other identifying mark of the certifying agent which certified the production or handling operation producing the finished product and any other certifying agent which certified production or handling operations producing raw organic product or organic ingredients used in the finished product: *Provided,* That, the handler

producing the finished product maintain records, pursuant to this part, verifying organic certification of the operations producing such ingredients, and: *Provided further,* That, such seals or marks are not individually displayed more prominently than the USDA seal.

(b) Agricultural products in packages described in §205.301(a) and (b) must:
(1) For products labeled "organic," identify each organic ingredient in the ingredient statement with the word, "organic," or with an asterisk or other reference mark which is defined below the ingredient statement to indicate the ingredient is organically produced. Water or salt included as ingredients cannot be identified as organic.

(2) On the information panel, below the information identifying the handler or distributor of the product and preceded by the statement, "Certified organic by * * *," or similar phrase, identify the name of the certifying agent that certified the handler of the finished product and may display the business address, Internet address, or telephone number of the certifying agent in such label.

§ 205.304 Packaged products labeled "made with organic (specified ingredients or food group(s))."

(a) Agricultural products in packages described in §205.301(c) may display on the principal display panel, information panel, and any other panel and on any labeling or market information concerning the product:
(1) The statement:

(i) "Made with organic (specified ingredients)": *Provided,* That, the statement does not list more than three organically produced ingredients; or

(ii) "Made with organic (specified food groups)": *Provided,* That, the statement does not list more than three of the following food groups: beans, fish, fruits, grains, herbs, meats, nuts, oils, poultry, seeds, spices, sweeteners, and vegetables or processed milk products; and, *Provided further,* That, all ingredients of each listed food group in the product must be organically produced; and

(iii) Which appears in letters that do not exceed one-half the size of the largest type size on the panel and which appears in its entirety in the same type size, style, and color without highlighting.

(2) The percentage of organic ingredients in the product. The size of the percentage statement must not exceed one-half the size of the largest type size on the panel on which the statement is displayed and must appear in its entirety in the same type size, style, and color without highlighting.

(3) The seal, logo, or other identifying mark of the certifying agent that certified the handler of the finished product.

(b) Agricultural products in packages described in §205.301(c) must:

(1) In the ingredient statement, identify each organic ingredient with the word, "organic," or with an asterisk or other reference mark which is defined below the ingredient statement to indicate the ingredient is organically produced. Water or salt included as ingredients cannot be identified as organic.

(2) On the information panel, below the information identifying the handler or distributor of the product and preceded by the statement, "Certified organic by * * *," or similar phrase, identify the name of the certifying agent that certified the handler of the finished product: *Except,* That, the business address, Internet address, or telephone number of the certifying agent may be included in such label.
(c) Agricultural products in packages described in §205.301(c) must not display the USDA seal.

§ 205.305 Multi-ingredient packaged products with less than 70 percent organically produced ingredients.

(a) An agricultural product with less than 70 percent organically produced ingredients may only identify the organic content of the product by:

(1) Identifying each organically produced ingredient in the ingredient statement with the word, "organic," or with an asterisk or other reference mark which is defined below the ingredient statement to indicate the ingredient is organically produced, and

(2) If the organically produced ingredients are identified in the ingredient statement, displaying the product's percentage of organic contents on the information panel.

(b) Agricultural products with less than 70 percent organically produced ingredients must not display:

(1) The USDA seal; and

(2) Any certifying agent seal, logo, or other identifying mark which represents organic certification of a product or product ingredients.

Source: *Federal Register* 65(246) (December 21, 2000).

2004 • 128 • Food Allergen Labeling and Consumer Protection Act

Introduction: *An estimated 2–5 percent of Americans suffer from food allergies that can cause mild discomfort to severe medical problems, including in a few cases death. The problem was that most processed foods did not identify food allergens. In 2004 Congress passed the Food Allergen Labeling and Consumer Protection Act, which requires food manufacturers to disclose on the label whether the product contains major food allergens. As a result of this law, most manufacturers list allergens on labels separate from ingredient labels.*

Food Allergen Labeling and Consumer Protection Act of 2004 (Public Law 108-282, Title II)

Congress finds that—

(1) it is estimated that—

(A) approximately 2 percent of adults and about 5 percent of infants and young children in the United States suffer from food allergies; and
(B) each year, roughly 30,000 individuals require emergency room treatment and 150 individuals die because of allergic reactions to food;

(2)

(A) eight major foods or food groups—milk, eggs, fish, Crustacean shellfish, tree nuts, peanuts, wheat, and soybeans—account for 90 percent of food allergies;
(B) at present, there is no cure for food allergies; and
(C) a food allergic consumer must avoid the food to which the consumer is allergic;

(3)

(A) in a review of the foods of randomly selected manufacturers of baked goods, ice cream, and candy in Minnesota and Wisconsin in 1999, the Food and Drug Administration found that 25 percent of sampled foods failed to list peanuts or eggs as ingredients on the food labels; and
(B) nationally, the number of recalls because of unlabeled allergens rose to 121 in 2000 from about 35 a decade earlier;

(4) a recent study shows that many parents of children with a food allergy were unable to correctly identify in each of several food labels the ingredients derived from major food allergens;

(5)

(A) ingredients in foods must be listed by their "common or usual name";
(B) in some cases, the common or usual name of an ingredient may be unfamiliar to consumers, and many consumers may not realize the ingredient is derived from, or contains, a major food allergen; and
(C) in other cases, the ingredients may be declared as a class, including spices, flavorings, and certain colorings, or are exempt from the ingredient labeling requirements, such as incidental additives; and

(6)

(A) celiac disease is an immune-mediated disease that causes damage to the gastrointestinal tract, central nervous system, and other organs;
(B) the current recommended treatment is avoidance of glutens in foods that are associated with celiac disease; and
(C) a multicenter, multiyear study estimated that the prevalence of celiac disease in the United States is 0.5 to 1 percent of the general population.

Section 203. Food Labeling; Requirement of Information Regarding Allergenic Substances.

(a) In General.—Section 403 of the Federal Food, Drug, and Cosmetic Act (21 U.S.C. 343) is amended by adding at the end the following:

(1) If it is not a raw agricultural commodity and it is, or it contains an ingredient that bears or contains, a major food allergen, unless either—

(A) the word 'Contains', followed by the name of the food source from which the major food allergen is derived, is printed immediately after or is adjacent to the list of ingredients (in a type size no smaller than the type size used in the list of ingredients) required under subsections (g) and (I); or

(B) the common or usual name of the major food allergen in the list of ingredients required under subsections (g) and (I) is followed in parentheses by the name of the food source from which the major food allergen is derived, except that the name of the food source is not required when—

(i) the common or usual name of the ingredient uses the name of the food source from which the major food allergen is derived; or

(ii) the name of the food source from which the major food allergen is derived appears elsewhere in the ingredient list, unless the name of the food source that appears elsewhere in the ingredient list appears as part of the name of a food ingredient that is not a major food allergen under section 201(qq)(2)(A) or (B).

(2) As used in this subsection, the term 'name of the food source from which the major food allergen is derived' means the name described in section 201(qq)(1); provided that in the case of a tree nut, fish, or Crustacean shellfish, the term 'name of the food source from which the major food allergen is derived' means the name of the specific type of nut or species of fish or Crustacean shellfish. Federal Register, publication.

(3) The information required under this subsection may appear in labeling in lieu of appearing on the label only if the Secretary finds that such other labeling is sufficient to protect the public health. A finding by the Secretary under this paragraph (including any change in an earlier finding under this paragraph) is effective upon publication in the Federal Register as a notice.

(4) Notwithstanding subsection (g), (I), or (k), or any other law, a flavoring, coloring, or incidental additive that is, or that bears or contains, a major food allergen shall be subject to the labeling requirements of this subsection. . . .

. . . The term 'major food allergen' means any of the following:

(1) Milk, egg, fish (e.g., bass, flounder, or cod), Crustacean shellfish (e.g., crab, lobster, or shrimp), tree nuts (e.g., almonds, pecans, or walnuts), wheat, peanuts, and soybeans.

(2) A food ingredient that contains protein derived from a food specified in paragraph. . . .

Source: Food Allergen Labeling and Consumer Protection Act of 2004 (Public Law 108-282, Title II).

2010 • 129 • Nutrition Labeling of Standard Menu Items at Chain Restaurants

Introduction: *In 2010 the U.S. Congress passed the Patient Protection and Affordable Care Act, signed into law on March 23, 2010 (sometimes called Obamacare due* *to its creation and promotion under President Barack Obama's administration). The act includes a provision that creates a national, uniform nutrition-disclosure standard for restaurants. Chain restaurants, drive-thrus, convenience stores, vending machines, and retail stores with 20 or more locations are required to post nutrition information in plain sight. Stores must also display "a succinct statement concerning suggested daily caloric intake." The standards went into effect in 2011. These federal standards replace the differing regulations and laws that a growing number of cities, counties, and states have passed during recent years.*

Nutrition labeling of standard menu items at chain restaurants.

(i) GENERAL REQUIREMENTS FOR RESTAURANTS AND SIMILAR RETAIL FOOD ESTABLISHMENTS.—Except for food described in subclause (vii), in the case of food that is a standard menu item that is offered for sale in a restaurant or similar retail food establishment that is part of a chain with 20 or more locations doing business under the same name (regardless of the type of ownership of the locations) and offering for sale substantially the same menu items, the restaurant or similar retail food establishment shall disclose the information described in subclauses (ii) and (iii).

(ii) INFORMATION REQUIRED TO BE DISCLOSED BY RESTAURANTS AND RETAIL FOOD ESTABLISHMENTS.—Except as provided in subclause (vii), the restaurant or similar retail food establishment shall disclose in a clear and conspicuous manner—

(I)(aa) in a nutrient content disclosure statement adjacent to the name of the standard menu item, so as to be clearly associated with the standard menu item, on the menu listing the item for sale, the number of calories contained in the standard menu item, as usually prepared and offered for sale; and

(bb) a succinct statement concerning suggested daily caloric intake, as specified by the Secretary by regulation and posted prominently on the menu and designed to enable the public to understand, in the context of a total daily diet, the significance of the caloric information that is provided on the menu;

(II)(aa) in a nutrient content disclosure statement adjacent to the name of the standard menu item, so as to be clearly associated with the standard menu item, on the menu board, including a drive-through menu board, the number of calories contained in the standard menu item, as usually prepared and offered for sale; and

(bb) a succinct statement concerning suggested daily caloric intake, as specified by the Secretary by regulation and posted prominently on the menu board, designed to enable the public to understand, in the context of a total daily diet, the significance of the nutrition information that is provided on the menu board;

(III) in a written form, available on the premises of the restaurant or similar retail establishment and to the consumer upon request, the nutrition information required under clauses (C) and (D) of subparagraph (1); and

(IV) on the menu or menu board, a prominent, clear, and conspicuous statement regarding the availability of the information described in item (III).

(iii) SELF-SERVICE FOOD AND FOOD ON DISPLAY.—Except as provided in subclause (vii), in the case of food sold at a salad bar, buffet line, cafeteria line, or similar self-service facility, and for self-service beverages or food that is on display and that is visible to customers, a restaurant or similar retail food establishment shall place adjacent to each food offered a sign that lists calories per displayed food item or per serving.

(iv) REASONABLE BASIS.—For the purposes of this clause, a restaurant or similar retail food establishment shall have a reasonable basis for its nutrient content disclosures, including nutrient databases, cookbooks, laboratory analyses, and other reasonable means, as described in section 101.10 of title 21, Code of Federal Regulations (or any successor regulation) or in a related guidance of the Food and Drug Administration.

(v) MENU VARIABILITY AND COMBINATION MEALS.—The Secretary shall establish by regulation standards for determining and disclosing the nutrient content for standard menu items that come in different flavors, varieties, or combinations, but which are listed as a single menu item, such as soft drinks, ice cream, pizza, doughnuts, or children's combination meals, through means determined by the Secretary, including ranges, averages, or other methods. . . .

Vending Machines.—

(I) in General.—In the case of an article of food sold from a vending machine that—

(aa) does not permit a prospective purchaser to examine the Nutrition Facts Panel before purchasing the article or does not otherwise provide visible nutrition information at the point of purchase; and

(bb) is operated by a person who is engaged in the business of owning or operat*ing 20 or more vending machines,*

the vending machine operator shall provide a sign in close proximity to each article of food or the selection button that includes a clear and conspicuous statement disclosing the number of calories contained in the article. . . .

(xi) Definition.—In this clause, the term "menu" or "menu board" means the primary writing of the restaurant or other similar retail food establishment from which a consumer makes an order selection.

Source: The Patient Protection and Affordable Care Act (2010), Public Law 111-148; 124 Stat. 119 through 124 Stat. 1025.

• Glossary •

alcohol: The most common alcohol is ethanol, a flammable liquid that boils at 173°F. Alcohol has been consumed by humans for thousands of years in various forms, such as ale, beer, wine, and spirits.

alcohol proof: A measure of how much alcohol (ethanol) is contained in a beverage. Alcohol proof works on a scale of 0–200, where 0 proof is no alcohol and 200 proof is pure alcohol. Alcoholic content is also measured by percent, where 0 percent is no alcohol and 100 percent is pure alcohol. Beer usually contains 3–12 percent alcohol, wine contains 9–16 percent, fortified wines have 15–20 percent alcohol, and spirits can range from 20 percent to 95 percent alcohol.

ale: A type of beer brewed from malted barley. Ale employees warm fermentation and brewers' yeast, which ferments quickly, giving the ale a sweet fruity taste.

aquaculture: The cultivation, under controlled conditions, of aquatic organisms, including fish, crustaceans, mollusks, and plants, such as seaweed and algae. These aquatic organisms are farmed in oceans, bays, estuaries, lakes, ponds, rivers, and inland saltwater wells. Saltwater aquaculture is also called mariculture.

bar: A commercial establishment that sells alcoholic beverages. Also, a long counter on which alcoholic beverages are served.

blood alcohol level: The percentage of alcohol in the blood. Blood alcohol level is used as a legal and medical measure of intoxication.

bouillabaisse: A French stew popularized in America by Creoles in Louisiana. Traditional ingredients include fish, onions, garlic, fish, tomatoes, and herbs.

bourbon: An American whiskey made using a corn-based mash. Bourbon originated in and around Bourbon County, Kentucky.

brandy: Distilled wine that typically contains at least 35 percent alcohol.

brewing: The process whereby a starch source, such as barley, millet, wheat, or corn, is fermented with yeast. This process usually produces liquids with an alcoholic content of 3–12 percent.

burgoo: Burgoo has two different meanings. The first is a Scotch burgoo, which is a pudding or mush made with oatmeal. The second meaning is a thick stew that originated in Kentucky and Tennessee during the 19th century but quickly spread throughout the

South and Southwest. Burgoo stew could contain almost any combination of meats and vegetables. Squirrel, wild turkey, pigeons, and fish were frequent ingredients, and the vegetables might include tomatoes, celery, turnips, and corn.

caffeine: A bitter alkaloid that is metabolized in the liver. Caffeine is a mild stimulant commonly found naturally in cocoa, coffee beans, tea leaves, and kola nuts. Caffeine appears in many junk foods, including chocolate, coffee, tea, colas, power and sports drinks, and energy bars. Consumed in small doses, caffeine can increase alertness, relieve drowsiness, and improve coordination. In large doses, caffeine can cause anxiety, insomnia, nervousness, and hypertension. Caffeine is a diuretic, and it can relieve some headaches and hence is found in many pain relievers.

calories: In the 1890s, chemist Wilbur O. Atwater analyzed the nutritional components of food (proteins, fats, and carbohydrates) and measured the caloric value of each of the groups. In the early 1900s, Russell Chittenden, a chemist at Yale University, took Atwater's idea of assessing food in terms of calories—the amount of heat required to raise the temperature of one gram of water 1 degree Centigrade—and applied it not only to energy taken in but also to energy burned in exercise. Thus, calorie counting was born. Lulu Hunt Peters's book *Diet and Health, with Key to the Calories* (1917) advocated calorie counting as a method of weight reduction. The book introduced the so-called scientific principle that calorie control equated weight control. Those who were unable to control their weight were judged to have no self-discipline, and obesity became a sign of moral weakness.

carbohydrates: One of the major dietary components. The primary function of carbohydrates is to provide energy for the body. The most important carbohydrates include simple sugars, starches, glycogen, and fiber. Complex carbohydrates are ultimately broken down into simple sugars that the body can easily metabolize.

carbonization: The process in which carbon dioxide (CO_2) gas is dissolved in a liquid. This creates the fizz in soft drinks, beer, champagne, sparkling wine, and some mineral waters.

cookbook: Traditionally, a published collection of recipes. While cookbooks continue to be published, they are also now online, in E-books, and in culinary apps.

cookbooklet: A small paper-covered booklet with recipes. Cookbooklets are frequently published by manufacturers of culinary equipment or commercial products and are intended to promote products.

chains: Multiple restaurants owned by the same company or franchisers.

cholesterol, blood: The body manufactures cholesterol in the form of dietary cholesterol. High levels of blood cholesterol increase the risk of heart disease. Cholesterol travels in the blood in little packages of fat and protein called lipoproteins. Cholesterol in high-density lipoproteins (HDL) is the so-called good cholesterol. Cholesterol in low-density lipoproteins (LDL) is bad because it is headed for your artery walls.

cholesterol, dietary: A crystalline substance found in animal tissues. The body normally synthesizes dietary cholesterol in the liver. The level of dietary cholesterol in the bloodstream can be influenced by heredity and through the consumption of certain foods. Cholesterol can cause atherosclerotic plaque and heart disease.

chowder: A fish-based soup or stew, often flavored with salt pork, potatoes, corn, and onions.

co-branding: The displaying of more than one brand name on a product or location. Also, the marketing or distribution of co-branded products or services. A co-branding arrangement has potential benefits for both sides.

continuous processing: A common way of manufacturing food. Continuous processing is more efficient and is less costly than batch processing. Most large food manufacturers have installed continuous processing machines that process their products with little human intervention.

denatured: During Prohibition, alcohol to be used for manufacturing purposes was denatured, a process that adulterated the alcohol, making it unfit for human consumption.

distilling: The process of separating mixtures based on the boiling point of liquids in the mixture. Impurities from water can be removed by boiling the water and condensing the steam. Since alcohol's boiling point is lower than that of water, alcohol can be removed from a mixture by keeping the temperature of the mixture below the boiling point of water (below 212°F) but above the boiling point of alcohol (162.5°F).

Dutch oven: An iron pot with a lid, legs, and a handle. Hot coals are placed under the legs or on a recessed lid for cooking and baking.

ethanol: Alcohol. Ethanol is a component in all alcoholic beverages and is used as a fuel in some cars.

fast casual restaurant: Restaurant where the average amount for a meal is between $8 and $15 and there is no need to leave a tip.

fast food: Inexpensive foods served in restaurant chains where orders are served promptly at a counter. Most fast foods are high in calories and low in nutritional value, but fast-food chains are increasingly serving a few healthier foods that are relatively low in calories and high in nutritional value.

fat, dietary: There are five major types of dietary fats: saturated, unsaturated, polyunsaturated, monounsaturated, and partially hydrogenated vegetable oil. Saturated fats are saturated with hydrogen atoms. In the United States, they are mainly found in dairy products, meat, poultry, and vegetable shortening made with coconut oil, palm oil, and/or palm kernel oil. Saturated fats can raise blood cholesterol levels, whereas unsaturated fats do not. Polyunsaturated fat molecules are missing hydrogen atoms. Sources of polyunsaturated fats are corn oil, cottonseed oil, safflower oil, soybean oil, and sunflower oil as well as some fish oils, margarine, mayonnaise, almonds, and pecans. Monounsaturated fats are dietary fats with one double-bonded carbon in the molecule; they are commonly found in poultry, shortening, meat, dairy products, and olive and canola oils. Partially hydrogenated vegetable oils are harder and more stable than other oils. Companies mix them with hydrogen, which increases the amount of saturated fat and creates transfat, which raises blood cholesterol.

fermentation: A process in which yeast interacts with sugar to create ethanol and carbon dioxide (CO_2). Fermentation is used in baking as well as in making alcoholic beverages.

fiber, dietary: The indigestible portion of plants. Dietary fiber, also known as roughage or bulk, is mainly found in fruits, vegetables, whole grains, and legumes. Fiber increases bulk and shortens transit time through the intestinal tract. Fiber also relieves or prevents constipation and lowers cholesterol. Medical researchers maintain that high-fiber diets lower the risk of diabetes and heart disease.

filé: A powder made from the dried sassafras leaves. Filé is traditionally used in Creole cookery.

fortified wine: Wine with a distilled spirit added. Fortification increases the alcoholic content. Typical fortified wines consumed in American history include Madeira, sherry, and port.

franchise: The authorization granted to an individual or group by a company to sell its products or services in a particular area.

fructose: A monosaccharide sugar occurring in many fruits, vegetables, and honey. Fructose is commonly used as a sweetener in food because it is much sweeter than glucose. When chemically combined with glucose, fructose forms sucrose, or common table sugar.

gelatin: A substance made from collagen in animal bones and skin. Gelatin is used as a gelling agent in food preparation. The most iconic product with gelatin is Jell-O.

globalization: The increase in the connection between peoples in the world through trade, travel, immigration, and communication.

graham flour: A flour is made from whole wheat flour. Graham flour was popularized by Sylvester Graham and other food reformers of the 19th century.

gumbo: A Creole stew. Gumbo is often made with poultry or seafood and thickened with okra or filé.

hasty pudding: A common dish served in America until the early 19th century. Hasty pudding typically consists of baked cornmeal, milk, molasses, and spices.

haute cuisine: A term from French meaning "high food." Historically, haute cuisine was an elaborate, complex, and expensive meal with many courses.

hominy: Dried kernels of corn steeped with an alkali.

homogenization: Milk is an emulsion of fat molecules in water. If allowed to sit, the cream will separate from milk. Homogenization is a process that reduces the size of the fat globules and thus reduces separation.

hoppin' John: A traditional African American food typically made with ham hocks and black-eyed peas.

hops: A dioecious, herbaceous plant. The female cone or flower cluster of hops (*Humuluslupulus*) is are used as a bitter flavoring and as a stability agent in beer.

intoxicating beverage: The Volstead Act defined intoxicating as any beverage containing more than 0.5 percent alcohol.

Irish stew: A traditional stew made in Ireland and England and consisting of mutton (usually neck), potatoes, onions, and parsley, although some cooks added turnips or parsnips, carrots, and barley. In Ireland, mutton was the dominant ingredient because of the economic importance of sheep milk and wool.

junk food: Foods high in calories, fat, caffeine, sugar, and/or salt with little nutritional value.

lager beer: Lager beer is made with *Saccharomyces pastorianus,* a yeast that settles to the bottom of the vats in brewing. The initial fermentation required 10–12 days, and then secondary fermentation took another few weeks, during which the beer had to be kept in a cool place. The resulting beer, known as lager, could be kept for a longer time without spoiling. Today, lager is America's dominant beer.

lard: Rendered and clarified pork fat.

leavening: Various substances, such as yeast, pearlash, saleratus, and baking soda, that are added to dough to make it rise.

liquor: A beverage that contains distilled ethanol.

mariculture: The cultivation, under controlled conditions, of aquatic organisms, including fish, crustaceans, mollusks, and plants in saltwater.

mashing: The process in brewing and distilling whereby a combination of milled grain and water is heated. This process allows enzymes to convert the starch in the grains into sugars, such as maltose. The liquid from the mashing process creates the wort.

Mason jar: A glass bottle with a screw cap used for preserving fruit. The Mason jar was invented by John Mason in 1858.

microbrewing: The process of making craft beer by small and independent brewers.

molasses: Historically, a by-product in the manufacturing of sugar. Traditionally, the juice from sugarcane was extracted and then boiled, which produced crystallization of the sugar. The liquid removed was molasses. In colonial times, molasses made in the Caribbean was barreled and sold or traded to British North American colonists, who used it as a sweetener or to make rum.

moonshine: The illegal distillation of whiskey. Moonshine is made in an unlicensed still and is usually not aged and often contains impurities.

multinational corporation: A corporation that operates in more than one country.

mush: Corn meal boiled in water and frequently eaten with milk or syrup.

organic foods: Foods produced in accordance with the National Organic Program. Restrictions for organic foods include that they cannot be grown or raised with synthetic fertilizers, pesticides, and hormones.

pasteurization: The process of heating a liquid to a specific temperature for a particular period of time to reduce the number of pathogens that might cause disease.

phylloxera: An aphid-like parasite that lives on the roots and sometimes the leaves of grape vines. The native American grape vines east of the Rockies are generally immune to the disease caused by the parasite.

posset: A spiced drink of hot milk curdled with an alcoholic beverage or other ingredients.

prohibition: A ban on the sale, manufacture, and/or transportation of alcohol at the local, state, and/or national levels. Prohibition existed in the United States from 1920 to 1933.

proteins: Molecules that consist of one or more amino acids. Twenty-two amino acids have been identified are necessary for health. Proteins are essential to building, maintaining, and repairing body tissue, such as skin, internal organs, bones, and muscle. Proteins often function as enzymes, hormones, and antibodies and are commonly found in many foods, such as eggs, cheese, meat, poultry, and fish.

pudding: Historically, a food boiled in an intestine, stomach, or pudding bag made of cloth. Pudding can be either sweet or savory.

Saratoga potatoes: Thin-sliced pieces of potatoes, the forerunner of potato chips.

scrapple: A traditional Pennsylvanian specialty consisting of pork scraps, corn meal, buckwheat flour, and herbs and spices.

sparkling wine: Any wine, such as champagne, that contains a high level of carbonation.

spirits: Alcoholic beverages, such as rum, whiskey, brandy, etc., made by distillation. Spirits tend to be higher in alcoholic content than beer and wine.

still: An apparatus used to make distilled alcoholic beverages, such as rum, whiskey, brandy, etc.

succotash: A traditional dish made from corn and lima beans. Succotash purportedly derives from American Indian cookery.

syllabub: A beverage made with curdled milk (or cream), wine, cider, or other ingredients.

tavern: Taverns, also called public houses and ordinaries, were places were alcohol and usually food were served.

teetotaler: A person who does not consume any alcoholic beverage.

trademark: A distinctive word, phrase, symbol, or design (or a combination or words, symbols, and designs) that distinguishes an individual, business, or other legal entity from others. Trademarks are usually employed to promote services or products. In the United States, trademarks have been registered since 1870. Today, trademarks are administered by the U.S. Trademark and Patent Office.

trencher: A wooden dish or platter on which food was served.

trust: Historically, a legal entity that tried to consolidate power and create monopolies that could control prices and generate profits.

wort: The liquid produced by the mashing process. Brewers and distillers add yeast to the wort to ferment the sugar and produce alcohol.

• Appendices •

A. Food History Organizations and Associations

Academic associations and organizations, such as the Association for the Study of Food in Society and the Association of the Study of Food and Society, have emerged, and many culinary history groups, such as the Culinary Historians of Washington (CHoW), the Culinary Historians of Boston (CHoB), and the Culinary Historians of New York (CHNY), have formed in many cities across America. Many culinary associations and groups are listed below.

Academic Associations

Agricultural History Society

The Agricultural History Society was founded in Washington, D.C., in 1919 "to promote the interest, study and research in the history of agriculture." Incorporated in 1924, the society began publishing a journal, *Agricultural History,* in 1927. From the site: "The term 'agricultural history' has always been interpreted broadly, and the Society encourages research and publishes articles from all countries and in all periods of history. Initially affiliated with the American Historical Association, the Agricultural History Society is the third oldest, discipline-based professional organization in the United States. Currently the membership includes agricultural economists, anthropologists, economists, environmentalists, historians, historical geographers, rural sociologists, and a variety of independent scholars."

Website: http://www.aghistorysociety.org/

Agriculture, Food & Human Values (AFHVS)

From the site: "Founded in 1987, AFHVS promotes interdisciplinary research and scholarship in the broad areas of agriculture and rural studies. Growing out of W. K. Kellogg Foundation–supported projects to promote interaction between liberal arts and agricultural disciplines, AFHVS provides a continuing link among scholars working in cross-disciplinary studies of food and agriculture. From a base of philosophers, sociologists and anthropologists, AFHVS has grown to include scientists, scholars and practitioners in areas ranging from agricultural production and social science to nutrition policy and the humanities. AFHVS provides a forum for

examining the values that underlie various visions of food and agricultural systems, and it offers members the opportunity to meet and discuss programs and research ideas of common interest. AFHVS encourages participation by the growing community of researchers and professionals exploring alternative visions of the food system, including regional food policies, community supported agriculture, and issues of local and global food security. AFHVS does not advocate or endorse specific policies or political platforms, and it welcomes participation from persons with views across the entire political spectrum."
Website: http://www.afhvs.org/

Association of the Study of Food and Society (ASFS)
From the site: "The ASFS was founded in 1985, with the goals of promoting the interdisciplinary study of food and society. It has continued that mission by holding annual meetings; the first was in 1987. Working with BERG Publishers, the organization produces the quarterly journal, *Food Culture & Society.*"
Website: http://www.food-culture.org/

International Association of Culinary Professionals
From the site: "The International Association of Culinary Professionals (IACP) is a worldwide forum for the development and exchange of information, knowledge, and inspiration within the professional food and beverage community. First coming together in 1978 as a small but determined group of cooking school owners and instructors, IACP—then known as the Association of Cooking Schools (ACS)—. . . laid a foundation for food culture not only in America, but well beyond. Now with nearly 3,000 members from more than 32 countries, IACP is engaged in and committed to excellence in all aspects of the culinary industry at every level, local, national, and global."
Website: www.IACP.com

Culinary History Organizations

Culinary Historians of Ann Arbor
Website: www.culinaryhistoriansannarbor.org

Culinary Historians of Boston
Email: historian@culinaryhistoriansboston.com
Website: www.culinaryhistoriansboston.com

Culinary Historians of Chicago
Website: www.culinaryhistorians.org

Culinary Historians of New York
Website: www.culinaryhistoriansny.org/

Culinary Historians of Northern California
Website: www.groups.yahoo.com/group/CHoNC

Culinary Historians of Southern California
Website: http://chscsite.org/

Culinary Historians of Washington DC
Website: www.chowdc.org

Culinary History Enthusiasts of Wisconsin (CHEW)
Website: http://www.chewwisconsin.com/

Foodways of Austin
Website: http://www.main.org/foodways/

Genesee Valley Food History Guild
Website: http://www.geocities.ws/denrie13/history.html

Historic Foodways Society of the Delaware Valley
Website: http://historicfoodways.org/

New Orleans Culinary History Group
Website: www.tulane.edu/~wclib/culinary.html

B. Important Culinary History Listservs and Websites

Many groups studying America's culinary history have developed websites and listservs. Some prominent examples are listed below.

Civil War Interactive Cookbook
Articles and recipes from the 19th century.
Website: www.civilwarinteractive.com/cookbook.htm

19th Century Foodways (Yahoo Group)
From the site: The purpose is "to explore the diverse foodways of the 19th century for living historians, historic house museum programs and anyone interested in foodways of this time period. Come on in, sit down and let's talk food. . . . This is a place to learn and share information about 19th century foods, cooking and dining."
Website: http://groups.yahoo.com/group/19thcenturyfoodways/?yguid=177241131

Feeding America: The Historic American Cookbook Project
From the site: "The Feeding America project has created an online collection of some of the most important and influential American cookbooks from the late 18th to early 20th century. The digital archive includes page images of 76 cookbooks from the MSU Library's collection as well as searchable full-text transcriptions. This site also features a glossary of cookery terms and multidimensional images of antique cooking implements from the collections of the MSU Museum." This collection "hopes to highlight an important part of America's cultural heritage for teachers, students, researchers investigating American social history, professional chefs, and lifelong learners of all ages."
Website: http://digital.lib.msu.edu/projects/cookbooks/

The Food Timeline
From the site: "The Food Timeline was created by Lynne Olver, reference librarian with a passion for food history. Information is checked against standard reference tools for accuracy. All sources are cited for research purposes. As with most historical

topics, there are some conflicting stories in the field of food history. We do our best to select and present the information with the most documented support."

"Since we launched in March 1999, The Food Timeline's scope has grown from a single page with a sprinkling of links to 50+ web pages offering a wealth of historic information, primary documents, and original research. As of November 24, 2011 we served 26.5 million readers and answered 23 thousand questions. . . . The Food Timeline is recognized by the American Library Association (ALA) as a Great Website for Kids and was reviewed in ALA's academic publication *Choice*, July 2009."
Website: www.foodtimeline.org

SavoryFare2 (Yahoo Group)
From the site: "This list focuses on the historic foodways of the 18th Century, specifically the period during the American War for Independence (the Revolutionary War). Discussions on this list will include receipts (recipes) and appropriate documentation, ingredients (both finding original and possible modern substitutes), measurements, cooking methods, foodways background and relevant material culture of colonial America, including immigrants of the period and their contribution. Anyone who has an interest in the foodways of the mid to late 18th century is welcome to subscribe! . . . This list is an adjunct to the RevList, an active community of living historians, but anyone with an interest in the food and related history of this time period is both wanted and welcome!"
Website: http://groups.yahoo.com/group/SavoryFare2/

C. Food Newsletters, Periodicals, Journals, and Magazines

Newsletters, journals and magazines now include information and articles about food history. These include *Gastronomica: The Journal of Food and Culture,* published by the University of California Press, and *Food and Society,* published by the Association for the Study of Food and Society. Other good examples are listed below.

The Art of Eating
The Art of Eating, which first appeared as a food letter in 1986, is published four times a year. There is no advertising. Along with in-depth articles are recipes, letters, a wine review ("Why This Bottle, Really?"), restaurant reviews, book reviews, and addresses for exceptional open-air markets, individual growers and craftsmen, bakers, cheese makers, wineries, olive oil mills, charcutiers, chocolatiers, and restaurants (from haute cuisine to very simple).
Website: www.artofeating.com/

Flavor & Fortune
Flavor & Fortune is a quarterly publication of the Institute of the Science and Art of Chinese Cuisine. The journal specializes in information about Chinese cuisine and includes informative articles along with book, food, and restaurant reviews.
Website: www.flavorandfortune.com/index.html

Food and Foodways: Explorations in the History and Culture of Human Nourishment
Food and Foodways is a refereed, interdisciplinary, and international journal devoted to publishing original scholarly articles on the history and culture of human nourishment. The journal publishes works by academics and and others who use food as a lens of analysis.
Website: http://www.tandfonline.com/action/pricing?journalCode=gfof20&

Gastronomica: The Journal of Food and Culture
From the site: Since 2001, *Gastronomica* has been "renewing the connection between sensual and intellectual nourishment by offering readers a taste of passionate inquiry through scholarship, humor, fiction, poetry, and exciting visual imagery. With its diverse voices and eclectic mix of articles, *Gastronomica* uses food as an important source of knowledge about different cultures and societies, provoking discussion and encouraging thoughtful reflection on the history, literature, representation, and cultural impact of food." *Gastronomica* is published by the University of California Press.
Website: www.gastronomica.org/

D. LIBRARIES WITH LARGE CULINARY OR AGRICULTURE-RELATED COLLECTIONS

Libraries around the country have begun to develop major culinary collections. The following are examples of selected libraries with extensive culinary collections.

Albert R. Mann Library
Cornell University
Website: www.mannlib.cornell.edu/
This library has excellent agricultural and home economics collections.

American Antiquarian Society
185 Salisbury St.
Worcester, Massachusetts 01609
(508) 755-5221
Website: http://www.americanantiquarian.org/
This library has an excellent collection of cookbooks published mainly before 1876.

City College of San Francisco
Alice Statler Library
Room 10, Statler Wing
50 Phelan Ave.
San Francisco, CA 94112
(415) 239-3460
Fax: (415) 239-3026
Email: aniosi@ccsf.edu
Website: http://www.ccsf.edu/NEW/en/library/research-help/subject-guides/culinary_arts.html

The Alice Statler Library is a small specialized library that serves the Culinary Arts and Hospitality Studies Department. The website offers subject guides on culinary topics as well as links to hundreds of culinary- and food-related websites.

Culinary Archives and Museum
Johnson & Wales University
315 Harborside Boulevard
Providence, Rhode Island 02905
(401) 598-2805
Website: www.culinary.org/
This library includes more than 250,000 cookbooks, periodicals, manuscripts, and menus. It is the largest collection of culinary works and manuscripts in the United States.

Culinary Institute of America
Conrad Hilton Library
1946 Campus Drive
Hyde Park NY 12538-1499
(845) 452-9600
Website: http://library.culinary.edu/
This library has 86,000 works, many focused on culinary topics. It also has a large culinary menu collection from 1883 to the present.

Esther B. Aresty Collection of Rare Books on the Culinary Arts
Van Pelt-Dietrich Library
University of Pennsylvania
3420 Walnut Street
Philadelphia, PA 19104-6206
(215) 898-7088
Website: http://www.library.upenn.edu/exhibits/rbm/aresty/aresty1.html
This collection includes 576 cookbooks and 13 manuscripts that span the last five centuries. Other culinary collections at the library include the Laurie Burrows Grad Cookbook Collection, with more than 6,000 cookery titles primarily from the late 20th century, and the Chef Fritz Blank Culinary Archive and Library, with thousands of cookbooks and cookery-related books in the collection that span the 17th to 21st centuries.

Fales Library and Special Collections
Fales Food and Cookery Collection
Bobst Library, New York University
70 Washington Square South
New York, NY 10012
(212) 998-2596
Email: fales.library@nyu.edu
Website: http://www.nyu.edu/library/bobst/research/fales/foodcookery.html
The Fales Food and Cookery Collection has more than 55,000 cookbooks and culinary works.

Indiana University
Lilly Library Collections
Food and Drink Collection

200 E. Seventh St.
Bloomington, IN 47405-5500
(812) 855-2452
Email: liblilly@indiana.edu
Website: http://www.indiana.edu/~liblilly/collections/overview/food.shtml
The Food and Drink Collection of the Lilly Library includes a wide range of American and European cookbooks and culinary works. Many of the works are annotated in William R. Cagle, *American Books on Food and Drink: A Bibliographical Catalog of the Gernon Collection Housed in the Lilly Library* (1998), and William R. Cagle, *A Matter of Taste: A Bibliographical Catalogue of International Books on Food and Drink in the Lilly Library* (1999).

Kansas State University Library
Cookery Collection in the Richard & Marjorie Morse
Department of Special Collections
506 Hale Library
Manhattan, KS, 66506-1200
(785) 532-7455
Email: rarebooks@ksu.edu
Website: www.lib.ksu.edu/depts/spec/rarebooks/collections/cookery.html
A large collection of cookbooks, many of which are noted in G. A. Rudolph, comp., *Receipt Book and Household Manual* (1968).

Library of Congress
Washington, DC
Website: http://www.loc.gov/rr/rarebook/coll/028.html
The Rare Book and Special Collections Reading Room of the Library of Congress includes several culinary collections, including the Katherine Golden Bitting Collection of more than 4,300 publications, including manuscripts on gastronomy from the 15th through 20th centuries. Many are listed in Katherine Bitting, *Gastronomic Bibliography* (1939). The Library of Congress's general collection includes a wide selection of culinary works, periodicals, and photographs. Some are digitized and are available online.

Longone Center for American Culinary Research
William L. Clements Library
University of Michigan
909 University Ave.
Ann Arbor, MI 48109-1190
(734) 764–2347
Email: clementslibrary@umich.edu
Website: http://www.clements.umich.edu/longone-archive.php
The Longone Culinary Archive includes cookbooks as well as a wide diversity of materials from the 16th to early 20th centuries—books, ephemera, menus, magazines, graphics, maps, manuscripts, diaries, letters, catalogues, advertisements, and reference works.

Los Angeles Public Library
Rare Books Department

630 W. Fifth Street
Los Angeles, CA 90071
(213) 228-7350
Email: rarebook@lapl.org
Website: http://www.lapl.org/collections-resources/lapl-indexes/cookery-ephemera-index
The Rare Books Division includes a large number of cookbooks and more than 2,500 promotional booklets on food and cooking from commercial and noncommercial sources dating from the late 19th century.

Napa Valley Wine Library
PO Box 328
St. Helena, CA 94574
(707) 963-5244 or (707) 963-5145
Email: info@napawinelibrary.org
Website: www.napawinelibrary.org
The collection includes wine books from the 19th century to the present, particularly from the 1950s to the present, and also includes transcripts of oral interviews of local individuals involved in the wine business.

New York Academy of Medicine
1216 Fifth Ave, and 103rd St
New York, NY 10029
(212) 822-7200
The New York Academy of Medicine has an unusual array of early cookbooks and culinary manuscripts, including a copy of the ninth-century cookery manuscript attributed to Marcus Apicius. The general collection includes many early works on cookery and medicine.

New York Public Library
42nd Street and Fifth Avenue
New York, NY 10029
Website: www.nyam.org/library/about/
For menus, go to http://menus.nypl.org
The New York Public Library includes a wide range of cookbooks and culinary periodicals and an excellent menu collection, many of which can be examined online.

New York State Historical Association
Research Library
Website: www.library.nysha.org
The collection includes a large number of cookbooks and manuscripts, mainly from New York.

Schlesinger Library
Radcliffe Institute
10 Garden Street
Cambridge, Massachusetts 02138
Website: http://www.radcliffe.harvard.edu/schlesinger-library/collections
The collection includes a wide range of cookbooks as well as archival materials and personal papers of many culinary luminaries, such as Julia Child.

The Shields Library Special Collections
University of California at Davis
100 North West Quad
Davis, CA 95616-5292
(530) 752-1621
Website: http://www.lib.ucdavis.edu/dept/specol/about/visitors.php
Shields Library has an excellent collection of works on wine. Its Special Collections includes many works on temperance, prohibition, and beverages.

Sonoma County Wine Library
Healdsburg Regional Library
Piper and Center Streets
Healdsburg CA 95448
(707) 433-3773
Website: www.sonoma.lib.ca.us/wine
The collection includes 5,000 books dealing with wine making, grape growing, wine marketing, and the history of wine, with a special emphasis on Sonoma County.

Texas Women's University Library
Cookbook Collection
P.O. Box 425528, 1200 Frame
Denton, TX 76201
(940) 898-3701
Fax: (940) 898-3764
Email: lib_admin@twu.edu
Website: http://www.twu.edu/library/cookbook-collection.asp
The collection includes cookbooks, menus, vendors' pamphlets, and recipe books dating from 1624.

University of California at San Diego
American Institute of Wine and Food's Culinary Collection and Mandeville Special Collections Library
UCSD Libraries, 0175S
9500 Gilman Drive
La Jolla, CA 92093-0175
(858) 534-2533
Email: spcoll@ucsd.edu
Website: http://libraries.ucsd.edu/locations/mscl/collections/american-institute-of-wine-and-food-culinary-collection.html
The American Institute of Wine and Food's Culinary Collection and Mandeville Special Collections Library includes a wide range of culinary works dating from the 16th century and specializes in Latin American and Californian cookbooks and other culinary works.

University of Houston
Hospitality Industry Archives
229 C. N. Hilton Hotel and College
Houston TX 77204-3028
(713) 743-2470

Email: cbaird@uh.edu
Website: http://www.hrm.uh.edu/RESOURCES/Library-and-Archives-/Hospitality-Industry-Archives/
The Hospitality Industry Archives includes more than 3,000 linear feet of archives focused on hospitality leaders' and leading brands' corporate and personal papers, historical documents, and memorabilia.

University of Iowa Library
Szathmary Culinary Archives
Department of Special Collections
Iowa City IA 52242-1420
(319) 335-5921
Email: lib-spec@uiowa.edu
Website: http://www.lib.uiowa.edu/spec-coll/
The Szathmary Culinary Archives contains more than 20,000 items, including more than 100 manuscript recipe books.

University of Washington
Special Collections
University Archives, Pacific Northwest Collection
Allen Library
Box 352900
Seattle, WA 98195-2900
(206) 543-19292
Fax: (206) 543-1931
Email: speccoll@u.washington.edu
Website: www.lib.washington.edu/Specialcoll
The cookery portion of the collection specializes in the Pacific Northwest.

Vorhoff Library
Culinary Collection
Newcomb College Center for Research on Women
Tulane University
New Orleans, LA 70118
(504) 865-5762
Website: http://tulane.edu/newcomb/vorhoff-collections.cfm
The Culinary Collection includes more than 2,000 works related to the culinary life of New Orleans, Louisiana, and the South in general.

E. Food-Related Museums

Yet another dimension of culinary history has been living museums and historical sites, such as Plimouth Plantation in Massachusetts and Colonial Williamsburg in Virginia, that now include significant historical cooking programs. Most states and communities have such museums.

Virtual Museums

New York Food Museum
Website: www.nyfoodmuseum.org/

The Potato Museum
Website: www.potatomuseum.com/

Museums and Historical Sites with an Interest in Historical Cookery
Major museums include the following.

Colonial Williamsburg

From the site: "The Colonial Williamsburg Foundation operates the world's largest living history museum in Williamsburg, Virginia—the restored 18th-century capital of Britain's largest, wealthiest, and most populous outpost of empire in the New World. Here we interpret the origins of the idea of America, conceived decades before the American Revolution. The Colonial Williamsburg story of a revolutionary city tells how diverse peoples, having different and sometimes conflicting ambitions, evolved into a society that valued liberty and equality. . . . In Colonial Williamsburg's 301-acre Historic Area stand hundreds of restored, reconstructed, and historically furnished buildings. Costumed interpreters tell the stories of the men and women of the 18th-century city—black, white, and native American, slave, indentured, and free—and the challenges they faced."
Website: www.colonialwilliamsburg.com

Plimoth Plantation

From the site: "With help and support from friends, family and business associates, Henry Hornblower II started the Museum in 1947 as two English cottages and a fort on Plymouth's historic waterfront. Since then the Museum has grown to include Mayflower II (1957), the English Village (1959), the Wampanoag Homesite (1973), the Hornblower Visitor Center (1987), the Craft Center (1992) and the Maxwell and Nye Barns (1994). Today, Plimoth Plantation provides an engaging and experiential outdoor and indoor learning environment on its main campus and at the State Pier on Plymouth's waterfront. Our permanent exhibits tell the complex and interwoven stories of two distinct cultures—English and Native. The main exhibits are enhanced with an exciting menu of special events, public programs and workshops that offer a rich and diverse exploration of the 17th-century."
Website: www.plimoth.org

For a complete list of museums that offer food and drink history in the United States, check the Association for Living History, Farm and Agricultural Museums (ALHFAM).
From the site: This association "serves those involved in living historical farms, agricultural museums and outdoor museums of history and folklife. Since its founding in 1970, ALHFAM has been at the forefront of the growth and professionalization of the use of living history techniques in museum programs. ALHFAM members and member institutions can be found across the United States and Canada and in many other countries."
Website: www.alhfam.org

F. Universities with Food Studies Programs

Many culinary arts schools also offer history classes, and food studies programs have been initiated at several universities, including New York University, Boston University, and Indiana University.

Boston University
Program in Culinary Arts
Website: www.bu.edu/foodandwine/culinary-arts/

Indiana University
Indiana University PhD Track in the Anthropology of Food
Website: http://www.indiana.edu/~anthro/grad/foodStudies/index.shtml

New School
Food Studies Program
Website: www.newschool.edu/continuing-education/food-studies

New York University
Department of Nutrition, Food Studies, and Public Health
Website: www.steinhardt.nyu.edu/nutrition

University of Vermont
Master of Science in Food Systems
Website: www.uvm.edu/foodsystems/mfs/

• Selected Bibliography •

As a result of the interest in the history of American food and drink, the number of books published on food-history topics has mushroomed. Several university presses, such as those at the University of Iowa, the University of North Carolina, the University of South Carolina, the University of Illinois, Columbia University, and the University of California, have developed extensive lists of scholarly works on food, and hardly a week goes by without a commercial press releasing yet another work on some topic related to culinary history. Many of these books are listed below.

Adamson, Melitta Weiss, and Francine Segan, eds. *Entertaining from Ancient Rome to the Super Bowl: An Encyclopedia.* Westport, CT: Greenwood, 2008.

Alamillo, José M. *Making Lemonade Out of Lemons: Mexican American Labor and Leisure in a California Town, 1880–1960.* Urbana: University of Illinois Press, 2006.

Albala, Ken. *Beans: A History.* Oxford, UK, and New York: Berg, 2007.

Albala, Ken. *Pancake: A Global History.* London: Reaktion, 2008.

Alexander, Kelly, and Cynthia Harris. *Hometown Appetites: The Story of Clementine Paddleford, the Forgotten Food Writer Who Chronicled How America Ate.* New York: Gotham Books, 2008.

Allen, Frederick. *Secret Formula: How Brilliant Marketing and Relentless Salesmanship Made Coca-Cola the Best-Known Product in the World.* New York: HarperBusiness, 1994.

Allen, Gary. *Herbs: A Global History.* London: Reaktion, 2012.

Allen, Gary, and Ken Albala, eds. *The Business of Food: Encyclopedia of Food and Drink Industries.* Westport, CT: Greenwood, 2007.

Amerine, Maynard A. *Vermouth: An Annotated Bibliography.* Richmond: Division of Agricultural Sciences, University of California, 1974.

Amerine, Maynard A., and Axel E. Borg. *A Bibliography on Grapes, Wines, Other Alcoholic Beverages, and Temperance: Works Published in the United States before 1901.* Berkeley: University of California Press, 1996.

Amerine, Maynard A., and Herman Phaff, comps. *Bibliography of Publications by the Faculty, Staff, and Students, of the University of California, 1876–1980, on Grapes, Wines, and Related Subjects.* Berkeley: University of California Press, 1986.

Amerine, Maynard A., and Louise B. Wheeler. *A Checklist of Books and Pamphlets on Grapes and Wine and Related Subjects, 1938–1948.* Berkeley: University of California Press, 1951.

Arndt, Alice, ed. *Culinary Biographies: A Dictionary of the World's Great Historic Chefs, Cookbook Authors and Collectors, Farmers, Gourmets, Home Economists, Nutritionists, Restaurateurs, Philosophers, Physicians, Scientists, Writers, and Others Who Influenced the Way We Eat Today.* Houston, TX: Yes Press, 2006.

Aronson, Marc, and Marina Budhos. *Sugar Changed the World: A Story of Magic, Spice, Slavery, Freedom and Science.* Boston: Houghton Mifflin Harcourt, 2010.

Asbury, Herbert. *The Great Illusion: An Informal History of Prohibition.* Garden City, NY: Doubleday, 1950.

Balinska, Maria. *The Bagel: The Surprising History of a Modest Bread.* New Haven, CT: Yale University Press, 2008.

Baron, Stanley. *Brewed in America: A History of Beer and Ale in the United States.* New York: Arno, 1972.

Behr, Edward. *Prohibition: Thirteen Years That Changed America.* New York: Arcade, 1996.

Belasco, Warren. *Meals to Come: A History of the Future of Food.* Berkeley: University of California Press, 2006.

Belasco, Warren J. *Appetite for Change: How the Counterculture Took on the Food Industry, 1966–1988.* New York: Pantheon, 1989.

Benson, Abraham Benson, ed. *Penn Family Recipes: Cooking Recipes of William Penn's Wife Gulielma.* York, PA: Shumway, 1966.

Berzok, Linda Murray. *American Indian Food.* Westport, CT: Greenwood, 2005.

Beyer, Mark. *Temperance and Prohibition: The Movement to Pass Anti-liquor Laws in America.* New York: Rosen, 2006.

Bitting, Katherine. *Gastronomic Bibliography.* San Francisco: Halle-Cordis Composing Room/Trade Freeroom, 1939.

Blanding, Michael. *The Coke Machine: The Dirty Truth behind the World's Favorite Soft Drink.* New York: Avery, 2010.

Blocker, Jack S. *American Temperance Movements: Cycles of Reform.* Boston: Twayne, 1989.

Blot, Pierre. *Hand-Book of Practical Cookery.* 1869; facsimile reprint, New York: Arno, 1973.

Bower, Anne L., ed. *African American Foodways: Explorations of History & Culture.* Urbana: University of Illinois Press, 2007.

Bower, Anne L., ed. *Recipes for Reading: Community Cookbooks, Stories, Histories.* Amherst: University of Massachusetts Press, 1997.

Brenner, Joël Glenn. *The Emperors of Chocolate: Inside the Secret World of Hershey and Mars.* New York: Broadway, 2000.

Brown, Eleanor, and Bob Brown. *Culinary America: Cookbooks Published in the Cities and Towns of the United States of America during the Years from 1860 through 1960.* New York: Roving Eye, 1961.

Brown, John Hull. *Early American Beverages.* Rutland, VT: Tuttle, 1966.

Brownell, Kelly D., and Katherine Battle Horgen. *Food Fight: The Inside Story of the Food Industry, America's Obesity Crisis, and What We Can Do about It.* Chicago: Contemporary Books, 2004.

Bryan, Lettuce. *Kentucky Housewife.* 1839; reprint, Columbia: University of South Carolina Press, 1991.

Bullock, Tom. *173 Pre-Prohibition Cocktails.* Jenks, OK: Howling at the Moon, 2001.

Burns, Eric. *The Spirits of America: A Social History of Alcohol.* Philadelphia: Temple University Press, 2004.

Cagle, William R., and Lisa Killion Stafford. *American Books on Food and Drink.* New Castle, DE: Oak Knoll, 1998.

Campos, Paul. *The Obesity Myth: Why America's Obsession with Weight Is Hazardous to Your Health.* New York: Gotham Books, 2004.

Capital City Cookbook. 3rd ed. Madison, WI: Grace Church Guild, 1906. Published with *Midwestern Home Cookery* (Originally titled *Presbyterian Cookbook* [Dayton, OH: Thomas, 1875]); facsimile reprint, New York: Arno, 1973.

Carlin, Joseph. *Cocktail: A Global History.* London: Reaktion, 2012.

Carson, Barbara G. *Ambitious Appetites: Dining, Behavior, and Patterns of Consumption in Federal Washington.* Washington, DC: American Institute of Architects Press, 1990.

Carson, Gerald. *Cornflake Crusade.* New York: Rinehart, 1957.

Carson, Gerald. *The Social History of Bourbon: An Unhurried Account of Our Star-Spangled American Drink.* New York: Dodd, Mead, 1963.

Chambers, Thomas A. *Drinking the Waters: Creating an American Leisure Class at Nineteenth-Century Mineral Springs.* Washington, DC: Smithsonian Institution Press, 2002.

Chapple, Francis H. *Wellsprings: A Natural History of Bottled Spring Waters.* New Brunswick, NJ: Rutgers University Press, 2005.

Chazanof, William. *Welch's Grape Juice: From Corporation to Co-operative.* Syracuse, NY: Syracuse University Press, 1977.

Cinotto, Simone. *Soft Soil, Black Grapes: The Birth of Italian Winemaking in California.* Translated by Michelle Tarnopolski. New York: New York University Press, 2012.

Civitello, Linda. *Cuisine and Culture: A History of Food and People.* 2nd ed. Hoboken, NJ: Wiley, 2011.

Clarke, Tony. *Inside the Bottle: An Expose of the Bottled Water Industry.* 2nd. ed. Ottawa: Canadian Centre for Policy Alternatives, 2007.

Cochran, Thomas C. *The Pabst Brewing Company: The History of an American Business.* New York: New York University Press, 1948.

Coe, Andrew. *Chop Suey: A Cultural History of Chinese Food in the United States.* New York: Oxford University Press, 2009.

Cohen, Rich. *Sweet and Low: A Family Story.* New York: Farrar, Straus and Giroux, 2006.

Collins, Kathleen. *Watching What We Eat: The Evolution of Television Cooking Shows.* New York: Continuum, 2009.

Conaway, James. *Napa: The Story of an American Eden.* Boston: Houghton Mifflin, 1990.

Conlin, Joseph R. *Bacon, Beans, and Galantines: Food and Foodways on the Western Mining Frontier.* Reno: University of Nevada Press, 1986.

Conrad, Barnaby, III. *The Martini: An Illustrated History of an American Classic.* San Francisco: Chronicle Books, 1995.

Conroy, David. *In Public Houses: Drink and the Revolution of Authority in Colonial Massachusetts.* Chapel Hill: University of North Carolina Press, 1995.

Cook, Margaret. *America's Charitable Cooks: A Bibliography of Fund-Raising Cook Books Published in the United States, 1861–1915.* Kent, OH: n.p., 1971.

Corbett, Theodore. *The Making of American Resorts: Saratoga Springs, Ballston Spa, and Lake George.* New Brunswick, NJ: Rutgers University Press, 2001.

Coulombe, Charles. *Rum: The Epic Story of the Drink That Conquered the World.* New York: Citadel Press, 2004.

Covey, Herbert C., and Dwight Eisnach. *What the Slaves Ate: Recollections of African American Foods and Foodways from the Slave Narratives.* Santa Barbara, CA: Greenwood/ABC-CLIO, 2009.

Cummings, Richard O. *The American and His Food: A History of Food Habits in the United States.* Chicago: University of Chicago Press, 1940.

Cummings, Richard O. *The American Ice Harvests: A Historical Study in Technology, 1800–1918.* Berkeley: University of California Press, 1949.

Curtis, Wayne. *And a Bottle of Rum: A History of the New World in Ten Cocktails.* New York: Crown, 2006.

Cushing, C. H., and B. Gray, comps. *The Kansas Home Cook-Book.* 5th ed., with introduction and suggested recipes by Louis Szathmáry. 1886; reprint, New York: Arno, 1973.

Czarra, Fred. *Spices: A Global History.* London: Reaktion, 2009.

Dabney, Joseph Earl. *Smokehouse Ham, Spoon Bread & Scuppernong Wine: The Folklore and Art of Southern Appalachian Cooking.* Naperville, IL: Cumberland House, 2010.

Dallas Free Kindergarten and Training School. *Lone Star Cook Book.* 1901; reprint, with an Introduction by Andrew F. Smith, Bedford, MA: Applewood Books, 2005.

Davidis, Henriette. *Pickled Herring and Pumpkin Pie: A Nineteenth-Century Cookbook for German Immigrants to America.* Edited by Louis A. Pitschmann. Madison: University of Wisconsin, 2002.

DeGroff, Dale. *The Craft of the Cocktail.* New York: Clarkson Potter, 2002.

Deutsch, Jonathan, and Rachel D. Saks. *Jewish American Food Culture.* Westport, CT: Greenwood, 2008.

DeWitt, Dave. *The Founding Foodies: How Washington, Jefferson, and Franklin Revolutionized American Cuisine.* Naperville, IL: Sourcebooks, 2010.

Diamond, Becky. *Mrs. Goodfellow: The Story of America's First Cooking School.* Yardley, PA: Westholme, 2012.

Dillon, John J. *Seven Decades of Milk: A History of New York's Dairy Industry.* New York: Orange Judd, 1941.

Diner, Hasia R. *Hungering for America: Italian, Irish, & Jewish Foodways in the Age of Migration.* Cambridge, MA: Harvard University Press, 2001.

Eden, Trudy. *Cooking in America, 1590–1840.* Westport, CT: Greenwood, 2006.

Edge, John T. *Apple Pie: An American Story.* New York: Putnam, 2004.

Edge, John T. *Donuts: An American Passion.* New York: Putnam, 2006.

Edge, John T. *Fried Chicken: An American Story.* New York: Putnam, 2004.

Edge, John T. *Hamburgers and Fries: An American Story.* New York: Putnam, 2005.

Elias, Megan J. *Food in the United States, 1890–1945.* Santa Barbara, CA: Greenwood/ABC-CLIO, 2009.

Epstein, Becky Sue. *Champagne: A Global History.* London: Reaktion, 2011.

Estes, Rufus. *Good Things to Eat as Suggested by Rufus.* Edited by D. J. Frienz. 1911; reprint, Jenks, OK: Howling at the Moon, 1999.

Ettlinger, Steve. *Twinkies, Deconstructed.* New York: Hudson Street, 2007.

Eustis, Celestine. *Cooking in Old Creole Days.* 1904; reprint, New York: Arno, 1973.

Farmer, Fannie Merritt. *Boston Cooking-School Cook Book.* 1896; facsimile reprint, New York: Weathervane, 1986.

Firth, Grace. *Secrets of the Still: A Zesty History of How-To for Making Spirits, Fragrances, Curables, Gasohol and Other Products of the Stillroom.* McClean, VA: EPM, 1983.

Fisher, Mrs. Abby. *What Mrs. Fisher Knows about Old Southern Cooking.* With historical notes by Karen Hess. 1881; reprint, Bedford, MA: Applewood, 1995.

Foss, Richard. *Rum: A Global History.* London: Reaktion, 2012.

Franklin, Linda Campbell. *300 Years of Kitchen Collectibles.* 5th ed. Iola, WI: Krause, 2002.

Freedman, Paul, ed. *Food: The History of Taste.* Berkeley: University of California Press, 2007.

Freidberg, Susanne. *Fresh: A Perishable History.* Cambridge, MA: Belknap Press of Harvard University Press, 2009.

Fuller, Robert C. *Religion and Wine: A Cultural History of Wine Drinking in the United States.* Knoxville: University of Tennessee Press, 1996.

Funderburg, Anne Cooper. *Sundae Best: A History of Soda Fountains.* Bowling Green, KY: Bowling Green State University Popular Press, 2002.

Furnas, J. C. *The Life and Times of the Late Demon Rum.* London: W. H. Allen, 1965.

Fussell, Betty. *Raising Steaks.* Orlando: Harcourt, 2008.

Fussell, Betty. *The Story of Corn: The Myths and History, the Culture and Agriculture, the Art and Science of America's Quintessential Crop.* New York: Knopf, 1992.

Gabaccia, Donna R. *We Are What We Eat: Ethnic Food and the Making of Americans.* Cambridge, MA: Harvard University Press, 1998.

Gabler, James M. *Passions: The Wines and Travels of Thomas Jefferson.* Baltimore: Bacchus, 1995.

Gabler, James M. *Wine into Words: A History and Bibliography of Wine Books in the English Language.* Baltimore: Bacchus, 1985.

Gdula, Steven. *The Warmest Room in the House: How the Kitchen Became the Heart of the Twentieth-Century American Home.* New York: Bloomsbury, 2008.

Geraci, Victor W., and Elizabeth S. Demers, eds. *Icons of American Cooking.* Santa Barbara, CA: Greenwood, 2011.

Gitlin, Marty, and Topher Ellis. *The Great American Cereal Book: How Breakfast Got Its Crunch.* New York: Abrams, 2011.

Gleick, Peter H. *Bottled and Sold: The Story behind Our Obsession with Bottled Water.* Washington, DC: Island Press, 2010.

Graham, Sylvester. *Treatise on Bread and Bread-Making.* 1837; reprint, Milwaukee: Lee Foundation for Nutritional Research, n.d.

Grimes, William. *Straight Up or on the Rocks: The Story of the American Cocktail.* New York: North Point, 2001.

Grivetti, Louis E. *Chocolate: History, Culture, and Heritage.* Hoboken, NJ: Wiley, 2009.

Gusfield, Joseph R. *Symbolic Crusade: Status Politics and the American Temperance Movement.* 2nd ed. Urbana: University of Illinois Press, 1986.

Gutman, Richard J. S. *American Diner, Then and Now.* Baltimore: Johns Hopkins University Press, 2000.

Haber, Barbara. *From Hardtack to Home Fries: An Uncommon History of American Cooks and Meals.* New York: Free Press, 2002.

Hamilton, Alissa. *Squeezed: What You Don't Know about Orange Juice.* New Haven, CT: Yale University Press, 2009.

Hamilton, Carl. *Absolut: Biography of a Bottle.* New York: Texere, 2000.

Hancock, David. *Oceans of Wine: Madeira and the Emergence of American Trade and Taste.* New Haven, CT: Yale University Press, 2009.

Haraszthy, Arpad. *Wine-Making in California: With an Introduction by Ruth Teiser and Catherine Harroun.* San Francisco: Book Club of California, 1978.

Harwell, Richard Barksdale. *The Mint Julep.* Charlottesville: University Press of Virginia, 1975.

Haworth, Alan, and Ronald Simpson, eds. *Moonshine Markets: Issues in Unrecorded Alcohol Beverage Production and Consumption.* New York: Brunner-Routledge, 2004.

Hays, Constance L. *The Real Thing: Truth and Power at the Coca-Cola Company.* New York: Random House, 2005.

Hearn, Lafcadio. *La Cuisine Creole: A Collection of Culinary Recipes from Leading Chefs and Noted Creole Housewives, Who Have Made New Orleans Famous for Its Cuisine.* 1885; reprint, Baton Rouge, LA: Pelican/Moran, 1967.

Helstosky, Carol. *Pizza: A Global History.* London: Reaktion, 2008.

Hendricks, Edwin. *Liquor and Anti-Liquor in Virginia.* Durham, NC: Duke University Press, 1967.

Hess, John, and Karen Hess. *The Taste of America.* New York: Grossman, 1977.

Hill, Mrs. A. P. *Mrs. Hill's New Cook Book.* New York: Carleton, 1872. Reprinted with *The Confederate Receipt Book.* Birmingham, AL: Oxmoor, 1985.

Hilliard, Sam Bowers. *Hog, Meat and Hoecake: Food Supply in the Old South, 1840–1860.* Carbondale: Southern Illinois University Press, 1972.

Himelstein, Linda. *The King of Vodka: The Story of Pyotr Smirnov and the Upheaval of an Empire.* New York: Harper, 2009.

Holian, Timothy J. *Over the Barrel: The Brewing History and Beer Culture of Cincinnati, 1800 to the Present.* St. Joseph, MO: Sudhaus, 2000.

Holland, Leandra Zim. *Feasting and Fasting with Lewis and Clark: A Food and Social History.* Emigrant, MT: Old Yellowstone, 2003.

Hooker, Richard J. *A History of Food and Drink in America.* Indianapolis: Bobbs-Merrill, 1981.

Hooker, Richard J., ed. *A Colonial Plantation Cookbook: The Receipt Book of Harriott Pinckney Horry, 1770.* Columbia: University of South Carolina Press, 1984.

Hopkins, James T. *Fifty Years of Citrus: The Florida Citrus Exchange.* Gainesville: University of Florida Press, 1960.

Horowitz, Roger. *Putting Meat on the American Table: Taste, Technology, Transformation.* Baltimore: Johns Hopkins University Press, 2006.

Horsman, Reginald. *Feast or Famine: Food and Dink in American Westward Expansion.* Columbia: University of Missouri Press, 2008.

Inness, Sherrie A., ed. *Kitchen Culture in America: Popular Representations of Food, Gender and Race.* Philadelphia: University of Pennsylvania Press, 2001.

Jacobson, Michael F. *Liquid Candy: How Soft Drinks are Harming Americans' Health.* Washington, DC: Center for Science in the Public Interest, 2005, at: http://www.cspinet.org/new/pdf/liquid_candy_final_w_new_supplement.pdf

Janer, Zilkia. *Latino Food Culture.* Westport, CT: Greenwood, 2008.

Janik, Erica. *Apple: A Global History.* London: Reaktion, 2011.

Jenkins, Virginia Scott. *Bananas: An American History.* Washington, DC: Smithsonian Institution Press, 2000.

Jones, Judith. *The Tenth Muse: My Life in Food.* New York: Knopf, 2007.

Josselyn, John. *New-England Rarities Discovered.* 1672; reprint, Boston: Massachusetts Historical Society, 1972.

Kahn, E. J., Jr. *The Big Drink: The Story of Coca-Cola.* New York: Random House, 1960.

Kamp, David. *The United States of Arugula: How We Became a Gourmet Nation.* New York: Broadway Books, 2006.

Kander, Mrs. Simon, and Mrs. Henry Schoenfeld, comps. *The "Settlement Cookbook": The Way to a Man's Heart.* 1903; facsimile reprint, New York: Grammercy, 1987.

Katz, Solomon, ed. *Encyclopedia of Food and Culture.* 3 vols. New York: Scribner, 2003.

Kerr, K. Austin. *Organized for Prohibition: A New History of the Anti-Saloon League.* New Haven, CT: Yale University Press, 1985.

Kessler, David A. *The End of Overeating: Taking Control of the Insatiable American Appetite.* Emmaus, PA: Rodale, 2009.

Kinsley, H[erbert] M. *One Hundred Recipes for the Chafing Dish.* 1894; facsimile reprint, New York: Arno, 1973.

Kiple, Kenneth F., and Kriemhild Conèe Ornelas, eds. *The Cambridge World History of Food.* 2 vols. New York: Cambridge University Press, 2000.

Kirtland, Elizabeth Stansbury. *Six Little Cooks.* 1879; facsimile reprint, New York: Arno, 1973.

Kobler, John. *Ardent Spirits: The Rise and Fall of Prohibition.* Boston: Da Capo, 1993.

Kosar, Kevin. *Whiskey: A Global History.* London: Reaktion, 2010.

Kraig, Bruce. *Hot Dog: A Global History.* London: Reaktion, 2009.

Kraig, Bruce, and Patty Carroll. *Man Bites Dog: Hot Dog Culture in America.* Lanham, MD: AltaMira, 2012.

Krebs, Roland. *Making Friends Is Our Business: 100 Years of Anheuser-Busch.* St. Louis, MO: n.p., 1953.

Krondl, Michael. *Sweet Invention: A History of Dessert.* Chicago: Chicago Review Press, 2011.

Kuh, Patric. *The Last Days of Haute Cuisine: America's Culinary Revolution.* New York: Viking, 2001.

Kurlansky, Mark. *The Big Oyster: History on the Half Shell.* New York: Random House, 2006.

Kurlansky, Mark, ed. *The Food of a Younger Land: A Portrait of American Food—Before the National Highway System, Before Chain Restaurants, and Before Frozen Food, When the Nation's Food Was Seasonal, Regional, and Traditional—From the Lost WPA Files.* New York: Riverhead Books, 2009.

Ladies' Auxiliary, Y.M.C.A. *El Paso Cookbook.* Introduction by Andrew F. Smith. 1898; reprint, Bedford, MA: Applewood Books, 2005.

Lappé, Frances Moore. *Diet for a Small Planet.* New York: Friends of the Earth/Ballantine, 1972.

Lappé, Frances Moore, and Anna Lappé. *Hope's Edge: The Next Diet for a Small Planet.* New York: Jeremy P. Tarcher/Putnam, 2003.

Lathrop, Elise. *Early American Inns and Taverns.* New York: Tudor, 1937.

Lawson, Annie H., and Jon Deutsch, eds., *Gastropolis: Food & New York City.* New York: Columbia University Press, 2008.

Lea, Elizabeth Ellicott. *A Quaker Woman's Cookbook: The Domestic Cookery of Elizabeth Ellicott Lea.* Edited with an introduction by William Woys Weaver. Philadelphia: University of Pennsylvania, 1982.

Lee, N. K. M. *The Cook's Own Book.* 1832; reprint, New York: Arno, 1972.

Lee, Paula Young, ed. *Meat, Modernity and the Rise of the Slaughterhouse.* Lebanon: University of New Hampshire, 2008.

Lender, Mark Edward, and James Kirby Martin. *Drinking in America: A History.* Revised and expanded ed. New York: Free Press, 1987.

Lerner, Michael A. *Dry Manhattan: Prohibition in New York City.* Cambridge, MA: Harvard University Press, 2007.

Leslie, Eliza. *Directions for Cookery: Being a System of the Art, in Its Various Branches.* 10th ed. 1848; reprint, New York: Arno, 1973.

Leslie, Eliza. *Indian Meal Book.* Reprinted under title *Corn Meal Cookery: A Collection of Heirloom Corn Meal Recipes Dating from 1848.* Hamilton, OH: Burns, 1998.

Levenstein, Harvey A. *Paradox of Plenty: A Social History of Eating in Modern America.* New York: Oxford University Press, 1993.

Levenstein, Harvey A. *Revolution at the Table: The Transformation of the American Diet.* New York: Oxford University Press, 1988.

Levine, Susan. *School Lunch Politics: The Surprising History of America's Favorite Welfare Program.* Princeton, NJ: Princeton University Press, 2008.

Levinson, Marc. *The Great A&P and the Struggle for Small Business in America.* New York: Hill and Wang, 2011.

Levy, Esther. *Mrs. Esther Levy's Jewish Cookery Book.* 1871; reprint, Cambridge, MA: Applewood, 1988.

Lincoln, Mrs. D. A. *Boston Cooking-School Cook Book.* With an introduction by Janice Longone. 1887; reprint, Mineola, NY: Dover, 1996.

Long, Lucy. *Regional American Food Culture.* Santa Barbara, CA: Greenwood, 2009.

Longone, Janice B., and Daniel T. Longone. *American Cookbooks and Wine Books, 1797–1950.* Ann Arbor, MI: Clements Library/Wine and Food Library, 1984.

Louis, J. C., and Harvey Yazijian. *The Cola Wars: The Story of the Global Corporate Battle between the Coca-Cola Company and PepsiCo.* New York: Everest House, 1980.

Lowenstein, Eleanor. *Bibliography of American Cookery Books, 1742–1860.* Worcester, MA: American Antiquarian Society, 1972.

Luchetti, Cathy. *Home on the Range: A Culinary History of the American West.* New York: Villard, 1993.

Mariani, John. *America Eats Out: An Illustrated History of Restaurants, Taverns, Coffee Shops, Speakeasies, and Other Establishments That Have Fed Us for 350 Years.* New York: William Morrow, 1991.

Martin, Laura C. *Tea: The Drink That Changed the World.* Tokyo and Rutland, VT: Tuttle, 2007.

Maurer, David W. *Kentucky Moonshine.* Lexington: University Press of Kentucky, 2003.

McCoy, Elin. *The Emperor of Wine: The Rise of Robert M. Parker, Jr. and the Reign of American Taste.* New York: ECCO, 2005.

McLean, Alice L. *Cooking in America, 1840–1945.* Westport, CT: Greenwood, 2006.

McMillan, Tracie. *The American Way of Eating: Undercover at Walmart, Applebee's, Farm Fields and the Dinner Table.* New York: Scribner, 2012.

McNamee, Thomas. *Alice Waters and Chez Panisse: The Romantic, Impractical, Often Eccentric, Ultimately Brilliant Making of a Food Revolution.* New York: Penguin, 2007.

McWilliams, James E. *A Revolution in Eating: How the Quest for Food Shaped America.* New York: Columbia University Press, 2005.

Meacham, Sarah Hand. *Every Home a Distillery: Alcohol, Gender, and Technology in the Colonial Chesapeake.* Baltimore: Johns Hopkins University Press, 2009.

Mendelson, Anne. *Milk: The Surprising Story of Milk through the Ages.* New York: Knopf, 2008.

Mendelson, Anne. *Stand Facing the Stove: The Story of the Women Who Gave America the Joy of Cooking: The Lives of Irma S. Rombauer and Marion Rombauer Becker.* New York: Henry Holt, 1996.

Mendelson, Richard. *From Demon to Darling: A Legal History of Wine in America.* Berkeley: University of California Press, 2009.

Merlo, Catherine. *Heritage of Gold: The First 100 Years of the Sunkist Growers, Inc., 1893–1993.* [Los Angeles: Sunkist Growers, n.d.]

Mitchell, William Frank. *African American Food Culture.* Westport, CT: Greenwood, 2009.

Mittelman, Amy. *Brewing Battles: The History of American Beer.* New York: Algora, 2007.

Moss, Maria J. *A Poetical Cook-Book.* 1864; reprint, New York: Arno/New York Times, 1972.

Moss, Michael. *Salt Sugar Fat: How the Food Giants Hooked Us.* New York: Random House, 2013.

Mullins, Paul R. *Glazed America: A History of the Doughnut.* Gainesville: University Press of Florida, 2008.

Myers, E. G., comp. *The Capitol Cookbook: A Facsimile of the Austin 1899 Edition.* Austin, TX: State House Press, 1995.

Nestle, Marion. *Food Politics: How the Food Industry Influences Nutrition and Health.* 3rd ed. Berkeley: University of California Press, 20013.

Nestle, Marion. *What to Eat: An Aisle-by-Aisle Guide to Savvy Food Choices and Good Eating.* New York: North Point, 2006.

Noling, A. W., comp. *Beverage Literature: A Bibliography.* Metuchen, NJ: Scarecrow, 1971.

Noon, Mark A. *Yuengling: A History of America's Oldest Brewery.* Jefferson, NC: McFarland, 2005.

Odegard, Peter H. *Pressure Politics: The Story of the Anti-Saloon League.* New York: Columbia University Press, 1928.

Ogle, Maureen. *Ambitious Brew: The Story of American Beer.* Orlando: Harcourt, 2006.

Okrent, Daniel. *Last Call: The Rise and Fall of Prohibition.* New York: Scribner, 2010.

Oliver, J. Eric. *Fat Politics: The Real Story behind America's Obesity Epidemic.* New York: Oxford University Press, 2005.

Oliver, Sandra L. *Food in Colonial and Federal America.* Westport, CT: Greenwood, 2005.

Oliver, Sandra L. *Saltwater Foodways: New Englanders and Their Food at Sea and Ashore, in the Nineteenth Century.* Mystic, CT: Mystic Seaport Museum, 1995.

O'Neill, Molly. *Mostly True: A Memoir of Family, Food, and Baseball.* New York: Scribner, 2006.

O'Neill, Molly, ed. *American Food Writing: An Anthology with Classic Recipes.* New York: Literary Classics, 2007.

Ozersky, Josh. *Hamburgers: A Cultural History.* New Haven, CT: Yale University Press, 2008.

Paarlberg, Robert. *Food Politics: What Everyone Needs to Know.* New York: Oxford University Press, 2010.

Peck, Garret. *The Prohibition Hangover: Alcohol in America from Demon Rum to Cult Cabernet.* New Brunswick, NJ: Rutgers University Press, 2009.

Pendergrast, Mark. *For God, Country and Coca-Cola.* 3rd ed. New York: Scribner, 2013.

Pendergrast, Mark. *Uncommon Grounds: The History of Coffee and How It Transformed Our World.* New York: Basic Books, 2010.

Pennell, Elizabeth Robins. *The Delights of Delicate Eating.* Introduction by Jacqueline Block Williams. Urbana: University of Illinois Press, 2000.

Pépin, Jacques. *The Apprentice: My Life in the Kitchen.* Boston and New York: Houghton Mifflin, 2003.

Pinckney, Eliza Lucas. *Recipe Book.* Charleston: Committee on Historic Activities of the South Carolina Society of the Colonial Dames of America, 1969.

Pinney, Thomas. *A History of Wine in America.* 2 vols. Berkeley: University of California Press, 1989.

Polan, Dana B. *Julia Child's the French Chef.* Durham, NC: Duke University Press, 2011.

Pollan, Michael. *In Defense of Food: An Eater's Manifesto.* New York: Penguin, 2008.

Pollan, Michael. *The Omnivore's Dilemma: A Natural History of Four Meals.* New York: Penguin, 2006.

Quinzio, Jeri. *Of Sugar and Snow: A History of Ice Cream Making.* Berkeley and Los Angeles: University of California Press, 2009.

Randolph, Mary. *The Virginia Housewife.* Edited by Karen Hess. 1824; facsimile reprint, Columbia: University of South Carolina Press, 1984.

Ranhofer, Charles. *The Epicurean.* 1893; reprint, New York: Dover, 1971.

Reardon, Joan. *M. F. K. Fisher among the Pots and Pans: Celebrating Her Kitchens.* Berkeley: University of California Press, 2008.

Reardon, Joan. *M. F. K. Fisher, Julia Child, and Alice Waters: Celebrating the Pleasures of the Table.* New York: Harmony Books, 1994.

Reardon, Joan. *Poet of the Appetites: The Lives and Loves of M. F. K. Fisher.* New York: North Point, 2004.

Regan, Mardee Haidin. *The Bartender's Best Friend: A Complete Guide to Cocktails, Martinis, and Mixed Drinks.* New York: Wiley, 2003.

Reichl, Ruth. *Garlic and Sapphires: The Secret Life of a Critic in Disguise.* New York: Penguin, 2005.

Riley, John J. *A History of the American Soft Drink Industry: Bottled Carbonated Beverages, 1807–1957.* Washington, DC: American Bottlers of Carbonated Beverages, 1958.

Rimas, Andrew, and Evan D. G. Fraser. *Beef: The Untold Story of How Milk, Meat, and Muscle Shaped the World.* New York: William Morrow, 2008.

Ritzer, George, ed. *The McDonaldization: The Reader.* 2nd ed. Thousand Oaks, CA: Pine Forge, 2006.

Ritzer, George. *The McDonaldization of Society.* Revised ed. Thousand Oaks, CA: Pine Forge, 1996.

Roberts, Paul. *The End of Food.* Boston: Houghton Mifflin, 2008.

Rodengen, Jeffrey L. *The Legend of Dr. Pepper/Seven-Up.* Ft. Lauderdale, FL: Write Stuff Syndicate, 1995.

Rombauer, Irma S. *The Joy of Cooking.* 1931; facsimile reprint, New York: Scribner, 1998.

Rose, Peter. *The Sensible Cook: Dutch Foodways in the Old and the New World.* Syracuse, NY: Syracuse University Press, 1989.

Roth, Rodris. *Tea Drinking in 18th-Century America: Its Etiquette and Equipage.* Paper 14. Contributions from the Museum of History and Technology, 1961.

Rovell, Darren. *First in Thirst: How Gatorade Turned the Science of Sweat into a Cultural Phenomenon.* New York: American Management Association, 2006.

Rowley, Matthew B. *The Joy of Moonshine!* New York: Lark Books, 2007.

Royte, Elizabeth. *Bottlemania: How Water Went on Sale and Why We Bought It.* New York: Bloomsbury, 2008.

Rubel, William. *Bread: A Global History.* London: Reaktion, 2011.

Sack, Daniel. *Whitebread Protestants: Food and Religion in American Culture.* New York: St. Martin's, 2000.

Salem, Frederick William. *Beer: Its History and Its Economic Value as a National Beverage.* Hartford, CT: F. W. Salem, 1880.

Salinger, Sharon V. *Taverns and Drinking in Early America.* Baltimore: Johns Hopkins University Press, 2002.

Schlosser, Eric. *Fast Food Nation: The Dark Side of the All-American Meal.* Boston: Houghton Mifflin, 2001.

Seely, Mrs. L. *Mrs. Seely's Cook Book.* Edited by Shirley Abbot. 1902; reprint, Birmingham, AL: Oxmoor, 1984.

Sen, Colleen. *Curry: A Global History.* London: Reaktion, 2009.

Shapiro, Laura. *Julia Child: A Penguin Life.* New York: Penguin, 2007.

Shapiro, Laura. *Perfection Salad: Women and Cooking at the Turn of the Century.* New York: Holt, 1987.

Shapiro, Laura. *Something from the Oven: Reinventing Dinner in 1950s America.* New York: Penguin, 2004.

Sheraton, Mimi. *Eating My Words: An Appetite for Life.* New York: Harper Perennial, 2006.

Simmons, Amelia. *American Cookery.* With an essay by Mary Tolford Wilson. 1796; facsimile reprint, New York: Oxford University Press, 1958.

Sinclair, Andrew. *Era of Excess: A Social History of the Prohibition Movement.* New York: Harper and Row, 1964.

Sismondo, Christine. *America Walks into a Bar: A Spirited History of Taverns and Saloons, Speakeasies and Grog Shops.* New York: Oxford University Press, 2011.

Skilnik. Bob. *The History of Beer and Brewing in Chicago, 1833–1978.* St. Paul, MN: Pogo, 1999.

Slavicek, Louise Chipley. *The Prohibition Era: Temperance in the United States.* New York: Chelsea House, 2008.

Smith, Andrew F. *American Tuna: The Rise and Fall of an Improbable Food.* Berkeley: University of California Press, 2012.

Smith, Andrew F. *Drinking History Fifteen Turning Points in the Making of American Beverages.* New York: Columbia University Press, 2012.

Smith, Andrew F. *Eating History: 30 Turning Points in the Making of American Cuisine.* New York: Columbia University Press, 2009.

Smith, Andrew F. *Hamburger: A Global History.* London: Reaktion, 2008.

Smith, Andrew F. *Junk Food and Fast Food: An Encyclopedia of What We Love to Eat.* Santa Barbara, CA: Greenwood, 2011.

Smith, Andrew F. *Peanuts: The Illustrious History of the Goober Pea.* Urbana: University of Illinois Press, 2002.

Smith, Andrew F. *Popped Culture: A Social History of Popcorn in America.* Columbia: University of South Carolina Press, 1999.

Smith, Andrew F. *Potato: A Global History.* London: Reaktion: 2011.

Smith, Andrew F. *Pure Ketchup: A History of America's National Condiment.* Columbia: University of South Carolina Press, 1996.

Smith, Andrew F. *Sugar: A Global History.* London: Reaktion, forthcoming.

Smith, Andrew F. *The Tomato in America: Early History, Culture and Cookery.* Columbia: University of South Carolina Press, 1994.

Smith, Andrew F. *The Turkey: An American Story.* Urbana: University of Illinois Press, 2006.

Smith, Andrew F., ed. *The Oxford Encyclopedia on Food and Drink in America.* 2nd ed. New York: Oxford University Press, 2012.

Smith, Andrew F., ed. *The Oxford Companion to American Food and Drink.* New York: Oxford University Press, 2007.

Smith, Frederick H. *Caribbean Rum: A Social and Economic History.* Gainesville: University Press of Florida, 2008.

Smith, Gregg. *Beer in America: The Early Years, 1587–1840: Beer's Role in the Settling of America and the Birth of a Nation.* Boulder, CO: Siris Books, 1998.

Solmonson, Lesley Jacobs. *Gin: A Global History.* London: Reaktion, 2012.

Spaulding, Lily May, and John Spaulding. *Civil War Recipes: Receipts from the Pages of Godey's Lady's Book.* Lexington: University Press of Kentucky, 1999.

Stavely, Keith, and Kathleen Fitzgerald. *America's Founding Food: The Story of New England Cooking.* Chapel Hill: University of North Carolina Press, 2004.

Steinberg, Ellen F., ed. *Learning to Cook: A Chicago Culinary Memoir.* Detroit: Wayne State University Press, 2007.

Stern, Jane and Michael Stern. *Two for the Road: Our Love Affair with American Food.* Boston and New York: Houghton Mifflin, 2006.

Sullivan, Charles L. *Napa Wine: A History.* San Francisco: Wine Appreciation Guild, 1994.

Taber, George M. *Judgment of Paris: California vs France and the Historic 1976 Paris Tasting That Revolutionized Wine.* New York: Scribner, 2005.

Thomas, Lately. *Delmonico's: A Century of Splendor.* Boston: Houghton Mifflin, 1967.

Thompson, Peter. *Rum Punch and Revolution: Taverngoing and Public Life in Eighteenth-Century Philadelphia.* Philadelphia: University of Pennsylvania Press, 1999.

Thornton, P. *The Southern Gardener and Receipt Book.* 1845; reprint, Birmingham, AL: Oxmoor, 1984.

Townsend, Elizabeth. *Lobster: A Global History.* London: Reaktion, 2011.

Ude, Louis Eustache. *The French Cook.* 1828; reprint, New York: Arco, 1978.

Ukers, William H. *All about Coffee.* 2nd ed. New York: Tea and Coffee Trade Journal Company, 1935.

Ukers, William H. *All about Tea.* New York: Tea and Coffee Trade Journal Company, 1935.

Warner, Deborah Jean. *Sweet Stuff: An American History of Sweeteners from Sugar to Sucralose.* Washington, DC: Smithsonian Institutional Press, 2011.

Washington, Martha. *Martha Washington's Booke of Cookery.* Edited by Karen Hess. New York: Columbia University Press, 1981.

Weasel, Lisa H. *Food Fray: Inside the Controversy over Genetically Modified Food.* New York: American Management Association, 2009.

Weaver, William Woys. *Sauerkraut Yankees: Pennsylvania German Foods and Foodways.* Philadelphia: University of Pennsylvania Press, 1983.

Webb, Lois Sinaiko, and Lindsay Grace Roten. *Holidays of the World Cookbook for Students.* Updated and revised ed. Santa Barbara, CA: Greenwood, 2011.

Webb, Lois Sinaiko, and Lindsay Grace Roten. *The Multicultural Cookbook for Students.* Updated and revised ed. Santa Barbara, CA: Greenwood, 2009.

Webster, Mrs. A. L. *The Improved Housewife.* 6th ed. 1845; facsimile reprint, New York: Arno, 1973.

Weiss, Harry B. *The History of Applejack or Apple Brandy in New Jersey from Colonial Times to the Present.* Trenton, NJ: New Jersey Agricultural Society, 1954.

Weiss, Laura. *Ice Cream: A Global History.* London: Reaktion, 2011.

Wheaton, Barbara Ketcham, and Patricia Kelly. *Bibliography of Culinary History: Food Resources in Eastern Massachusetts.* Boston: Hall, 1987.

Wilcox, Estelle Woods, comp. *Centennial Buckeye Cook Book.* Reprinted with an introduction and appendices by Andrew F. Smith. Columbus: Ohio State University Press, 2000.

Williams, Elizabeth M., ed. *The A–Z Encyclopedia of Food Controversies and the Law.* Santa Barbara, CA: Greenwood, 2010.

Williams, Ian. *Rum: A Social and Sociable History of the Real Spirit of 1776.* New York: Nation Books, 2005.

Williams, Jacqueline B. *The Way We Ate: Pacific Northwest Cooking, 1843–1900.* Pullman: Washington State University Press, 1996.

Williams, Susan. *Food in the United States, 1820s–1890.* Westport, CT: Greenwood, 2006.

Williams, Susan. *Savory Suppers and Fashionable Feasts: Dining in Victorian America.* Knoxville: University of Tennessee Press, 1996.

Wilson, David Scofield, and Angus Kress Gillespie, eds. *Rooted in America: Foodlore of Popular Fruits and Vegetables.* Nashville: University of Tennessee Press, 1999.

Woloson, Wendy A. *Refined Tastes: Sugar, Confectionery and Consumption in Nineteenth-Century America.* Baltimore: Johns Hopkins University Press, 2002.

Worth, Richard. *Teetotalers and Saloon Smashers: The Temperance Movement and Prohibition.* Berkeley Heights, NJ: Enslow, 2009.

Wyman, Carolyn. *Jell-O: A Biography; The History and Mystery of "America's Most Famous Dessert."* San Diego: Harcourt, 2001.

Wyman, Carolyn. *SPAM: A Biography; The Amazing True Story of America's "Miracle Meat"!* New York: Harcourt Brace, 1999.

Yenne, Bill. *American Brewery: From Colonial Evolution to Microbrew Revolution.* St. Paul, MN: MBI Publishing, 2003.

Zanger, Mark H. *The American Ethnic Cookbook for Students.* Phoenix, AZ: Oryx, 2001.

Zanger, Mark H. *The American History Cookbook.* Westport, CT: Greenwood, 2003.

Ziegelman, Jane. *97 Orchard: An Edible History of Five Immigrant Families in One New York Tenement.* New York: Smithsonian Books/HarperCollins, 2010.

Ziemann, Hugo, and Mrs. F. L. Gillette. *The White House Cookbook.* New York: Saalfield, 1903.

• About the Author and Contributors •

Author

Andrew F. Smith has taught the history of American food and drink at the New School University in New York for the past 18 years. He was formerly a high school teacher and for three decades organized in-service education programs for secondary and undergraduate educators. Smith is the author or editor of 24 books, including Greenwood's *Junk Food and Fast Food: An Encyclopedia of What We Love to Eat* (2012), and he has written more than 300 articles in academic journals, popular magazines, and newspapers. He has served as consultant to several television series on the history of American food and beverages and is the editor of the Edible Series of books that focuses on the history and culture of food and drink. His website is andrewfsmith.com.

Contributors

Zilkia Janer teaches Latin American and Latino literature and culture at Hofstra University. She is the author of *Puerto Rican Nation-Building Literature: Impossible Romance* (2005) and has published a number of articles on Latin American and South Asian culinary cultures.

Lucy M. Long is an instructor in international studies and American cultures studies at Bowling Green State University. She is the editor of *Culinary Tourism: Eating and Otherness* (2004) and has written on food and folklore.

· Index ·